The publisher gratefully acknowledges the generous
contributions to this book provided by:

The Gladys Krieble Delmas Foundation

The Sonia H. Evers Renaissance Studies Endowment
Fund of the University of California Press Foundation

The Margarita Hanson Publication Endowment Fund
of the American Musicological Society

MONTEVERDI'S LAST OPERAS

MONTEVERDI'S LAST OPERAS

A Venetian Trilogy

ELLEN ROSAND

UNIVERSITY OF CALIFORNIA PRESS

Berkeley   Los Angeles   London

FRONTISPIECE. Claudio Monteverdi, portrait by Bernardo
Strozzi, ca. 1630. (Sammlungen der Gesellschaft der Musik-
freunde in Wien)

University of California Press, one of the most distinguished university presses
in the United States, enriches lives around the world by advancing scholarship
in the humanities, social sciences, and natural sciences. Its activities are supported by the UC Press Foundation and by philanthropic contributions from
individuals and institutions. For more information, visit www.ucpress.edu.

University of California Press
Berkeley and Los Angeles, California

University of California Press, Ltd.
London, England

© 2007 by The Regents of the University of California

Library of Congress Cataloging-in-Publication Data

Rosand, Ellen.
   Monteverdi's last operas : a Venetian trilogy / Ellen Rosand.
      p.   cm. — (Evers Renaissance studies)
   Includes bibliographical references and index.
   ISBN 978-0-520-24934-9 (cloth : alk. paper)
      1. Monteverdi, Claudio, 1567–1643. Operas.   2. Opera—Italy—17th century.
      I. Title.

ML410.M77R67   2007
782.1092—dc22   2007002313

Manufactured in the United States of America

16   15   14   13   12   11   10   09   08
10   9   8   7   6   5   4   3   2

This book is printed on Natures Book, which contains 50% post-consumer
waste and meets the minimum requirements of ANSI/NISO Z39.48–1992 (R 1997)
(*Permanence of Paper*).

For my husband, David Rosand

CONTENTS

ILLUSTRATIONS

FIGURES

TABLES

MUSICAL EXAMPLES

PREFACE

Il ritorno d'Ulisse in patria and *L'incoronazione di Poppea* have fascinated scholars and listeners alike, from the late nineteenth century, when they were first rediscovered, to the
present day, when performance has brought them into the operatic mainstream. My own
fascination with these works predates my musicological career. I trace its beginnings to
two encounters in the early 1960s: one, a production of *Incoronazione* staged at the
Roman amphitheater in Aix-en-Provence, which my husband and I happened upon in
the summer of 1961, while on our honeymoon; the other, a performance of the prologue
and opening scene of *Il ritorno d'Ulisse* at Harvard's Lowell House in 1962, during Nadia
Boulanger's residency at the university, in which, appropriately, as it turned out, I sang
the role of Fortuna. The rest, we might say, is history.

In the nearly half-century since those first encounters, *Ritorno* and *Incoronazione* can
hardly be said to have been ignored, either by performers or scholars. They have been
studied in the context of Monteverdi's life and work in general, in that of his secular music and his theatrical works, in the larger context of seventeenth-century Venetian opera,
and as individual works of art. I have made my own contributions to the literature, returning to the operas again and again, like many of my colleagues, in an attempt to account for their power, trying to see them from different angles and to fathom their
extraordinary effect in the theater, all the while straining to keep up with the burgeoning
literature they stimulated. Even since 1990, when I realized I was writing this book, the
contributions of many authors have broadened and deepened our understanding of the
operas. The glacial rate at which my own work progressed made it possible for me to
build on those contributions, but it also made it necessary for me to engage with them

critically. Irritating as this may have been at times, the long gestation has given me the opportunity to take a broader view. In addition to being able to incorporate recent discoveries of an archeological nature (namely, new sources), I have profited from the insights brought about by the development (and also the decay or assimilation) of new critical approaches in musicology—the isms of the 1980s and 1990s. New methods of textual criticism, gender and genre studies, narrative, cultural, and critical theory have all had some impact on (some might say taken their toll of) the study of Monteverdi's late operas. The works have been subjected to deconstruction, and the status (and authority) of both author and text repeatedly called into question. But they have also been rendered ready to be reconstituted, rehabilitated, their value to be reaffirmed.

This, in fact, is my aim. The explosion of scholarship on Monteverdi's operas justifies taking another, deeper look. In works as thoroughly studied as these have been, but for which basic questions still remain unanswered—as basic as those involving chronology and authorship itself—any new piece of information or new perspective can alter the picture considerably, clarifying or obscuring it further. We have witnessed this with respect to the sources: a newly discovered libretto of *Incoronazione* and a score of Francesco Sacrati's *La finta pazza* have caused us to modify our view of the chronology and authenticity of the former. Here I examine the Venetian works from a new perspective, concentrating on what can be gleaned from considering them as a group—not merely as a pair, but as constituents of a trio, a trilogy that includes the opera that came between them, but for which we have no music, *Le nozze d'Enea*. Indeed, I would regard as a particularly significant contribution of this book the introduction of this neglected work into the literature on Monteverdi's Venetian operas. The presence of *Nozze* as the middle element of what I have called a Venetian trilogy has had implications for every aspect of my study. It has opened up new prospects on everything from the sources to the interpretation of meaning to questions of authorship raised by the other two works. It has helped to determine which are the "best" sources, that is, which librettos can be taken as closest to those the composer was given and how the scores might be read to reveal his values in the setting of those texts. It has, finally, enabled me to realize my main objective: to come closer to understanding the distinctiveness of *Ritorno* and *Incoronazione* and their place within the creative life of their author, Monteverdi.

My reasoning is in some sense circular, because although I cannot prove beyond a shadow of a doubt that Monteverdi wrote all the music in the scores—he didn't—I do believe that the general principles governing the relationship between the scores and librettos are consistent with a composer of great dramatic imagination and demonstrate his art. Indeed, considered as a trilogy, the last Venetian works reaffirm their composer's claim to a special place in the history of opera. Together they distinguish him from his immediate successors, such as Francesco Cavalli, whose responsibility for the exploration of conventions that enabled the development of opera as a genre was more direct, more practical, but whose handling of his texts was entirely different. Seen against one another, and as a group, the three members of the Venetian trilogy highlight the consistency in

Monteverdi's attitude towards his librettos, deepening what we know about his values as a composer of opera: that he was prepared to rearrange, cut, and otherwise manipulate text in the pursuit of his goal of creating music drama.

Individually and as a group, these three operas may indeed be unique within the context of Venetian opera—especially in comparison with those of Cavalli and other contemporaries—but they are neither unique nor surprising within the context of Monteverdi's own works in other genres; they embody the same attitudes toward words, participating in the same ruthless rewriting of text, and the same determined search for emotional expression. The composer who wrote Monteverdi's madrigals, his letters, his motets, and his masses also wrote these operas. The Venetian trilogy affirms Monteverdi's authorship of its constituent parts.

I am well aware that my conclusions regarding Monteverdi's authorship of these works depend on the analysis of sources whose connection with the composer has long (if not always) been regarded as questionable at best. But the trilogy perspective has actually helped me to clarify the relationships among these sources and to locate Monteverdi more confidently within them.

In arguing for Monteverdi as author of these works, I nonetheless embrace many of the current caveats regarding *Incoronazione:* that he may not have written "Pur ti miro" and some other parts of the music we have (in both scores), though I draw the line at Ottone, to my mind perhaps the most "Monteverdian" of all the characters in the opera. But I confess to being tired of the recent temporizing, of the constant reminders of the contingent aspects of the sources, by scholars readier to dismantle than construct, to puncture rather than reify or reinscribe. Contingent they may be—none of the scores actually bears Monteverdi's handwriting, and only that of *Ritorno* can even plausibly be assigned to Monteverdi's lifetime—but, considered together, these sources nonetheless demonstrate the hand of a master musical dramatist. Together they represent the works of a composer who had lived a lifetime with the challenges of setting texts to music, and had found characteristic, and stylistically coherent ways of meeting them.

⁂

A kind of trilogy itself, my book comprises three distinct but related parts, each, as much as possible, maintaining a focus on the three operas as a group. Following the opening chapter, a prologue that introduces the cast of characters and describes the setting, the first part of the book (Chapters 2–4) is largely bibliographical. Chapter 2, on the reception of *Ritorno* and *Incoronazione,* lays out some of the issues that have kept and continue to keep these remarkable works alive as scholarly and musical objects. In Chapters 3 and 4 I move to a consideration of the sources of all three works, textual and musical, and of the questions of authenticity they raise. This is certainly the most difficult section of the book, the one that will require the most intense concentration on the part of readers to follow the intricacies of my argument, particularly regarding the *Incoronazione* sources.

But playing the sources of the three operas off against one another leads to new insights regarding their chronology, form, and function.

The second part, which consists of a single long chapter (Chapter 5, "Ancients and Moderns"), is a crux of the book. After considering their contrasting dramatic structures, I again play the three works against each another, and through comparative analysis attempt to recover a sense of the missing music of *Nozze*. The third part (Chapters 6–8), then, takes a critical approach to the librettos and their setting. Here, interactions between text and music remain at center stage, and the nature of Monteverdi's responsibility for the dramatic impact of the works is investigated. Chapter 6 ("Master of Three Servants") explores Monteverdi's aesthetics, as adumbrated in his letters, and then considers the ways in which the three Venetian librettists attempted to satisfy him by providing the kinds of conventional dramatic situations and texts he sought in librettos. The last two chapters are devoted to the analysis of characters, both as individuals (Chapter 7: "Constructions of Character") and in comparison to one another (Chapter 8: "The Philosopher and the Parasite"). This final chapter uses an analysis of the text and music of two central figures, Seneca and Iro, to construct a debate that epitomizes the contrast between the works and elucidates their meaning. The conclusions are then expanded to include *Nozze,* and the chapter ends with a consideration of the meaning of the trilogy as a whole. A brief epilogue places Monteverdi, the dramatist, within the context of the history of opera, as initiator of and participant in the grand tradition that links him with such figures as Handel and Mozart, and especially his *co-nazionale*—and near namesake—at the other end of that tradition, Giuseppe Verdi.

⁊⬥

This book brings together and synthesizes some of my previous studies, published and unpublished: the published essays on individual operas drawn upon here include "Seneca and the Interpretation of *Poppea*" (1985), "Iro and the Interpretation of *Ritorno*" (1989), "Monteverdi's Mimetic Art" (1989), "*Il ritorno d'Ulisse* and Classicism" (1990), "The Bow of Ulysses" (1993), "*Il ritorno d'Ulisse* and the Power of Music" (1993), and "Did Monteverdi Write *L'Incoronazione di Poppea,* and Does it Matter?" (1995). My most original and most productive inspiration, the idea of considering the three operas together, was born when I delivered the Una Lectures in the Humanities at the University of California, Berkeley (1991). In the intervening decade and more, I have explored the implications of this idea in lectures at Princeton, UCLA, Eastman, the University of Oslo, the University of Pennsylvania, and Indiana University; and in 2000 I tested much of this material in a series of lectures at the University of Cremona.

The list of my debts to institutions, colleagues, students, friends, and family incurred over the course of the past fifteen years, since I began writing this book, is Leporellian. I only hope I can remember them all here. Fellowships from the American Council of Learned Societies and the Guggenheim Foundation in 1990–91, just as I had finished my previous book, provided the support and time to contemplate and explore the dimensions of a new project. A grant from the Rockefeller Foundation (1992) afforded a blissful month of uninterrupted writing at Bellagio, at the perfect time. By then, I had begun teaching at Yale, where I was able to test various aspects of the subject in seminars with a series of extraordinary students, many of whose ideas have had a significant impact on my work, and many of whom helped with the practical tasks of bringing the project to fruition, even as they themselves were becoming professional musicologists: Roger Freitas, my incredibly precise research assistant in the 1990s; Nathan Link, who literally worked around the clock to prepare the musical examples while he was finishing his dissertation; and Zachariah Victor, my 24/7 resource for computer and other technical problems. Mauro Calcagno not only supplied me with innumerable photocopies of far-flung articles during his graduate student days at Yale, but has read drafts, checked translations, and served as a sounding board for many of my ideas since then. I treasure our regular Sunday afternoon telephonic colloquies.

Several other colleagues have read and commented on drafts of individual chapters: Jonathan Glixon, Paolo Fabbri, and Lorenzo Bianconi. And I am grateful to my readers for the University of California Press, James Haar and Gary Tomlinson, who viewed the manuscript from complementary—and exceedingly helpful—perspectives. Bonnie Blackburn, whose collaboration as copy editor I requested and was mercifully granted by the editors at the Press, surpassed my fondest hopes in the care, insight, and energy she brought to her task. I cannot count the number of ingenious solutions she offered to problems that had stymied me even into my final draft. My project editor, Rose Vekony, identified and resolved a host of other problems that had slipped below my proofreading radar.

Joseph Kerman, my friend for more than thirty years, is all over this manuscript. He read (and rewrote) it repeatedly, in part and in whole, summer and winter, on east and on west coasts, and especially in cyberspace—always trusting it was for the last time. His enthusiasm for the project, for the operas themselves, and for my efforts, helped to sustain me throughout these long years.

Valerie Oltarsh, my precious college roommate, did not read a word of this manuscript and now sadly will never do so, but she was my cheerleader the entire time, providing the kind of support that human beings need from one another to get through life, not just the writing of books. Most of all, I cannot imagine this book without my husband, David, who lived it with me from the very beginning, before it was anything but a gleam in my eye. His passion for the operas of Monteverdi was born and grew with mine, and his own deepening understanding of Venetian art and culture has nourished my thinking for nearly half a century. This book is as much his as mine, and I lovingly dedicate it to him.

EDITORIAL PROCEDURE

In transcriptions from *Il ritorno d'Ulisse* and *L'incoronazione di Poppea,* I have used the editions of Alan Curtis and Jane Glover as well as the manuscript sources. Bass figures are provided only where the harmony is ambiguous, whether or not they are included in the sources. For reasons of space, I have superimposed multiple strophes on the same bass where possible. In some—but not all—cases, rhythmic values are reduced, as indicated. Although I have generally adhered to one or another of the manuscript sources of *Incoronazione,* I have transposed the two stanzas in Example 17 to provide a more reasonable tonal relationship between them. I have generally identified tonal centers exclusively by pitch—using capital and small letters for major and minor, respectively—to avoid the implication of a system of tonality not yet in effect in this period.

In transcriptions of the Italian text, I have generally adhered to the rules given in *Libretti d'opera italiani dal Seicento al Novecento,* ed. Giovanna Gronda and Paolo Fabbri (Milan: Mondadori, 1997), pp. 1809–10. Accordingly, I have distinguished *u* from *v,* altered final *j* to *i,* and changed *et* and *&* to *e* before consonants and *ed* before vowels. Otherwise, I have regularized apostrophes and accents, and, more cautiously, punctuation, and have indicated the beginning of each poetic line by capitalizing its initial letter. Textual repetitions and intercalations introduced by the composer are given in italics. Libretto passages omitted in the musical setting, as well as substantive textual variants—between different librettos or between librettos and score—are placed in brackets. Refrains are underlined. The musical examples preserve the textual readings of the scores, rather than those of the librettos.

With respect to Italian verse, as discussed herein, two identifying features are noteworthy: the number of syllables per line and the position of the final accent. The free mixture of seven- (*settenario*) and eleven-syllable lines (*endecasillabo*) known as *versi sciolti* characterizes recitative poetry. Lines with five (*quinario*), six (*senario*), and especially eight syllables (*ottonario*) are more typical of aria poetry. Final accents can fall either on the penultimate syllable (*piano*), the final syllable (*tronco*), or the antepenultimate syllable (*sdrucciolo*).

In identifying scene numbers, I have generally adhered to those given in the librettos, as indicated in Tables 6, 14, and 15, even though they may differ from those in the scores.

ABBREVIATIONS

AcM	*Acta musicologica*
AMw	*Archiv für Musikwissenschaft*
CM	*Current Musicology*
COJ	*Cambridge Opera Journal*
DBI	*Dizionario biografico degli italiani*
DTÖ	Denkmäler der Tonkunst in Österreich
EM	*Early Music*
EMH	*Early Music History*
JAMS	*Journal of the American Musicological Society*
JM	*Journal of Musicology*
JRMA	*Journal of the Royal Musical Association*
MD	*Musica disciplina*
Mf	*Die Musikforschung*
ML	*Music & Letters*
MQ	*Musical Quarterly*
MR	*Music Review*
MT	*Musical Times*
NG	*The New Grove Dictionary of Music and Musicians*, 2nd ed., ed. Stanley Sadie. London: Macmillan, 2001
NGO	*The New Grove Dictionary of Opera*, ed. Stanley Sadie. London: Macmillan, 1992
NRMI	*Nuova rivista musicale italiana*

RIM	*Rivista italiana di musicologia*
RMI	*Rivista musicale italiana*
RQ	*Renaissance Quarterly*
SIMG	*Sammelbände der Internationalen Musik-Gesellschaft*
SM	*Studi musicali*
StOpIt	*Storia dell'opera italiana*
VfMw	*Vierteljahrsschrift für Musikwissenschaft*

LIBRETTOS

Library sigla are those used in *RISM (Répertoire international des sources musicales)* and listed in *NG II (The New Grove Dictionary of Music and Musicians*, 2nd ed. [New York: Grove's Dictionaries, 2000]).

F	*La Coronazione di Poppea.* I-FN Magl. VII. 66
LN	*Il Nerone overo L'incoronatione di Poppea drama musicale* (Naples: Mollo, 1651)
LV	*L'incoronatione di Poppea,* di Gio. Francesco Busenello. Opera musicale rappresentata Nel Teatro Grimano l'Anno 1642, in Busenello, *Delle hore ociose* (Venice: Giuliani, 1656)
R	*La Coronatione di Poppea.* I-RVI Silvestriani 239
SV	*Scenario dell'opera REGGIA Intitolata La Coronatione di POPPEA. Che si rappresenta in Musica nel Theatro dell'Illutr. Sig. Giovanni Grimani* (Venice: Pinelli, 1643)
T	*La Popea.* I-TVco Rossi 83
U1	*La Coronatione di Poppea.* I-UDc 55
U2	*Coronatione di Poppea.* I-UDc Fondo Joppi 496
V	*La Popea.* I-Vmc Cicogna 585
W	*Nerone.* PL-Wn BOZ 1043

I

Orpheus in Venice

Prologue

Claudio Monteverdi has long been celebrated as the first great composer of opera; he was acknowledged as such during his lifetime. Although his star waned in the interim, since the late nineteenth century it has been rising again, and he has fully reclaimed that status today.

Such a reputation was easier to assert, if not to explain, in a musicological vacuum, that is, so long as the operas of his contemporaries and immediate followers in Venice remained unknown. But now that many of those operas have been recovered, analyzed, performed, and recorded, Monteverdi stands even taller. Although other seventeenth-century composers may have written more operas, and their direct impact on day-to-day operatic developments may have been greater at the time, their works seem somehow trivial next to those of Monteverdi. His contemporaries' view of him as the animating spirit of opera, the figure responsible, as one of them said, for making "known to the world the true nature of theatrical music, which was not well understood in modern compositions," has indeed been confirmed by history.[1] Monteverdi's is a voice that sounds most resonantly over the centuries. Two products of his last years in Venice, *Il ritorno d'Ulisse in patria* and *L'incoronazione di Poppea*, are the only operas before Handel's, maybe even

---

1. "Io me ne chiamo sodisfatissimo et ella deve restarne contenta poi che ha fatto conoscere al Mondo qual sia il vero spirito della Musica teatrale non bene intesa da Moderni compositioni." From the author's prefatory letter to the libretto of *Il ritorno d'Ulisse*, given in full in Appendix 1.

before Mozart's, that have succeeded in becoming part of the standard repertory of today's operatic mainstream.[2]

In light of this stature, it is sobering to remember that more than half of Monteverdi's operas are actually lost to us. Whereas his contemporaries knew him as the composer of theatrical entertainments numbering a dozen or more, his current operatic reputation rests on three very different works: *La favola d'Orfeo* (1607) from the early period of his career in Mantua, and *Il ritorno d'Ulisse in patria* (1640) and *L'incoronazione di Poppea* (1643) from his twilight years in Venice. The Mantuan and Venetian works are so different, in fact, that the great Italian musicologist Nino Pirrotta was moved to propose that a study of them be titled "Opera from Monteverdi to Monteverdi."[3]

There is no great mystery here, of course. These differences are readily explained as the result of different times and different systems of patronage: *Orfeo* was a court opera whereas *Ritorno* and *Incoronazione* were designed for the Venetian public theater. We can also comprehend the differences as the result of a composer's natural development over the course of three and a half decades, a development that could not help but take into consideration the achievements of other composers of opera, the changing world of the art itself.

But Monteverdi's two surviving Venetian works, although written only three years apart, also differ markedly from one another (so much so, indeed, that they were once thought to be by different composers, as we shall see). Many of the differences derive from the contrasting nature of their librettos—one based on epic narrative, the other a drama of intrigue, one built largely of free recitative, the other brimming with closed forms, one celebrating the triumph of virtue, the other its defeat. They differ too in their narrative strategies, in the interaction between characters, and in the composer's musical characterizations. The most notable and still disturbing difference, however, lies in the contrasting moral ethos of the two works, between a world of emotional propriety and restraint and one of hedonistic abandon. And this difference is magnified in the musical style: ascetically speech-like in *Ritorno*, sensuously melodic in *Incoronazione*.

In any effort to comprehend the relationship between these two contrasting works, it is essential to take account of the work that came between them, Monteverdi's third Venetian opera: *Le nozze d'Enea e Lavinia*, staged in 1641, one year after *Ritorno* and two years before *Incoronazione*—essential, even though no score has survived. Ironically, despite—or perhaps even because of—the absence of a score, the documentation of Monteverdi's authorship is actually more secure than for either of the other Venetian

---

2. Among recent mainstream productions, the series in 2002 at the Brooklyn Academy of Music was exemplary. See Joseph Kerman, "The Full Monte," *New York Review of Books* 49, no. 10 (13 June 2002): 36–38.

3. Nino Pirrotta, "Monteverdi e i problemi dell'opera," in *Studi sul teatro veneto fra Rinascimento ed età barocco,* ed. Maria Teresa Muraro (Florence: Olschki, 1971), 337; repr. in Nino Pirrotta, *Scelte poetiche di musicisti* (Venice: Marsilio, 1987), 211; translated as "Monteverdi and the Problems of Opera," in Nino Pirrotta, *Music and Culture in Italy from the Middle Ages to the Baroque: A Collection of Essays* (Cambridge, MA: Harvard University Press, 1984) (hereafter *Essays*), 235–53.

works. But even without the score, there is much to be gleaned about this opera from other kinds of sources. Read carefully, contemporary librettos and descriptions can reveal a great deal about *Nozze,* and they also shed new light on its fellows. On one level, consideration of *Nozze* helps to explain some of the discrepancies and inconsistencies among the sources of *Ritorno* and *Incoronazione,* which have caused considerable confusion and controversy, and which have been read as casting doubt on the authenticity of both works. And on another, by rationalizing and placing in perspective some of the most striking contrasts between *Ritorno* and *Incoronazione, Nozze* illuminates their relationship— and, not incidentally, their meaning. The three operas, then, benefit from being considered as a group, for each serves to illuminate the others. Taken together, they distinguish Monteverdi from his contemporaries even as they more precisely define his own contribution to the evolving art of opera.

A particular dramatic vision links *Ritorno* and *Incoronazione* to one another and to *Nozze.* This ghost opera joins with the two survivors to form a coherent body of works that attests to Monteverdi's position within the world of Venetian opera as a whole. For these operas form more than a merely fortuitous group; they constitute a trilogy—indeed, as I will argue, a self-consciously Venetian trilogy. Following a trajectory from Troy through Greece to Rome, together they stand witness to the myth of Venice, rehearsing the course of empires that will culminate in the foundation of the Serenissima.

A New Ulysses

One of the most distinctive aspects of Monteverdi's three Venetian operas is that their librettos are known to have been written specifically for him, as part of an effort to lure him back to the musical theater, from which he had been conspicuously absent for some time. Their authors, all members of the same Venetian circle, seem to have participated in a program for the renewal of the still young art of musical drama, and that renewal involved the co-opting of its originating musical dramatist.

In 1640, the Venetian nobleman Giacomo Badoaro, writing anonymously, prefaced his libretto of *Il ritorno d'Ulisse in patria* with an open letter addressed to the "very illustrious and very reverend Signor Claudio Monteverdi."[4] He was writing in the full flush of success, after Monteverdi's setting of the opera had been performed ten times, he tells us. He had embarked upon this libretto, his first substantial literary effort, for the sole purpose of tempting the composer out of his operatic retirement and encouraging him to display his operatic mastery to the city of Venice. Until now, Badoaro explains, Venetian audiences had been deceived by mere appearances. The emotions they had seen portrayed on stage left them cold and unmoved, because they were warmed by

---

4. The letter and libretto are unsigned, but Badoaro's authorship is established in a published document of 1640 and later in his own libretto of 1644, *Ulisse errante* (see below, n. 47). See Appendix 3.

a painted sun; only the great master Monteverdi, the true sun, radiates sufficient heat to truly ignite the passions.[5]

Badoaro was a figure of considerable standing in Venice, a leading member of a distinguished patrician family—he was to serve several terms in the Collegio, the chief advisory body to the Doge, and subsequently was one of two Capi to the powerful Council of Ten.[6] As such, he lent enormous prestige to the operatic enterprise. By the time he penned his letter to Monteverdi, though, opera was already a burgeoning cultural phenomenon in Venice. Three years earlier, an industrious band of five traveling musicians from Rome, headed by Benedetto Ferrari, librettist and theorbist, and Francesco Manelli, composer and singer, had produced the first opera on the lagoon, to great acclaim. They performed at the Teatro S. Cassiano; the theater, owned by the Tron family, had presented plays earlier in the century but fallen into disuse and was then restored for the purpose of presenting opera. Their cast was supplemented by local musicians, some from the San Marco chapel. The travelers repeated their success at the same theater the following season, with a new opera, and in the next year, 1639, they moved to a newly constructed theater at SS. Giovanni e Paolo, owned by the Grimani family, where they offered not one but two productions. Meanwhile, another company had taken over at S. Cassiano, this one headed by a local musician, Francesco Cavalli, second organist of San Marco. Cavalli was to provide annual operas for S. Cassiano for the next decade, moving then to a succession of other theaters, launching an operatic career that spanned some thirty years. Ferrari and Manelli kept up the pace, extending their activities to still a third theater, S. Moisè, owned by the Giustiniani family. They produced their own as well as others' operas simultaneously there and at SS. Giovanni e Paolo, beginning in 1640. But their contribution ceased when they left Venice for Emilia Romagna in 1644.[7]

By 1640, then, the phenomenon that was to become commercial opera as we know it was already well on its way to being established. It must have seemed only a matter of time until Monteverdi, the most renowned musician in Venice, would become caught up in the activities. For more than a quarter-century, since his arrival from Mantua in 1613, Monteverdi had served as *maestro di cappella* at San Marco, certainly the most prestigious musical position in Italy, if not the world. The composer was something of an *éminence grise* as far as opera was concerned. He was probably the best-known composer of dramatic music in all of Italy, but he seemed in no hurry to join in the frenetic activity that characterized the Venetian opera world at this time. Although his most famous works, *Orfeo* and *Arianna*, dating from his Mantuan years, were decades old, he had continued to fulfill operatic

---

5. "Per eccitare la virtù di V.S. a far conoscer a questa città che nel calore degl'affetti vi è gran differenza da un sol vero a un sol dipinto mi diedi da principio a compore il Ritorno d'Ulisse in patria."

6. Marco Barbaro, "Albori de' patritii veneti," cited in Beth L. Glixon and Jonathan Glixon, *Inventing the Business of Opera* (New York: Oxford University Press, 2006), 110, n. 4.

7. The full history is detailed in Ellen Rosand, *Opera in Seventeenth-Century Venice: The Creation of a Genre* (Berkeley and Los Angeles, 1991) (hereafter *OSV*), chap. 3.

commissions for private patrons—at Mantua, Parma, and Piacenza, as well as in Venice itself—ever since his arrival on the lagoon.[8] In any case, his absence from the initial phase of operatic activities in Venice did not go unnoticed. Indeed, as early as 1638, one of his contemporaries expressed the hope that the composer would soon surprise them by producing an opera on a Venetian stage, as everyone else seemed to be doing. And even if he never actually produced such a work, continued this observer, his voice would nonetheless be heard, since he was so powerfully behind the whole operatic venture in the first place.[9]

Whether Monteverdi was loath to join the commercial stampede of public opera out of a sense of decorum—he was not only *maestro di cappella*, but had taken religious orders—or, more likely, because of the indifference or exhaustion of old age, the reluctant composer evidently needed to be persuaded.[10] The responsibility for undertaking this task was claimed by Giacomo Badoaro, and he could hardly have been more successful. Monteverdi responded with a tremendous surge of activity, producing the three new operas for Venice in as many years, all of them for the Grimani theater, SS. Giovanni e Paolo: *L'incoronazione di Poppea* reached the stage only a few months before the composer's death in 1643.[11]

This list does not include the revival of Monteverdi's *Arianna*, written for Mantua in 1608, which inaugurated the third Venetian opera house, S. Moisè, in 1640. Apparently it ran concurrently with *Ritorno* at SS. Giovanni e Paolo. We have very little information about this remarkable event—remarkable because *Arianna* was vastly different in genre

---

8. Most recently, his *Proserpina rapita*, a kind of dramatic cantata on a text by Giulio Strozzi, had been performed in 1630 at the Palazzo Mocenigo, the same performance venue as his *Combattimento di Tancredi e Clorinda* six years earlier. For a survey of Monteverdi's theatrical activities after his arrival in Venice, see Tim Carter, *Monteverdi's Musical Theatre* (New Haven and London: Yale University Press, 2002), chaps. 7 and 8.

9. "Dio voglia non se avanzi anco sopra delle scene dove tutti li altri sono per capitare una di queste sere con una Comica, et musicale rappresentatione. . . . E se non vi sarà in atto vi potrà essere in potenza perché haverà consigliato forte il tutto." For the context and dating of this passage, see Ellen Rosand, "Barbara Strozzi, *Virtuosissima cantatrice:* The Composer's Voice," *JAMS* 31 (1978): 241–81, at 251, n. 34; also *OSV*, 16–17, with translation.

10. Monteverdi's contract with the *procuratori* of San Marco did not specifically forbid commercial activities, but those of Giovanni Croce and Giulio Cesare Martinengo, his immediate predecessors as *maestro di cappella*, did. See Gastone Vio, "Ultimi ragguagli monteverdiani," *Rassegna veneta di studi musicali* 2–3 (1986–87): 347–64, at 360. The composer's infirmity during the last year of his life—he was seventy-four—is an issue in Alan Curtis's analysis of *Incoronazione* (see Alan Curtis, "*La Poppea impasticciata,* or, Who Wrote the Music to *L'Incoronazione* (1643)?," *JAMS* 42 [1989]: 23–54, at 25). Monteverdi was also busy with other projects at this time: he signed the dedication to the *Selva morale*, a publication that has been shown to be of special, personal importance to him, on 1 May 1641, some months after *Ritorno* and *Nozze* were performed. According to Robert Holzer ("Monteverdi's *Rerum vulgarium fragmenta:* The Italian-Texted Pieces of the *Selva morale et spirituale,*" unpublished manuscript), the volume reveals that he was preparing for his death. Nino Pirrotta made a great deal of Monteverdi's reluctance to compose operas for Venice ("Early Venetian Libretti at Los Angeles," in *Essays,* 321–22), but he exaggerated its extent, since he was mistaken about the chronology of *Ritorno,* thinking it did not receive its premiere in Venice until 1641, rather than a year earlier. See below, Chap. 3, for a full discussion of the chronology of the *Ritorno* performances.

11. For evidence that *Ritorno* was performed at SS. Giovanni e Paolo rather than S. Cassiano, as formerly thought, see below, Chap. 3.

and style from anything else on the boards at the time. Perhaps the revival had not yet taken place when Badoaro undertook to write his libretto, for if the production had been part of his campaign to lure the composer back to the stage, one might expect that he would have mentioned it. In 1640 *Arianna* may have been no more than a *succès d'estime*, perhaps even a disappointment. Ariadne's famous lament must have been cheered, but other aspects may well have puzzled or bored audiences entranced by the facile melodious novelties of Manelli and Ferrari.[12] The libretto printed in 1640 shows that very few changes were made in an opera originally designed for the Mantuan court, an esoteric elite. It may very well not have appealed to the new Venetian public.[13] (Perhaps we can trace another persuasive influence here, that of Ferrari, for it was his company—now companies—that probably produced *Arianna* at S. Moisè, as well as all three of the Monteverdi operas at SS. Giovanni e Paolo.)[14]

It is clear, in any case, that by its very creation, Badoaro's libretto for *Ritorno* was designed as a challenge to the composer. Monteverdi would reveal to the world the difference in warmth between the real and painted sun and display his superiority over the younger composers whose works had so far dominated the Venetian stage. In emphasizing Monteverdi's skill in portraying the affections, Badoaro reveals his awareness of the composer's special strengths, an awareness that informs many aspects of his libretto. But, as he explains in his prefatory letter, in order to make sure that his text would suit the composer, he submitted drafts of some scenes to Monteverdi so that he could alter them, perfecting them in a way that would allow him to release his musical inspiration.[15] The modest hope that

---

12. The "melodious novelties" are described in the prefaces to the librettos of *Andromeda* and *La maga fulminata,* and illustrated in Manelli's and Ferrari's contemporary monody books. See Alessandro Magini, "Le monodie di Benedetto Ferrari e *L'incoronazione di Poppea:* Un rilevamento stilistico comparativo," *RIM* 21 (1987): 266–99; also John Whenham, *Duet and Dialogue in the Age of Monteverdi,* 2 vols. (Ann Arbor: UMI, 1982), esp. chap. 9.

13. The libretto was published twice in Venice: in 1639, as a purely literary reprint of the 1608 text, without the composer's name (*L'Arianna: Tragedia del signor Ottavio Rinuccini . . . rappresentata in musica* [Angelo Salvadori]); and again in 1640, when it was clearly associated with Monteverdi's music and with a performance at S. Moisè (*L'Arianna del Sig. Ottavio Rinuccini, posta in musica dal Sig. Claudio Monteverdi, rappresentata in Venetia l'anno 1640* [Antonio Bariletti]). Among the (few) alterations, the choruses were to be omitted, as indicated by a series of inverted commas ("virgolette") in the margins, the standard means of marking libretto passages that were cut in performance. See *OSV,* 17, n. 20, and 18, n. 22.

14. Given his apparent reluctance to join the operatic fray, it may surprise us that Monteverdi did not restrict his activities to mere composition, but entered into the business end of things as well. He was apparently involved in the hiring of singers for the 1640–41 season at SS. Giovanni e Paolo, when both *Ritorno* and *Nozze* were performed; he owed money to the scenographer of S. Moisè, the venue of the *Arianna* revival in 1640; and, as indicated in a document of 28 February 1641, he was a creditor of Ferrari, whose company had certainly produced *Ritorno* and probably also *Nozze* and *Arianna.* See Gastone Vio, "Musici veneziani dei primi decenni del Seicento: Discordie e bustarelle," *Rassegna veneta di studi musicali* 5–6 (1989–90): 375–85, and, especially, Beth Glixon, "Scenes from the Life of Silvia Gailarti Manni, a Seventeenth-Century *Virtuosa,*" *EMH* 15 (1996): 97–146, esp. 113–16.

15. "Perfetionate al fine a lei le donai acciò con il mio poetico perfetionasse, sfogasse il suo musicale furore." For possible evidence for Monteverdi's early intervention in Badoaro's text, see Chap. 3, n. 40.

Monteverdi's musical setting will permit his poor text to pass as respectable;[16] he has no hesitation in ascribing all of the opera's success to the composer, even going so far as to confess (somewhat facetiously, no doubt) his inability to recognize his own creation in its Monteverdian guise.[17] His Ulysses, he concludes, gallantly, is more greatly indebted to the composer than the real Ulysses was to the goddess Minerva.[18] Badoaro closes his letter less modestly, declaring himself extremely satisfied with his handiwork—and hoping Monteverdi is, too—since it has enabled the composer to demonstrate to the world the true nature of theatrical music, which other composers either did not understand or failed to project—yet another only partly veiled denigration of the younger generation.[19]

Monteverdi's first public opera was indeed a great success. In addition to the ten Venetian performances specifically mentioned in Badoaro's letter, each of them before an equally crowded and enthusiastic audience,[20] *Ritorno* was taken on the road shortly afterward by the Ferrari–Manelli troupe, for a series of performances in Bologna.[21] Most unusually, it was then repeated in Venice the next year, 1641—this in spite of the already evident Venetian resistance to such revivals. In fact, *Ritorno* was not only the first, but also the last Venetian opera to be heard in successive seasons throughout the entire seventeenth century.[22] For one brief, resonant historical moment, the 1640 and 1641 seasons, Monteverdi dominated the operatic scene in Venice. Four of the ten operas produced in those years were by him: of the remaining six, there were two each by Ferrari and Cavalli, and one each by Manelli and Francesco Sacrati. (See Table 1 below.)

The most concrete testimony to the impact of *Ritorno d'Ulisse*, however, is provided not by any comparative performance statistics but by Monteverdi's next opera, also performed

---

16. "Sperai i miei versi racoloriti dall'Armonia di lei fossero portati a passare per riguardevole."

17. "Ammiriamo con grandissima maraviglia i concetti così pieni, non senza qualche conturbatione, mentre non so più conoscere per mia quest'opera."

18. "[Mio] Ulisse è più obbligato a V. S. che non fu il vero Ulisse alla sempre Gratiosa Minerva."

19. See above, n. 1.

20. "Hora veduta . . . rappresentar l'opera dieci volte sempre con eguale concorso della Città." We do not know how many performances were normal for this period, but ten must have been a large number, since the librettist made so much of it. Slightly later in the century, some operas were performed as many as thirty-five times. See Glixon and Glixon, *Business,* app. 7, which provides performance statistics for several seasons during the 1650s and 1660s.

21. The Bologna production is documented in *Le glorie della musica celebrate dalla sorella poesia, rappresentandosi in Bologna la Delia e l'Ulisse nel teatro de gl'Illustriss. Guastavillani* (Bologna: Ferroni, 1640). This important volume was first introduced into the literature in Wolfgang Osthoff, "Zur Bologneser Aufführung von Monteverdis 'Ritorno di Ulisse' im Jahre 1640," *Mitteilungen der Kommission für Musikforschung* 11 (1958): 155–60.

22. For data on revivals, see Cristoforo Ivanovich, "Memorie teatrali di Venezia," in his *Minerva al tavolino* (Venice: Pezzana, 1681); 2nd ed. (1688) repr. *Memorie teatrali di Venezia,* ed. Norbert Dubowy (Lucca: Libreria musicale italiana, 1993), and subsequent chronologies, primarily those of Carlo Bonlini (*Le glorie della poesia e della musica contenute nell'esatta notitia de teatri della città di Venezia* [Venice: Bonarigo, 1730; repr. Bologna: Forni, 1979]) and Antonio Groppo (*Catalogo di tutti i drammi per musica recitati ne' teatri di Venezia dall'anno 1637 in cui ebbero principio le pubbliche rappresentazioni de' medesimi, fin all'anno presente 1745* [Venice: Groppo, 1745; repr. Bologna: Forni, 1977]). There were a few revivals, but apparently not in successive years (though *Giasone* may have been revived during Ascension following its premiere in carnival 1649).

in 1641, for which *Ritorno* was the acknowledged model: *Le nozze d'Enea e Lavinia.* The libretto, also issued anonymously, was by a friend of Badoaro's, recently identified, after years of mystery, as one Michelangelo Torcigliani.[23] Since the music for this opera has not yet surfaced, we owe virtually all of our information about its origins and substance to a scenario that was published in conjunction with the performance, or, rather, to the preface to that scenario, written in the form of a letter "ad alcuni suoi amici" from the librettist. In it, the author, anxious to identify himself as an aristocratic novice like Badoaro, reveals that he had conceived his text in response to the 1640 premiere of *Il ritorno d'Ulisse.* He had completed it for performance in the present year (1641) to follow the revival of Badoaro's

---

23. Though contemporary manuscript copies of *Nozze* ascribe the libretto to Badoaro, the text of the prefatory letter excludes this possibility. See Thomas Walker, "Gli errori di *Minerva al tavolino:* Osservazioni sulla cronologia delle prime opera veneziane," in *Venezia e il melodrama del Seicento,* ed. Maria Teresa Muraro (Florence: Olschki, 1976), 7–20, and Anna Szweykowska, "Le due poetiche venete e le ultime opere di Claudio Monteverdi," *Quadrivium* 18 (1977): 145–57, who demonstrate the untenability of that attribution, but without offering any alternative. The matter is resolved in Nicola Michelassi, "Michelangelo Torcigliani è l'Incognito autore delle *Nozze di Enea con Lavinia*," *Studi secenteschi* 48 (2007): 381–86. Michelassi bases his identification on the aesthetic positions taken in Badoaro's second libretto, *Ulisse errante* of 1645, published under his academic alias, especially as articulated in the author's prefatory letter, which is addressed to Torcigliani. This letter reveals that Badoaro had designed *Ulisse errante* as a response to *Le nozze d'Enea,* just as the latter had been designed as a response to *Il ritorno d'Ulisse* (see below, n. 47).

A connection to Monteverdi is established in Leonardo Querini, *I vezzi d'Erato* (Venice: Herz, 1649), which is dedicated to Torcigliani. During the course of his lengthy dedication (following folio 6, pages are unnumbered), signed on 29 September 1649, Querini mentions some of Torcigliani's friends—including Badoaro and Giovanni and Antonio Grimani, owners of the Teatro SS. Giovanni e Paolo, as well as Girolamo Lando, a Venetian nobleman heavily involved in the gestation of another Venetian theater, the Teatro Novissimo (see Glixon and Glixon, *Business,* pp. 78–80, 85–88). During the course of a lengthy passage in praise of Torcigliani's writings in various genres, Querini unexpectedly mentions Monteverdi's opinion of him, indicating clearly that his poetry had been set by the great master, now deceased (fol. 3): "Ma dove rimaneansi quelle sue brillantissime gratie, lequali sì mirabilmente campeggiano nell'habito della musica? Il divino Claudio Monteverde soleva dire; benché maestro unico delle harmonie; che dalle medesime n'apparava egli le più recondite finezze del canto, e che 'l canto pure, cui dava loro, non era altramenti un darlo, ma un restituirlo: imperciocché le note, delle quali vestivale, erano tutte levate dale viscere di quello spirito harmonico, che insitamente le informa, e che dentro di quelle odesi tacitamente a cantare da chiunque ben lo ascolta coll'attentione dell'anima." Rather than adding his music, according to Querini, when Monteverdi set Torcigliani's poetry he was restoring its own innate music. Querini then touches on Torcigliani's dramatic writings: "O se 'l suo dramatico socco venisse giammai a passeggiare sopra le scene, so ben'io, che gli affetti necessitate a seguitare i moti di quello, confesserebbono all'hora di non haver mai più sentita sì gagliarda, ma ne sì dolce tentatione al lor cuore. E non le saranno eternamente debitrici le muse? Non riconosceranno dalla sua richissima vena i loro aumenti più nobili; mentre fra per l'accennate eccellentie, e per quelle ancora delle sue stupende, e quasi, non che impareggiabili, impossibili foggie di verseggiare, vedonsi entro di quella così ampliati i confini del proprio imperio? Siamene grande, e chiara testimoniatrice la sua aurora fra le Nereidi . . ." Finally, in an extended passage directly relevant to the absence of a printed libretto for *Le nozze d'E-nea,* Querini attempts to counter Torcigliani's disinclination to publish his works: "Ma quando o mio Signor Torcigliani, quando vedremo manifestate alle genti; le divinità de' suoi fogli? Permeterà dunque, che le sue compositioni, quasi notturne cerimonie d'Isside, rimangano sempre involte fra l'ombre, senza comparer giammai alla luce?" And he bolsters his argument by citing the many authors who, though perhaps equally disinclined, nonetheless were convinced to publish by the promise of fame. Although it is not conclusive, Querini's text certainly strengthens the attribution of the text of Monteverdi's penultimate opera to Torcigliani. For further on

much applauded work—though Torcigliani expects that his admittedly inferior effort will seem even weaker when so directly juxtaposed with Badoaro's (see Appendix 2 [b]).[24]

Nozze is deliberately constructed to resemble *Ritorno* in many particulars, particulars that distinguish both librettos from contemporary Venetian practice. It too is epic in subject, based on the *Aeneid* as its model, *Ritorno,* was on the *Odyssey;* moreover, taking advantage of an Aristotelian expedient, it too is subtitled "tragedia di lieto fine."[25] Accordingly, it likewise is in five rather than the more typical three acts, and makes unusually extensive use of choral commentaries. But whereas all of these similarities might be regarded as generic—the result of a shared commitment to following the "rules" of tragedy—there is one similarity that cannot be so understood.

The author of *Nozze* specifically describes his search for a parallel to one of the most memorable characters in *Ritorno,* the parasite Iro. (This explicit instance of modeling makes others all the more likely.) The poet found Iro's successor—or thought he did—in Numanus, squire of Aeneas's rival Turnus, although in portraying Virgil's "strong man" as a *persona giocosa* he admits to having been forced to diverge somewhat from his literary source, something his model, Badoaro, had not done. As Torcigliani apologetically explains, he sought to introduce a comic character because he knew that many spectators preferred jokes to seriousness, which was evident from the delight that greeted Monteverdi's Iro; and he settled upon Numanus because he could not find a more suitable candidate in Virgil (see Appendix 2 [l]). Whether or not he actually succeeded in imitating Iro (the question is explored later), his intention is straightforward enough: he wanted his work to enjoy the same success as Badoaro's.

This said, the most significant link between the libretto of *Nozze* and its model, and the one that surely inspired the emulation, is that it was written for the same composer, and just as carefully and consciously designed to please him. Like Badoaro before him, Torcigliani goes out of his way to offer us a view of Monteverdi's role in the shaping of the libretto, revealing at the same time his own understanding of the composer's special gifts. To begin with, he says, he avoided abstruse thoughts and concepts, concentrating

Torcigliani, see Edoardo Taddeo, "La cetra e l'arpa: Studio su Michelangelo Torcigliani," *Studi secenteschi* 34 (1992): 3–60; idem, "Torcigliani e Delfino, patriarca atomista," ibid. 40 (1999): 83–95; and Michelangelo Torcigliani, *Echo cortese o vero resposte date da più, e diversi Signori a M. A. T. con altre Lettere ecc. publicate da Salvestro Torcigliani suo fratello* (Lucca: S. Marescandoli, 1680); idem, *Echo cortese parte seconda con l'Iride posthuma o vero veri residui di diversi componimenti di M. A. T. publicati . . .* (Lucca: Marescandoli, 1681); and idem, *Echo cortese parte terza con la parte seconda dell'Iride posthuma* (Lucca: I Paci, 1683).

24. Extensive excerpts from Torcigliani's letter are given in Appendix 2. The full text is transcribed in Maria Paola Sevieri, *Le nozze d'Enea con Lavinia* (Recco: De Ferrari, 1997), 94–99; it is transcribed as well as translated by Tim Carter in *Composing Opera: From Dafne to Ulisse Errante*, ed. Tim Carter and Zygmunt M. Szweykowski (Kraków: Musica Iagellonica Katedra Historii i Teorii Muzyki Uniwersytetu Jagiellońskiego, 1994), 147–79. A facsimile of Badoaro's preface to *Ulisse errante* is available in Alessandra Chiarelli and Angelo Pompilio, *"Or vaghi or fieri": Cenni di poetica nei libretti veneziani (circa 1640–1740)* (Bologna: CLUEB, 2004), 123–27.

25. For the significance of the designation "tragedia di lieto fine," see *OSV,* 41–42. It is discussed further in Chap. 5 below.

instead on the affections, in deference to Monteverdi's wishes. At a later stage, in order to appeal to the composer's taste for clarity of expression—evidently after having submitted a draft to him as his predecessor had done—he changed and omitted many things he had originally included (see Appendix 2 [n]). Even so, like Badoaro, he feared that his libretto was unworthy of such a great man and that the musical setting would only emphasize the infinite disparity between poet and composer (see Appendix 2 [b]). In the end, however, he admits that he need not have worried. Monteverdi had covered the weaknesses of the libretto with his glorious music, once more confirming his preeminence (see Appendix 2 [u]). And, he concludes, theatrical music will forever be in Monteverdi's debt for having been restored to a state more perfect than it ever was, even in ancient Greece (see Appendix 2 [v]). Unlike *Ritorno,* whose success is amply documented, we know nothing about the public response to *Nozze.* It is clear, however, that by imitating his predecessor's efforts to cater to the composer's tastes, even going so far as to model his work directly on Badoaro's, Torcigliani did his best to ensure a similar reception.

Monteverdi's final Venetian opera, *L'incoronazione di Poppea,* was certainly the most successful of the three. It was revived more than once in later years, probably in Venice as well as Naples, and perhaps even Paris. Its librettist, Francesco Busenello, already with a pair of operatic texts to his credit, was far more skilled as a dramatist than the other two, and although he left no explicit indication of having molded his text to suit Monteverdi, he must have done so, since *Incoronazione* differs markedly from both Busenello's two previous librettos and his two later ones, all of them written for another composer, Cavalli.[26]

Notwithstanding the librettists' efforts, the composer found neither *Ritorno* nor *Incoronazione* precisely to his liking. This we can tell from his editing of the texts he was presented with, as I shall demonstrate in some detail in Chapter 7. Monteverdi's alterations to *Ritorno* in particular were nearly extensive enough to justify Badoaro's claim that he failed to recognize his drama in the theater—though there may have been a wry subtext behind the seemingly jocular modesty of his remark.[27] But whatever its shortcomings as an operatic text, Badoaro's libretto did challenge Monteverdi in a particularly powerful way, not in any individual aspect of the text but in its subject matter. In choosing to cast this particular portion of the *Odyssey*—the tale of Ulysses' return to his homeland to reclaim his wife and kingdom from the Suitors—as a libretto for Monteverdi, Badoaro enlisted rhetoric, example, and metaphor in his cause.

---

26. Busenello's other librettos were *Gli amori di Apollo e Dafne* (1640), *La Didone* (1641), *La prosperità infelice di Giulio Cesare dittatore* (1646), and *La Statira* (1656), all published in *Delle hore ociose* (Venice: Giuliani, 1656). Unlike the *Incoronazione* scores, those of *La Didone, Apollo,* and *Statira* do not differ substantially from Busenello's printed text. This suggests not only that Cavalli's editorial interventions were comparatively minimal, but that Busenello's printed texts—presumably including *Incoronazione*—were essentially those he submitted to the composer. Cavalli's editing of *La Didone* is discussed in Chap. 3.

27. As far as *Nozze* is concerned, too, it is likely that Monteverdi did not leave the text unedited in "covering its weaknesses with his glorious music." This point is discussed in Chap. 5.

Indeed, we recall the librettist's avowed aim of luring the aged composer from his operatic retirement, and the terms in which he expressed it—comparing Monteverdi's real solar heat to painted imitations, and urging him to reveal the true nature of dramatic music, which was not understood by other composers. In this context it is certainly tempting to read a personal meaning into Ulisse's speech at the end of act 3, in his great scene of confrontation with the Suitors. They have failed in their efforts to draw his bow and win his wife. Now the hero, still disguised as an old man, picks up the weapon and with feigned modesty challenges the upstarts, as he begins to reclaim his domain:

Gioventù superba,	Proud youth
Sempre valor non serba	is not always valorous
Come vecchiezza humile	just as humble age
Ad'ogn'hor non è vile.	is not always despicable.
Regina, in queste membra	Queen, in these limbs
Tengo un'alma sì ardita	I hide a soul so bold
Ch'a la prova m'invita.	that it urges me to the trial.
Non perché poi vincendo	Not because in winning
Chiedessi in guiderdon bellezze e regni,	I would ask beauties and kingdoms as reward
Che Fortuna, et etade	since fortune and age
Mi vieta il prender sì gran ricchezze,	prevent me from accepting such great riches,
Mi contende il goder sì gran beltade.	forbid me to enjoy such great beauty.
Il giusto non eccedo.	I will not exceed what is right.
Rinoncio il premio, e la fatica io chiedo.	I renounce the prize and ask only for the effort.[28]

Can we not hear Monteverdi's own voice in these words—the old man, returned after a long absence to reclaim his domain, the operatic stage, from the younger composers, his cocky would-be usurpers ("gioventù superba")?

Monteverdi's contemporaries surely could; the identification of the composer with the ancient Greek hero finds explicit expression in a sonnet written on the occasion of the performances of *Il ritorno d'Ulisse* in Bologna in 1640.[29] Bearing the rubric "Per l'Ulisse, opera musicale del Sig. Claudio Monteverdi," the sonnet concludes with the following sestet:

A tender l'arco arma d'Ulisse intatta	To bend Ulisse's unyielding bow
Mentr'ei l'incurva a sostener lo scettro,	while he holds it fast to maintain his scepter
Proci, la vostra man non ben s'adatta.	is beyond your hand, o Suitors.

---

28. Ironically, perhaps, this passage is one of those omitted from Monteverdi's setting.

29. The sonnet, signed Ber[?] Mar[?], appears in *Le glorie della musica*, 6. For the full text, see Appendix 8, B. 4.

Claudio a cui ride il lauro, a cui l'elettro	Claudio, on whom the laurel smiles, on whom
Sudan le pioppe, e i pini, oggi non tratta	poplars and pines shower their amber resin, today
Alcuno eguale a voi l'arco del plettro.	you have no peer in stretching the bow of the plectrum.

In returning to the stage in a blaze of glory after a silence of more than "quattro lustri," with *Il ritorno d'Ulisse*, then *Le nozze d'Enea*, and finally *L'incoronazione di Poppea*, Monteverdi reclaimed his birthright, reasserting his *padronanza* in the field of opera, not as a memory from decades past, but in the present and for the future.

The Myth of Venice

A Venetian audience of the early 1640s had reason to perceive a general connection between *Ritorno* and *Nozze*. It would have recognized both operas as epic subjects. Within the brief history of opera in Venice thus far, this was unusual: before *Ritorno*, all the operas presented on stage had been mythological pastorals. But *Ritorno* was based on the *Odyssey*, and *Nozze* was based on the *Aeneid*, Virgil's imitation of the Homeric epic. The link between the two librettos is closer still. As we have already noted, the author of *Nozze* had Badoaro's *Ritorno* firmly and specifically in mind when he wrote his text.

The similarities between the two librettos are indeed striking (I shall discuss them at length later). In addition to scouring his source for a parallel to Iro, the librettist of *Nozze* modeled other characters as well as the overall structure of his libretto on those of his predecessor. In both operas the hero is first seen landing from the sea, to be greeted by a chorus of Nereids; more substantially, both heroes have sons, prominent protagonists in the action and symbolic of future generations. And the resolution of both plots is engineered by Jove, who settles a dispute between Venus and Juno.[30]

But *Nozze* was more than merely an imitation of *Ritorno*. It was a literal sequel to it, purposefully continuing its grand narrative in the same way that the *Aeneid* had taken up where the Homeric epic had left off, and both sequences pointed ahead to a world of the future.[31] The implications of the sequential relationship between the librettos are spelled out in the final scene of *Nozze*, in a speech by Hymen, the god of marriage (given below). Here is how the scene is described in the printed scenario:

---

30. It may be worth noting that the landing of both protagonists after a sea voyage and the resolution of both plots in Giove's realm would have allowed for the use of the same sets in the two productions. Sevieri, *Le nozze*, 54, lists a number of other parallels. Some of them merely echo parallels in the sources, while others are not particularly convincing. The Silvia–Elminio pair, for instance, has little relationship to Eurimaco–Melanto.

31. Badoaro's *Ulisse errante* of 1645 was actually a prequel to his *Ritorno*. For aesthetic theories expounded there, see below, Chap. 5.

Following the marriage [of Enea and Lavinia], Hymen takes the opportunity of recounting the origin and greatness of Rome, and then the birth of our Venice, certainly an event of no less significance, since this most noble city began at the time when Rome fell under the yoke of the Barbarians, who, by invading Italy, forced many of her inhabitants to take refuge in these lagoons in order to escape their fury; and in this way they founded the city . . . which through the valor of our fathers attained the greatness for which we admire her now. And may it please God that she conserve herself, as by means of sustaining Virtue, no doubt she will. (Appendix 2 [t])

What we have here, in its essential form, is an explicit retelling of the genealogical myth of Venice, a sequence of events that was fundamental to the way Venetians viewed themselves and their history. This particular strand, which had been woven over the course of previous centuries, saw the Serenissima as the culmination of a historical line running from the fall of Troy through the foundation, rise, and fall of Rome. According to the myth, the union established by Aeneas with the Latins developed into the Rome of history, then the Republic, which matured into the full glory of empire only to succumb to inevitable decline. Once mighty Rome fell to the invading barbarian hordes, and from the ruin of one great historical epoch there arose a new, divinely ordained republic founded in Christian liberty. The successor to the pagan state created by Aeneas was the Republic of St. Mark, which, favored by God, was destined to surpass Rome in power and vastness of dominion, glory, and abundance. Venice, according to this myth, was the successor to ancient Rome, the culmination of a long history that led from the fall of Troy to the emergence of the Serenissima. Ulysses' return to his homeland from Troy and Aeneas's marriage to Lavinia can both be readily viewed as steps on the way to the founding of Venice.[32]

Although novel in 1640–41, neither this subject matter nor its disposition across two separate librettos is unique among Venetian operas of this period. The same legendary sequence provided the thematic material for another pair of librettos just slightly later than those being considered here: *La finta pazza* (1641) and *La finta savia* (1643), both by the same author, Giulio Strozzi, though set by different composers and played in different theaters. While our two works are linked clearly enough but only by implication, the latter two are explicitly related to one another as well as to the first stages of the myth of Venice. In the scenario to *La finta pazza*, the author concludes his description of act 1, scene 4 with a direct reference to the myth: "Venus, learning that Fate decrees that Troy

---

32. There were actually two versions of the myth, both originating in Troy. In the first version, the founding of Venice is parallel to the founding of Rome: Antenor and Aeneas both leave Troy, the former to found Venice, the latter Rome. For the role of Troy in the mythic foundation of Venice, see Edward Muir, *Civic Ritual in Renaissance Venice* (Princeton: Princeton University Press, 1981), 65–74; Patricia Fortini Brown, *Venice and Antiquity: The Venetian Sense of the Past* (New Haven and London: Yale University Press, 1996), 30–33, 70–74, et passim; and Craig Kallendorf, *Virgil and the Myth of Venice: Books and Readers in the Italian Renaissance* (Oxford: Oxford University Press, 1999), 26–27. See also *OSV*, chap. 5.

will eventually go down in flames, consoles herself, saying that she is justified in being proud of the outcome, that from Trojan blood will emerge the Romans and the glorious Venetians." And, as Venus says, when the time comes: "I know the fate of Asia requires that I be conquered in the end, but destiny will make amends for the great sorrow of my losses. Venetian and Roman will not from the Greek Achilles spring, but from good Trojan blood: and thus I have good reason to be proud."[33]

Strozzi's preface to *La finta savia,* the second work, spells out its sequential relationship to the first: "*La finta pazza* contains a Greek story, *La finta savia* a Latin one; the former leads toward the destruction of Troy, the latter refers to the future founding of Rome." The author then promises a third work, to be called *Romolo e Remo,* which will round out the sequence: "[These two poems], in the coming years, God willing, we are preparing to complete. . . . The real name of the *finta savia* was Anthusa . . . which was the third name of the city of Rome. . . . The second name of Rome was Amaryllis, drawn from the loves of Ilia and Mars, which will be expounded by me in the future drama of *Romolo e Remo.*"[34]

This third work was indeed produced two years later (at SS. Giovanni e Paolo). It provided Strozzi with the occasion for completing his narration of the myth begun with *La finta pazza* and explaining the purpose of his project as a whole. He did this in the prologue and final scene of the work, the action of which he describes in the scenario. In the prologue "Aeneas descends on the chariot of his mother, Venus, and seeing Fame drowsy among the clouds, he invites her to broadcast for many centuries the works of his glorious descendants for the future founding of Rome, of whose valor the Most Serene Republic of Venice has remained the eternal heir."[35] And in the final scene, Numitore, Flora, Remo, and Ilia "come together to pray to heaven for their prosperity and invite their people, who were of noble Trojan blood, as the Venetians still are, to applaud their deeds."[36]

---

33. "Venere, ancorché sappia, che per decreto del Fato, deva Troia finalmente andar in cenere, si consola, e dice, d'haver giusta, che doveranno fare dal sangue Troiano, i Romani, ed i Veneti popoli tanto gloriosi . . ." (Giulio Strozzi, *La finta pazza* [Venice: Surian, 14 January 1641], scenario). "So, ch'il Fato d'Asia vuol, / ch'io rimanga vinta alfin, / ma ristora il grande mal / delle perdite mie anco il destin. / Deve il Veneto, e 'l Roman / non d'Achille Greco uscir, / ma dal buon sangue Troian: / onde ho giusta cagion d'insuperbir" (*La finta pazza,* 1.4).

34. "Questi Drami [*La finta pazza* and *La finta savia*] son Poemi imperfetti: e l'uno contiene una Historia Greca, e l'altro una Latina: L'uno mira alla distruttione di Troia, l'altro accenna la futura fondatione di Roma, che negli anni venture, a Dio piacendo, andiamo apparecchiando. . . . Il vero nome della Finta Savia fu Anthusa, che noi per leggiadria diverso, habbiamo in Aretusa cangiato: e 'l nome di Anthusa fu il terzo nome della città di Roma. . . . Il secondo nome di Roma era d'Amarillide tratto dagli Amori d'Ilia, e di Marte, che nel futuro Drama di Romolo, e di Remo saranno da me spiegati" (Giulio Strozzi, *La finta savia* [Venice: Leni e Vecellio, 1 January 1643]; Afterword, p. 188).

35. "Scende Enea sul carro di Venere sua Madre, e veduta la Fama sonnacchiosa tra le nugole l'invita a portar' intorno per molti secoli l'opre de' suoi gloriosi Nipoti per la futura fondatione di Roma, del cui valore è rimasta eterna herede la Serenissima Republica di Venetia" (Giulio Strozzi, *Romolo e Remo* [Venice: Surian, 1645], scenario, p. 8).

36. "Vengono a cose stabilite a pregar il Cielo per le loro prosperità, ed invitano i lor Popoli ch'erano del nobil sangue Troiano, come sono i Veneti ancora, ad applaudere alle lor'Opre (*Romolo e Remo,* scenario, p. 36).

La finta pazza, La finta savia, and *Il Romolo e Remo,* three librettos recounting three successive stages of the genealogical myth of Venice, were explicitly conceived as a trilogy by their patriotic author. Strozzi would have been heavily invested in dramatizing the myth of Venice on stage. As the author of the encomiastic epic *Venetia edificata,* published in 1624, the most recent and elaborate retelling of the myth, Strozzi was publicly committed to assuring that it would be kept alive for centuries to come. His poem, in twenty-four cantos, which was republished numerous times during the course of the century, assumed a kind of biblical resonance in Venetian political circles of this time.

Although the relationship between *Ritorno* and *Nozze* may not have been planned as deliberately as that among Strozzi's works, it *was* planned and it is certainly no less compelling.[37] Moreover, by its very existence Strozzi's trilogy suggests possibilities for interpreting Monteverdi's last opera, *Incoronazione,* as the completion of an analogous trilogy. For *Incoronazione* can indeed be seen as depicting a third stage of the prehistory of Venice: the moral weakening of the Roman Empire that left it prey to barbarian invasion. We might paraphrase Strozzi's description of his trilogy to describe Monteverdi's: *Ritorno* contains a Greek story, *Nozze* a Latin one; the one follows from the destruction of Troy, the other deals with the founding of Rome; a third opera will tell of the destruction of Rome, whose greatness will live once again in the Most Serene Republic of Venice. Such a reading of *Incoronazione,* what we might call a political reading, would be a step toward resolving the vexing issue of interpretation raised by the problematic work. It would explain the unpalatable victory of sensual passion and raw ambition over reason and morality as a justification for the founding of Venice.[38]

To be sure, the political program for *Ritorno,* the first of the operas, is not explicit—we have no printed libretto or scenario that lays it out. Nor does the text itself contain any pointed references to Venice. But that of *Nozze* could not be clearer. In addition to the passage already quoted from the author's preface to the scenario, we have his description of the final scene: "Hymen . . . with Venus and Juno . . . unites the happy couple, foretelling from such a marriage the greatness of Rome, and the birth and marvels of the city of Venice. Here the opera ends."[39] One of the surviving manuscript librettos even

---

37. The first member of Strozzi's trilogy was performed at the Teatro Novissimo, the second and third at SS. Giovanni e Paolo. This affirms the connection between the two theaters and also the possibility that all three works need not have been performed at the same theater to be perceived as a group (though Monteverdi's were). On the connections between the Novissimo and SS. Giovanni e Paolo, see Glixon and Glixon, *Business,* chap. 4, esp. pp. 127–33.

38. An interpretation I originally proposed in Ellen Rosand, "Seneca and the Interpretation of *L'incoronazione di Poppea,*" *JAMS* 38 (1985): 34–71.

39. "Sopragiunge Latino, ed accogliendo Enea le riconferma la figliuola per moglie, eccitando li Troiani e Latini ad invocar Himeneo, il quale con Venere e Giunone comparendo congiunge li Sposi felici presagiendo da tal maritaggio le grandezze di Roma e la nascita e maraviglie della Città di Venetia. Qui restando terminata l'opera" (*Le nozze d'Enea,* Argomento e scenario, p. 36).

provides us with the text of Hymen's speech: "From this lofty and beautiful marriage / I see with the passing years / a city proudly raise its wings to the stars. / But though the august empire will suffer / under the unjust yoke of barbarians, / it will have a fortunate end, / whereby, phoenix-like, / from the fire, in water born, / a city happy and virgin will emerge. / And though all things are mortal in the end, / she alone is perpetual and immortal, / her honors of pure faith."[40]

So the full and explicit articulation of the myth of Venice in *Nozze* legitimizes in retrospect the interpretation of Badoaro's work as the first part of a Troy–Rome narrative, and in prospect that of *Incoronazione* as the third.[41] Does the connection to *Incoronazione* seem rather more of a reach? Consider another tale of Roman decadence published at just this time, *L'imperatrice ambiziosa,* a novel about Agrippina, Poppaea's mother-in-law, written by Federico Malipiero, a compatriot and literary colleague of all three of Monteverdi's librettists (as well as Strozzi). Expounding upon the demise of the depraved Empress Agrippina, the author extracts the following lesson: "This was the greatness of a woman, incomparable in every way. Thus did she fall from supreme eminence to the darkest depths because the higher mortals rise, the more they are subject to uncertainty. Empires are transformed in a flash, like human happiness, which can collapse and be extinguished in a single moment. Often the tombs of one kingdom have become the cradles of another, and from the ruins of a fallen republic have arisen the magnificence of a new one."[42] Inspired by the fate of Agrippina, Malipiero's words could

---

40. "Da l'alte nozze e belle, / Qual veggio, in girar d'anni, / Città sino alle stelle / Erger superba i vanni. / Ma che del mondo avrà l'impero augusto, / Da sotto il giogo in fin, barbaro ingiusto, / Caduta fortunata, / Onde, qual suol fenice, / Dal rogo in acqua nata, / Sorga città felice, / Vergine, e dove è tutto al fin mortale, / Ella sola perpetua ed immortale, / Di pura fe' gli onori." The text is in libretto I-Vmc 564 (no. 5 in Table 4 below, Chap. 3).

41. Admittedly, there is no evidence that Busenello considered his *Incoronazione* the final limb of a trilogy, begun with *Ritorno;* but he may have thought of it in connection with his own Virgilian work—*Didone* (*Aeneid,* bk. 4)—performed the previous season (cf. Table 1, below). He wrote a second Virgilian libretto, *Enea nell'inferno,* based on an episode from Book 6 of the *Aeneid.* Though it was never set to music, or published, it is in effect a sequel to *La Didone* (and perhaps also a prequel to *Incoronazione* as well as to *Giulio Cesare*). That Busenello thought of his own *Enea,* at least, within the context of the myth of Venice is indicated by the dialogue between Anchise's ghost and Enea in the final scene. Having heard his father's prediction of his marriage to Lavinia and the founding of the Empire, Enea asks: "E sarà qui finita / La nostra linea, o padre?" to which Anchise responds: "No, sorgerà più gloriosa, e fia / Nell'Adria un nuovo mondo in cerchio augusto / Dalla man degli dei su l'onde eretto. / Quivi i Veneti eroi, togata gente, / Dilateranno dalle stelle istesse / L'accarezzato e sempre giusto impero." Enea contínues, asking: "E come bellicoso e come grande / S'innalzerà quel riverito nome?" and Anchise answers: "volerà dirempetto al sol nascente / Un alto leone; / Stringerà l'Ellesponto / Con forza militare; / Ma con le glorie illustri, / Da molti invidiate, / Dilaterollo e in poco volger d'anni / Debellerà, soggiogherà i tiranni." Enea then bows in reverence before the Venetian heroes mentioned by Anchise, because "di Venetia brama e venerar e vagheggiar gli eroi" (Arthur Livingston, *La vita veneziana nelle opere di Gian Francesco Busenello* [Venice: V. Callegari, 1913], 207–208). One copy of the manuscript libretto of *Enea nell'inferno* is in I-Vnm It. IX, 493 (= 6660). Badoaro, too, may have conceived of his own three librettos—*Il ritorno d'Ulisse* (1640), *Ulisse errante* (1644), and *Helena rapita* (1653)—as a trilogy, but one written in reverse order.

42. "Queste dunque descritte fur le grandezze d'una Donna inarivabile in tutte le cose. Così trabboccò dall'eminenza al profondo, perché quanto più le mortali cose sono ellevate, tanto più sono all'incertezza assoggettate.

serve equally well for her son, Nero. And they spell out the implied moral of the coronation of Poppaea as a step in the proleptic unfolding of the myth of Venice.

Any Venetian audience could be counted on to supply the culmination of that mythic history: the magnificent Republic itself—whose glory was nowhere more in evidence in 1643 than in its proliferating opera houses. The myth was literally featured on Venetian stages during the first decade of operatic activity. A glance at the repertory of this period (Table 1) reveals that a rather large proportion of operas was based on Homeric and Virgilian themes. *Le nozze di Teti e di Peleo* (1639) is concerned with the prehistory of the Trojan War, the marriage of the parents of Achilles; *La finta pazza* (1641) follows that hero's adventures in Skyros, where he has been sent by his mother to protect him from being killed at Troy. Other operas concerned the aftermath of the war: *Il ritorno d'Ulisse* (1640), as we have seen, and *Ulisse errante* (1644) describe Ulysses' travels and his efforts to return home; *La Didone* and *Le nozze d'Enea* (both 1641) together present successive stages in Aeneas's journey from Troy to Rome (the former following him as far as Carthage, the latter taking up his story as he lands in Rome).[43] In fact, in one opera season (1641), an enthusiastic tourist could have taken in four distinct stages of the genealogical myth in three different theaters; *La finta pazza* at the Novissimo, *Il ritorno d'Ulisse* at SS. Giovanni e Paolo, *La Didone* at S. Cassiano, and later in the season *Le nozze d'Enea*, once again at SS. Giovanni e Paolo. Only one of the five operas performed in that season—Ferrari's *La ninfa avara* at S. Moisè—did not participate in the story. The librettos set by Monteverdi were thus very much in the cultural mainstream of Venetian opera at the time. And it is hardly a coincidence that all three of them—along with the second and third of Strozzi's texts—were performed at the Grimani theater of SS. Giovanni e Paolo, the theater that, along with the Novissimo, was most obviously associated with efforts to promulgate the myth of Venice during this period.[44]

One may wonder about the coherence of Monteverdi's trilogy, in view of the fact that its constituent librettos are by different authors. But the three librettists were known to each other and part of a single, coherent intellectual milieu. Two of them, Badoaro and Busenello, were lifelong friends, who maintained an active and mutually flattering

Gli imperi si mutano a momenti, come la felicità humana traccolla, e fornisce in un punto. Le tombe spesso d'un regno fur le culle d'un altro, e sopra le rovine d'una caduta Republica insorsero le magnificenze d'una novella." Federico Malipiero, *L'imperatrice ambiziosa* (Venice: Surian, 1642), 184.

43. In referring to the ghosts of Priam, Anchise, Ettore, and Creusa in the prologue, the scenario of *Le nozze* invokes memories of an earlier aspect of Enea's story, related in the contemporary (and competing) *Didone* (Argomento e scenario, p. 20; Sevieri, *Le nozze*, 37). Torcigliani acknowledges the melancholy effect of beginning his *Nozze* with ghosts, but justifies it as enhancing the contrast with the happy ending ("E se paresse che con quest'ombre il principio fosse malinconico, io dico, che forse non sta male in questo modo per far tanto maggior il passaggio all'allegrezza del fine"). On the term "malinconico," see below, Chap. 3, n. 22.

44. The Grimani theater was the largest and most spectacular in Venice. It also boasted the longest continuous tradition of operatic performances of the seventeenth century. In a letter dated January 1656, presenting his most recent libretto, *La Statira*, to Giovanni Grimani, owner of SS. Giovanni e Paolo, Busenello thanks him for having welcomed his "melodrammi" for the past thirteen years (see Livingston, *Busenello*, 370).

TABLE I
Venetian Opera Chronology, 1637–1645

1637

S. Cassiano	*Andromeda,* Ferrari/Manelli

1638

S. Cassiano	*La maga fulminata,* Ferrari/Manelli

1639

S. Cassiano	*Le nozze di Teti e di Peleo,* Persiani/Cavalli
SS. Giovanni e Paolo	*La Delia,* Strozzi/Manelli
	L'Armida, Ferrari/Ferrari

1640

S. Cassiano	*Gli amori d'Apollo,* Busenello/Cavalli
SS. Giovanni e Paolo	*L'Adone,* Vendramin/Manelli
	Il ritorno d'Ulisse, Badoaro/Monteverdi
S. Moisè	*L'Arianna,* Rinuccini/Monteverdi
	Il pastor regio, Ferrari/Ferrari

1641

S. Cassiano	*La Didone,* Busenello/Cavalli
SS. Giovanni e Paolo	*Il ritorno d'Ulisse,* Badoaro/Monteverdi
	Le nozze d'Enea e Lavinia, Torcigliani/Monteverdi
S. Moisè	*La ninfa avara,* Ferrari/Ferrari
Novissimo	*La finta pazza,* Strozzi/Sacrati

1642

S. Cassiano	*La virtù de' strali d'amore,* Faustini/Cavalli
SS. Giovanni e Paolo	*Il Narciso ed Ecco immortalati,* Persiani/Marazzoli
	Gli amori di Giasone, Persiani/Marazzoli
S. Moisè	*L'amore innamorato,* Fusconi/Cavalli
	Il Sidonio e Dorisbe, Melosio/Fontei
Novissimo	*Il Bellerofonte,* Nolfi/Sacrati
	L'Alcate, Tirabosco/Manelli

1643

S. Cassiano	*L'Egisto,* Faustini/Cavalli
SS. Giovanni e Paolo	*L'incoronazione di Poppea,* Busenello/Monteverdi

TABLE I *(continued)*

Novissimo	*La finta savia*, Strozzi/Various
	La Venere gelosa, Bartolini/Sacrati

1644

S. Cassiano	*L'Ormindo*, Faustini/Cavalli
SS. Giovanni e Paolo	*Il prencipe giardiniero*, Ferrari/Ferrari
	L'Ulisse errante, Badoaro/Sacrati
Novissimo	*La Deidamia*, Herrico/Cavalli?

1645

S. Cassiano	*La Doriclea*, Faustini/Cavalli
	Il Titone, Faustini/Cavalli
SS. Giovanni e Paolo	*Il Bellerofonte*, Nolfi/Sacrati
	Il Romolo e Remo, Strozzi/Cavalli?
Novissimo	*Ercole in Lidia*, Bisaccioni/Rovetta

correspondence over more than thirty years.[45] Badoaro was also a friend of Torcigliani, who repeatedly refers to him as such, though without mentioning his name, in his preface to the scenario of *Nozze*.[46] Among their more formal links, all three men were members of the most important literary academy in Venice: the Accademia degli Incogniti—an academy that Giulio Strozzi had helped to found, and for which his *Venetia edificata* was a kind of gospel.[47]

---

45. Their poems to one another, among them some in Venetian dialect, appear in a number of contemporary manuscripts, especially I-Vmc Cod. Cicogna 1082. These include a lengthy tribute by Busenello on Badoaro's death (pp. 59–71)—seventeen stanzas of thirteen verses each. Several of their reciprocal poems are given in Livingston, *Busenello*, 119–22. It is appealing to imagine that, like Badoaro and Torcigliani, in Michelassi's view, the two friends might have included the aesthetics of the opera libretto among the topics they discussed.

46. He refers several times to *Il ritorno d'Ulisse* as the work of "our most illustrious and most virtuous friend" (nostro illustrissimo e virtuosissimo amico) and to "him whom I love so much" (mi sarei volontieri rimaso ad applauder cogli altri [in the audience] a chi tanto amo [Badoaro], le cui lodi più mi piacciono delle mie perché sono più meritate) (scenario preface, Appendix 2 [b]).

47. Both Busenello and Torcigliani were publicly linked to the Incogniti. Their biographies are included among those of the forty most illustrious members in *Le glorie degli Incogniti* (Venice: Valvasense, 1647), and Torcigliani is identified as a member in Badoaro's preface to *Ulisse errante* (addressed to "Signor Michel'angelo Torcigliani, l'Assicurato Academico Incognito"). As for Badoaro, his academic affiliation is revealed in his second libretto, *Ulisse errante*, ascribed on its title page to L'Academico Incognito. As I show in Chap. 3, the preface to that work makes it clear that it is by the same author as *Il ritorno d'Ulisse* ("Feci già molti anni rappresentare il ritorno d'Ulisse in Patria"). Although Badoaro is listed as the author in many of the manuscript copies of the *Ritorno* libretto, those attributions are not necessarily trustworthy (see Chap. 3). But his authorship of *Ritorno* (and therefore *Ulisse errante*) is confirmed by a sonnet addressed to him in the Bologna volume *Le glorie della musica* ("Per l'Ulisse, Drama dell'Illus.mo Sig.

The importance of the Incogniti for opera has been extensively documented over the past several decades.[48] In brief, the academy comprised a group of mostly aristocratic writers united by libertine attitudes; they debated moral, political, and social issues at weekly meetings and in streams of publications—religious pamphlets, philosophical tracts, and novels. Their innumerable writings conveyed their commitment to the exploitation of history for political purposes. They investigated the lives of ancient rulers as models of good government, applicable to present-day circumstances. And they sought moral exempla in literature of the past, which they subjected to a variety of treatments, ranging from straightforward translations to freely embellished reinterpretations.

The writings of one particular member of the group, Federico Malipiero, are specially linked to our trilogy. We have already mentioned one of his books in connection with *Incoronazione, L'imperatrice ambiziosa,* a novelistic moral investigation of the life of the empress Agrippina. A similar volume, on the subject of Ulysses *(La peripezia d'Ulisse overo la casta Penelope)* is even more obviously connected to *Ritorno,* as we shall see. According to Malipiero's preface, his book was actually inspired by the opera. In this same period, he also produced translations of the *Iliad* and the *Odyssey,* a heavy task Malipiero justified by emphasizing Homer's unquestioned cultural significance for modern society.[49] Although it was published posthumously, and without an authorial

---

Giacomo Badoero, e Musica del Sig. Claudio Monteverdi"), 7, signed by one Clotildo Artemii (given in Appendix 8, B4). The two men Badoaro mentions as having requested that he write the *Ritorno* libretto, Pietro Loredano and Gasparo Malipiero, are not the more famous Incogniti Francesco Loredano and Federico Malipiero, but probably relatives (one of them the scene or costume designer). In addition to Giorgio Spini, *Ricerca dei libertini: La teoria dell'impostura delle religioni nel Seicento italiano* (Rome: Editrice universale, 1950; 2nd ed. Florence: La nuova Italia, 1983), there are several recent bibliographical sources on the Incogniti. They include: Agnès Morini, "Sous le signe de l'inconstance, la vie et l'oeuvre de Giovan Francesco Loredano (1606–61)" (Thèse de Doctorat d'État, University of Paris, 1994); Mario Infelise, "*Ex ignoto notus?* Note sul tipografo Sarzina e l'Accademia degli Incogniti," in *Libri, tipografi, biblioteche: Ricerche storiche dedicate a Luigi Balsamo,* ed. Istituto di Biblioteconomia e Paleografia (Florence: Olschki, 1997), 207–23; Monica Miato, *L'Accademia degli Incogniti di Giovan Francesco Loredan, Venezia (1630–1661)* (Florence: Olschki, 1998); Tiziana Menegatti, *Ex Ignoto Notus: Bibliografia delle opere a stampa del Principe degli Incogniti: Giovan Francesco Loredano* (Padua: Il Poligrafo, 2000); and Nina Cannizzaro, "Studies on Guido Casoni (1561–1642) and Venetian Academies" (Ph.D. diss. Harvard University, 2001).

48. The connection was first recognized by Lorenzo Bianconi and Thomas Walker, "Dalla *Finta pazza* alla *Veremonda:* Storie di Febiarmonici," *RIM* 10 (1975): 379–454, esp. 410–24. I explored it further in *OSV,* esp. chaps. 2–5. Most recently, Wendy Heller has extended the discussion to issues of gender and sexuality in *Emblems of Eloquence: Opera and Women's Voices in Seventeenth-Century Venice* (Berkeley and Los Angeles: University of California Press, 2003), esp. chap. 2.

49. "Omero è un essemplare da copia, di cui s'hanno servito tutti li andati, e serviransi tutti li viventi scrittori. Grande ma grave insieme è la lettura d'Omero. Bella ma utile ancora è la invenzione d'Omero. Io leggo Omero, come essemplare che mi precetta somma dottrina. Presi, e scelsi a trapportar Omero dal suo Greco nel nostro Toscano linguaggio, perche sperai non tanto di giovar a molti, che non intendono 'l Greco, ne il Latino, quanto d'imparar quelle cose (che per esser io civilmente nato) vò fiutandole, come cane da caccia faccia tra i boschi una lepre, ò una Dramma" (*L'Iliada d'Omero trapportata dalla Greca nella Toscana lingua da Federico Malipiero* [Venice: Baglioni, 1642], Lettore). On Malipiero, see also pp. 55–56 below.

preface, the *Odyssey* translation, too, seems also to have been influenced, if not inspired, by the opera.[50]

Beyond these specific connections, the Incogniti were particularly interested in opera, and many of them wrote librettos. They found in the ambiguous new genre—half music, half drama—an ideal arena for exploring their ideas about antiquity, politics, and morality. And an ideal agent of propaganda on behalf of Venice. Indeed, possibly the strongest bond linking the members of this group was their Venetian patriotism. All of their literary efforts were informed by a profound commitment to the welfare and fame of the Republic, a commitment that animates the political agenda of the trilogy written for Monteverdi.

A somewhat later, even more pointedly political trilogy is suggestive in this connection—this one for the spoken theater and based exclusively on Roman history, planned by the Incognito playwright Pietr'Angelo Zaguri. Following *La Messalina* (1656), which deals with the empress Messalina's adultery and death, and *Le gelosie politiche, e amorose* (1657), detailing Agrippina's efforts to gain the throne for Nero by engineering his marriage to Octavia, Zaguri's trilogy too was intended to conclude with the episode of Nero and Poppaea. As the author explained in a note to the reader of *Le gelosie politiche:* "Here I am, ready to confirm, with my second work, my weakness. Wait to see, with the continuation of the story, the cruelty of Nerone for the love of Poppea in a drama suited to your taste, if I can violate mine, disinclined as it is to such an exercise."[51] This third work was apparently never published, possibly never written, but the idea of a trilogy was clearly still in the air, an acknowledged formula for a sequence of theatrical entertainments designed to extract political lessons from historical models.

Although Monteverdi's trilogy may not have been initially intended toward such ends, its three parts are bound together by the shared cultural background and values of their librettists, which made a political interpretation all but inevitable. But we must not forget the most important link of all: their composer. Not only did Monteverdi set all three librettos to music, but the first two of them, at least—and arguably the third as well—were specifically designed to suit him. And if the three librettists did not always get things just right—as suggested by the many alterations and revisions, large and

---

50. Some of Malipiero's expansions of the Homeric text seem to take into account particular moments in the opera. See below, Chap. 5.

51. "Eccomi . . . a confermare con la seconda compositione le mie debolezze. . . . Attendi di vedere con il proseguimento dell'Historia la crudeltà di Nerone per gl'Amori di Popea in un Drama secondo il tuo genio, se però potrò violentar il mio, non inclinato a simil essercitio." Pietr'Angelo Zaguri, *Le gelosie politiche* (Venice: Pinelli, 1657), "A chi legge," pp. 7–8. On the political significance of Zaguri's trilogy, see Wendy Heller, "Tacitus Incognito: Opera as History in *L'incoronazione di Poppea*," *JAMS* 52 (1999): 39–96, esp. 59–62, and *Emblems*, 150–52. It is possible that Zaguri was not actually a member of the Incogniti, since his name does not appear in any of the standard membership lists, in *Le glorie degli Incogniti* or Girolamo Ghilini, *Teatro aperto d'huomini letterati* (Venice: Guerigli), both published in 1647. It could be that he became a member only after 1646, when his family bought their membership in the nobility, too late to be included in the lists. See Glixon and Glixon, *Business*, 110, n. 5.

small, which Monteverdi made to the texts, as detailed in the following pages—all three of them managed to provide the composer with characters and situations that challenged him to exercise the full range of his creative abilities as a musical dramatist. Thanks to the fortunate set of circumstances surrounding the emergence of public opera in Venice—the demand created by successful productions, the economic potential of theater and box ownership, and the vision of a group of patriotic writers who saw opera as a means of promoting the myth of Venice—an already great and famous composer gained a more resonant and monumental arena in which to demonstrate his art.

2

Discoveries and Reception

Scholarship

Monteverdi's *Ritorno d'Ulisse* and *Incoronazione di Poppea* are the best-known operas of the seventeenth century—those most thoroughly studied and most often performed. In fact, their discovery just over a century ago may have stimulated more sustained interest from both scholars and performers than any other individual works in the history of music. That interest has not abated to the present day. Every decade since their discovery has made its mark on the history of their scholarship, and on their performance.

Indeed, they have inspired a sequence of studies that parallels the development of musicology itself, both chronologically and nationally, attracting some of the main figures in the burgeoning discipline and exemplifying its evolving methodologies. Initially the province of the most important German scholars in the 1890s and opening years of the past century, they sparked the interest of the French in the 1910s and 1920s, and of the Italians in the 1930s and 1940s.[1] By the 1950s and 1960s, with the coming of age of Anglo-American musicology, *Ritorno* and *Incoronazione* had essentially become

---

1. The French could not resist pointing out that they were compensating for the lack of Italian interest in their own heritage. See Vincent d'Indy, preface to his edition of *Incoronazione* (1908) (Paris: Rouart, Lerolle, c. 1922): "the opera had remained ignored even—one might say, above all—in its country of origin." Cited in Jeremy Barlow, "The Revival of Monteverdi's Operas in the Twentieth Century," in *The Operas of Monteverdi*, ed. Nicholas John, English National Opera Guide 45 (London: John Calder, 1992), 193.

common international property, with German, Italian, English, and American scholars all making important contributions to their understanding.

Scholarship at every stage was and continues to be accompanied or stimulated by performances and/or editions, which likewise trace the development of performance practice over the course of the century. Indeed, *Ritorno* and *Incoronazione* stand as a barometer at the intersection of musicology and performance, a potent reminder of their interdependence. The lengthy roster of editors and performers of these works includes a remarkable array of distinguished composers—D'Indy, Dallapiccola, Krenek, Malipiero, Henze—their interest evidently piqued by what they perceived as creative spaces within them.[2]

Developing scholarship has also been characterized by the gradual uncovering of phantoms, the dismantling of a series of myths surrounding the works, some of them present from the beginning of their historiography, others accidental, even comical, accretions along the way. These include Badoaro as author of *Le nozze d'Enea,* the existence of a Viennese revival of *Ritorno* in the seventeenth century, an earlier version of *Ritorno* by Monteverdi (1630), and the presence of the composer's handwriting in the Venetian score of *Incoronazione.*[3]

❧

Monteverdi's last operas aroused curiosity in the early nineteenth century as part of the awakening interest in a composer whom German musicology's "Urvater" Ernst

---

2. If we consider those who "edited" or "arranged" *Orfeo,* the list is even longer. It includes Hindemith, Orff, Berio, and Maderna. See Barlow, "The Revival." The most recent "arrangement" of a Monteverdi opera, which is of necessity nearly a new work, is Alexander Goehr's *Arianna* (1994–95). Dallapiccola explained his attitude toward editing *Ritorno* in his essay, "Per una rappresentazione de *Il ritorno di Ulisse in patria* di Claudio Monteverdi," *Musica* 2 (1943): 121–36. He thought of his edition as a translation, and expected that like most translations, though appropriate for the time in which it was undertaken, it would not suit the future: "Il lavoro mio dev'essere considerato essenzialmente *pratico:* una *traduzione musicale* . . . come le traduzioni . . . hanno una vita limitata—perché più o meno rispecchiano il gusto della loro epoca—e, scomparendo, cedono il posto ad altre traduzioni più conformi al gusto delle nuove generazioni, così avviene, così deve avvenire per le traduzioni musicali" (pp. 32–33). Henze's edition has been characterized as "appropriazione produttiva" or "elaborazione" "di una grande opera della storia della musica da parte di un compositore moderno" (Hans-Klaus Jungheinrich, "Arrivi e partenze: Hans Werner Henze e la sua elaborazione del *Ritorno d'Ulisse in patria* di Monteverdi," in *Il ritorno d'Ulisse in patria,* program book, 50th Maggio Musicale [Florence: Cassa di Risparmio, 1987], 81).

3. These myths will be dismantled over the course of the following chapters. One (first proposed by Osthoff) that still survives in some of the literature is that Anna Renzi, the Venetian Ottavia in *L'incoronazione di Poppea,* also sang the role in Naples. Although it was put to rest by omission in, among other places, *NGO,* Carter, *Musical Theatre,* 294, leaves the question open. The most extensive recent treatment of Renzi, in Beth L. Glixon, "Private Lives of Public Women: Prima Donnas in Mid-Seventeenth-Century Venice," *ML* 76 (1995): 509–31, does not mention Renzi in connection with Naples, but she does cite evidence that the singer collaborated with Giovanni Battista Balbi in 1649 (pp. 516–17). Balbi was certainly involved in operatic productions in Naples in the early 1650s, but probably not until after *Incoronazione* had been produced there (see Nicola Michelassi, " 'Musici di fortuna' e 'pellegrini architetti': *La Finta pazza* tra Venezia e l'Europa," introduction to *La doppia Finta pazza: Un dramma veneziano in viaggio nell'Europa del Seicento,* ed. Nicola Michelassi [Florence: Olschki, 2008]).

Ludwig Gerber had called "the Mozart of his time."[4] Many of Monteverdi's works, including *Orfeo,* were already known through editions printed during his lifetime, but not the Venetian operas. They seem to have fallen into a black hole soon after the composer's death. Writing shortly after the middle of the eighteenth century, the first English music historian, Charles Burney, mentioned Monteverdi in connection with opera in Venice, but only in a very general way. Though he was aware of the revival of *Arianna* there, he apparently knew nothing of the other works.[5] And yet, though the scores had disappeared, the operas had left traces of their existence in published literature of the time, publications that were presumably available to at least some early musicologists.[6]

That Monteverdi had written operas for the Venetian stage was certainly known to Burney's Italian predecessors, even if their knowledge was imperfect and rather confused. To appreciate the difficulties surrounding the subsequent reception of these works, it is worth examining these first imperfect accounts and confusions, particularly because they provided the starting point for the efforts of modern scholars to clarify their understanding of Monteverdi's operatic production.

The first to chronicle Monteverdi's contribution to the development of Venetian opera seems to have been the seventeenth-century librettist and historian Cristoforo Ivanovich. As an appendix to his book *Minerva al tavolino* (1681), Ivanovich published a chronology entitled "Le memorie teatrali di Venezia." He based his information primarily on extant librettos, most of them published, and also, probably, on hearsay. Having arrived in Venice from his native Dalmatia in 1657, Ivanovich undoubtedly knew many Venetians who had seen the operas listed in his chronology. But he attributed only two operas to Monteverdi: *Ritorno* in 1641, and *Incoronazione* in 1643, for which he also listed a revival in 1646.[7] With respect to the composer's other operas, he made a number of mistakes, some of which continued to occlude the historical record until fairly recently. (Thomas Walker, in a classic study, was the first to uncover many of these errors.) For instance, he attributed the Venetian revival of *Arianna,* Monteverdi's most famous opera during his lifetime, not to Monteverdi but to Sacrati; and he mistook the year, placing it in 1641 rather than 1640. And he attributed *Le nozze d'Enea e Lavinia* to Cavalli, erroneously assigning the libretto to Giacomo Badoaro. These mistakes seem particularly

---

4. Ernst Ludwig Gerber, *Neue-historisch-biographisches Lexikon der Tonkünstler* (Leipzig: A. Kühnel, 1812–14), 3 (1813): cols. 450–52.

5. See Charles Burney, *A General History of Music, from the Earliest Ages to the Present Period (1789),* ed. Frank Mercer (New York: Dover, 1935), 2:543 on *Arianna* in Venice.

6. Authors ranging from Padre Martini (1771) and Ernst Ludwig Gerber (1790) to Karl von Winterfeld (1834) and Robert Eitner (1871) were very likely acquainted with *Orfeo;* they probably also had access to the seventeenth- and eighteenth-century chronologies, and possibly even librettos of Monteverdi's Venetian operas.

7. Ivanovich, "Memorie teatrali"; 2nd ed. (1688) repr. *Memorie teatrali,* ed. Dubowy. Dubowy's introduction contains biographical information on Ivanovich. Skepticism regarding the 1646 Venetian revival of *Incoronazione* dates from the 1970s. See below, n. 55.

inexplicable, because Ivanovich presumably had access to the libretto of *Arianna* as well as the scenario of *Nozze,* both printed, in which Monteverdi was clearly identified as the composer.[8]

Several of these errors—among the "circa quaranta" noted by another early chronicler of Venetian opera, Carlo Bonlini—were corrected in subsequent chronologies by Bonlini himself (1730), Antonio Groppo (1745), and Leone Allacci (1755), though they all maintained the inaccurate ascription of the *Nozze* libretto to Badoaro.[9] But Bonlini, and then the others, introduced a new error, attributing Francesco Manelli's *Adone* to Monteverdi, an attribution that persisted in the literature until quite recently.[10] Like most early Venetian operas, however, *Ritorno* and *Incoronazione* remained shadows (without musical bodies—librettos only) until the 1880s. Then, within a couple of years of one another, scores for both were rediscovered. Their fates have remained intertwined ever since.

Ritorno surfaced first, when a score was identified by the Austrian music historian August Wilhelm Ambros at the Vienna State Library, an identification based on certain earlier statements made by his uncle R. G. Kiesewetter.[11] After announcing the discovery in the second edition of his *Geschichte der Musik* (1881), Ambros provided a general description of the manuscript's appearance and handwriting, concluding that the alterations indicated by a second hand—a different act division and the cut of a scene in act 5 ("Scena 2nda la si

---

8. See Walker, "Gli errori di *Minerva al tavolino,*" for Ivanovich's overemphasis on Cavalli. As far as *Nozze* is concerned, Ivanovich probably took the erroneous Badoaro attribution from one of the early manuscript librettos (listed in Table 5 below, Chap. 3) but must have relied on his own predilection for Cavalli when it came time to attribute the music.

9. [Bonlini], *Le glorie della poesia:* "Ma questo Catalogo [of Ivanovich] . . . non è giunto a quella perfezione, che sarebbe desiderabile in una tale materia. E per verità fattone un rigoroso rincontro con i Libretti ch'abbiamo in stampa, vi si scorgono circa quaranta sbagli di non poco rilevo" (p. 5); Groppo, *Catalogo di tutti i drammi per musica,* and Leone Allacci, *Drammaturgia di Leone Allacci accresciuta e continuata fino all'anno MDCCLV* (Venice: Giambattista Pasquali, 1755). They may have been critical of Ivanovich, but continued to perpetuate many of his errors.

10. *Adone* was one of Ivanovich's many misattributions to Cavalli, so that in reascribing it to Monteverdi, Bonlini et al. must have thought that they were correcting a typical error. See Anna Amalie Abert, *Monteverdi und das musikalische Drama* (Lippstadt: Kistner & Siegel, 1954), 128. Even Leo Schrade, *Monteverdi, the Creator of Modern Music* (New York: Norton, 1950), 357 accepted the attribution (somewhat skeptically), though Vogel had already questioned it as early as 1887. See below, n. 16.

11. Codex Class. IV, 18763, Nationalbibliothek, from the private library of Leopold I. Cf. August Wilhelm Ambros, *Geschichte der Musik,* 2nd ed., ed. Hugo Leichtentritt (Leipzig, 1881), 362–3: "Von diesen Spätlings-Opern [*Adone, Enea, Ritorno,* and *Incoronazione*] ist nur der Ulisses durch einen glücklichen Zufall erhalten." Alois Franz Simon Joseph Molitor (1766–1848), a Viennese composer, guitarist, and collector of manuscripts with a renowned private library of music manuscripts, may have been the first to identify the anonymous score in Vienna as Monteverdi's opera. His name is cited in the original entry on *Ritorno* in the catalogue of the Nationalbibliothek: [*Il ritorno d'Ulisse in Patria.*] *Drama musicum trium actuum, carens inscriptione. In fol. 1a adnotavit Iosephus Haupt: "Auctor musicus est Cl. Monteverde iudicibus Kiesewetter, Molitor et Ambros. Libellus genuinus, quem Iacobus Badoaro composuit, retractatus et in brevius redactus est; discrepant initium et finis ab originali."*

lascia fuora per essere maninconica")—must be ascribed to Monteverdi himself.[12] He then went on to explain the circumstances of its identification in a footnote, concluding, touchingly, that in view of its importance, he had copied the score out in its entirety, "so that the world might have a second copy."[13]

Intriguing though this newly discovered score must have been, its authenticity was suspect from the very beginning. It not only lacked both title page and author's name; more disturbingly, it diverged substantially from what was then the only known libretto, a Venetian manuscript dated 1641, which named Monteverdi as the composer.[14] Indeed, in a publication of 1887, one of the first Monteverdi scholars, Emil Vogel, punctured the enthusiasm generated by Ambros's discovery. Basing his opinion purely on the documentary evidence, Vogel concluded, with palpable disappointment, that he could not share Ambros's optimism about the score: "According to Ambros, the score of *Ritorno* can be found in the State Library in Vienna, in a well-preserved exemplar furnished with notations in Monteverdi's own hand. If this statement were correct, we would fortunately possess at least one of the late operas of Monteverdi and thus a most valuable treasure. Unfortunately, however, we cannot agree with Ambros's assertion."[15] He then demonstrated that the score did not correspond to the Venetian libretto of 1641, which was ascribed to Monteverdi, identifying as the most important differences the number of acts (5 vs. 3) and the texts of the prologue and final scene (see below). Though he suggested that Badoaro himself could have revised the libretto for Monteverdi or that

---

12. "Der Deckel ist mit dem in Gold eingepressten Bilde des Kaisers bezeichnet, eine Ehre, welche diese Partitur z.B. mit Cavalli's Autograph des 'Egisto' theilt. Von anderer Hand als der des Copisten sind Aenderungen in der ursprünglichen Eintheilung der Akte beigeschrieben, und bei der weggelassenen zweiten Scene des dritten Aktes, welche vermuthlich den Selbstmord des Bettlers Irus enthielt, steht die seltsame Bemerkung: 'Scene [sic] 2da si lascia fuora per essere maninconica.' Diese Zusätze können schwerlich von einer andern Hand sein, als von jener Monteverde's selbst" (Ambros [1881], 363).

13. "Der Schatz lag lange unbeachtet in der kais. Bibliothek, da das Titelblatt fehlt und die Partitur ursprünglich als 'unbekannte Oper' catalogisirt war. Kiesewetter sah sie, erkannte sie ganz richtig als Werk Monteverde's—seine Erklärung wurde im Katalog beigesetzt—er selbst aber machte, was nur bei der an Phlegma streifenden Gelassenheit meines Oheims Kiesewetter erklärlich wird, von dem kostbaren Funde keine weitere Erwähnung, keinen weiteren Gebrauch! Ich habe die Partitur, obschon ich sie in Wien täglich sehen kann, für mich eigenhändig copirt, damit doch noch ein zweites Exemplar in der Welt sei" (Ambros [1881], p. 363, n. 1). A postscript reflecting the authenticity debate was added to this note in the third edition (see n. 20 below).

14. Listed by Robert Haas ("Zur Neuausgabe von Claudio Monteverdis *Il Ritorno d'Ulisse in patria*," *Studien zur Musikwissenschaft* 9 [1922]: 3–42), 10, as Dramm 908–30018? [probably 909.2 because 908 does not correspond to a copy of *Ritorno*, but 909.2 is in fact the only copy that ascribes the music to Monteverdi on the title page] (see Table 4 below, Chap. 3). It is uncertain whether other scholars disturbed by inconsistencies with the score were looking at the same libretto, since they failed to give a shelf-mark, but it would not have mattered, since, as we shall see, all of the librettos are essentially the same.

15. Emil Vogel, "Claudio Monteverdi: Leben, Wirken, im Lichte der zeitgenössischen Kritik und Verzeichniss seiner im Druck erschienenen Werke," *VfMw* 3 (1887): 315–450, at 403–4: "Die Partitur des *Ritorno* soll nach Ambros' Versicherung in einem wohl erhaltenen Exemplare, mit anmerkungen von Monteverdi's eigener Hande versehen, in der k.k. Hofbibliothek zu Wien aufbewahrt sein. Waren diese Angaben richtig, so besassen wir wenigstens eine der Spätlingsopern Monteverdi's und durften uns dieses hochst werthvollen Schatzes wegen glücklich preisen. Leider aber können wir den Ambros'schen Angaben nicht unbedingt zustimmen."

the score might represent the composer's setting of an earlier version, he rejected both possibilities for lack of evidence. Since the alterations in the score were not, as Ambros had thought, in Monteverdi's hand, he reasoned that it could just as well be by another composer.[16] In any case, it was not demonstrably by Monteverdi.[17] Vogel's doubts were shared by two of the heaviest hitters of nineteenth-century musicology, Hermann Kretzschmar[18] and Hugo Riemann;[19] they were also mentioned by Ambros in his third edition.[20]

However, they were roundly dismissed by another, slightly younger member of the "great generation" of German musicologists, Hugo Goldschmidt (1903), who reasserted Monteverdi's authorship, essentially on stylistic grounds.[21] His evaluation depended to some extent on the discovery, in the meantime, of *Incoronazione*, with which he found many common elements. With Goldschmidt's imprimatur, *Ritorno* was eventually published with great fanfare (and accompanied by a lengthy, if somewhat defensive essay) by Robert Haas in 1922. (Haas made the claim that alterations visible in the score indicated that it had served for a performance in Vienna. He supported this with evidence from another contemporary score likewise in the Leopold I collection of the Nationalbibliothek, Cavalli's *Egisto*, noting that both scores involved simplification of scenic demands.)[22] Haas's edition was soon followed by two others: one by the French composer Vincent d'Indy (1925), the other by the Belgian musicologist Charles van den Borren (1926), both designed for performances, in Paris and Brussels respectively.[23] Finally, in 1930, Francesco Malipiero's edition for the Collected Works (vol. 12) appeared; for more than half a

---

16. Vogel, "Monteverdi," 392–93, was aware that a putative earlier *Ulisse* by Monteverdi had been identified, but did not think it could be associated with the Vienna score. "Ob also wirklich die Wiener Partitur Monteverdi zuzuschreiben is, bleibt mindestens zweifelhaft; ein sicheres Resultat, wenn es überhaupt möglich, wird sich erst nach genaueren Untersuchungen herausstellen" (pp. 403–4). Vogel (p. 402), incidentally, was also presciently skeptical of the attribution of *Adone* to Monteverdi, since the libretto he knew—the only one—did not mention him. Had he pursued his doubts further, he might have noticed that the actual composer of the work, Manelli, had signed the dedication of the libretto.

17. "Dieses mit der 1641 in Venedig aufgeführten Oper *Ritorno* nicht identisch ist" (Vogel, "Monteverdi," 404).

18. Hermann Kretzschmar, *Geschichte der Oper* (Leipzig: Breitkopf & Härtel, 1919), 63: "die Echtheit dieses Werkes ist im hohen grade Zweifelhaft."

19. Hugo Riemann, *Handbuch der Musikgeschichte* (Leipzig: Breitkopf & Härtel, 1904–23), 2/2: 276: "ob die . . . in Wien erhaltene Partitur . . . Monteverdis ist, scheint zweifelhaft."

20. Ambros, *Geschichte der Musik*, 3rd ed. (1909), 4: 591, n. 1 summarizes the authenticity debate: "In neuerer Zeit sind Zweifel um die Echtheit des Ulisse aufgetaucht. Vogel hielt die Echtheit für nicht begnügend belegt. Hugo Goldschmidt trat gegen Vogel für die Echtheit ein und hat für seine Behauptung einen umfangreichen Beweis angetreten."

21. Hugo Goldschmidt, "Monteverdi's *Ritorno d'Ulisse*," *SIMG* 4 (1902–3): 671–76, and 9 (1907), 570–92. "Dieser 'genaueren Untersuchung' habe ich mich unterzogen und kann als ihren Erfolg mitteilen, dass die Wiener Partitur mit Monteverdi's Ritorno identisch ist" (p. 671).

22. Claudio Monteverdi, *Ritorno d'Ulisse in Patria*, ed. Robert Haas (Vienna: Universal-Edition; Leipzig: Breitkopf & Härtel, 1922 (DTÖ, Jahrgang 29, Band 57). In Haas's article, "Zur Neuausgabe," which appeared in the same year, pp. 12–20 are devoted to comparison of the two sources. On the question of scenic demands, see pp. 1–2.

23. For a review of Van den Borren's edition, see *Revue de l'Université de Bruxelles* 30 (1924–25): 353–87.

TABLE 2
Editions

Il ritorno d'Ulisse in patria

1922	Robert Haas (*Denkmäler der Tonkunst in Österreich,* 57, Vienna: Universal)
1925	Charles van den Borren (MS, Brussels)
1925	Jack Westrup (MS, Oxford?)
1926	Vincent d'Indy (Paris: Heugel)
1929	Francesco Malipiero (Collected Works, 12)
1942	Luigi Dallapiccola (Milan: Suvini Zerboni)
1972	Raymond Leppard (London: Faber?)
1982	Hans Werner Henze (Mainz: Schott)
1998	Clifford Bartlett (Huntingdon, UK: King's Music)
2002	Alan Curtis (London: Novello)

L'incoronazione di Poppea

1904	Hugo Goldschmidt (*Studien zur Geschichte der italienischen Oper im 17. Jahrhundert,* 2, Leipzig: Breitkopf, repr. Hildesheim: Olms, 1967)
1908	Vincent d'Indy (Paris: Schola cantorum; Paris: Lerolle, 1922)
1914	Charles van den Borren (Brussels: n.p.)
1931	Gian Francesco Malipiero (Collected Works, 13, Vienna: Universal)
1937	Giacomo Benvenuti (Milan: Suvini Zerboni; repr. 1965)
1937	Ernst Krenek (Vienna: Universal)
1938	Giacomo Benvenuti, Venice facsimile (Milan: Bocca)
1953	Giorgio Federico Ghedini (Milan: Ricordi)
1954	Gian Francesco Malipiero (Paris: Heugel)
1958	Hans F. Redlich (Kassel: Bärenreiter)
1960	Walter Goehr (London: Universal)
1965	Riccardo Nielsen (Bologna: Bongiovanni)
1966	Raymond Leppard (London: Faber; rev. ed. 1968)
1969	Sergio Martinotti, Venice facsimile (Forni: Bologna)
1977	Raymond Leppard (London: Faber)
1989	Alan Curtis (London: Novello)

century, it was the preferred (only) source for both scholars and performers. A modern performing score, edited by Alan Curtis, was finally published in 2002. (See the list of editions, Table 2.)

Meanwhile, shortly after Ambros's discovery of *Ritorno,* the Venetian librarian Taddeo Wiel identified one of the anonymous manuscripts in the Contarini Collection of the Biblioteca Marciana as the long-lost *Incoronazione di Poppea.* Although a different title, *Nerone,* was affixed to the spine of the manuscript, partly obscuring the composer's name (which also appears inside, on fol. 2r), and although the score diverged in a number of respects from the known libretto, printed in 1656, the work was immediately accepted as Monteverdi's.[24]

The unearthing of "Monteverdi's dramatic testament" was greeted with unreserved enthusiasm by Kretzschmar, who rejoiced in the fact that the composer's true contribution to music drama of the seventeenth century could now be understood. The opera, he concluded, was the purest expression of the spirit of music drama sought by the Florentine Hellenists.[25] Like *Ritorno,* but a great deal sooner (eighteen years sooner, to be precise), *Incoronazione* was published (by Goldschmidt in 1904)[26] and performed: by d'Indy (Paris, 1905 and 1913),[27] Van den Borren (Brussels, 1914), and Jack Westrup (Oxford, 1927). Malipiero issued his edition for the Collected Works (vol. 13) in 1931; a facsimile was published in 1938. (It should be pointed out, as evidence of the contrasting reception of the two sister works, that until 2007 there was no facsimile of *Ritorno.*)[28]

Having coincidentally resurfaced at around the same time, it was inevitable that *Ritorno* and *Incoronazione* should be measured against one another. Some scholars used *Incoronazione* to shore up the attribution of *Ritorno*—Westrup invoked stylistic kinship,[29] and Van den Borren noted analogous discrepancies in the sources,[30] while Goldschmidt gave equal weight to both factors.[31] But others were struck by the dissimilarities between the two works, or rather, by the inferiority of *Ritorno,* which they took pains to explain:

24. Wiel's discovery was published in his Contarini catalogue in 1888 (Taddeo Wiel, *I Codici musicali contariniani del secolo XVII nella R. Biblioteca di San Marco in Venezia* [Venice: F. Ongania, 1888, repr. Bologna: Forni, 1969]). Regarding the spines of the Contarini volumes, see below, Chap. 3, n. 52. For a history and description of the Contarini Collection, see Thomas Walker, "*Ubi Lucius*: Thoughts on Reading *Medoro,*" in Francesco Lucio, *Medoro,* Drammaturgia musicale veneta 4 (Milan: Ricordi, 1984): cxxxi–clxiv; esp. cxli–cxlvii.

25. Hermann Kretzschmar, "Monteverdi's *Incoronazione di Poppea,*" *VfMw* 10 (1894): 530: "dasjenige Werk, das den Geist aus dem im Kreise der Florentiner Hellenisten das Musikdrama hervorging, am reinsten und sichersten ausspricht."

26. Hugo Goldschmidt, *Studien zur Geschichte der italienischen Oper,* 2 (Leipzig: Breitkopf & Härtel, 1904; repr. 1967), 33–203. The volume comprises a scene-by-scene analysis, the libretto, and excerpts from the score.

27. On the basis of a Schola Cantorum edition (Paris, 1904), issued in piano reduction in 1908 and published in 1922 (Paris: Lerolle).

28. *Il ritorno d'Ulisse in patria,* facsimile, ed. Sergio Vartolo (Florence: SPES, 2007).

29. Basing his opinion on a BBC broadcast of d'Indy's edition, Westrup concluded: "It is true that there is no external evidence that Ulysses is by Monteverde. But no one hearing it with a knowledge of the other two works could have a moment's doubt as to its authenticity" ("Monteverdi's *Il ritorno d'Ulisse in patria,*" *Monthly Musical Record* [2 April 1928]: 106).

30. Charles Van den Borren, "Il ritorno d'Ulisse in patria," *Revue de l'Université de Bruxelles* 3 (1924–25): 353–87, at 361 adduced the differences between the *Incoronazione* sources to justify the troubling discrepancies between those of *Ritorno,* concluding that Monteverdi "a pratiqué ici [in *Ritorno*], sur une large échelle, ce qu'on lui verra faire, un an plus tard, dans *l'Incoronazione.*"

31. Goldschmidt ("Monteverdi's *Ritorno d'Ulisse*") invoked specific stylistic similarities between the works (even forgiving Vogel's negative assessment of *Ritorno* for having been made before the discovery of *Incoronazione*). They include, interestingly, a similar cut of the chorus in the final scene so as to end with a love duet. He also pointed out that the score does not have a word that is not in the libretto (p. 672), that there are as many omissions in *Incoronazione* as in *Ritorno,* and, finally, that the editing, so much like that of *Incoronazione,* proves rather that Monteverdi wrote the work ("Kein anderer Komponist jener Zeit verfährt so eigenartig mit seinem Libretto" [p. 675]).

it was written in haste, the subject was dull, Monteverdi was tired,[32] the score was only a sketch.[33]

Ritorno remained problematic, its unevenness to be excused, the discrepancies between its sources to be explained away, but Monteverdi's authorship was generally accepted until the early 1940s, when performances in Florence, at the Maggio Musicale (on 23 and 26 May 1942), in an edition by Luigi Dallapiccola, brought the issue once more to the fore. And again, *Incoronazione* set the standard for comparison. Apparently in anticipation of these performances, the musicologist Giacomo Benvenuti published an article in the Venetian daily newspaper *Il Gazzettino* (7 May 1942) under the provocative headline: "Il ritorno d'Ulisse non è di Monteverdi." Relying on his intimate knowledge of the composer's style, gained through editing *Orfeo* (1934) and publishing the facsimile of *Incoronazione* (1938), and following what he described as a minute comparison with all of his other works, Benvenuti declared *Ritorno* to be absolutely without value and therefore not by Monteverdi.

Responses to Benvenuti were predictably defensive, once again focusing on the perceived unevenness of the *Ritorno* score. At a pre-concert lecture at the Società Leonardo da Vinci, Florence, on 21 May 1942, some weeks after the *Gazzettino* article but before the performance, Dallapiccola himself questioned Benvenuti's premise, suggesting for the first time that the issues of authorship and quality might be separated—an important distinction that was to have broad application in the subsequent debate on *Incoronazione*. Warning that it was not enough to say that *Ritorno* could not be by Monteverdi simply because it is less beautiful than *Incoronazione,* he minimized the importance of attribution altogether in his praise of the work. *Il ritorno d'Ulisse,* he concluded, deserved to be performed even if Monteverdi were not the author.[34]

Other critics responding to Benvenuti were satisfied to temporize on the issue of quality or else to continue justifying its lack in *Ritorno.* Though he found that it "abounds in *longueurs,* superfluities, and indolence, and is uninspired" (abbonda di lungaggini, del superfluo, e dell'ozioso, fatto per fare), Guido Pannain doubted that *Ritorno* was really so ugly as to be unworthy of Monteverdi, and he trotted out the usual instances of similarities with *Incoronazione* to support Monteverdi's authorship, concluding that "*Ritorno*

---

32. Louis Schneider, *Un précurseur de la musique italienne aux XVIe et XVIIe siècles: Claudio Monteverdi. L'homme et son temps* (Paris: Perrin, 1921), 215: "n'est-il pas permis au bon Homère de sommeiller parfois; et Monteverdi n'a-t-il pas le droit d'avoir été moins inspiré par le sujet?" On p. 306, calling it "une œuvre inégale," he asks: "Faut-il attribuer cette infériorité partielle à la hâte avec laquelle Monteverdi a écrit son ouvrage, au sujet qui était un peu fade, à une fatigue momentanée du compositeur? Ce qu'il importait de montrer, c'est que la partition n'est pas indigne du maître. On aurait tort de la juger par comparaison avec l'*Orfeo* ou l'*Incoronazione,* dont elle n'a ni le souffle ni la maîtrise."

33. Henry Prunières, *La vie et l'œuvre de Claudio Monteverdi* (Paris: Librairie de France, 1926; trans. as *Monteverdi: His Life and Work.* [New York: Dutton, 1926]), 176: [*Ritorno*] "must be considered not as a work finished at leisure but as a kind of improvisation of genius, a vast sketch, certain parts of which have been elaborated, while others are of set purpose only roughly indicated."

34. The lecture was published as the essay cited above in n. 2 ("Per una rappresentazione").

d'Ulisse is an opera that is only half successful. But the negative elements that testify to its inferiority with respect to the other two Monteverdi operas that have come down to us are no reason to impugn its authenticity."[35] The musicologist Adelmo Damerini also joined the debate, admitting the work's unevenness and suggesting, for some of the duller moments, that "il genio dormitabat." He also raised the intriguing possibility of collaboration, proposing that "another hand, perhaps that of a student, might have intervened momentarily, to help the Master finish the opera more quickly, as often happened in the workshops of the great painters and sculptors."[36]

The idea of collaboration gained support from other scholars as well. Domenico De' Paoli, for instance, conceding that the work was flawed by a "fundamental disequilibrium . . . where, together with many pleasing pages one finds others of absolute insignificance," suggested that, because the composer was so busy in 1641—he was presumably working on *Le nozze d'Enea* and the revival of *Arianna* at the time—he might have incorporated material from a hypothetical earlier opera, an *Ulisse* said to have been composed in 1630. The result, as De' Paoli quaintly put it, was a collaboration between Monteverdi and himself.[37] De' Paoli's hypothesis was extended by Hans Redlich, author of the first substantial German monograph on Monteverdi, who posited the intervention of a younger composer (Manelli?) to explain the stylistic unevenness of the score. Redlich, in fact, who dubbed the opera "the *Schmerzenskind* of Monteverdi scholarship," on the basis of its "doubtful authenticity," even declined to provide "a detailed analysis" of the work.[38] Claudio Sartori likewise found its dubious authenticity—and many defects— grounds for omitting *Ritorno* from discussion and moving straight to *Incoronazione* in his survey of the operas: "If many of its qualities can make one think of Monteverdi, its numerous defects have caused scholars to consider it either an inferior work of the master or even the creation of an imitator or student. Given these doubts, we skip *Ritorno* and come finally to *L'Incoronazione*."[39]

---

35. Guido Pannain, "Claudio Monteverdi nell'opera in musica," *Musica* 2 (1943): 35–50: "Si può concludere che Il Ritorno d'Ulisse sia un'opera riuscita a metà. Ma gli elementi negativi che testimoniano della sua inferiorità rispetto alle altre due che ci sono giunte del Monteverdi non sono la ragione di farne impugnare l'autenticità" (p. 45).

36. Adelmo Damerini, "Aspetti dell'VIII Maggio musicale fiorentino," *Musica* 2 (1943): 207–13: "o che altra mano, di qualche allievo per esempio, sia intervenuta, momentaneamente, ad aiutare il Maestro per compiere l'opera in più breve tempo, come accadeva nelle 'botteghe' dei grandi pittori e scultori" (p. 209).

37. Domenico De' Paoli, *Monteverdi* (Milan: U. Hoepli, 1945), 318: "Si vorrebbe sottoporre alcuni 'fatti esterni' i quali potrebbero aiutare a spiegare le ragione dello squilibrio fondamentale di quest'opera e come in essa, vicino a parecchie pagine geniali se ne trovino altre assolutamente insignificanti . . . in un epoca quando la collaborazione tra musicisti alla stessa opera era d'uso corrente, Monteverdi poteva ben collaborare con se stesso."

38. Hans Ferdinand Redlich, *Claudio Monteverdi, Leben und Werk* (Olten: O. Walter, 1949), 120. On stylistic inequalities, see p. 111.

39. Claudio Sartori, *Claudio Monteverdi* (Brescia: La Scuola, 1953), 207: "Se per molti caratteri può far pensare al M., per numerosi difetti ha indotto gli studiosi o a ritenerla opera inferiore del maestro stesso o addirittura creazione di un imitatore o di un allievo. . . . Nel dubbio trascuriamo dunque *Ritorno* e veniamo finalmente all'*Incoronazione*."

This hypothetical *Ulisse* of 1630, initially mentioned and dismissed by Vogel, was actually a phantom, otherwise known as *Delia e Ulisse*. Such a work had first been identified by a certain Gaetano Giordani (librarian at Bologna) on the basis of what he thought was a libretto published in 1630, a volume entitled *Le glorie della musica celebrate dalla sorella poesia*.[40] But the identification turned out to be mistaken in every conceivable way: the date of publication of the little volume was actually 1640; the opera in question was in fact two, one *(Ritorno)* by Monteverdi, the other *(Delia)* by Manelli; the book was a collection of poetry in honor of the performers, not a libretto, and so on. Nevertheless, the possibility that such an opera might have been related to the Viennese score of *Ritorno* remained alive until the late 1950s, when the young German scholar Wolfgang Osthoff proved its speciousness.[41]

Osthoff brought new professionalism to Monteverdi studies—and new sources (including six additional manuscript librettos of *Ritorno* as well as the above-mentioned Bolognese publication of 1640—not 1630—*Le glorie della musica*, which documented a performance of the opera in Bologna). His work, among other things, marks a new stage in the authenticity debate, what we might call the return of Ulysses to the canon. In addition to unmasking the Bologna ghost as a reference to a performance of Monteverdi's opera in 1640, he compared the six manuscript librettos he had discovered with the one that was already known, identifying many variants, some of them closer to readings in the score. These findings helped to diminish the importance of the disparities that had originally undermined confidence in Monteverdi's authorship. Moreover, through comparison with manuscripts in the Contarini Collection, he showed that the score was certainly written in the seventeenth century (rather than the eighteenth, as De' Paoli had thought), and proposed that similarities to the score of Cavalli's *Apollo e Dafne*, performed at S. Cassiano in the same year, pointed to a similar date of copying.[42] Osthoff's comprehensive musical analysis, finally, established numerous connections with other compositions by Monteverdi, madrigals as well as *Incoronazione*. All this reinforced the claim that *Ritorno* was by the same composer.[43]

---

40. See Gaetano Giordani, *Intorno al Gran Teatro del Comune e ad altri minori in Bologna* (Bologna: Società tipografica bolognese e Ditta Sassi, 1855), 62. The full title of the volume, already mentioned in chap. 1, is *Le glorie della musica celebrate dalla sorella poesia Rappresentandosi in Bologna la Delia, e l'Ulisse nel Teatro de gl'illustriss. Guastavillani* (Bologna: Ferroni, 1640).

41. Abert, *Monteverdi*, 44 also doubted that Monteverdi had written an earlier *Ulisse*.

42. Wolfgang Osthoff, "Zu den Quellen von Monteverdis *Ritorno di Ulisse in patria*," *Studien zur Musikwissenschaft* 24 (1960): 67–78. But see Jane Glover, *Cavalli* (London: Batsford, 1978); Peter Jeffery, "The Autograph Manuscripts of Francesco Cavalli" (Ph.D. diss., Princeton University, 1980); and Walker, "*Ubi Lucius*," who argue that *Apollo e Dafne* was copied later. Glover (*Cavalli*) identifies *Apollo* as one of two Cavalli MSS copied by hand "x"; Walker ("*Ubi Lucius*") as "C" (placing it among the MSS copied by Cavalli's équipe); and Jeffery as being unique, though sharing characteristics with some other Cavalli scores, including partial watermarks and one rubric in Cavalli's hand. As far as S. Cassiano is concerned, *Ritorno* was probably never performed there. See Chap. 3.

43. Wolfgang Osthoff, *Monteverdistudien: Das dramatische Spätwerk Claudio Monteverdis* (Tutzing: Schneider, 1960), 183–205.

Thanks to Osthoff's clarification of the situation, *Ritorno* is now generally accepted as genuine. Far from impugning the authenticity of the opera, the disparities between the sources are now regarded as evidence of Monteverdi's characteristic brand of editing, to be discussed more fully in the following pages, especially Chapters 6 and 7.[44]

⚡

In contrast to *Ritorno*, *Incoronazione* enjoyed an excellent press from the moment of its discovery. Kretzschmar's initial enthusiasm for the work found echoes in the comments of every subsequent critic, perhaps none louder than those of Leo Schrade, for whom it represented the culmination of a grand teleology: the defining work of Monteverdi's entire output. *Incoronazione* "has been regarded as the supreme music drama of the epoch.... What Monteverdi presumably set out to accomplish, he realized: the synthesis of his art, of the art of his time, and, prophetically, of the art of the seventeenth century. There were operas that in many ways were the equals of his, but of genuine music dramas there was none." Then, following a lengthy disquisition on the perfection of the final duet, "Pur ti miro," Schrade concluded: "In this last work Monteverdi attained the perfection he had been striving for from the beginning, in which art fulfills its nature, and form and expression are one."[45] Likewise, Sartori saw *Incoronazione* as the achievement of Monteverdi's goal: "The opera is but the culmination of his creative efforts, the fulfillment of a lifelong quest. . . . It is the masterpiece desired and prepared for over an entire lifetime."[46]

Predictably, critics were struck by the freshness of the work, its "radiant youth,"[47] marveling that it could have been written by a seventy-four-year-old composer. In the words of Sartori, "though born of a seventy-five-year-old musician, it retains all of the prodigious freshness of a youthful work, but without the inexperience of a young man."[48] Praising the composer's uncanny ability to penetrate the psyches of his characters, critics paid it the ultimate complement of linking it to the most highly regarded works in the history of opera, from *Boris Gudonov*[49] to the masterpieces of Mozart and Verdi.[50]

In keeping with their enthusiasm, the authenticity of *Incoronazione* was regarded as beyond question, in part, no doubt, because of the look of the Venetian score, the one score that was known at the time. If the copyist's hand—or, rather, hands—were not

---

44. Abert, *Monteverdi*, 45, was one of the first scholars to maintain that the differences between the libretto and the score of *Ritorno* were characteristic of Monteverdi's style of editing.

45. Schrade, *Monteverdi*, 357–58, 367.

46. "La sua opera è solo la conclusione della sua creazione, il compimento della sua ricerca durata tutta la vita.... È il capolavoro sognato e preparato durante tutta una vita" (Sartori, *Monteverdi*, 227).

47. "Aujourd'hui encore, l'oeuvre reste vivante et rayonne de jeunesse" (Prunières, *Monteverdi*, 154).

48. "per questa nata da un musicista settantacinquenne, mantiene tutta la prodigiosa freschezza di un'opera giovanile, pur senza l'inesperienza della creazione di un giovane" (Sartori, *Monteverdi*, 227).

49. André Tessiers, "Les deux styles de Monteverde," *Revue musicale* 3 (1922): 223–54, at 253.

50. Denis Arnold, *Monteverdi* (London: Dent, 1960), 130.

Monteverdi's, the performance indications at least showed every evidence of being the composer's.[51] Though substantial differences between score(s) and librettos (now, thanks to Osthoff, five others had been discovered) were noted, admittedly less troubling than those of *Ritorno*, these were adduced as evidence of Monteverdi's handiwork, and his authorship was never questioned—until recently.

The unearthing of a second score at the Conservatorio S. Pietro a Majella in Naples by the librarian Guido Gasperini, however, had posed something of a problem. Not only was this score clearly linked to a libretto published in conjunction with a performance in Naples in 1651, eight years after Monteverdi's death, but it contained more music than the Venice score (and more text than the published libretto of 1656).[52] This made the relationship of the two exceedingly difficult to explain. It would seem that the work was somehow expanded rather than contracted for the Naples revival. But eight years after his death, Monteverdi could hardly have been responsible for the additions. Although Malipiero recognized that some Naples readings were closer than those in Venice to Busenello's libretto, Benvenuti, probably the work's most ardent champion, and with a proprietary interest in the Venice score, having recently published it in facsimile, rejected the Naples readings out of hand: "these musical passages . . . contrary to what Malipiero believes, reveal not even the slightest artistic value. They were probably interpolated on the occasion of the performance of Poppea in Naples in 1651 and are neither Monteverdian nor by Cavalli, nor do they have even the most distant Venetian scent."[53] Fortunately for scholars, Malipiero included the major Naples variants and additions in an appendix to his Complete Works edition of 1931.

It is rather ironic that while Osthoff's research in the 1960s helped to buttress the case for *Ritorno*, it was also responsible for beginning to undermine that for *Incoronazione*. He discovered that some of the music in the Venetian score, namely, the overture, was probably by Cavalli, that Cavalli had edited the score for performance, and that it was copied by one of Cavalli's regular copyists active exclusively during the early 1650s (later this hand was identified—by Peter Jeffery—as that of Cavalli's wife, who died in September 1652).

---

51. Schneider, *Un précurseur*, 272, thought acts 1 and 3 were autograph, as did Gian Francesco Malipiero (*L'incoronazione di Poppea*, in *Tutte le opere*, vol. 13 [1931], preface), whereas Giacomo Benvenuti, "Il manoscritto veneziano della *Incoronazione di Poppea*," *RIM* 41 (1937), 176–84, at 180, thought only the editorial interventions were.

52. The existence of the Naples libretto was first noted by Benedetto Croce, *I teatri di Napoli* (Naples: Pierro, 1891), 131. Gasperini's discovery of the score (described in Guido Gasperini and Franca Gallo, *Catalogo delle opere musicali: Città di Napoli, Biblioteca del R. Conservatorio di Musica di S. Pietro a Majella*, Pubblicazioni dell'Associazione dei musicologi italiani, serie 10 [Parma: Officina Grafica Fresching, 1934], 259) was reported in Malipiero (*L'incoronazione di Poppea* [1931], preface); see also Benvenuti, "Il manoscritto veneziano," 176.

53. "Queste musiche . . . contrariamente a quanto crede il Malipiero, non rivelano nessun neppure modesto pregio artistico. Esse furono probabilmente interpolate in occasione della rappresentazione della Poppea a Napoli nel 1651 e non sono né monteverdiane né del Cavalli, né hanno un qualche lontano sentore di veneziano" (Benvenuti, "Il manoscritto," 177). His condescending tone in referring to Malipiero's ideas regarding the Naples score is quite characteristic. See esp. p. 182 f. Benvenuti's edition of *Incoronazione* was published a year before the facsimile (Milano: Suvini Zerboni, 1937); cf. Table 2 below.

This train of facts led to an inevitable conclusion: since both the Naples and Venice scores were copied after Monteverdi's death, neither could be associated with the first performance of the opera in 1643. (Osthoff assumed that the Venice score was for the Venetian revival of 1646.) The connection to Monteverdi was now open to question, especially since none of the known sources reliably ascribed the work to him.[54]

The doubts awakened by Osthoff's discoveries deepened in the following decade, when a philological study by Alessandra Chiarelli of all the sources then known concluded that both scores of *Incoronazione* probably descended from a lost original, that they were both connected to the Neapolitan production of 1651 rather than to a Venetian revival of 1646, which, she suggested, probably never took place, and that even more of the music—not just the overture—was probably not Monteverdi's.[55] Ironically, though the shock has diminished by now, the rejected music included what was undoubtedly the most famous part of the opera, the notoriously sensuous final duet "Pur ti miro," the text and possibly the music of which Lorenzo Bianconi had already tentatively attributed to Ferrari.[56] (I shall consider the question of authenticity more fully in the next chapter.)

Briefly, the argument is as follows: Present in all of the manuscript sources (scores and librettos of uncertain date, most of them posthumous), "Pur ti miro" is missing from both of the printed (and securely dated) texts, which are also posthumous. The significance of this discrepancy is heightened by the fact that the text had appeared in print, in another libretto, of another opera, by another author, which was published and performed before the premiere of *Incoronazione*. The author of the libretto and the music of this opera, *Il pastor regio,* performed both in Venice (1640) and Bologna (1641), was Benedetto Ferrari. (That the duet text appeared in the Bologna edition only suggested that it was added after the Venetian production.) To complicate the matter further, the same text appeared six years later in the libretto for *Il trionfo della fatica* (Rome, 1647), a *carro musicale* that was set to music by Filiberto Laurenzi, another composer with strong connections to opera in Venice, particularly during the year of the *Incoronazione* premiere.[57]

---

54. To this day, there is only one such source, the Udine libretto, which was discovered only a decade ago. See Chap. 3.

55. Alessandra Chiarelli, "*L'incoronazione di Poppea o Il Nerone,*" *RIM* (1974): 117–51. For her doubts about a 1646 production, based on inconsistencies in the Bonlini and Groppo chronologies and inaccuracies in Ivanovich, see p. 125. Bianconi and Walker, "Dalla *Finta pazza,*" 416–17, n. 154, noting the absence of any printed librettos in 1646, suggest that no performances took place in that year because carnival activities were suspended on account of the war of Candia. But John Whenham, "Perspectives on the Chronology of the First Decade of Public Opera at Venice," *Saggiatore musicale* 11 (2004): 253–302, at 272, argues that only certain theatrical activities were suspended, not necessarily all operas (and he adduces *Ercole in Lidia,* which John Evelyn reported seeing in 1646, as evidence). Moreover, as I show in Chap. 4, the relationship among the sources of *Incoronazione* makes a performance in 1646 quite likely. For further on Whenham's argument, see Chap. 4, n. 116.

56. Cf. Chiarelli, "*L'incoronazione,*" 149–51.

57. See Lorenzo Bianconi, *Music in the Seventeenth Century* (Cambridge: Cambridge University Press, 1987), 194–96, for a summary of the whole story.

However, since Chiarelli's and Bianconi's work, new evidence has emerged showing that, though its text may not have been written by Busenello, "Pur ti miro" was probably part of the original production of *Incoronazione*. This comes from the manuscript libretto discovered by Paolo Fabbri in Udine, the one libretto that seems clearly to reflect that production: it contains "Pur ti miro."[58] This discovery permitted the hypothesis that Ferrari or Laurenzi, or both, were somehow involved with the original production.[59] When he identified the music of still another younger composer, Francesco Sacrati, in *Incoronazione*, Alan Curtis concluded that the 1643 Venetian production of *Incoronazione*, like *La finta savia*, an opera performed during the same season, at the same theater, presumably by the same troupe, must have been a collaborative effort, a pasticcio. (The pasticcio hypothesis helped to justify Curtis's doubts concerning the authenticity of various other passages in the score, which were based on what he considered anomalous musical and notational features.)[60]

Ironically, this was the same hypothesis that had been advanced more than a half-century earlier, with much less evidence, to explain some of the puzzling anomalies in *Ritorno*. It is ironic, too, that the youthfulness so prized in *Incoronazione*, especially in its final duet, could turn out to have been just that: but not Monteverdi's. "Pur ti miro" (and possibly more than that) may well be the work of a composer who was really young at the time it was composed, as were Sacrati, Ferrari, and Laurenzi.

This argument has recently been taken up once again, this time by Anthony Pryer, in the context of debates regarding authentic performance practices.[61] He leans toward authenticity. Arguing on the basis of stylistic rather than documentary evidence, he points out that none of the traits Curtis identifies as non-Monteverdian (minim triple, cadential tic, and so on) occur in "Pur ti miro." This leads him to suggest that there could have been two versions of the music—one by Monteverdi (in *Incoronazione*), the other by Ferrari (in *Il pastor regio*)—noting as confirmation that the two composers had set another text, "Voglio di vita uscir," differently. He also counters the claim that the progressive form of the duet—often touted as an early example of da capo—made Monteverdi an unlikely composer, by citing another such form in an uncontested earlier portion of *Incoronazione*.

---

58. Paolo Fabbri, "New Sources for *Poppea*," *ML* 74 (1993): 16–23. Recently, in liner notes for a recording of *Incoronazione* conducted by Sergio Vartolo (Brilliant Classics 2004), Lorenzo Bianconi has expressed skepticism concerning the date of the Udine libretto. I discuss this whole matter in Chap. 3 below.

59. A document of 28 February 1641, indicating Monteverdi to be a creditor of Ferrari (cited above, Chap. 1, n. 14), certainly supports the notion that the two were involved in opera production together in the early 1640s—presumably for *Il ritorno d'Ulisse* and *Le nozze d'Enea*, when Ferrari managed both SS. Giovanni e Paolo and S. Moisè. That this joint activity extended to the 1642/43 season is thus highly likely.

60. Curtis, "*La Poppea Impasticciata*," 32–35. Anomalies identified by Curtis include so-called "minim-triple" notation, passages with missing text and/or music, indications for transposition, and certain kinds of ornaments and cadences that are atypical of Monteverdi. This material is considered later.

61. Anthony Pryer, "Authentic Performance, Authentic Experience, and *Pur ti Miro* from *Poppea*," in *Performing Practice in Monteverdi's Music*, ed. Rafaello Monterosso (Cremona: Fondazione Claudio Monteverdi, 1995), 191–213.

In the most recent monograph on Monteverdi's operas, Tim Carter tries to have it both ways: taking account of—and even adding to—Pryer's arguments for authenticity, but generally favoring Curtis's against it, he concludes that "if 'Pur ti miro' is not by Monteverdi, it is a much closer imitation of him than is currently assumed."[62] My own view is that the piece may indeed not be by Monteverdi, but that it may not matter.[63] I shall consider "Pur ti miro" again in the next chapter, as part of the authenticity debate that continues to surround both *Incoronazione* and *Ritorno*, deriving from the peculiar nature of the source material of the two works.

Performance

At the very time when the seeds of doubt concerning *Incoronazione* were being planted, the opera, along with its hardy predecessor *Ritorno*, was finally beginning to earn a place on the modern stage. This it did in a series of productions beginning in the 1960s that embodied the developing narrative of early music performance as it threaded its way between deference to the supposed tastes of modern audiences and increasing respect for the conditions and values of the original performance. (See discography, Table 3.)

Two particularly important productions of the 1960s epitomize the historical performance debate as it existed at the time. The first and initially more influential of the two was the Glyndebourne production (1962) conducted by John Pritchard, in a version edited (or "realized," as he termed it) by Raymond Leppard. Leppard addressed himself to the Glyndebourne public, an audience used to the operas of Mozart, Rossini, and Verdi. Keeping in mind the tastes of that audience and the capabilities of the performers, Leppard added, cut, and changed many things in the original score. He reorchestrated it for a large ensemble that included harps as well as lutes, and transposed the original soprano and alto castrato roles to be sung by tenor and baritone. He also restructured the drama, dividing it into two rather than three acts in order to accommodate the traditional single Glyndebourne intermission. A recording was issued in 1963 and the edition was published the following year, both of which inspired and facilitated many subsequent productions in Europe as well as in the United States.[64] The edition, in fact, remains in print and is still used, especially in peripheral centers; the orchestral parts are available for rental.

---

62. Carter, *Musical Theatre*, 233.

63. See Ellen Rosand, "Did Monteverdi Write *L'incoronazione di Poppea* and Does It Matter?" *Opera News* 59, no. 1 (July 1994): 20–23.

64. As is evident from Table 3, there were several earlier recordings. See Barlow, "The Revival," 193–207; also Giuseppe Rossi, "Il taccuino del discofilo," in the program book from a production in Florence, 1992, and Jürg Stenzl, "Claudio Monteverdi nell'epoca della riproducibilità tecnica," in *L'esperienza musicale: Teoria e storia della recezione*, ed. Gianmario Borio and Michela Garda (Turin: EDT, 1989), 166–84; a longer version of this article may be found in *Rezeptionsästhetik und Rezeptionsgeschichte in der Musikwissenschaft* (Laaber: Laaber-Verlag, 1991), where figures 2 and 3 (p. 299) provide a complete list of recordings up to 1982. For a list

The second crucial production of the 1960s was conducted at the University of California at Berkeley by Alan Curtis, then a young harpsichordist, soon to make his way in the world of Baroque opera. Representing the opposite pole in the historical performance debate, it could not have been more different from the Glyndebourne production, with its modest orchestra—only three violins and continuo—and use of original vocal ranges (Nerone and Ottone were sung by soprano and alto). Though first performed and recorded in 1966, Curtis's edition itself did not appear in print until 1989, following a second recording issued in 1980. A comparison of the two recordings indicates how much Curtis himself modified and reconsidered his edition during the intervening years. The late appearance of Curtis's edition in print, with respect to Leppard's, meant that it could not exercise the same influence on subsequent performances, at least until recently. Though it requires considerable work on the part of potential conductors, Curtis's score promotes musicology in the theater. The editor has chosen among different readings, basing his choices on philological criteria, and he has explained those choices to satisfy potential performers. His score represents a major achievement in recent Monteverdi studies.

A third highly influential edition of *Incoronazione*, by Nikolaus Harnoncourt, one of the prime movers in the early music movement, was performed and recorded in Vienna in 1974. What remained the most complete version until very recently—it is almost uncut—was subsequently reduced for a production in Zurich in 1982, also conducted by Harnoncourt, which was directed by Jean Pierre Ponelle. That production was filmed in the early 1980s, along with *Orfeo* and *Ritorno*, and was seen by audiences around the world, including millions in the United States on public television. Monteverdi's operas had become (almost) a household commodity.

In keeping with the role of stepchild it had played since the discovery of *Incoronazione*, *Ritorno* was neither performed nor edited as often during the early period. No performances are documented for twenty years after that of the Dallapiccola edition at the Maggio Musicale of 1942. The 1960s saw only a couple of productions (one of Dallapiccola's edition at the Piccola Scala [1963] and two others, in Stuttgart and London, in 1965, based on an edition [or adaptation] by one F. Marshall), and only one recording (Ewerhart, 1964).[65] Though Harnoncourt had actually performed and recorded *Ritorno* before *Incoronazione*, in 1971, and again with Ponelle in 1977—the project entailed performance of the three operas in chronological order, beginning with *Orfeo*—Leppard did not reach it at Glyndebourne until 1972 (recorded only in 1979), a full decade after his

of *Incoronazione* recordings and performances up to 1988, see Christophe Capacci, "Discographie," in *Monteverdi: Le Couronnement de Poppée, L'Avant-scène opéra* 115 (December 1988): 154–61, and Michel Pazdro, "L'œuvre à l'affiche," ibid., pp. 162–65. For a review of recent DVDs of *Ritorno* and *Incoronazione*, see Roberto Giuliani, "Monteverdi Opera on DVD," *Early Music* 34 (2006): 702–706.

65. For various editions and performances of *Ritorno* up to 1994, see *Monteverdi: Le retour d'Ulysse, L'Avant-scène opéra* 159 (1994), especially Denis Morrier, "Un retour aux sources d'*Ulysse*," pp. 110–115; Pierre Michot, "Discographie-Vidéographie," 120–26; and Josée Bégaud and Germain Fauquet, "L'oeuvre à l'affiche," 128–33.

TABLE 3

Discography

Il ritorno d'Ulisse in patria

1962	Rudolf Ewerhart (Vox DLBX 211 and DLLX 5211, stereo)
1971	Nikolaus Harnoncourt (Telefunken 6.35.376)
1973	Raymond Leppard (Pickwick Screen Legend)
1979	Raymond Leppard (CBS 79 332)
1982	Nikolaus Harnoncourt (Telefunken 6.35.592)
1985	Jeffrey Tate, Salzburgh Festival, Henze version (video: Kultur 0053; DVD: RM Associates)
1992	Alan Curtis (Nuova Era)
1992	René Jacobs (Harmonia Mundi)
1998	Gabriel Garrido (K617)
2002	Nikolas Harnoncourt, Zurich Opera (Arthaus Musik DVD)
2002	William Christie, Aix-en-Provence (Virgin Classics DVD)
2005	Pierre Audi (Opus Arte 0926)
2005	Anthony Rolfe-Johnson, Amsterdam Opera (Opus Arte DVD)
2006	Sergio Vartolo (Brilliant Classics)

L'incoronazione di Poppea

1952	Walter Goehr (Classic/Concert Hall CHS 1184, mono)
1954	Nino Sanzogno (Fonit Cetra Arkadia N. Ark 103 [14])
1963	Rudolf Ewerhart (Vox, SVBX 5212)
1963	John Pritchard/Raymond Leppard (EMI Seraphim 6073)
1966	Alan Curtis (Cambridge CRS B 1901)
1974	Nikolaus Harnoncourt (Teldec 6.35.247)
1978	Julius Rudel (Legendary Records 160; Lyric Distribution DVD)
1980	Alan Curtis (Fonit Cetra LMA 3008; Lyric Distribution DVD)
1982	Nikolaus Harnoncourt (Teldec)
1984	Jean-Claude Malgoire (CBS)
1984	Raymond Leppard (Castle Opera DVD)
1986	Michel Corboz (Lyric Distribution DVD)
1988	Richard Hickox (Virgin Classics VCT 7 90775–2/4)
1988	Alberto Zedda (Nuova Era 6737/39)
1990	René Jacobs (Harmonia mundi HMC 901330.32)
1993	René Jacobs, Schwetzinger Festspiele (Arthaus Musik DVD; also Lyric Distribution DVD)
1996	John Eliot Gardiner, Queen Elizabeth Hall, London (Archiv)
1998	Ivor Bolton, Munich Opera Festival 1997 (Farao Classics)
1998	Herbert Von Karajan, Wiener Staatsoper 1963 (DGG)
2000	Carlo Franci, Firenze, Maggio Musicale 1966 (Allegro)
2000	Gabriel Garrido (K617)

TABLE 3 *(continued)*

2005	Sergio Vartolo (Brilliant Classics)
2005	Christophe Rousset, Amsterdam Opera, 1994 (Opus Arte DVD 0924)
2005	Mark Minkowski (Bel Air Classiques DVD)

This list does not include the more recent videos of live performances of *L'incoronazione di Poppea* issued by House of Opera, including Venice, 1985, Lausanne, 1986, and Welsh National Opera, 1998.

Incoronazione, and Curtis not until 1990, in Berkeley (recorded in 1992), nearly a quarter-century after his *Incoronazione.* Although it has since nearly caught up in terms of performances, *Ritorno* has still not been recorded as frequently. Three recordings were issued in the 1990s, however (Curtis, 1992; Jacobs, 1992; and Gabriel Garrido, 1998) and another in 2006 (Vartolo), and a scholarly edition by Alan Curtis, a pendant to his *Incoronazione,* finally appeared in 2002.[66]

During the past several decades *Incoronazione,* in particular, has presented a challenge to some of the best-known early music conductor/editors. In addition to the recordings of Harnoncourt and Curtis, those of Jean-Claude Malgoire (1984), Richard Hickox (1988), Jacobs (1990), John Eliot Gardiner (1996), Ivor Bolton (1998), Gabriel Garrido (2000), and Sergio Vartolo (2005) offer a compendium of the performance choices available in the late twentieth century. The most basic decision confronting any conductor or editor involves establishing a musical text. The obvious options would be either to rely on one or another of the extant manuscript scores (Hickox chose the Venice score; Malgoire, Gardiner, and Garrido the Naples score); or to combine elements of both (like Curtis 1980 and Jacobs). As we shall see, the choice is not as straightforward as it might seem, because it necessarily implies certain assumptions that may not be completely conscious, let alone valid: namely, that one or another of the manuscripts is "closer" to Monteverdi's original, or represents a particular early performance; or that the combination of elements from both best reproduces the attitudes and procedures of the original performers. Sources other than the scores—contemporary librettos and the scenario—would certainly need to be taken into consideration to clarify this situation.

Then there are the cuts: of characters, of individual scenes, and of shorter passages within scenes. Even for modern audiences inured to Wagnerian length, these operas have almost always been deemed too long.[67] Needless to say, even minor cuts can affect the way the work is perceived by an audience. But major cuts were routinely made in the 1960s

---

66. Jane Glover also edited the score, based on Bartlett's transcription (Monteverdi, *Il ritorno d'Ulisse in patria* in a new performing edition by Jane Glover, based on the transcription by Clifford Bartlett). Cf. Table 2 above.

67. Until recently, Harnoncourt's first version was the most comprehensive. That honor has been assumed by Sergio Vartolo with his recording for Brilliant Classics. A comparative analysis of the cuts and other interventions in the various versions of the two operas would make a valuable contribution to the history of the early music movement.

productions of *Incoronazione*. Ottavia's nurse was eliminated in Leppard, Ewerhardt, Goehr, and Fracci; Valletto and/or Damigella in Curtis 1980 and Ewerhart; the prologue was omitted in Leppard, Fracci, Ewerhart, and Goehr; and the entire mythological component of the final scene was cut in most of the earlier versions. These would be considered too extreme in today's early music climate, an impoverishment of the dramatic meaning of the work. Indeed, all of the more recent recordings include the prologue, and most also include Ottavia's nurse, but cuts are still taken in the final scene of the opera (within the dialogue of Venus and Cupid), and most recordings still eliminate numerous brief passages within the text.[68]

The more recent conductors are all certified members of the so-called historically-informed performance movement; they are committed to "authenticity," but they construe their authenticities differently.[69] However complex the issue, it is clear that authenticity cannot be measured by absolute fidelity to original sources, even if those sources could be fully recovered: we cannot recreate the original performance conditions, even if we knew precisely what they were. And so it is no surprise that every one of these conductors makes compromises, interpreting the sources in light of particular performance exigencies. Every conductor, no matter what his attitude toward the sources, has had to decide how to realize the harmony and deploy the continuo instruments, decisions that would originally either have been self-evident or intentionally left to be worked out in rehearsal—the players themselves now, as then, would be responsible for realizing the continuo parts. Among those who interpret the sources most liberally only a few have felt the need to add completely new material, such as instrumental sinfonie and ritornelli taken from other operas, even by other composers (especially Jacobs). Most conductors add parts for instruments that are not called for either by the early scores or by contemporary pay records (such as flutes and trumpets). In almost all of the recordings, instruments are used in ways not dictated by the sources (string parts, for instance, are routinely added to the basso continuo line to accompany lyrical passages: Jacobs does this in almost forty different places).

For the past decade many of these decisions have been facilitated by Curtis's edition; nonetheless, most conductors still need to make their own choices based on the nature and traditions of the performance space (size of theater, number of intermissions), the availability of performers (countertenors or women for castrato roles; Baroque or modern instruments), the expectations of the audience for which the production is intended, and even constraints of time. As such, their responsibility is not so different from that of the original performers. Operatic productions have always depended on such contingencies.

If the compromise between the desire for authenticity and specific performance considerations is more difficult to achieve with *Ritorno* and *Incoronazione* than with other

---

68. I discuss those involving Seneca in Chap. 8.

69. For a thorough rehearsal of the issues, historical and critical, surrounding the concept of "authenticity," see Richard Taruskin, *Text and Act: Essays on Music and Performance* (New York: Oxford University Press, 1995), especially the introduction.

operas in the repertory, that is partly owing to historical distance and the absence of a continuous (or, indeed, any) performance tradition. But it is also because the surviving sources are unusually laconic, incomplete, and, as a result, inadequately understood. We do not quite know what they represent; all that is clear is that on their own they are insufficient as a basis for performance, authentic or not. *Any* effort to present these operas with a clear aesthetic vision must confront the challenge of the sources and recognize their implications for the understanding of the works.

The increase in performances and recordings of *Ritorno* and *Incoronazione* over the past several decades has made them almost familiar to modern audiences. They are produced in the world's leading opera houses, in the company of the canonical works in the operatic repertory. That very familiarity has raised questions beyond the technical ones of performance practice, questions about the meaning of these operas, both to their original audience and to a modern one. Such questions have stimulated interest in the conditions of their early production and inspired the development of new contexts for their interpretation; they have been studied within the context of the specifically Venetian cultural milieu and within the broader context of the history of opera. That larger vision should serve to guide basic editorial decisions; it should alert editors to the implications of their choices and how they affect the communication of meaning.

Of the two, *Ritorno* would seem to present fewer problems of interpretation than its sister work, partly because there is only a single extant score, but also because it remains faithful to its canonical literary source, Homer's *Odyssey*. Although different productions have cut various portions of the lengthy text—scenes of the Olympian gods, for instance—and reconfigured the acts in various ways, the opera remains essentially what its title says it is: a reenactment of Ulysses' return to his homeland.

Meaning in *Incoronazione,* on the other hand, is congenitally elusive. Not only have two quite different contemporary scores come down to us, but, far from adhering to any single established literary source, the opera conflates and rearranges several unfamiliar ones. Furthermore, it was also known under a different title, *Il Nerone,* which only confirms a sense of ambiguity, suggesting that problems of interpretation were inherent from the beginning of its history. One version would presumably emphasize the emperor Nerone as protagonist, whereas the other would underscore Poppea's achievement of her goal. A desire to privilege one of these readings over the other could well influence the editing of the text. The implications for interpretation opened up by such a seemingly minor disparity between sources are indeed major. And there are many such disparities.

A most telling example is offered by "Pur ti miro," the possibly "inauthentic" duet with which the opera ended in at least some of its early performances. Although the sources might justify omitting it as not by Monteverdi—as we have noted, it is missing in both printed librettos—its absence in performance would shift the weight of the opera, not only the conclusion but the ultimate meaning of the work. It would end with a mythological triumph, the crowning of Poppea by Amore and Venere. Without "Pur ti miro," we would be deprived of the sensual sound of an endlessly repeating, seductive ostinato, a piece that mimes the intimacy of lovers, their hypnotically intertwining lines encircling one another to the point of exhaustion. The notoriously shocking effect of *Incoronazione,* its intense sexuality, would be less palpable, tamed and contained within a decorous mythological frame.[70]

Another significant omission that might be justified by adhering to a particular source is that of Seneca's farewell to his followers, a scene missing in the Naples libretto of the opera. Without this scene, Seneca's death would appear much less shocking: he would simply disappear, unnoticed. The effect of his death would be softened, too, if it were not directly followed by the ironically contrasting love scene between Valletto and Damigella (as in Curtis 1980; the scene is moved in Leppard's version, so that rather than commenting on Seneca's death, it precedes it.) Our perception of Seneca's character would also be affected if the speech in which the Valletto mocks his pedantry were cut, as it is in three of the libretto sources. Clearly, then, editing of the sources can have a crucial impact on the effect of these works in the theater, on the meanings conveyed to an audience.

After more than a century of study and half a century of performance, Monteverdi's Venetian operas have not yet yielded up all their secrets. Some of the most basic questions about them remain to be answered. Scholars continue to wrestle with the ambiguities of meaning, especially those posed by *Incoronazione.* The problem is exacerbated by an inadequate comprehension of the sources: we still do not have a valid text, or even "texts," because we still do not know what the sources actually represent, how they relate to one another, and where they fit within the complex chronology of the creation and performance of the operas. The establishment of such a basic text, in turn, depends upon an understanding of the cultural and historical milieu in which these operas were created and performed, of the contingencies of their original production(s). The task of interpretation is philological as well as historical.

---

70. The only recorded version I know of to have omitted "Pur ti miro," to interesting effect, was conducted by Nino Sanzogno for RAI (1954). Malipiero's performance edition of the work (1954) also cut "Pur ti miro."

3

Sources and Authenticity

Three Librettos

That *Ritorno* and *Incoronazione* continue to raise more problems of interpretation than any other operas of the period is due in part to the nature of their source material. For no other contemporary opera are the surviving sources so numerous, so varied, and so complex as those of Monteverdi's Venetian operas, and this includes *Le nozze d'Enea* as well as the other two. These sources comprise manuscript scores, manuscript and printed librettos of several kinds, with diverse relationships to one another, and printed scenarios. The very survival of these sources, as well as their unique character and complexity, results from the confluence of a number of fortunate and probably independent historical accidents.

First, the operas were written and performed during the early 1640s, the formative years of Venetian opera, before printed librettos had become conventional accessories for theatergoers; if they were published at all, it was after the performance, as a kind of memento or historical record. Instead of printed librettos, audiences of the period were provided with shorter, cheaper publications called scenarios, which enabled them to follow the drama by summarizing the plots. Librettos do survive, but in manuscript form. Second, their librettists were aristocrats who preferred anonymity and purposely refrained from seeking the financial rewards or fame of publication.[1] Third, the librettos were written for a composer notorious for altering his texts. And, finally, rather than being discarded and forgotten after a single season, like most other operas of the time, two of them—*Ritorno*

---

1. Technically, Busenello was a *cittadino ordinario*, a member of the highest level of the *cittadino* class, rather than an aristocrat. See Glixon and Glixon, *Business*, 176 and appendix.

and *Incoronazione*—were revived under conditions that probably explain the survival, and certainly the nature, of the scores. Both of the *Incoronazione* scores, as I have noted, can be associated with a revival, and the same may be true of the single *Ritorno* score, as we shall soon see. At least one of the individuals responsible for the *Incoronazione* revival was, fortunately, Francesco Cavalli, Monteverdi's great disciple—fortunately, because Cavalli evidently prized his own scores highly enough to arrange for their copying and preservation.[2] It is probably thanks to his impulse toward preservation, unique in the period, that the Venice manuscript of *Incoronazione* survived. As I have mentioned, not only is Cavalli's hand evident in its numerous alterations, but the score is partly in the hand of his primary copyist, his wife.[3]

All these conditions have broad implications. As far as the librettos are concerned, the uniqueness of the situation is worth emphasizing: aside from those for Monteverdi's three works, almost no manuscript librettos of Venetian operas have survived.[4] Those for Monteverdi's works—twelve for *Ritorno*, eleven for *Nozze*, seven for *Incoronazione*—are listed in Tables 4, 5, and 6 below. The librettos of all the other operas produced in Venice during the seventeenth century were published. Initially they appeared soon after the performance, in commemorative editions recording a past event—the relationship to the performance was often signaled by the use of the verb in the past tense on title pages: "rappresentato." But gradually, for practical reasons, librettos began to be published sooner, when performance was still in the future—"da rappresentare" was the telltale title-page formula. When issued in advance, librettos could not only aid the public in following the plot at hand, but they could also attract audiences to an imminent production. The librettos usually carried the name of their authors and were printed at their expense.[5]

The scenarios that were published in their stead during the early years, whose sole purpose was to outline the plots, were much shorter and thus less expensive to produce. (They could also be produced quickly, in the days—or even hours?—before a performance, and are therefore more likely than librettos to provide details about a particular production.) Issued anonymously, probably by the impresario, scenarios might or might not have been followed, eventually, by librettos. Because they were actually used, and had no pretense to literary value, their survival rate is predictably low: many more of them

---

2. Cavalli may have been motivated by a sense of history, or, more likely, by a desire to increase the value of his estate. He certainly treated the scores as property in his testament, bequeathing them to his most prized student, Giovanni Caliari. See Taddeo Wiel, "Francesco Cavalli (1602–1676) e la sua musica scenica," *Nuovo archivio veneto*, 3rd ser., 18 (1914): 106–50; also Glover, *Cavalli*, 32, and Walker, "*Ubi Lucius*," 72.

3. See Jeffery, "The Autograph Manuscripts," 169–75.

4. The exceptions prove the rule. Manuscripts of two other librettos by Busenello, *Apollo e Dafne* and *La Didone*, both of them early works, have survived in multiple copies. See below, n. 14. (Presumably they were copied before the publication of *Le hore ociose*, the collected edition of Busenello's librettos [Venice: Giuliani, 1656], or else if no copies of that publication were available to the potential collector.)

5. On the conventions of libretto publication, see Glixon and Glixon, *Business*, chap. 5, "The Librettist"; *OSV*, 81–88; and Whenham, "Perspectives," who questions the reliability of verb tense as a key to performance chronology.

must have been published than are extant.[6] Carlo Bonlini, one of the early chroniclers of Venetian opera, explained the distinction between librettos and scenarios in his entry for *Andromeda* (1637), the first opera libretto published in Venice, which appeared several months after the performance:

> This drama was not printed, as normally happens now, before the performances, for the greater convenience of the spectators, who pay greater attention when they can see the libretto, which makes manifest what they listen to. For this reason, its publication was useless, since it only appeared two months afterwards, and only served to render more obvious the vain ostentation of its author; an example that is still followed, if only by a few. I believe, however, that the listeners of that time were satisfied with the simple publication of the scenario, which was very much the custom in the early years; the many scenarios of the oldest dramas in circulation among collectors, even today, either separately or affixed to the libretto of the same drama, which contain the argomento and the action of the whole opera, provide clear evidence of this.[7]

Printed scenarios were probably issued for all three of Monteverdi's Venetian operas, although exemplars of only those for *Nozze* and *Incoronazione* have survived; but the librettos for *Ritorno* and *Nozze* were never published at all, either before or after the productions.[8] In contrast, the libretto of *Incoronazione* was eventually printed with the author's name, but only in 1656, more than a decade after the original performance, in a collected edition of Busenello's librettos. (Another libretto was printed anonymously in Naples in 1651, in connection with the Neapolitan revival of the opera; see below.)

---

6. Since many scenarios survive in only a single exemplar, it is probable that others have disappeared completely. See Ellen Rosand, "The Opera Scenario, 1638–1655: A Preliminary Survey," in *In Cantu et in Sermone: For Nino Pirrotta on his 80th Birthday,* ed. Fabrizio Della Seta and Franco Piperno (Florence: Olschki, 1989), 355–46; also Gloria Staffieri, "Lo scenario nell'opera in musica del XVII secolo," in *Le parole della musica II: Studi sul lessico della letteratura critica del teatro musicale in onore di Gianfranco Folena,* ed. Maria Teresa Muraro (Florence: Olschki, 1995), 3–31.

7. "Questo Drama non fu stampato, come d'ordinario si pratica, in tempo che ne seguivano le Recite, a maggior commodo de' Spettatori, che stanno con l'attenzione più risvegliata, quando abbino sotto l'occhio il libretto, che faccia lor fede di quanto ascoltano. Perciò la sua impressione fu infruttuosa, mentre si vidde solo circa due mesi dopo, e non servì ch'a rendere più palese la vana ostentazion del suo auttore. Esempio, che non lasciò d'imitarsi ancora, se ben da pochi. Credo però che l'uditorio all'ora restasse pago con la semplice stampa dello scenario, come era molto in uso negl'anni primi, facendo di ciò ben chiara testimonianza, molti scenari de' più antichi drami, che vanno vagando per mano de' più curiosi, anche al giorno d'oggi, o sciolti, o annessi al libretto del drama istesso, ne i quali si contiene l'argomento, e l'azione di tutta l'opera" (Bonlini, *Le glorie della poesia,* 35–36).

8. Wolfgang Osthoff noted a reference to a scenario for *Ritorno,* the existence of which he was unable to verify ("Zu den Quellen," 69, n. 14). Groppo (*Catalogo di tutti i drammi,* 17) mentions a scenario for *Ritorno,* but it is unclear whether it was printed or manuscript, since he fails to note the size, information he includes for all the other scenarios. The closest thing we have to a scenario for *Ritorno* is the argomento found in two of the manuscript librettos (see Table 4 below, and Appendix 5). For *Incoronazione* in 1642, Bonlini notes that the libretto was not published, but that the performance was accompanied by a scenario, "come è seguito fin'ora di tutti gl'altri di quest'Autore [e.g., *Apollo e Dafne* and *Didone*] che sono stati accompagnati in Scena solamente

The exceptional position of our three librettos—their survival either in manuscript only or in a much later publication—is a function of the shared social background of the authors. They were aristocrats whose elevated social status apparently discouraged professional engagement in operatic activities. Giacomo Badoaro, the author of *Ritorno,* even (explicitly) disclaimed personal ambition in the letter to Monteverdi from which I have already quoted, which prefaces one of the manuscript copies of his libretto (see Appendix 1): His aim in writing *Ritorno d'Ulisse,* he says, was emphatically not to compete with those talents [*ingegni*] who had recently been presenting their compositions publicly in Venetian theaters. He hoped, rather, as we have seen in Chapter 1, to lure Monteverdi out of operatic retirement. Significantly, this letter was unsigned, though the libretto to which it is affixed (see no. 5 in Table 4 below)—the only one of the *Ritorno* manuscripts even close to contemporary with the first performance—identifies Badoaro by his initials on its title page.

All but one of the eleven other manuscript copies are also ascribed to Badoaro on their title pages, but, as we shall see, ten of these date from the eighteenth century, and thus could have drawn their information as to the author (as well as other things) from a later source. In fact, it was not until 1644, some four years after the premiere of *Ritorno,* in the preface to his second operatic text, *Ulisse errante,* which he published under an academic alias, "Assicurato Academico Incognito," that Badoaro acknowledged his authorship of the earlier libretto—and thus, indirectly, of the prefatory letter to Monteverdi: "Feci già molti anni rappresentare il ritorno d'Ulisse in Patria. . . . Hora fo vedere l'Ulisse Errante."[9]

Like his friend Badoaro, the author of *Nozze,* with equivalent modesty, and carefully maintaining his anonymity—almost to this day, it would seem—explains in the long letter introducing the printed scenario that he has never seen fit even to admit to the public that he is a writer, let alone display his works: "though drawn by inclination to poetry I have written many things, even though terrified by the difficulty of so divine a faculty, and even more by the weakness of my own wit, I have hidden my compositions from the sight of others, so that only a few closest friends even knew that I composed a single

con un breve Scenario in Stampa" (p. 42). Although one copy of the *Didone* scenario has survived (I-Vnm 908.4), none is extant for *Apollo and Dafne.* This confirms that the surviving scenarios do not represent all of those that were printed. Four copies of the *Nozze* scenario are known: I-Mb Racc, Dramm. 527; I-Vnm Dramm. 909.3 and 3449.10; and I-R Biblioteca dell'Istituto nazionale d'archeologia e storia dell'arte, Misc. Teatr. 11/11. Both of the known scenarios for *Incoronazione* are in I-Vnm: Dramm. 910.8 and 3450.11. A third exemplar, once located in Paris (by Osthoff, and listed in Claudio Sartori, *I libretti italiani a stampa dalle origini al 1800: Catalogo analitico con 16 indici* [Cuneo: Bertola & Locatelli, c. 1990–c. 1994], 5, 140), appears to be lost. Salvioli (Giovanni Salvioli and Carlo Salvioli), *Biblioteca universale del teatro drammatico con particolare riguardo alla storia della musica italiana* 1 [Venice: Ferrari, 1903], col. 261), lists a scenario for *Apollo e Dafne,* but only for the putative revival of 1647.

9. Badoaro was identified as L'Assicurato Accademico Incognito in Lione Allacci's entry on *L'Ulisse errante* in *Drammaturgia di Lione Allacci,* 826: "*L'Ulisse errante* . . . poesia dell'Assicurato Accademico Incognito, cioè, Giacomo Badoaro, Patrizio Veneto." In any case the ascription of both librettos to Badoaro is assured by that sonnet in the little Bologna volume cited above in Chap. 1, n. 21.

verse" (Appendix 2 [c]). Although all but two of the eleven manuscripts of *Nozze* ascribe the text to Giacomo Badoaro (nos. 2 and 6 in Table 5 below are anonymous), it is clearly by someone else. This is confirmed in the scenario letter, in which the author refers to Badoaro in the third person.[10]

The existence of multiple manuscript copies of *Ritorno* and *Nozze*, then, most of them preserving quite similar readings, is a direct result of their not having been published in the first place. Most of our information about Venetian librettos comes from comprehensive collections that now survive in various libraries around the world (the Biblioteca Marciana, Library of Congress, and elsewhere). When these collections were in the process of being formed, during the eighteenth century, *Ritorno* and *Nozze* had to be copied by hand in order to be included. One of the collectors was the aforementioned Bonlini, who noted that although *Ritorno* and *Nozze* had not been printed, "manuscript copies can easily be had, though hardly free of errors."[11]

At present, we have no way of knowing what sources the copyists used. Thus the authenticity of the information on their title pages as well as of their textual readings (especially if shared) is always open to question. On the other hand, they are more likely to preserve an earlier, more purely literary version of the text than their printed counterparts of later years, which were specifically designed to present the finished product: what the audience could expect to hear in the theater, the version already edited by the composer.[12] The manuscript librettos, then, offer at least the possibility of being unedited, of representing the stage at which the composer received them. It is this feature of the *Ritorno* librettos in particular that is so important. It seems evident, even from a superficial comparison, that the much fuller text of the librettos is earlier than that in the score. Even though the title pages of most of them indicate that they were actually copied after the performance ("rappresentato"), they clearly preserve the text as it was before the composer edited it.[13] There was no printed performance text to copy from, only the original

---

10. See Chap. 1, nn. 23 and 46.

11. Bonlini, *Le glorie della poesia*, 40: "Tanto questo Drama *[Nozze]*, quanto il suo precedente *[Ritorno]* non furono mai stampati. Possono però aversi facilmente Manoscritti, se ben poco degl'errori purgati." Bonlini's libretto collection is one of the four that ended up in the Biblioteca Marciana—Groppo's are the 900 series, Giovanni Rossi's the 100s, and Apostolo Zeno's the 3000s. The Zeno collection is catalogued in Marinella Laini, *La raccolta zeniana di drammi per musica veneziani della Biblioteca nazionale marciana, 1637–1700* (Lucca: Libreria musicale italiana, 1995). For another such collection, see Irene Alm, *Catalogue of Venetian Librettos at the University of California, Los Angeles* (Berkeley: University of California Press, 1993).

12. The efforts of printers of librettos to incorporate last-minute changes introduced in the text in conjunction with performance are discussed in *OSV*, 204–209; see also Glixon and Glixon, *Business*, 125–28.

13. In the preface to his edition of *Ritorno* (London: Novello, 202), p. ix, Alan Curtis makes the intriguing (but ultimately unconvincing) suggestion that "the libretto text might represent a later version, with additions and revisions by Badoaro (or someone else!), which may or may not ever have been set to music and performed." The distinction between the author's text and the performance text is an important one in the history of opera. See the discussion in Maria Grazia Accorsi, "Varietà: Problemi testuali dei libretti d'opera fra Sei e Settecento," *Giornale storico della letteratura italiana* 166 (1989): 212–25. The issue is treated more extensively in Lorenzo Bianconi, "Hors-d'oeuvre alla filologia dei libretti," *Saggiatore musicale* 2 (1995): 143–54.

pre-Monteverdi version. Thus, when measured against the score, the librettos allow us to observe Monteverdi, the dramatist, at work—to see how and where he intervened in the poetic text. (I return to this subject in Chap. 7.)

A similar comparison is obviously not possible in connection with *Nozze*. Without a score, there would seem nothing to measure the manuscript librettos against. In fact, however, as we shall see, one of the librettos is different enough from the others to suggest a different, later, stage in the process by which the literary libretto was transformed into a text for performance. And this, combined with information from the printed scenario, may allow us to glimpse Monteverdi's editing, as if through a scrim.

The situation for the third of these librettos, *Incoronazione*, is somewhat different, for it survived in printed as well as manuscript form. Its author, Gian Francesco Busenello, was not quite an operatic novice like Badoaro; he had already supplied two librettos for Cavalli by the time of *Incoronazione* (*Gli amori di Apollo e di Dafne* [1640] and *La Didone* [1641]—which were also not published in conjunction with the performances).[14] But he too was an aristocrat for whom publication, particularly in connection with such an overtly commercial venture as opera, may have been deemed inappropriate. His name is certainly missing from most of the manuscript librettos as well as from two of the three printed sources of *Incoronazione* (see Table 6 below). But he must have overcome whatever scruples had initially stood in his way, for he eventually published *Incoronazione*, along with his two earlier Cavalli librettos and several later ones, in a collection entitled *Le hore ociose* (1656), ostentatiously dedicating the volume to Cardinal Pietro Ottoboni, the future Pope Alexander VIII.[15]

The availability of this publication presumably obviated the necessity for later collectors to have *Incoronazione* (and Busenello's other librettos) copied by hand, for, unlike those for the other two operas, all of the *Incoronazione* manuscripts appear to be early—some of them, at least, from before 1656. (Interestingly, some manuscript copies of Busenello's early Cavalli librettos, *Didone* and *Apollo e Dafne*, have survived in collections that also contain *Incoronazione* manuscripts.)[16] Indeed, the distinctive history of the opera suggests a somewhat different role for the *Incoronazione* manuscript libretto.

---

14. It is no coincidence that manuscript versions of these two librettos have also survived. These include I-TVco Cod. Rossi 29: *Gli Amori d'Apollo e di Dafne Opera recitata in musica nel Theatro di S. Cassano In Venetia l'Anno 1640* (no author's name); I-RVI Silvestriani 244 (Cod. 7–1-30), Mazzatini no. 66: *Gl'Amori d'Apollo e Dafne del Businello. Rappresentata in musica nel' Theatro di S. Cassano di Venetia Anno 1640* (no author's name); I-Pu MS 40: *La Dafne opera che si rapresentò in musica nel teattro di San Cassano, L'Anno 1639* [sic], *del Eccmo Sig. Gio: Francesco Businello, honorata con la musica del Ille & Illto Rdo Sig.* [blank] *in Venetia*. Copies in Venice (I-Vnm Ital. Cl. 9) include *Apollo e Dafne*, n. 591 (= 10407) and *La Didone*, n. 465 (= 6386), both with the author's name, though it is missing in the fragment of *La Didone* in I-Fn Magl. VII. 129. There are two further fragments of *La Didone* in I-Vmc: Cicogna 1229 (fols. 216–19, act 3, scene 7), and Correr 270 (fols. 394–403).

15. *Le hore ociose* contains five librettos: *Apollo e Dafne, La Didone, L'incoronazione di Poppea, La prosperità infelice di Giulio Cesare dittatore,* and *La Statira*. At least one of Busenello's librettos, *Enea nell'inferno*, remained unpublished—it was probably never set to music. In his dissertation for Yale University (in progress) Pietro Moretti considers the significance of Busenello's publication of his librettos.

16. Notably in Treviso, Rovigo, Florence, and Venice, Museo Correr.

Of our three operas, only *Incoronazione* is known to have been revived some years after its first performance. The differences among the manuscript librettos, many of them considerably more substantial than those for the other two operas, and between them and Busenello's printed text, suggest that they may reflect not only the original production, but possibly intermediate stages between it and the revival(s). As will soon become clear, several of the manuscript librettos are not collectors' copies of a definitive authorial text but rather working documents, preserving different versions of an evolving or changing text.

Whatever the reason, Busenello's delay in publishing his *Incoronazione* libretto had an impact on the state of the surviving sources, and should influence our understanding of them: the considerable time lag between the first performance (1643) and *Le hore ociose* (1656) allows for the possibility that Busenello edited his text in the interim and that the printed libretto does not represent his original version. The publication must represent the text in the form in which the author wanted it known then—but not necessarily the form in which he gave it to Monteverdi.[17] On the other hand, Busenello may have wished to reassert his authorship of a text that had been mauled and mutilated—and published anonymously in Naples—in its various operatic incarnations by publishing it in its original form. Such a desire certainly motivated his colleague, Giulio Strozzi, to reissue his libretto of *La finta pazza* three years after its original publication.[18] There is evidence, in fact, to which I shall return, that Busenello's printed text (like Strozzi's?) may actually be closer to the version given to the composer than any of the other librettos.[19]

In part because of their unusual profusion, the sources for all three of these operas are particularly difficult to reconcile with one another; reconciliation in each instance requires hypotheses regarding function and chronology. Interestingly, however, and, as it turns out, helpfully, the sources for each of the operas present a different profile, and each of these profiles is useful in understanding the others. It is somewhat paradoxical that fuller understanding of these sources does not necessarily confirm Monteverdi's authorship of the operas—on the contrary, as we have seen in the previous chapter, it might weaken his claim. But it does help to explain the nature of his contribution to the works. And it clarifies as well as confirms their distinctive position within the context of Venetian opera as a whole.

---

17. Note that the Naples score includes more of *Le hore ociose* than the Venetian score does. Could the printed libretto have been expanded to include Naples material, or was that material present from the beginning and cut from the Venetian score? See Chap. 4.

18. "I willingly undertook this third printing of the true *Finta pazza* because I saw that some wandering musicians have had it reprinted it elsewhere in various ways, and that they go around performing it as if it were their own" (Venni volontieri a questa terza impressione della vera Finta Pazza, perché ho veduto, ch'alcuni musici di fortuna l'hanno variamente fatta ristampar altrove, e la vanno rapresentando, come cosa loro); Giulio Strozzi, *La finta pazza*, terza impressione (Venice: Surian, 1644), Preface. He was of course referring to the Febiarmonici, who had been performing the opera up and down the Italian peninsula and had published a libretto in Codogno in 1644, without reference either to Strozzi or to the Venetian origins of the work. See *OSV*, iii.

19. In establishing the text of his edition, Curtis operated on the assumption that Busenello continued to revise his text, at least in small ways, until he published it in 1656. See Claudio Monteverdi, *L'incoronazione di Poppea*, ed. Alan Curtis (London: Novello, 1989), xi.

Almost from the moment the score of *Ritorno* was discovered in the Vienna National Library, more than two centuries after its Venetian premiere, Monteverdi's authorship was in doubt. The text in the score differed too radically from the single manuscript libretto then known (Biblioteca Marciana, Dramm 908, *recte* 909.2), a manuscript that seemed to document the first performance by virtue of naming the date of performance and theater as well as the composer on its title page. The uncovering of eleven additional manuscript librettos, however, has helped to clarify the situation, though not in any way that might have been predicted. These sources are listed in Table 4.[20]

It turns out that only one other libretto (no. 12) names the composer (though he is also identified in the prefatory letter to no. 5); this weakens the significance of that feature as a determinant for the authenticity of the libretto over that of the anonymous score. Indeed, the absence of Monteverdi's name in nine of the twelve librettos is not surprising, especially since they appear to have been literary rather than performance redactions, a distinction to be discussed presently. The same is also true of the *Incoronazione* librettos: Monteverdi's name appears in only one of the seven manuscripts and none of the printed sources. Indeed, that he is mentioned in almost all of the *Nozze* librettos is noteworthy, but only as an indication that they were copied from the same exemplar or a group of closely related ones. Because librettos were the property of their authors, and published for their gain, composers' names were not normally included, unless their prominence would have enhanced the prestige of the work.[21]

As far as date and venue are concerned, the librettos disagree among themselves, and therefore the authority of any one of them is undermined by the others. These disagreements can be used to advantage, however. They afford insight into the relationship among the sources, allowing us to privilege some of them over the others. But their points of agreement are even more significant: indeed, despite numerous small textual differences among the *Ritorno* librettos, they all confirm the major discrepancies with the score. Their title pages may be far from uniform, but the texts themselves agree in most important particulars.

The major differences between the librettos and the score are as follows: a different

---

20. As far as my numbering of the sources is concerned, I have adopted that first given in Osthoff, "Zu den Quellen," 69 as expanded in Sevieri, *Le nozze d'Enea*, 25–26, rather than Curtis (*Ritorno*, preface, x), who lists them alphabetically according to RISM sigla, because it retains a sense of the order in which these sources were discovered. One of these manuscripts, namely no. 12, has only recently come to light, thanks to Professor Emilio Sala, who generously provided me with a photocopy. This suggests that the list could expand at any time. I use numbers for the purpose of quick reference. In more extensive discussions of individual librettos, I identify them by location.

21. The exceptions are interesting. In addition to *Arianna*, advertised as a comeback for Monteverdi, and clearly *not* published under the auspices of the librettist, they include Sacrati in *Ulisse errante* (1644) and a few Cavalli operas. See below, n. 41, and also Glixon and Glixon, *Business*, chap. 5.

TABLE 4
Manuscript librettos of *Il ritorno d'Ulisse*

	Librettist	Genre/perf.	Theater	Composer	Date	Misc. notes
1. I-Vnm 909.2	Badoaro	Rappresentata	S. Cassiano	Monteverdi	1641	Groppo's hand
2. I-Vnm 1294.1		Drama per musica, rappresentato	SS. Giovanni e Paolo		1641	probably 18th c.
3. I-Vnm 3449.9	Badoaro				1641	Zeno collection; same scribe as 9
4. I-Vmc 3330	Badoaro G.V.	Tragedia di lieto fine, Rappresentata	SS. Giovanni e Paolo		1641	probably 18th c.
5. I-Vmc 564	D.G.B.G.V.					only secure 17th-c. copy
6. I-Vmc Cicogna 220.1	Badoaro N.V.	Drama, Rappresentato	S. Cassiano		1641	18th c.
7. I-Mb 3077	Badoaro	Tragedia, Rappresentata	S. Cassiano		1641	probably 18th c.
8. I-Pci H 48575	di G.B.		SS. Giovanni e Paolo		1641	18th c.
9. I-Rig Rar. Lib. Ven 13	del N.H. S.r Badoaro				1641	18th c.
10. US-LA II, 17	(D.G.B.G.V.)					possibly mid-17th c., because of florid script (Curtis)
11. I-Vcg S. Cassiano I.5	Badoaro N.V.	Drama, Rappresentato	S. Cassiano		1641	18th c.
12. I-Mb 5672	Giacomo Badoaro	Dramma per musica, Rappresentato	SS. Giovanni e Paolo crossed out, replaced by S. Cassiano	Monteverdi	1641	18th c. [1642 on cover]

NOTE: Eleven of the twelve librettos are ascribed to Badoaro: eight with his name (nos. 1, 3, 4, 6, 7, 9, 11, 12); three with initials only (nos. 5, 8, 10). Only one is completely anonymous (no. 2). Two include an identical Argomento (nos. 6, 11). Four indicate S. Cassiano (nos. 1, 6, 7, 11), four SS. Giovanni e Paolo (nos. 2, 4, 8, 12; in one case, 12, that name is crossed out and replaced by S. Cassiano.) Two are undated (nos. 5, 10). The title pages of seven of them—nos. 1, 2, 4, 6, 7, 11, and 12—indicate that the performance had already taken place. The remaining four are silent on the subject.

number of acts—the librettos are all in five acts, while the score is in three; a different prologue—the librettos all have the same prologue, for Il Fato, La Prudenza, and La Fortezza, whereas that of the score features Humana Fragilità, Il Tempo, La Fortuna, and Amore; and a different ending—the librettos all conclude, following the love duet between Ulisse and Penelope, with the renewal of their marriage vows, celebrated by a chorus of Ithacans that draws a brief moral referring back to the prologue, whereas the score ends with the love duet. In addition, many passages in the librettos, ranging from an entire scene to individual lines, are either omitted or completely rearranged in the music. (The omitted scene is 5.2 [Deserto. Ombre de' Proci, Mercurio]: "la si lascia fuora per esser maniconicha.")[22] Although the differences between score and libretto(s) once inspired skepticism regarding the authenticity of the work, the nature of at least some of these differences is now one of the strongest arguments in support of Monteverdi's authorship. They reveal the kinds of tightening and recasting of text familiar from his other works.[23] (I shall return to this.)

The sheer number of the librettos might seem to lend greater weight to their textual readings, as opposed to those of the single score, but the librettos are too closely related to one another to represent independent sources. As I have suggested above, with one or possibly two exceptions (no. 5, and perhaps no. 10), they appear to have been copied many years after the performance, in the eighteenth century.[24] It is even possible that most, if not all, of the eighteenth-century manuscripts were copied from a single exemplar.

Some of the many minor differences between the librettos and the score can presumably be ascribed to musical exigencies: these would include various rearrangements and cuts of textual passages. But the more substantive differences, namely, the different prologue, ending, and act division, cannot simply reflect the composer's intervention: they require some sort of historical explanation. Indeed, as we shall see, they suggest that there were at least two distinct versions of the text, one set by the composer, the other perhaps a purely literary one.[25]

Differences among the libretto title pages might suggest a resolution. While they are nearly unanimous in attributing the text to Giacomo Badoaro, by name or initials (only no. 2 is anonymous), and in dating the work to 1641 (only nos. 5 and 10 are undated), they disagree on

---

22. This passage is quoted from the score, fol. 107r (see Facsimile 18). "Maniconic[h]a" or "malinconico" was evidently a term of criticism associated with ghosts, as it is in the preface to *Nozze*, when the author defends the presence of Priam, Anchise, Ettore, and Creusa in his prologue: "And if it might seem that with these ghosts the beginning was too melancholy, I say that it is perhaps not bad in this way to make that much greater the passage to happiness of the ending, as with a sad ending it is good to begin with happiness, so that the decay is all the more miserable" (Appendix 2 [p]). This omission from *Ritorno* is discussed in detail in Chaps. 4 and 8. Interestingly, and possibly for similar reasons, a parallel scene for Seneca and the Virtues following Seneca's death was also omitted in both scores of *Incoronazione*. Were these scenes simply too difficult to stage? See Chap. 8 (the texts of these scenes are given in Appendix 7).

23. It should be noted that, although no music has survived for them, two choruses in act 1 (scenes 3 and 6) and a ballo in act 3 (scene 6) were clearly intended to be performed, as indicated by the rubrics in the score, whereas act 5, scene 2 was not. See below, Chap. 4.

24. Of the sources he knew (nos. 1–5), Osthoff identified only no. 5 as from the seventeenth century. The UCLA copy (no. 10), not known to Osthoff, has also been assigned to the seventeenth century, by Sevieri, citing "caratteristiche secentesche" (*Nozze*, 27). But she also mistakenly assigned no. 7 to the seventeenth century and no. 5 to the eighteenth. Curtis (*Ritorno*) also dates no. 10 to the middle of the seventeenth century, on the basis of its florid script, and he regards no. 5 as roughly contemporary with the premiere in 1640, noting that it is closer to the score than any of the other librettos (p. ix). (He identifies it as the only manuscript without a date on its title page, but no. 10 lacks a date as well.) The implication may be that only those copyists intent on completing their collections well after the fact (in the eighteenth century) would have insisted on precise (even if incorrect) details.

25. For a recent comparison of the score and the libretto (or librettos), see Norbert Dubowy, "Bemerkungen zu einigen Ulisse-Opern des 17. Jahrhunderts," in *Claudio Monteverdi und die Folgen. Bericht über das*

the theater; five give S. Cassiano (nos. 1, 6, 7, 11, 12), three SS. Giovanni e Paolo (nos. 2, 4, 8), and four no theater at all (nos. 3, 5, 9, 10). Two of these, 5 and 10, which are also undated, are special, and specially related to the *Nozze* librettos, as we shall soon see.[26]

Two of these features are noteworthy, and possibly connected: the agreement on the date of 1641 and the disagreement on the theater. First, the date: Even though 1641 is given by Ivanovich (who, of course, normally drew his information from librettos), we can now be certain that the premiere actually took place in 1640. *Ritorno* was certainly performed in Bologna in that year. We know this from the little commemorative volume published in 1640 in Bologna, *Le glorie della musica celebrate dalla sorella poesia,* which Osthoff brought into the discussion, and to which I have already referred several times.[27] The date is confirmed in another publication of 1640 that has also been mentioned several times, namely, the *Argomento e scenario* for *Nozze.* As we recall, the author of the scenario speaks of two sets of performances of *Ritorno,* one the previous year, and one in the present one. (Since the *Argomento* was published late in 1640 ["Già s'avicina il finir dell'anno"], "the previous year" must have referred to the season of 1639–40, and "the present one" to 1640–41. See below.)

Although Osthoff admitted that the *Nozze* preface could have referred to the Bologna performance of 1640, he preferred to posit a prior performance in Venice, during carnival of the same year, that is the 1639–40 season; but Nino Pirrotta, still influenced by the unanimity of the libretto dates, could not accept 1640 as the date of the Venetian premiere. According to him, the Bologna performance was the first, an "out of town" tryout for a *maestro di cappella* unenthusiastic about risking his reputation on the highly visible—and secular—stages of Venice.[28]

While Monteverdi does seem to have shown some reluctance to engage in public operatic activities in Venice, the Bolognese performance of *Ritorno* cannot be adduced as evidence. There is no longer any doubt that it was preceded by the Venetian premiere: Osthoff has been proved right. The Venetian production of 1640 is confirmed by yet another Venetian publication of that year, the already mentioned *La peripezia d'Ulisse overo la casta Penelope* by the Incognito writer Federico Malipiero, who claimed to have seen *L'Ulisse in patria* in a Venetian theater ("ne' Veneti Teatri"). So greatly had he been pleased by the "prodigious efforts of Homer's hero presented in recitative," that he decided to

---

Internationale Symposium Detmold 1993, ed. Silke Leopold and Joachim Steinheuer (Kassel: Bärenreiter, 1998), 215–43, esp. 232–43. He ascribes some of the discrepancies between them to a transformation from what was originally conceived as a five-act *festa teatrale* to a three-act *dramma per musica.* He sees Monteverdi's influence on the transformation (which included some cuts), concluding that it resulted in a more concentrated and improved drama. While recognizing that Badoaro's five-act conception is purposeful and stronger and that Monteverdi originally wrote a five-act version, he questions (p. 238) whether Monteverdi enhanced or worked against Badoaro when he strengthened the affects of his characters.

26. Curiously, in one of the librettos, no. 12, SS. Giovanni e Paolo is crossed out and replaced by S. Cassiano. This is the same libretto that bears two conflicting dates: 1642 on the cover and 1641 on the title page (= 1640, 1641?). These discrepancies may indicate that the copyist had more than one exemplar before him.

27. Osthoff, "Zur Bologneser Aufführung."

28. Pirrotta, "Monteverdi and the Problems of Opera," 251.

"present them in prose."[29] And thus was born his book. From this it becomes clear that there were indeed two Venetian productions of *Ritorno d'Ulisse,* in two successive seasons, 1640 and 1641. This fact, nearly unique for the entire seventeenth century, is just one of the many indications of the composer's extraordinary prestige within the world of opera in Venice. The manuscript librettos, then, with their date of 1641, might reflect only the second of the two productions—but in fact they don't. The situation is considerably more complicated, as we shall see.

Clarification of the chronology, however—that is, the evidence of two productions in two successive seasons—may in turn shed light on some of the discrepancies between the librettos and score, especially the substantive ones already mentioned. These can now perhaps be interpreted as reflecting two different productions of Monteverdi's opera, possibly the premiere of 1640 and the revival of 1641—or even the Venetian and the Bologna performances.[30] It is clear from cancellations in the score, for instance, that a setting in five acts (for 1640?) preceded the one in three (1641?).[31] But the possibility of documenting a revival is not adequate to explain the two different theater designations, since Venetian operatic chronology simply does not support S. Cassiano as a possible venue for either production. (See Table 1 above, Chap. 1.)

As we can determine from various documents, including librettos and chronologies, the first Venetian theaters began by presenting one opera each season. This was true of S. Cassiano (1637, 1638, 1639) and S. Moisè (1639). But when SS. Giovanni e Paolo opened in 1639, to much fanfare, it trumped the competition by presenting two operas. This is emphasized in the afterword to the *Argomento e scenario* of the first of them, *La Delia,* by Giulio Strozzi.[32] It seems that this feature, of presenting two rather than one

---

29. "Ella fù una fatica motivatami . . . da una Musa, e da un Cigno, ch'entrambi abitando l'arene dell'Adria, ne formano appunto un richissimo Parnaso di meraviglia. M'apportò 'l caso ne' Veneti Teatri a vedere l'Ulisse in Patria descritto poeticamente, e rappresentato Musicalmente con quello splendore, ch'è per renderlo memorabile in ogni secolo. M'allettò così l'epico della Poesia, com'il delicato della Musica, ch'io non seppi rattenerne la penna, che non lasciassi correrla dietro 'l genio. Viddi d'Omero le prodigiose fatiche rapportate dalla Grecia nella Latina Lingua. L'udii recitativamente rappresentate. L'ammirai poeticamente nella Toscana ispiegate. Parvemi, che lo portarle nella prosa fosse appunto fatica adeguata, a cui pretende co 'l fuggir l'ozio d'involarsi alla carriera de' vizii" (Federico Malipiero, *La peripezia d'Ulisse overo la casta Penelope* [Venice: Surian, 1640], Lettore).

30. This is certainly what Osthoff thought ("Zur Bologneser Affuhrung"). Curtis, *Ritorno,* ix, is still skeptical about a 1641 performance, but his reasons seem to me unfounded. He mistrusts the evidence from the *Argomento e scenario* of *Le nozze d'Enea,* concluding that "a document of 1640 can hardly provide proof of an event in 1641." But he fails to recognize that the date of the *Argomento* was probably *more veneto* (Venetian style), with the new year beginning on 1 March rather than 1 January, and therefore actually 1641. The question is whether we can assume that the librettos represent one version and the score another. This is certainly possible: the prologue and other material unique to the librettos might have served what Dubowy calls the original *festa teatrale,* but could have been altered or cut when the show was taken on the road to Bologna.

31. The evidence in the score is considered in detail in Chap. 4.

32. "Signor Giovanni Grimani. . . [ha] eletta [*La Delia*] ad esser la prima [opera], che comparisca in quel nobilissimo Teatro. . . . nel quale ancora intendo, che si destina di recitare quest'anno una segnalata fatica del Signor Benedetto Ferrari . . . una nuova Armida" (Giulio Strozzi, *La Delia* [Venice: Pinelli, 1639], Argomento e Scenario, preface, p. 25).

opera per season, continued to distinguish SS. Giovanni e Paolo from the other theaters throughout the first decade of operatic activity in Venice.[33]

Under these conditions, then, only SS. Giovanni e Paolo could have accommodated *Ritorno* in either 1640 or 1641. (The chronologies list one other opera for each of these seasons at SS. Giovanni e Paolo, though two in the surrounding seasons, so that *Ritorno* could have been the second in both cases. Similarly, the chronologies list an opera for each of these seasons at S. Cassiano.) As a venue for either of the *Ritorno* productions, then, S. Cassiano is probably a mistake.

Another kind of evidence supports this conclusion. We know from *Le glorie della musica* that it was the company of Benedetto Ferrari and Francesco Manelli that brought *Il ritorno d'Ulisse* to Bologna for the performance in 1640, evidently the same company that had produced it earlier that season in Venice, and that would revive it in the following season. We also know that the Ferrari troupe had left S. Cassiano by 1639, after two seasons, moving to S. Moisè and SS. Giovanni e Paolo in 1640. It is thus exceedingly unlikely that an opera with which they were so closely associated would have appeared in a competing theater, S. Cassiano, which had in the meantime been taken over by a company headed by Francesco Cavalli. All the librettos of *Ritorno* that mistakenly identify S. Cassiano as the theater, then, may have been copied from the same (erroneous) exemplar. One of them (no. 12), as we have seen, even compounds the error by replacing the correct theater, SS. Giovanni e Paolo, with the incorrect one, S. Cassiano.

It is interesting that the only two librettos lacking both date and theater designation (nos. 5 and 10) are also the only ones that were copied in the seventeenth century. And one of these, no. 5, appears to be roughly contemporary with the production.[34] Correr 564, in fact, may be our closest witness to Badoaro's original libretto. (It is also marginally more closely related to the score than any of the others, though not as close as Curtis would like to think.) Although it agrees with the other manuscripts in its prologue and five-act structure, and in most of its text, Correr 564 was heavily edited—there are cancellations and additions on practically every page. The copyist evidently had great difficulty deciphering his exemplar. Not only did he misread numerous individual words, especially abbreviations, but he also inadvertently dropped entire lines—many of which he subsequently inserted in a smaller script.[35] On a couple of occasions he even mistook

---

33. Although the number of productions in S. Moisè and the Novissimo occasionally rose to two in subsequent seasons, this did not happen at S. Cassiano until 1645, when it was specially signaled by the impresario, Giovanni Faustini. The operas were both on his own librettos: his preface to the first of them, *La Doriclea*, suggests that it was supposed to have been presented in a previous season, but had not been. See *OSV*, 171–72.

34. Curtis identifies it as stage 1 of his hypothetical chronology, dating it to c. 1639 (*Ritorno*, preface, pp. ix, xi). Carter, *Musical Theatre*, 240, n. 2, points out that it must date at least from after the premiere, since Badoaro's preface mentions ten performances having already taken place.

35. For example, in a speech for Nettuno toward the end of 1.5 and in one for Melanto near the beginning of 2.1.

performance rubrics and character names for lines of text.[36] By far the greatest part of the alterations rectify such mistakes. Some, however, offer viable alternative readings—even improvements—suggesting that the librettist himself was responsible for them, and that they represent his second thoughts.[37] Most of the revisions bring the text into line with the other librettos (since they were copied later, they could easily have incorporated the librettist's improvements), but a few produce readings that are found only in the score.[38] These observations confirm the importance of Correr 564 as a source. They allow us to conclude that although it contains many misreadings, some of which were never corrected,[39] it transmits an earlier layer of text than any other libretto, and that it may have been revised on the basis of the text from which the composer worked, or even possibly that of the score itself.[40]

---

36. In 4.3 he crossed out the rubric "fa prova e non può," which had been included in one of the Suitors' texts, rewriting it in smaller letters in the left margin. And he did the same with the designation "Coro in cielo" in 5.7.

37. All of the corrections in the prologue are of the authorial type, as are the following in the main body of the text: "[si piange pria ma al fin] quella ha loco," becomes "la gioia ha loco" (1.2); "[l'uman voler] tenaci e forte" becomes "sien fermi e forte" (1.7); "Ninfe ridate le gemme et altri" becomes "Ninfe serbate le gemme e gl'ori" (1.8); "[Pastor se non fia ver] ch'al primo vello" becomes "ch'al tardo passo" (2.6); "[Lieta e soave gloria, cara e] dolce memoria" becomes "dolce vittoria" (4.3); "Armalo in pace [un dì]" becomes "Tornalo in pace" (5.7) "alla vecchia cauta [anco si neghi]" becomes "alla vecchia nutrice" (5.9); "tacendo parlar" becomes "tacer o parlar" (5.8).

38. In 1.3, "la deitade offesa" is inverted to "dell'offesa deitade," which corresponds to the score but not to any of the other librettos. And in 1.2, two final vowels, not set to music, are crossed out in the first stanza of Melanto's aria text "desiri" and martiri."). Two lines that appear only in Correr 564 and the score were probably missing from the exemplar(s) used for copying the other librettos. Both must have been omitted by mistake, since they are crucial to the sense of the passages in question and rhyme with previous lines ("mal pratico d'inganni" in 1.8 rhymes with "tenero negl'anni," and "de' viventi amatori" in 2.1 rhymes with "A che sprezzi gl'ardori"). (Another line, or partial line, probably omitted by mistake in *all* of the librettos, occurs in 2.12 in the score: the phrase "di ciò che dona" is added to the line "ti lascia in testimon," creating a rhyme with the preceding "questa regal corona." See Curtis, *Ritorno,* 167 n. 1.) A different kind of parallel between the score and Correr 564 involves a line missing from both, replaced in the libretto by an ellipsis. Although the line does appear in some librettos (nos. 6 and 11), it is replaced by ellipses in others, so that in this instance Correr 564 is no closer to the score than a number of other librettos (see Curtis, *Ritorno,* 127, n. 1). This particular passage occurs within a series of speeches for the Suitors, which demonstrate Badoaro's inexperience as a poet. Though the sentiments expressed by the three are parallel, the forms of their speeches are not. A more experienced librettist would probably have treated them strophically. (For Monteverdi's corrections of similar irregularities, see Chap. 7.) The problems caused by this scene in the score are discussed in Chap. 4, pp. 77–82: "The Ninth Gathering."

39. Some patent errors that remained in Correr 564 include "honesta rimembranza" (originally possibly a misreading of "funesta rimembranza," which should have been, as in the score, "o mesta rimembranza"); "Senza periglio i miei pensieri" instead of "senza pensiero i miei perigli" (half corrected in the score and illegibly corrected in Correr 564); and "ceda l'obbedienza alla pietà" instead of "ceda all'obbedienza la pietà (corrected in the score though not in Correr 564). See Curtis's discussion of the various alterations, *Ritorno,* preface, p. xi.

40. Although some of the corrections in Correr 564 could have been made on the basis of the text in the score (such as those in 1.3 and 1.2, mentioned in n. 38), Carter's contention that the libretto reflects details of Monteverdi's musical setting—analogous to the Naples and Udine librettos of *Incoronazione* discussed below— cannot be substantiated (*Musical Theatre,* 240–41). His prime example, the duet between Telemaco and Ulisse, which is laid out line by line rather than according to poetic form, is not unique to Correr 564, and he is forced

As we have noted, for Monteverdi's second Venetian opera, as for his first, to which it is linked in so many ways, the only surviving librettos are manuscripts. For the most part, they are found in the same collections, some of them even bound together (Table 5).

Like those of *Ritorno*, most of the *Nozze* librettos preserve very similar readings, and therefore—with one important exception (as we shall see in Chap. 5)—were probably copied from a single exemplar or a group of closely related ones. Thus, even the agreement of their title pages on such facts as date, authorship, theater, and so forth is not necessarily significant or even reliable. Most tellingly, as we have seen, all but two of them (nos. 2 and 6) list Giacomo Badoaro as their author—an attribution that is borne out neither by the style of the work nor by any independent documentary evidence. The near unanimity of the title pages on this point, as on others—all but no. 3 mention the Teatro SS. Giovanni e Paolo; eight of eleven mention Monteverdi; all but two indicate that the performance had already been "rappresentato"—merely reinforces their descent from the same (faulty?) source.[41]

In fact, as I have mentioned, the attribution to Badoaro is contradicted by a more trustworthy source, the printed scenario. The information conveyed by these pamphlets, because they were printed and for a particular purpose, to accompany the performances of a specific opera, is inherently more reliable and also often fuller than that in many manuscripts. Issued late in 1640, while the opera was still "da rappresentarsi," this remarkable document comprises two distinct and very unequal parts. The scenario proper, a nine-page running description of the action, is introduced by a twenty-six page unsigned "lettera dell'autore ad alcuni suoi amici," from which I have already quoted several times, and which is found in Appendix 2. Although much of this "lettera" is devoted to an elaborate disquisition on the aesthetics of opera, it also contains specific historical information unavailable elsewhere. It is from this "lettera dell'autore," for instance, that we learn of the success of *Ritorno*, that a revival was being planned for the following season, that *Nozze* was designed to follow that revival, and, through references to Badoaro in the third person, that the two librettos were by different authors. Most significant of all, the "lettera" and the scenario proper provide many descriptive details about the production

---

to justify the many counter-examples—such as all of the other duets—on the basis of a putative earlier version of Monteverdi's score. (One could of course hypothesize a fuller score than the one we know—as in the case of *Incoronazione*, to be discussed presently—a predecessor that might also have contained the original prologue and ending, but I will argue below that our score essentially reflects both the original and the three-act revision.) It is possible, though, that the line-by-line arrangement of the Telemaco–Ulisse duet reflects one of the alterations the librettist confessed to have made after submitting his first draft to the composer.

41. In view of its absence from the title pages of most of the *Ritorno* librettos and all but one of the *Incoronazione* librettos, the presence of Monteverdi's name on a preponderance of title pages in *Nozze* is certainly worth noticing. He is also mentioned prominently within the text of the printed scenario. His collaboration, then, must have been considered a selling point. Cf. above, n. 21.

TABLE 5

Manuscript librettos and printed argomento and scenario of *Le nozze d'Enea e Lavinia*

	Librettist	Genre/perf.	Theater	Composer	Date	Notes
1. I-Vnm 909.4	Badoaro	Tragedia di lieto fine, Rappresentata	SS. Giovanni e Paolo	Monteverde	1641	from Groppo Collection
2. I-Vnm 1294. 2, 3		Drama per musica, Rappresentata	SS. Giovanni e Paolo		1641	18th c.
3. I-Vnm 3449.11	Badoaro	Tragedia di lieto fine				18th c.
4. I-Vmc 3330	Badoaro	Tragedia di lieto fine, Rappresentata	SS. Giovanni e Paolo		1641	18th c.
5. I-Vmc 3331	Badoaro	da Recitarsi	SS. Giovanni e Paolo	Monteverdi	1641	17th c. "onorato di Musica dal Sig. Claudio Monteverdi," three acts, mistakenly ascribed to 18th c. (Sevieri)
6. I-Vmc 3332		Tragedia di lieto fine, Rappresentata	SS. Giovanni e Paolo	Monteverde	1641	18th c.
7. I-MB 4457	Badoaro	Tragedia di lieto fine, Rappresentata	SS. Giovanni e Paolo	Monteverde	1641	18th c. Mistakenly ascribed to 17th c. (Sevieri)
8. I-Pci H 48576	Badoaro	Tragedia di lieto fine, Rappresentata	SS. Giovanni e Paolo	Monteverde	1641	probably 18th c.
9. I-Rig Rar. Lib. Ven 14	Badoaro	Tragedia di lieto fine, Rappresentata	SS. Giovanni e Paolo	Monteverde	1641	probably 18th c.
10. US-LAu II, 18	Badoaro	Tragedia di lieto fine, Rappresentata	SS. Giovanni e Paolo	Monteverde	1641	"17th-c. copy," similar to no. 7 (Sevieri)
11. US-Wc 6596.12	Badoaro	Tragedia, Rappresentata	SS. Giovanni e Paolo	Monteverde	1641	"probably 17th c." (Sevieri)
12. Argomento et Scenario		Tragedia di lieto fine, da rappresentarsi			1640	printed, Venice: 1640

NOTE: Adapted from Sevieri, *Le nozze d'Enea*, 24–25. Some information is also given in Osthoff, "Zur Bologneser Aufführung." Sevieri (pp. 26–27) dates nos. 7, 10, and 11 to the seventeenth century, the others to the eighteenth. But she is surely mistaken about no. 5, which, like *Ritorno* no. 5, appears to be the earliest of all the manuscripts; and nos. 7 and 11, which appear to be eighteenth-century copies.

Librettos 1–3 and 6–11 have the title *Le nozze d'Enea con Lavinia;* 4 and 5 have the title *Le nozze d'Enea e Lavinia.* The scenario has the title *Le nozze d'Enea in Lavinia..*

of the opera. As we shall again see in Chapter 5, this publication, along with the manuscript librettos of *Nozze*, particularly when read in conjunction with the sources for the other two operas, affords at least some indication of what the lost music was like.

L'incoronazione di Poppea

The source situation for Monteverdi's final opera, *L'incoronazione di Poppea*, is much the most complicated of the three works—far more complicated, in fact, than that of any other Venetian opera of the period. For not only have a greater number of sources survived, but they are of more kinds: not one manuscript score, but two, which preserve two different versions of the opera, both very likely related to the revival in Naples in 1651; not a number of closely related manuscript librettos, but two distinct groups with significant variants between them. These are listed, along with the printed sources—two librettos and a scenario—in Table 6. One group, representing a shortened version of the text, is closer to the scores and the scenario (nos. 1, 3, 7, 8), while the other group is closer to the full version of the text published by the librettist (nos. 2, 5, 6, 9, 10). A different possible grouping, which takes into consideration all of the sources—scores and librettos, printed and manuscript—distinguishes between those most directly related to performance(s), that is, the two scores and nos. 7, 8, and 9, and all of the others, nos. 1–6 and 10, which transmit the literary version of the text. Still another grouping would distinguish the sources that can be associated with the Naples revival (the two scores and no. 9) from all of the others.[42] These various ways of categorizing the sources help us to reconstruct the complex history of *Incoronazione*, with the eventual aim of resolving questions of authenticity.

As we have seen, most of the librettos for *Ritorno* and *Nozze* were literary versions copied later to fill out libretto collections, and bear—rightly or wrongly—the name of the author, Badoaro. With one possible exception, no. 2, however, the purpose of the *Incoronazione* manuscripts does not seem to have been either bibliographical or commemorative.[43] Only two of the other six provide any information other than the title (nos. 3 and 7); four of the seven are anonymous (nos. 1, 4, 5, and 6); all date from the seventeenth century, and all are

---

42. These groupings are based on distinctions made by Chiarelli, "*L'incoronazione di Poppea*," 117–51. See also Fabbri, "New Sources," 16–23 for a discussion of the relationships among these sources, two of which were not considered by Chiarelli, since he discovered them after her article was published.

43. Although the title page of the Rovigo manuscript (no. 2) seems to indicate that it was copied before the work was performed ("opera musicale *da rappresentarsi* nel teatro di SS. Giovanni e Paolo . . . 1642"), according to Chiarelli ("*L'incoronazione di Poppea*," n. 6), this annotation covered another, more accurate one, which indicated that the work had indeed already been performed ("rapresentata in SS Gio e Paolo Di Fran Businello / L'anno 1642"). It is noteworthy that the copyist of the Rovigo *Incoronazione* also copied *Apollo e Dafne*, in the same collection. Printed copies of both of these librettos (from *Le hore ociose*) are missing from the Silvestri collection, which otherwise appears to be chronologically complete. This suggests that the collector had the two texts copied for the sake of filling out his collection (because he did not own a copy of *Le hore ociose*). The motivation for both Rovigo manuscripts thus appears to have been commemorative.

TABLE 6
Manuscript librettos and printed sources of *L'incoronazione di Poppea*

Manuscript librettos	Librettist	Title	Genre/perf.	Theater	Date	Notes
1. (F) I-Fn Magl. VII. 66		*La Coronatione di Poppea*				
2. (R) I-RVI Silvestriani 239	Busenello	*La Coronatione di Poppea*	Opera musicale, da rappresentarsi	SS. Giovanni e Paolo	1642	Description corrected
3. (T) I-TVco Rossi 83	Busenello	*La Popea*			1640	
4. (U1) I-UDc 55		*La Coronatione di Poppea*				Fragment
5. (V) I-Vmc Cicogna 585		*La Popea*				
6. (W) PL-Wn BOZ 1043		*Nerone*	Opera			
7. (U2) I-UDc, Fondo Joppi 496	Busenello	*Coronatione di Poppea*	Recitata in Musica	SS. Giovanni e Paolo	1642	Monte Verde

Printed sources

8. **SV** Scenario dell'opera REGGIA Intitolata La Coronatione di POPPEA. Che si rappresenta in Musica nel Theatro dell'Illustr. Sig. Giovanni Grimani (Venice: Pinelli, 1643)
9. **LN** *Il Nerone overo L'incoronazione di Poppea drama musicale* (Naples: Mollo, 1651)
10. **LV** *L'incoronazione di Poppea*, di Gio. Francesco Busenello. Opera musicale rappresentata Nel Teatro l'Anno 1642, in Busenello, *Delle hore ociose* (Venice: Giuliani, 1656)

different: that is, they preserve readings different enough from one another to suggest at least several different stages in the evolution of the opera, both before and after the initial Venetian production.

The importance of one of these manuscripts far exceeds that of the others. The Udine manuscript (no. 7), discovered by Paolo Fabbri a decade ago, is the only contemporary source to attribute the opera to Monteverdi. Recall that the absence of such an attribution was a key piece of evidence in the case against authenticity.[44] Far from being a mere literary document, this libretto fairly bristles with the immediacy of a performance. In addition to the composer's name, it reports all of the most important facts about the production—librettist, composer, theater, date—much more than any other libretto, and these at the end of the text rather than on the title page: "Fine della coronatione di Poppea. Del Sig Busenello. Recitata in Musica del Sig Monte Verde nel theatro da cha Grimani a San Gio, e Paolo l'anno 1642." It is as if the copying took place as the performance

---

44. As late as 1990, the absence of Monteverdi's name in any contemporary source still encouraged Curtis to think of *Incoronazione* as a pastiche ("*La Poppea impasticciata*"). For a modern edition of the Udine libretto, see *Libretti d'opera italiani dal Seicento al Novecento*, ed. Giovanna Gronda and Paolo Fabbri (Milan: Mondadori, 1997), 1: 49–105, also notes, pp. 1814–16.

transpired, and came to an end at the same time. This effect is strengthened within the text itself. In contrast to the only occasional descriptive rubric in the other librettos, in this one, the visual effect of many scenes—certainly every scene change—is precisely described, almost as if its intention were to convey the experience of seeing the production. For instance: "Aerial scene with low horizons" (prologue); "We see Ottavia, who departs by boat for exile" (act 3, scene 6); "The prospect closes, and Rome returns" (3.7); and "The scene changes to the city of Rome in the distance" (3.8).[45] The final 4½ folios are devoted to an extended encomiastic poem addressed to the singer of the role of Poppea (unfortunately unnamed), reinforcing the impression that the copyist was actually present at the performance (the lengthy text is transcribed in Appendix 8, A). What is most intriguing, however, is that this libretto was clearly copied from a score. In addition to repeated words and irregular or incomplete poetic lines, which distort the poetic form and could not have come from a literary text, it contains the intercalations between scenes and between individual speeches, the extra refrains, and the fragmented, speechlike dialogue for which Monteverdi's score is so highly prized, and which are absent from all the other manuscript librettos. And if this were not enough, it turns out that the score from which it was copied was most likely that of the premiere, a score we do not have: the Udine manuscript, then, is a crucial witness to that event. We will explore this possibility further in the next chapter.

Finally, three of the *Incoronazione* sources are printed. One, a scenario (like that of *Nozze*), is characteristically—and demonstrably—linked to the original production, and as such is most closely related to the Udine manuscript (no. 7).[46] A significant parallel between the scenario and Udine libretto involves the stage directions, which in Udine are

---

45. A number of the rubrics in Udine are the same as those in the scenario. Those that are unique to the libretto are given in italics. Prologue: *Scena aerea con orizonti bassi. Fortuna, Virtu, e Amor in Aria sopra nuvole.* 1.1: Si muta la scena nel palazzo di Poppea. 1.5: Si muta la scena in città di Roma. 2.1: Si muta la scena nella villa di Seneca. 2.4: Si muta la scena nella città di Roma. 2.11: Si muta la scena nel giardin di Poppea. 3.1: Si muta la scena nella città di Roma. 3.6: *Si vede Ottavia, che se ne va in barca all'esiglio.* 3.7: *Si serra il prospetto e torna Roma.* 3.8: *Si muta la scena nella città di Roma con lontananza.* The complete scenario is reproduced in Appendix 4.

46. Interestingly, in both known copies of the scenario, pen lines in brown ink have been drawn at the beginning and end of the same scene—act 2, scene 6, for Poppea and Nerone. This suggests that the scene was not performed at the premiere (see Curtis, *Incoronazione*, xvii, n. 4). The Udine libretto (no. 7), presumably copied from the score of the premiere, is the only short libretto that includes this scene, though the longer librettos all have it. Librettos nos. 1 and 3 have a much shorter scene for Nerone and Poppea (thirteen lines of recitative instead of forty lines of recitative and aria), while no. 9 replaces it with a scene for Ottavia. It may be that the score for the premiere had included it, but that it was cut (or substituted) at the last minute, after the scenarios had been printed (and after no. 7 had been copied). Nos. 1 and 3, then, with their new text, may have been copied later, after no. 7. But it is difficult to know where they would have found their new text, since it is not in Busenello's printed libretto (no. 10). Aside from "Pur ti miro," this is one of *only three instances* in which text found in any manuscript libretto is missing from Busenello's printed text. Nos. 1, 3, and 7, and 5 (that is, three short librettos and one long one) have a second stanza for Nutrice's aria in act 2, scene 10 that is missing from Busenello. In nos. 2, 5, and 6 (three long librettos), act 2, scene 9 ends with an added two-stanza aria for Ottavia; but this is also found in the Naples score and libretto. In the final scene, nos. 2, 5, 6, and 7 (three long librettos and one short one) add eight lines for Poppea and Nerone leading into "Pur ti miro." These are also

not only unusually detailed for a libretto, as we have noted, but are often concordant with those in the scenario as regards both the scenes described and the manner of their introduction. (Other librettos have far fewer and fail to agree with one another.) Further parallels include the sequence of scenes and the descriptions of characters in many of them. ("Poppea con Arnalta vecchia sua consigliera discorre" in the scenario, 1.4, is matched in the libretto by "Poppea, Arnalta vecchia sua consigliera"; "Mercurio in terra mandato da Pallade" in the scenario becomes "Seneca, e Mercurio in terra" in the libretto, and so on.)[47]

The other two printed sources for *Incoronazione* are librettos, with two clearly different purposes, origins, and dates, as well as many divergent readings: one of them was issued anonymously in conjunction with the production in Naples in 1651, the other by the author himself, in the already mentioned collected edition of his librettos published in 1656, that is, fully thirteen years after the work was first performed on the Venetian stage. Although clearly neither of the printed librettos preserves the text of the original production, both of them are authoritative in a number of ways that reciprocally illuminate the other Monteverdi sources—not only those of *Incoronazione* itself but those of *Nozze* and *Ritorno* as well. For example, like the Udine manuscript, the Naples print shows strong evidence of having been copied from a score[48]—presumably a version of the one performed in Naples. It displays the same kinds of intercalations, refrains, repetitions, and hypermetric textual organization noted in the Udine manuscript, strengthening the possibility that librettos for the other two works might have had similar origins. This is particularly suggestive for one of the *Nozze* librettos, as we shall see. On the other hand, the text published by Busenello in 1656, which preserves poetic forms, multiple strophes, and symmetries, offers a clear model for a literary version of a libretto, one that can help to analyze and categorize the multiple manuscripts of *Ritorno* and *Nozze*. This version has been assumed to embody Busenello's second, or final, thoughts, possibly a revision of the text set by Monteverdi.[49] But, as I have already suggested, it might instead represent the original state, the form in which the composer would have first seen it.[50] This is an important point, because our interpretation of Monteverdi's editing procedures depends on it.

We can extrapolate from Busenello's other librettos in *Le hore ociose*, which were set by Cavalli. In all instances, even for the operas most distant in date from the publication,

---

found in the Naples score, but the Naples libretto has something else. Where would the extra text have come from? What is the importance of these insertions for the chronology of the libretto sources?

47. See Fabbri, "New Sources," 21–22, and also n. 45 above, as well as Appendix 4.

48. See Wolfgang Osthoff, "Die venezianische und neapolitanische Fassung von Monteverdis *Incoronazione di Poppea*," *AcM* 26 (1954): 88–113, at 93–94 and Chiarelli, "*L'incoronazione di Poppea*," 127.

49. By Osthoff, "Die venezianische und neapolitanische Fassung," 93; also Curtis, *Incoronazione*, xi. A modern edition of Busenello's text may be found in *Drammi per musica dal Rinuccini allo Zeno*, ed. Andrea della Corte (Turin: Unione tipografico-editrice Torinese, 1958; 2nd ed., 1970), 1: 430–509.

50. See above, p. 51 and n. 18.

namely *Apollo e Dafne* (1640) and *La Didone* (1641), the text in Cavalli's scores agrees almost completely with that of the printed librettos.[51] If the texts Busenello gave to Cavalli in the early 1640s were so close to those he eventually published in 1656 in *Le hore ociose*, we might expect to be able to say the same for *Incoronazione*.

AUTHENTICITY

Because they are so complicated, and the potential practical rewards of untangling them so great, the *Incoronazione* sources have naturally been studied more exhaustively than those of the other two operas—no modern performance could be attempted without coming to grips with the numerous variant readings—and consequently much has been learned about the work. Thanks especially to the efforts of Wolfgang Osthoff and Alessandra Chiarelli, we have come closer to understanding what the sources represent, both individually and in conjunction with one another. Whether such understanding can bring us any closer to resolving the authenticity question, however, is another matter. Indeed, ironically, greater knowledge of the sources over the past several decades has rendered Monteverdi's authorship increasingly questionable.

The major arguments against authenticity have included the virtual absence of any mention of Monteverdi in the contemporary documents, the clear evidence that both scores date from well after the composer's death, and the identification in them of specific music by other composers (Cavalli and possibly Sacrati, Ferrari, and Laurenzi).[52] Some recent discoveries, however, have tipped the balance slightly in the direction of authenticity. Foremost among them, as we have noted, is the Udine libretto, which appears to reflect the original production of 1643, and it alone of all the librettos ascribes the music to Monteverdi.[53] But other discoveries have strengthened the case against it. A score of Francesco Sacrati's *La finta pazza*, unearthed at Isola Bella by Giovanni Morelli and Lorenzo Bianconi several decades ago, shares some music with *Incoronazione*, and may confirm the presence of Sacrati's

---

51. Of course Cavalli omits some text, usually within long dialogue passages; he also cuts some stanzas from lengthy strophic arias; and he sets some ostensible aria material as recitative and vice versa. But he never changes Busenello's forms, introduces refrains, or intercalates the text of two characters for dramatic reasons.

52. Curtis hypothesized that "Monteverde" was replaced by "Il Nerone" on the spine of the Venice score when it was recognized that so much of the music was by other composers (*Incoronazione*, n. 10). But it is more likely that the substitution was intended to bring the score into line with the other Contarini volumes, which are organized by title. The change may date from the time when the volumes were shelved in the Marciana. See Walker, "*Ubi Lucius*," 146–47. Jeffery, "The Autograph Manuscripts," 172 identifies the hand that added "Monteverde" on fol. 2 of the manuscript as P3, which also appears elsewhere in the score.

53. Another contemporary document, discovered by Margaret Murata, certainly implies that Monteverdi's music was heard in the Venice 1643 production. The letter, dated 25 March 1643, from a French diplomat, addressed to Mazarin, recommended that an Italian opera company be engaged for Paris, that it include Anna Valeria and "Annuccia" [= Anna Renzi?], who had distinguished themselves in the previous season in Venice, and that the music "all be by Mondevergo." See Margaret Murata, "Why the First Opera Given in Paris Wasn't Roman," *COJ* 7 (1995): 87–106, esp. 100–102.

music in the *Incoronazione* score—in the coronation scene, possibly including the final duet.[54]

Beyond these general arguments, the close scrutiny and comparison of all of the sources initiated by Osthoff, pursued by Chiarelli and others, and most recently reconsidered by Curtis, has revealed a number of problematic passages in the scores (suggesting that they were added or altered after Monteverdi's death, presumably for Naples). Until recently the most significant of these was "Pur ti miro," but there are several others. These include musical material accounted for neither in the scenario nor in the Udine libretto, which presumably represent the first production, and that is also missing from Busenello's printed text;[55] and passages that show evidence of revision (cuts, transpositions) or of having been copied from an earlier score (containing errors, corrections, inconsistent or incomplete transcription of text and/or music).

As Curtis has pointed out, most of these passages (as well as all of the music in the Naples score that does not appear in the Venice score) are associated with a more modern style of metric notation than that used in the rest of the scores—what he characterized as minim-triple rather than semibreve-triple—suggesting that they represent the intervention of younger composers, or, at least, younger copyists. Indeed, these spots include all of the material specifically identifiable as by other composers (Cavalli's overture, "Sacrati's" music in the coronation scene, and Ferrari's—or Laurenzi's or "Sacrati's"—"Pur ti miro").[56] The most substantial questionable material, according to Curtis's criteria, involves the role of Ottone—nearly all of his music has been transposed to a higher range, some of it incorrectly or inconsistently, and is notated in minim-triple—and the final scene of the opera, site of the infamous "Pur ti miro."

Although careful examination of the sources has succeeded in calling Monteverdi's authorship of *Incoronazione* into question, to the point where some scholars refer to the

---

54. Curtis, "*Poppea impasticciata*," 41 and 47. But see Pryer, "Authentic Performance," 191–213. Lorenzo Bianconi, "La finta pazza," *NGO*, 2: 213 and "La finta pazza ritrovata," in *La finta pazza, Gran Teatro La Fenice, programma di sala* (1987), 972, cautions against comparative attribution of the music shared by *Incoronazione* and *La finta pazza*. Given the fact that, like the Venice *Incoronazione*, it is a later touring version of *La finta pazza* (1644 or later) that has survived rather than the original of 1641, it is impossible to ascertain which parts are in fact by Sacrati. For this reason, in further references to music from *La finta pazza*, "Sacrati" appears in quotation marks.

55. Some Naples music is closer than the parallel passages in the Venice manuscript to Busenello's text, but some is even more likely than anything in Venice to be by another composer. See Eric Chafe, *Monteverdi's Tonal Language* (New York: Schirmer, 1992), 412, n. 3. Material missing from Busenello's printed text is listed above in n. 46. (See also Chap. 4.)

56. It is interesting that Cavalli's overture and "Sacrati's" *Finta pazza* music are found only in the Venice score and were probably added after the original production, at a time closer to the date of copying, that is 1651 (Cavalli's overture comes from *Doriclea* of around 1645, and "Sacrati's" from a touring score of 1644, at the earliest). Ferrari and Laurenzi were more likely collaborators in the original production; in contrast to Cavalli and Sacrati, who were engaged in operatic productions elsewhere at the time—Cavalli at S. Cassiano, Sacrati at the Novissimo—Ferrari and Laurenzi were both involved at SS. Giovanni e Paolo in 1643, Ferrari as impresario, and both he and Laurenzi as composers of *La finta savia*.

work's author as "Monteverdi," in quotation marks, source criticism alone cannot resolve the issue. Stylistic analysis ought to play at least a confirming role. Indeed, we recall that style represented an important, if tacit, consideration in the early modern reception of both *Ritorno* and *Incoronazione*. Their association with Monteverdi justified the interest they evoked, and their authenticity—and value—was judged on the basis of stylistic comparison with one another and with the composer's other works. But the question of style remained peripheral to the subsequent evaluation of the sources; scholars found enough evidence for doubt without addressing it.

Lately, however, style has become an explicit issue, invoked to support the evidence of the sources. Curtis isolated a number of stylistic idiosyncrasies in the scores, present in the doubtful passages, that were uncharacteristic of Monteverdi, and which he associated with a range of younger composers.[57] The pervasive presence of one of these traits—a cadential "tic"—in the recently discovered score of *La finta pazza*, the only extant work attributed at least in part to Sacrati, and not in any of the known music of either Ferrari or Laurenzi, clinched the case, as far as Curtis was concerned: he concluded that, at the very least, *Incoronazione* was a collaboration, a pasticcio. And he compared it to *La finta savia*, the opera that shared the stage of SS. Giovanni e Paolo with *Incoronazione* in 1643, to which six different composers are known to have contributed (including Ferrari and Laurenzi, though not Sacrati or Cavalli).[58] Believing the collaborator to be primarily a single composer, Sacrati, Curtis published his edition of *Incoronazione* under the joint authorship of Monteverdi and Sacrati.[59]

Eric Chafe added further style-analytical evidence to the case. Considering *Incoronazione* within the context of a tonal-allegorical practice developed by Monteverdi over the course of his entire career, Chafe identified several anomalous passages—passages with key signatures of two or three sharps, which Monteverdi rarely or never used. All of them coincide with passages identified as doubtful by Curtis, with one major exception: those within the role of Ottone. Indeed, Chafe argues convincingly that, although parts of that role might have been transposed and copied by a younger scribe or composer, its tonal structure and text setting link it closely to Monteverdi's characteristic style. Further, although his analysis confirms the presumed "inauthenticity" of parts of the prologue and the coronation scene, he finds enough musical and allegorical links between them and other, unquestionably authentic material in the opera to suggest that

---

57. Curtis, "*La Poppea impasticciata*," 35, 38–41.

58. See above, Chap. 2, p. 37, for what I called Curtis's "pasticcio hypothesis." For a discussion of the *Finta savia* pasticcio, see *OSV*, 219.

59. As already mentioned (Chap. 2, p. 37), Pryer, "Authentic Performance," 204–207, punctures Curtis's argument by pointing out that the stylistic tics identified by Curtis as typical of Sacrati do not occur in the music for "Pur ti miro." Moreover, he questions Curtis's pairing of "Pur ti miro" with a trio in "Sacrati's" work ("Il canto m'alletta," 1.6, facsimile in Curtis, "*Poppea impasticciata*," 51), which is built on the same bass—a descending major tetrachord ostinato—suggesting that, if anything, the trio might have come *after* the duet (since the *Finta pazza* score clearly dates from 1644 or later).

these sections (including "Pur ti miro") were written under Monteverdi's supervision or, in any case, reflect his intent.[60]

We may never fully resolve the question of authorship, though the fact that clarifying discoveries have emerged so recently encourages hope that the answer may one day be found. In the end, though, it may not matter. Chafe's argument that our *Incoronazione* corresponds to Monteverdi's intention will comfort all those who cannot dare to imagine the work without "Pur ti miro." His analysis, combined with the evidence of the new Udine manuscript, establishes the likelihood that some of the "inauthenticities" were already part of the initial production—not introduced just for the Neapolitan (or some other) revival—and that the opera we know corresponds substantially to the *Incoronazione* experienced by the audience at the Teatro SS. Giovanni e Paolo in 1643. A closer look at the musical sources will help to clarify this situation.

---

60. "Factors of interpretation can seldom be expected to settle questions of authorship where source-critical methods seem to lead in the opposite direction. Since the latter have not provided a conclusive answer in the case of 'Pur ti miro,' I will argue on the basis of its demonstrably perfect suitability to *Incoronazione*, that while Monteverdi's authorship of the duet may be doubted, its presence at the end of the work is a touch that seems, however unlikely it may now appear on the basis of its history, wholly Monteverdian, and its placement there might still reflect his intent" (Chafe, *Tonal Language*, 300). For a recent interpretation that questions the musical suitability of the duet to the previous characterization of Poppea and Nerone, and therefore its authenticity, see Rachel A. Lewis, "Love as Persuasion in Monteverdi's *L'incoronazione di Poppea:* New Thoughts on the Authorship Question," *ML* 86 (2005): 16–41.

4

Two Scores

Il ritorno d'Ulisse in patria

Our single surviving score for *Ritorno* (Vienna, National Library, Mus. Ms. 18763) was subjected to fairly close analysis by Robert Haas in 1922, Wolfgang Osthoff in 1956, and Norbert Dubowy in 2000, and it has since come under the discerning eye of Alan Curtis in connection with his 2002 edition of the opera. But the manuscript has still not been treated to the kind of philological study that would be required in order to answer some fundamental questions it raises.[1] Hypotheses regarding its provenance, date, function, and connection with Monteverdi have been advanced over the years, but we still lack a satisfactory explanation for many of its idiosyncrasies. The information gleaned from Peter Jeffery's study of the Cavalli manuscripts and the various philological investigations of the *Incoronazione* manuscripts is not especially relevant to the *Ritorno* score, even though certain observations from those studies may prove of some use in trying to understand its special nature.[2]

Most of the questions raised by the manuscript are connected: its proximity to the composer, its differences from the librettos, the many corrections and inconsistencies within it, its provenance and dating, and its presence in Vienna. Although I cannot pretend definitively to resolve any of these questions, I can propose certain hypotheses on

---

1. *Ritorno*, ed. Haas; Osthoff, "Zu den Quellen"; Dubowy, "Bemerkungen"; *Ritorno*, ed. Curtis.

2. Jeffery, "The Autograph Manuscripts"; Chiarelli, "*L'incoronazione di Poppea.*" Likewise, efforts to understand the peculiarities of the *Ritorno* score can shed light on the *Incoronazione* scores.

the basis of analysis of the score, comparison with librettos, and investigation of the historical situation surrounding the known performances of the work.

The manuscript consists of 136 folios in seventeen numbered gatherings, all but two comprising eight folios *(ottonari)*.[3] It preserves a version (or several versions) of the opera that differs from the libretto Monteverdi was presumably given by Badoaro, differences to which the author seems to allude in his letter to the composer in the libretto Correr 564 (see no. 5 in Table 4 above, Chap. 3; and Appendix 1). As already noted, these include a different number of acts, a different prologue and ending, and some substantial excisions, one of them comprising an entire scene (act 5, scene 2). This list does not take into consideration the many smaller differences that might be ascribed to a composer's revisions, to be discussed in the following chapters—the cuts and rearrangement of text. The five-act and three-act divisions can be seen in Table 7.

From this comparison, scholars have concluded that there were essentially two versions of the work: Badoaro's five-act libretto and Monteverdi's three-act score. Accordingly, it has been assumed, if tacitly, that the conversion from five to three acts and the replacement of the original prologue and ending took place at the same time. But the score clearly shows that it was originally in five acts, that it was subsequently converted to three, and that the new prologue and ending were present *before* the conversion—that is, in the exemplar for this score. The end of the new prologue and beginning of act 1 occur on the same page (fol. 8v), in the same hand, with nothing to indicate that the prologue was copied at a different time from what follows (see Facsimile 1, following page 86).

The score, in fact, represents more than a single version of the opera. It is a fluid document that not only shows two versions simultaneously, the five-act original and a three-act revision, but demonstrates how and at what point—though not why—the one was transformed into the other. It also provides information about how it was copied and the reasons for some of its alterations and inconsistencies. What is more interesting, we can see that much of the editing was made to prepare or facilitate the actual process of production and performance. I will discuss this aspect at some length later in the present chapter.

The two versions of the opera that can be teased out of the score entailed at least three (possibly four) passes through the manuscript, stages—or layers—that can be clarified by different shades of ink: medium, light, and dark.[4] All three passes appear to have been the

---

3. Sixteen of the seventeen gathering numbers are clearly visible at the upper right-hand corner of every ninth folio. For the exception, the ninth gathering, which comprises twelve folios, see below. In addition to the original gathering numbers, modern numbers appear on every tenth folio, but beginning with fol. 2.

4. Debowy, "Bemerkungen," 233, too, posits several steps in the editing of the score for performance—turning what he assumes to have been a five-act *festa teatrale* into a three-act *dramma per musica*. First, he claims, material characteristic of the *festa teatrale* was cut: this would have included some choruses (in 1.3) and the Moor ballet, act 3, scene 3. (Though the music for these portions is indeed missing, rubrics in the score indicate to me that this material was not intended to be cut in performance.) Then, the act and scene numbers of the three-act version were added, some of them new, others clearly replacing those of the five-act version. Although he observes (n. 7) that some material written in lighter ink was added later, he does not pursue the significance of ink shades for the chronology of the copying of the score.

TABLE 7
Il ritorno d'Ulisse: comparison of three- and five-act structure

Three Acts	Setting	Characters	Musical articulations	Five Acts
Act 1				Act 1
1	Court	Penelope–Ericlea	"Di misera regina"	1
2		Melanto–Eurimaco		2
3	Sea	Nereidi		3
4		Feaci		4
5		Nettuno		5
6		Feaci		6
7	Land	Ulisse		7
8		Ulisse–Minerva		8
9		Ulisse–Minerva–Niadi	"O fortunato"	9
				Act 2
10	Court	Melanto–Penelope		1
11	Woods	Eumete		2
12		Iro–Eumete		3
13		Eumete–Ulisse		4
Act 2				
1	Sky	Telemaco–Minerva		5
2	Woods	Eumete–Ulisse–Telemaco		6
3		Telemaco–Ulisse	"Vanne alla madre"	7
				Act 3
4	Court	Melanto–Eurimaco		1
5		Suitors–Eurimaco–Penelope	"Non voglio amar"	2
6		Ballo		3
7		Eumete–Penelope		4
8		Proci–Eurimaco		5
9	Woods	Ulisse–Minerva		6
10		Eumete–Ulisse	"Godo anch'io"	7
				Act 4
11	Court	Telemaco–Penelope	"Memoria così trista"	1
12		Antinoo–Eumete–Iro–Ulisse–Telemaco–Penelope		2
[13]		Antinoo–Eumete–Iro–Ulisse–Telemaco–Penelope	"Battaglia"	3
Act 3				Act 5
1	Court	Iro		1
2	Desert	Mercurio		2
3	Court	Melanto–Penelope		3
4		Melanto–Penelope–Eumete		4
5		Melanto–Penelope–Eumete–Telemaco		5
6	Sea	Minerva–Giunone		6
7		Minerva–Giunone–Nettuno–Giove–Coro		7
8	Court	Ericlea		8
9		Ericlea–Penelope–Telemaco–Eumete		9
10		Ericlea–Penelope–Telemaco–Eumete–Ulisse	"Sospirato"	10

work of a single scribe, whose hand has not been identified in other known manuscript of this period.[5]

STAGES OF COPYING

Pass 1

In medium brown ink, the copyist produced what might be called a continuity draft of the full five-act version of the score, including the new prologue and ending—text and music—with material inessential to continuity left to be filled in later: upper string parts for the instrumental movements, second stanzas of song texts, multiple texts of ensembles, some characters' names (notably the Suitors on fol. 65v [see Facsimile 9] and fol. 71r), music and text for some choruses, and scene designations. The copyist also left some empty staves for the future insertion of instrumental movements.[6] His concern with the economical use of paper sometimes led to awkward dispositions of material that required subsequent clarification.[7]

Despite several anomalies, the original draft could have been copied from a single source, possibly the autograph. Monteverdi could—indeed, presumably would—have omitted the same material as the copyist, because it was extraneous to composition and could even have been filled in by an apprentice. This is true even of the most puzzling anomaly, the change in range halfway through the role of Eumete, indicated by a shift from tenor to soprano clef (beginning on fol. 72v: act 3, scene 4 / or act 2, scene 7) (see Facsimile 13).[8] Unlike the several other clef changes within individual roles that were made in pass 1, which involve only slight alterations in range—such as soprano to alto clef for Humana Fragilità[9]—this one has to mean that the original singer was replaced.

---

5. Haas, "Zur Neuausgabe," 5–6, thought he saw two different hands, but Curtis discerned one main one, as I do, though he thinks that a second "inexperienced, somewhat clumsy" scribe was responsible for some of the corrections in the manuscript, notably on fols. 3v–4v (*Ritorno,* preface, p. viii).

6. For example, the four staves on fol. 2v, blank except for their clefs, were presumably intended to accommodate a reprise of the introductory sinfonia following Humana Fragilità's opening speech. Space was evidently also left, and subsequently filled in, for the Phaeacians' sinfonia on fol. 27r (1.6; see Facsimile 3), though the bass was provided on fol. 27v. Clefs only were provided on fol. 32r for four of the five parts of Minerva's sinfonia (see Facsimile 5), which was filled in later. The blank space on fol. 69r–v (see Facsimiles 10–11) has another explanation, for which see the discussion of the ninth gathering below. As indicated by its pale ink, the entire "tocco di guerra" concluding act 4 (or act 2) (fols. 101v–103r) was evidently added at a later stage. See Facsimiles 16 and 17.

7. Clarification often took the form of paired letter designations indicating material to be inserted at particular points. See below, p. 84.

8. The fact that this change comes at the end of a problematic section of the manuscript, right after the heavily edited first scene between Penelope and the Suitors, may eventually help to explain it.

9. The copyist was evidently unsure whether to write the part of Humana Fragilità in soprano or alto clef. Two soprano clefs on fol. 5r seem to have replaced alto clefs. For analogous clef problems with the role of Ottone in the Venetian score of *Incoronazione,* see below.

Such cast changes, presumably in mid-composition or mid-revision, were not uncommon during this period; Jane Glover noted several instances in operas by Cavalli, including one in an autograph score.[10] Monteverdi could have planned to rewrite the earlier material prior to fol. 72 in the proper range, or simply to take care of the problem in rehearsal. Or perhaps the soprano Eumete was the original one, and the more complicated material, involving ensembles, was rewritten for the tenor, but the transposition of the less complicated recitative material of the second part of the opera was left for rehearsals. It has also been proposed that our scribe was copying from two exemplars, one featuring a tenor, the other a soprano Eumete, but there is no other suggestion of, let alone evidence for, this.[11]

Pass 2

In a lighter ink, the material omitted in Pass 1, which would have been needed for a performance—supplementary texts, string parts, some entire ritornellos, and most of the five-act scene designations (only through act 4, scene 1), though not the choruses—was filled in. A couple of performance rubrics were introduced, and certain ambiguities in the notation or succession of movements were clarified. Indeed, the distinctive shade of ink alerts us to what was considered inessential to composition, but essential to performance. (The different layers are clearly visible in Facsimiles 15 and 16.) This material could have come from a second layer of the autograph or could even have been provided by the copyist himself, since it did not actually involve composition.[12]

---

10. The copyist could have begun copying the role in its original form and then found that he had to transpose it because of a cast change, or, as in *Incoronazione*, he could have forgotten to transpose, or could have been copying from an exemplar that failed to transpose consistently. Glover's examples ("The Teatro Sant'Apollinare and the Development of Seventeenth-Century Venetian Opera" [Ph.D. diss., Oxford University, 1975], 79–80) are drawn from Cavalli's scores for *Oristeo, Eritrea, Scipione affricano, Egisto* (Dema is first soprano, then alto), *Rosinda* (Rudione begins in alto, continues in bass), *Apollo e Dafne* (Alfisibeo is bass, from act 2 tenor), and *Nozze di Teti* (Discordia is alto, but when disguised as Nereo becomes tenor). See also Ziani's *Alessandro Magno* (Cleandro is first a tenor, then a bass) and Boretti's *Ercole in Tebe* (Sifone is bass in act 1, then alto). Interestingly, most of these instances involve comic—or at least secondary—characters. The only composing score among these is *Rosinda*, but it shows clear evidence of Cavalli accommodating a cast change that occurred during the compositional process—the score contains multiple versions of some passages, in two different clefs. Alterations in cast could be accommodated during the copying as well as composing process. (Some other, temporary, clef changes within individual roles of *Ritorno* were probably just copying mistakes. Anfinomo and Pisandro switch between alto and tenor for their second appearance: on fols. 91r and 97r Anfinomo is written in tenor instead of alto clef; on fol. 96v Pisandro is written in alto clef instead of tenor. The situation is rectified later in the score.)

11. This is what Carter surmises (*Musical Theatre*, 239). Curtis, *Ritorno*, xv, does not consider the implications of the clef change for the source situation, but assumes that it indicates a change in cast at some point in the run of the opera.

12. On the possible sign of the copyist's incompetence as manifested in the upper parts of the Suitors' sinfonia at the end of act 2, see *Ritorno*, ed. Curtis, 176, n. 2; also Dubowy, "Bemerkungen," 232, n. 37.

Pass 3

In this pass, the copyist transformed the score into the three-act version. He or she re-placed most of the original scene designations, which were in light ink, with new, much darker ones applied with a heavily loaded pen. (This is particularly noticeable beginning at fol. 72v [see Facsimile 13, the point at which the part of Eumete changes clef: the dark 7 is an emphatic replacement for the earlier scene 4 beneath it.) Many of the five-act designations were erased or otherwise obscured by their replacements (see, e.g., fol. 42r: Facsimile 7); some were crossed out (such as those indicating the end of the original act 1 and beginning of act 2, fols. 41v–42r), while others were left in place by mistake (such as fol. 48v ["scena 4ta"] and fol. 65r ["scena 2da"; see Facsimile 8], though the new scene desig-nation ["quinta"] appears on the next folio) (see Facsimile 9). But as I have already noted, during pass 2 (in light ink) the copyist stopped entering the five-act designations after act 4, scene 1, so in pass 3 there was nothing more to be replaced. The last erasure occurs on fol. 82v ("fine de l'Atto 3, Atto 4," replaced by "Scena Xi"), the next designation, "xii, An-tinoo," on fol. 85v, cannot be seen to have replaced anything, and the indication for the next scene—which should be [act 2] scene xiii (or act 4, scene 3, fol. 91r)—is missing altogether.[13]

Although there should be no evidence of alteration in the scene designations of the final act—since it is the same in both five- and three-act versions (see Table 7 above)—the opening scene is marked act 3, scene 1 in the dark ink of the third pass, fol. 103v. (Could this mean that the conversion to three acts took place before this scene was copied?)[14] But the designation for scene 2, and for all the remaining scenes, as we would expect, is in the light ink of pass 2. Likewise, there should be no evidence of replace-ments through the ninth scene of act 1 (again, the same in both versions), but there is: there are two different designations for act 1, scene 1 (see fol. 8v, Facsimile 1); the desig-nation for scene 7 evidently replaced something else (see fol. 29r, Facsimile 4); and that for scene 8 (fols. 32v–33r) is peculiar in several respects. The original designation—on fol. 32v (see Facsimile 6)—as is characteristic of pass 2, is very light, and a second darker one (pass 3), on fol. 33r, which lacks a number altogether, was evidently entered by mis-take, since it does not mark the beginning of a scene (this is Minerva's entrance scene; see below).

A curious procedure, but one that sometimes clarifies the various layers, is a difference in protocol between the scene designations of pass 2 and pass 3. Most of the five-act des-ignations (pass 2)—certainly in the first act, sporadically later—list all characters in the

---

13. The scene designation is not strictly necessary here, since the new scene simply involved the addition of a few characters to those already on stage.

14. The ink appears to be the same as that of the new rubric indicating the end of the previous act ("fine del secondo atto") (fol. 103r). Since 3.1 was the only scene of the third act labeled in the dark ink of the third pass, it may not have received a designation at all in the five-act version.

scene in order of their appearance, whereas the three-act designations (pass 3) list either just the one who sings first (early in the score), or else none at all (beginning within act 3). Sometimes it is even apparent that character names subsequent to the first were erased or crossed out when the three-act designations were entered. On fol. 23r, scene 5, for Neptune and Jove (see Facsimile 2), the presumably original designation "Nettuno, Giove" in light ink is replaced in dark ink by "Nettuno," corrected, "Giove," crossed out, and "Nettuno" again. The second "Nettuno," in light ink, was intended to preface the actual voice part in the five-act version. (Cf. the discussion of this spot below.) In other places, the name of the first speaker is distinguished from the others by being gone over in the dark ink of pass 3 (as is Eumete on fol. 72v; see Facsimile 13).

This distinction in the way the characters are indicated in the two versions clarifies a unique passage in the score: two lines for Penelope at the opening of 2.1 (on fol. 42r; Facsimile 7), the only passage not accounted for in any libretto. As indicated by the rubric "[Atto secondo], scena [prima], Reggia, Penelope, Melanto," in pale ink, the passage was part of the five-act version. The copyist attempted to edit the old rubric by crossing out the material in brackets and inserting the new scene designation "Xma" above the old one. But the new designation for the three-act version is repeated and clarified following Penelope's speech: "Scena Xma, Reggia," indicating that the speech was intended to be cut, even though it is not crossed out. Melanto now initiates the scene. Penelope's speech may have been deemed less necessary to the three-act version (perhaps because the scene no longer opened an act), and so it was probably omitted.[15]

⁂

To summarize: three chronological layers can be discerned in the *Ritorno* manuscript: Pass 1, in medium ink, provided a continuity draft of the five-act version that omitted inessential material such as instrumental parts (and some whole movements), leaving space for them. Pass 2, in light ink, filled in that material in preparation for a performance, adding rubrics, instrumental parts, and texts. Also added were the capital letters A, B, and others—we will discuss these in some detail later—which clarify the order of material for the performers and could also have been intended to facilitate the copying of instrumental parts. Pass 3, in very dark ink, prepared a three-act performance, adding further rubrics and new scene designations.

---

15. The significance of Penelope's speech for the structure of the five-act drama is discussed in Chap. 5; also Chap. 7, n. 7. The fact that the editor failed to cross it out when he created the three-act version supports the idea, raised in connection with Eumete's role, that material in the score was sometimes left to be corrected during rehearsals. But the absence of this passage from the librettos remains mysterious. Perhaps it was introduced in the score to solve a problem encountered during rehearsals, as Carter surmises (*Musical Theatre*, 243), but only at the beginning of the second act in the five-act version, *not* in 1.10, as he assumes. Curtis (*Ritorno*, ix) misinterprets this passage by assuming it was added (rather than subtracted) for Bologna.

An understanding of the sequence of layers sheds light on some other differences between the score and the librettos, in particular the omission from the score of substantial textual material. Some of this material must eventually have been included, such as the "Coro di Nereidi" and "Coro di Sirene" in 1.3 and the Moors' "ballo greco" in 3.3 (or 2.6). Both scenes are announced by rubrics in the light ink of Pass 2, but no music is provided (Facsimiles 2 and 12). (The latter rubric, "Qui escono 8 mori che fan un ballo Greco," is on the right-hand margin of fol. 72r, which was folded over and cannot be seen in microfilm reproductions.) It is likely that the music for these scenes—and for the Naiads' chorus in 1.9—was left to be composed later, and would have been written on loose sheets.[16] (That loose sheets were used in connection with readying scores for performance—hardly a surprising fact—is clearly attested in the Venetian score of *L'incoronazione di Poppea*, as we will see shortly.) A rubric for another scene omitted in the first two passes, for 1.4, was added later in dark ink (Pass 3) and is relevant to performance: "Qui esce la barca de' Feaci, che conduce Ulisse, che dorme, e perché non si desti, si fa la seguente sinfonia toccata soavemente sempre su una corda" (Here the Phaeacians' ship appears on stage, carrying the sleeping Ulysses; and, so that he doesn't awaken, the full sinfonia should be played smoothly and softly, always on the same harmony). The rubric is followed by the rudimentary bass for the sinfonia, also in dark ink (of pass 3) (see below, on Ulisse's entrance, and Facsimile 2).

Only one entire scene seems to have been definitively—and explicitly—omitted from the score, the much discussed act 5, scene 2, a supernatural scene for Mercurio and the Suitors' ghosts, "lasciato fuora" because it was too melancholy. Some time ago I suggested that this scene was omitted by the composer for dramatic reasons, and that the rubric explaining the omission reproduced the rubric in the exemplar from which the score was copied.[17] Dubowy thought the scene was present in the exemplar, but that it was cut along with the original prologue and ending—and the choruses and balli—when the work was transformed from a five-act *festa teatrale* to a three-act *dramma per musica*. As I have already observed, however, the original prologue and ending had already been replaced when the five-act score was copied.[18]

Indeed, whereas the rubrics designating the choruses and the ballo indicated that the material in question would eventually be filled in, that for act 5, scene 2 closes off such

---

16. Many of Cavalli's scores omit music for the balli (and choruses). On this subject, see Irene Alm, "Winged Feet and Mute Eloquence: Dance in Seventeenth-Century Venetian Opera," *COJ* 15 (2003): 216–80. According to Alm, p. 224, although rubrics call for ballets in virtually all of the hundred-odd opera scores in the Contarini Collection, less than half contain music for them.

17. Ellen Rosand, "Iro and the Interpretation of *Il ritorno d'Ulisse in patria*," *JM* 7 (1989): 141–64.

18. In maintaining that this scene was probably present in Monteverdi's original, but was cut by the copyist, presumably because it was an underworld scene that would have presented difficulties in staging, Dubowy ("Bemerkungen," 233–34) overemphasizes certain parallels between the first two scenes of acts 1 and 5—Penelope/Iro (both laments), Melanto/Mercurio (both mention desert). Had the scene already been missing in the exemplar, he reasons, the copyist would have said "manca" rather than "si lascia fuora." And if it had been

a possibility. The rubric is actually even more ambiguous than it seems at first glance (see Facsimile 18). It was written in the light ink of the second pass (the one that inserted the five-act designations—but remember, this would have been scene 2 in both the five- and three-act versions, and so would not have needed correction for the three-act version)—and then edited in what looks like the same pass. The earlier layer is barely visible beneath a later one, which scratches out the material shown in square brackets: "Scena 2a [et 3a], la si lascia[n] fuora per esser maninconic[he]." It seems clear that the original rubric referred to the two parts of scene 2—the one for Mercurio, the other for the Suitors—as two separate scenes (hence the plural verb), a mistake that was subsequently corrected.[19] Presumably, the copyist would not have made such a mistake with this rubric if he were inventing it himself, rather than copying it from somewhere else. Nor could he be expected to offer such a value judgment on the content of the scene. Since the supernatural scene had already been omitted in the five-act version—the first pass—its omission must have been unrelated to the transformation into three acts, the third pass. Either the supernatural scene *or* the five-act structure, then, but not both, was integral to Dubowy's putative *festa teatrale*. The reason for omitting 5.2 must not have had to do with the genre, and therefore was not connected, as Dubowy claimed, to the replacement of the original prologue and the conversion to three acts.

It seems likely, then, that act 5, scene 2 was cut at the same time as the new prologue and ending were introduced, that is, before the five-act version of the score was copied, and not after. But other smaller cuts appear to have been made later, after the initial score had been copied—at the time it was converted to three acts. One such cut, involving the first of the Suitors' three scenes, certainly took place after the manuscript was compiled, since it caused a rupture in its otherwise completely regular gathering structure. In fact, two of the Suitors' three scenes appear to have been more heavily edited than any others in the score, suggesting that they may have presented a problem, not only to the composer, but in the staging of the opera as well.

The Ninth Gathering

In the setting of act 3, scene 2 (=2.5, fols. 65v–72r), the first of three scenes between the Suitors and Penelope, twenty lines of text are omitted, comprising one five-line stanza for Penelope and one each for the Suitors (lines 30–49 in Table 8, text given in brackets is omitted in the score, and text in italics is added by the composer). This cut, which may

---

missing, he continues, the copyist would have called it "superfluo" rather than "maninconico." These linguistic distinctions appear to be anachronistic as well as overly literal. The scribe was probably simply copying what was in the exemplar. I agree with Dubowy, however, that the scene could have been omitted because it was too difficult to stage.

19. Dubowy's elaborate explanation for the change from plural to singular in the rubric ("Bemerkungen," n. 38), that the copyist had first wanted to cut scene 2 as well as either 1 or 3 but then decided on just 2, is unconvincing. It is unlikely that the plural could have referred to either 5.1 or 5.3, since both are central to the drama and neither could have been judged "maninconico." (On "maninconico," see Chap. 3, n. 22.)

TABLE 8

Il ritorno d'Ulisse, 3.2 [or 2.5], Antinoo, Anfinomo, Pisandro, Penelope
[Eurimaco included in score and librettos but is silent]

ANTINOO

   1 Sono l'altre regine   65v

   2 Coronate di servi, e tu d'amanti:

   3 Tributan questi regi

   4 Al mar di tua bellezza un mar di pianti.

ANFINOMO, PISANDRO, ANTINOO *(a tre)*

   5 [1] Ama dunque, sì, sì;   66r

   6 Dunque riama un dì.

PENELOPE

   7 Non voglio amar, no, no;   66v

   8 Ch'amando penerò.

[I PROCI]

Ama dunque, sì, sì;

Dunque riama un dì.   VI =

PENELOPE

   9 Cari tanto mi siete

  10 Quanto più ardenti ardete;   67r

  11 Ma non m' appresso all'amoroso gioco

  12 Ché lungi è bel più che vicino il foco.

Non voglio amar, no, no;   67v

Ch'amando penerò.

PISANDRO

  13 La pampinosa vite,

  14 Se non s'abbraccia al faggio

  15 L'autun non frutta, e non fiorisce il maggio.

  16 E se sfiorita resta

  17 Ogni mano la coglie,   68r

  18 Ogni piè la calpesta.

ANFINOMO

  19 Il bel cedro odoroso

  20 Vive, se non s'incalma,

  21 Senza frutti e spinoso,

  22 Ma se s'innesta poi,

  23 Figliano frutti e fior li spini suoi.   68v

ANTINOO

  24 L'edera che verdeggia

  25 Ad onta anco del verno

TABLE 8 *(continued)*

26 [Adorna, si vagheggia]*a*

27 D'un bel smeraldo eterno,

28 Se non s'appoggia, perde

29 Fra [l']erbose ruine il suo bel verde.　　　　　　　　　　69r

PENELOPE

30 [L'edra, il cedro, e la vite

31 Altre leggi non han, che di natura

32 Ogni suo pregio oscura

33 Bella, donna, e Regina

34 S'a natura s'inchina.

PISANDRO

35 Tutta di pompe illustre

36 Va ricca primavera

37 Ma ciò che ride il dì piange la sera.

38 In fin ogni bel fiore

39 Colto, o non colto more.

ANFINOMO

40 Non ha beltà più ferma

41 La rosa nel suo stelo

42 Benché latte divin beva dal cielo,

43 Non colta non si serba

44 Ma cade in grembo all'erba.

ANTINOO

45 Beltà donnesca e bella

46 Più che fior, più che rosa

47 Ma porta in un balen fuga noiosa.

48 Goduta o non goduta

49 Tosto anch'ella è perduta.]

ANFINOMO, PISANDRO, ANTINOO *(a tre)*　　　　69v–70r

50 Ama dunque, sì, sì;

51 Dunque riama un dì.　　　　　　　　　　　　　= DE

PENELOPE

52 [2]　Non voglio amar, non voglio.　　　　　　　70v

53 Come sta in dubbio un ferro

54 Se fra due calamite

55 Da due parti diverse egli è chiamato,

56 Così sta in forse il core

57 Nel tripartito amore;

(continued)

TABLE 8 *(continued)*

58 Ma non può amar

59 Chi non sa, chi non può

60 Che piangere e penar.

61 Mestizia e dolor

62 Son crudeli nemici d'amor.

ANFINOMO, PISANDRO, ANTINOO *(a tre)*

[3] All'allegrezze dunque, al ballo, al canto!   71r–72r

Rallegriam la regina;

Lieto cor ad amor tosto s'inchina.

BALLO

Qui escono otto Mori che fanno un ballo greco cantato con li seguenti versi   72r

[Atto terzo, scena terza][b]

[4] Dame in amor belle e gentil,

Amate allor che ride april;

Non giunge al sen gioia o piacer

Se tocca il crin l'età senil.

Dunque al gioir, lieto al goder.

Dame in amor belle e gentil

Vaga ne' spin la rosa sta,

Ma non nel gel bella è *[la]* beltà:

Perde il splendor torbido ciel.

Ciglio in rigor non è più bel.

NOTE: VI = DE indicates the cut in the score.

[a] Curtis, 127 n. This line, missing from the score, is found in libretto nos. 6 and 11.

[b] The scene is missing in libretto no. 11.

---

once have been even more extensive, falls within an anomalous section of the manuscript: the ninth gathering is one of only two sections that fail to conform to the regular gathering structure. As mentioned earlier, all but two of the seventeen gatherings consist of eight folios. This one has twelve; the other exception, less disruptive since it occurs at the end, is the final gathering, which has only three.

This anomalous section was created when two nested bifolios were inserted between the eighth and what was originally the ninth gathering, and the original numbering changed to include the new bifolios as part of a now-expanded ninth gathering (Figure 1). The old signature marking for the ninth gathering (upper right-hand corner) can still be discerned on 70r (see Facsimile 11); it was scratched out and the number 9 introduced on the first of the new folios (66r) (see Facsimile 9), resulting in a gathering of twelve rather than eight folios (66r–77v). Although the inserted bifolios provide music for a shortened version of Badoaro's text (omitting twenty lines, as we have noted), the fact that it was a late insertion—requiring renumbering of the ninth gathering—suggests that the music it contains was also originally intended to be cut. The cut would thus have comprised all of the

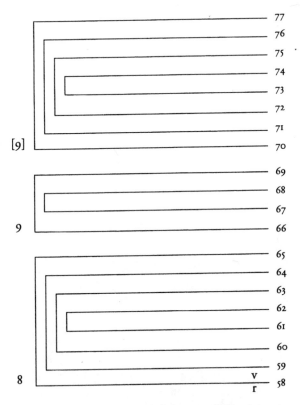

FIGURE 1. Ninth gathering of *Il ritorno d'Ulisse in patria*

Suitors' solo music in addition to some of Penelope's, that is, everything between fols. 65v and 69v, comprising forty-four lines of text (lines 9–51; see **vi** = **de** in Table 8 above). (Possibly the original singers of the roles were deemed competent enough for ensemble work, but not for solos.) Originally, then, it would seem that the score went from the trio "Ama dunque" [1] (fol. 65v) to Penelope's "Non voglio" recitative [2] (fol. 70v), and thence to the "Allegrezze" trio [3] (fol. 71r) and Moor ballet [4] (fol. 72r). (The numbers correspond to those in Table 8.) At some point during the preparation of a production (possibly during the conversion from five to three acts), some of the omitted material was restored (lines 9–29 in Table 8). It is worth noting that the inserted bifolios contain two substantial lacunae (on fol. 69r–v: six staves on fol. 69r [see Facsimile 10] and four on fol. 69v) and that all of fol. 69v would have been blank, if the opening of the chorus "Ama dunque" had not been re-copied onto it from fol. 65v (compare Facsimiles 9 and 11). The presence of the lacunae suggests that all of the omitted material—all forty-four lines—was to be restored, but that the composer or editor changed his mind, omitting only the twenty lines that might have seemed most redundant—second stanzas of parallel texts for Penelope and the Suitors (bracketed in Table 8). (The dramatic redundancy of the Suitors is considered in Chap. 7. Perhaps Monteverdi's first impulse was to cut the whole scene, since the Suitors sing again only two scenes later.)

The instability reflected in this portion of the manuscript regarding the Suitors extends to their subsequent appearances as well, especially their final one at the climax of the opera, where they are slaughtered by Ulisse. That scene involved cuts as well as additions of material that was not copied (because not yet composed?) in the first pass.

The copyist was evidently forced to develop various strategies to deal with a difficult exemplar here. At one point (fol. 96v; see Facsimile 14) he wrote Pisandro's vocal part below the bass, introducing the letter B (in the light ink of pass 2) to clarify the situation; this indicates that the name and text were not included in the original pass. In another case (fol. 97v; see Facsimile 15), the copyist sketched a few new string parts above the staff for the cadence of a sinfonia that had appeared several folios earlier.[20] In still another, he wrote straight across an opening (fols. 102v–103r) to accommodate the setting of Ulisse's battle cry, "Alle morti, alle stragi," with string accompaniment, even though that accompaniment was not entered until the second pass (see Facsimile 17). (He had to do the same for Iro's music in the previous scene, on fols. 89v–90r.) Although the scoring requirements forced him to copy some material out of order—Ulisse's battle cry was written above his invocation of Minerva, which actually preceded it—he clarified the order of the material by means of letters and lines of connection.

All in all, the final folios of the act must have been difficult to copy. The first pass was unusually sketchy. And the large amount of material left to be added in the second pass did not always fit in the allotted space: the staves reserved for the "tocco di guerra" had to be extended into the right margin of an already very crowded page to accommodate it (fol. 102r) (see Facsimile 16). And in the case of Ulisse's final battle cry (fols. 102v–103r; Facsimile 17), the necessity of distributing music occupying six staves on eight-staff paper produced an awkward arrangement that required clarifying rubrics, letters, and other signs. All of these irregularities, but especially the ad hoc strategies for clarification adopted by the copyist, leave the impression that the completion of this scene may have depended on last-minute decisions, perhaps regarding staging.[21]

Indeed, the most tantalizing aspect of this score—aside from the music itself, of course—is its evident proximity to performance. Both the second and third passes through the manuscript show specific concern with performance—presumably first of the five-act, then of the three-act version. This includes the insertion of new music, of rubrics indicating repetition of already existing music, clarification of the order of various numbers, and specific stage directions. (Some of this material even shows signs of having been introduced during rehearsals.)

---

20. Curtis (*Ritorno*, 176, n. 2) points out that the new, incompetent cadence was required to effect a transposition from Pisandro's key, D, to Anfinomo's, C.

21. Material omitted in the first pass included: the Suitors' amazed response to seeing Ulisse in his own clothes ("meraviglia, stupore, prodigi estremi," fol. 101v [Facsimile 16]); the five-part "Sinfonia da Guerra" (announced by a rubric on the same folio, 101v); and the instrumental accompaniment for Ulisse's battle cry "Alle morti," for which four staves were left empty (fols. 102v–103r, Facsimile 17).

At least two sets of performance rubrics can be discerned, one in the lighter ink associated with pass 2, the other in the darker ink of pass 3, presumably added for further clarification or precision.[22] Rubrics in both inks describe stage effects: two (in pass 2 light ink) are found in Ulisse's scene with Telemaco (2.7), "Scende dal cielo un raggio di foco sopra il capo d'Ulisse onde s'apre la terra, ed Ulisse si profonda" (A lightning bolt descends from the sky over Ulysses' head, whereupon the earth opens and Ulysses sinks) (fol. 57v) and "qui risorge Ulisse in sua propria forma" (here Ulysses appears in his true form) (fol. 59r). A similar indication occurs in 3.2 (fol. 76r): "qui vola sopra il capo de' Proci un'Aquila" (here an eagle flies over the Suitors' heads), provoking Eurimaco's fear of a bad omen. The actions of the Suitors in trying to string Ulisse's bow in 4.3 are described in some detail: first Pisandro (fol. 97r): "Pisandro s'apparecchia di caricar l'arco e non può" (Pisandro readies himself to string the bow and cannot), then Anfinomo (fol. 98r): "qui finge di caricar l'arco e non può, tratanto si pausa coll'istromento, e poi seguita" (here he pretends to string the bow and cannot, during which [the continuo player] pauses with his instrument, and then continues), and finally Antinoo (fol. 99r): "s'affatica caricare l'arco e non può" (strains to string the bow and cannot).[23]

Only a few dark rubrics from pass 3 prescribe stage action, for instance "Iro che fa alla lotta" (Iro who makes to fight) in 4.2 (fol. 89v). But others concern aspects of vocal performance. The directive "qui si ride da dovero in sin a qua" (here he laughs for real up to this point) appears above Ulisse's speech on fol. 81r, and "qui cade in riso naturale" (here he falls into natural laughter) above Iro's in 5.1 (fol. 105r). Other rubrics pertain to tempo and dynamics, suggesting that the passages concerned were considered either especially ambiguous or especially important by the composer. Those in light ink include "Allegro," for the opening sinfonia (fol. 2r) "pian, forte, più forte" over a long-held note for Eumete on fol. 53r–v, to indicate a crescendo; "presto, adagio, presto, adagio" for the Suitors' trio on fols. 75v–76r; and "presto" for two passages in Iro's monologue on fols. 105v and 106r.[24]

Those in the darker ink include a *trillo* for Iro (on fol. 106v); "presto" and "tardo" for Eurimaco (on fol. 20v, a strange passage in which the text is underlaid beneath a series of undifferentiated longas, signaling the singer's responsibility for the rhythm);[25] and "alle-

---

22. There is some ambiguity about a few performance indications (such as fol. 33r: "Ulisse fra se parla, e dice"), which look as if they were included in the first pass through the manuscript.

23. The description of Anfinomo's actions is clearly directed toward the accompanying instrument(s). Similarly performative rubrics accompany the entrances of the main characters (see below). In the librettos the Suitors' rubrics are uniform and simpler: "si prova" or "fa prova di carricar l'arco, e non può."

24. This monologue is analyzed in Chap. 8.

25. The notation resembles that of "Sfogava con le stelle" in Book 4 of Monteverdi's madrigals. There are other places like this in the score, most notably the Suitors' stunned reaction to Ulisse's successful stringing of his bow: "meraviglie, stupori, prodigi estremi" under a series of six breves (fol. 101v: see Facsimile 16).

gra" for Minerva's entrance on fol. 32v (see Facsimile 6) (possibly referring to her mood rather than her tempo). A third category of indications that would have been made in connection with a performance involves the labeling of ambiguous passages, particularly ritornellos or sinfonias. Letters (all of them in the light ink of the second pass) are frequently introduced to clarify the order of material. In the prologue (fol. 4v), "ut supra A" is added to the bass marked "Sinfonia prima," and a corresponding A, plus a rubric, "Sinfonia avanti il Prologo," is added to the previous sinfonia (fol. 2r). The opening sinfonia of 1.2, marked "B" in light ink, begins on the top five staves of fol. 14r and is continued on the verso, as indicated by the rubric "si volta la carta." This is followed by the rubric "si torna una carta in dietro Duri e penosi," to indicate that the aria with that incipit begins on the previous folio; following the aria, which continues onto fol. 15r, a rubric indicates a return to the opening sinfonia: "Sinfonia antecedente B et poi la seconda strofa." The "B" is lighter than the rest of the rubric, indicating that it was added for clarification, in the second pass. (The letter "B" is also used to clarify an awkwardness in the notation of Pisandro's vocal part on fol. 96v, which, as we have seen [see Facsimile 14], is temporarily written *beneath* the bass part.)[26]

On fols. 28v–29r, ambiguities are caused by the copyist's desire to save space (see Facsimile 4). Having no room on fol. 28v to finish copying the chorus of the Feaci—he needed four staves but only two were left—he continued it across the opening (marked A), where he followed it with Nettuno's curse on the Feaci; he then used the two staves remaining on fol. 28v to copy Nettuno's next speech, marked "NB B," which he likewise continued across the opening, onto fol. 29r. A rubric following the curse clarifies what has become a messy situation: "Dopo mutata la nave segue Imparino NB B" (After the scene of the ship, "Imparino" follows).

And sometimes other letters besides A and B are used. In a rubric at the end of act 4 (= act 2, fol. 103r) the letter "S" refers the copyist back to Ulisse's battle cry on the preceding folio (see Facsimiles 17 and 16). And in the penultimate scene of the opera (fols. 120v–123r), a five-part sinfonia follows the first of Ericlea's four stanzas, introduced by the rubric "seguita la sinfonia" (fol. 120v). The sinfonia itself is labeled "H" in light ink (on fol. 121r). Although her second and third stanzas run together, without any indication that they were separated by a repeat of the sinfonia (possibly a mistake), the third and fourth stanzas are followed by the bass line of the sinfonia, accompanied by the rubric "ritornello ut supra," with "H" added in lighter ink (on fol. 122r).[27]

---

26. Clarifiying another kind of anomaly, the bass line on fol. 19r, ambiguous because notated in tenor clef, is labled "basso continuo," in lighter ink.

27. But see Chap. 6, p. 200, for the potentially positive effect of omitting the ritornello here. Interestingly, an extra treble part is added over the bass following stanza 3, which does not agree with any of the parts of the original sinfonia (see *Ritorno*, ed. Curtis, 22, n. 1, also Dubowy, "Bemerkungen," 232, n. 37). Note the clear distinction between the use of "sinfonia" (the first time) and "ritornello" (all of the returns to the sinfonia). Ritornello is more like a verb than a noun. One wonders whether the use of different letters here and elsewhere might suggest that they refer to individual musical numbers in orchestral parts.

Particular care was evidently taken with the initial entrances of the three main characters: Penelope, Ulisse, and Minerva. In all three cases, the relevant material was added or clarified after the first—even after the second—pass through the manuscript (perhaps at rehearsals). Penelope's entrance, on fol. 8v, is the most difficult to reconstruct (see Facsimile 1). The facsimile shows the last two bars of the final trio of the Prologue and the bass line of the Prologue's repeated sinfonia, crammed onto the second half of two successive staves (presumably so as not to interfere with the space allocated for the opening of act 1), accompanied by the rubric "Sinfonia ut supra," followed by the letter "A." (The sinfonia and rubric appear to be in the normal ink of pass 1, the letter A in the light ink of pass 2, as if there was some ambiguity surrounding that sinfonia, possibly an implication that it might have belonged to the ensuing rather than the previous action. Clarification is provided by another light A at the head of the Sinfonia.) This is followed by the first three bars of Penelope's monologue, preceded by the bass of her introductory sinfonia, two bars of repeated Cs (shorthand for "vamp till ready"). There are two scene designations here, one at the top (in light ink), the other in the middle of the folio (in dark ink). The second, more concise designation ("Atto primo, scena prima, Penelope") was obviously not required simply for the conversion to three acts since the act and scene number remain the same in both versions, but it was clearly intended to replace the fuller first one ("Reggia, Penelope, Ericlea"), possibly because the placement of the first one, *above* the prologue sinfonia, was ambiguous.[28] Indeed, the new designation is followed by an explanatory rubric, which seems to have been entered at the same time: "finita la presente sinfonia in tempo allegro s'incomincia la seguente mesta, alla bassa sin che Penelope sarà gionta in Scena per dar principio al canto" (When the present sinfonia in allegro tempo is finished, the following sad one begins, softly, until Penelope has arrived on stage to begin singing). Beneath this, furthermore, and to the left, just above Penelope's bass, there is another rubric that appears to be in the same hand and shade of ink, though it is partly redundant: "questa sinfonia [referring to Penelope's bass line] si replica tante volte insinche Penelope arriva in scena" (This sinfonia is repeated until Penelope arrives on stage). It looks as though both rubrics, however redundant, were added during the third pass (for the three-act version) to clarify the staging of Penelope's entrance.

The staging of Ulisse's entrance, in 1.4, shows similar signs of attention (fol. 23r; see Facsimile 2). Here, the same repeated pitch, C, intended to accompany Ulisse's entrance, asleep, is introduced by the rubric we have already mentioned: "Qui esce la barca de' Feaci che conduce Ulisse che dorme, et perché non si desti si fà la seguente sinfonia toccata soavemente sempre su una corda." Again, since it is written in very dark ink, the rubric, and possibly the shorthand, vamp-till-ready sinfonia bass too, were introduced in pass 3. The same appears to be true for the following scene designation, "Scena 5ta." Indications

---

28. Recall the protocol of simplifying an initial rubric to include just the first singer.

for the two previous scenes, 3 and 4, in contrast, are written in the light ink of pass 2. The original designation for scene 5 is no longer visible, though the character names that accompanied it—Nettuno, Giove, etc.—can still be seen, in their edited form.

Minerva's entrance in 1.8 (fol. 32r; see Facsimile 5) was also clarified by material added after the first pass, which seems to have allocated space (four staves, and clefs), but no bass line, for an introductory sinfonia. (The bass line did appear subsequently, in the ritornello following the first stanza of Minerva's song.) When the music for the sinfonia was filled in, in pass 2, an extra staff had to be drawn at the bottom margin of the page to accommodate the bass. Like Penelope's and Ulisse's entrance music, this sinfonia, designated "A," is introduced by a lengthy performance rubric, "Minerva in habito da Pastorello esce con passi ordinati al suono della presente sinfonietta" (Minerva dressed as a shepherd enters with her steps coordinated with the sound of the present sinfonietta). Interestingly, the original scene designation was not entered until after the sinfonia, at the top of the next page (fol. 32v; see Facsimile 6), perhaps confirming that the sinfonia was not initially included as part of the scene.[29]

All of these observations regarding the various layers of the manuscript, considered in conjunction with evidence derived from the librettos and other documents, suggest a possible chronological framework for the score. I would propose that the five-act version (first and second passes), including the new prologue and revised final scene and presumably excluding the scenes of the libretto that were cut either entirely ("maninconico") or partially (i.e., the Suitors' scene in the ninth gathering), was prepared for the Venice premiere of 1640; and that it was then transformed into three acts, the Suitors' scene enlarged, and additional performance rubrics introduced (third pass). Since all the passes are in the hand of a single copyist, it is perhaps most likely that this performance was the premiere, and that the five-act version was never mounted. On the other hand, the Bologna revival was close in time—probably only a few months after the Venetian premiere—and it would be natural to expect the limitations of a traveling company or different audience expectations to have required exactly the sort of revisions we have been examining, so the three-act version could have been intended for Bologna.[30]

---

29. A subsequent scene designation was entered by mistake (the scene number was later erased) at the beginning of Minerva's second stanza, in the third pass. Analogous to Minerva's sinfonia, that of the Feaci on fol. 27r (Facsimile 3) is all in light ink (as was the designation for scene 6—folded over, perhaps invisible, which may be why scene 7 had to be corrected [Facsimile 4]). Empty staves with clefs, presumably intended to be filled in with instrumental parts, can be seen in the prologue, fol. 2v—though there is no bass staff or clef. Empty staves were also left for the accompaniment of Penelope's final aria (fol. 133r), which were never filled in, and probably never intended to be. (This situation is discussed in Chap. 7.)

30. This is essentially Curtis's interpretation (*Ritorno*, preface, p. ix). One obvious advantage of three over five acts for a traveling company, of course, would have been the reduction in the number of intra-act intermedi from four to two.

FACSIMILE 1. *Il ritorno d'Ulisse*, fol. 8v. Vienna, Österreichische Nationalbibliothek, picture archives, Cod. Mus. Hs. 18.763.

FACSIMILE 2. *Il ritorno d'Ulisse*, fol. 23r. Vienna, Österreichische Nationalbibliothek, picture archives, Cod. Mus. Hs. 18.763.

FACSIMILE 3. *Il ritorno d'Ulisse,* fol. 27r. Vienna, Österreichische Nationalbibliothek, picture archives, Cod. Mus. Hs. 18.763.

FACSIMILE 4. *Il ritorno d'Ulisse,* fols. 28v–29r. Vienna, Österreichische Nationalbibliothek, picture archives, Cod. Mus. Hs. 18.763.

FACSIMILE 5. *Il ritorno d'Ulisse*, 32r. Vienna, Österreichische Nationalbibliothek, picture archives, Cod. Mus. Hs. 18.763.

FACSIMILE 6. *Il ritorno d'Ulisse*, fol. 32v. Vienna, Österreichische Nationalbibliothek, picture archives, Cod. Mus. Hs. 18.763.

FACSIMILE 7. *Il ritorno d'Ulisse,* fol. 42r. Vienna, Österreichische Nationalbibliothek, picture archives, Cod. Mus. Hs. 18.763.

FACSIMILE 8. *Il ritorno d'Ulisse,* fol. 65r. Vienna, Österreichische Nationalbibliothek, picture archives, Cod. Mus. Hs. 18.763.

FACSIMILE 9. *Il ritorno d'Ulisse,* fols. 65v–66r. Vienna, Österreichische National-bibliothek, picture archives, Cod. Mus. Hs. 18.763.

FACSIMILE 10. *Il ritorno d'Ulisse,* fol. 69r. Vienna, Österreichische Nationalbibliothek, picture archives, Cod. Mus. Hs. 18.763.

FACSIMILE 11. *Il ritorno d'Ulisse,* fols. 69v–70r. Vienna, Österreichische Nationalbibliothek, picture archives, Cod. Mus. Hs. 18.763.

FACSIMILE 12. *Il ritorno d'Ulisse,* fol. 72r. Vienna, Österreichische Nationalbibliothek,
picture archives, Cod. Mus. Hs. 18.763.

FACSIMILE 13. *Il ritorno d'Ulisse,* fol. 72v. Vienna, Österreichische Nationalbibliothek, picture archives, Cod. Mus. Hs. 18.763.

FACSIMILE 14. *Il ritorno d'Ulisse,* fol. 96v. Vienna, Österreichische Nationalbibliothek, picture archives, Cod. Mus. Hs. 18.763.

FACSIMILE 16. *Il ritorno d'Ulisse,* fols. 101v–102r. Vienna, Österreichische National-bibliothek, picture archives, Cod. Mus. Hs. 18.763.

FACSIMILE 15. *Il ritorno d'Ulisse,* fol. 97v. Vienna, Österreichische Nationalbibliothek, picture archives, Cod. Mus. Hs. 18.763.

FACSIMILE 17. *Il ritorno d'Ulisse,* fols. 102v–103r. Vienna, Österreichische Nationalbibliothek, picture archives, Cod. Mus. Hs. 18.763.

FACSIMILE 18. *Il ritorno d'Ulisse*, fol. 107r. Vienna, Österreichische Nationalbibliothek, picture archives, Cod. Mus. Hs. 18.763.

FACSIMILE 19. *L'incoronazione di Poppea,* pp. 178–179. Naples, Biblioteca del Conservatorio di Musica S. Pietro a Majella, MS Rari 6.4.1.

FACSIMILE 20. *L'incoronazione di Poppea,* fol. 8r. Venice, Biblioteca Nazionale Marciana, It. IV, 439 (=9963).

FACSIMILE 21. *L'incoronazione di Poppea*, fol. 8v. Venice, Biblioteca Nazionale Marciana, It. IV, 439 (=9963).

FACSIMILE 22. *L'incoronazione di Poppea,* fol. 55r. Venice, Biblioteca Nazionale Marciana, It. IV, 439 (=9963).

FACSIMILE 24. *L'incoronazione di Poppea,* fols. 65v–66r. Venice, Biblioteca Nazionale Marciana, It. IV, 439 (=9963).

FACSIMILE 23. *L'incoronazione di Poppea*, fol. 62v. Venice, Biblioteca Nazionale Marciana, It. IV, 439 (=9963).

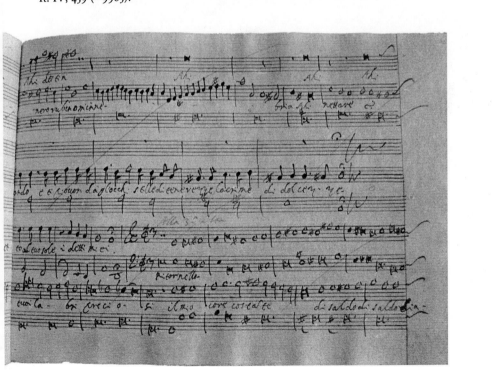

FACSIMILE 25. *L'incoronazione di Poppea,* fols. 66v–67r. Venice, Biblioteca Nazionale Marciana, It. IV, 439 (=9963).

FACSIMILE 26. *L'incoronazione di Poppea,* fol. 93v. Venice, Biblioteca Nazionale Marciana, It. IV, 439 (=9963).

FACSIMILE 27. *L'incoronazione di Poppea,* fols. 104v–105r. Venice, Biblioteca Nazionale Marciana, It. IV, 439 (=9963).

FACSIMILE 28. *L'incoronazione di Poppea*, p. 221. Naples, Biblioteca del Conservatorio di Musica S. Pietro a Majella, MS Rari 6.4.1.

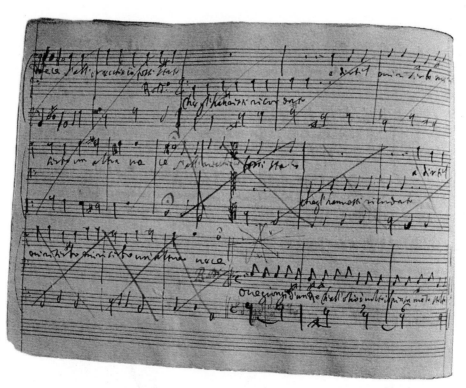

FACSIMILE 29. Francesco Cavalli, *Veremonda,* fol. 21v. Venice, Biblioteca Nazionale Marciana, It. IV, 439 (=9963).

FACSIMILE 30. Francesco Cavalli, *Veremonda,* fol. 27v. Venice, Biblioteca Nazionale Marciana, It. IV, 439 (=9963).

Although the manuscript is not dated, there is some external evidence to support a date close to the Venetian premiere and the two known revivals (in Bologna and Venice). Osthoff came to this conclusion a half-century ago on the basis of its five-part string textures, which he found characteristic of Venetian operas performed during the 1640s, and from the fact that he thought the hand of its copyist resembled that of Cavalli's *Apollo e Dafne,* an opera also performed in 1640.[31] Jeffery implicitly disputes this. According to him, the copyist of *Apollo e Dafne* is unique to that manuscript.[32] Moreover, since it is a fair copy and not a performance score, it cannot be reliably dated to 1640. And yet, since it was not among the (many) early Cavalli scores recopied for purposes of preservation during the 1660s, a date close to its Venetian premiere is at least possible. Even if a connection to the *Apollo* manuscript can never be established, however, internal evidence, as we have seen, strongly indicates that the score of *Ritorno* was compiled around 1640, during the years surrounding its first performance and revivals.

As far as the provenance of the score is concerned, the situation is considerably murkier. At present it is impossible to know how it ended up in Vienna—along with some other Venetian opera scores, including Cavalli's *Egisto.*[33] According to Jeffery, the *Egisto* score was copied around 1650–51, by the same two copyists as *Oristeo* and *Calisto,* one of whom was Maria Cavalli, possibly in conjunction with Italian theatrical performances in Vienna beginning in 1651.[34] We know that it was around this time that Ferrari traveled to that city to begin his service as instrumentalist and director of court festivities under Ferdinand III. Since he and Manelli had been responsible for producing *Ritorno* in Bologna (and also probably in Venice), perhaps he brought the score with him to Vienna. He could also have brought *Egisto;* not only had he produced Cavalli's opera in Genoa in 1645, but he made his own setting of the same libretto for Piacenza in 1651.[35]

---

31. Osthoff, "Zu den Quellen," 76–77. This was to counteract Domenico De' Paoli's opinion, apparently communicated privately to Redlich (Redlich, *Monteverdi,* 110), that the score was from the eighteenth century.

32. See above, Chap. 2, n. 42. Glover, *Cavalli,* 72, was the first to point out the uniqueness of the copyist of *Apollo e Dafne,* not only among Cavalli's scores, but within the Contarini Collection as a whole. It is not clear whether Jeffery included the *Ritorno* manuscript in his sample of copyists, though he must have seen the score, since he comments on the watermarks ("The Autograph Manuscripts," 160, n. 431).

33. Most recent scholars, including Dubowy, reject the possibility of a revival in Vienna ("Bemerkungen," 232 and n. 36), though Walter Pass, "Monteverdis Il ritorno d'Ulisse in patria," in *Performing Practice in Monteverdi's Music,* ed. Rafaello Monterosso (Cremona: Fondazione Claudio Monteverdi, 1995), 175–81 suggests— unconvincingly, in my view—that because of its strong moral message (as articulated in the original prologue), it could have formed part of the tradition of performance of Jesuit dramas in the Vienna of Leopold I.

34. See Jeffery, "The Autograph Manuscripts," 165–68.

35. Ferrari's setting of *Egisto* was performed in Piacenza on 22 January 1651. He arrived in Vienna some ten months later, on 12 November, after passing through Innsbruck, to begin his service under Ferdinand III. On Ferrari's setting of *Egisto* for Piacenza, see Bianconi and Walker, "Dalla *Finta pazza,*" 433, n. 220. They claim surprise at the idea that Ferrari set *Egisto,* since the libretto corresponding to the Piacenza production fails to mention a composer, and since *Egisto* was one of the Cavalli operas that was altered least in its numerous revivals. Could the document they cite have been wrong? Could it have meant that Ferrari *produced Egisto* in Piacenza on that date? If this were the case, that is, if it was *Cavalli's* score, newly copied, it would jibe with the dating of the Vienna score of *Egisto* (Jeffery, "The Autograph Manuscripts," 165–68), namely around 1651–52.

Curtis has suggested several other possibilities. On the basis of the oval emblematic decoration on the cover of a number of seventeenth-century opera scores now in the Vienna National Library, which replaced an earlier medallion portrait of the emperor Leopold and his first wife, he dates the arrival of the *Ritorno* manuscript (and the others associated with it in the same collection) to sometime after 1673, when the emperor's wife died. He suggests that both scores could have arrived via Innsbruck, having been presented to Archduke Ferdinand Karl, either by Ferrari, Cavalli, or Ziani, all of whom passed through the city between 1651 and 1662.[36]

All this must remain in the realm of speculation, however. We will have occasion to revisit the relationship between this score and the various librettos of *Ritorno* in succeeding chapters, in connection with more specific analysis of the composer's reaction to the text.

L'incoronazione di Poppea

Ideally, a discussion of the *Incoronazione* scores should aim to clarify their meaning and their place within the early history of the opera. It should allow us to understand how they relate to the Venetian premiere and to the Naples revival. The most important question, however, will be more difficult to answer—how faithfully do these scores transmit Monteverdi's music? This they cannot fully reveal. What they do reveal is that the music and text of the premiere—to say nothing of the revival(s)—were some considerable distance away from the composer's original conception.

Whereas much evidence suggests that the *Ritorno* manuscript was contemporary with the original production, this cannot be said of the *Incoronazione* scores. At the earliest, they were copied nearly a decade after the first performance, one certainly, the other probably in connection with the Naples revival of 1651. Although not an autograph, *Ritorno*, as we have seen, reveals several layers in the copying process that allow a hypothetical original to be reconstructed and provide evidence of alterations presumably made in the process preparing a performance—including the transformation from five to three acts. The score also communicates a vivid sense of the exigencies of a production, with its performance indications and last-minute additions and cuts.

Neither of the *Incoronazione* scores can provide this kind of information on its own. But the existence of two scores that differ from one another in potentially significant ways compensates to some extent for their chronological distance from the first performance. So does the survival of other kinds of materials associated with the premiere, missing for *Ritorno*, in particular the scenario and the Udine libretto (U2), which can be used in conjunction with the scores to reconstruct, however speculatively, the original work. As will soon become clear,

---

36. See Curtis, *Ritorno*, preface. For a description of the emperor Leopold's library, the "Schlafkammerbibliothek," see Josef Gmeiner, "Die Schlafkammerbibliothek Kaiser Leopolds I," *Biblio* 43 (1994): 3–4.

when considered all together, these sources indicate that the opera must have been revived at least once between the Venetian premiere of 1643 and the Naples performance of 1651. At the present time, two possibilities suggest themselves: Venice 1646, and/or Paris 1647.

๛

The two *Incoronazione* scores represent different functions and stages in the evolution of the opera. The first to be identified,[37] the Venice score (I-Vnm It. IV, 439 [= 9963], hereafter Vp), is a complex manuscript involving the collaboration of a number of different scribes—as many as seven, Benvenuti thought—including Cavalli as well as his wife Maria. Two copyists were responsible for the main text. Maria Cavalli wrote out acts 1 and 3, and a still unidentified scribe copied act 2.[38] Among the other scribes, by far the most significant was Cavalli himself, who edited the score for performance. Since his wife is known to have been active as a copyist only between 1650 and her death in mid-September 1652, we can be fairly certain that at least her part of the *Incoronazione* score falls within this two-year span. This dating is supported by the watermarks Vp shares with three other Contarini manuscripts from the same period, Cavalli's *Rosinda, Calisto,* and *Veremonda,* and the Vienna *Egisto.*[39] As for the second act, its chronological proximity to the rest of the score is attested by the presence of Cavalli's interventions throughout.[40]

Cavalli's performance indications in the score, closely resembling those in his own operas, certainly suggest that he was involved in the production. We can presume that he at least helped to prepare the performances of his operas that took place in Naples under his name at around the same time, including *Didone* in 1650, *Egisto* and *Giasone* in 1651, and *Veremonda* in 1652.[41] It thus seems likely that the Venetian score was indeed intended for

---

37. By Wiel, *I codici musicali contariniani.* See Chap. 2.

38. Benvenuti, "Il manoscritto veneziano"; id., preface to *Incoronazione,* facsimile; Osthoff, "Die venezianische und neapolitanische Fassung"; id., "Neue Beobachtungen zu Quellen und Geschichte von Monteverdis' *Incoronazione di Poppea,*" *Mf* 11 (1958): 129–38; and Jeffery, "The Autograph Manuscripts," 169–73. Osthoff first noticed that the scribe of acts 1 and 3 of *Incoronazione* also copied a number of Cavalli manuscripts. Glover, *Cavalli,* 71, designated this as Hand B, and Jeffery later identified it as that of Maria Cavalli.

39. See Jeffery, "The Autograph Manuscripts," 174. Interestingly, *Veremonda,* which was performed in Naples in 1652, is the only Cavalli score to share both a watermark and a copyist with *Incoronazione* (the earliest of the three Neapolitan manuscripts of *Giasone* shares watermark, but not copyist; see below, n. 56).

40. Curtis, "La Poppea impasticciata," 30, n. 18, however, thinks it might have been copied later, though hardly as late as 1720 or 1725, as suggested by Schneider (*Un précurseur,* 272).

41. Cavalli's actual presence in Naples cannot be proven. Indeed, Dinko Fabris thinks it unlikely, preferring to credit Giovanni Battista Balbi with the responsibility of having produced all of the Cavalli operas there. See Dinko Fabris, "*Statira* da Venezia a Napoli," in *Francesco Cavalli: La circolazione dell'opera veneziana nel Seicento,* ed. Dinko Fabris (Naples: Turchini edizioni, 2005), 165–94; also Bianconi and Walker, "Dalla *Finta pazza* alla *Veremonda,*" and Irene Alm, "Balbi," *NG.* According to Michelassi ("Musici di fortuna," nn. 65–66), however, another impresario and erstwhile colleague of Balbi, Curzio Manara, was responsible for the first three Neapolitan productions of Venetian operas in 1650 and early 1651, that is, *Didone, Incoronazione,* and *Egisto,* and Balbi's Neapolitan activities began only with the production of *Giasone* on 6 September 1651.

Naples. Although the opera may well have enjoyed other revivals the Neapolitan performance of 1651 is at present the only one that is securely documented and that matches the approximate date of the copying of Vp.[42]

The Naples score (I-Nc Rari 6, 4, 1, hereafter Np), identified some years after Vp, "among the refuse in the library of the conservatory of San Pietro a Maiella," has been relatively ignored in the literature. Probably, as Curtis has suggested, this was because the Venice score had the unkempt look of (and was thought for many years to be) an autograph and was therefore regarded as more authentic.[43] Np, in contrast, was a fair copy, judged by some to date from well after the middle of the century.[44] The assumption of Vp as the autograph obscured the fact that the Naples score presents a fuller—and therefore presumably earlier—version of the music, one closer to Busenello's text, as represented by the libretto he published in 1656 (LV).[45] Unlike the Venice score, whose link to the Naples revival is largely chronological and circumstantial, with external features—copyists and watermark—supporting a date of around 1651, it is the textual content of the Naples score that affirms its association with the same revival, as documented by the libretto published in Naples in 1651 (LN). The libretto, however, designed to be used by the audience, is probably closer to the text actually performed in Naples. That the score survives in the Naples library is also suggestive, though of course this is not necessarily

---

42. The number of surviving manuscript librettos with significantly different readings suggests that there may have been performances that we do not know about between 1643 and 1651—and even after. Though acts 1 and 3 of the Venice score had to be finished by 1652, when Maria Cavalli died, they contain markings of a copyist whose activity may not have begun until 1657. This would suggest a later performance. Some scholars have speculated that it could even have been performed as late as the 1680s at the Contarini villa at Piazzola, which might explain the presence of the score in the Contarini Collection. But, according to Walker ("*Ubi Lucius*," cxlvi), the *Incoronazione* manuscript probably entered the collection along with the Cavalli manuscripts in the same hand (his Hand C), none of them associated with performance at Piazzola. Curtis, *Incoronazione*, n. 12a, mentions several "phantom," that is, poorly documented, revivals at Piazzola in the 1680s (citing Paolo Camerini, *Piazzola* [Milan: Alfieri & Lacroix, 1925]) and Genoa in 1681 and 1682 (citing Remo Giazzotto, *La musica a Genova* [Genoa: Società industrie grafiche e lavorazioni affini, 1951]). There is no credible evidence for either of these.

43. It was Malipiero who described it as having been "abbandonato fra i rifiuti della Biblioteca nel R. Conservatorio di San Pietro a Maiella" (*Claudio Monteverdi, L'incoronazione di Poppea*, in *Tutte le opere*, vol. 13, preface). See also Curtis, "La Poppea impasticciata," 27. The Naples codex was described for the first time in Gasperini and Gallo, *Catalogo delle opere musicali: Città di Napoli*, 259. See Chap. 2, n. 52.

44. Mauro Amato, "Le antologie di arie e di arie e cantate tardo-seicentesche alla Biblioteca del Conservatorio S. Pietro a Majella di Napoli," 2 vols. (Ph.D. diss., Scuola di Paleografia Musicale di Cremona, a.a. 1996–97), 1:76, dates it after 1665. Anna Mondolfi Bossarelli, "Ancora intorno al codice napolitano della Incoronazione di Poppea," *RIM* 2 (1967): 294–313, erroneously proposed a much earlier date. The most complete description of the situation is found in Domenico Antonio D'Alessandro, "L'opera in musica a Napoli dal 1650 al 1670," in *Seicento napolitano: Arte, costume e ambiente*, ed. Roberto Pane (Milan: Edizioni di Communità, 1984), 409–30, esp. 413 and n. 36, also n. 19.

45. This conclusion is based on the assumption, argued in Chap. 3, that Busenello's text represents the one originally set by the composer. See Osthoff, "Die venezianische und neapolitanische Fassung," 95, and Chiarelli, "*L'incoronazione di Poppea*," 141, on the editing down of a fuller text; also Chap. 3, p. 61, on the distinction between the longer and shorter librettos.

indicative of provenance.[46] It remains to be explained—or, rather, investigated—why, if both scores were intended for the Neapolitan revival, they differ so much from one another.

Given their late date and their connection to a posthumous revival, the relationship of both scores to Monteverdi's original opera is also questionable, certainly more so than in the case of the *Ritorno* manuscript. Indeed, as we have already seen, both scores have been shown to contain material added after the first production, some of it surely by other composers. This is especially true of Np, which sets several textual passages found only in the Naples libretto:

1. Act 2, scene 5 [=2.7]), Ottavia, following Nerone–Lucano scene, hatches murder plot

   Eccomi quasi priva

2. Act 2, scene 7 [=2.9], Ottavia (following line 1075), 2 stanzas (also in R, W, and V), but not set as strophic aria. LN omits two lines (italics), and casts text as recitative.

      Mora, mora la Rea
   Già, già la punta a un cotel la svena
   [*Scelerata Poppea,*
   Verrà teco in sepolcro ogni mia pena.]
   Risanarà il mio duolo
   Del tuo sangue odiato un sorso solo;
      Gioirò vendicata,
   Nascerà il mio seren da la tua morte.
   E uccisa te, o mal nata,
   Non sarà più tiranno il mio consorte?
   E tornerà giocondo
   Il popolo, il senato, e Roma, e 'l mondo.

3. Act 3, scene 8: Finale, following line 1592, leading to "Pur ti miro" (also in U2, R, V, but not LN)

   In Venere ed Amore
   Lodi l'alma, esalti il cor.
   Nessun fuga
   L'aurea face,
   Benché strugga

---

46. Lorenzo Bianconi warns against establishing a connection to Naples based only on this fact in "Funktionen des Operntheaters in Neapel bis 1700 und die Rolle Alessandro Scarlattis," in *Colloquium Alessandro Scarlatti. Würzburg 1975,* ed. Wolfgang Osthoff (Tutzing: Hans Schneider, 1979), 43.

Sempre pace.
In Venere ed Amor
Lodi l'alma, esalti il cor.

Much of this is extra material for Ottavia, including one whole scene (2.5) as well as a strophic aria text inserted at the end of her scene with Ottone (2.7). A brief recitative passage preceding this aria, however, though absent in both Vp and U2, is present in Busenello's libretto (lines 1071–75), which means that it was probably not introduced only for Naples. In fact, it could have existed in the autograph and then been cut out for the premiere.[47] Another strophic aria for Ottavia, inserted within her opening monologue in 1.5, is not set in Np. It appears only in LN (see item 3 in Table 9 below, p. 98). The Naples score also adds instrumental accompaniments that are far from the style of Monteverdi (or Cavalli) to several vocal passages, including one for Ottone at the end of 1.11 (lines 595, 597–99) and another for the final stanza of Amore's aria at the end of 2.13 (lines 1235–38).[48] The Ottone passage is especially curious. Omitted in Vp (though present in U2 as well as LN), it is an aria setting of what was originally a recitative text, slightly modified: the second of Busenello's original five lines is cut and the first transformed from an objective statement to a more passionate utterance: "Ahi, chi ripon sua fede in un bel volto," becomes "O dio, chi, chi si fida in un bel volto." This is one of several examples of an agreement between U2 and Np that excludes Vp.[49]

---

47. Osthoff and others have noted the expanded role for Ottavia, which was signaled in the preface to the Naples libretto (see Appendix 4, C). Other passages in Np, such as lines 768–75 for Liberto, are missing from Vp and U2 but present in both LN and LV, indicating that they too probably existed before the Naples revival and could have been cut for the Venetian premiere. (If they are present in LV but missing from U2, they presumably were not in the premiere, just in the autograph.) Table 10 below (p. 101) lists those agreements between Np and LV that exclude Vp. Line numbers, based on those in Busenello's print, are taken from Thomas Walker's unpublished edition of the *Incoronazione* librettos (on file in the Yale Music Library). An expanded version of Walker's edition, undertaken by students in my *Incoronazione* seminar of 2006, is also on file in the Yale Music Library. The line numbers differ considerably from those in the edition by Andrea della Corte (Gio. Francesco Busenello, *L'incoronazione di Poppea* in *Drammi per musica dal Rinuccini allo Zeno*, ed. Della Corte, 2nd ed. [1970], 1: 430–509), because Della Corte sometimes counts a line divided between two characters as two separate lines and fails to count some of Busenello's refrains. The Udine libretto has been edited by Paolo Fabbri in *Libretti d'opera italiani*, 1: 49–105. See also notes, pp. 1814–16.

48. Instrumental parts are also sketched as an accompaniment to a duet in 2.6 between Petronio and Tigellino (lines 931–34), which is omitted in Vp.

49. *Busenello's original text* — *Naples score and Udine libretto*

Busenello's original text	*Naples score and Udine libretto*
Ahi, chi ripon sua fede in un bel volto	O dio, chi chi si fida in un bel volto
Predestina se stesso a reo tormento,	
Fabrica in aria e sopra il vacuo fonda,	Fabrica in aria, e sopra il vacuo fonda
Tenta palpare il vento,	Tenta palpar il vento
Ed immobili afferma il fumo e l'onda.	E immobile afferma il fumo e l'onda.

LN has a less emphatic variant of Busenello's first line: "Ahi, chi si fida / In un bel volto." Curiously, however, Ottone's little speech occurs *twice* in LN, at the end of both 1.11 and 1.12. Np sets it only the first time. The duplication could have been intentional, representing a refrain, or else it was included the second time by mistake. These two scenes are slightly different in LN and Np from elsewhere. In LV, a speech for Arnalta following

One further non-Monteverdian, even non-Venetian, element in Np involves the instrumental ritornellos. Not only are there more of them than in the Venice manuscript, but they are invariably scored for four-part strings rather than the three or five parts characteristic of Venetian operas. Furthermore, almost all the parts are written out.[50] It is worth noting, in connection with the relationship between the scores, that even in those much rarer cases where string parts are written out in Vp, the top part hardly ever agrees with that of Np.[51] The four-part realizations—along with the music setting text that is unique to LN—were probably provided by a Neapolitan composer. As far as the additional ritornellos are concerned, these doubtless reflect staging decisions in Naples, though we should perhaps leave open the possibility that they could have stemmed from the first production and were cut out in Vp.[52]

To be sure, the Venice score has its doubtful passages as well, or at least passages that do not appear to have figured in the original production, as suggested by their absence from U2. These have been worried over by numerous critics concerned especially with their authenticity, during the past half-century or more. They revolve around just a few characters, Ottone, Valletto, and Damigella, and one particular scene, the final one. Conversely, a few passages omitted in Vp but included in Np were clearly also present in the original performance score.[53] (I will return to these issues later in connection with new evidence from the scores.) Chiarelli is surely right to conclude that, rather than deriving from one another in some way, the two scores share a common parent—or grandparent, perhaps. Curtis even argues that since Vp and Np have their own versions of some of the same mistakes, "we may posit the existence of *at least* one intervening copy between an autograph original and the two surviving scores."[54] He assumes that the autograph would not have contained mistakes, and thus the intervening copy would have been the direct

---

Ottone's outburst (600–607) closes the scene, whereas in LN and Np Arnalta's speech initiates the new scene. The absence of Arnalta's speech in both U2 and Vp is further evidence of the proximity of Np to the putative autograph, as opposed to the score for the first performance. But agreements with U2 that exclude Vp suggest that Np might not only be closer to Monteverdi's autograph, but that it might also reflect elements of the premiere that were subsequently cut in the exemplar for Vp. Another agreement between U2 and Np that excludes Vp—but also, in this case, LN—occurs in the Finale. See below, p. 95.

50. Exceptions include one instance of the rubric "rit ut supra" (on fol. 32), a couple of rubrics without music in the final scene, and two unrealized bass lines. For the first of these, "per me guerreggia," see below, n. 52. The second is the passacaglia in the final scene; see below, n. 87.

51. Again, there are a couple of exceptions. The sinfonia at the end of act 2 is *a 4* in both scores—the only four-part scoring in Vp—and the parts are the same. This could be evidence of a common source for the two scores; other evidence is provided by the correspondence of deletions and lacunae. See below.

52. Np inserts a ritornello following Nerone's "In un sospir," p. 27, that is absent from Vp. Another, bass only, follows Poppea's "Per me guerreggia." This same bass is crossed out in Vp, suggesting either that it was the source for the bass in Np or that both were copied from the same source. Significantly, perhaps, the music of this aria differs somewhat in the two scores.

53. For example, eight lines in the final scene, shared with U2 and R but not Vp (item 3 above, p. 91). See above, nn. 47 and 49.

54. Chiarelli, "*L'incoronazione di Poppea*," 139; Curtis, "*La Poppea impasticciata*," n. 23.

source of the two scores. But, as I hope to show, it is more likely that the two scores had two different—or even two different sets of—parents.

Despite the fact that some of the textual readings in Np are actually superior to those in Vp (as we shall see, some of the Venice text is corrupt, and some is missing), and that it represents a more complete—indeed, more than complete—version of the opera, scholars can be forgiven for focusing on the latter, for it is by far the more interesting score. Indeed, its method of assembly, layers, and multiple hands tell a much more involved and compelling story. It is this story that will occupy us for most of the remainder of the present chapter. But it is one that is clarified by insights provided by its "poor 'Neapolitan' cousin"[55] and it will be convenient to discuss this before returning to its more problematic and intriguing relative.

THE NAPLES SCORE

Compared with Vp, the Naples score is reticent. It promises to tell us little about how, for what purpose, and from what kinds of sources it was compiled. As a fair copy, with formal act and scene designations boasting elaborate capital letters, it presents a relatively unblemished appearance, an opaque public façade. The manuscript was produced by a single copyist, who appears to have worked straight through, laying out the pages carefully, yet economically, and leaving few details to be filled in later. Nearly all the ritornellos are realized in four parts. Indeed, there is some paper-wasting redundancy in the copying of these, since even those ritornellos that are repeated tend to be written out, sometimes three or four times, rather than indicated by shorthand rubrics. This score has the look of a presentation copy.[56] As we shall see, it tends to agree more than Vp with the Naples libretto, but not completely (cf. above, pp. 91–92, and Table 9 below).[57]

But the unblemished façade is something of an illusion. This well-planned and smoothly copied score contains several surprising blank spots. These lacunae—mostly consisting of staves left conspicuously empty—turn out to be quite revealing about the exemplar from which the score was presumably copied, among other things. And all of them coincide with ambiguous passages in the other sources, passages that are directly connected to questions

---

55. The expression is Curtis's ("*La Poppea impasticciata*," 27).

56. D'Alessandro, "L'opera in musica a Napoli," 413 and n. 36, observes that Np shares its copyist and a watermark with another manuscript in the Naples Conservatory Library, namely the oldest of the library's three copies of Cavalli's *Giasone* (MS 33.1.21bis), which can be dated around 1651, the year the opera was performed in Naples. Amato, "Le antologie," 76 confirms the identity of the watermark but not the copyist. According to him, the *Incoronazione* hand is not found in any contemporary manuscript. The manuscript appears to lack foliation, but page numbers were introduced at some point in the past.

57. The differences between Np and LN indicated to Chiarelli, "L'incoronazione di Poppea," 136–37 that Np did not see LN. Conversely, LN shows signs of having seen Np but only somehow in conjunction with Vp (that is, it saw a score that preceded both of ours, possibly *C* (for Copy) in the stemma, Figure 2 below).

of authenticity. They involve two characters who are known to have undergone changes, Ottavia and Ottone, and the one scene whose original form has continued to resist satisfactory reconstruction, the Finale.

Among the empty staves, several were obviously reserved for ritornellos, two in the added scene for Ottavia (pp. 137, 139—four staves, without clefs, but with a decorative R for ritornello) and three in the opera's final scene (pp. 216, 217), marked "ritornello si piace" and "ritornello":

Vp	U2	Np	
~~Ritornello a 3~~ (fol. 102r–v)		1	"Ritornello si piace" ("entrance")
1563–70 (Consoli) (fols. 103–4)	1563–70		1563–70 (Consoli) (pp. 214–16)
~~Ritornello a 3~~ (fol. 104r–v)		2	"Ritornello" ("exit") (p. 216)
			1571–74 (pp. 216–17)
		3	"Ritornello" (p. 217)
		4	1575–83 (pp. 218–20)
~~1584–92~~ (fol. 104v–105v)	1584–86		1584–88 (p. 220)
	1589–92		1589–92 (p. 221)
	1592a–h		1592a–h (also R, V) (pp. 222–23)
			Ritornello bass only (p. 223)
			1593–97 (pp. 224–27)
			Ritornello a 4 (p. 227)
1597a–i ("Pur ti miro")	1597a–i ("Pur ti miro")		1597a–i ("Pur ti miro")

One of these (3) follows a textual passage that is omitted in Vp (lines 1571–74), while the other two (1 and 2) correspond to material that is crossed out in Vp (the ritornellos introducing and following the Consoli chorus: we might term them entrance and exit ritornellos).

Following the exit ritornello (2), Np proceeds with the text as given in Busenello's libretto, but adds two passages not found there: the already-mentioned eight lines (1592a–h) that also occur in U2 (as well as two of the longer manuscript librettos, Rovigo [R] and Venice [V]; and the text of "Pur ti miro" (1597a–i). Following the crossed-out exit ritornello, in contrast, Vp omits lines 1571–83 and continues with 1584–92, but this passage is also crossed out.[58] It then proceeds directly to "Pur ti miro," omitting the intervening lines 1593–97. (Some of the crossing out can be seen in Facsimile 27.)

---

58. Unlikely as it may seem, given the chronological disparity between the sources, Venere's music (lines 1589–92), crossed out in Vp (fols. 104v–105r), looks as though it was copied exactly from Np, but without the scribe noticing that the bass line was written first in alto, then in tenor clef, which she then sloppily corrected (on fol. 105r: compare Facsimiles 27 and 28). Can this indicate, once again, that both of our scores descend from C [*1646*]? Cf. previous note.

The (unusual) substitution of rubrics for ritornellos in this scene of Np, a score characterized by its superabundance of fully realized ritornellos, and the (also unusual and therefore significant) crossing out in Vp are evidently connected in some way to the uncertainties surrounding the authenticity of the Finale, principally the instability of its text. It may be that these ritornellos were missing (or crossed out) in the exemplar from which Np was copied.[59] If they were missing, we might reasonably conclude, it is because their contexts (or function) had not yet been fully worked out. If crossed out, they were perhaps no longer needed.[60]

The most striking—and largest—empty space in Np, however, was not intended to accommodate a ritornello and is not in the Finale. It too raises a question about the exemplar from which the score was copied. It comprises eight empty staves within Ottone's speech in act 2, scene 13 (pp. 178–79) (see Facsimile 19), a space that would accommodate a ten-line passage of recitative (lines 1257–66) that is omitted in Vp and U2—because cut from the premiere?—but retained in LN (and R). The coincidence of lacuna and omission suggests several possibilities. The ten-line passage could originally have been set to music in the exemplar for Np (from the autograph?), but subsequently marked for deletion.[61] In laying out his pages, the copyist might originally have allowed space for it, but if it was then cut, he would have had to leave that space blank in order to finish the scene on the pages he had planned for it. Perhaps, on the other hand, the passage was missing from the exemplar, but the copyist, alerted to its presence in the Naples—or another—libretto (as noted, R also has it), reserved space for it.[62] (Recall that it is LN rather than Np that most likely represents the material actually performed in Naples; see below.) The Naples libretto must have been copied from a score that included this passage, a score closer to the autograph than Np (i.e., not the Naples score, but not the Venice score either). (The Naples libretto diverges in other important ways from the Naples score, as we will see in a moment. Indeed, though it is certainly closer to Np than to Vp, it is different enough to indicate that, as Chiarelli concluded, it was copied from another source [*1651*; see Figure 2 below], possibly even the same source or combination of sources that served for Np, but at a different time, namely, closer to the time of performance.)

The lacunae in Np, then, offer a clue to the nature of the exemplar from which it was copied, in a sense confirming what we already know, namely, that its source was not the condensed version of the opera represented (somewhat differently) by Vp and U2, but a longer version closer in content to Busenello's original as it appears in the 1656 print (i.e.,

---

59. The fact that the entrance and exit ritornellos are the ones found in "Sacrati's" *La finta pazza* can hardly be irrelevant to the situation. See Bianconi, "La finta pazza ritrovata," 972. The issue is explored below.

60. These examples (a cross-out in Vp accompanying a lacuna in Np) might reinforce the idea that Vp was designed for copying. But see below for another interpretation of the crossed-out passages.

61. The absence of this passage would confirm Curtis's idea that the role of Ottone underwent major changes from the original autograph/production.

62. On the subject of saving space to be filled in later in a manuscript, see Jeffery, "The Autograph Manuscripts," 133, re Cavalli's *Orimonte*, which leaves space for arias that were perhaps intended to be inserted later.

Monteverdi's autograph?) To this, however, special Neapolitan material must have been added, since it is not found in Busenello's original or in any known manuscript, but only (if at all) in the Naples libretto (see above, pp. 91–92).

We learn more about Np—about its relationship to the Naples production—from LN, in which material was both added and eliminated (Table 9). Some of the additions clearly responded to exigencies of casting or staging. Two lines for Arnalta toward the end of 1.4, within a new nineteen-line passage following line 239, tell us that Arnalta and Nutrice were played by the same singer: "ond'io che sono, D'Ottavia, e di Poppea cara Nutrice." ("Virgolette" at the beginning of this added passage suggest that not all of it was sung in the performance.) The doubling of these roles may be reflected in Cavalli's editing of Vp, when he introduces rubrics directing the music of both Arnalta and Nutrice to be transposed up a fourth (and this is possibly another indication that Vp as edited was intended to be used for Naples parts). Moreover, new text for one of the soldiers at the end of 1.2, following line 142—"Anzi mi parto a volo. / In riguardo del resto, ch'ei s'imposa. / Tu qui rimanti, intendi / E nuovi ordin suoi fors'hora attendi"—may have been introduced to cover his exit. Perhaps he had to change costume in order to perform another role.[63]

Similar considerations, namely, the unavailability of sufficient singers, could have caused the omission of an entire scene in the Naples libretto (but not in the Naples score, or in any other source): the scene of Seneca and his followers. But given the centrality of this scene for the drama, it could also be that its subject matter, the celebration of suicide, a direct affront to Catholic dogma, was deemed inappropriate for a Neapolitan audience. The potential sensitivity of the religious authorities to moral and ideological references is indicated by the replacement in the libretto of allusions to religion or kingship by ellipses.[64] These are covered by the disclaimer at the end of the libretto: "Words found in this work such as Deity, Fate, Fortune, Heaven, Soul, and Paradise were introduced by the author for reasons of poetic fancy rather than for any other purpose inasmuch as with true feeling he submits himself to the censorship and correction of the Holy Roman Church" (Italian text in Appendix 4, C). Analogous omissions, presumably ascribable to censorship,

---

63. Chiarelli mentions these spots ("L'incoronazione," 143). The soldier may have been called upon to double Mercurio, now a tenor, or even Lucano. Another explanation for the soldier's additional lines might be to justify the presence of at least one soldier in the following scene with Poppea and Nerone. On the possibilities of double casting, see Carter, Musical Theatre, 104–107, who, however, does not consider the implications of a tenor Mercurio.

64. Such as Arnalta, 1.4 : "la prattica coi [Regi] e pericolosa" and "Il [Grande] spira honor"; 1.12: "La calunnia da [grandi] favorita." Ottone, 2.6: "Saro dannato, sì, ma in [paradiso]"; 2.12: "la macchiata [coscienza]." Drusilla, 3.3: "Lo sa la mia [coscienza]," "A coprir co 'l mio sangue i tuoi [peccati.]". Nerone, 3.8: "Homai comincia a divenir [beato]"? One wonders, in this connection, about the omission in LN (as well as in both scores, but not the other librettos), of two of Nutrice's lines: "Ottavia, o tu dell'universe genti / Unica Imperatrice"—the reference to empress of all peoples. Osthoff ("Die venezianische und neapolitanische Fassung," 97) raises the question of censorship in connection with the Seneca death scene. See also Chiarelli, "L'incoronazione," 143–44.

1. 1.2 Soldato 1 (after line 142):

> Anzi mi parto a volo
> In riguardo del resto ch'ei m'imposa.
> Tu qui rimanti, intendi
> E nuovi ordini suoi fors'hora attendi.

2. 1.4 Arnalta (after line 239 "Ben sei pazza"):

> (**virgolette**) Ma che stolti consigli
> Rapporto a Donna risoluta, e bella
> E per bellezza amata
> Da lui chi so'l ne l'universo impera?
> Mente vana, e leggiera.
>   Ottavia, datti pace;
> Poppea, prevali a te;
> Nerone, troppo audace,
> Ad ella giura fe; ond'io che sono,
> D'Ottavia, e di Poppea cara Nutrice,
> Presupposta Poppea imperatrice,
> A lei salda m'appiglio, e non ricuso
> In un mar di tormenti
> Seguir Ottavia tra dubbioso eventi.
>   L'interesse vuol così: sì, sì, sì.
> Questo mi da ragione,
> L'utile io propone,
> Ond'io sagace e scaltra,
> Se piangi l'una, riderò con l'altra.

3. 1.5 Ottavia, aria after "Disprezzata Regina"
   (before Nutrice interruption, after line 279):

> Lingua mia, non tanto ardire,
> Cela, e taci il tuo dolore;
> Mal conviensi a regio core,
> Negli oltraggi inlanguidire:
> Ma geloso timor non so suffrire.
>   Dal mio cor non sa partire
> L'empio duol, che m'avvelena,
> Incomincia all'hor la pena,
> Che promette di finire,
> Gelosia tu, che puoi fammi morire.

TABLE 9 *(continued)*

4. Finale: final hymn (replaces item 3 on
   p. 91, following line 1592):

   Felicissimo dì,
   Hoggi stretto s'unì,
   Con laccio indisolubile, e soave
   Neron, Poppea, sol fortunate amanti,
   Onde ciascuno i lor trionfi hor canti.

are evident in the Naples librettos of Cavalli operas as well. Cuts in *Didone* involved supernatural scenes and dialogue that was too pagan or lascivious. In *Egisto* they involved a scene for Amore and several theological references.[65]

One further notable omission in the Naples libretto, of "Pur ti miro" (missing in LV as well, but present in both scores and all the manuscript librettos), indicates, somewhat ironically, that this famous duet, which we can now accept as having been performed at the Venetian premiere, may not have been performed in Naples. Indeed, the libretto ends instead with a unique and sanitizing hymn to the happy couple, "a quattro voci": "Felicissimo dì / Hoggi stretto s'unì / Con laccio indisolubile, e soave / Neron, Poppea sol fortunati amanti, / Onde ciascuno i lor trionfi hor canti" (Most happy day, today were tightly united with a sweet and indissoluble knot Nerone and Poppea, most happy lovers; let all now sing of their triumphs). This puts a distinctly positive spin on the otherwise ethically questionable outcome of the work, perhaps another bow to moral sensitivity.

⁂

Some tentative hypotheses may be in order at this point (see the preliminary stemma, Figure 2). The Naples score represents the Neapolitan production, but not its final stage, which was probably closer to LN. Given its clarity and the leisure with which it was copied, it most likely constitutes a kind of ideal "ricordo" of a production that was subsequently

---

65. In 1.8 and 2.1. These have been pointed out by Bianconi and Walker, "Dalla *Finta pazza*," 380–81, and nn. 7 and 8. Unfortunately, the only known copy of the *Egisto* libretto from Naples (London, British Library 905.a.3.1) has disappeared. The alterations in *Didone* are inconsistent. The word "paradiso," for example, although used twice, is replaced by ellipsis only once. Certain cuts or changes avoid erotic words; but other such changes are more ambiguous, suggesting that they may reflect slight differences in the exemplars for the sources. The most substantial cuts seem to have been made primarily to reduce an excessively lengthy text to more manageable dimensions. Interestingly, some of these agree with cuts in the only known score of *Didone* (I-Vnm It. IV, 355 [=9879]), suggesting that this score, like those of *Incoronazione*, may reflect the Neapolitan rather than Venetian production. This could explain differences from the scenario. See Rosand, "The Opera Scenario," 341–42.

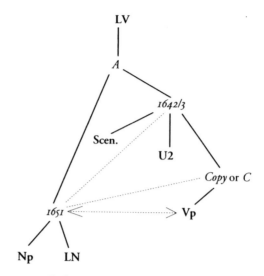

FIGURE 2. Preliminary stemma of *L'incoronazione di Poppea*

KEY:

bold = extant sources
italics = hypothetical sources
LV = Busenello's printed libretto (1656)
A = hypothetical autograph score
1642/3 = hypothetical first performance score
Scen = printed scenario (1642)

U2 = Udine libretto
C = hypothetical source of **Vp**
Vp = Venice score
1651 = conjectured Naples performance score
Np = Naples score
LN = Naples printed libretto (1651)

modified to suit last-minute performance exigencies. It was probably copied in Naples from a rougher performance score (one physically more like Vp) in which the ritornellos were realized and added text was set to music by a local composer. That rougher performance score (*1651* in the stemma) in turn could have been copied from (1) Monteverdi's autograph (*A* in the stemma: the conjunctive readings between Np and LN listed in Table 10 would reinforce this); (2) the shortened performance score of 1642/3 (the exclusive relationships between Np and U2 would reinforce this); or (3) both—or else, as we will see (4), the same source from which Vp seems to have been copied, marked *Copy* or *C* in the stemma. The Venice score was probably copied under Cavalli's auspices somewhat earlier than Np, as a performance score intended for Naples. Cavalli could have sent it to Naples, where it was edited further to suit the specific conditions of the performance (material added, subtracted). Neither of these hypotheses is completely satisfactory. Although the putative date and the presence of Cavalli's hand in Vp seem to point to the Neapolitan performance, or at least a performance at around the same time, only the Arnalta/Nutrice transposition suggests modification for that particular performance. We are still left with the problem that neither score entirely agrees with the Naples libretto, that is, what must have been the Naples performance.

TABLE 10

Conjunctive readings between Np and LV of *L'incoronazione di Poppea*
documenting derivation of Np from the autograph as opposed to the first performance

1. 1.5, Poppea, lines 202–207: "Se a tue promesse credo" (absent in Vp and U), not set as second strophe.
2. 1.11, Ottone, lines 595, 597–99: "Ahi, chi ripon"
3. 1.11, end, or beginning of 1.12, lines 600–607: "Infelice garzon"
4. 2.2, Liberto, lines 768–75 (not in Vp, U, F, T)
5. 3.3, Seneca, lines 801–10, "Supprimete i singulti" (not in F, T, or U)
6. 2.5, Valletto–Damigella, some text missing in Vp (lines 859–610, also in F, T, U, different music in Vp); lines 867–95 replaced in Vp by "O cara/caro." Complete music in Np, not Vp.
7. 2.6, Tigellino–Petronio, lines 927–34 (missing in F, T, U)
8. 2.6, Nerone, lines 941–46, second aria stanza (missing in F, T, U)
9. 2.9, Ottavia, lines 1071–75 plus new text (see p. 91, item 2)
10. 3.8, Finale: lines 1571–83

THE SCORES AND THE PREMIERE

The same situation, unfortunately, obtains with respect to the Venetian premiere: it is reflected in neither score. Although Vp certainly comes closer than Np, it fails to conform with the sources most closely associated with the premiere, namely U2 and the scenario. Several features—both omissions and additions—confirm the distinction. The omissions, listed below, include one full scene (item 5) and one aria (item 2) that are both found in U2:[66]

1. Poppea's aria in 1.4, second stanza (lines 202–207)
2. End of 1.10 (lines 468–81, 537–52), including Poppea's canzon "Se mi conduci Amor" (set in Np)
3. End of 1.11 (lines 595–99): Ottone's lines: "O Dio, che si fida in un bel volto" (set in Np)
4. Nerone's aria in 2.6, second stanza (lines 941–46)
5. 2.7: Poppea, Nerone
6. 3.8, Finale: Vp omits lines added in U2 (and elsewhere): "In Venere ed Amore" (set in Np, omitted in LN)

---

66. The scenario describes the missing scene, 2.7 (=2.6), as follows: "Nerone e Poppea esaltano i loro Amori dimostrandosi l'uno dell'altro ardentemente accesi." Np lacks this same material; it replaces the Nerone/Poppea scene with the new solo scene for Ottavia, as does LN. T and F replace it with a shorter dialogue. It has already been noted (Chap. 3, n. 46) that ink lines are drawn around this scene in both known copies of the scenario, suggesting that it was cut for the premiere (though it may have been present in the performance score, which would explain its presence in U2). Poppea's aria text is omitted in three librettos, R, W, and LN. The order of the penultimate two scenes in U2 and the scenario (as well as in other sources, including LV)—Ottavia/Arnalta—is reversed in both scores and LN, possibly for reasons of staging.

Vp also includes some material that is missing in U2, and thus was presumably added after the first production (though it could have been restored from the autograph), namely some of Valletto's role, including a new duet with Damigella.[67] Much of this material is found in the notoriously confusing final scene of the opera.

By and large, however, numerous exclusive agreements with U2 (and the scenario) make Vp the more reliable witness to the original production. In addition to many shared word variants or inversions in word order,[68] these include about a dozen cuts ranging from one or two lines to longer textual passages. Table 11 lists those textual passages from Busenello's libretto omitted in both U2 and Vp.[69]

Two areas of disagreement between U2 and Vp in fact reinforce their proximity. These are particularly significant, because they involve portions of the opera that have traditionally been considered of questionable authenticity: the role of Valletto and the final scene of the opera. Judging from U2, Valletto's role in act 1, scene 6 was much smaller in the original production than in the version represented by the Venice score (or any other source, for that matter):

	Busenello		Np, LN	U2	Vp
		OTTAVIA	*369–76*	*369–76*	*369–76*
VALLETTO	348–50 (recitative)	VALLETTO	*348–50*	—	*348–56*
	351–68 (aria)		*351–68*	*361–62*	~~357–68~~
OTTAVIA	369–82	OTTAVIA	*377–82*	*377–82*	*377–82*
VALLETTO	383–86	VALLETTO	*383–86*	*383–86*	*383–86*

U2 reduces Busenello's quite substantial text—consisting of a three-line recitative (lines 348–50), a three-strophe aria (lines 351–68), and, following fourteen lines for Ottavia, a scene-closing quatrain (lines 383–86)—to a mere six lines now intercalated within Ottavia's speech. Following her first eight lines (369–76), he sings a saucy couplet extracted from the second stanza of his aria text (lines 361–62), and then, after she finishes her speech (377–82), he closes the scene as in Busenello, with his quatrain. (The other short librettos, F and T, also omit most of the same material.) The interesting point here, and one that will shed light on the function of the Venice score, is that although Vp contains music for Valletto's full text, some of it is crossed out (namely, that for lines 357–68, two stanzas of the aria). The deletion brings Valletto's role in Vp more closely (though not exactly) in line with U2—though it is still larger. It also confirms that—as Osthoff, Chiarelli, and Fabbri have observed, or at least

---

67. Also included is the Valletto material in 1.6.

68. Such as 114: "giorno, hora" instead of "hora, giorno"; 236: "non temo" instead of "mi fido"; 447: "acquistarsi" instead of "guadagnare"; 466: "dolci" instead of "stretti"; 1267: "badi/tardo."

69. With one exception, F and T (but none of the other sources) share all of these cuts. (For item 10, F and T include Drusilla's four lines, but move them to later in the scene, following line 1380.)

TABLE II

Omissions shared by the Udine libretto and the Venice score of *L'incoronazione di Poppea*

1. Lines 121–22: 1.1, Soldier's text
2. Lines 202–206: 1.4, Poppea's second stanza
3. Lines 600–607: 1.11, Arnalta: "Infelice ragazzo"[a]
4. Lines 768–75: 2.2, Liberto
5. Lines 801–10: 2.3, Seneca
6. Lines 866–95: 2.5 Valletto/Damigella duet
7. Lines 927–34: 2.6, Tigellino, Petronio
8. Lines 941–46: 2.6, Nerone's 2nd stanza[b]
9. Lines 1071–75: 2.8, Ottavia, replaced by repeat of lines 1040–42 as refrain
10. Lines 1371–74: 3.3, Drusilla[c]

[a] Np and LN set this text at the beginning of the next scene, 2.12.
[b] While the text is found in Np, it is not treated as the second stanza of Nerone's aria. See below, n. 89.
[c] Lines found exclusively in U2 and Vp (but not Np) include Ottone's lines 992–94. Among other exclusive relationships, Vp and U2 are both correct in giving line 162, "vanne ben mio," to Poppea rather than Nerone (as in LV). Here the exemplar of U2 (the autograph or, more likely, first performance score) must have had the correct version.

implied—the source from which Vp was copied could have predated U2.[70] The crossing out of this material gains even greater significance when considered in connection with the other deleted passages in the Venice score, a topic that will be addressed shortly.

It is probably relevant in this connection that one of the most substantial omissions shared by U2 and Vp also involves Valletto: specifically, his lengthy dialogue and brief duet with Damigella in act 2, scene 5 (lines 866–95 in the remarkable "hor che Seneca è morto" scene) (item 6 in Table II above). This material is also absent in F and T, though present in LN as well as Np (which, we recall, probably descends more directly from the autograph). Though Vp omits most of the scene, it replaces the closing duet with another, longer one, on a different text ("O caro/cara"), which is found in no other source. (Indeed, the text is barely found in Vp either, as only the first and last words are provided.) It is difficult to guess where this duet might have come from and why it was substituted. (It is unlikely to have come from the autograph, since the text is not found in LV.) Being able to trace its source would undoubtedly reveal something very important about the derivation of Vp.

The famously problematic final scene of the opera presents an analogous (though reversed) situation (see above, p. 95).[71] Here the deletions in Vp upset an initial exclusive near

70. Osthoff ("Die venezianische und Neapolitanische Fassung") and Chiarelli ("*L'incoronazione*") had no knowledge of the U2 libretto, but they thought the exemplar for Vp could have preceded the first performance. Fabbri, "New Sources," 23, discusses revisions possibly having taken place in connection with the premiere. If the exemplar for Vp preceded U2, it could have been the autograph. In light of the putative *copy* (or *C*), from which Vp could have been copied, one could say that the source of *that* score was the autograph, that is, bypassing the shortening represented by the scenario and U2.

71. Also Curtis, "*La Poppea impasticciata*," facsimile 1, pp. 36–37.

congruence between it and U2 (except for lines 1592a–h; cf. p. 95). *Initially* both sources omitted lines 1571 to the end, except for 1584–92, but this segment was later cancelled in Vp. U2 replaces 1593–97 with 1592a–h (a new duet for Nerone and Poppea), which is not set in Vp but does occur in Np. (I shall return to this later.) As one of the few passages not included in Busenello's print, this text has the same status as "Pur ti miro." It was probably not in the autograph, but added for the first production. R and V, both long librettos, have this text too, which must have been taken from an earlier source, though not Busenello's print, but they also include Busenello's three final lines (1595–97) as a bridge to "Pur ti miro." (The fact that Np has finale material that is missing from Vp indicates, obviously, that it was copied from a score that had the music. Once again, it could have been the autograph.)[72]

As we have seen, consideration of the physical characteristics of the Naples score, unremarkable as they may seem, reinforced by comparison with some of the other sources, especially Vp, U2, and LN, affords some insight regarding the exemplar from which it was copied. It also helps to shed light on its function with respect to both the autograph and the original production as well as the Naples revival. A closer look at the Venice score proves equally revealing.

THE VENICE SCORE: STRUCTURE AND COPYISTS

Compared with the Naples score, as we have noted, the Venetian manuscript has a somewhat untidy appearance, owing to the presence of multiple scribes and copying procedures, a variety of notational shortcuts (such as "ritornello ut supra"), and numerous editorial markings, including indications for transpositions and cuts. All these features have implications for our understanding, not only of this manuscript, but of the evolution of the opera from premiere to revival(s). More like the *Ritorno* manuscript than Np, Vp is an active, fluid, and somewhat unstable text, embodying within itself the processes by which page moved to stage. It resembles a work in progress rather than a finished product, the impression left by the Naples score. (The question of which stage, of course, cannot be resolved definitively, but, as we have seen, Naples was one likely destination.)

---

72. Note that after describing Poppaea's crowning by the Consuls and Tribunes, the scenario says "Love likewise descends from Heaven with Venus, the Graces, and Cupids, and at the same time crowns Poppaea as goddess of beauty on earth, and the opera ends" (see Appendix 4, B). This indicates that the scene in U2 is incomplete, because it lacks the Graces and Cupids. The fact that no final love duet is mentioned in the scenario has been used to confirm the absence of "Pur ti miro" from the original production. But we now assume otherwise. Indeed, the presence of "Pur ti miro" in U2 suggests that the scenario may not actually represent the last word as far as the Venetian premiere is concerned. We should remember that U2 was copied *from a score*, presumably the score that was performed at the premiere. (And that it is probably later than the scenario, which was probably printed *before* the premiere.)

The manuscript comprises eight gatherings, four in act 1 and two each in acts 2 and 3.[73] The fact that each act is self-contained in this way would have permitted them to be copied separately, perhaps even in different locales, and then joined together. Gatherings 1–3 are *ottonari*, the first with an extra partial sheet tipped in at the beginning, and gathering 4 is a *quaternario*, with the second half of each sheet trimmed off at the spine (fols. 50–53).[74] Short stubs are visible deep in the gutter margin. The pages to which they were originally attached might have accommodated the beginning of act 2, but would have been rendered unnecessary (or redundant) when act 2, occupying its own pair of gatherings, was inserted. (Perhaps they were cut off at that time.)[75] The fifth and sixth gatherings (act 2) are also *ottonari*, but the latter (fols. 70–81) is truncated by having the second half of the outer two folios cut off. (Again, these extra folios could once have accommodated the beginning of act 3.) The seventh gathering is unusually long, a *duodecenario* (fols. 82–105), and the eighth unusually short, a pair of bifolios, with the second half of the outer folio cut off in the gutter margin (fols. 106–108). Once again, the final gathering could originally have been much longer, to accommodate the full final scene as given in Busenello's libretto.[76]

As we have already noted, the manuscript shows evidence of a number of different hands. The two principal copyists were Maria Cavalli, responsible for acts 1 and 3 (Benvenuti's no. 2, Jeffery's O1), and the unidentified scribe of act 2 (Benvenuti's no. 4, Jeffery's P2).[77] These two portions of the manuscript differ radically from one another. Maria Cavalli, clearly the more competent of the two scribes, copied her portion in a fairly straightforward manner, writing from top to bottom on each folio, cueing the beginnings of gatherings with guide words,[78] and indicating each new scene clearly by number. The less proficient copyist of act 2 adopted the more unusual procedure of writing across each

---

73. Benvenuti, *Incoronazione* facsimile, intro., p. 5: "se il primo e il terzo atto sono formati di fascicoli irregolari il secondo è addirittura composto con due grossi fascicoli, l'uno di sei e l'altro di sette fogli" (quoted in Osthoff, "Die venezianische und neapolitanische Fassung," 92).

74. According to Jeffery, "The Autograph Manuscripts," 123, both of these arrangements are irregular. For normal gathering structure, see his pp. 114–15—oblong quartos in gatherings of two conjugate pairs each = four leaves or eight pages. I am grateful to Jonathan Glixon for examining the gathering structure of this manuscript for me.

75. This could support the theory that act 2 was copied later than act 1, but it could just as well have been copied earlier, and the outer acts accommodated.

76. "Pur ti miro" begins at the bottom of the last verso of the seventh gathering and continues onto the first recto of the short eighth gathering. It could have replaced music on a normal *ottonario* gathering. Such shortening might explain the inclusion among the characters listed at the beginning of the scene of a "Choro d'Amori" and "Gratie," neither of which appears in the score as it stands (or in U2, as mentioned in n. 72). This would be analogous to what happened in the ninth gathering of *Ritorno*, when the Suitors' material was excised.

77. Regarding the instances of different copyists for different acts or gatherings of a single work, see Jeffery, "The Autograph Manuscripts," 263, who points out a similar mixture in several Cavalli scores, including *Xerse* and *Artemisia*.

78. On fols. 17v, 33v, and 49v in the first act and fol. 105v in the third.

opening rather than on one folio at a time.[79] Following scene 2 (fol. 55v), he failed to indicate new scenes until scene 7 (fol. 75v), at which point he resumed scene designations, but without their accompanying numbers.[80] And he failed to cue the end of his first gathering (there are only two) with a guide word. He also seems to have had occasional difficulty deciphering his exemplar, omitting words and even music in a number of places, as we shall see.

The other hands contributed additional layers to the score: one of them, Jeffery's P3 (thought by Benvenuti to be the same as Cavalli, i.e., his no. 1), wrote out the introductory three-part sinfonia on a loose sheet tipped into the score as fol. 1. (The bass of this sinfonia had already appeared at the top of what is now fol. 2, in Cavalli's hand, but was crossed out.)[81] The same copyist was also responsible for the upper parts of some of the ritornellos in the first two acts, which he designated with the abbreviation "Ritor" (When Maria wrote the abbreviation she seems to have doubled the t, as 'Rittor.') In addition, he wrote the name "Monteverde" on fol. 2 and the rubric "questa e l'istessa sinfo" (this is the same sinfonia) on fol. 44v.[82]

Still another copyist wrote out the prologue duet (Benvenuti's no. 3, Jeffery's P1), apparently inserted in a gap left for it by Maria Cavalli. It begins in the middle of a page already copied by Maria Cavalli (fol. 4v), and ends at the top of an otherwise blank page (fol. 5v). The size of the empty space suggests that a longer piece was anticipated. The prologue in the missing exemplar may indeed have been longer, to judge from U2, as well as T and F, which, in addition to containing three verses missing from both scores (lines 15–17), repeated the initial verses of Fortuna and Virtù as refrains, unlike either of our scores but characteristic of the prologues in other operas of this period. It is possible that the whole prologue (like many of Cavalli's) was a late addition. The final hand, Benvenuti's no. 1, belongs to Cavalli, who readied the score for performance. In addition to supplying directions for the copying of parts, including transpositions and cuts, he corrected some of the mistakes of the other scribes, and provided miscellaneous missing details. (As did P3 as well.)

A closer look at the copying of this score, particularly in conjunction with the other sources, can shed light on its relationship not only with the Naples score and performance,

---

79. The *Ritorno* score occasionally displays the same procedure, but only when there were simultaneous parts too numerous to fit comfortably on single folios.

80. Once again, this is reminiscent of the *Ritorno* score, where scene designations, like ritornello realizations, were left for a second pass through the manuscript.

81. Osthoff ("Neue Beobachtungen," 132–22) first pointed out the resemblance of this sinfonia to the opening sinfonia of Cavalli's *La Doriclea*. (This is the copyist Jeffery identifies as not having begun working until 1656.) See next note.

82. Jeffery, "The Autograph Manuscripts," 172; on p. 247 he implies that this copyist, whose hand is found in Contarini manuscripts dating from after 1656 [*Artemisia*], might have been Marco Contarini (see his p. 128 and also n. 709). But he also suggests that his notations might have been addressed to P3, the scribe who made fair copies of some of Cavalli's scores: Glover's Hand D. This copyist actually seems to have composed—and corrected—some of the realizations of the ritornellos. Could he have been one of Cavalli's students?

but with the original performance and perhaps others as well. In the end, it may also tell us something about Monteverdi's lost autograph. Maria's text is cleaner and more complete than that of the anonymous copyist of act 2, and her notational habits more organized. The contrast is evident from a comparison of their copying of the ritornellos. In act 1, Maria's usual procedure was to write out the bass, leaving one or two blank staves with treble clefs above it for the upper string parts. Ritornello repetitions, unless replaced by rubrics, such as "ritornello ut supra," were treated similarly. Then the parts of the initial ritornello, but not those of the repetitions, were filled in, either immediately by Maria herself or later, by P3 (the copyist of the introductory sinfonia).[83] Only occasionally did Maria slip; the two empty staves following Poppea's speech on fol. 15r ("Vanne ben mio"), for example, were sufficient for the bass only; likewise the single staff following Nerone's speech on fol. 15v ("Si rivedrem ben tosto"); and after reserving space for Arnalta's ritornello on fol. 22r, she neglected to supply it. (Np repeats Arnalta's previous ritornello at this spot.)

In contrast to Maria, the copyist of act 2 usually left a single empty staff above his ritornello basses, but the upper parts were rarely filled in. (In Seneca's death scene, he left three and two empty staves for the successive ritornellos.). He himself wrote out the parts in only three cases: once for Nerone ("Son rubini," *a 2*); and twice for Amore ("O sciocchi, o frali," *a 2* for both the ritornello and its repetition, and the final sinfonia of the act, in four parts, which is highly unusual for this score). It is worth remembering that this final sinfonia is the only one for which Vp and Np share the same realization, and both are in four parts. This must mean that the four-part ritornello was already written in the score(s) from which our scores were copied. The string parts for two further ritornello bass lines, Ottone's on fol. 67v and Nutrice's on fol. 72r, were filled in by P3, but others, such as the one in Seneca's death scene and one for Valletto, remained unrealized.

The situation regarding the ritornellos in the third act is even more curious. All told, there are only three of them, and they are all in the final scene. The first is a passacaglia bass, above which only a single empty staff is provided—for each of its three statements. The other two, for which Maria herself wrote out the two upper parts, were subsequently crossed out (see below). (As mentioned, these were replaced by rubrics in the Naples score. See above, p. 96)

The evident attention in Vp to saving paper and effort by not recopying ritornello repetitions is in stark contrast to Np. As we have seen, the Naples scribe was almost profligate in recopying fully realized ritornellos each time they occurred. This reinforces the idea, suggested earlier, that Np was a formal record of a performance that had already taken place rather than a source for parts, an incomplete score.

In addition to a number of unrealized or missing ritornellos, Vp contains some puzzling lacunae involving missing text, music, or both, many of them in act 2. Such omissions

---

83. Analogous to what happened in the *Ritorno* manuscript in Pass 2. But cf. the sloppy realization—by Cavalli?—of Arnalta's ritornellos on fols. 20v, 25v, and 72r, which look as if they could have been composed on the spot.

might be further evidence of that copyist's carelessness or the illegibility of his exemplar. But some of them seem rather to reflect another kind of problem with the sources. This is clearly the case with all of the omissions associated with Valletto, whose role shows many signs of instability. We have already noted (above, p. 102) the crossing out of music from his scene with Ottavia and Seneca in the first act (1.6: fols. 31r–32r), which brings the score into near conformity with U2. But other irregularities are associated with him as well. The final measure of the crossed-out passage lacks music in both sources (cf. Np, p. 59, Vp, fol. 32r). In addition, in Np, the first bar of that same passage lacks the proper text (p. 57). This might indicate a common (incomplete) source for both scores—or a common error in two different sources.[84]

The instability of Valletto's role encompasses his scene with Damigella, fols. 61v–62r ("Hor che"). Not only is one of Damigella's lines missing (856), but three of Valletto's lines (859–61) as well as nearly all the text of their duet are also missing. (I have already referred to this in the section above on Naples lacunae.) Most strikingly, also omitted are the vocal parts for the final six measures of the scene (fol. 63r). This irregularity is reinforced by the fact that the music of this scene is so different in Np. Indeed, it is specifically the music lacking text in Vp that coincides with different music in Np—the setting of lines 860–65: "Dunque amor . . . Dimelo, dì?" The inconsistencies undoubtedly reflect ambiguity in the exemplar(s) from which the scores were copied, as if the text and music were still in flux. (The exemplar seems not to have provided a legible version of this material; perhaps it lacked the music altogether. How else can we explain the wholesale and much abbreviated replacement of the text and music of the Valletto/Damigella duet [lines 867–95] in Vp?)[85]

Some of the other missing text in Vp might seem more accidental: In act 2, scene 1, for Seneca and Mercurio, several passages are without text, including four measures at the end of Seneca's first speech (fol. 54r) and the final line of Mercurio's long closing speech (seven bars of music, fols. 55v–56). But this scene, too, was apparently problematic. As we learn from a rubric in Cavalli's hand, the role of Mercurio was intended to be transposed up a fifth, that is, scored for tenor instead of the original bass. But instead of the regular "alla quinta" marking that he places before each of Mercurio's previous speeches—cancelled by "come sta" each time for Seneca—Cavalli indicated that the final speech would be found on a separate sheet of paper ("va scritto questo su la carta") (see Facsimile 22, bottom left corner of the folio). Evidently he did not trust the copyist to transpose such a lengthy, musically elaborate passage on his own, choosing instead to write it out himself, elsewhere. (Perhaps the copyist, knowing the passage was to be rewritten elsewhere, did not bother to underlay the text. Presumably the full text would have been copied on that extra sheet.) This is an important piece of evidence regarding the relationship of this score to the Naples performance, which is discussed below.

---

84. Like the one mentioned by Curtis ("*La Poppea impasticiata*," 23), as cited above, at n. 54.

85. Or else shortening was necessary and the simple, generic text was left to be rewritten later. The use of two-sharp keys in both versions suggests that this was later music. See Chafe, *Tonal Language*, 291.

Among other lacunae of this kind, a few occur in Ottone's music. Since his is one of the most problematic roles in the scores and it evidently underwent rather complicated transposition as well as perhaps some rewriting, it is possible that, though minor, the omissions in his text and music reflected difficulties in reading or translating the exemplar.[86] The difficulties with Ottone's role, however, are much more serious than this. Understanding them is critical to our understanding of the place of the Venetian manuscript in the evolution of the opera. In fact, certain idiosyncrasies of the Venetian manuscript may be responsible for creating the problem, but they can also help to resolve it.

CAVALLI'S INTERVENTIONS

We have already had occasion to consider several of Cavalli's interventions in the score: two excisions (in Valletto's scene and in the final scene of the opera) and a transposition (for Mercurio), cued by an explanatory rubric. These and other such interventions help to clarify our understanding of the function of this score. All of them appear to be directed toward the copyist(s) responsible for preparing materials for a performance.

Excisions

In all, including the Valletto and the final scene excerpts, six passages of varying lengths were excised from the score, that is, crossed out:

1. prologue sinfonia bass
2. 1.4, ritornello bass ("Per me guerreggia")
3. 1.6, Valletto passage ("Madama . . . ciò che si dica")
4. 2.6, Lucano–Nerone
5. 3.8, two ritornellos
6. 3.8, Amore: "Madre sia con tua pace" through Venere, "Io mi compiaccio . . . titolo di dea."

Some of these, as we shall see, also involved transposition. And some of them coincide with anomalies in the Naples score.

As we have noted, the deletion in Valletto's scene with Ottavia (item 3) and that of material for Venere and Amore in the final scene of the opera (item 6) appear to reflect modification of the music and text at some point after the initial production (cf. above, p. 102 and n. 72). Cavalli also crossed out two instrumental bass lines: the first (item 1),

---

86. These include missing text (on fol. 67v, one word—"isvieni," perhaps the copyist could not read it; fol. 73v, one bar: "Di Poppea"), and missing bass notes (on fol. 78v: three measures, in a very chromatic passage).

on fol. 2r, copied in his own hand, initially represented the opening sinfonia. It must have been crossed out when it was no longer needed, namely, at the time when the fully scored version of the sinfonia, on a separate sheet, now folio 1, was tipped into the manuscript. The second crossed-out bass line, in 1.4 (fol. 19r, item 2), was never replaced. It was intended to function as a ritornello following Poppea's refrain, "Per me guerreggia." Instead of filling in this ritornello, Cavalli directed the copyist (or performer) to repeat a ritornello from earlier in the scene ("ritornello da capo"), one associated with different text ("Speranza, tu mi vai"). Curiously, this same unrealized bass line also occurs in Np; though it is not crossed out there (nothing is), it is anomalous in remaining unrealized, one of only two such basses in the entire score.[87] (Once again, this parallelism between the scores confirms a kind of provisional status for the passage in question.) It suggests either that the Naples copyist was somehow influenced by Cavalli's deletion, or else that both copyists were responding to the same exigency (the ritornello wasn't needed; it was too difficult to realize; it gave undue emphasis to Poppea's refrain?). Most likely, though, the bass was included in the exemplar(s) for both Vp and Np, but never made it into the Naples performance.

Cavalli also crossed out two complete ritornellos, both of them in the final scene of the opera (item 5). As already mentioned, these ritornellos, preceding and following the chorus of Consoli e Tribuni, would originally have served as their entrance and exit music. Though the entrance music still seems necessary (Nerone notes the entrance of the group—"Ecco vengono i Consoli . . ."; Here come the Consuls), the exit music may not have been, once the dialogue between Venere and Amore leading to "Pur ti miro" had been eliminated (see above, p. 104). The final duet then would presumably have taken place in the presence of the Consoli and Tribuni. Again it is interesting that, though it includes music for the entire final scene, the Naples score has neither of these ritornellos: as I have already pointed out, it leaves (too little) space for the first, marked "ritornello," and for the second substitutes a highly unusual rubric, "ritornello si piace" (ritornello if wanted). Once again, an unstable area of the text (or the instability of a portion of the text) is confirmed by anomalies in both scores.[88]

Nerone and Lucano. By far the most curious of Cavalli's deletions involves an entire scene, and one of the most striking in the whole opera: the scene between Nerone and Lucano following Seneca's death (2.6). It may be that this excision was associated with the reworking of the previous scene for Valletto and Damigella (2.5). That reworking, as we noted, which involved the addition of new music and was incompletely copied in the score, shares an opening in the manuscript with the Lucano scene, fols. 64v–65r. It should also be noted that the Lucano scene, like that for Valletto/Damigella, was also unstable, having

---

87. The other is the already mentioned passacaglia bass in the final scene. See above, n. 52.

88. It is also interesting, as noted above (n. 59), that the music of these two ritornellos, but in the opposite order, is found in *La finta pazza.*

TABLE 12

L'incoronazione di Poppea, 2.6, Nerone–Lucano
(omitted text in italics; Cavalli's subsequent deletions struck through)

		"questo si lascia"	(fols. 62v–63r)
		[NERONE] a 2	
		Hor che Seneca e morto,	
		Cantiam, cantiam, Lucano,	
		Amorose canzoni	
		In lode d'un bel viso	
	900	*Che di sua mano// amor nel cor m'ha inciso*	(fols. 63v–64r)
		LUCANO (E NERONE)	
		Cantiam Signor, cantiamo,	
		Che spira glorie et influisce amori,	
		Di quell viso beato	
	905	In cui l'Idea miglior se stessa pose,	
		E seppe su le nevi,	
		Con nova mara/viglia,	(fols. 64v–65r)
		Animar, incarnar la granatiglia.	
STAGE I		[NERONE] TUTTI DOI	
		Cantiam di quella bocca	
	910	A cui l'India e l'Arabia	
		Le perle consacrò, donò gli odori:	
		Bocca, ahi destin, che, se ragiona o ride,	
		Con invisibil arme punge e all'alma	
		Dona felicità mentre l'uccide.	
	915	Bocca che, se mi /porge,	(fols. 65v–66r)
		Lascivando il tenero rubino,	
		M'inebria il cor di nettare Divino.	
		[PETRONIO] LUCANO	
		Tu vai, Signor, tu vai	
		Nell'estasi d'amor deliciando,	
	920	*E ti piovon dagl'occhi*	
		Stille di tenerezza,	
		Lagrime di dolcezza	
		NERONE *"alla 4ta alta"*	
		Idolo mio, Poppea,	
		Celebrarti io vorrei,	
	925	*Ma son minute fiacole e cadenti*	
		Dirimpetto al tuo Sole i detti miei.	

(continued)

TABLE 12 (*continued*)

"Ritornello alla 3a alta"

TIGELLINO

O Beata Poppea,
Signor, nelle tue lodi.

PETRONIO

O beato Nerone
930   In grembo di Poppea.

TIGELLINO

Di Neron,

PETRONIO

   Di Poppea cantiamo i vanti.

LUCANO

Apra le cattaratte il Ciel d'Amore,

PETRONIO, TIGELLINO

E diluvi et inondi a tutte l'hore

TUTTI

Felicità sovra gl'amati amanti.

NERONE *"alla 3a alta"*

935   ~~Son rubini amorosi~~
         ~~Tuoi labri pretiosi,~~
         ~~Il mio core costante~~
         ~~E di saldo dia//:~~

         ~~Son rubini amorosi,~~   (fols. 66v–67r)
STAGE 2   ~~Tuoi labri pretiosi,~~
         ~~Il mio core costante~~
         ~~E di saldo diamante~~
         ~~Così le tue bellezze et il mio core~~
940   ~~Di care gemme ha fabbricato amore.~~

Son rose senza spine
Le tue guancie divine;
Gigli e ligustri eccede
Il candor di mia fede:
945   Così tra il tuo bel viso et il mio core
La primavera sua divide Amore.

TABLE 12 *(continued)*

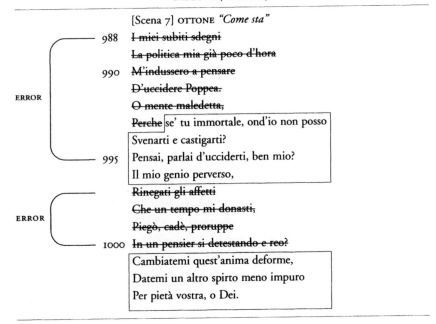

[Scena 7] OTTONE *"Come sta"*

988 ~~I miei subiti sdegni~~
~~La politica mia già poco d'hora~~
990 ~~M'indussero a pensare~~
~~D'uccidere Poppea.~~
~~O mente maledetta,~~
Perche se' tu immortale, ond'io non posso
Svenarti e castigarti?
995 Pensai, parlai d'ucciderti, ben mio?
Il mio genio perverso,
~~Rinegati gli affetti~~
~~Che un tempo mi donasti,~~
~~Piegò, cadè, proruppe~~
1000 ~~In un pensier sì detestando e reo?~~
Cambiatemi quest'anima deforme,
Datemi un altro spirto meno impuro
Per pietà vostra, o Dei.

ERROR (bracket for lines 988–995)
ERROR (bracket for lines following 996–1000)

already been edited to eliminate Petronio and Tigellino, as well as the second stanza of Nerone's aria "Son rubini preziosi." (See above, Table 11 [p. 103], items 7 and 8.)[89] The full text of the scene is given in Table 12.

The scene occupies five openings, beginning at the bottom of fols. 62–63 and ending in the middle of fols. 66–67. (Recall that the scribe of this act copied across each opening rather than down each page.) The excision is indicated in three different ways (see Facsimile 23): with the rubric "questo si lascia" ("this is to be omitted"; fol. 62v); with an asterisk (also on fol. 62v—somewhat problematic, as we will see in a moment), and by the crossing out of the entire first, fourth, and fifth openings. Then the six sheets were sewn together, totally burying their contents: tiny holes are visible in the margins of all of the folios, including those that were not crossed out, left by the pin or thread used to attach them together.[90]

89. In this score and in U2, but not in Np. Nerone's "Son rubini" is not set as a second stanza in Np, however, but as a different aria, perhaps by a Neapolitan composer. Monteverdi would have recognized the strophic structure and set it accordingly—like the first stanza. As noted above, this scene had already been shortened for the Venetian premiere, when Petronio and Tigellino were omitted. A comparison with Busenello's printed text of 1656, presumably close to the one Monteverdi received, and U2, presumably the text sung at the first performance, indicates that some of the lines originally given to Petronio (918–22) were transferred to Lucano, but that others, such as all of Tigellino's and Nerone's second strophe, were cut (lines 927–34). This material is absent in Vp, but it is present in Np and LN, though Petronio's and Tigellino's text is given to Nerone and Lucano. (Np presents "Nerone, Lucano, e Corte," which could have included Petronio and Tigellino.)

90. I observed these pin holes when examining the manuscript at the Biblioteca Marciana, Venice, with Alan Curtis in February 2003. Some Cavalli scores (notably *Xerse* and *Artemisia*) still had such thread in place when I examined them at the same time.

This action also buried a mistake that Cavalli, or whoever did the sewing, must have noticed: forgetting that the scribe had written across the openings, Cavalli had canceled that portion of the following scene for Ottone and Ottavia written at the bottom of the opening fols. 66v–67r. Evidently, when he saw Ottone's name on fol. 67r, which he marked with the rubric "come sta," he assumed that everything on fol. 66v belonged to the previous scene, which he was discarding, when in fact some of it was a continuation of Ottone's music in the new scene (see Facsimile 25). The mistake may have been encouraged by the scribe's failure, here and elsewhere, to indicate the beginning of the new scene.

Although the crossing out, the pin holes, and the rubric "questo si lascia" clearly indicate that the entire scene was to be deleted, the meaning of the asterisk is more ambiguous and quite interesting. A second asterisk, on fol. 65v, three folios after the first, just after the end of the duet for Lucano and Nerone, suggests that the cancellation occurred in two stages (see Facsimile 24). Like our modern vi=de, the pair of asterisks appear to indicate that at one point—in a first stage—only the duet was to be omitted, that is, approximately the first half of the scene (lines 896–922).[91] Perhaps this cut was made in order to eliminate Lucano's role—he appears nowhere else in the opera; perhaps no appropriate singer was available for the performance in Naples. At this stage, the rather stunted remainder of the scene, comprising only Nerone's four-line recitative "Idolo mio" and his single aria stanza "Son rubini," was surely still intended to be performed, since Cavalli introduced rubrics for transposition: "alla 4ta alta" for the recitative and "alla 3a alta" for the aria (see Facsimile 24), a transposition that he went on to cancel in his normal way at the beginning of the next scene, by marking Ottone's entrance "come sta."[92] See Facsimile 25, folio 67r.

If only the duet was cut in a first stage of editing, something must have happened to precipitate Cavalli's extension of the deletion to the entire scene, and this may well have been the necessity of transposing Nerone's part, as indicated by the rubrics in the scene's second half. This raised the prospect of actually having to rewrite the duet with Lucano, not merely transpose it, a complex project that would have required new, replacement sheets.[93] In any case, by this time, errors and transpositions had turned this part of the score into something of a mess. The scribe actually copied one section of the music twice in succession: first where it belonged, across the bottom of fols. 65v–66r (see Facsimile

---

91. In Cavalli's scores, asterisks often indicate the end of a cut (as in *Veremonda*, fol. 21v [Facsimile 29, three measures before the end]) or an addition (*Veremonda*, fol. 27v [Facsimile 30, just before Scena Settima, "Qui va il duetto su la carta"]). See also *Xerse*, fol. 57r and *Ercole amante*, fol. 131r (facsimiles in Hendrik Schulze, "Cavalli Manuscript Scores and Performance Practice," in *Francesco Cavalli: La circolazione dell'opera veneziana nel Seicento*, ed. Dinko Fabris (Naples: Turchini edizioni, 2005), 39–58, at 43 and 49. On the function of Cavalli's asterisks, see Jeffery, "The Autograph Manuscripts," 137 and esp. 179 on *Veremonda*.

92. The first transposition would have moved Nerone's music from D to G; the second from e—which did not agree with either version of the preceding recitative—to g, which goes well with the first transposition. In addition to raising the range of Nerone's part to encompass some high Gs, possibly to suit a new singer, transposition actually improved the tonal coherence of this scene. On the importance of such considerations for understanding transpositions or cuts, see below.

93. See above, p. 108, on Mercurio.

24), and a second time immediately afterward, across the next opening (top of fols. 66v–67r) (see Facsimile 25; compare bottom brace of Facsimile 24 with top brace of Facsimile 25).[94] This sort of recopying was customary when music intended to be performed had been unintentionally or unavoidably obscured by a cut or paste-over. The first version has all the transposition markings and the full text, while the second lacks transpositions and is missing some words; though it may originally have been intended as a replacement (as perhaps suggested by the asterisk placed precisely next to the first version—on fol. 65v, as we have noted), it was left unfinished and was crossed out *before* the remainder of the scene. The deletion strokes on the top staves of fols. 66v–67r are short, dark, and purposeful, covering only the staves in question—in contrast to the long, light, irregular strokes visible in the remainder of the scene. Whatever the explanation for the duplication, it added one more element of confusion for the potential copyist of the parts.

Whatever the explanation, there is no denying needle and thread: the end result was the excision of the whole scene, one of the most sensational in the score and certainly one loaded with dramatic meaning. While we have seen cuts and changes in various sources possibly made to satisfy the Neapolitan censor, this cannot have been one of them—the scene is present in the Neapolitan libretto.[95] But was it really excised? I feel sure that the Nerone/Lucano scene was never intended to be left out of any planned performance. It was crossed out in the score not because any particular portion was actually to be omitted, but because the various corrections, changes, scribal errors, and transpositions would have made it illegible; a fair copy, on separate sheets, had replaced it. The rubric "questa si lascia" (Facsimile 23) would then refer to the entire scene and would have been added last, at the same time that the whole scene was crossed out because it was to be found elsewhere. This is what happened, after all, with the opening sinfonia. The first version was crossed out when the second version was substituted for it on a separate sheet—and in this case we have that sheet, attached to the manuscript as fol. 1. We have noted (p. 108) an analogous situation in the Mercurio/Seneca scene where, although it was not crossed out, Mercurio's lengthy final speech was to be rewritten on a separate sheet instead of being transposed, like his shorter speeches in that scene. Here Cavalli was explicit: "va scritto questo su la carta."

This protocol would also explain the otherwise mysterious and barely legible rubric "su l'altra carta" ("on the other page") at the top margin of fol. 93v, though it is unclear what music is being referred to there (but see below) (see Facsimile 26). Finally, as I will soon show, the concept of "altre carte" will also help to resolve the problems raised by the final scene.

---

94. Actually the second version is slightly longer, as it includes the cadence to B minor, with which the continuation begins. I discuss this material somewhat differently in my article "L'incoronazione di Poppea di Francesco Cavalli," in *Francesco Cavalli: La circolazione dell'opera veneziana nel Seicento*, ed. Dinko Fabris (Naples: Turchini edizioni, 2005), 119–46.

95. For an exhaustive study of the political as well as the erotic implications of this scene, which could have provoked censorship, see Heller, "Tacitus Incognito."

Transpositions

The matter of transposition is crucial to an understanding of the function of this score, since it is one of the chief indications that it was revised for a new cast, and this has an impact on one of the most troubling aspects of the authenticity question: the role of Ottone. Transpositions affect nearly every character in the opera, some more than others; only Drusilla and Seneca are exempt. They fall into two groups: those, like Nerone's, which introduce small adjustments of range in portions of a role to suit a particular singer (even perhaps the original singer); and those more substantial transpositions that clearly reflect a cast change, like the one that turned Mercurio from bass to tenor. These changes were presumably made after the score was copied, in connection with preparing it for the Neapolitan performance, and were cued by Cavalli's rubrics. But the transpositions involving Ottone evidently occurred earlier; either before the score was copied or during the copying process itself—and also before Np was copied, since that score incorporates them as well. Either the copyist made the transpositions herself, or failed to do so consistently, thus necessitating Cavalli's corrections. In a small number of instances, a transposition seems unreasonable, either because it creates awkward tonal relationships between dialoguing characters or because it moves a voice into an unnaturally high register. Part of the problem lies in the inconsistency with which the indications are applied—the difficulty of knowing how long the transposition is intended to be in effect, caused by Cavalli's frequent failure to cancel it with "come sta."

We have already discussed the most straightforward kind of transposition, the one illustrated by the transformation of Mercurio from bass to tenor, possibly in response to a cast change.[96] For once, Cavalli's markings are consistent. In his dialogue with Seneca, all but one of Mercurio's entries are marked "alla quinta alta," and all of Seneca's are marked "come sta." The exception, as I have already suggested, Mercurio's final, most musically elaborate speech (fol. 55r), was to be written out on a separate sheet ("va scritto questo su la carta") because it was too complicated for the copyist to be expected to transpose at sight. This offers an example of a situation in which transposition was intended, but was not expected of the copyist.[97] Although the transposition of his role altered Mercurio's tonal relationship to Seneca in every one of their exchanges, the results were generally within conventional bounds.[98]

---

96. This role was undoubtedly doubled, possibly by one of the soldiers. One wonders which singer would have doubled the role in the earlier productions, since the only other bass role in the opera is Seneca's—and the two characters appear in the same scene.

97. It was presumably this kind of complicated transposition that led to the rewriting Curtis perceives in Ottone's music. But to pursue Curtis's argument further, would this necessarily mean that Mercurio's part would have to be rewritten by a younger composer, or could it simply have been worked out more carefully on a separate sheet? When this score was copied, of course, Monteverdi had been dead for some time, and so would not have been available (or needed?) to rewrite Mercurio's speech.

98. Seneca's first speech is in d, Mercurio's is transposed from g / B-flat to d / F. Seneca continues in d / g; Mercurio answers in C instead of F. Seneca then continues in d, and Mercurio's final speech is in G /D instead of C / G.

Not so with the transposition for Amore in the final scene of act 2. Following Ottone's cadence on V of d, Cavalli's rubric, "un tuono più alto," moves the opening of Amore's speech from F to G, replacing an effective deceptive cadence to III with an ineffective one to IV. On the one hand, the awkwardness suggests that tonal relationships may not have been as important as a comfortable range for a singer. But, on the other, the key of G fits better than F with Poppea's response to Amore's speech, which is also in G. (In any case, the difference in tessitura is too minimal to have made much of a difference to the singer, suggesting that perhaps Amore's role was transposed to accommodate one more transposition for Ottone that Cavalli had failed to indicate.)

A cast change for Naples evidently required the upward transposition of at least one other role, that of Nutrice, from alto to soprano. Cavalli's markings, "alla 4ta alta," are consistent in both of the scenes in which she appears, 1.5 with Ottavia and 2.10 with Drusilla and Valletto. As it happens, these transpositions do not introduce any awkward tonal juxtapositions with the other characters—in fact, some of the new relationships are even smoother: tonic to tonic rather than tonic to dominant. It is worth remembering that portions of the other alto nurse's role, Arnalta's, were also transposed up a fourth—though less consistently. The transposition begins with her five-strophe recitative in her first scene with Poppea (1.4) and includes the repeated ritornello. Though Cavalli does not mark every stanza, the entire piece should obviously be transposed. This is confirmed by the cancellation rubric, "come sta," for Arnalta's triple-meter aria "Mira, Poppea," which comes next, though upward transposition is once again indicated for her humorous conclusion to the scene, the aria-like "Ben sei pazza." It is difficult to fathom why the aria too was not transposed, since its tonal relationship to Poppea's ensuing speech would actually be smoother if it were a fourth higher. Perhaps the tessitura of the aria, generally higher than the rest of Arnalta's music here, would not have created difficulties for a soprano.

Arnalta's role was once again transposed in her scene with Poppea in act 2 (scene 8), but incompletely, and by a smaller interval. Cavalli indicates that the introduction to her lullaby, "Adagiati Poppea," should be transposed up a tone, from c to d, thus smoothing its relation to the lullaby itself, also in d, which is marked "come sta." Arnalta's brief appearances in scenes 2 and 3 of act 3 are not marked for transposition, but the beginning of her final solo scene, 3.6, is once again marked "alla 4ta alta," this single designation clearly intended to cover the entire scene. Though he applied his markings inconsistently, it seems evident that Cavalli's intention was to convert Arnalta's role from alto to soprano. As I have already suggested, the transposition of both nurses' roles may have been a response to the reduction in cast size for Naples, when they were both played by same singer—a soprano rather than an alto.

While these relatively consistent transpositions are probably motivated by cast changes, sporadic alterations within other roles, most notably those of Poppea and Nerone, are more difficult to understand. A question arises in connection with Poppea's very first appearance with Nerone in act 1, scene 3, which is marked "alla 4ta." Since this is the only transposition indicated in the scene, it could mean, like Arnalta's in 3.6, that the entire scene—including all of Nerone's music—was to be transposed up a fourth. But this would raise the tessitura of both roles to an uncomfortable level, requiring a number of high Cs for Nerone. Clearly it must mean something else. In this case, it would seem that the transposition applies only to Poppea's opening speech, lower than the rest of her music in this scene. Part of the bass line has already been transposed to accommodate the transposition of Poppea's music up by a fourth, but a hastily drawn tenor clef in bar 4 (fol. 13v) cancels that transposition, bringing the bass into proper relationship with Poppea's untransposed melody. The problem recurs in their next scene together, act 1, scene 10, again marked "alla 4ta" at the beginning. Presumably this transposition remains in force until it is cancelled (or partly cancelled) toward the end of the scene, when, inspired by Poppea, Nerone becomes agitated at the thought of Seneca's control over him. Three of Nerone's statements during his rapid-fire dialogue with Poppea are marked "come sta," implying that hers should still be transposed "alla 4ta." His fourth statement, however, communicating his decision to order Seneca's suicide, is again marked "alla 4ta." The effect of Poppea's manipulation is actually intensified by the contrast in range between the two characters here, a contrast that dissipates once she has achieved her goal—she remains on top until that point.

The remaining scenes between Nerone and Poppea have no transposition markings, implying either that they are missing or that the earlier markings were intended originally for purposes other than to suit new singers. Their absence, though, could explain the previously mentioned puzzling rubric "su l'altra carta" on the folio (fol. 93v) containing their duet in act 3, scene 5, "Non più" (see Facsimile 26). Perhaps, like Mercurio's speech, the duet—too complicated for mere mechanical transposition a fourth higher—would have been transposed (or rewritten?) on the "altra carta."[99]

Ottone. As with Mercurio and Nutrice, the role of Ottone was evidently transposed to suit a new singer—in this case, too, one with a higher voice, though only slightly higher. This is clear not from rubrics in the score, but from inconsistencies in the notation of the role. Indeed, those inconsistencies would have called for Cavalli's intervention—only some received it. Like the other transposed roles, this one required a new clef, in this case mezzo-soprano instead of alto. The fact that the new clef was not always the one written

---

99. It seems difficult to believe that Nerone's part could be transposed any higher than it is already. But there is some suspicion that Nerone may have been a tenor at some point. In that case, perhaps the transpositions were done by rote (purely by clef change) and then had to be modified. "Alla quarta alta" might have been intended to signify a clef change. Or perhaps the entire duet on fol. 93v was to be rewritten in a different key. Interestingly, in Np, Poppea's arioso "Idolo del cor mio" in this scene lacks the melismatic ornamentation of Vp. Perhaps the Vp passage was further modified on the "altra carta," and became more like Np. One further rubric for Nerone, "come sta," in a scene with Drusilla, Arnalta, and Littore (fol. 85v), is really impossible to explain, because there are no indications that anything in the scene was transposed and needed cancellation (unless it was assumed that all of Nerone's previous music was to be transposed).

down first, and that the copyist did not always remember to correct it when it was not, complicates the situation considerably. One can imagine that she wrote out the (original alto) clefs after scanning the exemplar, and then simply reproduced mechanically the pitches she saw, rather than remembering to change to mezzo-soprano clef every time Ottone sang.[100] She retained the alto clef—and presumably the original notes—for several of Ottone's exchanges with other characters (in 1.2 with the Soldati and 3.4 with Drusilla and Nerone), possibly because their brevity made transposition unnecessary. On a few other occasions (fols. 8v–10v) she mistakenly kept pre-written soprano clefs but notated the music in mezzo-soprano clef—she corrected the mistake by changing the clef on 8r, but not subsequently (compare Facsimiles 20 and 21), so that the music is actually wrong. (This same kind of mistake can be observed in Arnalta's aforementioned scene with Poppea, where Maria has obviously laid out the pages with soprano clefs for Poppea, forgetting to change them to alto for Arnalta's part [fol. 20r and especially fol. 20v]).[101]

The score reveals other instances of errors in the transposition of Ottone's role, which are notorious for having caused difficulties in editing the work.[102] The first of them occurs in his very first scene, where his opening arioso, "E pur io torno," is in D, but the following ritornello is in C, a tone lower.[103] This discrepancy is surely due to the fact that the arioso was directed to be transposed "un tuono più alto" in the exemplar for this manuscript, but the ritornello was left in its original key, to be altered mechanically in the parts (or by rubric). The use of D major here, with its two-sharp signature, is unusual for this period (and this score), so much so that the copyist failed to continue the signature after the second brace of Ottone's part, providing only one sharp in the third brace and none in the next two (on fol. 6v).

100. For an example of a scribe having copied mechanically from a manuscript written in a different clef and forgetting to make the appropriate transposition, see Jeffery, "The Autograph Manuscripts," 151. Also, cf. the Vp and Np final scene, where clefs were corrected only *after* the music had been copied exactly. For evidence that Cavalli's *Oristeo* was used as exemplar for making copies, see ibid., 151–52. Jeffery, p. 163, suggests that clef changes could have been intended for the ease of the continuo player rather than the copyist. On this point, see Schulze, "Cavalli Manuscript Scores."

101. On at least one occasion, Maria failed to indicate that she was notating a bass line in tenor clef (see n. 106 below).

102. Curtis, "*La Poppea impasticciata*," 29–31, discusses the problem of Ottone; see also id., *Incoronazione*, preface, pp. vi–vii.

103. Many scholars have noted this discrepancy but without coming to a definitive conclusion as to its meaning. Some have advanced what now seem fairly outrageous explanations, for instance Abert, *Claudio Monteverdi*, 70: "Möglicherweise wollte er mit dem fremden C-Dur und -moll das Fehlen jeglichen Widerhalls und das feindselige Schweigen des Hauses, in dem das Unheil auf Ottone lauert, symbolisieren" (Perhaps [Monteverdi] intended the strange C-major contrast to symbolize the absence of response and the hostile silence of the house in which calamity awaited Ottone). See also Wolfgang Osthoff, "Trombe sordine," *AMw* 13 (1956): 77–95, and Edward H. Tarr and Thomas Walker, "*Bellici carmi, festivo fragor*: Die Verwendung der Trompete in der italienischen Oper des 17. Jahrhunderts," *Hamburger Jahrbuch der Musikwissenschaft* 3 (1978): 154–56. Practical solutions to this problem have varied. While Malipiero maintains the discrepancy, Curtis retains the old key for stanzas and ritornello.

Curiously, the offending C-major ritornello first appeared at the end of the prologue, where a transposition "alla 4ta alta" was indicated, moving it to F. Though F was even less appropriate to the D-major arioso that followed—it worked better with C major, the original key of Ottone's music—it relates well to the end of the prologue, Amore's speech, which is in B-flat. It seems clear in any case, that the ritornello following Ottone's transposed arioso should also have been transposed "un tuono più alto."[104] The inconsistency continues into Ottone's strophic aria, which once again is in d (minor, this time) with the ritornellos still in c; they too need to be transposed "un tuono più alto."[105] (Considering that the score was presumably being prepared for the copyist of the parts, it was probably more important to have the vocal parts correct. The instrumental parts could wait until rehearsals.)

A similar problem arises in 1.11, the perplexing scene in which Ottone and Poppea sing the same strophic aria, but in different keys, Ottone in a, Poppea in c.[106] Here, however, Cavalli has compensated for Maria's failure to extend her transposition of Ottone's strophes to include his ritornellos (that is, those that introduce his strophes)—they are still in g, presumably the original key of the strophes—by marking each of them with the rubric "un tuono piu alto." And in order to clarify his intention, he marks each of Poppea's ritornellos "come sta."[107] But this was not enough. The tonal relationships in this scene are obscured by incomplete or inconsistent transpositions. The best hypothesis is that Ottone's and Poppea's strophes and ritornellos were intended to be a fifth apart—either in g and c or a and d, respectively—so that each of Ottone's final half-cadences would be resolved by the first upbeat chord of Poppea's ritornellos.[108]

---

104. Or else, both should be kept in C (Curtis's solution.) The use of the same ritornello in different keys is a distinctive feature of Ottone's scene with Poppea later in the act; see nn. 108, 109 below; also Chap. 7, n. 43.

105. I have already pointed out that Maria forgot to change to mezzo-soprano clef for the vocal part of Ottone's third stanza (compare Facsimiles 20 and 21), making it incompatible with the transposed bass.

106. Except for Poppea's third stanza, which, along with the preceding ritornello, is in d ("un tuono più alto"?)—the bass should be read in tenor rather than bass clef. In Np, though Poppea's third stanza is likewise in d, with the bass properly notated in the tenor clef, the preceding ritornello is in c like her others. Poppea's shift to d and the inconsistency between the two sources for her ritornello suggests that all three stanzas were originally in the same key and that the copyist simply forgot to transpose either the first two up to d or the third down to c. There are similar inconsistencies in Poppea's previous scene with Nerone, where transpositions appear to be almost randomly applied and cancelled. The discrepancy between Ottone and Poppea is compounded by the fact that in *both* scores their strophes are notated in different meters, Ottone in the more modern 3/2 (or minim triple) and Poppea in 3/1 (semibreve triple). See below, n. 109.

107. But this does not really make sense of the scene and the awkward juxtaposition of strophes of the same aria in two different keys. Jane Glover (*Claudio Monteverdi and Giovanni Francesco Busenello, L'incoronazione di Poppea*, performing edition [London: Cantata Editions, 2003]) has solved the problem by keeping all of the ritornellos in the same key, Ottone's a, and transposing Poppea's stanzas "un tuono più alto" (to d) until her final stanza, "Deh," sung at pitch. (She accepts the idea that Poppea's three stanzas were in the same key and opts for d rather than c.) As in his setting of the opening scene, Curtis transposes Ottone's stanzas down to g, the key of the ritornello. But he maintains the inconsistency in Poppea's, so that only her first two are in c, her third in d. Malipiero notes the discrepancy and reproduces it. I discuss this further in Chap. 7, n. 43.

108. This tonal relationship between his stanzas and her ritornellos underscores Ottone's psychological dependence on Poppea, discussed in Chap. 7. The relationship between her stanzas and his ritornellos is more

The inconsistencies in the copying and transposition of Ottone's role (not to mention the peculiarities in rhythmic notation, which Curtis has explored in great detail) are a function of the fact that, unlike the other transpositions, these were undertaken before or during the copying of this score: this copyist was required to implement them.[109] We can imagine similar difficulties occurring in the score or parts derived from Vp.[110] But perhaps we should not blame Maria entirely for these inconsistencies, since some of them— the untransposed ritornellos, though not the clef problems—also appear in Np.[111] Since we know that Np and Vp were not copied from one another, we must assume that Ottone's role was already edited to some degree in the exemplar(s) of both scores.

჻

The foregoing analysis of the irregularities in the *Incoronazione* scores tells us something about the evolution of the opera over the course of its active life—from Monteverdi's original version to the Naples revival (and even beyond). But are we any closer to answering the question posed at the beginning of this chapter: how could these scores, which differ so extensively from one another, both have served for the same Neapolitan revival? Indeed, to recapitulate, only a few pieces of evidence even suggest such a conclusion: The copying and watermarks of Vp point to the years 1650–52, and the transposition of the roles of both Arnalta and Nutrice from alto to soprano may reflect their having been performed by a single singer in Naples. There is no evidence that either score was copied from the other—in fact, as I have noted, there is evidence to the contrary. Certainly

<hr>

problematic; while two of his ritornellos in the Venice score begin with an upbeat d-minor chord, creating an awkward relationship to her final C, in the third the d is replaced by a c, which is smoother. In the Naples score the problem is avoided, since all three of Ottone's ritornellos open on G (the dominant of her C).

109. Curtis argues convincingly that, in addition to the transpositions, the use of more modern smaller note values in Ottone's music and at six other key points in the opera—minim triple rather than semibreve triple—indicates that these passages were written later than the rest of the score. The six other passages have already attracted our attention for other anomalous features, several of them linked to major differences—or unusual parallels—between the two scores: (1) the opening sinfonia (by Cavalli) was certainly added after the score was copied; (2) the Prologue contains a duet that was also added, in space left blank by the copyist (though minim triple appears elsewhere in the prologue); (3) the Mercurio / Seneca scene involves a transposition of Mercurio from bass to tenor and contains a number of untexted passages; (4) the ending of act 2, which differs radically in the two scores, lacks text and vocal parts for the closing duet; (5) the act 2 closing sinfonia is, atypically, *a 4* in both scores; (6) the content of the Finale differs markedly in the two scores. All of these passages indicate either that they were copied from a different, later (?) source than the rest of the score, or that, like Ottone's transpositions, they underwent transformation during the copying process. The fact that these metric distinctions are carried over into the Naples score, though, is another clue that they may have come from a shared distant ancestor, such as *C* in the stemma.

110. At the very outset of the opera, for instance, where the opening sinfonia and Fortuna's first speech are the only portions having a rubric for transposition "alla 4ta alta," but the rubric is never cancelled.

111. While the copyist of Np corrected the erroneous clefs in Ottone's role, he retained the inconsistencies between ritornellos and stanzas. This suggests that he was copying transpositions rather than implementing them.

Cavalli's transpositions were not carried over into the Naples score. Indeed, if we agree that the Naples libretto reflects that revival, then Np certainly comes closer to that revival than Vp. And yet, as we have seen, irregularities in the two scores coincide, indicating that they must have had at least something to do with one another. If we entertain the idea that, rather than indicating cuts, Cavalli's deletions refer to music on separate sheets, it may be possible to regard Vp as a kind of sketch for the revival, to which material corresponding to the Naples libretto was added—some of it newly composed by a Neapolitan (the added music for Ottavia, some instrumental accompaniments), but some of it possibly taken from an earlier, more complete score than Vp, a score possibly closer to Monteverdi's original autograph.

Such an interpretation would help to clarify one of the most mystifying portions of Vp, the final scene (fols. 104r–v, 105r–v) (cf. above, pp. 95–96). If we were to accept Cavalli's deletions at face value, that is, as cuts, this scene would go directly, and implausibly, from the Consuls and Tribunes chorus—in F and B-flat major—straight to "Pur ti miro," in G, without even an intervening ritornello. Not only would the ritornellos have been cut, but also a dialogue between Amore and Venere.[112] One might propose instead that, rather than being so radically shortened, the entire final scene, Cupids and all, was intended to be performed, as in LN and Np—which are in nearly complete agreement; and that the crossing out in Vp indicates that the fuller scene is to be found on separate sheets—except perhaps for "Pur ti miro." For, if we believe the Naples libretto, that duet was replaced by the already-mentioned hymn to the happy couple, "a quattro voci" (Table 13). This substitution, which effectively displaces the weight of meaning away from Poppea's triumph, may have had special significance in Naples. It reinforces what is perhaps the most distinctive alteration for that production: the new title. Indeed, that title, *Il Nerone,* which clearly deemphasizes Poppea's achievement, may be the ultimate bow to Neapolitan censorship. Or, to look at it another way, perhaps the emphasis on Poppea in the original title was uniquely suited to republican Venice, where courtesans and sexual license played an important social role, and where the corruption of Rome had political implications. In monarchical Naples, however, emphasis on the importance of the sovereign might have been deemed more appropriate.[113]

---

112. The harmonic conflict is not resolved even with the interpolation of the deleted passage, which also ends in F. Certainly this scene, even if it had included the deleted passages, would still have represented a much shortened version of Busenello's original scene. The clefs at the top of fol. 104v were written to accommodate the Consuls and Tribunes' chorus (TBB) rather than the ritornello that was copied there (two trebles and bass). In fact, there are several corrections of clef in the deleted passage, on fols. 104r and 105r. As we have seen in connection with Ottone, such corrections often signal transposition from an earlier or preceding version, or at any rate some difficulty with the exemplar.

113. I thank Lorenzo Bianconi for this observation. *Il Nerone* was also the title used for a possible production in Paris, another monarchy. See below.

TABLE 13
L'incoronazione di Poppea, Finale

Busenello libretto	Venice score	Naples score and libretto
AMORE Scendiam, scendiamo Compagni alati.		AMORE Scendiam, scendiamo Compagne alati.
CORO Voliam, voliamo A sposi amati.		CORO Voliam, voliamo A sposi amati

AMORE
Al nostro volo
Risplendano assistenti
  i sommi divi.
		AMORE
		A nostro volo
		Risplendano assistenti i
		  sommi divi.

CORO
Dall'alto polo
Si veggian fiammeggiar
  raggi più vivi.
		CORO
		Da l'alto polo
		Si veggian fiammeggiar
		  raggi più vivi.

AMORE
Se i consoli e tribuni,
Poppea, t'han coronato
Sovra provincie, e regni,
Hor ti corona Amor,
  donna felice,
Come sopra le belle,
  imperatrice.
O' madre, con tua pace
In ciel tu sei Poppea,
Questa è Venere in terra,
A cui per riverirla,
Ogni forma creata
  hoggi s'atterra.
	AMORE
	Madre, sia con tua pace,
	Tu in cielo sei Poppea,
	Questa è Venere in terra.
		AMORE
		Se i consoli e i tribuni
		Poppea, t'han coronato
		Sovra provincie e regni,
		Or ti corona Amor, donna
		  felice,
		Come sopra le belle
		  imperatrice.
		Madre sia con tua pace,
		Tu in cielo sei Poppea,
		Questa è Venere in terra,
		  e pur è Dea.

VENERE O figlio, io mi compiaccio Di quanto aggrada a te; Diasi pur a Poppea Il titolo di Dea.	AMORE Io mi compiaccio, o figlio, Di quanto aggrada a te, Diasi pur a Poppea Il titolo di Dea.	VENERE Io mi compiaccio, o figlio Di quanto aggrada a te, Diasi pur' a Poppea Il titolo di Dea.
		NERONE E POPPEA [Su, su], in Venere ed Amor Lodi l'alma esaldi 'l cor Nessun fugga l'aurea face

(continued)

TABLE 13 *(continued)*

AMORE		Ben che strugga, sempre piace,
Hor cantiamo giocondi,		Hor cantiamo giocondi
Festeggiamo ridenti		E in cielo il gioir sovrabondi
in terra, e in cielo		
Il gaudio sovrabbondi,		
E in ogni clima, in		In ogni clima, in ogni regione
ogni regione		
Si senta rimbombar		Rimbombar si senta
Poppea e Nerone		Poppea e Nerone
	NERONE E POPPEA	A QUATTRO VOCI [libretto only]
	Pur ti miro, pur ti godo,	Felicissimo dì
	Pur ti stringo, pur t'annodo.	Hoggi stretto s'unì,
	Più non peno, piu non moro,	Con laccio indisolubile, e soave
	La mia vita, o mio tesoro,	Neron, Poppea, sol fortunati amanti,
	Io son tua, tua son io,	Onde ciascuno i lor trionfi
	Etc.	hor canti

Since both scores, however related, were posthumous, our main aim has been to reconstruct their sources: to see what they can tell us about the original opera and its first performance. On the one hand, we have LN, copied from a score that was not Np, but possibly the same score from which Np itself was copied. That score had more music than Vp—including some written expressly for Naples. The differences between Np and LN can be explained by last-minute performance alterations in their source—carried over into LN, but not necessarily in the fair copy of the music. This common source for LN and Np might have looked something like Vp, but fuller, with material deriving from the autograph. Np may be a presentation score compiled (if not actually copied) before the Naples performance (or copied from a score that was compiled before the performance); but LN is closer to that performance, and was copied from a score (analogous to U2 and the scenario for the Venetian premiere). In fact, Np probably relates to the Naples performance (LN) in the same way as Monteverdi's (lost) autograph relates to the premiere (U2).

What then of Vp and its exemplar? As Paolo Fabbri and others have noted, the sources that correspond to the first production of Monteverdi's opera in 1643 are the scenario printed in that year and U2 (dated 1642), of which the Venetian score represents an abbreviated version.[114] But the score was also lengthened to include material not found in either the scenario or U2 though present in LV, Busenello's printed text of

---

114. See above, p. 101 and n. 66. It is worth emphasizing that most of the passages in U2 that are omitted in Vp appear in one or both of the Neapolitan sources.

1656.[115] The exemplar for Vp could thus have been the original performance score that was modified for a subsequent revival—the modifications including cutting some material from U2 and the scenario, restoring material from the autograph (Valletto), and transposing Ottone's role from alto to mezzo-soprano.

At this point it is worth considering the possibility of a performance of *Incoronazione* between the premiere and the Naples revival, namely the one in 1646 to which Ivanovich first referred and which figured in the subsequent chronologies. Though this possibility was rejected by Bianconi and Walker, information from the chronologies can now be reinforced by new evidence offered by John Whenham. He cites diplomatic dispatches that mention "the usual" operatic performances in two theaters in 1646 and suggests that the supposed prohibition against theatrical entertainments in that year was probably restricted to commedia dell'arte, and did not include opera.[116] This distinction would also help to explain the otherwise mysterious reference of the English traveler John Evelyn to having attended "three [*sic*] noble operas" in Venice in 1646.[117] Indeed, the chronologies list two operas for 1646, *L'incoronazione di Poppea* and *La prosperità infelice di Giulio Cesare dittatore*, at SS. Giovanni e Paolo and the Novissimo respectively. Since the Novissimo had closed by that time, the chronologies were probably confusing it with the Teatro Nuovo, another name for SS. Giovanni e Paolo, though this would make it difficult to identify the second theater referred to in the diplomatic correspondence.[118]

A performance of *Incoronazione* in 1646, which would have taken place at the Teatro SS. Giovanni e Paolo, might explain how Cavalli came to have Vp in his possession and how it came to include his sinfonia from *Doriclea*, an opera performed the previous year (at S. Cassiano). If SS. Giovanni e Paolo was indeed open in 1646, *Giulio Cesare* could also have been performed there in that year. Assuming that Cavalli was the author of *Giulio Cesare*, as Ivanovich claimed, we can surmise that he might have been playing an impresarial role at SS. Giovanni e Paolo (as he had previously done at two other theaters, S. Cassiano and S. Moisè), producing one original opera and filling out the remainder of the season with a revival. If Cavalli had the *Incoronazione* score in his possession from the revival of 1646, it would have been easy for him to have it recopied in 1650–52 by his wife. I would thus replace the hypothetical *C* (*Copy*) on Figure 2 with the hypothetical date 1646.

Finally, given that the Neapolitan sources make no mention of Monteverdi and that so

---

115. Especially passages for Valletto and Damigella.

116. For the claim that the theaters were closed for the 1646–47 season because of the war of Candia, see Bianconi and Walker, "Dalla *Finta pazza*," 416; also Chiarelli, "*L'incoronazione di Poppea*," 124–25. But according to Whenham, "Perspectives," 279–80, diplomatic dispatches of a certain Count Ferdinando Scotti dated 10 and 17 February 1646 (new style) refer to the "usual" operas being performed in two theaters, though he fails to name either the operas or the theaters. For another possible revival, in Paris in 1647, see below.

117. See John Evelyn, *Diaries*, ed. E. S. de Beer (Oxford: Clarendon Press, 1955), 2:473–75. Evelyn was more specific with respect to the previous year, when he reported seeing *Ercole in Lidia* during Ascension week. See ibid., 2:449–52; Glixon and Glixon, *Business*, 84–85; and Whenham, "Perspectives," 277.

118. The Novissimo and SS. Giovanni e Paolo were in any case linked during this period. See Glixon and Glixon, *Business*, 86–87.

many of Cavalli's operas were being performed in Naples during this period, it is surely worth wondering whether *Incoronazione* was not in fact presented as Cavalli's in Naples.[119]

EXCURSUS: PERFORMANCE IN PARIS

Recently, another possible performance of *Incoronazione* has come to light, between the Venetian premiere and the Naples revival, in Paris in 1647. This complicates but perhaps also helps to clarify the situation I have outlined. Such a performance is mentioned in a letter dated 3 January 1647 from the castrato Stefano Costa in Paris to his patron Cornelio Bentivoglio in Ferrara. Costa, who had arrived in Paris a week earlier ("il 26 del passato") to begin rehearsals for a production of *Orfeo* by Luigi Rossi and Francesco Buti, informs Bentivoglio that, since preparations for *Orfeo* were seriously behind schedule—the text and music of only the first act had been written—the company was thinking of performing *Nerone* instead, but in the small theater and without machines.[120] Costa would very likely have taken the role of Nerone in Paris, the role he probably sang at the Venetian premiere four years before. This can be inferred from two related facts: that he had performed a leading role in *La finta savia,* the opera that shared the stage of SS. Giovanni e Paolo with *Incoronazione* in 1642–43; and that theaters normally hired a company of singers for the entire season. Costa could also have sung the same role in the Venetian revival of 1646, though we have no information about this. We do know, from another letter in the Bentivoglio archive, dated September 1646, that attempts were being made to lure Stefano as well as two other Costas, the sisters Anna Francesca and Margherita (who was in Venice at the time) to Paris to perform in *Orfeo,* which they eventually did. Chances are they—and the rest of the *Orfeo* cast—would also have performed in *Nerone*.[121] Whether or not he had sung in Venice in 1646, Costa could have brought the 1643 score of *L'incoronazione di Poppea* (or *Nerone*) with him to Paris. There, it could somehow have gotten into the hands of Manara, whose connections with Paris dated from 1645, when he produced *La finta pazza* there.

---

119. This was certainly the case for Boretti's *Eliogabalo,* which is ascribed to Cavalli in the libretto published in Naples in conjunction with a performance in 1669. See Mauro Calcagno, "Fonti, ricezione e ruolo della committenza nell'*Eliogabalo* musicato da F. Cavalli, G. A. Boretti e T. Orgiani (1667–1687)," in *Francesco Cavalli: La circolazione dell'opera veneziana nel Seicento,* ed. Dinko Fabris (Naples: Turchini edizioni, 2005), 77–99.

120. Sergio Monaldini, *L'orto dell'Esperidi: Musici, attori e artisti nel patrocinio della famiglia Bentivoglio (1646–1685)* (Lucca: LIM, 2000), 13: letter of 3 January 1647 from Stefano Costa in Paris to Cornelio Bentivoglio in Ferrara: "In torno alla recita siamo addietro assai et non è con posto altro che il primo atto delle parole et anco della musica, et si crede che faremo il Nerone sicuro in anzi pero nel piciolo teatro senza machine, solo con le abiti belli, et doppo poi faremo l'opera grossa quale le parole sono del sig.r Buti." The "opera grossa" was finally performed on 2 March 1647.

121. There is no evidence that the Costa sisters were related to Stefano. Margherita Costa's presence in Venice in 1646 suggests that she could have performed in one or another of the operas of that season, possibly *Incoronazione.* The cast of *Orfeo* is listed in the manuscript scenario in I-Rvat, Barb. Lat. 4059, fol. 131. At least one of the Costa sisters, Anna Francesca (or "Ceccha") had performed in Paris in 1646, in Cavalli's *Egisto,* which, like *La finta pazza* the previous year, was produced by a traveling company led by Curtio Manara—the same Manara who produced *Incoronazione* in Naples four years later. See Michelassi, "Musici di fortuna."

All of this would be pointless speculation were it not that such a sequence of events offers another possible explanation for the fullness of Np with respect to Vp. Np could have been copied from the score used for the Paris 1647 production, which Costa had brought from Venice. Costa's score could have been either the one he had performed from at the premiere (i.e., *not* the autograph), close to the Udine libretto and scenario—that is, shorter than the autograph but longer than Vp—or the one he had sung in the revival of 1646, if he was in such a production. This score could then have been edited for Paris (shortened) and subsequently carried to Naples (by Manara), where it served as the exemplar for Np, to which material required by the conditions in Naples was added (material not in Busenello's libretto).

A Paris 1647 score, performed in the small theater without machines, might also help to explain some of the cuts in Vp, notably the omission of Venus, and the Graces and Cupids in the final scene. Without machines, these characters could not have descended from the heavens, as described in the Venetian scenario ("Amor . . . cala dal Cielo con Venere, Grazie ed Amori"). This omission, in turn, could also explain why the music of the final scene in Np seems stylistically so uncharacteristic of Monteverdi. If the scene was to be performed in Naples, and Monteverdi's music had been cut for Paris, another (Neapolitan) composer would have had to replace it. Finally, if a Paris 1647 score was in some sense an exemplar for both Np and Vp, this could also account for the mysterious parallels between them (lacunae, crossed-out passages, etc.).

It still remains to be explained why two different scores were prepared for Naples. Indeed, it could also be that Cavalli was preparing Vp for a performance somewhere else—in Florence, for instance, where several of his own operas were being performed during this very period, under the auspices of the same Curtio Manara.[122] Without further information, however, there is no way of confirming any of these hypotheses. I would only suggest here that a putative Paris 1647 score might be incorporated in the stemma.

❧

With the sources currently at our disposal, it is difficult to imagine getting any closer than this to Monteverdi's original. But our understanding of the material we have makes it possible to reconstruct a plausible version for performance and analysis. In doing so, we should distinguish among various possible alternatives: autograph, Venetian premiere, Neapolitan revival. We would come closest to the autograph by using the Venice score as a basis, restoring all the crossed-out passages, and adding everything from the Naples score that sets text found in Busenello's libretto (but also eliminating settings of any text that does not appear there, for example "Pur ti miro"). A score recreating the first performance, on the other hand, though also based on the Venice manuscript, would add material from Naples only if it was present in U2 or implied by the scenario. And it should subtract material not present in those sources. A reconstruction of the Naples production should obviously be based on the Naples score, but modified where possible

---

122. Bianconi and Walker, "Dalla *Finta pazza*," and Michelassi, "Musici di fortuna."

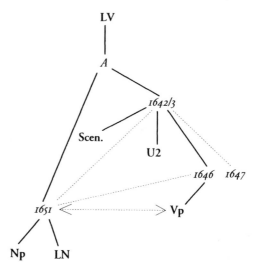

FIGURE 3. Stemma of *L'incoronazione di Poppea*

KEY:

bold = extant sources
italic = hypothetical sources
1642/3: same as U2? Adds *Finta pazza* ritornelli
Scenario (1642): from *1642/3*. Includes long finale (from autograph?), cuts 2.7
U2: from *1642/3*? Adds "Pur ti miro," reduces Ottone, cuts material from Table 11, reduces Valletto, cuts Tigellino and Petronio, cuts Amore at the end of act 2
1646: Cavalli edition of *1642/3*. Cuts 2.7, cuts Poppea's canzon, transposes Ottone incompletely, adds *Doriclea* sinfonia
1647: same as? *1646*, adds *Finta pazza* ritornelli?, shortens finale
Vp: from *1646/1647* (also *A*), restores some of Valletto, adds new duet with Damigella, shortends finale even further
1651: like LN. Material added specifically for Naples

(bold), other material (if not in U2 but in LV) from *A* or *1646/47*
LN: from *1651*. **Adds Ottavia material, combines Arnalta and Nutrice, cuts Seneca's death,** restores finale minus "Pur ti miro," **adds quartet,** restores Poppea's second stanza (1.4), restores Nerone's stanza (2.6), moves Arnalta from 1.11 to 1.12, restores Liberto (768–75), restores Ottone (1257–66), restores Ottavia (1071–75), restores Amore at end of act 2, replaces 2.7 with Ottavia
Np: from *1651*. **Replaces 2.7 with Ottavia, adds ritornelli.** Restores all of Valletto from *1642* (and Vp), restores full finale plus "Pur ti miro," but without ritornelli (rubrics only), restores Poppea's second stanza (1.4), restores Nerone's stanza (2.6), moves Arnalta from 1.11 to 1.12, restores Liberto (768–75), leaves lacuna for Ottone, restores Ottavia (1071–75), cuts Poppea's canzon

to agree with the Naples libretto (that is, by cutting Seneca and his followers.) The Venice 1646 production, if there was one, could perhaps be represented by the Venice score without Cavalli's editorial interventions.

☙

The stemma shown in Figure 3 has been revised to include putative *1646* and *1647* performances and summarizes the relationships among the sources that have been established during the course of this chapter. In contrast to those constructed by Chiarelli on the basis of a philological comparison of all of the sources (scores as well as librettos), this one incorporates only the scores and the librettos most closely associated with them.

5

Ancients and Moderns

Would that a third section of the previous chapter could have been devoted to the score of *Le nozze d'Enea*. Instead, in this one, I will attempt to say something about what such a score might have looked like, extrapolating from other information—librettos, scenario, and also, in the spirit of my trilogical approach, from the sources of the other two operas.

The implications of viewing Monteverdi's three Venetian operas together, as a trilogy, whose connections colored their original audience's experience of the works, are many and promising. We have already tested some of these implications in connection with the sources.[1] The *Nozze* sources help to clarify the chronology of *Ritorno*, and the parallels between the *Nozze* and *Ritorno* sources set in relief the distinctive profile of those of *Incoronazione*. Comparison of the sources, moreover, some of them closer to the composer than others, suggests that they may represent different stages in the evolution of the respective operas. And this in turn can even help to explain the stylistic disparities between the scores. But the real benefits of measuring the individual operas against one another extend to our understanding of the structure and meaning of the librettos and, more importantly, of their musical settings. The mere idea of considering the three as a group is critically liberating. It enhances our own more distant perception of common themes played off against one another, and it gives greater resonance to obvious parallels as well as differences. Sometimes similarities between two of the texts heighten a contrast with

---

1. For instance, the scores illuminate one another: copying procedures in *Ritorno* help to explain the different layers and omissions in the Venice score of *Incoronazione;* the distinctions between the literary and operatic versions of the *Ritorno* and *Incoronazione* librettos shed light on the librettos of *Enea,* discussed below.

the third. In other instances a difference may be mediated and thus diminished by the third. In still other cases, the three works may form a progression that highlights a particular issue or theme common to all of them.

A Question of Genre

The first two constituents of Monteverdi's Venetian trilogy, *Il ritorno d'Ulisse in patria* and *Le nozze d'Enea e Lavinia,* have many points in common, as might be expected of a work and its acknowledged imitation. Their similarities render *Incoronazione*'s differences all the more salient. To start at the very beginning, with the title pages: *Ritorno* and *Nozze* both bear the subtitle "tragedia," whereas *Incoronazione* is called, variously, "opera regia," "opera musicale," or "dramma musicale."[2] The difference is telling. "Tragedia" represents a conscious effort to invoke the venerable but exhausted tradition of Italian tragedy; "opera regia" or "dramma musicale" fully embraces the mixing of genres that had precipitated tragedy's demise, placing opera on a par with the other mixed genres of the period, such as tragicomedy and pastoral. "Tragedia," moreover, asserts a connection to serious, rule-bound literary drama, whereas the other terms imply the opposite: the accommodation of rules to the exigencies of performance by dilettantes and professionals. The term "opera regia" (royal or regal work, that is, one involving characters of royal or princely rank that was neither comic nor tragic), in fact, specifically evokes the scenarios of commedia dell'arte that were flooding Italy during this period, many of which bore that designation.[3]

The difference in subtitles had wide-reaching implications. It placed the authors on opposite sides of an undeclared but long-standing and active quarrel between the ancients

---

2. Cf. Tables 4, 5, and 6 above, Chap. 3. The designation "opera regia" is confined to the scenario of *Incoronazione*. The work is called "opera musicale" in nos. 2 and 10 and "dramma musicale" in no. 9. In nine of the librettos *Nozze* is called "tragedia di lieto fine"; in one (no. 11) it is just "tragedia," and in another (no. 2) it is "drama per musica." Only the three-act libretto (no. 5) lacks a generic subtitle altogether. Half (6) of the *Ritorno* librettos lack a generic subtitle (nos. 1, 3, 5, 8, 9, 10). One calls it a "tragedia" (no. 7), one a "tragedia di lieto fine" (no. 4), one (no. 6) simply "drama," and two (nos. 2 and 12), "drama per musica." (It is interesting that exemplars of both librettos bearing the atypical designation "drama per musica" are adjacent in the same collection, the Rossi collection, Marciana series 1294.1 and 1294.2, suggesting that the generic title may have been chosen by the collector/copyist.) This designation became conventional for opera librettos only after the middle of the century. "Tragedia di lieto fine," as defined in the *Argomento e scenario* of *Nozze* (pp. 3–4), is essentially one with a happy ending. See *OSV*, 41. The author must have been aware of the earlier, lengthier, and much more explicit definition in Giambattista Giraldi Cinthio, *Discorsi . . . intorno al comporre de i romanzi, delle comedie, e delle tragedie, e di altre maniere di poesie* (Venice: Giolitti, 1554). In regard to this subject, Louise George Clubb (*Giambattista Della Porta, Dramatist* [Princeton: Princeton University Press, 1965], 88–89) points out that Della Porta's *Penelope,* which he touted as the first Italian tragicomedy, followed all of Giraldi's rules for "tragedia di lieto fine."

3. On the term "opera regia," or "reggia," see Rosand, "The Opera Scenario"; also Staffieri, "Lo scenario," and especially *Il Solimano di Prospero Bonarelli,* ed. Roberto Ciancarelli (Rome: E&A, 1992), introduction, p. 37 (n. 46): "l'opera reggia fu una tipologia drammaturgica cui si accostarono dilettanti e professionisti." Strikingly, despite the opposing aesthetics that they imply, some scenarios juxtaposed the two designations *tragedia*

and the moderns, between the humanist values of a classical tradition and the adoption of a freer attitude toward drama of the kind displayed in the Spanish and Italian popular theater. The quarrel had been smoldering in academic circles since the Renaissance, and it was rekindled in seicento Venice by the newly arrived, commercially successful, and aesthetically ambiguous art of opera.[4] To invoke tragedy was to legitimize opera by recourse to ancient authority—in particular, Aristotle's "rules," as if those rules might mitigate the embarrassing awkwardness of speaking in song. All other subtitles affixed to librettos—including "opera regia" as well as "dramma per musica," "melodrama," "dramma musicale," and various combinations thereof—represented an explicit rejection of those rules, an embrace of the mixed genre of opera and of singing as an acceptable mode of dramatic expression.

This distinction between "tragedia" and the designations associated with *Incoronazione* hinges on two fundamental issues, one structural, the other thematic. The tragedies, in five acts, draw their subjects from material that is essentially mythical, from Homeric and Virgilian epic. "Opera regia," or the more generic "opera musicale," in three acts, draws upon history; its characters are chronologically and psychologically more proximate and thus more accessible to a modern audience. We will return to these distinctions.

It is to Michelangelo Torcigliani, the author of *Le nozze d'Enea,* and his "letter to his friends" that we owe the fullest explication of the rules of tragedy as applied to the opera libretto of this period. As he explains, they were designed to increase the moving power of the genre by enhancing its verisimilitude. Thus tragedies required heroes who were well known, because, as he put it, "those things believed to be true seem to move the affections more than those believed to be imaginary, and also stay in the memory longer" (see the original Italian in Appendix 2 [f]). And because they were so well known, the adventures of these heroes could not be altered without causing disbelief in the audience: the drama had to remain faithful to its source and any alterations required extensive justification. Convincing presentation of such "true stories," furthermore, required that the unities of time, place, and action be observed. The drama should be divided in five rather than three acts, so that the time represented on stage—that portrayed within the

---

and *opera regia*. Some recent writers have minimized the significance of the designation "tragedy" in connection with these works. Norbert Dubowy, "Bemerkungen," 225–31, argues that tragedy simply meant a drama in performance rather than one designed for reading, and he equates "tragedia" with "tragicommedia," *alla* Della Porta, preferring to call *Ritorno* an epic, in contrast to *Incoronazione*, which he terms "tragicommedia." Admittedly, as Silke Leopold points out (liner notes to Jacobs recording, Harmonia Mundi, 1992) *Ritorno* shows violence on stage (the deaths of the Suitors and Iro), a characteristic of epic that is eschewed in strict tragedy, but it follows the "rules" in most other respects. Indeed, the author of *Nozze* takes pains to distinguish his tragedy from the epic ("Tragedy is constrained to observe unity of time and action, whereas epic is not"; "Lettera," pp. 6, 9; see Appendix 2 [d and e].) By questioning the appropriateness of the designation "tragedia" for these early librettos, Dubowy minimizes the extent to which the librettists struggled to come to grips with the new genre. This struggle is explored in *OSV,* chap. 2.

4. For a convenient summary of the pressures that undermined Italian tragedy in the seventeenth century, see *Il Solimano,* ed. Ciancarelli, Introduction, pp. 25–29.

acts as well as that elapsed between them—might create the illusion of agreeing with real time. As our author explains it,

> Although the modern practice is to divide even spoken plays into three acts, I have preferred to divide mine into five . . . [in order] to adapt, at least in appearance, the time span of the imitation to the duration of what it imitates. Since the action of the play covers one day, it would seem that this is how long the play should last; but since this would be too inconvenient and tedious for the audience, the plot is divided into [five] acts, so that one can imagine that between one act and another more time elapses than actually does, and taken together, one can [reasonably] arrive at the span of one day. (See Appendix 2 [q])

Like the time represented on stage, so too should the action be mimetically convincing. This requires that each of the characters behave with decorum, or, in our author's words, that each "speak and act in accordance with his condition, sex, age, and mood." Enea should be strong; Ascanio, his son, generous; Turno, his rival, furious; Lavinia modest, and Amata, her mother, angry (see Appendix 2 [k]). The librettist even facilitated such decorum through variety of meter: *versi sdruccioli* for persons of low birth, the *tronco* (or *breve*) for angry ones, and so on (Appendix 2 [m]). Finally, tragedies should have prologues featuring allegorical characters that do not appear in the drama itself, but who introduce its subject and whose purpose it is to instruct the audience in the lesson to be learned (see Appendix 2 [o]).[5]

It is somewhat ironic that, although the author of *Nozze* aimed to follow "the rules" as closely as possible, their fullest realization occurred not in his own work, but rather in his model. Indeed, *Ritorno* may come closer to recreating the legendary effect of ancient tragedy than any other opera before or since. In writing his libretto, the *Nozze* author felt obliged to push against some of the prescriptions just outlined; *Ritorno* follows them with remarkable fidelity.

CLASSICS IN TRANSLATION

It should come as no surprise that our two tragedies share—and emphasize—a fidelity to their literary sources. Indeed, Badoaro's choice of the *Odyssey* was an implicit acknowledgment of obeisance to Aristotle, since the philosopher had cited the *Odyssey* more than once as exemplifying some of the most important features of tragedy.[6] Likewise, Torcigliani's choice of the *Aeneid* was legitimated by Virgil's own avowed relationship to his Homeric

---

5. Since Aristotle (and Torcigliani) emphasized the separation of prologue and drama, *Incoronazione* would have represented a departure from the rules: Amore is crucial to the denouement; see below, p. 180.

6. *Poetics* 1451^a–1452^b, 1459^a–1462^b (trans. in *The Complete Works of Aristotle*, ed. Jonathan Barnes [Princeton: Princeton University Press, 1985], 2:2316–40, paragraphs 8, 13, and 23–26). Giraldi Cinthio, *Discorsi*, 225 cites

predecessor. Giovanni Francesco Busenello, in contrast, flouts the very principle of fidelity, emphasizing his disregard for his sources—although, as we shall see, he tends to exaggerate the extent of his independence.

Il ritorno d'Ulisse

Despite its share of lengthy, meandering speeches, Badoaro's libretto is indeed a remarkably close adaptation of books 13–24 of Homer's *Odyssey*—or, more accurately, of the version through which Badoaro and his contemporaries were likely to have known the ancient Greek text: an Italian translation in *ottava rima* published in 1573 by Lodovico Dolce, one of the most active *poligrafi* in cinquecento Venice.[7] Like his versions of other classical texts, Dolce's *L'Ulisse* is a rereading, an interpretation filtered through his own literary experience. In addition to his *trasformazioni* of the monuments of ancient literature, that experience included editions and commentary on a whole range of Italian Renaissance texts, most notably Ariosto.[8] Dolce's *rifacimento* reduces the *Odyssey* to twenty cantos by a series of overlappings combined with some abbreviation, particularly in the second half, so that his final eight books cover the material in Homer's final twelve. The result is a more distilled and focused treatment of the last leg of Ulysses' homecoming, that part of the story adapted by Badoaro.[9]

---

both the *Iliad* and the *Odyssey* as examples of tragedies; the "unhappy" tragedies are more like the *Iliad*, whereas happy ones (= those with happy endings) are more like the *Odyssey*: "si per lo argumento, come per la mescolanza delle persone, che parue c'Homero in quiste due compositioni ci vulesse cosi dare l'essempio dell'una e dell'altra Tragedia . . . onde si vede quanto si siano ingannati coloro c'hanno ditto che la Iliade ci da la forma della Tragedia. . . . et l'Odissea quella della Comedia, dandoci insieme amendue l'essempio della Tragedia: quella della Tragedia del fine infelice; questa di quella di fin felice." See Ronnie H. Terpening, *Lodovico Dolce, Renaissance Man of Letters* (Toronto: University of Toronto Press, 1997), 226, n. 1, who cites Clubb, *Della Porta*, 88–89.

7. *L'Ulisse* (Venice: Gabriel Giolito de' Ferrari, 1573). There appear to have been only a few Latin translations of the *Odyssey* in the Renaissance. See Agostino Pertusi, *Leonzio Pilato fra Petrarca e Boccaccio: Le sue versioni omeriche negli autografi di Venezia e la cultura greca del primo Umanesimo* (Venice and Rome: Istituto per la collaborazione culturale, 1964), listing all known Latin versions on pp. 521–29. Dolce's was the first Italian translation to appear and remained the only Venetian translation of the *Odyssey* for seventy years, during which intense discussion of the *Poetics* heightened interest in the epic. (I thank Sara Van der Laan, a student in my Monteverdi seminar in 2003, for emphasizing this point.) See Howard Clarke, *Homer's Readers: A Historical Introduction to the Iliad and the Odyssey* (London: Associated University Presses, 1981).

8. There is a real question as to whether Dolce's editions should be called translations, "trasformazioni," "rifacimenti," or new works entirely. He himself is not always clear on the subject. See Turpening, *Lodovico Dolce*, chap. 1 and *passim*. The influence of Ariosto is striking in his *Iliad* (*L'Achille et l'Enea* . . . [Venice: Giolito, 1571]) as well as his *Ulisse*, not least at the ends of the individual cantos, where he adopts Ariostean strategies to maintain narrative suspense.

9. It must have been the liberties associated with the condensation that caused one nineteenth-century critic to judge the translation "tanto larga da non vedercisi più quasi niente dell'originale omerico" (Salvatore Bongi, *Annali di Gabriel Giolito de' Ferrari da Trino di Monferrato, stampatore in Venezia*, 2 vols. [Rome: Presso i principali librai, 1890–95], 2:335).

Dolce's editorial decisions—that is, the ways in which he shortens or minimizes certain incidents in favor of others or collapses intervening material—offer a key to his reading. Even more obvious clues are found in a series of *sentenze* at the head of the volume that extract major themes of the work, and an alphabetical table of "cose notabili." In addition, each canto is prefaced by an *ottava* summarizing the argomento as well as by a series of *allegorie* interpreting characters featured in the canto, several of which resonate with important themes in Badoaro's libretto. We will consider these later. Guiding the reader through the thicket of Homer's text, together Dolce's summarizing argomenti and his *allegorie* of books 13–20 read like a précis—we might even say scenario—of Badoaro's libretto. The argomento of the libretto (given in only two sources) makes the connection even clearer. (See Appendix 5, A and B.)

Beginning with Ulisse's appearance asleep on the Ithacan shore in 1.7 (the final scene of Badoaro's act 1), the sequence of events in the libretto follows that of Dolce's précis of books 13–17, though the librettist anticipates a few incidents that do not occur until books 18–20. Most of Dolce's argomenti cover two successive (but not necessarily contiguous) scenes of the libretto.[10] Although not all of Badoaro's scenes are accounted for in those argomenti—they contain no reference to any part of Badoaro's act 3, for instance—many of these occur in Dolce's text itself, usually in the same sequence.[11]

Those few scenes in Badoaro's libretto that are either not found or ordered differently in Dolce tend to amplify characters and situations and were clearly introduced for dramatic purposes, to provide opportunities for the characters to reveal themselves. Chief among these is Penelope's remarkable opening scene, which epitomizes her nightly ritual of lament as evoked more than once later in the epic (for instance, in Dolce's canto 15,

---

10. Thus canto 13 moves from Badoaro's 1.7 (Ulisse meets Minerva) to 2.4 (Ulisse, disguised as an old man, seeks out his faithful swineherd Eumete and advises him that his master is alive). Dolce's canto 14 presents the action of Badoaro's 2.5 and 6: Minerva magically influences Telemaco to return to Ithaca from Argos (scene 5), and to visit Eumete, where he meets Ulisse in disguise (scene 6). He fails to recognize him at first, but Minerva reveals his true identity. Act 2, scene 7 follows in canto 15, which then (leaving out for the present all of the scenes with the Suitors) skips forward to act 4, scenes 1 and 2: the first between Telemaco and Penelope, in which he recounts his travels and angers her, the second portraying Ulisse's appearance at court and the Suitors' disdain of him. Canto 16 continues the action of 4.2, describing Penelope's distress at the Suitors' mistreatment of her guest, and Iro's defeat at the hands of Ulisse. Canto 17 skips to 5. 8, which tells of Ulisse being bathed by his old nurse Ericlea, her observation of his scar, and her subsequent recognition of him. We backtrack in canto 18 to 4.3, which covers the contest with the bow as announced by Penelope, the Suitors' failure, and the beginning of Ulisse's murderous rampage against them. The slaughter continues into canto 19, in which he kills them all and is finally recognized by his wife. Libretto and translation begin to diverge in Dolce's two final cantos: two verses (3–4) in canto 19 and six in canto 20 are not treated in Badoaro's libretto.

11. In canto 13, for instance, Ulisse's encounter with Minerva is preceded by the dialogue between Giove and Nettuno and Nettuno's transformation of the Feaci's ship into a rock (Badoaro's 1.5–6). The sequence is strengthened by Dolce's omission of intervening Homeric material: the Feaci's prayers to Nettuno in lines 145–85. And five of the six scenes of act 3 appear in canto 15, where they belong (between the material summarized in verses 1–2 and 3–4 of the argomento: Suitors/Penelope [17–20]; Eumete/Penelope [21–22]; Suitors alone [12–16]; Ulisse/Minerva [21]; Eumete/Ulisse [24–30]).

stanza 33, addressed to Telemaco: "ho già pianto molti e molt'anni con mia grave offesa / Il padre tuo da me aspettato tanto").[12]

The relationship between Melanto and Eurimaco, also expanded, enables Badoaro to satisfy the particular theatrical convention of a second pair of lovers, but is based on Homer's characterizations.[13] Indeed, Dolce's allegory for Melanto in canto 17, though directed toward a dramatic situation not treated by Badoaro, captures nicely her attitude toward Penelope in the libretto: "Melanto . . . demonstrates the shamelessness of a tenant farmer who, wanting more than she is entitled to, wants to put herself in charge, and oppose what her mistress legitimately desires."[14]

The Suitors' material, too, is not wholly invented, but rather expands upon suggestions in Dolce's text, though Badoaro's reduction of their number to three is clearly justified by a musical consideration: the desirability of presenting them as a trio. Finally, in an operatic invention extrapolated from her promise to keep silent (Homer, 19.491–95, Dolce 17.23–24), Ericlea is given a solo scene (and aria), in which she debates whether to reveal Ulisse's secret, though the nature of that secret and the circumstances of its discovery are not mentioned until just before the denouement.[15]

Given its striking departure from Homer, we may wonder whether Badoaro's version of the denouement might not also have been inspired by Dolce. In Homer's memorable version, Penelope finally acknowledges Ulysses as her husband following his impassioned and extended description of the tree-fixed marital bed he himself had constructed (Odyssey 23.177–204). Dolce omits the entire exchange, relying solely on Penelope's rather bland allusion to private secrets between her and her husband (Odyssey 23.105–110) to promote the denouement. Badoaro, however, makes two crucial alterations to this scene, both directed toward the same goal. First, he replaces Homer's virtuoso description

---

12. Other references occur in canto 15, stanza 38, to her maid Eurynome, "Dapoi, che 'l Signor mio / Da me partissi, sei partì ogni bene, / Ne convien ch'io m'adorni, o che faccia io / Queste luci dolente unqua serene. / Né altro è il mio pensieri né il mio desio, / Che di morir, se tosto egli non viene"; and finally in canto 16, stanza 44, to Eurimaco: "Qual si sia / La mia beltà, quel dì che 'l mio consorte / Partì per Troia, tutta sparì via, / Ne più rimasa è in me cosa, ch'importe. / E s'ei tornasse, à me ritorneria / Gloria certo maggior, e miglior sorte." Emphasis on the keywords "tornasse" and "ritorneria" tempts the reader to find textual echoes of Badoaro (Penelope's "Torna, deh torna" in Badoaro's scene 1) in Dolce merely because they are both in Italian. Indeed, in many places, Dolce's Italian heightens our awareness of the extent to which Badoaro's language is derived from Homer. I am thinking particularly of Dolce's description of Ulisse's awakening in Ithaca and his subsequent dialogue with Minerva (canto 13, stanzas 10–11, and following). Badoaro's version of Penelope's opening speech includes a long passage, missing in Monteverdi's setting, in which she details her daily weaving and nightly unweaving of her cloth (Laertes' shroud) (Odyssey, bk. 19, 145–56; Dolce, canto 17, stanzas 9–10).

13. Both characters are much more fully drawn in Dolce (as well as in the Odyssey). Melanto, for instance, is an insidious traitor with a large role toward the end of the drama (in bk. 23), and Eurimaco is the most aggressive of the Suitors. Badoaro's characterization of these figures may have been influenced by those in Della Porta's Penelope. See below.

14. "Melanto . . . ci mostra la sfacciatezza d'una massara (massaia?) laqual volendo più di quell che s'appartiene a lei, vuol far la padrona, e contradir a quell che honestamente dalla padrona è voluto" (canto 17).

15. In Homer and Dolce, Ulisse warns Ericlea not to divulge his identity, but her struggle, in a solo scene, is Badoaro's expansion. (In Dolce, 19. 47, Homer, 23. 72, Ericlea finally tells Penelope about Ulisse's scar.)

of the bed with a much briefer description of its coverlet, embroidered with an image of Diana. Badoaro's introduction of a reference to the chaste goddess cannot have been casual. It underscores Penelope's greatest virtue, that same virtue broadcast in the subtitle title of Federico Malipiero's contemporary novel, *La peripezia d'Ulisse overo la casta Penelope.*[16]

Badoaro's second alteration was to shift responsibility for the denouement from Penelope to Ulisse. In Homer, we recall, Ulysses' description of the bed was provoked by a suspicious Penelope trying to trick him (by asking Eurykleia to move it). Badoaro's Ulisse comes up with the details of the coverlet on his own. Penelope's pretense is eliminated, her innocence, here too, reinforced. Badoaro's alterations have still a further purpose. Rather than merely confirming Penelope's emerging awareness of Ulisse's identity, an awareness minimized throughout the libretto, Badoaro postpones her recognition until after Ulisse's speech, thereby maintaining to the very end the remarkable tension systematically built up during the course of the opera. This tension is a crucial element in the structure of Badoaro's drama and, even more so, of Monteverdi's opera. Although Dolce supplies no model for Badoaro's denouement, his omission of its most memorable Homeric element may have left an opening for Badoaro's revisions.

Perhaps the most suggestive evidence of Dolce's importance to Badoaro, however, can be found in the allegories he extracts from the relevant cantos, especially his choice of characters to interpret. Most are straightforward enough: in canto 13, for example, Dolce highlights the three characters featured in his argomento, in the order in which they appear: Ulisse, Minerva, and Il Porcaro (Eumete, who is not named in Dolce). But it is interesting that Porcaro's allegory contrasts him with parasites and flies—for only in Badoaro's libretto, not in Homer, does this character confront Iro, the parasite: "From the Porcaro, who always maintained his love toward Ulisse . . . one understands that in the courts of princes more affection and faith is found in simple and lowly people than in ambitious and presumptuous courtiers, who show as much affection to the lord as they deem useful and profitable for themselves; but when fortune changes, they themselves change *like parasites and like flies,* which fly away once their food is taken away."[17] In canto 16, two of the six allegories are devoted to Iro: "From Iro, who taunts Ulisse, one understands the nature of parasites, who, in order to please those who support them, commit every insolence and

16. Venice: Surian, 1640. There was some controversy on the subject of Penelope's chastity. See Heller, *Emblems,* 33 and 307, n. 30; Giuseppe Passi, *I donneschi difetti* (Venice: Somascho, 1599), 85, refers to Angelus Sabinus and Pausanias for doubting Penelope's chastity. See also Lodovico Dolce, *Dialogo della institutione delle donne* (Venice: Giolito, 1547). On the emphasis on Penelope's chastity in the opera, see Chap. 7 below, pp. 253–54.

17. "Nel Porcaro, che mantenne sempre l'amore verso Ulisse, e verso la sua famiglia, si comprende, che nelle corti de' Principi, si trova più affettione, e fede nelle persone semplici e basse, che ne' Cortigiani ambitiosi e superbi, che tanto mostrano affetto al lor Signore, quanto vedono il loro utile, e commodo; ma mutandosi la fortuna, si mutan d'animo come i Parasiti e come le Mosche, le quali tolto via il mangiare, volan via ancor esse" (canto 13).

dispose themselves to injure any person, however honored" (16). "From the same Iro, who is almost killed by Ulisse, one understands how those who daringly test their strength against those they do not know deserve to be punished."[18]

There is nothing subtle about the moral drawn from these (or the other) allegories; the themes are almost banal, but Dolce's definition of Iro as a parasite is noteworthy, since that term, familiar from the Porcaro allegory just quoted, is not associated with him in any other version of the *Odyssey*.[19] Further, by endowing such an unheroic character with moral significance, of whatever quality, Dolce may have encouraged Badoaro to do the same.

Additional links to Badoaro can perhaps be traced in the *sentenze*—usually couplets or quatrains—extracted from the text and the list of "cose notabili" arranged alphabetically at the beginning of Dolce's book. One of the *sentenze* is enunciated by the allegorical figure Humana Fragilità, a character well known to us from the prologue to *Ritorno*. Allegorical figures are common in the literature of this time, and especially prominent in libretto prologues, but Humana Fragilità is actually quite rare. She does appear, however, in the standard iconographical handbook for allegorical representation, Cesare Ripa's *Iconologia*, where she is described as "an old, afflicted woman, poorly dressed, with an emaciated face, holding icicles in her hands that symbolize the fragility of human life."[20]

Humana Fragilità's *sentenza* comes from a speech by the disguised Ulisse addressed to the Suitors, immediately following his defeat of Iro (canto 16, 33; *Odyssey* 18.130):

Ma sappi, che non è sopra la terra	Know that in all the earth
Cosa de l'huomo più debole e frale.	there is nothing more weak and frail than man.

---

18. "In Iro, che si burla d'Ulisse, si comprende la natura de' parasiti, i quali per compiacer chi gli trattiene, fanno ogni insolenza e si mettono a ingiuriar ogni persona quantunque honorata." "Nel medesimo Iro, che resta quasi morto da Ulisse, si comprende come meritano d'esser gastigati coloro, che temerariamente si mettono a esperimentar le lor forze con le persone che non conoscono" (canto 16).

19. Malipiero (*La peripizia*), calls him a buffoon. Della Porta (*Penelope*) calls him a beggar ("mendico"); *Teatro*, vol. 1, *Le tragedie*, ed. Rafaelle Siri (Naples: Istituto Universitario Orientale, 1978). See below, Chap. 8, p. 339 and n. 37.

20. *Iconologia overo descrittione di diverse imagini cavate dall'antichità, e di propria inventione, trovate, e dichiarate da Cesare Ripa* (Rome: Lepido Faeii, 1603), 173 (originally published Rome, 1593). Ripa's description reads as follows: "Donna con faccia maciente, ed afflitta, vestita poveramente, tenga con ambe le mani molti di quei bamboli d'acqua aghiacciata, che pendono il verno da' tetti delle case, li quali bamboli dice il Pierio Valeriano che erano da gl'antichi Egitti posti per la fragilità dell'humana vita: non sarebbe anco disconveniente fare, che questa figura mostrasse, per la gravezza de gl'anni d'andare molto china appoggiandosi ad una fievole canna, per essere anch'essa vero simbolo della fragilità, come la vecchiezza alla quale quando un huomo arriva facilmente sente ogni minima lesione, e facilmente ne rimane oppresso. Notarono alcuni ancora la fragilità humana, con quelle bolle che fa l'acqua, che paiono in un subito qualche cosa, ma tosto spariscono, e non senza ragione." Humana Fragilità was also the subject of a painting by Salvator Rosa dating from the middle of the seventeenth century. For an interpretation, see Richard Wallace, "Salvator Rosa's *Democritus* and *L'Umana Fragilità*," in *Art Bulletin* 50 (1968): 21–32. In Salvator Rosa's depiction, the (young) lady is accompanied by representations of Fortune. Time and Fortune are part of the standard *vanitas* imagery stressing evanescence and death, and the vanity of worldly aspirations and achievements. For a recent exploration of the significance of these associations in Italian art of the seventeenth century, see Pierroberto Scaramella, "L'Italia dei trionfi e dei contrasti," in *Humana Fragilitas: I temi della morte in Europa tra Duecento e Settecento*, ed. Alberto Tenenti (Clusone: Ferrari, 2000), 25–98, esp. 73–84.

Humana Fragilità's allegorical associates, Time and Fortune, soon follow (references italicized).

Perciochè se ben mostra in pace e in Guerra	He can well show in peace and war
Invitto sorte, ed animo immortale;	an unconquered destiny and an immortal soul;
Nondimeno, se poi fato l'asserra	Nonetheless, if Fate
Averso, a segno d'ogni grave male.	turns against him, everything changes.
Cos'io pensai d'esser felice *un tempo*	Thus did I once think I was happy,
Hor mi ritrovo misero *col tempo.*	Now with time I find myself miserable,
Questo fa *la fortuna* ed il volere	Fortune does this and the will
De' sommi Dei: ma ben con veritate	of the highest gods; but truly
La giustitia del cielo è da temere	the judgment of heaven is to be feared
Contra l'altrui malitia e crudeltate. . . .	against others' evil and cruelty.

We are, in fact, very much in the world of Badoaro's (or rather Monteverdi's) prologue, where stanza by stanza Humana Fragilità decries her all too human struggle against the ravages of Time ("il tempo che mi crea, quel mi combatte"), Fortune ("frale vita è di Fortuna un gioco"), and Love ("al tiranno d'Amor serva sen giace / La mia fiorita età verde e fugace"). Odysseus's false exposition to the Suitors of his identity and travels, then, as rendered by Dolce, effectively elucidates the meaning of this prologue—and its relationship to (the moral of) Badoaro's drama.[21] Badoaro's Ulisse is indeed a frail human being, at the mercy of Time and Fortune, tossed and turned, subject to the whim of the gods.

This same passage also echoes, though perhaps less strongly, in Badoaro's original prologue, where Fortezza and Prudenza sing of their weakness in the face of Fato:

A trionfar s'arma Fortezza in vano,	To triumph, Fortitude arms itself in vain,
A trionfar Prudenza humana è frale.	To triumph, human Prudence is weak.
Forza, senno, valor ben poco vale,	Strength, wisdom, valor are worth little,
Che se il Fato dissente, è tutto vano.	For if Fate dissents, it is all in vain.

---

21. The parallel passage in Homer occurs in book 18, lines 130–42:

Of all creatures that breathe and walk on the earth, there is nothing
more helpless than a man is, of all that the earth fosters;
for he thinks that he will never suffer misfortune in future
days, while the gods grant him courage, and his knees have spring
in them; but when the blessed gods bring sad days upon him,
against his will he must suffer it with enduring spirit.
For the mind in men upon earth goes according to the fortunes
the Father of Gods and Men, day by day, bestows upon them.
For I myself once promised to be a man of prosperity,
but, giving way to force and violence, did many reckless
things because I relied on my father and brothers. Therefore,
let no man be altogether without the sense of righteousness,
but take in silence the gifts of the gods, whatever they give him.

.*The Odyssey of Homer*, trans. with an introduction by Richmond
Lattimore (New York: Harper & Row, 1965), 273.

Prudenza Humana would appear to be another allusion to Ulisse, whose traditional association with Prudence is emphasized by Dolce, once again, in allegories beginning three cantos of his *Ulisse* (7, 15, and 19; and two of his *Iliade*).[22] The arc of this drama is explicitly completed at the end of the libretto, in the Ithacans' chorus, which announces the triumph of Virtue, Strength, and Wisdom over Fortune:

Pugna spesso coll'uom Fortuna e sorte,	Fortune and fate often fight with man,
Spesso ei vede il destin di sdegno armato	He often sees destiny armed with anger,
Ma cede la Fortuna, e arride il Fato	But Fortune yields and Fate is propitious
Se s'arma di Virtù l'uom saggio, e forte.[23]	if a wise and strong man arms himself with Virtue.

This "plot" or moral, too, fits nicely enough on the shoulders of Ulisse. Through Minerva's help and his own wisdom and strength, he has fulfilled Fate's prophecy, announced in the prologue. Now that the unjust Suitors are dead, Neptune placated, and the Achaens suitably fearful, Ulisse can enjoy his homeland and his wife:

Vedrete hoggi mortali, Ulisse il forte	Today ye mortals will see strong Ulysses
Superar rischi, e valicar perigli,	conquer risks and overcome dangers,
Quinci la saggia Dea, co suoi consigli,	henceforth the wise goddess with her advice
Farsi per lui del mio voler consorte.	will make herself for him consort of my will.
Gode la patria al fin, gode la moglie,	He will finally enjoy his country and his wife,
Restan di vita i Proci ingiusti privi	The unjust Suitors will be deprived of life,
Nettun si placa, e temono gl'Achivi.	Neptune will be placated and the Achaeans fear.

Penelope, too, uses some of the imagery introduced by Humana Fragilità in her opening monologue: her "sol per me non raccoglie un fiato solo" echoes Fragilità's "un soffio sol m'abbatte"; her reference to "speranze non più verdi, ma canute all'invecchiato male" plays on the same theme as Humana Fragilità's "fiorita età verde e fugace" as she rages against the vicissitudes of Time:

L'aspettato non giunge:	The awaited one fails to arrive,
E pur fuggono gli anni;	and yet the years fly by.
La serie del penar è lunga, ahi troppo!	The series of punishment is long, oh, too much.
A chi vive in angosce il Tempo è zoppo.	To one who lives in anguish, Time is lame.

The years fly by, yet Time stands still. Has it even stopped Fortune's wheel from turning ("Cangiò forse Fortuna / La volubil ruota in stabil seggio") and her sail from being blown

---

22. The association with Prudence occurs not only in Dolce, but in virtually every allegorical reading of the *Odyssey*. Once again, I thank Sara Van der Laan for this observation.

23. This passage, of course, was cut when its complementary prologue was replaced.

about by the wind ("E La sua pronta vela / Ch'ogn'uman caso porta / Fra le incostanze a volo, / Sol per me non raccoglie un fiato solo")? Man may have a heavenly soul, she concludes, but his body is weak and quickly turns to dust ("L'uomo . . . porta un'alma celeste, un corpo frale: / Tosto more il mortale, / E torna il corpo in polve / Dopo breve soggiorno").[24] In a speech to Penelope at the beginning of act 2—a passage omitted by Monteverdi—Melanto, arguing on behalf of the third of Humana Fragilità's antagonists in the prologue, Love, returns to this same theme:

Fuggi pur del Tempo i danni,	Flee the ravages of Time,
Tosto vien nemica età.	Enemy age will soon arrive.
In passando i dì tiranni	By their passing tyrannical days
Fanno oltraggio a tua beltà.	commit outrage against your beauty.

(2.1)

And it sounds loudly once again in Mercurio's long speech to the Suitors' ghosts, which is summed up in an explicit moral addressed to the audience:

Vivi cauto o mortale,	Live cautiously, o mortals,
Che camina la vita, e 'l Tempo ha l'ale.	for life marches on and Time has wings,
E dove ingorda speme	And where hope grows greedy
Vivendo non s'acqueta,	it cannot be sated.
De l'humane pazzie quest'è la meta.	Of human madness, this is the dessert.

(5.2)

Although Dolce's *Ulisse* may have been the most widely available version of Homer's text from the late sixteenth century on, there were other Italian translations. One, by Girolamo Baccelli, in unrhymed *endecasillibi*, was printed in Florence in 1582. In his dedication to the Grand Duke of Tuscany, the author emphasized that his translation was the first into the Tuscan language, suggesting that it was addressed to a somewhat limited audience. Published in modest duodecimo format and with few illustrations, it lacked the apparatus of tables, summaries, allegories, and elaborate woodcuts that helped to render Dolce's imposing octavo volume reader-friendly.

Another, more recent, version of the *Odyssey* issued directly from Badoaro's orbit at around the time of *Ritorno*, Federico Malipiero's *L'Odissea d'Omero trapportata dalla greca nella toscana favella.*[25] Malipiero, we recall, was the fellow member of the Accademia degli Incogniti who claimed that his prose novel *La peripezia d'Ulisse overo la casta Penelope* (1640)

---

24. The full text of Penelope's lament is given in Chap. 7 (see Table 16).
25. Venice: Corradicci, 1643.

had been inspired by *Il ritorno d'Ulisse*. Indeed, Malipiero's published reference to the opera helps to establish that it was first performed in 1640. His *Odissea* did not appear until 1643, posthumously, but it was obviously written before then and must have been available to the Incogniti, as a source for their characteristic discussions and debates.[26]

In Malipiero's rambling prose *trasformatione* (or *trasportatione*), the Homeric source is expanded rather than contracted, and even while he preserves the original twenty-four books, Malipiero elaborates quite freely on Homer. Much as in Dolce, an introductory argomento and "tavola di cose notabili" give some idea of the important themes in each of the books, and there are intermittent marginal glosses with general comments identifying a speaker or topic of discussion, or with the indication "digressione," or "comparazione."[27] These mark authorial expansions: the extraction of a moral, the description of a setting, the explanation of a character's psychological motivation, or the amplification of a character's speech.

Although Malipiero proclaimed his debt to Badoaro and Monteverdi with respect to *La casta Penelope,* we cannot know how that debt would have manifested itself: only the first part of the novel was ever published, and it leaves off just before the libretto begins.[28] As it turns out, his posthumous *Odissea* may offer a clue. Indeed, some of Malipiero's expansions seem to reflect the characters (or even the staging) as presented in the operatic version.

To take one of many examples, his description of Melanto in book 18, glossed by the rubric "Melanto, disonesta Dama," reads like a summary of Badoaro's characterization, especially regarding her behavior toward Penelope and in the two scenes she shares with Eurimaco, which, we remember (p. 135), are themselves expansions and displacements of Homer and Dolce: "Melanto was a lovely but shrewd maiden. She was educated by Penelope herself, who kept her among all the royal delicacies as if she were one of her own daughters. Though Melanto received so many favors from Penelope, the immoral girl failed to shed tears for her mistress's affliction, but rather was accustomed to amusing herself lasciviously with her paramour, Eurimaco."[29] Malipiero's juxtaposition here of Melanto's failure to sympathize with Penelope's suffering and her unchaste behavior with Eurimaco seems almost a commentary on Badoaro's own juxtaposition of Penelope and Melanto in the first two scenes of act 1.

A similar forecast can be seen in Malipiero's description of Penelope earlier in the same book. Although occurring within the context of her confrontation with the Suitors,

---

26. Malipiero's translation of the *Iliad* had appeared in 1642. For a brief biographical sketch and a list of Malipero's works, see Pietro Angelo Zeno, *Memoria de' scrittori veneti patritii* (Venice: Baglioni, 1662), 77–78; also Rosand, "Seneca," nn. 36–38.

27. These, sometimes as many as four or five in a book, are conveniently listed in the tables of contents.

28. "Ho risoluto dividerle [le prodigiose fatiche d'Omero] in doi parti, sì per non apportar noia al lettore; sì per regolarmi nella seconda al gusto che n'havrà della prima il Mondo. In questa si contengono tutti li casi sofferiti da Ulisse. Nell'altra vi sarà descritto 'l suo ritorno in Itaca" (Malipiero, *La peripezia*, Lettore).

29. "Melanto era una damigella bellissima, ma avveduta . . . fu educata da Penelope medesima, e la tenne tra tutte le delicie regali come se fosse stata una sua vera figliuola. Melanto ricevuti tanti favori però da Penelope non secondava punto col pianto le di lei afflizioni, ma l'impudica innamorata d'Eurimaco soleva lascivamente trastullarsi con quell suo Drudo" (Malipiero, *Odissea,* book 18, p. 28).

it brings to mind the effect (and even the language) of her opening monologue, capturing her desperation:

> As she woke up the most beautiful lady began to yawn with her mouth, to stretch both arms, to rub both eyes with her hands, to rub her cheeks rosy, and to say these words to herself: "it is certain that, afflicted and inconsolable, I was overcome by sleep, which never can be paired with exhaustion and with the troubles of the soul. At least, instead of sleep, you, Death (who are its sister), if only you would take my soul from me, through which I am given that pain that can only be an endless torment for the memory of my dear, but lost, husband. Husband, to whom among all the Greeks there was none second, let alone equal." It is said that Penelope lamented in this manner; after getting up, accompanied by two maids who supported her between themselves, she left her bedroom and went, more beautiful than Beauty herself, to show herself to the Suitors . . . She had covered her head with the thinnest of veils, which not only covered her eyes, but—like a cloud of the finest vapor— veiled her cheeks, and these and those through the transparent veil appeared to be moons or stars in the heavens covered by a delicate, pure mist. At this unexpected appearance, the Suitors fell stunned upon the ground. Every one of her lovers at this point felt his heart pierced by a thousand amorous arrows, his soul lit by one thousand passionate flames.[30]

Given the vivid visual details, one might imagine Malipiero to have been inspired by the appearance of Badoaro's Penelope or even the reactions to her on the part of her audience: on stage and in the theater.

One further parallel involves Ericlea. As we noted, Badoaro constructs a soliloquy in which she gives voice to issues only implied in Dolce's text—her conflict about whether to reveal Ulisse's secret. Although Malipiero does not include an equivalent soliloquy, its text and affect resonate at several points within the much expanded dialogue between Ericlea and Ulisse on this subject, a dialogue that would have justified Badoaro's monologue. Following a moving description of Ericlea's response to recognizing Ulisse in the bath (1), Malipiero reports Ulisse's injunction to her (2). "Taci, imponi silenzio": these words echo loudly in Badoaro's soliloquy:

---

30. "Cominciò la bellissima isvegliata a sbadacchiar con la bocca, ad'estendere entrambe le braccia, a confiscarsi con le mani ambidue gl'occhi, a forbirsi le guancie di rose, ed a dire a se stessa queste parole: Per certo, ch'io afflitta e sconsolata. Fui vinta dal sonno, che tra la stanchezza, e fra i travagli dell'animo sempre mai suole star accoppiato. Almeno in vece di sonno, tu Morte, (che sei sorella di quegli) mi togliesti quest'anima, acciò fornissero in me que' dolori, che mi servono a perpetuo tormenti per la rimembranza del mio caro, ma perduto marito. Marito, che tra tutti gli Greci non si trovava a lui secondo, non che uguale. Così Penelope lagnando si diceva, e levata di letto, accompagnata dalle due Damigelle, tolta nel mezzo da loro uscì della sua stanza, ed andò più bella della stessa bellezza a farsi vedere a gli Proci. . . . Havea coperta costei la testa da un sottilissimo velo, il quale non solo le cuopriva gl'occhi, ma a guisa di nube, e di vapor tenuissimo le velava le guancie, e quegli, e queste così fuori del velo trasparivano, che parean Lune, o Stelle in Cielo adombrate da tenue, da candida nube . . . . Gli Proci a questa improvisa comparsa hebbero a cadere tramortiti tutti sopra la terra: Ogni amator di costei in questo punto sentissi da mille strali amorosi pugnere il cuore, da mille fiamme lussuose accendere l'alma nel seno" (Malipiero, *Odissea,* book 18, p. 25).

Ericlea, che vuoi far?	Ericlea, what will you do?
Vuoi tacer o parlar?	Will you be silent or speak?
Se parli tu consoli;	If you speak, you console;
Obbedisci, se taci.	you obey if you are silent.
Sei tenuta a servir,	You are compelled to serve,
Obbligata ad amar:	obliged to love:
Vuoi tacer o parlar?	will you be silent or speak?
	(5.8)

Her subsequent response to Ulisse's injunction (3) indicates her strength of character, and the effort that will be required to break her promise and reveal the truth to Penelope, an effort that surely comes through in Badoaro's text.[31]

The extent of Malipiero's explanations of character (Melanto), visual descriptions (Penelope), and expanded dialogue (Ericlea) exemplified here certainly suggests that, like his novel, his translation may well have been influenced by seeing *Ritorno* on stage. Indeed, Malipiero's text may offer, however indirectly, rare testimony regarding the production of Monteverdi's opera.

Whatever the specific relationship between Badoaro's libretto and Malipiero's *trasportazione*, it is certain that both authors' interest in the Homeric epic was sparked by the conviction, widely shared by members of the Incogniti, that the heroic exploits of ancient figures provided important models of virtue for modern readers. This was the motivation for a host of writings on a variety of heroic subjects—historical, biblical, mythological.[32]

Le nozze d'Enea

However filtered through Dolce's reading, the essential proximity of *Il ritorno d'Ulisse* to its classical source was highly significant—and hardly casual. It was a feature that Badoaro himself emphasized when comparing *Ritorno* to his second libretto, *L'Ulisse errante,* written four years later, which was also based on the *Odyssey.* His earlier text, he says, was a drama excavated precisely ("di punto") from Homer, a work recorded as outstanding ("ottimo") by Aristotle in his *Poetics.* Even then, he reports, complaints were

---

31. (1) "Euriclea in'un punto fu da due contrarii abbattuta, il dolor, l'allegrezza improvisamente assalironla. Pianse, e stillò lagrime da gl'occhi. . . . Non poteva la meschina formar più con la lingua parola, ma toccava con le mani, e blandiva la faccia d'Ulisse . . ."; (2) "Tu sola mi conosci in questo parto, dunque taci, imponi silenzio, né far, ch'altra persona sappi in questa Corte, ch'io sia arrivato . . . tu [se tacendo mi terrai celato] havrai la vita, la mia grazia, ed ogni favore in questa Corte"; (3) "adesso, adesso ti prometto essere nel silentio più dura d'un ferro, più soda d'un macigno, o d'uno scoglio" (Malipiero, *Odissea,* bk. 18, pp. 46–48).

32. This idea is explicit in the prefaces of many Incognito publications. See, for example, that of Malipiero's *L'Annibale eroe* (1640), quoted in Rosand, "Seneca," n. 37. Some idea of the range of Incognito publications on heroic subjects can be gleaned from Tomasso Bozza, *Scrittori politici italiani dal 1550 al 1650: Saggio di bibliographia,* Storia e letteratura 23 (Rome: Edizioni di "Storia e letteratura," 1949). A more recent, chronological list of just those works published by Francesco Valvasense, the chief "Incognito" publisher, is found in Miato, *L'Accademia degli Incogniti,* appendix 1.

heard ("udii abbaiar qualche cane")—we can guess that showing violence on stage was one of them; this was specifically ruled out by Torcigliani in the *Nozze* preface[33]—and now, in *Ulisse errante,* he grudgingly admits that he has "partly reduced the [number of] episodes, and partly expanded the subject with inventions that I judged to be necessary, without, however, departing from the essence of the story. It is true that the incidents that transpire during his travels are multiple actions; but the traveller's intention, which is to return to his homeland, is but a single action" (See Appendix 3 [a]).

No excuses were required in the case of *Il ritorno d'Ulisse.* Choosing the second half of the *Odyssey* as his source allowed Badoaro to fulfill virtually all of the Aristotelian "rules" as set forth in the *Nozze* preface. (Indeed, one might even entertain the attractive suspicion that the *Nozze* "rules" themselves were extrapolated from *Ritorno.*) It offered a well-known hero, lent itself to a unified action, and required little or no invention—all of the characters and events, numerous as they are, are derived from Homer. Indeed, Homer himself provided a rich and varied cast suitable to Venetian operatic convention: two pairs of lovers, servants, gods and goddesses, and the potential for comic relief. In addition, the *Odyssey* offered the possibility of realizing a central feature of tragedy that the *Nozze* author failed to mention: catharsis.[34]

The *Nozze* author was not as fortunate in his choice. For although the second half of the *Aeneid* could supply some of the required elements, it lacked certain others, as Torcigliani was well aware. He therefore felt compelled to take certain liberties with the "rules": to embellish a character, to modify a scene, and even to alter the plot. Most prominently, his libretto ends with the wedding of Enea and Lavinia, an event only alluded to by Virgil. And to that end, Lavinia's character is elaborated so that she falls in love with Enea during the course of the drama—because, as the author sweetly teaches us, such important marriages should be preceded by love (see Appendix 2 [j]).[35] In only one respect does *Nozze* follow classical doctrine more closely than *Ritorno:* it abjures showing violence on stage. Turno's death at the hands of Enea is reported by a chorus, whereas Ulisse slays the Suitors in full view of the audience.[36] The complex plot can be summarized as follows:

---

33. See below, n. 36.

34. *Incoronazione* has a parody of this. There, the catharsis is something to be anticipated with dread.

35. This is the second (and more significant) of the two major alterations of the Virgilian plot acknowledged by Torcigliani. The first involves Enea's interaction with the figure of Tebro, which in Virgil occurred at night ("in tempo, ch'ogn'uno quantunque travagliato finalmente riposa"), but which the librettist moves to day, changing the nature of the interaction to enhance its verisimilitude (see Appendix 2 [g–h]).

36. Cf. n. 3, above. Turno's death occurs at the end of act 4. Described in the scenario, it is indicated by rubric in the five-act libretto: "Turno fugge et seguito da Enea resta fuori di scena ucciso." Elminio's death occurs between scenes, and Amata's is omitted entirely, "so as not to trouble with sorrow so great a joy [as the wedding of Enea and Lavinia]". As the author explains it, "Non vedendosi l'altre morti di Turno, d'Elminio, e di Numano, *com'è gia noto* il precetto dell'arte di bandire la rappresentazione dell'atrocità anco dalle più malinconiche tragedie bastando, per intelligenza degli uditori, siano semplicemente riferite" (Appendix 2 [s]); italics mine. The choice of Della Porta to report rather than enact this scene in his *Penelope* was cited by Dubowy ("Bemerkungen," 230) to distinguish between tragicomedy and epic.

Virtù summons the ghosts of Priamo, Anchise, Ettore, and Creusa from the Elysian Fields to enjoy Enea's marriage (Prologue). Latino, King of Latium, concerned about the marriage of his daughter Lavinia, consults the oracle Fauno, who reveals that she is destined to marry a stranger (1.1). Nereids and Tritons celebrate Enea, who, having disembarked at the mouth of the Tiber, rejoices at his arrival in Italy. After noting the appearance of good omens, he sends some of his Trojan followers as ambassadors to Latino, and others to hunt for food (1.2). [Meanwhile, in Latium],Turno reveals himself to be in love and is reproved by Numano, who departs as Lavinia appears (1.3). After having inveighed against Love, she greets Turno's protestations of love with a stern response (1.4). Enea's ambassador Ilioneo asks for assurance from Latino, who not only provides it but offers his daughter's hand in marriage to Enea (1.5).

Giunone, angered at Enea's safe arrival in Italy, summons Aletto from the Underworld to sow discord between the Latins and the Trojans, which he readily does (2.1). Happily singing, the shepherds Elminio and Silvia, Tirreo's children, flee when come upon by Ascanio and the other hunters (2.2). Ascanio wounds Silvia's deer, and Tirreo, attracted by the noise, joins with the other shepherds to attack the Trojans, and they withdraw, fighting (2.3). Turno and Amata inveigh against Latino and the Trojans, expressing in words the effects caused by Aletto (2.4). Aletto reports to Giunone on the discord created by the death of the deer, and Elminio, and the fury of Turno and Amata (2.5).

Concerned for the fate of her son, Enea, Venere begs Vulcano to provide him with special armor (3.1). Latino is comforted by the prospect of peace with the Trojans and Lavinia's marriage. Tirreo appears, demanding vengeance for his slain son. Amata inveighs against the Trojans, and Turno attempts to have the Temple of Janus opened to declare war. When Latino refuses, retiring to his palace, Giunone descends and throws open the Temple herself. Turno and his Rutulian soldiers scream for war, and Numano celebrates having to kill all the Trojans (3.2). Lavinia, hearing rumblings of war, wonders what will become of her and retires to the walls to observe Enea in battle (3.3). Enea, not yet having heard rumors of the Latins' threats against him, and invited by the amenities of the place, lies down to sleep on the banks of the Tiber, who warns him of the imminent danger and encourages him to battle. Awakened, Enea laments his new difficulties and recalls his past misfortunes, but is soon reinvigorated (3.4). Venere presents Enea with his new armor. Turno, reaching the Trojan camp, calls his soldiers to arms, and Acate comes out to warn Enea, who enters his tent to arm himself (3.5). Turno encourages his soldiers and Numano calls *his* soldiers to battle; when the enemy appears, he flees. The two squadrons fight (3.6).

Turno, thinking he is being blamed for the evil, proposes a duel with Enea, while Amata attempts in vain to dissuade him from sending a herald to the enemy camp to challenge his rival. Numano wants to be the first to battle the Trojans (4.1). Amata urges Lavinia to stop Turno from fighting Enea, but regretting her actions, departs in a fury (4.2). After various doubts, Lavinia, having observed Enea fighting from the city walls, confesses her love for him, and is encouraged by her maidservant to pursue her love, both of them hoping for a happy ending (4.3). Giove urges Venere and Giunone, the one in favor of Enea, the other against him, to make peace, proposing a future duel to decide their conflict (4.4). Ascanio thinks the time has come to acquire fame. Numano returns to torment the Trojans and, wounded by Ascanio, flees (4.5). Enea, having accepted Turno's challenge, sets out to engage him in combat. Latino, present of necessity, retires before the onset of the fight. Tolunnio, inspired by the appearance of an omen, tries to interrupt the duel by inciting a full battle. Enea laments and calls for Turno to fight with him. After losing his sword, Turno flees, and, followed by Enea, is killed offstage (4.6).

Enea emerges triumphant, encouraging his son to glory by showing him the spoils of the defeated enemy (5.1). Drante, Latino's ambassador, invites Enea to enter the city and marry Lavinia, which he does, followed by the Trojans (5.2). Giove exhorts Giunone to relent toward Enea, which she readily does, moved by his bravery (5.3). Enea, having entered the city and met Lavinia, talks with her of love (5.4). Latino welcomes Enea and grants him Lavinia as his wife, exciting the Trojans and Latins to invoke Himeneo, who, appearing with Venere and Giunone, join the happy couple, predicting as the fruits of their marriage the greatness of Rome and the birth and marvels of Venice (5.5).[37]

There is good reason for thinking that, as with *Il ritorno d'Ulisse,* the relationship of *Le nozze d'Enea* to its classical source may have been mediated by Dolce, at least in part. His version of Virgil's text in ottava rima, *Achille et Enea,* was first published in Venice in 1570 and reprinted in at least two successive years. Although the numerous Renaissance editions of the *Aeneid* in Latin and Italian meant that there were many more choices to consult, including an earlier translation by Dolce himself, *Achille et Enea* would have served well as a pony because it was abbreviated, boiled down to some rich essence, very much like his *Ulisse.*[38]

The Virgilian portion of *Achille et Enea* comprises twenty-five cantos (30–55), two or more of them distributed over each of the twelve books of the *Aeneid.*[39] As in Dolce's *Ulisse,* each canto of *Achille et Enea* is prefaced by an argomento and a series of allegories that provide a running interpretation of various actions and characters appearing in the canto; those of cantos 41, 42, 43, 45, 47, and 55 (the last) cover material found in the libretto of *Nozze.* That of canto 42 parallels the action (of acts 1 and 2) most closely.

---

37. Based on the *Argomento e scenario.* See Appendix 6.

38. *L'Achille et l'Enea di Messer Lodovico Dolce.* For a list of Renaissance editions and translations of the *Aeneid,* see R. R. Bolgar. *The Classical Heritage* (New York: Harper, 1954), 538–41; and, more recently, Kallendorf, *Virgil and the Myth of Venice,* appendices 1 and 2. Sevieri, *Le nozze,* 35 assumes that the *Nozze* librettist used the translation by Annibal Caro, which became standard after its posthumous publication in 1581, but Dolce's version would have been more convenient because, like his *Ulisse,* it was abbreviated—and annotated.

39. I consulted the editions of 1571 and 1572. Two years earlier, another Virgil translation by Dolce was published (*L'Enea di M. Lodovico Dolce, tratta dall'Eneide di Vergilio, all'illustrissimo et eccellentissimo signor Don Francesco de Medici principe di Fiorenze e di Siena* [Venice: Varisco & compagni: 1568]). In his list of Dolce's writings, Terpening (*Dolce*) categorizes the two volumes differently: *L'Achille et Enea* as an original work, *L'Enea* as a translation. Perhaps because in this case Dolce's translation is even more discursive than the original, its relationship to the libretto is less striking.

Riceve il Re Latin benignamente	King Latino kindly receives
D'Enea gli ambasciatori, a quai cortese	the ambassadors of Enea, to whom courteously
Da quanto gli chiederon largamente.	he gives generously what they ask.
Manda Giunon a seminar cortese	Giunone sends Aletto to inspire discord
Tra i Rutuli e i Latin con foco ardente,	among the Rutulians and the Latins with burning fire,
Aletto, che al gran Turno il petto accese.	which ignites great Turno's breast.
Fiede di Silvia, Ascanio il vago cervo	Ascanio wounds Silvia's lovely deer,
Onde spinge a vendetta il cor protervo.	which pushes proud hearts to vengeance.

The sequence of discursive allegories that follows—for Re Latino, Giunone, Amata, Turno, and Silvia—highlights, in order, the most important plot elements in the first two acts of the libretto. They explain the motivations of the characters, summarize their relationships, and describe the action. (Excerpts from the original texts of the Allegories, juxtaposed with the relevant passages from the scenario, are given in Appendix 6.)

Re Latino, showing compassion for a person who has been persecuted by Fortune, happily accepts Enea's peace offerings, having decided, according to his "allegoria" in the previous canto, to award Lavinia in marriage to Enea rather than Turno.[40] Giunone, not yet tired of persecuting Enea, goes to the Underworld to find Aletto, who will sow discord among the Latins and inflame Amata against him.[41] Amata, who madly dismisses her husband's deliberations, shows how easily women believe and embrace the worst, with no other reason than having a bad impression of an enemy. This should warn us not to be too ready to believe those who, inspired by anger and self-hatred, place their own desires above the good of others.[42] Turno, suddenly inflamed with disdain, tries in every way to prevent Enea from obtaining Lavinia as his wife, demonstrating how much jealousy can do in a human breast, and how easily a lover can be convinced that someone wants to take away the woman who has been promised to him. This shows the power of Love, which, depriving man of reason, forces him to

---

40. "Per il Re Latino, che con liete accoglienze abbraccia gli oratori mandatigli da Enea, offerendogli gratiosamente quanto era in poter suo, Si comprende la vera grandezza d'animo, e l'alta bontà d'un valoroso e saggio principe, ch'havendo compassione d'una persona perseguitata dalla fortuna, dispone ogni sua forza, per sollevarla, mostrandosi ugualmente a tutti benigno, ed amorevole."

41. "Per Giunone, che ancor non satia di perseguitar Enea, va nell'inferno a ritrovar Aletto, per metter discordia tra i Latini e infiammar'il petto d'Amata, Si conosce come un'animo sdegnato non pensa in altro, fuor che in levar l'inimico, e repute a grand'honor'il soffocarlo per via di tradimenti, e che una Donna per l'odio conceputo non riguarda a ragion, se ben vedrà di vendicarlo d'un minimo sospetto, non che d'una offesa."

42. "Per Amata, che come pazza disprezza la deliberatione del marito, si dinota, quanto sien facili le donne a creder' ed abbracciar'il suo peggio, non havendo altra ragion, fuor che una pessima impressione di persona maligna, ed inimica. Il che ci devrebbe esser d'avvertimento, che non siamo così pronti a creder'a chi si muove per rabbia, e per odio di sé stessi, i quali prepongono il disiderio loro al ben d'altri."

desire his own ruin, as if it were good.[43] And, finally, Silvia, who, as if maddened, cries for revenge at the top of her lungs for her wounded deer, shows how women who fail to consider the consequences of their actions can ruin a whole kingdom for a small thing. This should be a warning not to resort to arms for mere appetite or for unrestrained desire.[44]

Several of the argomenti and allegories suggest that the librettist may have been influenced by them. The shepherdess Silvia, for instance, is highlighted by being allegorized in canto 42, as we have just noted. (She is allotted only a couple of sentences in Virgil.) This might help to explain her prominence in the libretto, where she is given an entire scene—and aria—to herself.[45] The most striking confluence between Dolce and the libretto, however, concerns the ending. While the wedding of Enea and Lavinia and its connection to future civilizations are only implied at the end of the *Aeneid*,[46] the two are specifically linked in the argomento of Dolce's final canto:

Canto 55 (p. 535)

Arde dal foco Ardea, piange la morte	Ardea burns with fire. Daunus laments the death
Danno del suo figliuol. Enea dissegna	of his son. Enea designs a
Nova città: Lavinia per consorte	new city, takes Lavinia for consort,
Prende; e del Re Latin nel seggio regna.	and reigns on the throne as Latin king.
Ode da Vener la felice sorte;	He hears from Venus of his happy fate,
De la sua descendentia illustre, e degna	of his illustrious and worthy descendants.
Purga d'Enea ne l'acqua il corpo, e prende	Venus cleanses Enea's body in water, and
Vener l'anima pura, e al ciel ascende.[47]	takes his pure soul and ascends to heaven.

43. "Per Turno, che di subito infiammato di sdegno, cerca in tutti modi, che Enea non ottenga Lavinia per mogliera, si vede quanto la gelosia possa in un petto humano, e quanto sia facile dar'ad intender'a un'innamorato, che altri voglia privarlo di quella donna, che a lui era stata promessa. Onde può sapere ognuno, quanto sieno potenti le forze d'Amore, che privando l'huomo di ragione, lo sforzano a desiderar sotto specie di bene la propria ruina."

44. "Per Silvia, che come forsennata ad alta voce grida vendetta del cervo feritole, si manifesta, che le donne per picciola cosa son cagione di ruinar'un Regno, non considerando esse il fine di ciò che tentano. Il che doverebbe ammonir più d'uno a non moversi all'armi così leggiermente per appetito, e sfrenato loro desiderio."

45. The Tiber scene in the libretto may have been similarly influenced. Cf. the librettist's remarks, discussed later, describing how the river Tebro speaks to Enea, rousing him from his slumber and convincing him to go to war. The Tiber is allegorized in Dolce's canto 43: "Per il dio del Tebro, che consigliando Enea l'assicura della Guerra con Turno, si dinota, che la candidezza dell'huomo nelle avversità e sempre mai favorita, ed aiutata de' cieli, non mancando essi di favorir' i preghi de' giusti, e de' buoni" (From the god of the Tiber, who advising Enea, reassures him about the war with Turno, one understands that the purity of man in adversity is always favored and aided by the heavens, who do not fail to favor the prayers of the just and the good).

46. The only mention of Lavinia at all in the final scene—"Lavinia is thine for wife"—occurs in line 937 (Virgil, *Aeneid,* trans. H.R. Fairclough, [Cambridge, MA: Harvard University Press, 1978], 2: 363).

47. The Venetian Dolce would certainly have been thinking of Aeneas's Rome as part of the prehistory of Venice. He interpolates a similar, but even more pointed non-Virgilian detail in his tragedy *La Didone,* act 2, scene 2. When Aeneas recounts Mercury's command that he leave Carthage in order to secure a glorious future for his descendants, Dolce adds a specific reference to Venice: "E i cui tardi nipoti, dopo molto / Girar di cielo, et

It was only a small step for the author of *Nozze* to turn this material into an effective *fin lieto* for his drama, one that paralleled that of *Ritorno*. Beyond that, more clearly than the Virgilian original, Dolce's final argomento provided the scaffolding on which the patriotic librettist could construct a particular political meaning for *Nozze*, as part of the myth of Venice.

Five Acts or Three

In airing the Aristotelian "rules" of tragedy, Torcigliani occasionally reveals the shortcomings of his own work, especially in comparison with his model, Badoaro's *Ritorno*. For the most part, however, he offers justification for some of the most distinctive shared "classical" features of the two librettos. Perhaps most striking is the five-act structure. This organizational scheme distinguishes *Ritorno* and *Nozze* immediately, not only from *Incoronazione* but from practically all other operas of the time.[48] As we have seen, Torcigliani was well aware that this classical scheme was old-fashioned, but he chose it anyway, as he explained, essentially to promote verisimilitude, the illusion of the passage of time. This has as much to do with the intervals between the acts as with the acts themselves, but a further justification for five-act structure—tacked on at the end of his explanation, almost as an afterthought—does relate to the internal organization of the acts: "It should be added that catastrophes do not work well within acts."[49] The implication is that if his libretto had been divided into three acts, one or another of the catastrophes would have had to occur within an act.[50] The author clearly conceived his drama in five carefully shaped acts (see Table 14 below, p. 160), which he outlines as follows:

In the first act . . . Enea is calmed by peace with Latino. In the second the furies spread the seeds of discord. In the third and fourth the consequences [of this action] are played out, ending with the death of Turno and the opposite catastrophe of the improvement of Fortune *[terminando con la morte di Turno con l'altra catastrofe contraria in miglioramento di Fortuna]*; which causes several peripeteias, not only in Enea, but in Lavinia, in Turno, and in Amata as well. The episode resolves in the fifth act with the recognition of Enea as truly the

---

lungo spatio d'anni, / A un'altra gran città initio / Con più felice augurio in mezzo l'acque / Ove la pace sempre, ove l'amore, / Ove virtude, ove ogni bel costume / Terranno il pregio in fin che duri il mondo." The passage is quoted in Kallendorf, *Virgil and the Myth of Venice*, 26–27. For the Trojan aspect of the myth of Venice, see above, Chap. 1, n. 32.

48. The exceptions include *Adone* (1639), *Arianna* (1640), *Ulisse errante* (1644), and *La prosperità infelice di Giulio Cesare* (1646), which is the only five-act libretto not subtitled "tragedia." See below, n. 66.

49. Discussed above (p. 132). "Che le catastrofe non paiono bene nel mezzo degli atti." The term *catastrofe* is Aristotle's. Of the three stages he advocates as necessary for catharsis in tragedy, the *protasi* prepares the tension; the *epitasi* brings the climax; and the *catastrofe* brings the resolution (*Poetics* 1450b), Barnes ed., para. 7.

50. See below for an analysis of three-act structure, in which act 1 = acts 1 + 2, and act 2 = acts 3 + 4; catastrophes, or resolutions, do indeed occur in the middle of acts.

one destined by Fate for the glory of Italy, whence he is more dearly welcomed by Latino, acclaimed by his former enemies, and with the concurrence of Giunone, formerly against him, the wedding is celebrated by Himeneo, god of marriage. (Appendix 2 [r])

In emphasizing the importance of the five-act structure to his own libretto, Torcigliani once again sharpens our perception of his model, *Ritorno*. The issue focuses attention on the troubling inconsistency among the sources of the earlier opera that we considered above. To recapitulate: although all of the known manuscript copies of Badoaro's libretto are in the classical five acts, these are reduced to three in the score. And it is in that three-act arrangement that the work is usually performed. Act 1 of the three-act version runs through the fourth scene of Badoaro's act 2; act 2 goes from 2.5 to the end of act 4; and the final acts of the two versions are the same.[51]

As we have already noted, the different act division is far from the only discrepancy between the sources of text and music of *Ritorno:* they also have two completely different prologues, and one full scene in the libretto is omitted in the score. In addition, many shorter passages of text are cut or reorganized in the music. The revision that transformed the five-act structure into three acts stands apart from all the other alterations, however. It could not have taken place before Monteverdi set the work since, as we have seen, the original five-act markings are still visible in the score. Nor could Monteverdi have been responsible for it, for, possibly even more than in *Nozze,* the five-act structure is intrinsic to *Ritorno,* and not only to the libretto but to Monteverdi's setting as well.[52]

---

51. Sergio Vartolo (Brilliant Classics, 2006) recorded the work in five acts. So did René Jacobs (Harmonia Mundi, 1992), but only because, in the three-act version, he judged the second act too long and the third too short. The work has also been performed in two acts, following Leppard's arrangement, and not only at Glyndebourne. Leppard's break occurs at the end of act 2 of the five-act version (2.4 of the three-act version) (see Table 7 above, Chap. 4, p. 71). Dubowy ("Bemerkungen," 237) justly points out that the only possible place to begin act 2 is between scenes 4 and 5, when the stage has emptied. (All the scenes before it and all those after it are linked.) Silke Leopold, *Claudio Monteverdi: Music in Transition* (Oxford: Oxford University Press, 1991), 201, thought the three-act structure good enough to have been Monteverdi's idea, but if so, it was certainly a second thought. Cf. Chap. 7 below, nn. 1, 3.

52. As I will show, this was probably not the case with *Nozze.* That music may have been written after the libretto was already reduced to three acts. Interestingly, the composer does seem to have been involved in deciding on the number of acts in one of his earlier works, *La finta pazza Licori,* which, however, was evidently conceived in three acts, but then expanded to five. This can be gleaned from various letters of 1627 from the composer to Alessandro Striggio concerning this project; all references in the letters are to the edition by Éva Lax (*Claudio Monteverdi, Lettere* [Florence: Olschki, 1994]; italics mine). No. 92 (1 May) speaks of the libretto as comprising "quattrocento versi"; no. 93 (7 May): "Lo porrà in ordine diviso *in 3 atti* o come piacerà a Sua Altezza Serenissima"; no. 98 (20 June): "l'ha ridotto *in cinque atti.*" Several of Monteverdi's remarks in no. 100 (10 July): "Ogni atto averà azzione nova da spiegare" and "la pazzia finta incomincerà nel terzo atto" suggest a concern for the shaping of individual acts that is reminiscent of the anonymous author of *Nozze.* (For further discussion of the Licori project, see below, Chap. 6.) On the reduction of another five-act drama to three acts, see Angelo Solerti, "Feste musicali alla corte di Savoia nella prima metà del secolo XVII," *RMI* 11 (1904): 675–724, at 689.

Perhaps the most remarkable quality of *Ritorno* is its dramatic momentum. Once launched, Ulisse's pursuit of his goal is unrelenting; resolution becomes increasingly inevitable. The drive toward that resolution is carefully planned to accelerate over the five acts, for each of them culminates with an action that marks a successive step in Ulisse's journey homeward (see Table 7 above, Chap. 4). Act 1 ends with his rejoicing at his arrival in Ithaca, act 2 with his reunion with Telemaco, act 3 with his vow to slay the Suitors, act 4 with his defeat of the Suitors, and act 5, of course, with his reunion with Penelope.[53]

Monteverdi's music forcefully supports this structure. Each action (and act) is sealed with expansive lyrical expression for Ulisse: the first with his aria "O fortunato," the second with his arioso "Vanne alla madre," the third with his joyous, indeed manic laughter, "Rido né so perche," the fourth with his impassioned battle cry, and the fifth with the love duet. Within the larger context of ascetic, speech-like exchanges that characterize so much of this score, these lyrical passages stand out and underline the significance of the crucial moments they mark. And it is the composer himself, and not the librettist, who is responsible for marking these particular moments with lyricism: with the exception of the final love duet, signaled in the text by a distinct change in metric structure (from *versi sciolti* to regularly rhymed and alternating *quinari*) and formal alternation of lines between Ulisse and Penelope, the act-closing lyrical emphasis was essentially Monteverdi's doing.

At the end of act 1, the composer converted Ulisse's shapeless eleven-line speech, with its irregularly recurring refrains (underlined), into the expansive strophic-refrain aria "O fortunato"(repetitions here and elsewhere in italics) (Example 1; the two "stanzas"— one comprising seven lines, the other four—are superimposed over the same bass):

<u>O fortunato</u>, *o, o, o, o fortunato* <u>Ulisse</u>,
Fuggi del tuo dolor
L'antico error;

---

53. Cf. Dubowy's diagram showing the convergence of Penelope's and Ulisse's two worlds ("Bemerkungen," 342–43). Dubowy too sees the five-act structure as intrinsic to Badoaro's drama, and presents a compelling analysis of the differences between it and the three-act version. Focusing on the shifting function of the staging, he concludes that the reviser changed to three acts not because it was the more modern structure, but because the five acts were unfeasible (pp. 235–37). He also argues that some of the cuts (like the Mercurio scene) were not Monteverdi's but the editor's, introduced when the work was transformed from a five-act *festa teatrale* to a three-act *tragicommedia*, or epic. His theory that these cuts were present in the exemplar from which our score was copied may be plausible, but his grammatical arguments in support of that hypothesis are not. In particular, he misunderstands the use of the plural in "maninconiche." In my view, the work was never a *festa teatrale*, but I agree with Dubowy that the transformation from five to three acts was largely a matter of convenience. On the meaning of "maninconiche," see above, Chap. 3, n. 22, and Chap. 4, n. 19; also below.

EXAMPLE 1. Ulisse, "O fortunato" (*Il ritorno d'Ulisse*, 1.9, mm. 315–62).

Lascia, *lascia* il pianto,
Dolce, *dolce* canto
Dal tuo cor lieto disserra;
<u>Non si disperi più</u>, *non si disperi più, non si disperi più* <u>mortale in terra.</u>

<u>O fortunato,</u> *o, o, o, o fortunato* <u>Ulisse,</u>
Dolce [*Cara*] vicenda si può soffrir, *si può soffrir,*
Hor diletto, hor martir, *hor martir,* hor pace, hor guerra, *hor guerra.*
<u>Non si disperi più</u>, *non si disperi più, non si disperi più* <u>mortale in terra.</u>

(O fortunate Ulisse, flee the pangs of your former woes, cease your lament. Let the sweet song release itself from your glad heart; despair no more, ye earthly mortals. O fortunate Ulisse, one can suffer sweet vicissitudes, now delight, now martyrdom, now peace, now war. Despair no more . . .)

The text supporting the arioso elaboration at the end of act 2 is even less formally suggestive, comprising merely a rhymed quatrain of three *settenari tronchi* and an *endecasillabo;* Monteverdi expands and intensifies this by extensive repetition of individual words and by a reprise of the opening, much repeated, line at the end for closure (Example 2):

Vanne, *vanne* alla madre, va'!
Porta, *porta* alla reggia il piè;
Sarò tosto con te, *sarò tosto con te,*
Ma pria canuto il pel ritornerà.
Vanne, vanne alla madre, và, vanne, vanne alla madre, va'.

(Go to your mother, go. Take foot to the royal palace. I will soon be with you, but first I will don my old-man's skin again.)

EXAMPLE 2. Ulisse, "Vanne alla madre" (*Il ritorno d'Ulisse,* 2.7 [or 2.3], mm. 158–68).

At the conclusion to act 3 (scene 7), Monteverdi shapes Badoaro's strongly metric but asymmetrical five-line text into a little bipartite aria, dilating with particular relish upon Ulisse's laugh (Example 3):

Godo anch'io, né so come.
Rido, *rido,* né so perché, *rido, rido, rido, rido, né so perché.*
Tutto gioisco,
Ringiovinisco,
Ben lieto, *ben lieto, lieto* affè.
Tutto gioisco,
Ringiovanisco,
Ben lieto, ben lieto affè.

(I too rejoice, but know not how. I laugh, but know not why. I rejoice in everything, I am rejuvenated, and very happy indeed.)

The already dramatic conclusion of act 4 is intensified by Monteverdi's vivid exploitation of the *stile concitato*. Here he divides Ulisse's five lines (two rhymed *settenario-endecasillabo* couplets, plus a final *endecasillabo*) into a pair of parallel two-line phrases separated by a *sinfonia di guerra*, culminating in a furious accompanied statement of the concluding line, much expanded through internal text repetition. This is presumably reiterated until the stage action has been completed and the Suitors lie mortally wounded (see Facsimiles 16 and 17 above, Chap. 4):

> Giove nel suo tuonar grida vendetta, *vendetta, vendetta,*
> Così l'arco saetta, *così l'arco saetta.*
> [*Sinfonia da guerra*]
> Minerva altri rincora, altri avvilisce
> Così l'arco ferisce, *così l'arco ferisce.*
> Alle morti, alle stragi, *alle morti, alle stragi,* alle *ruine* [rovine], *alle ruine, alle ruine.*
> *Alle morti, alle stragi, alle morti, alle stragi, alle ruine, alle ruine, alle ruine.*[54]

> (Giove in his thunder cries vengeance. Thus the bow shoots. Minerva encourages some, discourages others, thus the bow wounds. To death, to slaughter, to ruin.)

Highlighted by the composer, the five stages of Ulisse's progress are measured against Penelope's obdurate immovability. In opposition to Ulisse's motion, her stasis is reaffirmed at or near the beginning of each act. But what is so impressive is that the distance between the two characters, at its maximum in the first act, diminishes in each successive one. Ulisse moves closer to his intractable object, while Penelope remains unyielding until the very end of the opera.[55] At first, the characters inhabit distinct regions, the courtly hall that oppresses Penelope and the countryside of Ithaca that has welcomed Ulisse through its representative the swineherd; widely separated in the first two acts, these domains are linked for the first time in act 3 by Eumete's successive appearance in both.[56] In act 4, husband and wife finally occupy the same space, but she does not recognize him. Full recognition and reconciliation are postponed until the very end of act 5.

As he does for Ulisse, Monteverdi provides striking music for Penelope at all of these important formal junctures, though, significantly, as we shall see, her music is more impressive for its dour restraint than for its exuberance:[57] In act 1 her long opening lament sets the stage

---

54. This scene must have been shocking to its original audience. It certainly is to a modern one. See above, nn. 3 and 36, on the showing of violence on stage.

55. Recall how Badoaro's revision of Homer increases the effect of the final scene.

56. Dubowy ("Bemerkungen," 235) notices this and makes a nice point about the telescoping of the acts from 1 to 4, followed by a long fifth act. He suggests that the constant shifting of spaces indicates that the Ulisse and Penelope actions might be considered as taking place simultaneously until Eumete provides the connection by going from one realm to the next: at this point, narrative time takes on new urgency. The idea of simultaneity is reinforced by the argomento, in which several new scenes are introduced with the word "intanto" (in italics in Appendix 5, A). Penelope's opening monologue, for instance, is described *after* Ulisse's landing on Ithaca is reported.

57. See Ellen Rosand, "Monteverdi's *Il ritorno d'Ulisse in patria* and the Power of Music," *COJ* 4 (1992): 75–80; and Tim Carter, "'In Love's Harmonious Consort'? Penelope and the Interpretation of *Il ritorno d'Ulisse in patria*," *COJ* 5 (1993): 517–23.

for the entire subsequent action. In act 2 her dialogue with her lady-in-waiting Melanto jux-
taposes musically their two opposing points of view; while Melanto sings unstintingly, Penelope remains rooted in speech, renouncing all pleasure, musical as well as sexual. Monteverdi
expands the four-line refrain provided by Badoaro to close both of Melanto's speeches, creating a little bipartite aria whose phrases trail off into hedonistic melismas;[58] the pure sensu-
ousness of her wordless song heightens the contrast to Penelope's emphatically non-musical
expression, emphasizing the incompatibility of the two women and their views of love.

In act 3, Penelope counters the Suitors' "Ama dunque, sì sì / dunque riama un dì" with
an adamant couplet, "Non voglio amar, no, no / ch'amando penerò." These are the first
two of her six lines of text, greatly expanded through repetition and musical sequence.
(Cf. Table 8 above, Chap. 4.) The Suitors then repeat their request, whereupon she completes the remainder of her text, closing her statement with a return to her initial couplet
of refusal, expanded even further:

> Ama dunque sì, sì;
> Dunque riama un dì.
> *Ama dunque, sì, sì;*
> *Dunque riama un dì, dunque riama, dunque riama un dì, un dì.*
> Non voglio amar, no, no,
> *Non voglio amar, no, no, no, no, no, no, no, no,*
> Ch'amando penerò.
> *Non voglio, non voglio amar, no, no,*
> *Ch'amando penerò.*
> *Ama dunque . . .*
> Cari tanto mi siete
> Quanto più ardenti, *ardenti,* ardete;
> Ma non m'appresso, *non m'appresso* all'amoroso gioco
> Che lungi è bel più che vicino il foco, *che lungi è bel, è bel, è bel, più che vicino il foco.*
> Non voglio . . .

> (Love, then, yes, yes. And then love again, one day. I do not wish to love, no, no, for loving
> I will suffer. You are as dear to me as you ardently burn; but do not approach me in the game
> of love, for fire is more beautiful from afar than from near.)

Once again, Monteverdi has intensified the effect of her refusal not only by his emphatic musical setting of the lines but by providing an extra statement of them at the end
of her speech. The increase in interaction between Penelope and the Suitors caused by
this editorial intervention on the composer's part is a milder version of the kind of intercalation that is so prevalent in *Incoronazione*, as we shall see.[59]

---

58. Discussed and illustrated in Chap. 7, pp. 269–72. The refrain is inexact in all of the librettos but exact
in the score.

59. See Chap. 7. As noted below, there is some evidence of intercalation in *Nozze* too.

In act 4, Penelope's remonstrance with Telemaco is notable for its depressed immobility in contrast to her son's lengthy and enthusiastic, if not very tactful, description of Helen's beauty and Paris's delight in it. Penelope's reaction is cold and brief; her utterance lies at the very bottom of her range, moving repeatedly downward, and fixed solidly in d, her primary key. Her music literally dampens his enthusiasm.[60] Her most memorable—though least characteristic—music comes not at the beginning of act 5 but, appropriately, at the end: her joyful aria and duet with Ulisse.

In the three-act version of the opera this carefully planned musico-dramatic structure is obscured, not to say obliterated. As Ulisse's most expansive music no longer closes each act in turn, the inexorability of his stepwise progress is blunted,[61] and as Penelope no longer opens any act after the first, the sense of narrowing distance between her and Ulisse tends to be diluted. Other patterns in the five-act structure lose some of their impact in the revision as well, such as the regularly reiterated assault of Melanto and her lover Eurimaco on Penelope's values. Originally placed near the beginning of all but one of the acts, their lascivious view of love comes into direct conflict with her rigid chastity.[62] In the three-act version, however, two of these assaults occur in act 1 and one in the middle of act 2.

All of these observations assume that act division was more than a mere mechanical or literary device—that it entailed a pause of some kind, during which, as Torcigliani described it, the audience could appreciate the illusion of the passage of time. And indeed the scenario of *Nozze* (as well as all but one of the librettos of that work) confirms that its intervals were more than episodes of quiet time; they were filled with intermedi: a royal entertainment, a dance of the furies, a battle moresca, and a victory dance.[63] Whether or not the entr'actes of *Ritorno* were similarly filled—two intermedi are built into the drama, at the ends of acts 1 and 4[64]—some kind of articulation surely must have

---

60. See Chap. 7, p. 252, for the omission in this scene of her second speech. Monteverdi allows her only one.

61. Although the final act of both versions is the same, the others are different. The new first act consists of thirteen scenes: the original act 1 plus four scenes from act 2, ending with Eumete's welcome of Ulisse (it is Eumete's music that is the most memorable here, not Ulisse's). The second act (twelve scenes in all) then begins with Telemaco and Minerva and ends with the slaying of the Suitors. See Table 7 above, Chap. 4.

62. Melanto–Penelope in acts 2 and 5, Melanto–Eurimaco in acts 1 and 3 (Eurimaco disappears in act 4, presumably to die, as in Homer).

63. Only one intermedio is specifically called for in the three-act libretto, a "ballo di Furie e Mostri" at the end of act 1. Act 2 apparently ended without an intermedio. The intermedio that concludes act 3 of the five-act version, the battle moresca, would have come in the middle of act 2 of the three-act version. It is avoided by having the battle and Numano's flight take place together, earlier in the scene. The final battle cries of the warring armies are dampened somewhat in the three-act version: "Alle stragi, su, su" replaces "Alle stragi, su, su, alle morti." The intermedi of *Le nozze* are described in the argomento (see Appendix 6). Distinctions in the brief rubrics of the intermedi may help to clarify the relationships between manuscript librettos. For instance, among other similarities, the rubrics are exactly the same in five different librettos (nos. 3, 8, 9, 10, and 11), suggesting that they were copied from the same exemplar. See Table 5 above, Chap. 3.

64. And a third, a "ballo Greco" for eight moors, is indicated in the middle of act 3 (3.3). According to the rubric in the score (Facsimile 12, lower right margin), the ballo *was* to be performed, *pace* Dubowy, though, as is the convention in these scores, no music is given. See Alm, "Winged Feet."

occurred, if only because the work was so long. The intervals would have set into relief the individuality and careful shaping of each act.[65]

Ritorno was deliberately and effectively conceived in five acts, and then revised into three. As we have seen from the physical appearance of the score itself, in Chapter 4, the modification must have taken place some time after Monteverdi's original setting of 1640. The reasons for the alteration are more difficult to explain. Aside from the genre-change hypothesis proposed by Dubowy, or the possible streamlining for traveling purposes, it is likely that by 1641 five-act structure, already acknowledged as old-fashioned in 1640 (by Torgicliani), could no longer be sustained, even at the wealthiest of the Venetian theaters, SS. Giovanni e Paolo. This likelihood is strengthened by the fact that *Nozze*, too, seems to have undergone a revision that transformed it into three acts, possibly at around the same time. Given Torcigliani's emphasis on the necessity of five-act structure for his tragedy, this would seem a particularly egregious alteration.[66]

LE NOZZE D'ENEA: STRUCTURE AND PERFORMANCE

We have already noted that one of the eleven surviving manuscript librettos of *Nozze* differs substantially from the rest (no. 5 in Table 5 above, Chap. 3).[67] The most obvious distinguishing feature of many in this unique libretto is that it alone is in three acts. While it appears to be the earliest of the manuscript librettos—one of the two or three to have been copied in the seventeenth century rather than the eighteenth—it clearly represents a second version, a revision of the original five-act text.[68] Moreover, even though the scenario published in conjunction with the Venetian production of 1641 is in five acts, the three-act

---

65. The passage of time required in *Nozze* between acts 3 and 4 (where the battle of the Trojans and Rutulians takes place, the results of which are known and discussed in the very next scene, at the dawning of a new day) is lacking in the three-act version. Change of place or set is not possible because some of the same characters remain on stage (characters who have just fought [Turno], and one who has actually fled [Numano]). Atypically, the resultant strain on credulity is not compensated for in the three-act text. See the discussion of the three-act conversion below, pp. 166–67. In *Ritorno*, on the other hand, the new act break that falls between scenes 4 and 5 of act 2 works well: it separates the Eumete–Ulisse recognition scene in the woods from the scene between Telemaco and Minerva in the heavenly chariot. Nor do the missing act breaks between 2–3 and 3–4 interfere with the credible passage of time, since the changes of setting they allow are preserved within the new act 2.

66. It is just possible that, like *Ritorno*, the five acts were reduced to three in order to avoid the expenditures (for dancers, stage designs, even music and choreography) of two extra intermedi. I suggested in Chapter 4 that *Ritorno* could have been reduced for one or both of the revivals. That three-act structure was not yet conventional in these years is demonstrated by Giulio Strozzi's defense of it in his preface to *La Delia:* "Ho partita con qualche metodo l'opera in tre azzioni. Division commune di tutte le cose: principio, mezzo, e fine. Gli antichi ne formavano cinque, perché vi frammettevano il canto. Questa ch'e tutta canto, non ha dibisogno di tante posate" (pp. 6–7).

67. The degree of agreement among the others, as I noted, suggests that they were all copied from a single exemplar—or several closely related ones.

68. *Nozze* no. 5 is bound with *Ritorno* no. 5 in I-Vmc 3331, which is certainly a seventeenth-century manuscript.

libretto comes closer than any other source to the narrative it outlines. This becomes clear from a three-way comparison of the scenario with the five-act and three-act texts, which we need to consider in some detail (Table 14; see also Appendix 6).[69]

At first glance the correspondence seems close enough. Only one scene, for Silvia, was apparently added after the scenario was printed (**A**: act 2.5 = 1.12) and only one group of scenes in the scenario was omitted—the two successive scenes in act 4 (marked **B**): scene 4 for the Gods, in which Giove urges the warring goddesses Venere and Giunone to make peace, and scene 5, Ascanio's youthful attempt to show his bravery by wounding Numano. An earlier scene in the same act, scene 2, for Amata and Lavinia, is cut only in the three-act version (**C**), though Amata's final speech, lamenting the defeat of her hopes for Lavinia's union with Turno, is saved—tacked on to the end of the previous scene.

In a few cases all librettos break a scenario scene into several different scenes, but act 3, scene 4 corresponds to a single scene of the three-act libretto, whereas it accounts for three distinct scenes in the five-act version (**D**): Enea's sleep monologue (3.4), his conversation with Tebro (3.5), and his renewed commitment to fighting the Rutulians (3.6). The scenario's description of his actions, "Enea si duole de novi travagli, e rammemora le passate disgratie, ma tosto anco torna a rinvigorirsi" (Enea laments his new torments, and remembers his past suffering, but soon reenergizes himself), accords better with the three-act text than with the five-act version, where the memories of his past suffering are reduced from ten eloquent lines to a single generality: "O ciel dunque non basta / A raddolcir tuo sdegno / Ciò che soffersi ohimè d'empio, e d'indegno" (O Heaven, is the wickedness and indignity I have suffered not enough to soften your hatred?). This is one of several examples of the privileged relationship between the scenario and the three-act libretto. (This passage is discussed further below.)[70]

There are many other small differences between scenario and librettos, differences that seem to have nothing to do with the revision—in its scene divisions, for example. The description of act 2, scene 2 (Elmino and Silvia) mentions the arrival of Ascanio's hunting party, which does not take place in the librettos until the next scene, and the end of act 5 does not reflect the librettos because Latino is already present in scene 4 and does not "sopraggiungere" in scene 5. Some of these disparities may simply be the result of differing conceptions of scene division in the two kinds of sources: in librettos, characters' entrances usually indicate a scene change, whereas scenarios aim at a more efficient description covering dramatic units.

---

69. Although Savieri, *Le nozze*, acknowledges that no. 5 is probably closer to "l'evento teatrale" (p. 32), she adduces only minimal evidence, namely "la presenza di [un discreto numero di] indicazioni didascaliche," concluding that "per le sue caratteristiche è più vicino alla realizzazione scenico-operistico." In fact, no. 5 differs from the scenario in a number of ways besides the number of acts, cutting several scenes and rearranging others. With one exception, however (that of 4.2), the cuts are shared by all the other librettos; the rearrangements, though, seem to be connected to the reduction to three acts.

70. Enea's recital of his past suffering must have been an important part of the libretto, since it is also mentioned in the argomento (further evidence that the three-act version was the one performed) (see Appendix 2 [i]).

TABLE 14
Structure of *Le nozze d'Enea e Lavinia*

Scenario	Five Acts	Setting	Characters	Three Acts	Virgil/Dolce
	Prologue(s)			Prologue	
	Act 1			Act 1	
1	1	[Outdoors, kingdom]	Latino–Fauno	1	41
2	2	[Sea]	Tritons–Nereids	2	
	3	Land	Enea–Ascanio–Acate–Ilioneo–Trojans	3	42
3	4	Kingdom	[Latino]–Turno–Numano	4	
4	5	Garden	Lavinia–Turno	6	
5	6		Latino–Ilioneo	5	
		INTERMEDIO: *Giuochi*		5	
	Act 2				
1	1	Heaven	Giunone–Aletto	7	42
2	2	Forest	Silvia–Elmino	9	
3	3		Ascanio–Niso–Eurialo–Coro	10	
	4		[Ascanio–Niso–Eurialo–Coro] Tereo–shepherds	11	42
	5		A [Silvia, *not in scenario*]	12	
4	6	Kingdom	Turno–Amata	8	
5	7		Aletto–Giunone	13	
		INTERMEDIO: *Ballo dei furie e mostri*		5	
	Act 3			Act 2	
1	1	[Heaven]	Venere–Vulcano	1	44
2	2	[Kingdom]	Latino–Tereo–Amata–Turno–Giunone–Numano	2	
3	3		Lavinia	3	
4	4	[Outdoors]	Enea	4	
D(4)	5		Enea–Tebro		
D(4)	6		Enea–Tebro–Venere		43
5	7		Venere–Enea	5	45
6	8	[Battlefield]	Turno–Numano–Rutuli–Troiani	6	45
		INTERMEDIO: *Moresca dei soldati* E		5	
	Act 4				
1	1	Kingdom	Latino–Amato–Turno–Numano–Araldo–Venere?	7	
2	2		Amata–Lavinia [not in 3 acts]	—C	
3	3		Lavinia–Damigella	8	
4	—B	Heaven	Giove–Venere–Giunone [*scenario only*]		

TABLE 14 *(continued)*

	Act 5			Act 3	
5	—B		Ascanio–Numano [*scenario only*]		45
6	4		Enea–Turno–Troiani	9	
		INTERMEDIO: Ballo dei Troiani		5	
1	1	[Kingdom]	Enea–Ascanio–Acate–Troiani	1	50
2	2		Enea–Ascanio–Acate–Troiani–Drante	2	
3	3	[Heaven]	Giove–Giunone	3	
4	4	[Kingdom]	Lavinia–Enea–Latino–Rutuli–Troiani	4	
5	5		Lavinia–Enea–Latino–Rutuli–Troiani–Imeneo–Venere–Giunone–Amore	5	55

Although the scenario fails to describe a few important incidents at the point they occur, such as the death of Elminio in 2.3, it describes others for which there is no trace in any libretto. Once again in act 4, the lengthy description of Enea's confrontation with Turno in scene 6 refers to the ill omen of the swan: "Tolunnio augure all'apparir dell'augurio del cigno procura sturbar il duello con l'attaccar la battaglia universale" (Tolunnio, the augur, at the sight of the omen of the swan, interrupts the duel with a call to universal arms; *Aeneid*, 12.238 ff.), which is never mentioned in the text.

Most of the discrepancies with the scenario apply to all of the librettos equally, as we have seen. Some can be explained by the different goals of the two kinds of sources, as outlined in Chapter 3. Designed specifically to help the theater audience follow the action, and possibly also as advertisement for a prospective performance, the scenario aimed at a concise description of the action unfolding on stage. It was presumably published as close to the premiere as possible, so that it could incorporate whatever last-minute changes in the text—the reordering of scenes, the omission or addition of materials—might have been required by the stage director or the performers to suit the particular production. The librettos, on the other hand, are more likely to reflect the poetic text as the librettist wrote it, before being subjected to such modifications. This is evidently true of the five-act texts of *Nozze*, but, as we shall see, not the three-act version.

Indeed, discrepancies with the scenario that are restricted to the five-act version set the agreements with the three-act text in relief. The situation with act 4, scene 4—treated as a single scene in the scenario and three-act libretto, but broken into several scenes in the five-act one—has already been mentioned. The scenario and the three-act libretto are alone in omitting one of the most distinctive portions of the five-act text: a second prologue, spoken by Virgil's ghost. This item was evidently included for its purely literary

effect, rather than for any dramatic purpose—indeed, it is quite unlikely that such a prologue would ever have been sung.[71]

Even more significantly, the three-act libretto is the only one to conclude with Himeneo's political speech as described in the scenario, the speech that actually spells out the
relationship of the opera to the myth of Venice. This is a relationship, it goes without saying, that would have been especially relevant to a Venetian audience—but presumably to
no other. The omission of the speech in all the five-act librettos—and thus the omission of
the explicit connection to the myth—is another indication that these represent a more
generic literary version of the text, possibly intended for commemorative publication—or
conceivably for performance outside Venice.[72]

We should remember, finally, that the three-act libretto is the only one to share with
the scenario the telltale title-page formula indicating that performance is in the future:
"da recitarsi" in the libretto, "da rappresentarsi" in the scenario.[73] (No *Ritorno* librettos
have that designation: they either have "rappresentato" or no verb at all, and no *Incoronazione* librettos have it either.) In contrast, all but one of the five-act *Nozze* librettos
allude to performance in the past, "rappresentata." This confirms that the five-act manuscripts were copied later—after the performance—and therefore were essentially commemorative, not to say literary, in purpose. To be sure, their exemplar must have been
much earlier.[74] Most likely, it was the text as written by the librettist—and even as given to
the composer, the very same text that was subsequently revised into three acts. It is not hard
to guess when the transformation to three acts might have taken place: sometime between
the publication of the scenario and the performance itself. Indeed, the relationship between
this scenario and the three-act libretto suggests an analogy to that between the scenario

---

71. This is certainly suggested by the fact that only the first prologue is described in the scenario. According to Savieri, *Le nozze*, 66, n. 25, topical and encomiastic allusions in the second prologue suggest that the five-
act version may have been conceived for performance in another city—she proposes Turin or Ferrara—but we
have no record that the work was ever performed outside Venice. Indeed, this seems exceedingly unlikely, as
she herself implies earlier (p. 30), when she cites the double prologue as evidence that the five-act version represented a literary redaction, compiled for academic circulation. Dubowy ("Bemerkungen," 234) adduces this
underworld prologue to confirm that the underworld scene of *Ritorno* (5.2) was appropriate for an epic *festa
teatrale*.

72. That the three-act version is not wholly reliable, however, is indicated by the fact that it agrees with all
librettos but nos. 2 and 6 in ascribing the text erroneously to Badoaro. Other inaccuracies, such as mistakes in
characters' names (Drance for Drante; Carilao for Eurialo; Numanto for Numano), may be a more positive feature, helping to confirm its proximity to the "event" and distance from a literary source. See p. 163.

73. This whole issue is discussed in *OSV* and Chap. 3 above.

74. This is the conclusion reached by Sevieri as well. But see above, n. 71. For the distinction between practical and commemorative or literary librettos, see *OSV*, chap. 2, and Accorsi, "Varietà: Problemi testuali." Sevieri (*Le nozze*, 31) argues that the scenario had commemorative as well as the standard practical value of
detailing the action, noting that normal *scenari* were more concerned than this one with practical or specific aspects of the productions—name of theater, name of scenographer, etc. Its lengthy (twenty-six-page) prefatory
"Lettera" certainly distinguishes it from all other scenarios as a publication, but the scenario proper (pp. 17–36)
is pretty standard.

and the Udine libretto of *Incoronazione*: the one published shortly before, the other copied shortly after the premiere.

❧

It is probable, then, that by the time *Le nozze d'Enea* was performed at the Teatro SS. Giovanni e Paolo in 1641 it was already in three acts. Given the unique parallels between the scenario and the three-act libretto, it may already have been transformed by the time Monteverdi set the text to music. A closer look at the libretto indicates the hand of an editor rather than a mere copyist, one concerned specifically with issues of performance. The detailed alterations are subtly directed toward increasing character interaction and expressive intensity, as I hope to show; they give the impression that the editor had a stage performance in mind, even a musical stage performance. In fact, the kinds of differences between the three and five-act librettos—different line arrangements, dialogue instead of block texts, revised meter, the introduction of irregular stanzaic structure—suggests that the exemplar, like those for two of the *Incoronazione* librettos (the Naples print and the Udine manuscript), may not have been a text at all, but a score. This hypothesis is strengthened by certain inaccuracies in the three-act text. The mistakes in some characters' names (Drance for Drante; Carilao for Eurialo; Numanto for Numano), and an extraneous double letter in another (Lattino) suggest that the copyist was unfamiliar with the *Aeneid* and was reading from a poorly legible source, such as a score.[75]

Several other distinctive characteristics of the three-act text link it to staged performance rather than essentially literary production. Its list of characters, under the headings "Attori nel prologo" and "Attori nell'opera," differs significantly from those of the five-act sources—all labled more generically as "Interlocutori"—not only in the order in which the characters are named, but in their description. Whereas the five-act listings identify most of the characters exclusively as generalized historical figures, the three-act listing is more audience-friendly; it frequently includes personal details, specifying relationships in terms of this particular drama rather than mere historical roles. Thus, *Turno Prencipe de Retuli* becomes *Turno Re de Retuli, Amante di Lavinia; Enea Prencipe de Troiani* becomes *Enea amante di Lavinia; Numano millantatore Rutulo* becomes *Numan[t]o scudiere di Turno;* Acate is called *compagno d'Enea,* instead of being listed with Illioneo as *principali troiani.*[76] The three-act libretto is also distinctive in listing the characters more or less in order of their appearance on stage, rather than generically by social class: gods,

75. There are numerous such hypercorrections throughout the text, indicating the influence of a particular dialect. On those in the Udine libretto of *Incoronazione,* see Fabbri, "New Sources," 19. Note, however, that Drance and Drante may have been alternatives for the same name.

76. Niso, a Trojan soldier, is erroneously called *servo di Lattino,* and his companion Eurialo is misidentified as a shepherd (and grouped with Tereo and Elmino) in the three-act version, further evidence of the copyist's unfamiliarity with Virgil/Dolce.

royalty, secondary figures (the oracle Fauno coming at the very end).[77] Finally, the three-act libretto includes a number of scenic descriptions not present in the other versions.[78]

Although the reduction of five acts to three appears to be more mechanical than in the case of *Ritorno*—the original acts 1–2 are joined to make the new act 1, and the original acts 3–4 become the new act 2[79]—it nevertheless still obscures some of the careful symmetries built into the individual acts. This is a matter of some importance; we have seen how it plays out in *Ritorno*. Act 1 of the original *Nozze* both opens and closes with the same character on stage, Latino. The prediction of scene 1, that a new man will come to marry Lavinia, is fulfilled in the final scene (6) by the report that the Trojan hero Enea has indeed set foot on Italian soil. Act 2 begins and ends with the same characters, too, in this case Giunone and Aletto; an action set in motion in the opening scene is fulfilled at the close. Aletto's ill wind—invoked by Giunone to ruin Enea and her rival Venere—has poisoned the relationship between the Trojans and the native shepherds (the Trojans have killed Silvia's deer and her brother), and has inflamed Turno against Enea. Celebrating their success, the conspirators close the act by invoking a dance of the furies. Act 3 is devoted to Venere's side of the battle, as she implements her protection of her son, first by procuring arms for him from Vulcano, and then by warning Enea of Turno's plan: the grand confrontation between Turno and Enea begins at the end of the act. Act 4 opens with Latino trying to calm Turno's anger, Amata trying to discourage him from fighting, and begging Lavinia to do the same; she is unsuccessful because Lavinia, who is drawn to Enea, prays to Venere for his victory, which is achieved in the act's closing scene. Act 5, unchanged as act 3 of the new version, is also symmetrical. The two opening scenes celebrating the Trojan victory are separated from the two final scenes of resolution by a heavenly scene in which Giove negotiates with Giunone.

Not only does the three-act arrangement obscure these formal symmetries in the individual acts, it also creates some problems of its own. (Cf. Table 14 above.) The climactic battle between the Rutulians and the Trojans, which culminates in a moresca, no longer occurs in its proper place at the end of act 3, but instead interrupts act 2 (E); the idea of a mid-act battle, let alone a ballo, is certainly problematic (but recall the ballo for eight moors in act 3 of *Ritorno*). Here perhaps the awkwardness is mitigated slightly by the elimination of the moresca, if not the battle itself. But the appearance of Turno and Numano in the following scene strains credulity, since they were involved in the immediately preceding battle—Numano had even left the stage in flight.[80] Similar awkwardness is avoided in act 1, however, where scenes 5 and 6 are reversed and modified so as to short-

---

77. Beginning with Latino and the oracle Fauno—though Amata and Lavinia are out of order, as are Enea and his family.

78. For instance, 1.2: Coro di Tritoni e Nereidi *che guidano la nave d'Enea;* 1.3: Enea *che sbarca con* Ascanio, etc.; 1.4: *Stanze nella reggia* di Latino, etc.; 1.5: *Sala con Latino in trono*, Illioneo; and 1.6, *Giardino*, Lavinia, Turno. There is one unique description in Correr 3332 (no. 6), Silvia *piangente*.

79. The final acts of both versions are the same (as in *Ritorno*). Acts 3 and 4 are actually lumped together in the description of the plot in the "Lettera" (p. 23), though not in the scenario proper. Compare pp. 145–46 above with Appendix 2(r).

80. Cf above, n. 65.

circuit the celebratory dances that formed the intermedio to act 1. In the five-act original, scene 5, a private dialogue where Lavinia rejects Turno's advances, is followed by a big public display in Latino's throne room, in which he welcomes Illioneo, the Trojan emissary; it culminates in an intermedio, an elaborate entertainment presented for the delectation of the foreign guests. In the three-act version the scene of public display is rewritten so that it concludes differently—not with Latino's recognition, expressed in an aside, that the Trojan arrival represents the fulfillment of the oracle's prophecy, but with a passage transplanted from an earlier scene (scene 3) in which Illioneo presents precious Trojan relics as a peace-offering to Latino. The bringing of the gifts provides at least some sense of ceremony to replace the excised celebratory intermedio, and leads quite smoothly to the scene between Lavinia and Turno that had originally preceded it.[81]

In fact, this scene actually makes more sense after the Trojan scene than before it, for Lavinia's rejection of Turno's advances can now be understood in connection with her future relationship with Enea rather than as merely whimsical or flirtatious. The reversal of scenes occasions one more minor cut in the text, a few lines accompanying Numano's exit at the conclusion of his scene with Turno (1.4; 1.3 in the scenario). This scene had originally preceded Turno's scene with Lavinia, so Numano had to leave Turno alone on stage for Lavinia to find him in the next scene (1.5). But now that the men's scene is followed not by the scene for Lavinia but by one for Latino and the Trojan guests—a change of set—Numano's exit is unnecessary, and his lines could be cut.[82] Finally, one substantial cut is not accomplished without leaving some ends dangling. This is the stichomythic confrontation between Amata and Lavinia that comprises most of act 4, scene 2. As already noted, Amata's final speech of the scene, in which she decries the defeat of her plan to marry her daughter to Turno, is tacked onto the end of the previous scene in which Turno, in the presence of Amata, decides to do battle with Enea (2.7/4.1); thus what was originally an angry diatribe against Lavinia's stubbornness now serves as an effective forecast of Turno's doom. But Lavinia's opening lines in the following scene refer to what her mother has just said to Turno, lines she could not have heard in the three-act revision, her scene with her mother having been cut.[83]

---

81. "Queste reliquie intanto, / Delle patrie ricchezze / Che d'amistà fede; segni t'invia / La tua bontà non sprezze." These four lines referring to the precious objects carried away from Troy by the refugees compensate for a longer passage that was cut in scene 3: "Con Sergesto e Cloanto / Togli fuor de le navi / Quel ingemmato scettro, / Che fu di Priamo il Grande, / Re sventurato, e la corona, e 'l manto. / A la vicina Regia / Vanne con questi doni, indi procura / Per noi pace sicura." It is difficult to know which of the changes came first, the cut in scene 3 or the addition in scene 6. It may well be that the earlier, longer passage, with its reference to two extra characters, Sergesto and Cloanto, was cut first because those characters were not available in the cast of the three-act version; and then reference to the treasures was moved to a more opportune point in the drama. In any case, the two changes are clearly interrelated.

82. It may also be that the change in scene order was required by the necessity of preparing for the immediately following heavenly scene for Giunone and Aletto, without benefit of an intermedio.

83. The elimination of this scene also deprived Monteverdi of the opportunity of creating the kind of stichomythic (line-for-line dialogue) confrontation he exploited so powerfully in Incoronazione, between Seneca and Nerone.

Alterations like these indicate that the conversion of *Nozze* to three acts from five was not quite as straightforward as it might appear and that the effort involved more than the mere joining of acts 1–2 and 3–4 into acts 1 and 2, respectively. Indeed, they reveal a rather careful editor at work in the undertaking. Some alterations were clearly aimed at shortening the text: without affecting the plot, four lines are trimmed from the prologue (possibly an aria); more than twenty from 1.1 (for Latino); ten from 1.3 (the passage concerning the relics), and fourteen from 5.2 (now 3.2, from Drante's lengthy speech). One of these cuts, in the opening scene, seems to point up a revision in their source that the copyists of the five-act versions failed to see. It reduces a highly redundant twenty-four-line passage for Latino to its last seven lines (compare lines 1–6 with lines 18–24).

1 Già fu ch'un dì sperai,	I hoped one day,
2 Figlia, per tua mercé d'esser felice.	my daughter, thanks to you to be happy.
3 Or mi trovo infelice,	[But] now I find myself unhappy,
4 Mentre l'inferma mia terrena vista	because my infirm worldly sight
5 Non sa qual sia nel Cielo	knows not whether in heaven
6 Stella fatal per te severa, o trista.	your fateful star be cruel or sad.
7 Già de l'età su 'l verde,	Already in the green of your youth,
8 Su 'l terminar d'Aprile,	at April's end,
9 Braman altri in te cor quel fior gentile,	others desired to gather that gentle flower
10 Che se più tarda ogni vaghezza perde.	that, if postponed, loses all beauty.
11 Ma quai mostri, o portenti	But what monsters or portents
12 Fan ch'io non acconsenti?	make me not consent?
13 O fatidiche voci,	O prophetic voices,
14 Quai presaggite voi beate sorti?	do you predict a happy fate?
15 Dio, ruina, e morti?	God, or ruin and deaths?
16 Dove, dove rendete	Where, where will you reveal
17 Del'ignoto Destin, voi corsi obliqui? *end cut]*	of unknown destiny your oblique ways?
18 Padre son'io di figlia	I am father of a daughter
19 Ch'in seno ha beltà tale	who has in her breast such beauty
20 Che può farmi felice,	that can make me happy,
21 Ma mi rende infelice,	but makes me unhappy,
22 Ove l'inferma mia terrena vista	when my infirm worldly vision
23 Non sa se lieta, o trista,	knows not whether a happy or sad
24 Giri per lei nel ciel stella fatale.[84]	fatal star turns for her in the heavens.

---

84. This cut, in fact, may tell us more about the nature of the exemplar(s) from which the five-act texts were copied than about the editing of the three-act version. We are evidently dealing here with a text that had already been edited; both versions are preserved in the five-act librettos because whoever copied them must not have recognized that the passage had been revised, and that lines 18–24 were intended to replace 1–17, not to follow them.

Other alterations involved adding text to smooth over the awkwardnesses created by the reduction from five acts. Act 1, scene 8 (2.6) (Turno and Amata) was moved ahead and now follows immediately upon the scene in which Giunone calls upon Aletto to spread his evil influence. A substantial passage (fifteen lines) was inserted at the beginning to enable the characters to react to strange premonitions of disaster obviously resulting from the workings of Aletto's invisible poison.[85] Still other additions improve the drama in more subtle ways—independently, it would seem, of the conversion to three acts. Ten lines inserted just before the end of Enea's monologue in 2.4 display the hero at his most distressed. Recalling painful memories of his past, he invokes the ghosts of his dead family to witness how much that pain is exceeded by his present suffering. Recognizing that his torment will forever be linked to the underworld, he rails against the powers of Hell:

Spargesti, *o* cara patria,	You spread, o dear country,
Tant'anni il sangue a fiumi,	blood in rivers for so many years,
Cadendo in fin tradita,	falling in the end, betrayed,
Distrutta, incenerita.	destroyed, incinerated.
Voi de congiunti estinti ombre dolenti	You, sad shadows of extinct relations,
Ridire i miei tormenti,	repeat my torments,
Voi dell'atroce esilio men dogliosi	you, less pained by atrocious exile,
Ahi, che i miei guai penosi.	ahi, than my painful sufferings.
Non tollero l'Inferno	I will not bear Hell,
Benché sia con il suo, mio straccio eterno.	though to it be tied my eternal suffering.

These inserted lines of direct address, with their repeated invocations (italicized) culminating in blasphemy, heighten the effect of the volte-face that follows, justifying Enea's horror at his own emotional excess:[86]

Ma del usato ardir, quai novi accenti.	But in my customary boldness, what new accents are these?
L'impeto del dolore	The outburst of pain
Tragge dalla mia lingua, e non dal core.	came from my tongue, and not my heart.
Enea dunque si duole,	Enea now laments,
Che nel più fier sembiante	who in his proudest aspect
Rimirò morte, e si serbò costante?	stared at death, and remained constant?

---

85. Note that another libretto, Correr 3332 (no. 6), also reorders this text, but does not add the extra fifteen lines. There is other evidence of a link between 3332 and 3331 (nos. 6 and 5). Alone among all the five-act librettos it shares the idiosyncratic sequence of scenes in no. 5: 1.8–12 (or 2.2–6), in which Turno–Amata (1.8) follows Giunone–Aletto, which is in turn followed by the Elminio–Silvia sequence. "Silvia *pastorella piangente*" substitutes for Turno–Amata as the penultimate scene of the act. According to Sevieri (*Le nozze*), these two librettos also share at least one erroneous reading: that of line 1109 (numbers from Severi's edition of the libretto). This suggested to her (p. 34) that one contaminated the other.

86. This, of course, is a typical feature of lament texts, at least from the time of Arianna. See chap. 6, p. 228 and following.

No, no, pur imperversi il Cielo, il Fatto	No, no, no matter how contrary Heaven or Fate,
Sarà non mai languente	his heart will no longer languish;
Nelle perdite ancor il Core vincente.	even in loss will it be victorious.

While the modifications described thus far, whether cuts or additions, are aimed at strengthening the overall structure of the libretto, or that of individual scenes, a number of smaller alterations have a more localized effect. Words and phrases are often inverted, rearranged, replaced, or repeated to promote greater dramatic immediacy or rhetorical heightening. Almost always—though not invariably, as we will see—this means a shuffling of the metric scheme, something easily accomplished in Italian verse; adding a word or two can change an *endecasillabo* into two rhyming *settenari,* and so on. (A host of expressive repetitions affect the meter of single lines: the expansion of "Vergine, e regal sei" to "Vergine, e regal vergine ben sei" and the introduction of elision where there was none originally, in the transformation of "Ahi dove è gita" to "Ah dove, dove è gita.") In 1.5, an expressive repetition is added, turning Illioneo's single *endecasillabo* into a more urgently theatrical pair of *settenari:*

Tu nomar Troia udisti, ma che dico?	BECOMES	Tu nomar Troia udisti
		Ma che dico, che dico.

Near the end of 3.2 (5.2), an active verb (italicized) is emphasized through repetition, as a *settenario* quatrain becomes a more irregular tercet:

Entriamo pur mio figlio	BECOMES	*Entriam* mio figlio *entriamo*
Ne la cittade amica.		Nell'amica città ch'ivi nel tempio
Ivi nel tempio noi		Noi sciolgerem divoti.
Scioglieremmo divoti.		

Rhetoric is intensified too by the interpolation of expressive exclamations—"Lavinia, *ohime* con l'infocata guancia" from "Lavinia, ma la guancia"—and especially by the addition of personal or possessive pronouns, adjectives, and spatial or temporal adverbs that call attention to the speaker or the precise location or time of the action (all italicized).[87] Note, for instance, the shift from description to personal involvement in 1.2, when

---

87. What Roman Jakobson calls shifters, or deictic pointers, features of recited as opposed to contemplated text (see Roman Jakobson, "Closing Statement: Linguistics and Poetics," in *Style in Language,* ed. Thomas A. Sebeok [New York: Wiley, 1960], 350–77). For the significance of temporal, spatial, and personal deictics in Monteverdi's dramatic language, see Mauro Calcagno, "'Imitar col canto chi parla': Monteverdi and the Creation of a Language for Musical Theater," *JAMS* 55 (2002): 383–431.

Al aspettato ar[r]ivo	BECOMES	Al aspettato ar[r]ivo
D'orror lo scoglio privo, i sassi infiora.		D'horror *lo voglio* privo
		E sassi omai s'infiora;[88]

or the added metric emphasis on the speaker, "io" (italicized) in the following examples. In 1.1:

Ricorrer voglio a Fauno, il padre amato	BECOMES	Riccorrere vogl'*io*,
		A Fauno, al padre amato.

In 2.1 (3.1),

Tanto a punto, mia vita	BECOMES	Tal'*io* dolce mia vita
Da te mi promettea.		Da te spero aita.

And in 2.3 (3.3):

Qual è, se non son io l'infausta face	BECOMES	Qual è, se non son *io*
		La fatal dolorosa infausta face.[89]

In a related example, increased emphasis on the personal is achieved with "lui" replacing "quel" (italicized):

Su Troiani e Latini,	Su Troiani, e Latini in dolce canti,
Su, su in dolci canti	Ite invocando *lui*
Ite invocando *quel* che stringe i cori	Che stringe i cor di nodi onesti, e santi.
Di nodi onesti a santi.	

Further improvements to produce a clearer or more vivid rhetoric can be seen in the change to "Assai più d'altro grato" from "Più d'ogni altro assai grato"; "madre tua" from "figlio di lei," "ancor che" for "quantunque," "hora lo rendi" for "hor lo raccendi," "cento e cento" from "più di cento." Precision of place (in italics) as well as more personal action is marked in this expansion of a tercet to a quatrain:

Qui dove d'erbe, e fiori, e 'l fiume	Qui dove d'Erbe, e fiori
M'appresteran letto morbido, odoroso	*E 'l margine del fiume*
Chiudi gl'occhi al riposo	M'appresteran morbido letto, e adorno
	Gl'occhi racchiudo, e poso.

---

88. Note also the added adverb of time, "omai." This brings up the important issue of homonyms: scoglio/voglio. See below, n. 92.

89. Note the series of intensifying adjectives.

And time is emphasized in the change to "Pur *al fin* mi son cari" from "Pur mi son dolci, e cari," as well as in numerous instances when the adverb "omai" is inserted. The effects of repetition and shifter are combined in so slight a change as the contraction of "voi l'innocenza mia / mirate, e diffendete" to "*Voi* l'innocenza mia, *voi* diffendete."

While many metric changes seem incidental or accidental and others merely increase the emphasis on significant words, some seem devised to improve the poetry. Revision produces a tighter, more elegant metric structure in Numano's speech in 2.2 (3.2), where the rhyme between lines 1 and 3 is emphasized by the contraction of line 3 from an *endecasillabo* to a *settenario:*

Or si contento io stò
Nuotando in mar di latte
Poiché nuotar dovrò   [Poiche nuotar ben presto anco dovrò]
In' ampio mar di sangue
Delle genti da me vinte, e disfatte.

This particular change also increases the immediacy of the action by eliminating the delaying, modifying verbiage: "ben presto anco."

Patient analysis of this kind can seem compulsive, yet it builds a cumulative case for a conclusion of some importance: most of these alterations can be categorized as performative as opposed to literary. This suggests that while the five-act text was intended for silent reading, the three-act text was intended to be declaimed. Our librettos illustrate what linguists have characterized as the transformation from diegetic narration to mimetic representation: a shift from page to stage.[90] Two of the most striking interventions of this type occur in the shepherdess Silvia's beautiful strophic lament in 1.12 (2.4), itself an addition to the narrative as given in the scenario. In the first instance, the end of her third strophe is replaced by a much more expressive text:

Perché 'l bel cervo mio per voi spirò,   BECOMES   Se 'l cervo mio per voi *l'alma* spirò,
Perché 'l mio bell'Elmin per voi mancò   S'Elminio *hoimè* per voi *languì,*
                                                                                  mancò,

its rhetorical power enhanced by the exclamatory "hoimè," and the sequential doubling, "languì, mancò." A second change in the same piece, building in some sense on the first, is even more powerful. The first three strophes of this highly unusual text are comprised of three rhymed couplets: two *decasillabi tronchi,* two *quinari sdruccioli,* and two *endecasillabi tronchi* (or perhaps originally six *quinari*). In the fourth and final strophe Silvia interrupts this distinctive pattern to address her dead brother directly: "S'Elminio morto

---

90. On this distinction, see, among others, Keir Elam, *The Semiotics of Theatre and Drama* (London and New York: Methuen, 1980). The huge literature on the distinctions between read and spoken texts is summarized in Calcagno, "'Imitar col canto chi parla.'"

sei," inserting an extra *settenario* (italicized)—unrhymed—just before the final couplet. The sudden intrusion of direct address, evoking the poignancy of absence, immeasurably intensifies the effect of Silvia's grief.[91]

1 Piante, gettate le frondi al suol,
  Aure, spirate voci di duol.
  Fior disperdettevi,
  Herbe struggetevi
  Poi che il bel Cervo mio lassa finì.
  Poi che il mio bel Elminio ohimè morì.

Plants, cast your leaves to the ground,
breezes, breathe sounds of sorrow,
flowers, disperse yourselves,
grasses, destroy yourselves,
for my beautiful deer is no more;
for my beautiful Elminio, alas, has died.

2 Più non godrete quel volto bel,

  Più non vedrete quel corpo snel.
  Gl'augelli gemino,
  Le belve fremino,
  Poi che il bel Cervo mio spirato è già.
  Ch'il bel Elminio più vita non hà.

No longer will you delight in that beautiful
      face,
no longer will you see that nimble body.
The birds groan,
the beasts tremble,
for my beautiful deer has expired,
that beautiful Elminio no longer lives.

3 O man funeste, mani infernal,
  Che trar poteste quegl'empii stral,

  Inareditevi,
  Inceneritevi.
  Se 'l Cervo mio per voi l'alma spirò,

  L'Elminio hoimè per voi languì, mancò.

O fatal hands, infernal hands,
which could have extracted those wicked
      arrows,
wither,
burn.
If my deer yielded up its soul
      because of you,
Elminio, alas, because of you languished, is
      gone.

4 Silvia dolente pur straccia il crin,
  Chiama nocente crudo destin,
  Pietosi sietemi,
  Parche uccidetemi.
  S'Elminio morto sei
  S'il mio diletto Cervo morto fù
  Viver priva di lor non voglio più.

Unhappy Silvia tears her hair,
the innocent one calls out to cruel destiny,
have pity on me
ye Fates, kill me.
If you are dead, Elminio,
if my beloved deer was killed,
deprived of them, I no longer wish to live.

---

91. The role of Silvia may have been sung by the young Silvia Gailarti (born ca. 1629), and the aria added for her. She and her mother, Leonora Luppi, very likely appeared in either *Ulisse* or *Nozze*, or both, as indicated by an agreement signed by Monteverdi on 19 July 1640 that mentions several singers, including Silvia and Luppi. When Luppi later brought a lawsuit against Monteverdi for non-payment of wages, he attested that he had seen Silvia perform on stage, but had not arranged her contract. Perhaps Benedetto Ferrari had done so, as the impresario at SS. Giovanni e Paolo during the 1640 and 1641 seasons, since, according to a document of 28 February 1641, cited in Chap. 1, n. 14, he owed money to Monteverdi, possibly for having provided the music for *Le nozze*. See Glixon, "Scenes from the Life," 97–146, esp. 113–16, and 119 on the role of Silvia.

We have seen instances of rhetorical intensification through the addition of shifters, repetitions, and vocatives, as well as other alterations that seem less purposeful, offering simple variants, equally valid alternatives, with different spellings and word choices, and even word orders perhaps representing different local traditions. Certain of the altered rhyme schemes and line lengths even suggest that the source text was not entirely fixed and that the editor was attempting to improve the poetry. Some of the small variants are actually homonyms, raising the possibility of some oral component in the transmission of the text.[92]

But others, like Silvia's final strophe, offer the intriguing possibility of reflecting not only the generalized shift from page to stage, from a read text to one intended to be enacted, but an even further step along the road toward performance, the actual modifications introduced in the musical setting. These include the occasional dropping—or adding—of vowels at the ends of words (1.6: Core/Amore; 3.3: amor/furor) and the division of longer lines into shorter ones or vice versa (as in Numano's speech mentioned above). A musical choice seems especially implicated in the alteration that transforms Giunone's two *versi sdruccioli* and a *verso piano* (2.1) into three *versi sdruccioli* (1.7):

Ciò che provò già Troia hor senta	BECOMES	Ciò che provò già Troia hor
il Latio		senta il Latio
Lavinia sia nov'Elena		Lavinia sia nov'Elena
Paride novel l'odiato Enea		E l'odiato Enea novello Paride.

Likewise, the recasting of Damigella's pair of unrhymed *endecasillabi* (2.8) into four strongly rhymed *settenari tronchi* gives the distinct impression of reflecting a musical impulse to set the passage lyrically:

Non è, non è quel dianzi ne Lavinia	BECOMES	Non è quel dianzi, no,
Ah che non è chi fu che lei cangiò		Lavinia ah che non è.
		Com'ella uscì di sé,
		Che fù, che lei cangiò?

92. There are many examples. The following list includes alternatives as well as homonyms: prego/porgo, rischiara/tranquilla; svizzano/guizzano, m'inclina/m'inchino, vegliar/venir, priego/parlar, tratto il Gange/dal Gange uscito, celeste/sorgente, morte/Marte, confusi/profondi, serpe/aspe, munita/armato, ne vien/vientene, nemico/inimico, ragioni/cagioni, sdegno/foco, serpendo/scorrendo, sfratte/fuggite, coglierem/chiarirem, crudo/empio, germoglian/germoglia, tutto, e perturbato/perturbato il tutto, terrore/furor. Some possible misprisions (oral or written) include: accenda/asconda, vero/vano, tristo/presto, sospetti/sogetti, cede/cade, Resa/resta, Marte/morte, straniere/sentiero, preggi/freggi, invocato/invitato. The *Incoronazione* and *Ritorno* collations show many of the same kinds of variants (Chiarelli, "*L'incoronazione*," and Fabbri, "New Sources," both discuss this subject with reference to *Incoronazione*). Those for *Incoronazione* are noted in Thomas Walker's comparative edition of the *Incoronazione* librettos (unpublished manuscript in the Yale Music Library).

Perhaps most significantly, from the point of view of the musical setting, the three-act libretto divides a number of blocks of text into dialogues between characters. In 1.2 the text is divided between the Coro di Nereidi and the Coro di Trittoni; no such division is indicated in the five-act librettos.[93] Likewise, near the end of 1.7 (for Giunone and Aletto), Aletto tells how he will do Giunone's bidding in a succession of very short lines. While the five-act librettos designate the entire speech for Aletto, the three-act libretto involves Giunone in the dialogue. She eggs him on:

ALETTO: Ch'io porti
    Sconforti,
    Rie sorti,
[GIUNONE:] Sì, sì.
[ALETTO:] Scontenti,
    Spaventi,
    Tormenti
    Darò.

Finally, the text of the duet between Lavinia and Enea at the end of 3.4, indicated simply as *a 2* in all the five-act librettos, is distributed as follows in the three-act version:

ENEA: O fortunati affani,
LAVINIA: Aventurosi danni.
ENEA: O miei pianti e sospiri,
LAVINIA: Pene, doglie e martiri,
ENEA: S'indi nascer dovea si dolci effetti,
LAVINIA: Se tai produr dovean gioie e diletti.

Alterations such as these strongly suggest the connection of the three-act version to a stage performance—presumably of 1641, the only one we know of.[94] Even more intriguingly, they strengthen the idea, advanced above, that the text, like two of the *Incoronazione* librettos, may have been copied, not from another libretto, but from a score. This impression is reinforced by a special category of variants in the three-act version, which includes the rearrangement of pairs of short lines as single long ones and vice versa (cf. examples cited above). Typically, as we have seen, this results in a changed deployment of metrical lines. But in a few revealing cases the librettist created a-metrical lines, suggesting that he was following a musical source—or at least a source in which the text was not laid out metrically. For instance, the *endecasillabo* "Placano i flutti l'ire e i fieri venti" is split awkwardly into two shorter lines in the three-act version: "placano i flutti l'ire / e i fieri venti." The same sort of error is

93. The actual number of lines is not entirely clear, since there are some discrepancies among the sources.

94. There is one example of the reverse. In the five-act version of the Lavinia–Damigella scene, a substantial duet passage is distributed more specifically between the two characters.

produced when "Qual fai concordo al dir la mano o 'l piede" is transformed into "Qual fai concordo al dir / La mano o 'l piede"; and (in 1.6 [1.4]) "Perché dal Ciel fu sposa destinata," which becomes the incorrect couplet "Si che dal Cielo già fui / In sposa destinata."

These are just the sorts of variants that led Paolo Fabbri to conclude that the Udine libretto of *Incoronazione* was copied from a score. I have in mind what Fabbri calls suppressed vowels in contrast to elisions, conjunctive errors—namely shared mistakes, and omission or inclusion of refrains. An obvious example of a conjunctive error in *Nozze* is the one that gives the first four lines of act 5, scene 4 (=3.4) to Latino rather than Lavinia in all of the five-act librettos. This is strange, because it makes more sense if the entire first speech (all seven lines) is sung by Latino.[95]

If the three-act text of *Nozze* was indeed copied from a score, it brings us tantalizingly close to Monteverdi's music—not close enough, alas, but closer than we might have anticipated. Indeed, when considered in this light, a number of the changes already observed take on new resonance. The lines added to Enea's big solo scene in act 2 make it much more like the famous Lament of Arianna; this, as we will see in the next chapter, was the model for all of Monteverdi's late operatic laments. The rhymed quatrain of *settenari tronchi* for Damigella created from the unrhymed hendecasyllabic couplet (cf. p. 172 above) strongly resembles one of those ariosos that Monteverdi was so fond of carving out of recitative poetry in *Ritorno* and *Incoronazione*. Finally, there is Silvia. The dramatic irregularity imposed upon her aria in the three-act libretto is just the kind of formal liberty Monteverdi would have relished—and exploited—in setting a strophic text.

Modern Taste

Having established the strong possibility that the three-act libretto of *Nozze,* a revision of a five-act original, was closely tied to the opera as it was performed in 1641 and perhaps as originally set by Monteverdi, we return once more to its predecessor and model, *Ritorno,* which was also originally written in five acts but performed in three. It is tempting to imagine that the transformation in both operas took place at around the same time—after the Venetian premiere of *Ritorno* but before the Bologna revival. Although we cannot say for certain, it may well be that by 1641 the sheer number of three-act operas in competing theaters—less demanding on the audience's attention, certainly less pretentious and requiring fewer intermedi—made such transformation necessary. Notwithstanding both librettists' energetic defenses of five-act structure, it would seem that modern taste—or commercial exigency—had its way. Once more we are indebted to *Nozze*. The conflict

---

95. Lines 1119–25 in Sevieri, *Nozze,* 133. The situation is analogous to a notorious moment in *Incoronazione,* in which a number of sources agree on a mistake (the "Vanne" problem). See above, Chap. 4, Table 11, n. c. In attempting to establish a stemma for the text of *Nozze,* Sevieri, pp. 32–34, lists a number of significant variants and conjunctive errors. (She concludes that the two "best" texts are no. 10 for the literary version, and no. 5 for the performance version.)

between aesthetic theory and theatrical practice revealed in its sources affords us a sense of just how powerful were the pressures exerted by modern taste—powerful enough to force the revision of *Ritorno* as well.

Yet when all is said and done, whatever the damage inflicted on symbolism and structure, the alteration of these operas to three acts could not disguise their verisimilitude of plot, their adherence to the unities, or the decorum of their characters—in short, their essential classicism. Even in their three-act guises both works remain firmly on the ancient side of the old quarrel. But the change does indicate the extent of the tension between the ancients and the moderns. And it is worth noting once again here that our two "tragedies," among the first five-act Venetian librettos of the period, were also virtually the last.[96] All aspects of their classicism, not only its most obvious sign, were under siege.

It is no coincidence that the standard-bearer for the moderns was Busenello. In many ways his *Incoronazione* libretto can be read as a direct challenge to those of his friend Badoaro and Badoaro's friend Torcigliani. Busenello eschewed tragedy as his subtitle, adopting instead, as we have noted, the distinctly modern "opera musicale," redolent not of Aristotle but of the popular theater.[97] And he chose as a source for his drama not the epics, ancient and modern, nor the Ovidian mythologies enlisted by his contemporaries—although he had done so in the recent past—but Roman history as recorded by Tacitus.[98] Since his protagonists were not of such well-established heroic stature as Ulysses or Aeneas, he evidently felt less compelled to adhere closely to his literary source in portraying them; his disclaimer in the preface to his libretto fairly boasts of his freedom: "Nerone, enamored of Poppea, wife of Ottone, sent him under the pretext of embassy to Lusitania so that he could take his pleasure with her—this according to Cornelius Tacitus. But here we represent things differently." And he then goes on to outline his drama: "Ottone [is] desperate at being deprived of Poppea. Ottavia, wife of Nerone, orders Ottone to kill Poppea; he promises to do so, but lacking the spirit to deprive his beloved of life, he dresses in the clothes of Drusilla, who loves him. Thus disguised, he enters Poppea's garden. Love disturbs and prevents that death. Nerone repudiates Ottavia, in spite of the counsel of Seneca, and takes Poppea as his wife. Seneca dies, and Ottavia is expelled from Rome" (see Appendix 4, A).

---

96. The others are listed above, n. 48.

97. Other textual sources have different subtitles, as noted in Table 6 above, Chap. 3; and n. 2 above (this chapter). Although Busenello entitled the printed version of the libretto "opera musicale," it was published in 1656, well after opera had become established. We cannot be sure that the subtitle "opera regia" on the scenario had anything to do with him, since his name is not mentioned anywhere in it.

98. The relationship between *Incoronazione* and Tacitus is exhaustively explored in Heller, "Tacitus Incognito," 39–96; also ead., *Emblems*, chap. 4: "Disprezzata Regina," esp. pp. 145–52. See also Iain Fenlon and Peter Miller, *The Song of the Soul: Understanding Poppea* (London: Royal Musical Association, 1992); Cesare Questa, *L'aquila a due teste: Immagini di Roma e dei romani* (Urbino: Quattro Venti, 1998), 173–81; and id., "Presenze di Tacito nel Seicento veneziano," in *Musica, scienze e idee nella Serenissima durante il Seicento: Atti del convegno internazionale di studi, Venezia—Palazzo Giustinian Lolin, 13–15 dicembre 1993*, ed. Francesco Passadore and Franco Rossi (Venice: Fondazione Levi, 1996), 317–24.

The drama does indeed take liberties, especially with the historical sequence of events and the portrayal of characters.[99] The chronology according to Tacitus (dates are A.D.) is as follows:

58 Beginning of Nero's affair with Poppaea, Otho to Lusitania (*Annals* 13.46)

59 Death of Agrippina (instigated by Poppaea) (*Annals* 14.1–8)

62 Nero divorces Octavia, marries Poppaea, and banishes the former to Pandateria, where he then has her killed (*Annals* 14.60–64)

65 Seneca is forced to commit suicide for his supposed participation in a plot to overthrow the emperor (*Annals* 15. 60–64)

66 Nero kicks the pregnant Poppaea, accidentally killing her (*Annals* 16.6)

68 He himself is overthrown and commits suicide (*Lives of the Caesars* 6.49)

Busenello rearranges these events substantially, even more than his summary suggests. Agrippina's death is eliminated, replaced by Seneca's, which is also engineered by Poppea, but results from his opposition to Nerone's marriage rather than any presumed conspiracy; it thus occurs well before Ottavia's exile rather than after it. (Busenello's summary does not even hint that Seneca's death will be anticipated.) Ottone's transfer (actually he is banished rather than given a governorship) is postponed until just before the marriage of Poppea and Nerone, where it occurs concurrently with the announcement of Ottavia's exile. Both of these events take place before Poppea is crowned empress. (I explore the implications of anticipating Seneca's death in Chap. 8.)

Regarding his dramatis personae, Busenello adds one significant main character to the mix, Drusilla, presumably in order to join with Ottone to constitute the obligatory second pair of lovers.[100] And he develops several others well beyond their roles in Tacitus. Ottone becomes much more active in Busenello's version of the story. Rather than Tacitus's dissolute figure who is sent away at the beginning of the action, he appears throughout the libretto, precipitating some of the most important events; most significantly, he is enlisted to carry out Ottavia's dirty work: to kill Poppea. And Ottavia, too, assumes an active role in her eventual fate by conspiring to eliminate her rival. In another, highly ironic departure from Tacitus's characterizations, Busenello has Lucano rejoicing with Nerone immediately following Seneca's death, when in fact Lucan was Seneca's nephew and actually died with his uncle in the same purge of conspirators.[101]

---

99. See Robert Holzer, review of *The Song of the Soul: Understanding Poppea* by Peter Miller and Iain Fenlon, *COJ* 5 (1993): 79–80 and Heller, "Tacitus Incognito," table, p. 65.

100. Although Fenlon and Miller, *Song of the Soul,* 42–43 suggest that she was inspired by the eponymous character from Ariosto (*Orlando Furioso,* 37), known for her constancy, a crucial element in their interpretation of the opera, it seems just as likely that Busenello was thinking of the Drusilla who was Agrippina's sister (Nero's aunt); Suetonius, *The Twelve Caesars,* trans. Robert Graves (London: Penguin, 1957), 4.24. See Wendy Heller, "Chastity, Heroism, and Allure: Women in the Opera of Seventeenth-Century Venice" (Ph.D. diss., Brandeis University, 1995), 228, n. 8.

101. Heller makes a great deal of this alteration ("Tacitus Incognito," 86–90).

By citing Tacitus, though, Busenello may have intended to deflect attention away from a number of other sources, namely Suetonius (*The Lives of the Caesars*, 6, 8); Dio Cassius (*Roman Histories*, 61–2); and the anonymous tragedy *Octavia*, attributed at that time to Seneca himself.[102] Suetonius is indeed a likely source for some of Busenello's lighter moments, such as the opening scene, where Ottone comes upon Nerone's soldiers. Suetonius's Otho bars the bedroom door against Nero (8.3), and his reference to Otho's baldness (8.12) may be the source of Poppea's remark on that subject in 1.11 ("A te le calve tempie, / Ad altri il crin la Fortuna diede"). Dio Cassius, among other things, seems to have influenced Busenello's ambiguous characterization of Seneca. And the *Octavia* not only offers the prototype for the relationship of two nurses to their mistresses, one for each protagonist, but provides a template for the stichomythic debate between Nerone and Seneca in act 1, scene 9 of the libretto as well as for Ottavia's grand final lament (minus *coro*). It also provided specific linguistic inspiration for Ottavia's condemnation of Giove for his impotence in her first lament, "Disprezzata regina." Finally, it offered a model for including the gods in the drama (absent from Tacitus, of course).[103]

The translations of our friend Dolce would also very likely have figured in Busenello's reading. The *Octavia*, for instance, is among his ten translations of Senecan tragedies.[104] Two prefatory *argomenti* highlight important features of the Senecan text, several of

---

102. Edward Champlin (*Nero* [Cambridge, MA: Harvard University Press, 2003], 37–38) emphasizes the fact that Tacitus and Dio, historians, and Suetonius, biographer, the main sources for this material (aside from the *Octavia*), were independent of one another, and that none of them was an eyewitness to the events they reported. Busenello's inclusion of details unique to one or another of them thus suggests he was familiar with all three. Champlin's discussion of the sources (chap. 2: "Stories and Histories") provides interesting insight into some of Busenello's characterizations; see esp. pp. 46–48 and 103–104.

103. Much of the foregoing paragraph is based on Holzer ("Review"), 80. Heller also brings Lucan's *Pharsalia* into the mix ("Tacitus Incognito," 86–90). See also Carter, *Musical Theatre*, 274–76, who suggests the influence of Lucian. Robert Ketterer argues for the relevance of Ovid's *Amores* 1. 9 in "Militat omnis amans: Ovidian Elegy in *L'incoronazione di Poppea*," *International Journal of the Classical Tradition* 4 (1998): 381–95. He also sees Neoplatonic conceits reflected in Busenello's text in "Neoplatonic Light and Dramatic Genre in Busenello's *L'Incoronazione di Poppea* and Noris's *Il Ripudio d'Ottavia*," *ML* 80 (1999): 1–22. In arguing for their interpretation of *Incoronazione* as a Tacitean text, Fenlon and Miller (*The Song of the Soul*) widen the net by exploring a number of contemporary readings of Tacitus and Seneca, including those of Simone Luzzato, Johannes Lipsius, Montaigne, Traiano Boccalini, and Gianfrancesco Loredano. Questa (*L'aquila a due teste*, 174, n. 3) characterizes the relationship of the *Octavia* to *Incoronazione*, unacknowledged by Busenello, as that of a hypotext, in contrast to an archetype. The one is not necessarily a model, though it may share important features; the other is clearly part of the same tradition. On this distinction, see Gerard Genette, *Palimpsestes* (Paris: Editions du Seuil, 1982), 11–14; Eng. trans., *Palimpsests: Literature in the Second Degree* (Lincoln: University of Nebraska Press, 1997). The *Octavia* was the first (only?) drama of its period to be based on history rather than myth. As characterized in a recent review by Marina Warner, it "was dealing with stuff happening: it is a work of mythic roman self-portraiture, as well as 'an act of loyalty on behalf of the People of Rome.' Nero's wife had been much loved, but he had discarded her for Poppaea and, after the burning of Rome, had her murdered—all this only six years before the probable date of the play's first performance" (review of T. P. Wiseman, *The Myths of Rome* [Exeter: University of Exeter Press, 2004], *Times Literary Supplement* [15 April 2005], 8). Wiseman presents the historical events depicted in the *Octavia* in a section entitled "Grand Opera" (pp. 265–72).

104. *Le tragedie di Seneca tradotte da M. Lodovico Dolce* (Venice: Gio. Battista et Marchion Sessa, 1560).

which resonate with aspects of Busenello's libretto: In the first argomento, the description of Nerone's attitude toward Ottavia justifies her opening diatribe in Busenello, "Disprezzata regina": "Nerone, having become bored with dealing with her, speaking to his friends, opined that it should have been enough for her to have the title and ornament of wife. And having proposed several times to strangle her, rejected her for being sterile."[105] And his description of Ottavia herself, paraphrasing Tacitus, appropriately characterizes the goal of both of Busenello's laments: "And as Tacitus says, never was there a woman who more moved to pity the eyes of those who looked at her" (E come dice Tacito, non fu mai donna alcuna, che più movesse a pietà gl'occhi di coloro, che la miravano). The second, much shorter, argomento, which also mentions Ottavia's sterility, adds several further familiar elements: "He rejected her for being sterile. Now Ottavia regrets her most miserable fortune. Besides that, Seneca, Nerone's teacher, laments over the morals and disasters of his time. Finally, on Nerone's order, unhappy Ottavia, the Roman people who had long opposed it now in agreement, is lead to her death."[106] The emphasis on Ottavia's sterility, rather than the trumped-up charge of adultery, finds its way into Nerone's debate with Seneca, while the characterization of Seneca's thoughts aptly encapsulates the content of his critique of the court as "insolente e superba" (2.1) and his commentary on Ottavia's situation (1.7):

Le porpore regali, e Imperatrici,	The royal and imperial purple
D'acute spine, e triboli conteste	of sharp thorns and tribulations composed,
Sotto forma di veste	beneath their raiment
Sono il martirio a prencipi infelici;	are torments for unhappy princes.
Le corone eminenti	Eminent crowns
Servono solo a indiademar tormenti,	serve only to bejewel suffering;
Delle Regie grandezze	of royal grandeur
Si veggono le pompe, e gli splendori,	we see the pomp and splendors,
Ma stan sempre invisibili i dolori.	but the pain remains ever invisible.

Even more relevant for Busenello, however, is Dolce's often-reprinted translation of a contemporary work by a Spanish author, Pedro Mexía's *Historia imperial y Cesarea* of 1545 (*Le vite di tutti gl'imperadori romani da Giulio Cesare insino a Massimiliano*). Here, an account of Nero's reign is confined within a twenty-page narrative.[107] In this case, marginal glosses call attention to particular successive aspects of Nero's story—including

---

105. "Nerone venendogli a noia il praticar seco [with Ottavia] riprendendolo gl'amici, rispose, che bastar la doveva lo haver titolo ed ornamento di moglie. Et havendo più volte proposto di strangolarla, la rifiutò come sterile" (Dolce, *Seneca*, argomento).

106. "La rifiutò come sterile. . . . Hora adunque Ottavia si rammarica della sua miserissima fortuna. . . . Oltre a ciò, si duole Seneca maestro di Nerone de' costumi e della calamità del suo tempo. Finalmente di ordine di Nerone la infelice Ottavia, concedendolo il popolo Romano, che buona pezza lo haveva negato, e condotta alla morte" (Dolce, *Seneca*, argomento).

107. *Le vite di tutti gl'imperadori romani da Giulio Cesare insino a Massimiliano tratte per M. Lodovico Dolce dal libro spagnuolo del nobile cavaliere Pietro Messia, con alcune utili cose in diversi luoghi aggiunte*, first published

characterizations as well as incidents in the plot—e.g.: *Seneca maestro, S'inamora di Poppea, Superbia di Poppea, Si dilettava soverchiamente di musica, Rifiuta Ottavia e sposa Poppea, Ottavia sbandita da Nerone, Morte di Lucano e di Seneca, Morte di Poppea,* and so on. Although these glosses generally parallel Tacitus's ordering of events, their emphasis of some events and neglect of others shapes the material in a special way, providing a particular slant that is reflected in Busenello's drama. "Seneca maestro" (p. 86), for instance, describes the relationship between Seneca and Nerone that forms the background of their interaction in Busenello's text: "The good counsel of Seneca could suppress and restrain his evil inclinations for some time, and was the reason that, at the beginning of his reign, he behaved like a good prince" (Poterono i buoni consigli di Seneca reprimere qualche tempo, e tenere a freno le sue cattive inclinationi, e furono cagione, che ne' cominciamenti del suo Imperio facesse da buon prencipe). "S'inamora di Poppea" (p. 90) efficiently characterizes the motivations and actions of both Nerone and Poppea, as portrayed by Busenello:

> Allowing himself to be overcome by his cupidity ... he fell in love with the wife of his great friend Ottone, who, after some time had passed, was himself made emperor. Called Poppea Sabina ... she was a beautiful woman, but also unrestrained and immoral, who longing for Nerone to satisfy her desires without disturbing Ottone, her husband, as a reward for his good service he sent him to Spain as governor of Portugal, and began to make love to Poppea freely, forgetting and disdaining his own wife, Ottavia. This made Poppea so arrogant that, becoming ashamed at being a mere concubine, with great insistence she dedicated herself to procure and request from Nerone that he reject Ottavia and take her as his legitimate wife. And seeing that Agrippina was a great impediment to this, she managed to make sure that the incipient discord between mother and son became inflamed. Through the good offices of Poppea and through her own wickedness, the mother became so hated by Nerone that he decided to have her killed.[108]

If we replace Agrippina with Seneca, as Busenello did, this passage closely parallels the action of the libretto as a whole. Finally, two consecutive rubrics, "Rifiuta Ottavia e sposa

---

in 1558 (Venice: Giolito). The section devoted to Nero is found on pp. 85–104. Dolce's translation was reprinted at least thirteen times in Venice during the sixteenth and seventeenth centuries. See Mauro Calcagno, "Staging Musical Discourses in Seventeenth-Century Venice: Francesco Cavalli's *Eliogabalo*" (Ph.D. diss., Yale University, 2000), 118 and n. 71.

108. "Lasciandosi egli vincer dalle sue cupidigie ... si accese dell'amor della moglie del suo grande amico Ottone; che di poi in processo di tempo fu fatto imperatore, la quale era chiamata Poppea Sabina ... donna bellissima ... ma con tutto ciò incontinente, e disonesta: la quale bramando Nerone di recare a suoi desiderii senza disturbo dando ad Ottone suo marito questo guiderdone della sua buona servitù lo mandò in Ispagna governatore di Portogallo, e si mise liberamente ad amar questa Poppea, scordandosi, ed isprezzando la sua propria moglie, Ottavia.... Di ciò Poppea s'insuperbì tanto, che recandosi a vergogna l'esser concubina, con grande instanza si diede a procurare, ed a ricercar di Nerone, che rifiutando Ottavia, prenderse lei per sua legittima moglie. E veggendo che ciò era un grande impedimento Agrippina ... s'ingegnò di operare che le cominciate discordie tra la madre e 'l figlio s'infiammassero.... per la buona diligenza di Poppea, e per la sua propria malvagità, venne a Nerone la madre in così fatto odio, che deliberò di farla morire" (Dolce, *Le vite*, 90).

Poppea" and "Ottavia sbandita da Nerone" (both p. 94), describe actions in Busenello's text that are also consecutive, though essentially in reverse order.

Beyond Dolce, and more chronologically proximate to our libretto, are the various Incognito *novelle*, including Ferrante Pallavicino's *Le due Agrippine* and Federico Malipiero's *L'imperatrice ambiziosa*, both published in 1642. Although focused on Agrippina, Nerone's mother, these two volumes expand upon themes and characters associated with her (Nerone, Poppea, Ottavia, Seneca) in ways that resonate in Busenello's text.[109]

The important point about Busenello's (contradictory) attitude toward his sources is that he simultaneously flaunted his departure from and minimized his dependence on them. His purpose was clear. It was certainly in accordance with Incognito philosophy to keep one's sources hidden. It was equally appropriate for him to assume an anti-classical pose, as if in explicit defiance of the Aristotelian strictures regarding verisimilitude.[110] Indeed, as we shall see, it is precisely this attitude that energizes the debate between his modern work and its two eminently classical—that is, ancient—predecessors, *Ritorno* and *Nozze*.

But not all aspects of classicism were equally dispensable for Busenello. His prologue, for Fortune, Virtue, and Love, nearly follows Aristotle's requirements. It features its own allegorical characters, who introduce the subject of the drama and who instruct the audience in the lessons to be learned. (The fact that one of them, Love, eventually appears in the drama itself may be considered a slight stretching of the rules.) Busenello evidently found it expedient to observe the unities in *L'incoronazione di Poppea*, despite the license for their abuse provided by modern taste; otherwise he might have been expected to have flaunted his disrespect for them, too, as he had done in his previous libretto, *La Didone*. Of that work he had announced that "it reflects modern opinions," that "it is not constructed according to ancient rules but, following [modern] Spanish usage represents years rather than hours."[111] Not so *Incoronazione*, which, like *Ritorno* and *Nozze*, clearly transpires during a single revolution of the sun. Indeed, were there any doubt, the scenario proclaims the unity of time, assuring the audience on several occasions that the actions it is about to witness are taking place during that very day (2.1: Mercurio, sent by Pallade, announces to Seneca that he will certainly die *in quel giorno*; 2.13: Amor protests that besides saving Poppea, he wishes to crown her *in quel giorno*; 3.5: Nerone swears to Poppea that she will be his wife *in quel giorno*; see Appendix 4, B). Busenello was a pragmatic modernist. His choices depended on his needs; the rules were up for grabs, to be

---

109. The relevance of each of these sources to particular aspects of Busenello's libretto will be discussed in due course. Heller (*Emblems*), 147–52, mentions many other contemporary treatments of the Poppea subject, including Giovanni Francesco Loredano's dialogue "La Poppea," as well as various interpretations of Tacitus that Busenello would probably have known.

110. Mauro Calcagno would consider this attitude fully in keeping with the Incogniti's philosophy of Nothing. See his "Signifying Nothing: On the Aesthetics of Pure Voice in Early Venetian Opera," *JM* 20 (2004): 461–97, esp. 473. Note that the emblem of the Incogniti was the Nile, a river whose source was famously unknown.

111. "Quest'Opera sente delle opinioni moderne. Non è fatta al prescritto delle Antiche regole; ma all'usanza Spagnuola rappresenta gl'anni, e non le hore" (*La Didone*, preface).

used or abused according to necessity. He could just as well respect one of them—the unity of time—as he could reject another—the five-act structure.

But while Busenello opted for the modern three-act division in *Incoronazione*,[112] this was far from a casual choice motivated by a desire to seem "modern." The three-act structure can be seen to be fully as intrinsic to that work as the five-act structure is to the "classical" librettos (Table 15). Both of the intervals between the acts allow for the passage of imagined (rather than represented) time that is essential to the dramatic verisimilitude, in that each enables a crucial event that has just transpired to accumulate its full resonance. By the end of the first act, Seneca's doom is clearly sealed—as Poppea, who has suggested it, knows, as Nerone, who has ordered it, knows, and as Ottone, who has overheard Nerone's order, knows as well. Most important, the audience knows. But the key player in this particular intrigue, Seneca himself, has not yet been apprised of his fate. The pause before the second act heightens anticipation of what his response might be. (And, on a more mundane level, it allows for the passage of reasonable time for Nerone's messenger to reach him.)

The interval between the second and third acts works on the audience in a similar way. We have just witnessed the failure of Ottone's attempt on Poppea's life. Here, we expect the interval to provide time for the information to reach the other characters. Despite the passage of that time, however, when Drusilla opens act 3 she has not yet heard the news. Her ignorance is particularly ironic, since it is she who will be accused of the crime. This interval intensifies the poignancy of Drusilla's situation, a poignancy exacerbated by the excessive happiness of her song.[113]

But there is a larger structure in *Incoronazione*—what we might call a macro-structure, a binary division that interacts with and draws energy from the three-act division. Seneca's death bisects the action, positioned as it is close to the center of the middle act and representing the moment of catastrophe (or peripeteia), at which all of the accumulated tensions begin to resolve. In the first half of the libretto, while the stoic philosopher is alive, his position and influence act upon the other characters, most of whom show at least some signs of conscience: Ottavia's moral and religious beliefs prevent her from avenging herself, despite her rage against Nerone; Ottone cannot allow himself to yield to his anger; and even Arnalta cannot condone her mistress's ambition and feels pity for Ottone; most important, Nerone cannot bring himself to send Ottavia into exile, though he recognizes, with Poppea's prompting, that Seneca's death is a necessary prerequisite to such action and finally orders it. In the second half, after that death has taken place, the entire moral fabric of the world unravels: Ottavia plots a murder and blackmails Ottone to commit it;

---

112. The act division in *Incoronazione* may not have been specifically directed against the classical model. (His *Didone*, also in three acts, was equally modern. Since it was based on the same Virgilian source as *Nozze*, though treated much more freely, it was perhaps more blatantly in opposition.) Busenello chose five acts for *La prosperità infelice di Giulio Cesare*, but ostentatiously disobeyed other Aristotelian rules, notably those regarding the unities. See *OSV*, 51.

113. On Drusilla's characteristic naïveté, see Chap. 7; also Ellen Rosand, "Monteverdi's Mimetic Art: *L'Incoronazione di Poppea*," *COJ* 1 (1989): 113–37, esp. 122–23.

TABLE 15
Structure of *L'incoronazione di Poppea*

Act and scene	Setting	Characters
Prologue		
Act 1		
1	Poppea's palace	Ottone–Soldiers
2		Soldiers
3		Nerone–Poppea
4		Poppea–Arnalta
5	Rome	Ottavia–Nutrice
6		Seneca–Ottavia–Valletto
7		Seneca
8		Pallade–Seneca
9		Nerone–Seneca
10		Nerone–Poppea (*Ottone in disparte*)
11		Ottone–Poppea (*Arnalta in disparte*)
12		Ottone
13		Ottone–Drusilla
Act 2		
1	Seneca's villa	Mercurio–Seneca
2		Seneca–Liberto
3		Seneca–Famigliari (Death of Seneca)
[4]		[Seneca–Virtù]
5	Rome	Valletto–Damigella
6		Nerone–Lucano (Tigellino and Petronio)
[7]		[Nerone–Poppea]
8		Ottone
9		Ottavia–Ottone
10		Drusilla–Valletto–Nutrice
11		Ottone–Drusilla
12	Garden	Poppea–Arnalta
13		Amore–Poppea–Arnalta
14		Amore–Poppea–Ottone–Arnalta
[15]		[Amor]
Act 3		
1	Rome	Drusilla
2		Arnalta–Littore–Drusilla
3		Nerone–Drusilla–Arnalta–Littore
4		Ottone–Drusilla–Nerone–Littore
5		Nerone–Poppea
6		Ottavia
7		Arnalta
8	Nerone's palace	Nerone–Poppea–Consoli–Tribuno–Amore–Venere–Gratie–Amorini

NOTE: Brackets indicate scenes omitted in both musical settings.

Ottone, yielding to his anger and agreeing to kill Poppea, exploits Drusilla's love for him; Arnalta accepts Poppea's ambitious expediency; and Nerone repudiates Ottavia.

This grand bipartite structure, enlisting the momentum generated in the long first act to bridge the division between it and the second, contrasts with that of *Ritorno* with its much more deliberate, gradual, iconic accumulation of momentum. On the smaller scale of scene structure, the formal articulations and recurrences, the symmetries and reiterated emphases of *Ritorno* are replaced in *Incoronazione* by a much more natural flow of scenes—at one point, concluding act 1, nine in succession, without a break (cf. Table 15)—and by an easier and more relaxed interchange among characters.[114]

Those characters, too, are very different. The decorous emblematic protagonists of *Ritorno* and *Nozze*, painted in primary colors, who express themselves in their own individual ways—strong and steadfast Enea, modest Lavinia, wise Ulisse, faithful Penelope—yield in *Incoronazione* to figures of much greater complexity and chiaroscuro. Busenello's characters are ambivalent, uncertain, changeable, less fixed by their masks; their colors are shaded; no single adjective suffices to describe any one of them. Such characters were ideally suited to Monteverdi's well-known penchant for portraying emotional flux. Once again we can thank the author of *Nozze* for illuminating this point. In a now familiar passage from his scenario letter, Torcigliani explains that he himself felt compelled to depart from his Virgilian source, requiring Enea to pass quickly from calm to suffering, and thence to happiness. He did this in order to indulge Monteverdi's taste for rapidly changing emotions, thereby providing the composer with the opportunity to demonstrate the marvelous variety of his art (see Appendix 2 [i]).

The new psychological complexity of Busenello's characters could only have emerged from the kind of freedom manifested in his libretto as a whole, from the librettist's new attitude toward a new kind of source, from his self-conscious modernism. It is one of the most tangible fruits of his opposition to the ancients.

---

114. In a kind of cinematic juxtaposition, the two widely separated scenes in act 2 that begin with the same phrase, "Hor che Seneca è morto" (scene 5 for Nerone and Lucano, scene 10 for Poppea and Arnalta), can perhaps be thought of as occurring simultaneously. Dubowy ("Bemerkungen") made a similar observation with respect to *Ritorno* (see above, n. 56).

6

A Master of Three Servants

Monteverdi's Way with Words

Perhaps the most distinctive aspect of all three of the Venetian librettos is that they were designed for a composer notoriously exigent about his texts. Unlike his younger contemporaries in Venice, those neophytes "who failed to understand the true nature of theatrical music,"[1] Monteverdi had a proven track record, a long stylistic history, an established reputation for his way with words. In writing for him, the Venetian authors had that history to contend with, and the model of their predecessors to learn from: Alessandro Striggio, Ottavio Rinuccini, and Giulio Strozzi.

The composer's requirements were of various kinds. Some were explicit; Monteverdi discusses them forthrightly in his letters, as we will see, and his librettists were certainly as well apprised of them as we are today. Others, more implicit, they would surely have intuited from the works themselves, from his editorial intervention in the setting of famous texts as different from one another as the sonnets of Petrarch and the Vespers antiphons for the Blessed Virgin Mary. A prime example is "Hor che 'l ciel e la terra" from the Madrigals of 1638, in which the poetic form of the sonnet virtually disappears under the weight of musico-rhetorical expression. The composer left almost no text untouched: repetitions, elisions, fragmentation, and emphases rendered some of them almost unrecognizable in their Monteverdian transformations.

---

1. The phrase, cited in Chap. 1, n. 1, comes from Badoaro's letter to the composer given in Appendix 1.

Monteverdi's concern with the quality of the librettos he set is clear from his brusque dismissal of various texts offered to him, on miscellaneous pretexts. Actions speak louder than words; we can discount his professions of obedience to his patrons and willingness to comply with their suggestions and his disingenuous disclaimers of all knowledge of poetry.[2] He even declared, in a letter of 1627, that his very willingness to write an opera depended on the libretto being by an excellent poet. This was one of two prerequisites. The other was that there be adequate time available for the undertaking. Otherwise, he concluded, the task would be too difficult, would not appeal to him, and would undoubtedly cause him intense suffering, as he had learned from bitter experience. He was thinking of his masterpiece of 1608, *L'Arianna*, on a libretto by Ottavio Rinuccini, which had obviously fulfilled the first of these criteria, but not the second.[3]

His intervention in the librettos evidently began well before he actually set them. We recall that Badoaro submitted a draft of the text of *Ritorno* to the composer and then revised it according to his criticisms.[4] Even Rinuccini's *Arianna*, which Monteverdi found so congenial to his taste, most likely bears signs of the composer's influence; composer and librettist must have worked together on the project, particularly during the two periods of several months when Rinuccini was in Mantua, in late 1607 and then again in the following year.[5] Certainly both were involved in revisions to the work in response to the complaint of the Grand Duchess on 26 February 1608 that it was "too dry" (troppo asciutto). Originally scheduled for January, the opera was not performed until 28 May, after having been revised by composer and poet.[6]

---

2. As in the often-quoted letter no. 19 of 9 December 1616 dismissing "il librettino contenente la favola maritima delle *Nozze di Tetide*" by some nameless poet ("che non so il nome, e tanto più quanto che questa professione della poesia non è mia"). Unless otherwise indicated, the texts of the letters, and the numbers, are taken from *Claudio Monteverdi, Lettere*, ed. Lax. See also *The Letters of Claudio Monteverdi*, trans. and ed. Denis Stevens (London: Faber, 1980; rev. ed. Oxford: Clarendon Press, 1995).

3. "Vorei però pregar e supplicar Vostra Signoria Illustrissima che, dignandosi Sua Altezza Serenissima che mettessi in musica la comedia che Ella mi acenna, che si degnasse d'aver consideratione a duoi capi: l'uno che potessi aver tempo comodo per conporla, e l'altro che [the libretto] fosse fatta di mano eccellente, ché non men riceverei non poca fatica e poco gusto d'animo, anzi afflicione grandissima, in ponere versi in musica fatti alla bonissima, di quello farei nel breve tempo—ché la brevità del tempo fu cagione ch'io mi riducessi quasi alla morte nel scrivere l'*Arianna*" (1 May 1627; letter no. 92). On the excellence of the libretto of *Arianna*, see Gary Tomlinson, "Madrigal, Monody, and Monteverdi's *Via naturale alla immitatione*," *JAMS* 34 (1981): 60–108.

4. Chap. 1, p. 6 and n. 15. Torcigliani implies that he did the same thing (Chap. 1, pp. 9–10): "ho io schifati li pensieri e concetti tolti di lontano, e più tosto atteso a gli affetti, come vuole il Signor Monteverde, al quale per compiacere ho anco mutate, e lasciate molte cose di quelle, ch'io havea poste prima" (Appendix 2 [n]). See also below, p. 216.

5. See Angelo Solerti, *Gli albori del melodramma*, 3 vols. (Milan, Palermo, and Naples: Sandron, 1904–1905; repr. Hildesheim: Olms, 1969), 1: 80, 86, 92, 95–96. Tomlinson argues that Rinuccini's text inspired the development of Monteverdi's style, a point of view confirmed by Doni; see Tomlinson ("Madrigal," 86). Most recently on the circumstances surrounding the composition of *Arianna*, see Bojan Bujić, "Rinuccini the Craftsman: A View of his *L'Arianna*," *EMH* 18 (1999): 75–117.

6. Solerti, *Albori*, 1: 92, and Tomlinson, "Madrigal," n. 57. Bujić, "Rinuccini," 77, n. 9, suggests that the duchess, Leonora de' Medici, who probably remembered the elaborate Florentine intermedi of 1589 and the productions surrounding her sister Maria's wedding in 1600, would have found Arianna "dry" in comparison. On

Though he clearly esteemed the poet, and set a number of his texts in addition to *Arianna*—some of the most impressive late madrigals, such as "Ogni amante è guerrier" and the "Lament of the Nymph"—Monteverdi's approval was hardly unconditional. His disparaging comments on a later Rinuccini libretto, *Narciso*, which the author had hoped he would set, make it clear that he found it unsatisfactory: "[the work] does not have the force I would like, because of the many sopranos that would be needed for so many nymphs, and with many tenors for so many shepherds, and with no other variety, and then with such a tragic and sad ending."[7] The libretto lacked the requisite dramatic power, and in this case at least, that power involved the choice of vocal parts. The conventions of vocal scoring were clearly an issue for him: nymphs had to be sopranos, shepherds tenors. We can sense how he would have appreciated the variety of characters, of different ages and social classes, featured in all three of his Venetian librettos, and suspect also some possible dissonance with respect to the casting of *Incoronazione*, with its castrato heroes. The lead roles in *Orfeo* and *Ritorno* are tenors.[8]

Gary Tomlinson has argued that the libretto for *Orfeo* by Alessandro Striggio was less well suited to Monteverdi's style than Rinuccini's *Arianna*, and that a key number, Orfeo's "Tu sei morta," reveals the incompatibility of text and music—and between poet and composer. But Monteverdi seems to have respected Striggio's skill as a librettist. Not only did he collaborate with him on several subsequent projects—all unfortunately lost, including the eclogue-ballet, *Apollo*—but numerous letters addressed to the poet in his capacity as secretary to the Duke of Mantua exude confidence in his abilities. Several

Rinuccini's likely changes to the libretto, see Bujić, p. 95: "Rinuccini probably extended the opening conversation between Venere and Amore and added more material at the very end of the drama." Bujić, however, is skeptical of interaction between poet and composer, even in response to the dutchess's dissatisfaction (p. 107). See Tim Carter, "Lamenting Ariadne?" *EM* 27 (1999): 395–405, and id., *Musical Theatre*, 202–11, on the possibility that the lament was one of the additions intended to relieve the "dryness" of the first version.

7. "Esso signore, quando era in vita . . . me ne fece grazia dela copia non tanto, ma di pregarmi che la pigliassi, amando egli molto tal sua opera, sperando ch'io l'avessi a porre in musica. Holle dato più volte assalti, e l'ho alquanto digesta nella mia mente, ma a confessar il vero a Vostra Signoria Illustrissima, mi riuscisse, al parer mio, non di quella forza ch'io vorei, per gli molti soprani che gli bisognerebbe per le tante ninfe inpiegate, e con molti tenori per gli tanti pastori e non altro di variazione, e poi con fine tragico e mesto" (letter no. 93).

8. Nino Pirrotta ("Forse Nerone cantò da tenore," in *Musica senza oggettivi: Studi per Fedele D'Amico*, ed. Agostino Ziino [Florence: Olschki, 1991], 1:47–60; repr. in Nino Pirrotta, *Poesia e musica e altri saggi* [Florence: La Nuova Italia, 1994], 179–94), finds it difficult to accept the fact that Nerone and Ottone were originally played by castrati, as the two scores indicate. Finding support in the late date of the scores, he prefers to think that the role of Nerone, at least, was changed in one of the posthumous performances (1646, 1651). See also Roger Freitas, "The Eroticism of Emasculation: Confronting the Baroque Body of the Castrato," *JM* 20 (2000): 196–249, esp. 234–39. In support of Pirrotta's suspicions, it is worth noting that castratos indeed rarely portrayed heroes in the earliest years of Venetian opera, though they were known to play female characters, including goddesses and nurses. In operas beginning in 1643, however, which often featured two male heroes, one was generally played by a castrato, the other by a tenor or bass. Pirrotta's hypothesis might help to explain some of the problems with the transpositions in Vp, particularly in connection with Ottone and Nerone, though it is likely, as we have seen, that Stefano Costa, a castrato, played Nerone at the Venetian premiere.

times he urges Striggio to consider writing a libretto for him,[9] and he defers to his judgment on a number of operatic issues. (To judge from other instances, if some of Monteverdi's compliments can be ascribed to his natural deference toward a patron or social superior, he would have found it difficult to hide any qualms he might have had.) As early as 1620, for example, he reports on the positive reception of the Lament of Apollo, an excerpt of the above-mentioned eclogue by Striggio: "[Since] the Lament of Apollo pleased [the audience] in the manner of its invention, poetry, and music, they think . . . of having afterwards this fine idea of Your Lordship's put on a small stage." And then he asks for additional verses: "If I have to compose the ballet for this, would Your Lordship send me the verses as soon as possible? But if not, I shall add something of my own invention so that such a fine work of Your Lordship's can be enjoyed."[10] He liked Striggio's text for *Apollo*—and he also felt free to ask for fairly specific revisions. Further lines are requested to accommodate a strophic aria for Amore. He then amplifies his request in a passage that demonstrates the workings of his sense of drama: though he wished Amore's aria to have two stanzas, he was concerned that its cheerful mood might end up contrasting too strongly in affect with the immediately preceding lament of Apollo.[11]

Two weeks later Monteverdi sends Striggio a song for another character in the ballet, Peneo, which he says he composed "alla bastarda," knowing how effective such a style is when issuing forth from the mouth of the singer assigned to the role, a certain Signor Amigoni. Moreover, he adds, "it will also serve as contrast from the other songs [of the other characters] and will seem even more different if that god sings only once."[12] He is alert to the

---

9. "Non mancherò alla giornata di far qualche cosa in tal genere di canto rappresentativo, e più voluntieri se Ella maggiormente con Suoi bellissimi versi me ne farà degno" (letter no. 53); "Se dunque ci fosse tempo e poi che avessi l'opera o parto del nobillissimo ingegno Suo, sia sicurissima che ne sentirei giubilo infinito, perché so quanta facilità e proprietà Vostra Signoria Illustrissima mi aportarebbe" (letter no. 92).

10. "Qui da certi signori è statto udito il *Lamento di Apollo* e piaciuto in maniera nella invenzione, ne' versi e nella musica, che pensano, dopo un'ora di concerto che si suol fare da questi tenpi in casa d'un certo signore de casa Benbi, al'audienza del quale vengono principalissimi signori e dame, pensano, dicco, sopra una senetta far conparir questo bel pensiero di Vostra Signoria Illustrissima. . . . Se io doverò fare il ballo, m'invia Vostra Signoria Illustrissima quanto prima li versi; quando che no, gliene attacherò uno a mio caprizzio acciò si goda così bel'opera di Vostra Signoria Illustrissima" (letter no. 41, 1 February 1620). Does Monteverdi's readiness to supply some text himself here remind us of Verdi? With letter no. 45 (22 February 1620), he sends two further sections for the eclogue ("Ecco la sinfonia per Amore e l'altra per la entrata").

11. "Qui dove Amore incomincia a cantare, mi parrebbe bene che Vostra Signoria Illustrissima li agiongesse tre altri versetti di simile piede e simile senso aciò potessesi ripetere un'altra volta la medesima aria, sperando che questo coloretto di questa poca allegrezza non fosse per far mal effetto, seguitando per contrario il passato affetto dolente d'Apollo, e poi andar seguitando, come sta mutando modo di parlare, l'armonia, come parimente fa l'orazione" (letter no. 38, 9 January 1620).

12. "Il canto presente di Peneo è statto fatto da me così in tal genere come alla bastarda, perché so quanto vale tal modo in bocca del signor Amigoni; servirà anco per diversare dali altri canti, e parerà più la differenza in tal deità, cantando che una sol volta" (letter no. 43, 15 February 1620). "Alla bastarda" refers to a singing style that pushes the voice to exceed normal limits of range and capacity for diminutions. The term comes from the viola bastarda, an instrument Monteverdi played. See Richard Wistreich, *Warrior, Courtier, Singer: Giulio Cesare Brancaccio and the Performance of Identity in the Late Renaissance* (Aldershot: Ashgate, 2007), chap. 6.

strengths of a particular performer, and no less alert to the matter of affective contrast. Central to his conception of drama, this topic is one to which he returns repeatedly during the course of his correspondence.

Many other Monteverdi letters offer tantalizing insight into his concerns, both practical and aesthetic: with performers, venue, audience, text setting, and the conventions of operatic production. But two particular groups of letters, addressed to Striggio, and separated by a decade, reveal more consistently, completely, and forcefully his attitude toward opera, his aims as a musical dramatist. The first group concerns a libretto he did not like, Scipione Agnelli's *Tetide,* the second a work he did, Giulio Strozzi's *La finta pazza Licori.*

The six *Tetide* letters, written over a relatively brief period of six weeks from 9 December 1616 to 20 January 1617 (nos. 19–24), contain some of his most direct statements of artistic intent. From the very beginning, Monteverdi has difficulty disguising his positive disdain for the text—"il librettino contenente la favola maritima delle Nozze di Tetide." The subject matter is unsuitable for musical setting. It requires too many sopranos and tenors (nos. 19, 20). It has too few sung ballets, which anyhow are not in appropriate meters; it is too long, containing too much recitative speech and not enough dialogue or arias.[13] Suitable instruments, placed appropriately, will be too difficult to hear and will have to be tripled; likewise, the singers will have to shout rather than sing in a delicate voice. Still, he offers some tactful suggestions for improvement: "if all three Sirens have to sing their songs separately I'm afraid the work will be too long for the audience, and with too little contrast, since *sinfonie* will be required to separate them, runs to support the declamation, and trills, which will produce a certain similarity. So for this reason, and for overall variety, I would consider having the first two madrigals sung alternately, now by one voice, now by two together, and the third by all three voices."[14] Two further suggestions are directed toward enhancing the verisimilitude of the drama. He proposes that Venus's part, "which comes after Peleo's plaint and introduces the florid style of singing, that is with runs and trills," be sung by "Signora Andriana in a loud voice, and then by her two sisters [softly?], so that she is answered by an echo, since the text *(orazione)* contains the following line: 'And let the rocks and the waves tell of love.'" But before this the souls of the listeners should be prepared by an instrumental Sinfonia placed in mid-scene, which would likewise be a response to the text, since following his plaint Peleo says: "But what do I hear in the air? A most sweet celestial concert?" In both of these instances, Monteverdi's aim is to strengthen the link between text and music, to use music to imitate the action.[15]

---

13. Monteverdi's concern with the number of arias is highly relevant to his Venetian librettos; see below.

14. "Se averanno a cantar tutte tre separatamente, che troppo lunga riuscirà l'opera ali ascoltanti, e con poca differenza, poiché tra l'una e l'altra farà de bisogno sinfonia che tramezzi, tirate che sostentino il parlare, e trilli, e in genere riuscirà una certa similitudine, che perciò giudicherei, anco per variazione del tutto, che, interzatamente, li duoi primi madrigaletti or da una e or da due voci insieme fossero cantati e il terzo da tutte tre insieme" (letter no. 22, 6 January 1617). This sounds very much like a description of the prologues of both *Ritorno* and *Incoronazione.*

15. "La parte di Venere, parte prima che viene dopo il pianto di Peleo e prima ad essere udita nel cantar di garbo, cioè in tirate e trilli, averei giudicato per bene che dovesse essere cantata forsi anco dalla signora Andriana

But the crucial shortcoming of the libretto of *Le nozze di Tetide* is one that no amount of tinkering can correct. It is a shortcoming that goes to the very heart of Monteverdi's dramatic aims: the absence of convincing characters. The oft-quoted passage expressing Monteverdi's incredulity, verging on outrage, comes from the very first of the *Tetide* letters:

> I have noticed that the interlocutors are winds . . . And that the winds have to sing! . . . How, dear Sir, can I imitate the speech of winds, if they do not speak? And how can I, by such means, move the passions? Arianna was moving because she was a woman, and similarly Orfeo because he was a man, not a wind. Music can suggest, without any words, the noise of winds and the bleating of sheep, the neighing of horses and so on and so forth; but it cannot imitate the speech of winds because no such thing exists. . . . And as to the story as a whole . . . I do not feel that it moves me at all . . . nor do I feel that it carries me in a natural manner to an end that moves me. Arianna led me to a just lament, and Orfeo to a righteous prayer, but this fable leads me I don't know to what end.[16]

In this aesthetic credo, the composer states unequivocally that his aim is to move the passions, and that he cannot do so unless he himself is moved. When Monteverdi finally learned that *Le nozze di Tetide* was intended not as a full-length opera but as intermedi for a play ("commedia grande"), he was much relieved, and accepted the libretto with no further ado as worthy and most noble.[17] But his misprision (or Striggio's) had forced him into a clear statement of his intent, clarifying for us—perhaps even for himself—his goals as a musical dramatist and, not so incidentally, his sensitivity to genre.

Whereas the *Tetide* letters emphasized the shortcomings of Agnelli's libretto, those concerning Giulio Strozzi's *La finta pazza Licori* emphasized its strengths. This was a text the composer could take seriously, something he could work with, rather than dismissing it out of hand. The dozen letters, written sometimes weekly over the course of an extended

---

come voce forte, e dale due altre sue signore sorelle servita per risposte di eco, stando che l'orazione ha dentro questo verso: 'E sfavillino d'amor li scogli e l'onde', ma prima preparando li animi de li ascoltanti con una sinfonia di ustrimenti contenenti, se fosse possibile, mezza la sena, perché pervengono avanti questi duoi versi di Peleo, dopo fatto il pianto: 'Ma qual per l'aria sento / Celeste, soavissimo concento?' " (letter no. 22). The echo and the heavenly concert are phenomenal or literal music. On the musical imitation of action, see below, on *Licori* and also *Incoronazione*.

16. "Ho visto li interlocutori essere Venti, Amoretti, Zeffiretti e Sirene, e per consequenza molti soprani faranno de bisogno; e s'aggionge di più che li Venti hanno a cantare, cioè li Zeffiri e li Boreali! Come, caro signore, potrò io imitare il parlar de' venti, se non parlano? E come potrò io con il mezzo loro movere li affetti? Mosse l'Arianna per essere donna, e mosse parimente Orfeo per essere omo, e non vento. Le armonie imittano loro medesime, e non con l'orazione, e li streppiti de' venti, e il bellar dele pecore, il nitrire de' cavalli e va discordendo, ma non imitano il parlar de' venti che non si trova! . . . La favola tutta, poi . . . non sento che ponto mi mova, e con difficoltà anco la intendo, né sento che lei me porta con ordine naturale ad un fine che mi mova: l'*Arianna* mi porta ad un giusto lamento e l'*Orfeo* ad una giusta preghiera; ma questa—non so a qual fine" (letter no. 19, 9 December 1616).

17. "Confesso . . . che ella fosse cosa da essere cantata e rapresentata in musica come fu l'*Arianna*, ma dopo inteso dalla passata [lettera] di Vostra Signoria Illustrissima che ha da servire per intermedii de la comedia grande, sì come in quel senso primo io me la credevo di poco rilievo, così, per lo contrario, in questo secondo la creddo degna cosa e nobillissima" (letter no. 22, 6 January 1617).

period from 1 May to 18 September 1627, testify most eloquently to the kind of interaction Monteverdi sought with his poets, the kind of impact he wanted to have, and the values that governed his theatrical philosophy and imagination.[18] Strozzi, with whom Monteverdi was to collaborate several times, must have represented an ideal partner for the demanding composer, for not only did he qualify as an excellent poet ("poeta eccellentissimo" [nos. 92, 96]) and worthy colleague ("degno sogetto" [no. 98]), but he was showing himself willing and able to carry out Monteverdi's ideas.[19]

From his first mention of "un operina . . . assai bella e curiosa, [qual puo tirare da quattrocento versi]" (a little work . . . very beautiful and unusual [which runs to some 400 lines]; [no. 92]), it is clear that the *Licori* project appealed to the composer. He was perhaps particularly attracted by the challenge of imagining the brief original text of some 400 verses, designed by Strozzi in dialogue form as entertainment for a musical evening hosted by Girolamo Mocenigo, as a full-fledged opera, and by the promise of being able to influence the shaping of the text to suit his own dramaturgical purposes, or, as he put it, to his way of thinking ("a mia contemplazione") [no. 96].[20] It was his custom, he explains ("come me"), to suggest alterations—in this case enrichments of the poetic text by the addition of some extra, distinctive scenes.[21] Because Strozzi was so excellent in his profession, such a loyal friend, so anxious to please him, and on the spot, Monteverdi was confident of the results.[22]

Monteverdi wrote all of this not to Strozzi, of course, but to Striggio, himself an experienced librettist in his own right, and acquainted with the circumstances at court—the available singers, the other works being planned, the schedule of events. Striggio may even have been responsible for suggesting some of the alterations to Strozzi's libretto—for example, by making the composer aware that there were three major female singers to accommodate, rather than only one (cf. letter no. 96). But Monteverdi certainly played the major role here. His specific (and far-reaching) concerns with this work, taken together with those expressed

---

18. The letters are numbered 92–104 in Lax and Stevens. The final mention of *La finta pazza* occurs in letter no. 108 of 18 September. Monteverdi had been in contact with Strozzi at least since 1621, when he was commissioned by the "Florentine nation" to write a mass commemorating the death of Cosimo de' Medici. Strozzi, a Florentine, was the official chronicler of the ceremony, which was held at SS. Giovanni e Paolo on 21 May; for Strozzi's chronicle, see Paolo Fabbri, *Monteverdi* (Turin: EDT, 1985), 240; trans. Tim Carter (Cambridge: Cambridge University Press, 1994), 179.

19. "voluntieri conseguita con la sua gentillezza gli pensieri miei; la qual comodità mi rende assai più facile il porla in canto" (letter no. 98, 20 June 1627).

20. Other works commissioned by Mocenigo included *Il combattimento di Tancredi e Clorinda* (1624) and *Proserpina rapita* (1630). On the latter, see Luca Zoppelli, "Il rapto perfettissimo: Un'inedita testimonianza sulla *Proserpina* di Monteverdi," *Rassegna veneta di studi musicali* 3 (1987): 343–45; and Carter, *Musical Theatre*, 226–36.

21. "non voglio mancare . . . di seco [Strozzi] abocarmi e, come me, vedere che esso signore la inrichischi anco di altre variate e diverse sene, come ben gli dirò secondo il mio gusto" (letter no. 94, 22 May 1627).

22. "spero che con la comodità del poeta eccellentissimo che qui mi sarà vicino con desiderio di consolarmi, per essere molto mio signore e amico, di far qualche cosa che non dispiàcerà né a Sua Altezza Serenissima, né a Vostra Signoria Illustrissima . . ." (letter no. 96, 5 June 1627). Friendship, as well as proximity, may have been an important ingredient in these relationships. Badoaro, as we have seen, makes much of his friendship with the composer.

in connection with texts he found less congenial, adumbrate what we may recognize as the composer's "ars dramatica." Likening opera, in its vastness, to an epic poem ("una comedia cantata . . . tanto vol dire come un poema" [no. 92], as opposed to intermedi), he is concerned with every imaginable aspect of its construction, from the choice of subject matter and development of the plot to the sequence of scenes, selection of characters, and distribution of the dialogue ("le convenienze").[23] His first step was to assimilate the libretto as a whole—he uses the verb "digerire" repeatedly for this process—which enabled him to make judgments about it and facilitated his eventual setting.[24] La finta pazza Licori, he reports, is admirable for the beauty of its verse as well as the originality of its subject.[25] Not only is the subject "not bad," but so is the way it unfolds.[26]

This is in marked contrast to Rinuccini's ill-fated Narciso, the other libretto under consideration at the time. This Monteverdi also "digested," but, as we have seen, it did not strike him as strong enough, because of the poor choice of characters and an unappealing ending.[27] La finta pazza, with its thousand little comical situations and graceful plot that by means of a delightful stratagem culminates in a wedding, is infinitely to be preferred,[28] and it will appear far newer, more varied, and more delightful on stage.[29] Though he clearly preferred Strozzi's text to Rinuccini's Narciso for many reasons, one of them had to do with the characters: the fact that Narciso called for so many tenors bothered him, but the problem must have been the nature of the characters, their sameness. He was evidently not averse to having many tenors in another work—Ulisse—as we shall see.[30] Novelty and variety: this combination, which seems to motivate most of Monteverdi's editorial suggestions, comes up in almost every one of the Licori letters. (We saw it in those pertaining to Tetide as well.) In one of his most far-reaching interventions, addressing the fundamental issues of overall dramatic structure and distribution of the action, he urges Strozzi to enrich his text by adding new, varied, and different scenes, as well as characters, so that Licori isn't on stage so often.[31]

---

23. We should note his attention to these same categories in his editing of the Ritorno libretto: sequence of scenes, selection of characters, distribution of dialogue (see below). His conception of opera as epic ("poema")—in contrast to the simpler, less demanding genre of "intermedi per comedia grande"—suggests a further reason why the librettos of Ritorno and Nozze would have appealed to him.

24. For instance, "Già da me è digesta nel modo che tutta sta in maniera tale che so che in brevissimo tempo da me sarebbe posta in musica" (letter no. 95, 24 May 1627).

25. "e nella bellezza del verso e nella invenzione, io l'ho provato in atto dignissimo sogetto e prontissimo" (letter no. 93, 7 May 1627). He could be speaking of Strozzi rather than the text here.

26. "La invenzione non mi par male, né men la spiegatura" (also no. 93).

27. Passage from no. 93 quoted above, n. 7.

28. "doppo fatto mille invenzioncine ridiculose, si riduce al sposalizio con bel'arte d'inganno" (letter no. 92, 1 May 1627).

29. "riuscirà in sena e più nova e più varia e più dilettevole" (letter no. 94, 22 May 1627).

30. As already noted (p. 188), Monteverdi also criticized the libretto of Tetide for requiring too many tenors (and sopranos); see letter no. 20.

31. "Non voglio mancare . . . vedere che esso signore la inrichischi anco di altre variate e diverse sene, come ben gli dirò secondo il mio gusto; e vedere se la può inrichire d'altre novitate con aggionta de personaggi aciò la finta pazza non si vedda cotanto ad operare con frequenza" (letter no. 94).

Novelty and variety are desirable not only among the scenes and characters, but especially within the role of the main character. Every time Licori appears on stage, he assures Striggio, he will make certain that she produces new moods and fresh changes of music as well as gestures.[32] He says it again in the next two letters: his aim is that every time Licori is about to come on stage, she will bring new delight with new variety;[33] Strozzi should restrict her appearances and distinguish each of them by means of new inventions and actions.[34] The composer searches for greater novelty even within Licori's individual speeches, recommending that the poet rewrite some of them accordingly.[35]

Later Monteverdi indicates, not without some satisfaction, the extent to which the concepts of novelty and variety have permeated Strozzi's thinking, and, by implication, the extent to which the librettist has understood his desires. Not only will each of the five acts develop a new action,[36] each will contain a ballet that is different and strange.[37] He is pleased to report, finally, that the finished libretto is "full of many beautiful variations."[38] Monteverdi's incessant, even obsessive, quest for novelty and variety in Strozzi's libretto was not a matter of text alone, of course, but had strong musical implications. He tells us that Licori's successive appearances on stage were to be distinguished by different kinds of music ("nove differenze di armonie" [no. 94]), and his explanation of what he means offers an important key to the understanding of his style: In three of her appearances, he says, "I certainly think the effects will come off well: first, when the camp is being set up, hearing sounds and noises behind the scenes like imitations of her words should not (it seems to me) prove unsuccessful; secondly, when she pretends to be dead; and thirdly, when she pretends to be asleep, for here it will be necessary to use music suggesting sleep" (no. 95).[39]

Three different kinds of music; we can imagine what some of this might have sounded like by extrapolating from the composer's other works. The camp music, presumably in a fast tempo, might well have included military effects such as the rapid arpeggios and repeated notes of the *stile concitato,* similar to those featured in the war-like madrigals of Book 8. In the *Combattimento di Tancredi e Clorinda,* for instance, the orchestra echoes individual gestures of battle as described by the narrator. As for music suggesting sleep,

---

32. "ogni volta che uscisse in scena, aporti sempre novi gusti e nove differenze di armonie come parimente de gesti" (also no. 94).

33. "ogni volta che sia per uscire in scena, sempre abbi ad aportare diletto novo con le variazioni nove" (letter no. 95, 25 May 1627).

34. "la parte di Licori la farà uscire più tardamente e non così quasi ad ogni scena, e la farà uscire sempre con nove invenzioni e azioni" (letter no. 96).

35. "Al mio gusto dice benissimo in duoi o tre lochi, in due altri mi pare potrebbe dire meglio—non già per il verso, ma per la novitade" (letter no. 94).

36. "ogni atto averà azione nova da spiegare" (letter no. 100, 10 July 1627).

37. "Ci sarà un ballo per ogni atto e tutti diversi l'un dal'altro e bizzarri" (also no. 100).

38. "piena di molte belle variazioni" (letter no. 101, 24 July 1627).

39. "In tre lochi ben sì penso sortirassi l'effetto; l'uno di quando forma il campo, che, sentendosi dentro la scena gli soni e gli strepiti simili alle immitazioni dele sue parole . . . l'altro di quando finge essere morta; e terzo di quando ella finge dormire, dovendosi in tal loco adoperare armonie imitanti il sonno" (letter no. 95).

we need look no further than Arnalta's soporific, repetitive lullaby near the end of act 2 of *Incoronazione*, and Poppea's sleepy, halting response to it. In both instances, Monteverdi creates music that mimes—he would say imitates—the dramatic action, the movement of the body: In the first, music is both scenographic and narrative, simultaneously setting the stage and describing the action, the physical activity of a bustling military camp. In the second, music enacts the gradual relaxation of a body overcome by sleep.

The composer hopes to introduce still another novel musical style in connection with the same sleep scene, by having Licori's lover, Aminta, who evidently comes upon her asleep, speak in such a way as not to disturb her.[40] Once again, the aim is dramatic verisimilitude, to compose distinctive music that is directly inspired by the dramatic situation, only here, rather than describing an external action (a noisy camp) or state of being (drowsiness), music *is* the action: the soft voice, the whisper.

Monteverdi leaves somewhat less to the imagination in his description of what probably would have been the most striking musical novelty of the score: the portrayal of Licori's feigned madness, to which he devotes lengthy, notoriously thorny—and much debated—passages in two of his letters to Striggio (nos. 93, 100). In describing what he expects from "la signora Margherita," the performer assigned the role of Licori, Monteverdi manages to articulate the essential features of his theory of musical imitation, which lies at the core of his identity as a composer of opera. Variety, once again, is all-important, and it is in the portrayal of Licori's madness that variety plays its most crucial role. For although within a libretto as a whole it allows for contrasting affections, thereby engaging an audience, in the character of Licori the variety is both unusually constant and unusually intrinsic: it is the very embodiment of her madness. Here, in the unusual literalness of its imitations, music mimes madness.

Because there is so much variety in the role, he explains, implicitly distinguishing it from the other roles in the drama (perhaps any drama), it will require a special kind of singer, one capable of changing emotions (and character) with extreme rapidity, who will be able to portray first a man, then a woman with lively gestures and different (distinct) emotions ("separate passioni")—that is, distinct enough to make her characterization of each credible. He then goes on to explain how this should be done: the portrayal should focus on the specific situation and textual imagery at hand, not that of the past or future, and this focus should extend to the specific word being sung at any one time, ignoring the sense of the phrase in which it is embedded. Monteverdi's locution here, his directive that the imitation specifically ignore the sense of the phrase (in contrast to normal imitation, we might add), emphasizes the abnormality of the situation. Thus, when she speaks of

---

40. "E vorò che mi acomodi anco il ragionamento d'Aminta all'ora quando ella dorme, ché vorei che parlasse con fine che non avesse voce di poterla destare; che tal risguardo di dover parlar sotto voce mi darà occasione di portar nova armonia, e differente da le passate, al senso" (letter no. 94). This is reminiscent of the direction in the *Ritorno* score indicating that a sinfonia is to be played softly so as not to disturb the sleeping Ulisse. Cf. Facsimile 2.

war, she will have to imitate war, when of peace, peace, when of death, death, and so on. And because these transformations and imitations have to follow one another so rapidly, the singer of the role, who should move the audience to laughter and compassion (nearly simultaneously), should forswear all other imitation but that of the moment, suggested by the particular word she has to say.[41] Licori's madness, then, is expressed not by the music itself but in the way that music is attached to the words—its blinkered, obsessive, literal connection to the text's individual images.

In amplifying his description later (10 July), he explains that "signora Margherita will have to play now a soldier, now a ruffian, timid and bold by turns, and master perfectly the appropriate gestures (for each mood), without self-consciousness," because he is constantly aiming to have lively imitations of the music, gestures, and tempi take place behind the scenes (offstage? backstage? in the orchestra?); he believes such a performance will please Striggio because the changes from lively and raucous to gentle and sweet music will take place almost instantaneously so that the meaning of the text ("l'orazione") will really stand out.[42] Here, finally, the purpose of Monteverdi's variety is made explicit: rapid changes of musical style—tempo, melody, harmony—that is, of affect, focus attention on the changing text, conveying its meaning.[43]

And yet with all this, Monteverdi still worries. The words Licori sings must lend themselves to imitation. They cannot be bland or neutral, words that fail to suggest gestures, noises, or other imitative ideas. "In some other places, however, because the words cannot mimic either gestures or noises or any other kind of imitative idea that might suggest itself, I am afraid the previous and following passages might seem weak" [no. 95].)[44] The composer fears a letdown in Licori's role, and perhaps the drama as a whole. He seeks

---

41. "È vero che la parte di Licori, per essere molto varia, non doverà cadere in mano di donna che or non si facci omo e or donna con vivi gesti e separate passioni, perché, la immitazione di tal finta pazzia dovendo aver la considerazione solo che nel presente e non nel passato e nel futuro (per consequenza la immitazione dovendo aver il suo appoggiamento sopra alla parola e non sopra al senso dela clausola), quando dunque parlerà di guerra, bisognerà imitar di guerra, quando di pace, pace, quando di morte, di morte, e va seguitando, e perché le transformazioni si faranno in brevissimo spazio, e le immitazioni. Chi dunque averà da dire tal principalissima parte che move al riso e alla compassione, sarà necessario che tal donna lassi da parte ogni altra immitazione che la presentanea, che gli somministrerà la parola che averà da dire" (letter no. 93).

42. "Resterà solo che la signora Margheritta o divenghi soldato, bravo, o temi, o ardischi, inpadronendosi bene deli proprii gesti, senza tema e rispetto, perché vado tendendo che le immitazioni galiarde e de armonie e gesti e tempi, si rapresentino dietra la sena; e creddo che non dispiacerà a Vostra Signoria Illustrissima, perché si faranno passaggi in un subbito tra le galiarde e streppitose armonie e le deboli e soavi aciò ben bene salti fuori l'orazione" (letter no. 100).

43. This passage has been interpreted differently over the past several decades. Minimizing the composer's explicit reference to the musical depiction of madness, Tomlinson finds the description characteristic of what he regards as the marinesque treatment of text that marks Monteverdi's late works in general (*Monteverdi and the End of the Renaissance* [Berkeley and Los Angeles: University of California Press, 1987], 205). Most other commentators have recognized it as exceptional rather than characteristic (e.g., Bianconi, *Music in the Seventeenth Century*, 40).

44. "Ma in certi altri che le parole non ponno aver imitazione de' gesti o de' strepiti od altro modo d'immitazione che salti fuori, dubito che languiderebbe o il passato od il futuro" (letter no. 95).

continuously vivid dramatic situations that can be encapsulated in imitable words, thus allowing his music to do its affective work, to assert its expressive power.

❧

The feigned madness of Licori haunted or inspired Giulio Strozzi in his subsequent career as one of the most influential librettists in the early years of Venetian public opera. Closely involved with the Ferrari–Manelli troupe, he provided texts for the inauguration of two opera houses, *La Delia*, with music by Manelli, for SS. Giovanni e Paolo in 1639, and *La finta pazza*, set by Sacrati, for the Novissimo in 1641. The latter, as we have seen, initiated a trilogy analogous to Monteverdi's, and it became a vehicle for a series of traveling companies headed by Sacrati. Performed throughout Italy during the course of the 1640s, *La finta pazza* played an important role in spreading the fame of Venetian opera.

Although Strozzi may not have been a complete neophyte in 1627 when he began his first theatrical collaboration with Monteverdi (he had already written a couple of plays, including *Ersilda* in 1621), the composer's influence seems to have rubbed off on him. We gain some sense of this from a couple of remarks in his preface to the libretto of *La Delia*. He begins his note to the reader by declaring, in terms reminiscent of those used by Torcigliani in the preface to *Le nozze d'Enea*, that he has stayed away from easy "concetti" and metaphors, "the fake coin of eloquence" that is so easily produced today by those [writers] who fail to recognize that many years and great effort are required to produce the pure gold of a truly natural style.[45] Strozzi then moves to the topic of music, noting the importance of a close relationship to text:

> Music is only the sister of that poetry that wishes to enjoy a sibling relationship with it, but when they don't understand one another well, they are neither relatives nor friends. Song that soothes the soul can become unappealing in two ways: when it is forced to follow the false visions of the poet or when the word or the last syllable of the word fades away in the spaciousness of a theater, causing the listener to lose the thread of accumulated ideas. More in the mind than in the ear, and more declaimed than sung must those verses be, which are seasoned by musical harmonies. And the repetition of delightful things does not cause boredom.[46]

Finally, in a postscript to the scenario, Strozzi speaks briefly of the music of Manelli, his collaborator in *La Delia*, praising two particular characteristics of his style: "un'imitatione

---

45. "Io non infilzo concetti, né sono Alchimista di Metafore. Se sapessero alcuni con quanta poca fatica si fa la moneta falsa dell'eloquenza, che corre hoggidì, si arrossirebbono in darle cotanto spaccio e s'intendessero similmente quanto sta malagevole il formar l'oro puro d'uno stile facile insieme, e sostenuto, non si riderebbono di coloro, che doppo l'esercitio di molti anni arrivano quasi a saperlo fare" (Giulio Strozzi, *Delia*, preface, p. 5).

46. "La Musica è sorella di quella Poesia, che vuole assorellarsi seco, ma, quando non s'intendono bene tra di loro, non sono né attenenti, né amiche. Il canto, che raddolcisce gli animi riesce in due maniere un'abborrita cantilena, o quando s'ha da gir dietro alle chimere del Poeta, o quando dileguandosi la parola, o la finale d'alcuna

di parole mirable," and "un'armonia propria, varia, e dilettevole," qualities that figured among those valued by Monteverdi. It is almost uncanny to hear the phrases themselves echoing specific passages from Monteverdi's letters to Striggio regarding Strozzi's text.[47]

ə⁊

The loss of so many of Monteverdi's dramatic works is lamentable, and has been deplored for more than a century. One thinks especially of *Arianna*, so highly praised in its day, and *Le nozze d'Enea*, so proximate and integral to the two operatic masterpieces of the composer's last years. But in one sense, at least, one feels that the greatest loss of all is that of *La finta pazza Licori*. Not only are we deprived of an extraordinary work, the shaping of which sustained the composer's interest over a period of more than six months, but we must forgo the opportunity of fully appreciating Monteverdi's own analysis of the piece, as provided by his letters. To be sure, the correspondence offers some sketchy details about the work as a whole: we know that what began as a dialogue of some 400 verses (presumably for Licori and Aminta) had become, within six months, a five-act drama with ballets. We also know that it ended in a marriage, presumably between Licori and Aminta, that there were at least three striking scenes for Licori, a role played by the famous soprano Margherita Basile, and that there were parts for two other Mantuan prime donne (her sisters?) and possibly the "bassetto" Rapallino.[48]

We can tell something more from Strozzi's second libretto of madness—what we might call *La finta pazza Deidamia*, the libretto set by Sacrati in 1641, which probably incorporated material from the earlier work.[49] Both Strozzi's text and Sacrati's musical setting of Deidamia's feigned madness reflect qualities that Monteverdi emphasized in his letters to Striggio—vivid, sharply juxtaposed images, literal musical imitations, of war, sleep—but this must be a pale substitute for Monteverdi's own lost setting.

It is likely, as Tomlinson has argued, that Monteverdi never actually set—or even saw—Strozzi's full text of *La finta pazza Licori*. The opera probably never came to fruition.[50] But his epistolary critique offers at least some compensation. It serves not only

---

voce nell'ampiezza de' Teatri, smarriscono gli uditori il filo de gli ammassati concetti. Prima nella memoria, che ne gli orecchi; e più decantati, che cantati devon'esser que' versi, che si rivolgono nel condimento delle musicali armonie; e delle cose dilettevoli la repetitione non reca tedio" (Strozzi, *Delia*, preface, pp. 5–6).

47. "M'era scordato di dirle, come il Signor Francesco Mannelli Romani, che vestì di Musica . . . con molto applauso l'Andromeda, e la Maga Fulminata del Signor Benedetto Ferrari, ha questa volta mostrato un eccesso del suo affetto, & un sommo del suo valore in honorar la mia Delia: io so quel, che mi dico: stupirà Venetia in sentir a qual segno arrivi lo studio fatto in quest'Opera dal Signor Manelli: Ha un'imitazione di parole mirabile, un'armonia propria, varia, e dilettevole. In somma, come esca alle stampe questa fatica, si conoscerà, se ho parlato per interesse, o più tosto defraudato al vero" (Giulio Strozzi, *Argomento e scenario della Delia*, 26–27).

48. For Rapallino, mentioned in letters nos. 93–96, 98, and 118, see Richard Wistreich, "'La voce è grata assai, ma . . .': Monteverdi on Singing," *EM* 22 (1994): 7–19.

49. This argument is pursued in *OSV*, 349–50.

50. Gary Tomlinson, "Twice Bitten, Thrice Shy: Monteverdi's 'finta' *Finta pazza*," *JAMS* 36 (1983): 303–11.

to elucidate that specific lost work, but also those works that have survived. By extrapolating from the letters, we learn much about the composer's impact on (and attitudes toward) his other librettos. More important for our purposes, they allow us to evaluate the extent to which he found what he wanted in the texts of his Venetian trilogy. More explicitly than any music, if not more eloquently, the Licori correspondence, along with several other choice letters, reveals Monteverdi's aims as a musical dramatist.

Speech and Song, Recitative and Aria

As we have seen, by the time Monteverdi finally began to compose for the public theaters in Venice, his idiosyncrasies were widely recognized—much as he had revealed them to Striggio, his faithful correspondent. It must have been something of a commonplace that his central objective as a composer was to move the passions of his listeners. Badoaro and Torcigliani tell us anew of the composer's taste for simplicity, his aversion to abstruse thoughts and concepts, and his focus on portraying the affections, particularly contrasting ones, which provided him with the opportunity of displaying the full pathos of his art. These remarks are amplified by the composer's first biographer Matteo Caberloti, writing after Monteverdi's death. Caberloti describes the great emotional range and contrast displayed in the operas, which change from moment to moment: "now they invite laughter, which all at once is forced to change into crying, and just when you are thinking of taking up arms in vengeance, a marvelous change of harmony disposes your heart to clemency; in one moment you feel yourself filled with fear and in the next you are possessed by complete confidence."[51] But because Monteverdi's Venetian librettists worked with him directly, in the same place at the same time on productions in their own city, their interaction was never documented in letters that might providentially be preserved for later centuries. We are nonetheless afforded some insight into their collaboration by the unique circumstances surrounding the sources of the operas—the survival, as we have seen, of material representing multiple layers of the compositional process.

Within the commercial atmosphere that encouraged the development of public opera in Venice, it must have been standard procedure for librettists to conceive their texts for particular composers. We know that the author of the very first Venetian librettos, *Andromeda* and *La maga fulminata*, Benedetto Ferrari, wrote his texts for the composer Francesco Manelli. But the two men were members of the same troupe and collaboration took place in private, within the confines of the troupe's regular activities that culminated in the performance, and we have no evidence that sheds light on the interaction

---

51. "hora t'invitano al riso, il quale in un tratto sforzato dei cangiare in pianto, e quando pensi di pigliar l'armi alla Vendetta, all'hora appunto con miracolosa metamorfosi cangiandosi l'harmonia si dispone il tuo cuore alla Clemenza: in un subito ti senti riempire di timore, quando con altrettanta fretta t'assiste ogni confidenza." Matteo Caberloti, "Laconismo delle alte qualità di Claudio Monteverdi," in *Fiori poetici raccolti nel funerale del . . . signor Claudio Monteverde . . .* , ed. Giovanni Battista Marinoni (Venice: Miloco, 1644), 8.

between librettist and composer. There is no score, only librettos printed well after the performances—presumably in a form already edited by the composer. With operas whose scores have been preserved, such as Cavalli's, we are almost equally at a loss, for the differences between scores and librettos are necessarily negligible. Again, the librettos were presumably printed after the text was set, in a form already modified in connection with the composer's requirements. Indeed, many librettos show evidence of having been printed at the very last minute, in order to accommodate the exigencies of a particular performance. They cannot be relied upon to reflect the original text.

But as should be well known by now, Monteverdi's Venetian librettos have survived primarily in manuscript, and some of these certainly represent an earlier text than those of the scores, even though they may have been copied later. In the case of *Ritorno* and *Nozze,* as we noted, nearly all the librettos preserve a literary version of the text, presumably a version close to the one first presented to the composer (though we should probably take Badoaro seriously when he claims to have submitted even earlier drafts of some scenes to the composer for editing).[52] Only the three-act libretto of *Nozze* represents a later, edited text, equivalent to that in the *Ritorno* score. With *Incoronazione* the situation is more complicated. While Busenello's libretto as printed in the collected edition of 1656 probably transmits something close to the author's original text of 1643—analogous to the literary librettos of *Ritorno* and *Nozze*—most of the manuscript librettos are obviously later, though not necessarily later than 1651, the approximate date of the scores we have. The Udine libretto, as we have seen, was probably copied from the score for the original production version, and must therefore date from around 1643. Precisely because they are so varied, so unfixed, these sources provide a window into the composer's workshop. They allow us to observe Monteverdi's editing procedures at close range. The librettists' understanding of the composer's requirements can be measured by the material they gave him.

IL RITORNO D'ULISSE

In his letters, Monteverdi criticizes a dramatic text more than once for its overabundance of dialogue at the expense of expressive singing—what we might translate as a potential disproportion between action and emotional expression, or between recitative and aria.[53] This criticism is implicit in his setting of the *Ritorno* libretto, where he seems to have exploited every available opportunity for lyrical expansion, even rewriting recitative text to allow for lyrical setting.[54] But the librettists had to balance the requirement for lyrical

---

52. In his prefatory letter to Monteverdi (see Appendix 1).

53. The opposed terms in letter no. 19 are "parlare" and "cantar di garbo." In letter no. 20, the composer complains of too few dialogues between characters in a particular libretto, and the few there are, he continues, are spoken rather than sung ("e que' pochi parlano e non cantano di vaghezze").

54. I discuss this in *OSV,* 250–56. See also Carter, "'In Love's Harmonious Consort,'" and id., *Musical Theatre,* chap. 3.

expression with that of verisimilitude—a familiar Monteverdian desideratum, implied by his request for human characters that would be capable of moving him—and the audience—by their emotions, characters like Arianna and Orfeo. Underlying the requirement for verisimilitude was the knowledge, clearly articulated by Badoaro, among others, that human beings did not normally carry out their daily activities in song, particularly strophic song, in which the same music was repeated for changing text.[55] To be sure, there were exceptions. Certain characters—gods and goddesses, servants—were not governed by the same standards of realistic behavior as historical figures. Even historical figures, though, might be forgiven for expressing themselves lyrically under duress—but not formally, where repetition implied some kind of control that was antithetical to their heightened emotional state.

Accordingly, although Badoaro provided various points of repose within his *versi sciolti*, brief passages set apart by closed rhyme scheme and meter, the libretto of *Ritorno* has relatively few closed forms that explicitly call for lyrical setting—only eight strophic texts in all. In addition to a brief strophic duet for Melanto and Eurimaco, and two arias for the Suitors, these include arias for Melanto (1.2 and 2.1), Minerva (1.8), Iro (2.3), and Nettuno (5.5): a servant, a god and goddess, and a beggar, all characters for whom formal singing was either natural or forgivable. (Strophic arias for the Suitors and Moors are omitted in the score.)[56] But Monteverdi created a number of other occasions for lyricism, capitalizing on formal cues present in the libretto—a recurrent refrain, for instance, or a metrically coherent textual passage set off by its rhyme scheme, meter, or both. Such passages often coincide with the expression of characters' feelings, thereby justifying lyrical expansion or expressive singing ("canto di garbo"). The score is filled with passages like these.[57]

Monteverdi even constructed strophic arias out of non-strophic (or imperfectly strophic) material. In each case, rather than compromising verisimilitude, repetition of the same music to different text heightens the dramatic effect. In act 1, scene 9, in a passage we have already considered in Chapter 5, Ulisse has finally recognized that the land to which he has been transported is indeed Ithaca, his homeland. Monteverdi converts an exceedingly amorphous text into what comes across as a strophic aria, utilizing two irregularly spaced refrain lines to mark the opening and closing of each "strophe" (underlined).

---

55. In opera, "non possiamo fuggire un'inverosimile, che gli huomini trattino i loro più importanti negotii cantando." Giacomo Badoaro, *Ulisse errante* (Venice: Pinelli, 1644), preface, p. 12 (quoted in *OSV*, appendix I: 8.j). See also Appendix 3 [c].

56. With the exception of the two for the Suitors, which naturally include a stanza for each of them, all of the arias have two strophes. They are Minerva's "Cara e lieta gioventu" (1.8); Melanto's "Duri penosi" (1.2) and "Ama dunque" (2.1) (though the second strophe is replaced in the score by repeat of the first as a refrain); Iro's "Pastor d'Armenti puo" (2.3); and Nettuno's "So ben quest'onde" (5.7).

57. See Carter, *Musical Theatre*, table 3-1 and p. 254 for a list of lyrical "numbers" in *Ritorno*. Carter, "'In Love's Harmonious Consort,'" 7, also points out that Eumete's lyrically expansive "O gran figlio" sets a recitative text, the composer overriding the poetic form for dramatic reasons; but Eumete sings naturally, in any case, because he's a shepherd.

The composer expands the two refrain lines enormously through textual and musical repetition so that they end up comprising most of the aria; then, despite their unequal length, he treats the penultimate line of each "strophe" similarly, using the same extended melisma for the non-parallel words "lieto" and "guerra." Inspired by Badoaro's refrain as well as by the expressive content of Ulisse's words, which literally invite song, Monteverdi's lyrical setting effectively changes not only the weight but the form of the text. (See Example 1 above, Chap. 5).

O fortunato Ulisse,	O fortunate Ulisse,
Fuggi del tuo dolor	flee the old pangs
L'antico error;	of your former woes;
Lascia il pianto.	cease your lament;
Dolce canto	let the sweet song
Dal tuo cor lieto disserra;	release itself from your glad heart.
Non si disperi più mortale in terra.	Despair no more, ye earthly mortals.
O fortunato Ulisse.	O fortunate Ulisse.
Dolce [*Cara*] vicenda si può soffrir,	Sweet vicissitudes one may suffer—
Hor diletto, hor martir, hor pace, hor guerra.	now delight, now martyrdom, now peace, now war.
Non si disperi più mortale in terra.[58]	Despair no more, ye earthly mortals.

In another instance, toward the end of the opera, Ericlea wrestles with herself about revealing Ulisse's identity to Penelope. Monteverdi turns an irregular twenty-four-line text into a refrain form comprising four unequal sections of nine, four, five, and six lines, each closing with a *sentenzia* of self-justification (underlined). By adding a ritornello after sections 1, 3, and 4, and setting each final *sentenzia* to the same highly expanded music, the composer intensifies the formal implications—and the affect—of Ericlea's monologue. The music concretely marks her progress from her initial vow of silence (sections 1 and 2) through ambivalence (section 3), to her decision to speak. We may recall Torcigliani's observation: *Such changes of affection please our Signor Monteverdi very much because they allow him to display the marvels of his art* (see Appendix 2 [i]). As in Ulisse's aria, but by different means, Monteverdi superimposes a kind of strophic structure on the text and, far from sacrificing affective intensity, he increases it. The absence of a confirming ritornello after the second "refrain" (line 13) and consequent telescoping of sections 2 and 3 creates a sense of urgency that matches Ericlea's ambivalence (Example 4):[59]

---

58. See above, Chap. 5, pp. 151–53. Monteverdi's strophic setting is in some sense a correction of Badoaro's text. Indeed, the irregularities of rhyme and meter, failing as they do to reinforce the formal implications of the refrain, bespeak Badoaro's ineptitude as a poet; the text requires the composer's clarification. Eumete's "O gran figlio," in contrast, has no formal implications. Monteverdi's choice of lyrical setting is based on purely dramatic considerations.

59. The omission of the ritornello between sections 2 and 3 might have been a mistake; see Chap. 4, p. 84 and n. 27.

EXAMPLE 4. Ericlea, "Ericlea, Ericlea, che vuoi far?" (*Il ritorno d'Ulisse*, 5.8 [or 3.8]).

a. Section 1, mm. 1–34.

EXAMPLE 4 *(continued)*

b. Section 2, mm. 35–45

c. Section 3, mm. 51–61

d. Section 4, mm. 78–89

1 Ericlea, che vuoi far?	Ericlea, what will you do?
Vuoi tacer o parlar?	Will you be silent, or speak?
Se parli tu consoli,	If you speak, you will console;
Obbedisci se tacci.	you obey if you are silent.
Sei tenuta a servir,	You are compelled to serve,
Obbligata ad amar.	obliged to love.
Vuoi tacer, o parlar?	Will you be silent, or speak?
Ma ceda l'obbedienza alla pietà.	But let obedience yield to pity.
[all'obbedienza la pietà.]	
Non si dee sempre dir ciò che si sa.	We must not always tell what we know.
RITORNELLO	
2 Medicar chi languisce, o che diletto,	To minister to one who languishes, what delight!
Ma che ingiuria, e dispetto	But what injury, what spite,
Scoprir l'altrui pensier.	to disclose another's thoughts;
Bella cosa tal volta è un bel tacer.	at times silence is golden.
[ ]	
È ferità crudele	It is ferocious cruelty
Il poter con parole	to be able with words
Consolar chi si duole, e non lo far;	to comfort the grieving, and not do it;
Ma del pentirsi al fin	but repentance, in the end,
Assai lung'è il taccer più che il parlar.	far longer from silence than from speaking lasts.
RITORNELLO	
3 Del [Bel] secreto tacciuto	A fine secret wrapped in silence
Tosto scoprir si può,	can always be disclosed later;
Una sol volta detto	once said,
Celarlo non potrò.	hide it I can no more.
Ericlea, che farai, taccerai tu?	Ericlea, what will you do? Will you be silent?
[Che] in somma un bel tacer scritto non fu.	For, in sum, silence is not a law.
RITORNELLO	

But while he tended to accept every possible invitation to song that he found in Badoaro's libretto, Monteverdi did not always support or exploit textual symmetries with lyrical setting. He could also withhold lyricism for dramatic purposes—he does so in a number of instances, not only in *Ritorno* but in *Incoronazione* as well (in connection with Penelope, but also with Melanto and Ottavia, as we will see).

L'INCORONAZIONE DI POPPEA

Busenello's libretto, in contrast to Badoaro's, is remarkably rich in explicit closed forms, including some sixteen strophic texts as well as many prominent sestets, quatrains, couplets, and refrains.[60] The strophic texts are not only more numerous, but are distributed more democratically. Busenello offers them to the main protagonists as well as to secondary characters. Ottone has three, while Poppea, Nerone, Arnalta, Nutrice, and Valletto each have two,[61] and the *familiari,* Seneca, and Amore each have one.[62] Only Ottavia, significantly, has none.[63] A satisfying balance between dialogue and lyricism was thus more readily achieved in *Incoronazione* than in *Ritorno.* Even so, Monteverdi still tended to manipulate Busenello's forms, even his strophic ones, to wring greater dramatic veracity from them. (His revisions also combat Busenello's verbosity.)

Nutrice's aria in response to Ottavia's lament in act 1, scene 5 offers a striking example of the composer's flexible approach to strophic form (and his dramatic imagination). Following Ottavia's anguished speech, "Disprezzata regina," Nutrice urges her to listen to her advice, thus preparing the way for the conventional advice-aria that follows. The aria comprises two bipartite stanzas of four *ottonari* (in *rime alternate,* abab) plus a hendecasyllabic couplet (CC):

Se Neron perso ha l'ingegno	If Nerone has lost his wits
Di Poppea ne' godimenti,	in the enjoyment of Poppea,
Sciegli alcun, che di te degno	choose someone else worthy of you
D'abbracciarti si contenti.	who will enjoy your embraces.
Se l'ingiuria a Neron tanto diletta,	If injuring you so delights Nerone,
Habbi piacer tu ancor nel far vendetta.	take your pleasure in vengeance.
E se pur aspro rimorso	And even if harsh remorse
Dell'honor t'arrecca noia,	should trouble your honor,
<u>Fa riflesso al mio discorso,</u>	<u>reflect on my words,</u>
<u>ch'ogni duol ti sarà gioia.</u>	<u>that every woe may turn to joy.</u>
L'infamia sta gl'affronti in sopportarsi,	Infamy lies in accepting insults,
E consiste l'honor nel vendicarsi.	honor in avenging them.

But Monteverdi does not adhere to the strophic form. Instead, he interrupts the second stanza after the *ottonario* quatrain, intercalating two of Ottavia's lines from later in the scene (in italics and brackets), and then repeats the last two lines of the quatrain

60. Two of the strophic texts—one for Poppea in 1.10, the other for Seneca in 2.4—fail to appear in either score or in the Udine libretto; Monteverdi may never have set them to music. Carter, *Musical Theatre,* lists Busenello's closed forms (what he calls structured verse) in his Table 3–1, though unlike those for *Ritorno* listed in the same table, he fails to include texts not set by the composer.

61. The arias include Ottone: 1.1, 2.8, plus 1.11 with Poppea; Poppea: 1.4 and 1.10 (cut), plus 1.11 with Ottone and 2.7 with Nerone (cut); Nerone: 2.6 and 3.5, plus 2.7 with Poppea (cut); Arnalta: 1.4 and 2.12; Nutrice: 1.5 and 2.10; Valletto: 1.6 and 2.5 (not set strophically).

62. Famigliari: 2.3; Seneca: 2.4 (cut); Amore: 2.13.

63. For Heller (*Emblems,* 152–68), Ottavia's failure to engage in lyrical expression is connected to her sexuality and fundamental to her characterization. See also Carter, *Musical Theatre,* 290–96.

before continuing on to the nurse's closing hendecasyllabic couplet (word repetitions are in italics when text is in roman, and vice versa):

NUTRICE: E se pur aspro rimorso
 Dell'honor t'arrecca noia,
 Fa riflesso al mio discorso,
 Ch'ogni duol ti sarà gioia.
OTTAVIA: *[Così sozzi argomenti*
 Non intesi più mai da te, nutrice.]
NUTRICE: *Fa, fa, fa, fa riflesso al mio discorso,*
 ch'ogni duol, ogni duol, ogni duol,
 ogni duol, ogni duol ti sarà gioia,
 ti sara gioia, ti sara gioia.
 L'infamia sta gl'affronti in sopportarsi,
 E consiste, *consiste,* l'honor nel vendicarsi,
 nel vendicarsi, nel vendicarsi.

  And even if harsh remorse
  should trouble your honor,
  reflect on my words,
  that every woe may turn to joy.
  [Such dishonorable counsel
  I have never heard from you, my nurse.]

The composer's intervention not only enhances the verisimilitude of the interaction—Ottavia doesn't stand around waiting for her nurse to finish her lengthy song, but responds naturalistically, and impatiently, and directly instead—but her interruption causes Nutrice to repeat (and emphasize) her message: "Fa riflesso al mio discorso, / Ch'ogni duol ti sara gioia" (which Monteverdi expands to more than double its original length, through text repetition and melodic sequence, thereby strengthening its impact; Example 5a and b). The music of the two stanzas is quite different in other respects as well. Having created a memorable refrain, here, the composer brings it back once more, in still another, shorter and more telescoped version, at the conclusion of Nutrice's final sardonic speech to her mistress, comprising eleven lines. Most interestingly, although as *versi sciolti* they are clearly intended as recitative, Monteverdi sets the first two lines of that speech lyrically, the first to the music that opened the previous aria strophes, as if they were initiating a third stanza, an impression reinforced by the return of the refrain at the end (Example 5c).

Figlia, *figlia* e Signora mia, *signora mia,*
 tu non intendi, *no, no, non intendi, no,*
 no, no, no, non intendi
Della vendetta il principale arcano.
L'offesa sopra il volto
D'una sola guanciata
Si vendica col ferro, e con la morte.
Chi ti punge nel senso,
Pungilo nell'honore,
Se bene a dirti il vero,

My child and lady, you don't
 understand

the mysterious principle of vengeance.
The insult on the face
of a single slap
is avenged with the sword and with death.
He who wounds your feelings,
strike him in his honor.
To tell you the truth

Né pur così sarai ben vendicata;
Nel senso vivo te punge Nerone,

E in lui sol pungerai l'opinione.
Fa, fa, fa, fa riflesso al mio discorso,
Ch'ogni duol, ch'ogni duol, ogni duol ti
 sarà gioia, ti sarà gioia, ti sarà gioia.

not even this will bring you revenge.
Nerone has wounded your innermost
 feelings,
and you can only wound his reputation.

EXAMPLE 5. Nutrice, aria and recitative (*L'incoronazione di Poppea*, 1.5).

a. Mm. 108–31

EXAMPLE 5 *(continued)*

b. Mm. 131–60

EXAMPLE 5 *(continued)*

c. Mm. 195–230

EXAMPLE 5 *(continued)*

In this scene, then, Monteverdi has both undermined and developed Busenello's strophic structure for dramatic purposes. The form is a hybrid: the effect of the interruption depends on the fact that it occurs within the second stanza of an aria, after the first has been heard. Monteverdi then exploits that very effect to increase the formal coherence of the rest of the scene.

Although Busenello offered him many formal opportunities, Monteverdi did not always accept them fully. Indeed, his varied response constitutes a critique of Busenello's forms, often pointing up their failure to adhere to the composer's concept of verisimilitude. We might say that the composer read beyond the form of Busenello's texts, to their meaning, subjecting them to the test of verisimilitude.

This is evident in the very first scene of the opera, Ottone's opening monologue. Busenello structures the scene with great care. An initial hendecasyllabic abba quatrain, with built-in word and phrase repetition (A: a series of similes: "qual linea al centro," "qual foco a sfera," "qual ruscello al mare") is followed by four three-line abb stanzas comprised of a *settenario* and an *endecasillabo* couplet (B), which breaks off into *versi sciolti* (C) as Ottone notices Nerone's soldiers guarding Poppea's door and imagines what lies behind it. After Ottone angrily and ironically turns on himself, criticizing the futility of his own previous actions, he addresses the absent Poppea once more (D), and Busenello inserts a group of four short, pathetic lines (*quaternari*), before concluding the scene in *versi sciolti*, with nine mostly hendecasyllabic lines (E, below, p. 211) (sections A and D are illustrated in Examples 15 and 16 below, Chap. 7).

A: E pur io torno qui, qual linea a centro,

    Qual foco a sfera, e qual ruscello al mare,
    E se ben luce alcuna non m'appare,
    Ah so ben io, che sta il mio sol qui dentro.
    E pur io torno qui, qual linea a centro.

B: Caro tetto amoroso,
    Albergo di mia vita, e del mio bene,
    Il passo, e 'l core ad inchinarti viene.
      Apri un balcon, Poppea,
    Col bel viso, in cui son le sorti mie,

Thus do I return here, like a radius to its point,
like fire to the sun, and stream to the sea,
and if I see no light,
I know that my sun is within.

Beloved roof,
dwelling of my life, and my beloved,
My feet and heart come to bow before you.
    Open your window, Poppea,
with your beautiful face, in which my fate rests,

Previeni, anima mia, precorri il diè.	anticipate, precede the day.
Sorgi, e disgombra homai	Arise, and clear
Da questo Ciel caligini, e tenebre	the haze and shadows from the sky
Con il beato aprir di tue palpebre.	With the blessed opening of your eyelids.
Sogni, portate a volo,	Dreams, bear in flight,
Fatte sentir in dolce fantasia	in sweet fancy on your wings,
Questi sospiri alla diletta mia.	these sighs to my beloved
C: Ma che veggio infelice?	But what do I see, unhappy one?
· Non già fantasmi, o pur notturne larve,	these are not ghosts or nocturnal phantoms.
Son questi i servi di Nerone; ahi dunque	but Nerone's servants, ah thus
Agl'insensati venti	to unfeeling winds
Io difondo i lamenti.	do I divulge my laments.
Necessito le pietre a deplorarmi,	I urge the stones to weep for me,
Adoro questi marmi,	I adore these marble columns,
Amoreggio con lagrime un balcone,	I woo a balcony with tears,
E in grembo di Poppea dorme Nerone.	And Nerone sleeps in Poppea's arms.
Ha condotti costoro,	He brought these guards
Per custodir se stesso dalle frodi.	to protect himself against traitors.
O salvezza de Prencipi infelice,	Oh, unhappy safeguard of princes,
Dormon profondamente i suoi custodi.	His guards are fast asleep.
D: Ahi perfida Poppea,	Ah, faithless Poppea,
Son queste le promesse, e i giuramenti,	Are these the promises and vows
Ch'accesero il cor mio?	that inflamed my heart?
Questa è la fede, o Dio;	this the faith, oh God?
Io son[o] quell'Ottone,	I am that Ottone
Che ti seguì,	who followed you,
Che ti bramò,	who desired you,
Che ti servì,	who served you,
Che t'adorò.	who adored you.

Monteverdi accepts Busenello's invitation to set the opening quatrain lyrically, repeating the first line at the end to confer closure. But he does not begin the strophic aria with Busenello's first stanza, preferring instead to mark the distinction between that stanza and the remaining three, each of which begins with an invocation (italicized). In the opening quatrain, Ottone apostrophizes generally on his pleasure at returning to Poppea. Closing in then, in the first strophe, he directs his attention to Poppea's house. In the next two, he addresses Poppea herself: "Apri," "Sorgi"; and in the last, he asks his own dreams to fly to his beloved: "Sogni, portate a volo." By declining to set Busenello's strophic text completely strophically, Monteverdi has chosen meaning, that is, dramatic sense, over form.[64]

Constantly aiming to convey dramatic naturalism and psychological realism, both within individual characters and in interactions between them, the composer edited

---

64. This aria is discussed further in Chap. 7, pp. 304–8.

Busenello's libretto in many other ways, and not only in connection with arias. One of his most characteristic means of enhancing character interaction and maintaining dramatic pace, particularly in *Incoronazione*, was through textual intercalations, such as those between Nutrice and Ottavia just discussed. A similar procedure links Ottone's opening scene with the following one, as the composer anticipates several lines for the first soldier (indicated in italics and bracketed in the extract, left column); the two soldiers' lines are also intercalated, as indicated (original text in the right column):

E: Che per piegarti, e intenerirti il core
Di lagrime imperlò preghi devoti,
Gli spirti a te sacrificando in voti.
M'assicurasti al fine,
Ch'abbracciate haverei nel tuo bel seno
Le mie beatudini amorose,
Io di credula speme il seme sparsi,
Ma l'aria, e 'l Cielo a danni miei rivolto,
[Tempestò di ruine il mio raccolto.]

Scene 2

SOLDATO 1: *[Chi parla, chi parla]*
OTTONE: *Tempestò di ruine [SI: chi parla],*
il mio raccolto.
SOLDATO 1: *Chi va li, chi va li?*
SOLDATO 2: *Camerata, camerata?*
SOLDATO 1: *Ohimè, ancor non è dì?*
SOLDATO 2: *Camerata, che fai?*
Par che parli sognando.
SOLDATO 1: *Sorgono pur dell'alma i primi rai.*
SOLDATO 2: *Su, risvegliati tosto.*
SOLDATO 1: *Non ho dormito in tutta notte mai.*
SOLDATO 2: *Su, su, su, risvegliati tosto.*
Guardiamo il nostro posto.

Scene 2

SOLDATO 1: Chi parla, chi va li?
Ohimè ancora non è dì?

Sorgono pur dall'Alba i primi rai.
Non ho dormito in tutta notte mai.
SOLDATO 2: Camerata, che fai?
Par che parli sognando.
Su, risvegliati tosto,
Guardiamo il nostro posto

As with Badoaro's libretto, the composer also exploited Busenello's refrains, expanding and repeating them to create larger formal units. In sum, while *Incoronazione* contains many more unequivocal arias than *Ritorno*, including twice as many strophic texts, the difference is obscured by Monteverdi's sensitivity in both settings to the nuances of feeling in his characters. He does not hesitate either to ignore his librettists' formal cues or to create his own forms when it suits his dramatic purpose.

LE NOZZE D'ENEA E LAVINIA

With respect to the proportion of recitative to aria poetry, our middle opera, *Nozze*, stands somewhere in between its companions. It includes seven strophic texts, all of them justified from the point of view of verisimilitude—and none of them for protagonists. These comprise two for chorus (Nereids and Tritons in 1.2 and Trojans in 4.4), two for supernatural characters (Aletto in 1.7, and Venere in 3.7), one for the boy Ascanio (1.3), and two involving the shepherdess Silvia (a dance-duet with her beloved Elminio in 2.2 and an aria, three scenes later):[65]

1.2 Coro di Nereidi e di Tritoni: two irregular stanzas, "Vieni pur, vieni Enea" (irregular refrain form), a[ ]bCcdEE (internal rhymes for b in C and d in E), aAbCcdEE (same internal rhymes) aA (possible missing A line in first stanza).

1.3 Ascanio: two *settenario* stanzas, "Già l'amorosa stella," abab (each followed by sounds of a storm *qui tuona, qui folgora*)

1.7 Aletto: three *ternari* stanzas, "Ch'io porti," aaab, plus irregular single stanza (missing in three-act libretto): abcdEe (6 6 6 6 10 5)

2.2 Silvia–Elmino: two stanzas embedded in four-line irregular refrain, "Elmino, cantiamo," aabB ccd eed Baab (6 6 2 10, 6 6 5 6 6 5 10 6 6 2)

2.5 Silvia: four six-line stanzas, "Piante, gittate le frondi al suol," aabbcc (9 10 6 6 10 10)

3.7 Venere: two six-line stanzas: "Sia pure un cuor ferrigno," aabBcC

4.4 Coro di Troiani: two four-line *senario* stanzas, "Enea pur l'ha colto," plus third stanza in a different meter, ending the act: abba, cdcd; eefF (5 5 6 11)

In addition to the seven strophic pieces, there are more than twice that many single stanzas of specially organized poetry, some of which would have encouraged lyrical setting by virtue of their dramatic function:[66]

1.1 Oracolo di Fauno: "Già non pensare, o mia diletta prole (four *endecasillabi*, ABBA)

1.3 Acate: "Su compagne, in lieti accenti (four *ottonari*, abab)

1.4 Turno: "Ora non più m'alletta" (abbaCC, embedded in recitative passage)

2.2 Latino: "Così, così mia pace" (abaccDD)

3.2 Numano: "Or sì contento io sto" (abAcBdeEFgfG)

3.3 Lavinia: "Misera, qual io sento" (aabcbC); "Fiero destin fatale" (abaBcdDef or efe); "O placido riposo" (abBccDedeff); "Forse su l'alte mura" (abbccDD)

3.4 Enea: "Vieni sonno" (AbBAcddCeeFGgHh)

3.5 Tebro: "Enea, tu dormi? Ah ch'è dover ch'omai" (*ottava rima:* ABABABCC)

3.8 Numano: "O Troiani, o Troiani" (aAbBCCdDEE)

4.1 Numano: "Fien dunque senza me guerre e perigli" (AbbccdD)

---

65. An eighth strophic text occurs in the second prologue, for the Ombra di Virgilio. In four hendecasyllabic stanzas of four lines, it is typical of prologues and would probably have been set—if at all—as strophic variations, like the prologue of *Orfeo*.

66. Some of these, namely, those for Lavinia in 3.3 and 4.3 and Enea in 3.4, will be discussed below in connection with laments. The sequence of stanzas for Lavinia and her Damigella in 4.3 is structured with particular skill.

4.3 Lavinia–Damigella *a 2:* "Sì che de casti ardori (aabb); Lavinia: "Non posso altro, né vo'" (aabb); Damigella: "De la dea che innamora" (ababC); *a 2:* "Dunque se 'l vento freme" (cddeff); Lavinia: "Il paterno voler spira ad un segno" (EGG)

4.4 Enea: "Deh quanto è 'l mio contento" (ababcdcdEE)

4.4 Turno: "Te non imploro Amor" (aabbCC)

5.5 Enea: "O sol che già brev'ora" (aBbcA); Lavinia: "Aria, che dianzi piena" (deE); Enea: "Tu mar turbato" (fgG); Lavinia: "Tu terra aspersa" (hiI); Enea: "Voi mormorate" (jk); Lavinia: "Augei snodate" (jkk); *a 2:* "Cosa non sia" (lmmlN)

Acate's rhymed quatrain of *ottonari* in 1.3, for instance, is certainly an invitation to song:

Su compagne, in lieti accenti	Come, companions, in happy accents
Voi le lingue disciogliete,	loosen your tongues,
E agli auguri a noi ridenti	and for our happy omens
Acclamate ed applaudate.	cheer and applaud.

Fauno's hendecasyllabic abba quatrain in 1.1, on the other hand, as a speech addressed to his son, Latino, is clearly intended as recitative:

Già non pensare, o mia diletta prole	Do not think, o my precious offspring,
Genero destinarti a noi vicino.	to designate yourself father-in-law to one who is near.
Altri verrà lontano e peregrino,	Another will come from far, a pilgrim,
Che illustrerà tua stirpe al par del sole.	who will render your progeny equal to the sun.

Other single stanzas could have invoked lyricism because of their emotional content. Latino's seven-line speech in 2.2, for instance, which closes with a hendecasyllabic couplet, is a kind of prayer, or invocation:

Così, così mia pace	Thus, thus, my peace
Apparsa anco sparisci	appeared and disappeared
In un balen fugace.	in a lightning flash.
O speranze mortali,	Oh, mortal hopes,
Infide, vane e frali!	treacherous, vain, and frail!
Ma voi che a l'altrui fé, numi, assistete,	But you who others believe in, aid me,
Voi, l'innocenza mia, voi difendete.	you, defend my innocence.

Similarly, Enea's longer and even more regular speech in 4.4 ("Deh quanto è 'l mio contento"), a pair of rhymed *settenario* quatrains followed by a hendecasyllabic couplet, culminates in a prayer to Venere and Vulcano that would have been appropriate for lyrical expression:

Deh, quanto è 'l mio contento	Oh, how happy I am
Che sia dal sangue solo	that by blood only
Di Turno il foco spento,	Turno's fire was extinguished,
Acceso il commun duolo.	which caused communal suffering.
Bella madre d'Amore	Beautiful mother of love,
Onde quest'aure io godo,	because of whom I delight in these breezes,
Tu dio d'aspro furore,	and you, god of bitter anger,
Uniti in dolce nodo	united in a sweet knot
Ove d'armi e d'amor litigi han loco,	where arms and love entwined have a place,
Propizi a' voti miei, supplice invoco.	be propitious to my prayers, I beseech you.

Still other such passages, embedded in recitative speeches, suggest lyrical setting as a means of distinguishing them rhetorically from their surroundings. Turno's "Ora non più m'alletta" (1.4), a rhymed quatrain of *settenari* followed by a hendecasyllabic couplet, part of a much longer sequence of *versi sciolti*, expresses his surprise that his thoughts have turned from war to love:

Ora non più m'alletta	No longer am I enticed
Di tromba il suon feroce,	by the fierce sound of the trumpet,
Armi o battaglia attroce.	by terrible weapons or battle.
Un guardo mi diletta	Rather, a mere look delights me,
Di due begli occhi, e d'una bocca vaga	of two beautiful eyes, and from a lovely mouth
La dolce melodia viepiù m'appaga.	the sweet melody appeases me.
Ma lasso, che pur guerra ancor è questa,	But alas, this is still war,
In cui ferita ho l'alma	in which I have a wounded soul,
Che, se pugnar non resta,	which, if it cannot land a blow,
Più teme morte omai che speri palma.	fears death more than it hopes for victory.

Here the musical references—to the sound of trumpets and the sweet melody—contribute to the likelihood that this passage would have been set lyrically. Finally, a speech for Turno in 4.4 ("Te non imploro Amor") suggests lyricism, or anyhow distinctive, closed setting, primarily on account of its sharp metric profile: an emphatic sestet comprising four *settenari tronchi* rounded out with the usual hendecasyllabic couplet:

Te non imploro amor,	I do not implore you, Love,
Cagion del mio dolor,	cause of my pain,
Né men Lavinia te,	nor even you, Lavinia,
Ingrata a la mia fé.	ungrateful for my faith.

| Te chiamo genio mio funesto e cieco | I call upon you, my fatal and blind spirit, |
| Ove vuole il destin mi adduci teco. | to lead me wherever destiny wishes. |

Other single stanzas are longer and metrically more varied, but still imply lyrical setting, because of their content or position in the scene. Numano's twelve lines of *versi sciolti*, "Or si contento io sto," at the end of 3.2, suggest a comic exit aria (cf. below, p. 244).

Tight metric organization also characterizes a number of shared passages of text, clearly marking them for setting as lyrical duets, or, in one case, quartet. One such passage, a pair of rhymed *settenario* tercets for Lavinia and her Damigella, occurs in 4.3:

Dunque se 'l vento freme,	Thus though the wind shivers,
S'avvien che 'l mar s'adiri,	and the sea becomes angry,
Ardito il cor respiri.	boldly will the heart breathe.
Amor governa il legno	Love governs the boat,
Qual tramontana stella,	as the north star
Splende ciprigna bella.	beautiful Venus shines.

Another, the obligatory final love duet for Enea and Lavinia (5.4), comprises a rhymed quatrain alternating *settenari* and *endecasillabi* enclosed by a two-line refrain (underlined).

<u>O fortunati affanni,</u>	<u>O fortunate suffering,</u>
<u>Avventurosi danni,</u>	<u>eventful damage,</u>
Noie, pianti, sospiri,	troubles, cries, sighs,
S'indi nascer dovean sì dolci effetti.	from which such sweet effects were born.
Pene, doglie, martiri	Pain, suffering, martyrdom,
Se tai produr dovean gioie e diletti,	if you produce such joy and delight,
<u>O fortunati affanni,</u>	<u>O fortunate suffering . . .</u>
<u>Avventurosi danni.</u>	

The brief but equally obligatory final quartet for Himeneo, Venere, Amore, and Giunone, with the unusual metric structure of four *quinari* culminating in an *endecasillabo*, occurs in the last scene:

Dov'è bellezza	Wherever beauty,
Dov'è richezza,	wherever wealth,
Dov'è amor,	wherever Love,
Dov'è fede,	wherever faith is,
Ivi ogni gioia, ivi ogni ben risiede.	there all joy, there all happiness dwells.

One further textual element that attracts attention to itself and calls for special musical emphasis is the refrain. Although much more characteristic of both *Ritorno* and *Incoronazione,* exact or varied refrains recur in a few instances in *Nozze* to suggest some kind of musical structure. We have just seen an example in the love duet: the single stanza is en-closed by a two-line refrain of rhymed *settenari*. The whole text was undoubtedly intended to be set lyrically. In other cases, only the refrain calls for lyricism. A closed tercet for the Trojan chorus celebrating Enea's victory opens act 5, scene 1 and recurs after a long recita-tive dialogue between Enea and Ascanio:

O glorioso Enea,	O glorious Enea,
Del gran Dardano tuo germe ben degno,	worthy descendant of great Dardanus,
Mercé di cui godiam riposo e regno.	thanks to whom we enjoy peace and reign.

It recurs once again at the end of the next scene, following an even longer dialogue between Acate, Enea, and Drante that seals Enea's victory and his union with the Latins. Clearly intended to be set lyrically, as distinct from the intervening dialogue, the refrain provides appropriate formal and presumably musical punctuation at the climax of the opera.

Despite the relative infrequency of refrains, the large number of distinct and varied invitations to song in *Nozze,* including strophic structures as well as single closed poetic stanzas, suggests that Monteverdi may have found the libretto more naturally musicable than that of *Ritorno,* that is, clearer in its signals for "canto di garbo." We are sensitized to this fact, of course, by knowing how Monteverdi set the earlier libretto, the ways he had to expand and alter the text to infuse it with formal lyricism.

The Role of Meter

In addition to his more effective distribution of recitative and aria text, Torcigliani dis-plays extraordinary metric variety and subtlety. We noted earlier how he emphasized his effort to introduce metric contrast for the purpose of characterization, as Monteverdi surely would have liked, specifically choosing *versi sdruccioli* for low persons (Vulcano, Numano) and short lines and *versi tronchi* for angry ones (see Appendix 2 [m]).[67] Aletto's vengeful aria in 1.7, for instance, comprises three stanzas of *ternari* culminating in a longer stanza of *quaternari sdruccioli.* And the final confrontation between Enea and Turno at the end of act 4 concludes with short bursts of *quinari tronchi:*

TURNO: Or che farò?	Now what will I do?
Solo la fuga	Flight alone
Salvar mi può.	can save me.
ENEA: Non val fuggir,	It's not worth fleeing;
convien morir.	it's better to die.

---

67. See above, Chap. 5, p. 132. Short lines also characterize youth: Elmino and Silvia, for instance, ex-change groups of *senari* in their duet in act 2, scene 2.

In the final scene of the opera, several exchanges in *versi sciolti* terminate in symmetrical groups of *quinari*, as if short meter were serving a culminating effect. (Indeed, the last twenty lines of the libretto—arranged as a series of stanzas—are virtually all rhymed *quinari*.)

Beyond deploying distinctive meters and metric arrangements for particular characters and dramatic situations, Torcigliani takes great care in his distribution of rhymes and verse sequences, sometimes opting for long series of tight rhyming lines in the same meter (ten or twelve couplets), at other times avoiding rhyme and continuous meter altogether (as in Latino's huge opening narrative). (The prologue, with its mixture of *versi sciolti*, stanzas of rhymed *endecasillabi*, and *quinario* refrains, gives a good idea of the variety that characterizes this text.)

Perhaps the most striking example of the librettist's use of metric contrast for dramatic purposes occurs in the dialogue between Venere and Vulcano in act 3, scene 1, a remarkable tour de force, with its participants wonderfully characterized by their contrasting use of *piano* and *sdrucciolo* verse endings. Trading on Vulcano's sexual frustration, Venere manipulates her blacksmith husband so that he agrees to forge arms for Enea. Her seductive *versi piani*, punctuated by some well-placed *tronchi*, engage and parry his *versi sdruccioli*:

VULCANO: Così m'astringe l'obbligo	Thus does obligation press me
Di fabricare al sommo Giove i fulmini.	to make thunderbolts for great Giove.
Ma tu le voci hai placide,	But you have calm tones,
Poi meco hai fatti rigidi.	though you have rigid business with me.
VENERE: È vero, anima mia,	It's true, my soul,
Ma tu sei dio del foco,	but you are the god of fire,
E temo, se ti appressi,	and I fear that if I approach you,
Nova incauta Semele,	like a new, incautious Semele,
Arder a' cari amplessi.	I will burn with your dear caresses.
Basta, basta l'ardor	The ardor is enough
Che lungi gli occhi tuoi fan nel mio cor.	that from afar inspires my heart.
Più non m'accender tu,	Do not ignite me further,
Deh, vita mia, non più.	alas, my life, no more.
VULCANO: Serba queste blandizie	Keep this flattery
A quel tuo Marte armigero,	for your squire Mars,
A quell'Adon tuo florido,	for your blooming Adonis,
Che di Vulcan mi cangiano,	who from Vulcan
Ben spesso, in semicaprio.	often transform me into a half-goat.
VENERE: O bocca vezzosetta,	O charming mouth,
Che sì, che se non taci,	if you are not silent
Io prenderò vendetta	I will take vengeance
De l'onte de' tuoi baci.	on the shame of your kisses.
VULCANO: Sei su le tresche, Venere,	You are trying to deceive me, Venere.
Grazie vuoi tu richiedermi.	You want to ask me for my favors.
VENERE: Sì, ma quel che desio	Yes, but what I desire,
Nol mi negar, ben mio.	do not deny me, my beloved.

There is nothing like this in *Il ritorno d'Ulisse*. As far as subtleties of meter are concerned, Badoaro is clearly less resourceful than Torcigliani. But his libretto does introduce a certain amount of metric variety as a means of characterization (and to stimulate varied musical setting). For instance, he reserves his use of short meters—lines of five or fewer syllables—for the secondary characters: especially Melanto, Eurimaco, and Iro, while restricting his hero and heroine to *versi sciolti*. But on a number of occasions his poetry seems disturbingly irregular, his choices of meter and rhyme almost random, requiring special intervention on the part of the composer to render it dramatically viable.

Such would seem to be the case in act 1, scene 2. In this long dialogue between Melanto and Eurimaco (which comes as welcome relief from the somber mood established by Penelope's lament in the previous scene), each of the lovers' speeches is differently structured. Although only Melanto's first speech is a strophic aria, the composer sets the rest of the text lyrically as well, taking advantage of various cues provided by Badoaro: irregular refrains and distinct groups of short lines are suggestive for the musical shape of the scene—indeed, the composer simply omitted many lines having to do with plot development, which would have required recitative setting and interrupted the flow of his lyricism.[68]

Melanto's opening aria comprises two stanzas of six *quinari* rounded out by an hendecasyllabic couplet (abbaCC):

Duri e penosi	Hard and painful
Son gl'amorosi	are the cruel desires
Fieri desir[i];	of lovers.
Ma alfin son cari,	But in the end they become dear,
Se prima amari	though at first bitter,
Gli aspri martir[i].	these harsh torments.
[Che] s'arde un cor, è d'allegrezza un foco	If a heart burns, it is a fire of happiness;
Né mai perde in amor chi compie il gioco.	he who plays the game of love never loses.
Chi pria s'accende . . .	

Eurimaco responds with a single stanza of six lines, four *settenari* likewise rounded out by a hendecasyllabic couplet: abbaCC. (Monteverdi adds a refrain, italicized.)

Bella Melanto mia,	My beautiful Melanto,
Graziosa Melanto,	lovely Melanto,
Il tuo canto è un incanto,	your song is an enchantment,
Il tuo volto è magia,	your face is bewitching,

---

68. He may not have intended to omit those lines that explain that their love depends on Penelope accepting one of the Suitors ("Se Penelope bella / Non si piega alle voglie / De rivali Amatori / Mal sicuri saranno / I nostri occulti amori"). The omission is among those criticized by René Jacobs as casualties of sloppy editing (see Chap. 7, n. 1). For another possible explanation, see Chap. 7, n. 3.

<table>
<tr><td>

Bella Melanto mia.

E tutto laccio in te ciò ch'altri ammaga:

Ciò che laccio non è, fa tutto piaga.

</td><td>

My beautiful Melanto.

Everything in you is a snare that beguiles
others,
and whatever is not a snare, wounds
everything.

</td></tr>
</table>

This provokes another six-line stanza from Melanto that is more irregular in structure—rhyme scheme and meter fail to confirm one another—but still closed, abcBDd:

<table>
<tr><td>

Vezzoso garruletto,
Oh, come ben tu sai
Ingemmar le bellezze,
Illustrar a tuo pro d'un volto i rai.

Lieto vezzeggia pur con glorie mie
Le tue dolci bugie.

</td><td>

Loquacious flatterer,
oh, how well you know how
to adorn beauty,
to show the radiance of a face to your own
advantage.
Caress happily with my glories
your sweet lies.

</td></tr>
</table>

Eurimaco's next speech comprises five lines that are only partly rhymed and metrically irregular: abc(3)c(3)dd, to which Melanto responds with five more shapely lines of her own, abBcC:

<table>
<tr><td>

EURIMACO: Bugia sarebbe s'io
    Lodando non t'amassi:
    Che il negar
    D'adorar
    Confessata deità
    È bugia d'empietà.
MELANTO: De' nostri amor concordi
    Sia pur la fiamma accesa.
    Ch'amato il non amar arreca offesa
    Né con ragion s'offende
    Colui che per offese amor ti rende.

</td><td>

A lie would it be if
praising, I did not love you.
For to deny
adoration
of an acknowledged goddess
would be an impious lie.
Of our mutual love
let the flame be ignited.
For a love not returned causes offense,
nor is it right for him to offend
the one who renders love for offense.

</td></tr>
</table>

(Although these five lines were assigned to Melanto in the libretto, Monteverdi sets the first three as a duet and gives the last two to Eurimaco.) The lovers then divide a hendecasyllabic quatrain: abba, which culminates in a full duet. (The duet is not especially required by the form of the text but primarily by its meaning and position in the scene.)

<table>
<tr><td>

MELANTO [*Eurimaco*]:
    S'io non t'amo, cor mio, che sia di gelo
    L'alma ch'ho in seno a' tuoi begli occhi
        avante

</td><td>

If I do not love you, my heart,
let the soul in my breast freeze before
    your eyes.

</td></tr>
</table>

EURIMACO [*Melanto*]:

Se in adorarti il cor non ho costante	If in adoring you my heart is not constant,
Non mi sia stanza il mondo o tetto il cielo.	let me have no room on earth, no roof in heaven.

A DUE: Dolce mia vita sei,	You are my sweet life;
Lieto, mio ben sarai;	happily, you will be my beloved.
Nodo sì bel non si disciolga mai.	Such a beautiful knot will never be dissolved.

Though the remainder of the scene is drastically cut by the composer, reduced from twenty-nine lines to six, the final duet is repeated at the end.

One has the distinct impression in this scene that meter does not matter; that whatever Badoaro had intended, Monteverdi would have introduced lyricism because it suited a perceived need to contrast Penelope's melodic restraint and to portray the sexual relationship of the "second couple" of his drama. (In a sense, this is analogous to his construction of strophic arias discussed above. He transformed the text as he saw fit.)

Badoaro may have been less sensitive—and less inclined—to metric variety and contrast than Torcigliani. Yet, of our three librettos, *Incoronazione* is by far the least varied as far as meter is concerned, and no doubt intentionally so.[69] It is overwhelmingly comprised of *settenari* and *endecasillabi*, and not only for recitative. Most of the closed aria forms use those meters as well, alone and in combination. Only a few arias utilize another meter (predictably those of secondary characters), and then only at the beginning, all of them closing with a hendecasyllabic couplet. Nutrice's aria "Se Neron perso ha l'ingegno" (1.5) comprises four *ottonari* plus the couplet, Amore's "O sciocchi, o frali" (2.13) two *quinari* plus couplet, and his "Forsennato, scelerato" (2.14) eight *ottonari* plus couplet.[70] (Seneca's scene with the Virtues, cut by Monteverdi, is in *quinari*, and his followers' chorus is in *ottonari*.) A particularly effective use of *ottonari* enhances the flirtation between Valletto and Damigella in act 2, scene 5. Valletto opens a ten-line stanza in *rime alternate* by mixing *ottonari tronchi* and *piani*, which Damigella effectively reverses in her response.

VALLETTO: Sento un certo non so che,	I feel a certain I don't know what
Che mi pizzica e diletta.	that tickles and delights me.

---

69. Bruno Brizzi, "Teoria e prassi melodrammatica di G. F. Busenello e *L'Incoronazione di Poppea*," in *Venezia e il melodrama nel Seicento*, ed. Maria Teresa Muraro (Florence: Olschki, 1976), 51–74, at 62–63, examines the various verse forms in Busenello's text, distinguishing, for instance, descending (11, 7) from ascending (7, 11) final couplets.

70. Amore also inserts a couple of urgent *quaternari* in the recitative at the beginning of his descent to protect Poppea (2.13): "Ella non sa / Ch'hor hor verrà." And he uses *quinari* in the final scene, in his exchange with the chorus of Amorini. "Pur ti miro," too, is in *quaternari*.

Dimmi tu che cosa egli è,	Tell me what it is,
Damigella amorosetta.	you amorous maiden.
. . . .	. . . .
DAMIGELLA: Astutello, garzoncello,	You cunning little boy,
Bamboleggia Amor in te.	Love is playing games with you.
Se divieni amante a fè	If you really become a lover
Perderai tosto il cervello.	You will soon lose your mind.

Such manipulation of verse endings is typical of Busenello's aria texts, even those in the characteristic *settenario* and *endecasillabo* meters. In act 2, scene 10, for example, *settenari* and *endecasillabi tronchi*, mixed with *versi piani*, enhance the humor of Nutrice's disquisition on old age (the variety adds a kind of spice):

Il giorno femminil	The day of a woman
Trova la sera sua nel mezo dì.	finds its evening at midday.
Dal mezo giorno in là	After noon
Sfiorisce la beltà;	beauty begins to disappear.
Sol tempo si fa dolce	Only time can sweeten
Il frutto accerbo e duro,	bitter and hard fruit.
Ma in hore guasto vien quel ch'è maturo.	But within hours mature fruit becomes rotten.
Credetel pure a me,	Believe me,
O giovanette fresche in su 'l mattin.	you fresh maidens in the morning of life.

Predictably, Busenello's recitative hardly ever departs from *versi sciolti*. But when it does, the effect is striking—and purposeful. And, thanks to Monteverdi, memorable. (He obviously responded to this kind of variety too.) Two instances in the prologue stand out, one near the beginning of Fortuna's speech ("dissipata/disusata/mal gradita"), the other near the end of Amore's ("riveritemi/adoratemi"). In both instances, the interruption of *versi sciolti* with *quaternari*—*piani* in one case, *sdruccioli* in the other—inspired measured, sequential treatment by the composer. Such interruptions are used to particular dramatic effect early in the opera. In 1.1, the already-mentioned opening scene for Ottone, a sequence of four *quaternari* in the midst of an extended passage of *versi sciolti* (thirty-one lines) adds an element of passion to Ottone's appeal to Poppea: "che ti seguì / che ti bramò / che ti servì / che t'adorerò," a sequence that inspired exact, obsessive repetition in the music.

Ahi, perfida Poppea,
Son queste le promesse e i giuramenti
Ch'accesero il cor mio?
Questa lè la fede, o Dio!

Io son quell'Ottone
Che ti seguì,
Che ti bramò,
Che ti servì,
Che t'adorò.[71]

Che per piegarti e intenerirti il core	who to bend and soften your heart
Di lagrime imperlò preghi devoti,	with tears I adorned my devoted prayers,
Gli spirti a te sacrificando in voti.	sacrificing my spirits to you in vows.

Similarly, in 1.3, their first love scene, a pair of rhymed *ternari* inserted within a long passage of *versi sciolti* increases the intensity of Poppea's urging Nerone not to leave her: "deh non dir / di partir," an intensity that is magnified when the passage is repeated six lines later as part of a refrain. (This happens later in the scene, too: "Se ben io vò / Pur teco stò.")[72]

Busenello's text is metrically distinctive in other ways as well. Although nearly all speeches end in rhymed couplets, many consist of long sequences of unrhymed lines until then: of Fortuna's twenty-four opening lines, fifteen are unrhymed, as are eight of Virtù's eleven. In Arnalta's recitative in 1.4 six of eight are unrhymed. Nutrice's eleven-line recitative in 1.5 has only one rhyme, at the end. This pattern is particularly noticeable in Ottavia's lament (the first rhyme in her thirty-seven-line text does not occur until lines 12–13, an *endecasillabo* couplet) and in Seneca's speeches. (His speech in 1.6 continues for fifteen lines before being articulated by a rhyme.)[73] Lengthy unrhymed passages like these, especially sequences of *endecasillabi*, lend a sense of prose-like naturalness to the dialogue. When more strictly rhymed, like some of Seneca's other speeches, the dialogue can convey excessive formality.[74]

In some of the most passionate exchanges, poetic lines are divided between characters, so that only together do they complete the full line. The effect is one of urgent interruption, as if one character is unable, for some reason, to wait until the other has finished. Such exchanges are particularly memorable near the end of the first scene between Poppea and Nerone, where they effectively propel the encounter to conclusion. The first four elements together make up an *endecasillabo:* "Tornerai / Tornerò / Quando? / Ben tosto," followed immediately by two more, "Me 'l prometti? / Te 'l giuro," comprising a *settenario*, though Monteverdi's setting of this passage actually counteracts Busenello's dramatic rhythm by

---

71. Probably for reasons of phrase structure, the composer repeats text here, extending the line to a *settenario:* "*Quell'Ottone* che t'adorerò." This passage is discussed, quoted, and translated above, pp. 209–10.

72. Another effective interruption occurs, again as they prepare to separate, near the end of one of their subsequent scenes (2.7), "Tu di là, / Io di quà," a scene that appears in neither score. Drusilla's insertion of three *ternari*, "Se le mie veste / Havran servito / Per ben coprirlo," within her act 3 monologue indicates her impatience for the news that Ottone's murder of Poppea has been successful.

73. This point is explored further in Chap. 8.

74. See Brizzi, "Teoria e prassi," 62.

slowing it down through extensive repetition. A similar exchange enhances the shock in Ottone's response to Ottavia's suggestion that he kill Poppea, first a *settenario*, then an *endecasillabo*: "Che uccida chi?/ Poppea; / Quel che già prometesti / io ciò promisi?" And this too the composer slows down through repetition, thereby intensifying the psychological effect. Busenello suggests still another psychological effect when he uses the technique in a scene between Drusilla and Ottone. Here she is attempting to reassure herself that his sudden change of attitude means that he loves her, and he is all too anxious to reassure her: "M'ami adunque?/ Ti bramo," an exchange that is emphasized by being repeated within the space of five brief lines:

DRUSILLA:	M'ami, adunque?	You love me, then?
OTTONE:	Ti bramo.	I desire you.
DRUSILLA:	E come in un momento?	But how, all in a moment?
OTTONE:	Amor è foco e subito s'accende.	Love is a fire, and ignites in an instant.
DRUSILLA:	Sì subite dolcezze	Such sudden sweetness
	Hora gode il mio cor, ma non le intende.	My heart now enjoys, but does not understand.
	M'ami adunque?	You love me, then?
OTTONE:	Ti bramo.	I desire you.

Natural (or naturalistic) exchanges between characters are perhaps the most distinctive aspect of Busenello's dramatic language. This is particularly striking in the scenes of passionate confrontation, such as the one between Nerone and Seneca. Here the librettist famously adopts the Senecan technique of stichomythia to portray the escalating tension between the two men as they move from exchanges of four lines to two, and finally to a long series of single lines, which culminate in Nerone's declaration that Poppea will be his wife.

The prose-like immediacy of Busenello's dialogue, especially such rapid-fire interchanges as these that he built into the text, surely inspired one of the most characteristic features of Monteverdi's setting, the intercalations, most memorably in the scene between Seneca and Nerone just mentioned, but also between Nerone and Poppea. (Those between Nutrice and Ottavia in 1.5 and between Ottone and the Soldiers linking act 1 scenes 1–2 were mentioned above.) Although the other two librettos show evidence of having inspired some intercalation, particularly in the construction of duets, where block speeches naturally lent themselves to segmentation in order to reflect intimate communication, only in *Incoronazione* does the technique become critical to the unfolding of the drama.[75]

---

75. Although intercalations occur occasionally in *Ritorno*—Ulisse's "O fortunato" and Penelope's "Non voglio amar," for example, discussed in Chap. 4—and probably also in *Nozze* (see Chap. 5), they are especially characteristic of *Incoronazione*. This point is discussed more fully in Chap. 7, in connection with Poppea/Nerone, Seneca/Nerone, and Ottone/Drusilla.

Fashioning the "Just Lament": Arianna's Venetian Progeny

A just lament, a righteous prayer: we remember Monteverdi's phrase from his famous letter to Striggio. Moved by the human plight of Ariadne and Orpheus, the composer was able to tell their stories. And the telling revolved around two central moments: Arianna's lament and Orfeo's prayer. Monteverdi isolates the big scenes for the central characters as emblematic, marking them as crucial to the operas, as exemplifying or embodying their conviction, their verisimilitude.

We know from many sources that Arianna's lament was one of Monteverdi's favorite pieces—and not only his. We recall that it was regarded as "the most important part" of the opera by the original audience,[76] that every household with a keyboard instrument was said to have had a copy, that it inspired a host of imitations, and that Monteverdi himself extracted it from the opera and published it in three different forms—as a monody, a sacred contrafactum, and a five-voice madrigal cycle. We also know that he remembered it with special fondness years later, when he reported to the theorist Giovanni Battista Doni that it had enabled him to understand the art of imitating the affections.[77] It is to the reputation of Arianna's lament, of course, that we owe its survival; what was the most important part of the opera to its original audience—and its composer—is even more important to us: it is all we have.[78]

At least some of the credit for Monteverdi's extraordinary lament must be—and has been—ascribed to the poet, Ottavio Rinuccini, who created a text that so effectively matched the composer's rhetorical language. The long lament, in five unequal sections punctuated by brief choral responses,[79] is constructed essentially of *versi sciolti* that are articulated and shaped by a variety of rhetorical emphases: irregularly recurring refrains (particularly the poignant opening line, "Lasciatemi morire"), repeated locutions, questions,

---

76. Monteverdi identified it as such in his letter of 21 March 1620 to Striggio: "Mando anco il principio del *Lamento*, qual di già l'avevo in casa ricopiato sopra altra carta, aciò anco intorno a questo si avantaggia tenpo, essendo la più essenzial parte del'opera" (letter no. 51), one of a number of letters dealing with a planned revival of *Arianna* for Mantua in the spring of 1620. (This series of letters begins with no. 50, 17 March, and ends with no. 55, 18 April.) This was one of several planned revivals. The only one that seems to have taken place occurred in Venice in 1640 (see Chap. 1). Finding it dramatically redundant, Carter, *Musical Theatre*, 206–8, argues convincingly that the lament may have been added as a result of the opera having been judged "tropp'asciutta." See above, n. 6.

77. On the nature of the collaboration between poet and composer, see Fabbri, *Monteverdi*, 142 and n. 193 (trans. Carter, 96 and n. 157). On "la via naturale alla immitazione," see the letter of 22 October 1633 to Doni (no. 124). Tomlinson, "Madrigal," 86–87, gives particular credit to the poet for providing a text so well suited to Monteverdi's taste, a claim supported by a letter from Doni to Mersenne quoted in James Moore's review of *The Letters of Claudio Monteverdi*, ed. Denis Stevens (London, 1980), in *JAMS* 35 [1982]: 562–64.

78. There have been tantalizing rumors of the work resurfacing over the years, but nothing has yet come of them.

79. Eighty-four lines in Solerti's edition (*Albori*, 2: 782–862, including choral response of twelve lines, in four tercets). For corrections to Solerti's text, see Bujić, "Arianna," appendix 1. For a probable five-scene organization of *Arianna*, see Carter, *Musical Theatre*, table 8-1, p. 208.

and inversions inspire a setting characterized by huge emotional contrasts and accumulating tension. Arianna moves us by the intensity of her pain and by her efforts to deal with it, as she progresses from despair ("Lasciatemi morire," "O Teseo, O Teseo mio") to disbelief ("Dove, dove è la fede"), to fury ("O nembi, o turbi, o venti"), to shame ("Non son, non son quell'io"), and, finally, to resignation ("Mirate, ove m'ha scorto empia fortuna"). Monteverdi casts the lament entirely in recitative style, but he exploits Rinuccini's refrains, phrase and word repetitions, and patterns of rhyme and meter to create a strong sense of overall melodic and rhythmic shape. Although Arianna shares the scene with a responsive chorus and companion, she is not affected by them: her lament is completely self-motivated, generated by the ebb and flow of her own internal passions.

If Monteverdi sought other Ariannas, convincing human beings who could inspire him to the natural expression of suffering, he certainly found them in his Venetian texts. The Venetian librettists knew Arianna's lament not from its dead traces on the page, but from live performance on the stage, when the opera was revived at the Teatro S. Moisè in 1640. All three librettists offered him the opportunity of focusing their protagonists' suffering in a central, pivotal scene that was molded to the pattern of Rinuccini's great lament. Penelope, Enea, Lavinia, and Ottavia are all Arianna's heirs.[80]

Badoaro's imitation comes immediately, in the extraordinary opening scene of *Ritorno*, in which Penelope vents her suffering to her old nurse Ericlea. Resignation, anger, and hope succeed one another as she laments her twenty-year abandonment by Ulisse. The text itself is rather shapeless, a somewhat crude imitation of Rinuccini's strongly articulated text for Arianna, but it is adequate to Monteverdi's purpose; it provides him with raw material that he could transform into a lament of overwhelming power and conviction fully worthy of its model.[81] Monteverdi's editing of this scene, as we shall see in the next chapter, was essential to its final effect. It represents what is arguably his most substantial and successful intervention in all of his works.

Lacking the music for Monteverdi's second Venetian opera, *Nozze*, we are of course at a disadvantage in identifying analogies to Arianna's lament. But in fact the libretto contains several rather promising candidates in two lengthy monologues for Lavinia and one for Enea. The librettist himself calls our attention to the most prominent of these passages, Enea's soliloquy in act 3 (scenes 4–5), which he describes at considerable length in his "Lettera." His description emphasizes his keen awareness of Monteverdi's tastes and requirements (see Appendix 2 [h, i]).[82]

---

80. Tomlinson (*Monteverdi*) has already discussed the parallels between Arianna and her successors, Penelope and Ottavia, to the detriment, however, of the later heroines. See also id., "Music and the Claims of Text: Monteverdi, Rinuccini, and Marino," *Critical Inquiry* 8 (1982): 565–89.

81. This extensive transformation and its importance for the whole structure of the drama are discussed in Chap. 7. (Arianna resonates as well in Ulisse's first soliloquy, also discussed in Chap. 7.)

82. As already mentioned (Chap. 5, n. 35), the shaping of this scene—or rather these two scenes—entails some distortion or alteration of the Virgilian plot, which clearly disturbs our academic librettist, and the same is true of the other Ariadne-like scenes.

He has portrayed Enea first as happy about the prospect of peace with the Latins—we recall that he has stretched his Virgilian model by keeping his hero temporarily ignorant of their battle plans—but also tired from his past exertions, so that, lulled by the amenities of the landscape, he lies down to rest on the banks of the Tiber; the river, which will eventually owe its fame to him, then offers a friendly warning of the approaching dangers from the Rutulians, and exhorts him to combat.[83] At this unexpected news Enea awakens disturbed *(turbato)*, and, lamenting the persistence of his bad luck *(malvagia)*, recalls the details of his past misfortunes, which in part at least must have been known to the spectators.[84] Whereupon, as a strong man reinvigorates himself, so he, having passed from calm to suffering, now rejoices at the sight of his mother, Venus. "These changes of affection," the author emphasizes, "*which are always effective in poems like these, happen also to please our Sig. Monteverdi very much, because they give him the opportunity of displaying, with varied pathos, the marvels of his art.*"[85]

To be sure, the scene sequence requires the intervention of two other characters to inspire some of Enea's emotional shifts: in contrast to Arianna, whose emotions developed internally, Enea responds first to Tebro and then to Venere.[86] Still, his mood changes are forcefully projected in the poetry of his speeches. Like Arianna's, Enea's text is primarily in *versi sciolti;* and though it lacks the repetitive rhetorical structures that Monteverdi found so congenial in the earlier work—alliteration, assonance, anaphora, isocolon—it is replete with expressive imagery and strong metric patterns. Beginning with a textual passage that is somewhat more tightly rhymed than the norm, a pair of tercets: abB, cDD (but 7 7 11, 7 11 11), Enea tries to calm himself, urging his heart to banish all unhappy thoughts—to submerge them in the waters of Lethe. (Presumably the absence of metric confirmation of the rhyme scheme would have discouraged the composer from setting these lines as two parallel stanzas, though the repeated invocation in lines 3, 4, and 5—italicized here—might have suggested lyrical expression.)

Alle liete novelle	To the happy news
Da Illioneo recate,	brought from Ilium
Itene lunghi omai [ormai] cure mal nate,	be banished, ill-born worries,
Serenatevi o lumi,	calm yourselves, o eyes,
Tranquillati mio Cor; con dolce quiete	be tranquil, my heart; in sweet quiet
Ogni tristo pensier somergi in Lete.	let every sad thought be submerged in Lethe.

---

83. See Appendix 2 [g]. The intervention of the Tiber is not listed in the scenario, where a single scene number (3.4) covers all of this action—it comprises two scenes in the three-act libretto and three in the others (see Table 14 above, Chap. 5). A sleep scene like this was in the process of becoming something of a convention in contemporary Venetian opera; there is, of course, a very prominent one in *Incoronazione* (see below, n. 87).

84. The fact that the ten lines that rehearse Enea's past suffering appear only in the three-act libretto is further evidence of its proximity to the scenario, and thus the performance. (See Chap. 5, p. 159 and n. 70.)

85. "le quali mutationi d'affetti, come in sì fatti poemi, paiono sempre bene, piacciono poi molto al nostro Signor Monteverde per haver egli campo con una varia patetica di mostrar li stupori dell'arte sua" (see Appendix 2 [i]).

86. Enea's monologue actually ends before Venere's entrance, though their conversation inspires his final change of mood to happiness.

Enea then invokes sleep, beginning with a rhetorically heightened line, "Vieni o sonno, deh vieni oblio dei mali," which initiates a new closed group of lines, this time four, with the rhyme scheme abba. The apostrophic nature of this invocation, as well as the recurrence of a varied form of the opening line to round out the quatrain, lend a somewhat formal tone to this speech, suggesting the possibility of lyrical setting.

Vieni o sonno, deh vieni oblio de mali	Come, o sleep, do come, oblivion of evils,
Del nostro dì fuggace	of our days fleeting
Porto, ch'ai solo in te sicura Pace.	port, which alone offers secure peace.
Vieni, e sopra di me riposa l'ali.	Come, and over me rest your wings.

In the concluding twelve lines, Enea employs a panoply of standard natural images to affirm his peaceful mood, declaring his affinity with the beauties of nature: the rustling of the wind, the song of birds, the murmuring of the waves; finally, he succumbs to sleep (the expressive alliterations that mark this passage are underlined and significant textual variants are given in brackets):

Spiran tra fronde, e fronde	Between leaves and leaves breathe
I freschi venticelli,	fresh breezes,
Cantano i vaghi augelli	lovely birds sing,
Concordi ai suon del [Concorde il suono al]	in concord with the murmuring of
mormorar dell'onde,	the waves,
Cari dolci, e graditi,	dear, sweet, and pleasing
Al tuo venir inviti	invite your coming.
Ma le preghiere mie non porta il vento,	But the wind does not carry my prayers,
Di già vacilla il piè, s'aggrava il lume,	already my foot slips, the light dims,
Qui dove d'Erbe, e fiori, [e 'l fiume]	here, where grass, flowers,
[3331 only: E il margine del fiume]	and the riverbank
M'appresterà morbido letto, e adorno,	make ready for me a soft and ornate bed,
[letto morbido, odoroso]	
Gl'occhi racchiudo, e poso.	I close my eyes and rest.
[Chiudi gl'occhi al riposo]	

Here it is the musical imagery and the predominantly short, mostly rhymed lines that might suggest a lyrical setting of the first part of this text. As for the end of it—"Di già vacilla il piè"—recalling Monteverdi's remarks on sleep in the *Finta pazza* letters and the sleep scene in *Incoronazione*, we almost hear the composer portraying Enea's increasing drowsiness with hesitant rhythm, interspersed with rests, and descending melody.[87] This

---

87. As we have seen, Monteverdi had already assayed the imitation of sleep in *La finta pazza Licori*. Could he have requested such a scene from Torcigliani, or could the librettist have included it specifically to please him? The same question might be asked of the continuation of Enea's monologue, particularly given its resemblance to the lament of Arianna.

brief moment of repose is abruptly shattered by Tebro's warning of imminent war, to which Enea, rudely awakened, responds with agitation. Following his initial shock of disbelief, he cries out bitterly against heaven. Has he not suffered enough? Will his trials never end?

Luci mie, che vedeste?	Eyes of mine, what do you see?
Verace oggetto, o pur larva mendace?	A true object, or else a false shadow?
Fosti tu, di quest'onde [. . . humido dio]	Were you, of these waters a damp god,
Pietoso Nuncio a me del rischio mio?	pitying messenger of my risk?
O ciel dunque non basta	Oh heaven, it is not enough, then,
A raddolcir tuo sdegno	to sweeten your disdain
Ciò che soffersi ohimè d'empio, e d'indegno?	my cruel and undeserved suffering?
[3331 only: Spargesti, cara Patria	You shed, dear country,
Tant'anni il sangue a fiumi	rivers of blood for so many years,
Cadendo in fin tradita	falling in the end, betrayed,
Distrutta, incenerita.	destroyed, incinerated.
Voi de congiunti estinti Ombre dolenti	You sad shades of my dead relatives
Ridite i miei tormenti.	will rehearse my torments.
Voi dell'atroce esilio men dogliosi	You, less pained by atrocious exile,
Ahi, che i miei guai penosi.	alas, than my painful misery.
Non tollerò l'Inferno	I will not bear Hell
Benché sia con il suo mio straccio eterno.]	though to it be tied my eternal suffering.

Initially unrhymed and irregular, his poetry becomes increasingly measured and passionate, and filled with hard sounds (underlined); couplet follows upon rhymed couplet as shock becomes self-pity and then anger, culminating finally in a furious outburst. The rapidly shifting pronouns of his address, voi/miei/voi/miei/suo/mio (italicized), reflect his heightened emotion: he refuses to accept Hell's torments. But then, recognizing that he has overstepped the bounds of decorum, he abruptly takes hold of himself. Arianna-like, Enea regrets the intensity of his anger: pain was the cause of his excessive passion, his words came from his tongue, not his heart.[88] Pulling himself together, then, he is able to objectify his grief and in the final three lines of the scene he summons up his former courage: however contrary heaven and fate may be, his brave heart will be victorious:

Ma del usato ardir, quai novi accenti	But in my customary boldness, what
[voci indegne].	new accents are these.
L'impeto del dolore	The outburst of pain
Tragge dalla mia lingua, e non dal core.	came from my tongue, and not my heart.
Enea dunque si duole,	Enea now laments,

---

88. This, of course, is precisely what happens in Arianna's lament; it happens as well in Lavinia's scene with her Damigella, and Ottavia's with her nurse (see below), but not in Penelope's lament. Enea's about-face depends for its effect especially on the ten previous lines, unique to the performance libretto, which convey the escalation of his tension to the breaking point.

Che nel più fier sembiante	who in his proudest aspect
Rimirò morte, e si serbò costante?	stared at death, and remained constant?
No, no, pur imperversi il Cielo, il Fatto	No, no, no matter how contrary Heaven and Fate,
Sarà non mai languente	no longer will the victorious heart
Nelle perdite ancor il Cor vincente.	languish in its losses.

When Venere arrives in the following scene to bestow upon him the arms made for him by Vulcano, Enea rejoices. Reassured now that he will vanquish his enemies, he closes the scene with a quatrain expressing his newfound confidence. Although formally rather neutral, surely this final exuberant quatrain would have been set lyrically, as some kind of joyful aria.

Qual più lieto di me, qual più felice?	Who more joyous than I, who happier?
Cinto di sì bell'armi	Clothed in such beautiful armor
Pugnerò, vincerò palme, et allori,	I will fight, I will win palms and laurels;
Preparate al mio Crin fregi, et onori.	prepare adornments and honors for my hair.

One is reminded here of Ulisse's rejoicing at his good fortune in *Ritorno*, act 1: "O fortunato Ulisse," which the composer set as a formal strophic aria, even though the form of the text did not call for it.

Thus has Enea passed, to reiterate the librettist's words, from "quiete" to "travaglio" to "allegrezza"—from quiet, to suffering, to happiness—all within the space of a single (if admittedly lengthy) monologue: *such changes of affection please our Signor Monteverdi very much because they allow him to display the marvels of his art.*

❧

Not content with a single imitation of Arianna's lament, Torcigliani constructed two other scenes, for Lavinia, with similar attention to sharp affective contrasts and accumulating tension. One is a fifty-four-line soliloquy (3.3), the other a dialogue with her maid (3.8) in the manner of Penelope's (or Arianna's) lament. While it may not be as self-consciously constructed as Enea's, in Lavinia's soliloquy successions of expressive images and sudden changes of mood reveal her struggle to control her feelings, her anguish at having been the cause of so much bloodshed, and her fear for Enea's safety during his long anticipated confrontation with Turno (textual variants bracketed, expressive alliteration underlined).

1 Freme l'aria e rimbomba	The air trembles and thunders
2 All'orrido fragore	from the horrible roar
3 Della guerriera Tromba.	of the trumpet of war.
4 Rintuona il Cielo a gl'ululati, a i stridi	The sky resounds with howls and screams,

5 Onde al sangue, alle morti	while to blood, to death
6 Sciolto da' ferrei lacci, Italia sfida	dissolved by iron bonds Italy confronts
7 Il terrore [furor] omicida.	murderous terror.
8 Onde [Or di] sì fiere sorti	Now of such proud destiny,
9 Del suscitato ardor, ch'Italia sface,	of renewed passion that destroys Italy,
10 Qual è, se non sol io,[89]	what, if not I alone,
11 La fatal, dolorosa infausta face?	is the fatal, suffering, unlucky torch?
12 Infelici bellezze,	Unhappy beauties,
13 Che nate esser sembrate	who seem to have been born
14 Per dar altrui dolcezze	to give delight to others,
15 E sete di martir cagion spietate,	and have become the despised cause of martyrdom,
16 O frigio duce, o Enea,	O Phrygian duke, O Enea,
17 Da' desolati lidi	from the desolate shores
18 Della caduta patria, a chi [che] vogliesti,	of your fallen country, why did you turn,
19 Ver le sponde latine i lini arditi,	toward Latin shores your brave sails,
20 S'esser dovean per me così funesti?	if because of me they were to become so deadly?
21 *Misera*, qual io penso [sento]	Miserable one, how I think
22 Orror, tema, spavento?	horror, fear, fright?
23 *Palpita* il cor frequente,	My heart beats too fast,
24 Si turba il guardo fioco,	my feeble eyes are troubled,
25 *Vacilla* il piè cadente,	my falling step wavers
26 E ne le vene alterna or gelo or fuoco.	and my blood turns now to ice, now to fire.
27 Fiero destin fatale,	O proud and fatal destiny,
28 A che temer m'insegni	why do you teach me to fear
29 Tempesta più mortale	a more mortal storm
30 Di quell'ancor [amor] di cui rimiro i segni?	than that love, whose signs I recognize?
31 Ah che non è, non è	Ah, let not, let not
32 La bella Italia offesa:	beautiful Italy be offended:
33 Contro Lavinia, ohimè, volta è l'impresa,	Against Lavinia, alas, the effort is directed
34 Sì che altri senta esterna[90]	so that others feel externally,
35 Ed io nel sen doglioso	what I in my unhappy bosom
36 Più cruda guerra interna.	feel as a crueler internal war.
37 O placido riposo,	O peaceful rest,
38 Lassa, dove venisti? [ne gisti]	alas, where have you gone?
39 Dolce seren, o dio, come sparisti?	Sweet serenity, oh God, how did you disappear?
40 Or, agitata, parmi	Now agitated you seem

89. "Qual è, se non sol'io, l'infausta face," a combination of lines 10–11.

90. "Sì ch'altri senta, ed io nel sen doglioso," two *settenari* (34–35) joined to form an *endecasillabo*.

41	Esser rapita a l'armi.	to have been abducted to war.
42	Esser vorrei ne la crudel tenzone	I would like to be in the cruel combat
43	Per rimirar d'appresso	to see from nearby
44	Chi è del mio mal cagione.	the one who is the cause of my pain.
45	Ma ciò non è concesso	But that is not allowed
46	A pudor verginale,	by virginal modesty,
47	A maestà regale.	by royal majesty.
48	Forse su l'alte mura,	Perhaps on the high wall,
49	Infra le schiere sparte	within the spartan ranks
50	Del sanguignoso Marte,	of bloody Mars,
51	Vedrò chi più vorrei [vedo]	I will see the one I most wish to see,
52	Bench'esser io potrei	though I could be
53	Vie più che spettatrice,	more than spectator,
54	Spettacolo infelice.	the unhappy spectacle itself.

Lavinia's emotions undergo abrupt and frequent oscillation. Her powerful evocation of the images of war (ll. 1–11, note emphasis on hissing _f_s) is followed suddenly by the expression of her awareness of her personal stake in it (ll. 12–15), and then her description of her fear (ll. 21–26), and her longing for peace (ll. 37–39). Rapidly shifting address from Enea, to herself, to Destiny, and back to herself again, in the third and then the first person, she is at once subject and object, both spectator and spectacle of her own destruction. Such kaleidoscopic emotions and points of view, once again, are precisely what Monteverdi sought in a libretto; _they gave him the opportunity of displaying the marvels of his art._ Perhaps above all, Lavinia's vivid description of the physical manifestations of her emotional distress (ll. 21–26)—rapid heartbeat, blurred vision, unsteady gait, fever and chills, an unsteadiness conveyed by the alternating accents (_sdrucciolo/piano_ beginnings) of successive lines (_sdrucciolos_ italicized)—is made to order for a composer who strove so intently to imitate feelings.

It is worth pointing out that Lavinia's emotional shifts—from description to objectified thought ("Infelici bellezze"), to expression of feeling ("Misera qual'io sento"), to the questioning of destiny ("Fiero destin fatale"), to lamenting her lost peace, and culminating in hope ("Forse su l'alte mura")—are enhanced by the form of her poetry: various sections of her text are distinguished from one another not only by their expressive focus but by individually closed rhyme schemes—a rhymed sestet (ll. 21–26, "Misera, qual io sento," aabcbC) and septet (ll. 48–54: "Forse su l'alte mura," abbccdd)—or rhythmic structures that invite lyricism.[91] _Versi sciolti_ finally yield to a succession of twelve _settenari,_ mostly in rhymed couplets, which contribute to the accumulation of tension at the conclusion of her scene. More highly structured than either Enea's lament or Penelope's, Lavinia's monologue shows the extent to which Torcigliani was aware of Monteverdi's style: the premium

---

91. Sevieri, _Le nozze_, 138, nn. 69, 75 characterizes these as "canzonette meliche."

he placed on variety and contrast. *Such changes of affection please our Signor Monteverdi very much because they offer him the opportunity to display the marvels of his art.*

Though the impending war is still very much on her mind in her second (shorter) monologue, five scenes later, the source of Lavinia's distress is more specific and more internal: in the interim she has fallen desperately in love with Enea and is ashamed of her feelings. Here, her passionate outpouring, a lament, is mediated by a series of brief interjections from her lady-in-waiting, objective, descriptive remarks that are directed outward, to the audience: "this is not Lavinia. She has gone mad. What has changed her?" And then, "Alas, such gestures, such an appearance, what unsteady glances, never seen before; what will become of her?"[92] Finally, having understood that love is the source of her mistress's pain, Melanto-like, she encourages her not to fight but to accept it.

Lavinia's feelings of love may be exacerbated by her fear of Enea's death at the hands of Turno, but it is the feelings themselves that she is attempting to exorcize during the course of her monologue. Her speech, in three large sections, begins as a narrative, as she recalls how she was overcome with love for "il famoso Troiano" when he appeared on the city walls in battle dress (fourteen lines), and how her passion increased as she observed his confrontation with Turno (twenty lines). Now, she says, she cannot bear the thought of her beloved's death ("Ed hor"), ending her speech with a brief prayer to Venere. Finally, in the third and last segment of the speech she laments her situation:

Ma misera, infelice,	But miserable, unhappy me,
Per mal noto straniero	for an unknown foreigner
Prego, bramo, pavento;	I pray, burn, fear;
Di più piango, sospiro e mi lamento.	and more, I cry, sigh, and lament.
E quai son questi segni	And what are these signs
Che tentano l'entrata	that seek entrance
Del mio ritroso petto, affetti indegni?	within my shy breast, unworthy affections?
Che dico? Ah, troppo già l'han superata!	What am I saying? Ah, they have already overcome me.
Sento, sento ben io	I feel, well do I feel
Qual forza omnipotente	that an omnipotent force
Prese il mio cor repente,	suddenly took hold of my heart
De la passion rubelle	and with rebellious passion
Fa dura strage e se le rende ancelle.	slaughtered it and made it a servant.
Io amo, ohimè, che dissi? Ah, chi mi udì?	I am in love, alas, what did I say? Ah, who heard me?
Deh, disperdete voi, veloci venti,	Alas, scatter, you swift winds,
I mal proferti accenti.	my ill-uttered words.

---

92. Rather than Arianna's, the arrangement and content of this text call to mind another of Monteverdi's most memorable laments, the Lament of the Nymph.

It is particularly in this final section that the librettist engages typical lament rhetoric: Lavinia expresses and analyzes her feelings almost simultaneously, in sequences of highly expressive verbs ("prego, bramo, pavento: di più piango, sospiro e mi lamento") followed by repeated retractions: ("Ma che dico?, and later, "Io amo, ohimè, che dissi?"), finally, regretfully, begging the winds to dissipate her unwisely uttered words.

Like the two earlier soliloquies, Lavinia's speech is comprised almost exclusively of *versi sciolti*, which Monteverdi would probably have set in expressive recitative style. This is in contrast to Damigella's responses, all of which are more highly organized: the first a quatrain of *settenari tronchi*, the second an abb tercet of *ottonari*. Though her third response begins in *versi sciolti*, it culminates in a rhymed quatrain of *settenari*, cast as a duet with Lavinia. To judge from similar closed passages in the text of *Ritorno*, each of these more structured passages would probably have inspired lyricism from the composer.

⁂

All three of these monologues for Enea and Lavinia are striking not only for their general affective mobility, but for their pointed exploitation of contrasting images of love and war, a fundamental aspect of Monteverdi's late aesthetics. The composer's interest in the dichotomy of these two feelings—and their intersection—could hardly have been a secret to any librettist collaborating with Monteverdi in the early 1640s. It had formed the rhetorical skeleton (and raison d'être) of his most recent publication, the *Madrigali guerrieri et amorosi* of 1638. The war-like style, or *stile concitato*, was featured repeatedly in both parts of that collection as a means of conveying feelings associated with intense passions or of depicting descriptions of battle, either real or symbolic. Monteverdi, whose exploration of the style occupied him for much of his career, found many opportunities of deploying it in his Venetian operas; *Ritorno* and *Nozze* feature literal battles. The violent confrontation between Ulisse and the Suitors is matched by the battle between Enea's and Turno's forces at the end of act 3, initiated by the same battle cry: "Alle straggi, su, su" (though the battle is not actually finished until the end of the following act, when Turno is reported killed by Enea while attempting to flee). Surely Monteverdi would have used a similar battle sinfonia in both instances.

In laments, too, Monteverdi uses the *stile concitato* at a climactic moment to portray excessive anger that will soon boil over into contrition. The style is anticipated by Arianna when she reaches for percussive, rapid repeated notes at the height of her anger, close to the end of her lament (ll. 836–42):[93]

Ahi, che non pur risponde!	Ah, he still does not answer!
Ahi che più d'aspe è sordo a' miei lamenti!	Ah, more deaf than a viper is he to my lament!

---

93. On the (questionable) use of the term "concitato" to describe a panoply of percussive effects, see Massimo Ossi, *Divining the Oracle: Monteverdi's 'Seconda Prattica'* (Chicago: University of Chicago Press, 2003), 227, n. 21.

O nembi, o turbi, o venti,	O storms, o tempests, o winds,
Sommergetelo voi dentr'a quell'onde!	drown him beneath your waves!
Correte, orche e balene,	Hasten, whales and sea monsters,
E de le membra immonde	and with his foul limbs
Empiete le voragini profonde.	fill your deep abysses.
Che parlo, ahi! che vaneggio . . .	Ah, what am I saying? Am I delirious?

Ottavia invokes the full panoply of *concitato* elements at the climax of her lament (1.5) as she curses the Gods for failing to punish Nerone for betraying her, and then apologizes:

Se per punir Nerone	If to punish Nerone
Fulmini tu non hai,	you have no thunderbolts,
D'impotenza t'accuso,	I will accuse you of impotence,
D'ingiustizia t'incolpo;	I will charge you with injustice.
Ahi, trapasso tropp'oltre e me ne pento. . . .	Ah, I have gone too far and I repent. . . .

In what would seem like a similar call for the *stile concitato* in his great scena, already discussed, Enea's emotions reach excessive heights during the recital of his past woes, triggering the Arianna-like reversal (see p. 228 and n. 88 above).

Lavinia's war-like imagery is different, however. The first nine lines of her monologue (pp. 229–30) describe an external battle, the one she witnesses, rather than a symbolic, internal one that she feels. Monteverdi might have used the *stile concitato* here as well, but in a different, more objective manner: perhaps resembling his setting of the battle cries in *Ritorno*. Although later on she refers to suffering internal war—in fact, explicitly to the contrast between what she sees and what she feels (ll. 31–36)—in this scene at least, Lavinia never reaches the extreme passion that would either cause her to regret her words, or require the *stile concitato* to convey her feelings, even in our speculations. The same may be said of her scene with her Damigella. Perhaps the cause of her passion—her love for Enea is not even unrequited—is not serious enough to inspire real suffering. Though she does regret her words here, more than once, they never approach the excess of those of her sisters. Her suffering lacks the historical resonance—and conviction—of Arianna's, Penelope's, and Ottavia's. And this is no accident. We recall that Lavinia's monologues, like Enea's, involved departures from the *Aeneid* that the librettist justified as a means of enhancing the verisimilitude of his plot. Explicitly in the case of Enea, and implicitly for Lavinia, emotions were pumped up to provide the composer with suitable situations for "just lament and righteous prayer."

Note, finally, that while all three of the *Nozze* "lament" texts feature rapid changes of emotion, repeated locutions, and rhetorical emphases that would have suited Monteverdi's taste, they lack one of the most conspicuous expressive features of Arianna's lament, a refrain: "Lasciatemi morire," echoing throughout the long lament, in exact and inexact repetitions, is one of its chief structural/affective elements. The importance of refrains for the composer is underlined by his editing of Penelope's lament (as we shall see, his heightening of Badoaro's refrains is one of the main features of his revision), as well as his settings of other lament texts.

Alas, aside from guessing that he might have treated this or that passage lyrically, or used the *stile concitato* or imitated an action in another, without the score of *Nozze* we obviously have no way of knowing how Monteverdi actually set the texts we have been discussing. We cannot even know whether he set them as given in the libretto or altered them (by adding refrains, for instance). It is evident, though, from comparative analysis of the poetry, that despite their lack of refrains, the texts of all the big scenes in *Nozze* are more tightly structured—and more concise—than Penelope's lament from *Ritorno*. At least in this respect, his own disclaimers to the contrary, Torcigliani reveals himself to have been innately more skillful than his predecessor. Monteverdi may well have been more satisfied with these texts and felt no need to alter them. Or they may have been introduced or improved following his preliminary critique of the libretto. (We have noted above [n. 88] that the effect of the most Arianna-like passage of Enea's scena, the reversal, was strengthened by a textual passage found only in the performance libretto.) It could even be that Torcigliani had learned from Badoaro's mistakes.

The same may be said for Busenello, whose lament texts in *Incoronazione* Monteverdi surely must have found more congenial than Penelope's, since he apparently did not feel the need to alter them. Among the most striking monologues in this opera are those sung by Ottavia, in 1.5 and 3.6.[94] The first of them, much the longer and more varied of the two (thirty-seven lines as opposed to sixteen), displays greater affinity with those of both Arianna and Enea. In it, Ottavia reveals her ambivalence: self-pity, anger, and hurt alternate in rapid succession within her, reason and passion vying for primacy. Her text is replete with those *changes of affection that please Signor Monteverde very much because they allow him to display the marvels of his art.* Initially in the depths of depression, "disprezzata" and "afflitta," she soon becomes furious at Nerone and curses him, inciting herself to frenzy as she invokes Giove to strike her husband dead with his thunderbolts. But suddenly, as already noted, like Enea, Lavinia, and Arianna before her, she is surprised by the vehemence of her own anger and steps back from it, vowing to suffer in silence: "Ahi trapasso tropp'oltre, e me ne pento, supprimo e sepelisco in taciturne angoscie il mio tormento." The intervention of her nurse, with her encouragement to forget about Nerone and find a lover (reminiscent of Melanto's advice to Penelope in the scene following her lament), provokes a final sacrilegious outburst: If god did not exist she herself would claim god-like powers to right the wrongs she has suffered ("Se non ci fosse né l'honor né Dio, sarei Nume a me stessa, e i falli miei con la mia stessa man castigherei"). But instead she sinks back into herself, defeated, resigned to silent suffering. In

---

94. Ottone's opening soliloquy, discussed above, pp. 209–10, and in Chap. 7, also shares significant elements with Arianna's lament. Soliloquies were so intrinsic to Ottavia's character that a third one was added in the Naples production (see Chap. 4).

its lack of psychological progress, her soliloquy more closely resembles those of Arianna and Penelope than Enea's.

Although Monteverdi does not appear to have substantially rewritten Busenello's text for Ottavia—all of the versions in librettos and scores are essentially the same—his setting sharpens its contours, projecting its emotional shifts much more powerfully, heightening in various ways the contrasts already present. In contrast to his complete reworking of Penelope's lament, here he makes only two significant editorial changes, both for the purpose of intensification: one such change involves bringing a line back unexpectedly as an exclamatory refrain (l. 4, "O delle donne miserabil sesso," returns following l. 8—an affective insertion set to a rhythmically and melodically heightened version of the original passage, covering a diminished octave); in the other change, mentioned above, he intercalates Ottavia's final despondent lines of resignation with her nurse's attempt to comfort her. Otherwise, his chief method of rhetorical intensification is by means of repetition of individual affective words, and not once but three, four, and in one case five times. A list of the repeated words reads like an emotional précis of the monologue: "Disprezzata regina," "afflitta," and "Nerone," three times each; "il matrimonio," and "siam costrette" twice each, and "fulmini" five times in succession.[95]

1 OTTAVIA: Disprezzata regina, *regina, regina disprezzata, disprezzata regina*	Humiliated queen,
2 Del monarca romano afflitta, *afflitta, afflitta* moglie,	martyred wife of the Roman monarch,
3 Che fo, ove son, che penso, *che penso?*	What am I doing, where am I, what am I thinking?
4 O delle donne miserabile sesso;	Oh, miserable sex of woman:
5 Se la natura e 'l cielo	though nature and heaven
6 Libere ci produce,	created us free,
7 Il matrimonio, *il matrimonio* c'incatena serve.	marriage enchains us like slaves.
8 Se concepiamo l'uomo, *O delle donne miserabil sesso,*	In conceiving boys
9 Al nostr'empio tiran formiam le membra,	we form the limbs of our wicked tyrants,
10 Allattiamo il carnefice crudele	we nurse a cruel executioner
11 Che ci scarna e ci svena,	who tears at our flesh and tortures us,
12 E siam forzate, *siam forzate* per indegna sorte,	and we are forced by unworthy fate
13 A noi medesme partorir la morte.	to give birth to our own death.
14 Nerone, *Nerone,* empio Nerone,	Nerone, wicked Nerone,

---

95. The setting contrasts strongly in this respect with Arianna's lament, where repetition, whenever it occurs, is built into the text. Tomlinson emphasizes this point in contrasting Rinuccini's text with Striggio's for Orfeo's "Tu sei morta." For an analysis of the expressive possibilities inherent in word repetition, see Ivan Fónagy, *La repetizione creativa: Ridondanze espressive nell'opera poetica* (Bari: Dedalo, 1982), esp. 18–19. The composer utilizes exaggerated text repetition as an expressive device in Penelope's lament as well as Iro's. See Chap. 7. The nature of the words chosen for repetition here may be suggestive, in retrospect, for the texts in *Nozze*.

15 Marito, O Dio, *o Dio*, marito	husband, oh God, husband
16 Bestemmiato per sempre	blasphemed forever
17 E maledetto dai cordogli miei,	and cursed by my miseries,
18 Dove, *dove*, ohimè, dove sei?	where, alas, where are you?
19 In braccio di Poppea, *in braccio di Poppea, di Poppea*	In Poppea's arms
20 Tu dimori felice e godi, *felice e godi*, e intanto	you rest and take your pleasure, while
21 Il frequente cader de' pianti miei,	my endless tears
22 Pur va quasi formando	seem almost to form
23 Un diluvio di specchi in cui tu miri,	a flood of mirrors in which you see
24 Dentro alle tue delizie i miei, *i miei*, *i miei* martiri.	within your happiness my torments.
25 Destin, *destin*, se stai lassù,	Providence, if you are up there,
26 Giove ascoltami tu,	Jove, listen to me,
27 Se per punir Nerone	if to punish Nerone
28 Fulmini, *fulmini, fulmini, fulmini, fulmini* tu non hai,	you have no thunderbolts,
29 D'impotenza t'accuso,	I accuse you of impotence,
30 D'ingiustizia t'incolpo.	I charge you with injustice.
31 Ahi, trappasso tropp'oltre e me ne pento.	Ah, I go too far and I repent.
32 Sopprimo e seppelisco	I repress and bury
33 In taciturne angoscie il mio tormento.	in silent anguish my torment.
NUTRICE: Ottavia, Ottavia . . .	*Ottavia . . .*
34 OTTAVIA: O ciel, o ciel, deh, l'ira tua s'estingua,	O heaven, o heaven, quell your rage.
35 Non provi i tuoi rigori il fallo mio.	Do not let your severity punish my offense.
NUTRICE: Ottavia, Ottavia, o tu dell'universe genti Unica imperatrice . . .	*Ottavia, o you of the world sole empress*
36 OTTAVIA: Errò la superficie, il fondo è pio,	The surface erred, the foundation is pure.
37 Innocente fu il cor, peccò, *peccò* la lingua.	The heart was innocent, only the tongue sinned.
NUTRICE: . . . odi, odi	*. . . Hear, hear*
38 [Ottavia, o tu dell'universe genti	Ottavia, you of the world
39 Unica imperatrice]	sole empress
40 Di tua fida nutrice, odi gl'accenti.	Of your faithful nurse, hear the words.

As far as the musical setting of Ottavia's lament is concerned, the emotional contrasts in the text are underlined by the alternation of strongly consonant passages and lengthy sections of unresolved dissonance; abrupt metric shifts and the interruption of rapid successions of repeated notes with slower-moving passages interspersed with rests signal temporary changes of mood. As already noted, Monteverdi unleashes the full power of his *stile concitato* at the climax of Ottavia's building fury, as she repeatedly invokes

Giove's thunderbolts to strike Nerone down, starting at the top of her range and descending in sequence to the bottom. Rising back up again to accuse Giove of impotence, she becomes exhausted, and sinks gradually back down to the bottom of her range, ashamed at her outburst. In contrast to Penelope, whose overwhelming emotion is depression, Ottavia's is anger. As a result, her voice is harsher, the extremes of her range repeatedly exploited in brief paroxysms of octave-spanning phrases. Although his textual changes are few, through repetition, melodic structure, and rhythmic contrast Monteverdi brings this soliloquy to dramatic life, imbuing the listener with sympathy for Ottavia's plight.[96]

⧫

Of the legendary Arianna, we know that "not one lady [in the audience] failed to shed a tear at her plaint."[97] This must have been in large part due to the efficacy of Virginia Andreini Ramponi, who stepped in to perform the role after the sudden death of Caterina Martinelli, for whom Monteverdi had conceived it. That Arianna's Venetian successors were worthy of their model can be gleaned from contemporary reports of their performances. For instance, we know of several admiring poems and letters addressed to Giulia Saus Paolelli, the Roman singer who created the role of Penelope.[98] Although much of the information they provide is fairly generic, a few telling details emerge regarding her special vocal qualities. She, too, we learn from a sonnet in praise of her performance as Penelope, inspired tears in her audience:

---

96. Heller has raised the question whether the listener actually feels sympathy for Ottavia (*Emblems*, 152–77). By restricting her musical utterances to recitative, she argues, the composer limited her ability to express emotion. One small hint of this may perhaps be found in the description of Ottavia's first scene in the scenario of *Incoronazione*, where she is characterized as "exaggerating" her sufferings: "Ottavia imperatrice *esagera* gl'affanni suoi con la Nutrice, detestando i mancamenti di Nerone suo consorte." On the other hand, according to contemporary descriptions of the original Ottavia as performed by Anna Renzi, the despised queen clearly moved her audience, even to tears. (See below.) Beth L. Glixon (review of Heller, *Journal of the Society for Seventeenth-Century Music* 12, no. 1 [2006], www.sscm-jscm.org/jscm/) questions Heller's characterization of recitative as lacking in emotional effect, especially with respect to Ottavia.

97. The lament "fu rappresentato con tanto affetto e con sì pietosi modi, che non si trovò ascoltante alcuno che non s'intenerisse, né fu pur una Dama che non versasse qualche lagrimetta al suo pianto" (*Compendio dalle sontuose feste fatte l'anno MDCVIII nella città di Mantova di Federico Follino*), in Solerti, *Gli albori*, 2: 145. See Suzanne Cusick, "There Was not One Lady who Failed to Shed a Tear: Arianna's Lament and the Construction of Modern Womanhood," *EM* 22 (1994): 21–41; Carter, "Lamenting Ariadne," 395–405; and id., *Musical Theatre*, 202–11; also Bonnie Gordon, *Monteverdi's Unruly Women* (Cambridge: Cambridge University Press, 2004), 164–70.

98. See *I vezzi d'Erato, poesie liriche di Leonardo Quirini* (Venice: Hertz, 1649), 88–89. Querini addresses three rather generic poems to Giulia Saus Paolelli: "Per la Signora Giulia Saus Paolelli Cantatrice Divina," "Per la medesima. mentre canta l'Eneide di Virgilio," and "Per la medesima. Cantando il lamento di Didone descritto in quel divino poema." Though they tell us little about her voice, they do reveal that, in addition to Penelope, she sang the role of Didone, probably in Cavalli's opera in 1641. But if she also sang Penelope in Venice in 1641—as she certainly did in 1640—this means she would have been employed at *both* S. Cassiano

Per la Sig. Giulia Paolelli, Mentre rappresentava Penelope nell'Ulisse

Di Casta Moglie il maritale affetto	The marital affection of a chaste wife,
Giulia ci mostri, e con l'essempio approvi,	Giulia, you show us, and with your example you approve;
Mosse ella i lumi, e tu lo sguardo movi	she moved her eyes, and you move your gaze
L'anime entrambe a scarcerar dal petto.	to release both souls from their breast.
E di te, fu di lei regio l'aspetto,	And through you, did she appear regal,
Arse ella i Re, tu Regii cor commovi,	she enflamed kings, you moved royal hearts,
Ella fu di Virtù l'Idea, rinovi	she was the idea of Virtue, you renew
Tu di virtù l'epilogo perfetto.	the perfect epilogue of virtue.
Pianse a sospir di lei Itaca terra	She cried in sighs the true torments
Veri i tormenti, e a' tuoi finti dolori	of her Ithacan land, and to your feigned pain
Le luci al pianto Felsina disserra.	Felsina opened her eyes to tears.
Ma vinci lei, che cari hebbe i Tesori,	But you won over her, who held treasures dear,
Tu, a non macchiar l'onor, ch'in te si serra	you, not to stain the honor that in you is contained,
Sai fastosa sprezzar preghiere, ed ori.	know how splendidly to disdain entreaties and gold.

(Del Confuso Accad. Fedele)[99]

---

and SS. Giovanni e Paolo during the same season; this would have been extremely unlikely. Perhaps Querini was confused and the Virgilian opera was *Nozze* rather than *Didone;* perhaps Paolelli did *not* sing Penelope in 1641; or, finally, perhaps *Ritorno* was indeed revived at S. Cassiano, as some of the librettos indicate but I have dismissed (see Table 4 above, Chap. 3). Querini was also the author of poems on the deaths of Monteverdi ("O tu, che in nere spoglie" [p. 137]), Isabella Andreini, and Cesare Cremonini. Further on Saus Paolelli, see Fulvio Testi, *Lettere,* ed. Maria Luisa Doglio (Bari: Laterza, 1967), 1: 495–6, letter addressed to Francesco d'Este from Rome, 3 December 1633, one of six written on the same day, which also mentions Maddalena Manelli (see Appendix 8, B.1). According to the description of the performances of *Il Bellerofonte* by Francesco Sacrati, on a libretto by Vincenzo Nolfi, produced at the Teatro Novissimo in 1641–42, in which she sang the role of Queen Anthia, Giulia had been charming Venetian audiences for three years (*Descrittione de gli apparati del Bellerofonte di Giulio del Colle,* 1642) (text in Appendix 8, B.2). The only document that provides any concrete information about Paolelli's voice is Testi's letter, written from the point of view of the spectator.

99. *Le glorie della musica,* 19 (other texts in Appendix 8, B.4). Five of the remaining fifteen sonnets in the same volume (far more than for any other figure) refer to Paolelli in the title role of Manelli and Strozzi's *La Delia,* which shared the Bologna stage with *Ritorno* in 1640. Others are addressed to Guastavillani, the owner of the theater, Monteverdi, Badoaro, Ferrari (as theorbo player), Maddalena Manelli as Venere in *Delia* and Minerva in *Ritorno,* and there are two brief poems (the only non-sonnets) for Costantino Manelli (the Manellis' son) as Amore in *Delia.* Other poems relevant to the performance of *Ritorno* in Bologna include the following sonnets: "Per l'Ulisse, Opera Musicale del Sig. Claudio Monteverdi" (p. 6, partly quoted in Chap. 1) and "Per l'Ulisse, Dramma dell'Illustrissimo Sig. Giacomo Badoero, e Musica del Sig. Claudio Monteverdi" (p. 7), the document that clinches the attribution of the libretto to Badoaro.

A fulsome letter of admiration by the Incognito author Ferrante Pallavicino also reports on the audience's enthusiastic response to her performance, providing a few more specific details:

> And what affections (my thoughts said to themselves) would not be moved to pity in seeing the souls of those who hear you, already rapt by your harmony, now drawn out by a rapid fugue, now suspended in a sigh, now contained in a *groppo* of well-articulated runs, now assailed by the ordinance of musical voices; now finally tormented in various guises, while unexpectedly they stop, and impetuously push forward, gravely free themselves, and precipitously let go; they commit themselves, finally, to pursue one who with varied artifice has by rule to be always inconstant and restless? I would call these torments of Hell, if from your eyes, and in hearing your sweet accents, it were possible to feel anything but the delights of paradise.[100]

Although clearly an object of admiration, as a performer Paolelli remains a shadowy figure, particularly in comparison with her compatriot Anna Renzi, who created the role of Ottavia, among many others.[101] Found among a group of poems in her honor, published in Venice in 1644, the descriptions of Renzi as Ottavia are remarkably vivid. One of them actually traces the temporal *effect* of Renzi's performance of the lament. It begins by describing her appearance—her languid face, her sighs; and then moves to the effects of her singing—which caused Love itself to dissolve in tears from pain; and finally the verisimilitude of the performance—"were your suffering and tragic story real, and had your sad voice, sweet words, and loving sayings affected Nero as they did us, he would have become humble and pious."

E mentre fuori uscivi	And while you came out
Col tuo languido volto,	with your languid face,
Pria, che snodassi il canto,	before you unleashed your song
Con dolci ricercate	with sweet refinement
De' sommessi sospiri,	of subdued sighs
Palesavi ad'ogn'uno i tuoi martiri.	you revealed to everyone your torments.
Poi cominciasti afflitta	Then, afflicted, you intoned
Tue querele Canore	your melodious complaints
Con tua voce divina,	with your voice divine,

---

100. *Panegirici, epitalami, discorsi accademici, novella, et lettere amorose di Ferrante Pallavicino* (Venice: Gio. Battista Cester, 1652), 184–88; another edition (Venice: Turrini, 1652), 162–65. Letter no. 9: "Alla sig. Giulia Paulelli Romana. Per vaga cantatrice" (text in Appendix 8, B.3). This letter provides new information on some of Paolelli's other roles (relevant passages italicized in Appendix): the clearest reference is to Armida (presumably the title role of Ferrari's opera, Venice, SS. Giovanni e Paolo, 1639); Scilla is not a character familiar from any Venetian opera of around this time. Nor is it clear which opera Pallavicino's "straggi di Roma" refers to.

101. On Anna Renzi, in addition to Heller, *Emblems*, 174–77, see Glixon, "Private Lives," 512–19.

Disprezzata Regina,	"Disprezzata Regina,"
E seguendo il lamento	and continuing your lament
Facevi di dolore	you forced Love
Stillar in pianto, e sospirar Amore.	to burst into tears and sigh.
So ben'io, che se vero	Well do I know that,
Fosse stattu [sic] il cordoglio,	had the grief been true,
E l'historia funesta,	and the dolorous tale,
Alla tua voce mesta,	hearing your mournful voice,
Alle dolci parole, ai cari detti,	your sweet words, your endearing expressions,
Sì come i nostri petti	just as they filled our breasts
Colmaro di pietade, ah so ben'io,	with pity, ah, well do I know that
Neron s'haverebbe fato humile, e pio.[102]	Nero would have been rendered humble and compassionate.

Another poem focuses on specific musical aspects of Renzi's performance (in italic):

O di celeste spirto aspetto, e voce,	O appearance and voice of celestial spirit,
Del paradiso sol vaga Sirena,	only siren of paradise
Che *repudiato da Neron in scena,*	*who repudiated by Nero on stage*
Formi armonico misto, e dolce, e attroce.	*form a mixed harmony, sweet and terrible,*
Hor con tremula, hor lenta, hor con veloce	*now tremulous, now slow, now with rapid*
Fugga, e pausa si turba, e rasserena	*flights and pauses your soul becomes agitated, and calm,*
L'alma tua d'armonia tutta ripiena,	*all filled with harmony,*
Che se ben punge i cor, già pur non noce.	*which if it strikes the heart, it does not harm it.*
Mentre in esilio al mar tu doni il pianto,	*When, exiled on the sea, you deliver your lament*
Si ferma l'onda, e si raffrena il vento,	*the waves are stilled and the wind is checked*
Per coglier le tue perle, e 'l dolce canto.	*to collect your tears, and your sweet song.*
Anna lo stesso ciel io miro attento	Anna, the same heaven I see Aminte, attentive
A tuoi dogliosi accenti Aminte, e in tanto	to your mournful tones, and
In ruggiada stillarsi al tuo lamento.[103]	Drip with tears at your lament.

Ottavia's "just lament," in Renzi's voice, did not fail to stimulate tears of sympathy in her listeners.

---

102. "Abozzo di veraci lodi. Alla Signora Anna Renzi Cantatrice singolare Idilio d'incerto Autore," in Giulio Strozzi, *Le glorie della signora Anna Renzi romana* (Venice: Surian, 1644), 37–38. Translation from *OSV*, 385. Complete text in Appendix 8, C.2. See also Heller, *Emblems*, 174–77.

103. Strozzi, *Le glorie*, 30: "Per la Signora Anna Renzi Romana unica cantatrice nel teatro dell'Illustrissimo Signor Giovanni Grimani," signed by G. B. V. (=Giacomo Badoaro Veneto?).

The most complete and revealing description of Renzi's extraordinary qualities as a performer is found in the introduction to the volume, by Giulio Strozzi, *Elogio di Giulio Strozzi, tratto dal libro secondo de' suoi Elogii delle Donne virtuose del nostro secolo*. According to Strozzi, who had many occasions to observe and work with her, Renzi was noted even more for her acting abilities, stage presence, and dramatic intelligence than for her voice:

> The action that gives soul, spirit, and existence to things must be governed by the movements of the body, by gestures, by the face, and by the voice, now raising it, now lowering it, becoming enraged and immediately becoming calm again; at times speaking hurriedly, at others slowly, moving the body now in one, now in another direction, drawing in the arms, and extending them, laughing and crying, now with little, now with much agitation of the hands. Our Signora Anna is endowed with such lifelike expression that her responses and speeches seem not memorized but born at the very moment. In sum, she transforms herself completely into the person she represents. . . . She takes control of the stage, understands what she delivers, and delivers it as clearly as any ear could desire. She has a fluent tongue, smooth pronunciation, not affected, not too rapid, a full, sonorous voice, not harsh, not hoarse, nor one that offends you with excessive subtlety; which arises from the temperament of the chest and throat. . . . She has felicitous passages, a lively trill, both double and *rinforzato*. . . . She silently observes the actions of others, and when she is called upon to represent them, helped by her sanguine temperament and bile, which fires her . . . shows the spirit and valor learned by studying and observing.[104]

Surely, a singing actress with such great natural sensitivity, range, subtlety, intelligence, and dramatic skill would have excelled in conveying the human emotions that Monteverdi sought to communicate in his works. Some of these same qualities must have distinguished the performance of Ramponi as Arianna. As a leading member of the commedia dell'arte troupe I Fedeli, directed by her husband, Giovanni Battista Andreini, she was officially a singing actress, but evidently one very much in the Renzi mold. In another role, a few years later, Ramponi was once again specifically praised for being "così efficace spiegatrice degli affetti dell'animo che col pietoso canto mosse altri al pianto."[105] If, as

---

104. Translation from *OSV*, 232; text in Appendix 8, C.1. Renzi was indeed a special case. In addition to her obvious abilities, she was a pet of the opera publicists who wrote about her. Other references to her in the role of Ottavia are found in *Le glorie*, 28, 31, and 47 (given in Appendix 8, C.2).

105. Judith Cohen, "Giovan-Battista Andreini's Dramas and the Beginnings of Opera," in *La musique et le rite sacré et profane: Actes du XIIIe Congrès de la Société Internationale de Musicologie*, ed. Marc Honegger and Paul Prevost (Strasbourg: Université de Strasbourg, 1986), 2: 423–32, at 424, quoting *La Breve descrittione* of *Il rapimento di Proserpina* (Marigliani/Giulio Cesare Monteverdi, 1611): "Venne la famosa Sig. Florinda, Idea del bel dire, Gloria de' Comici, Pompa de' Teatri et così efficace spiegatrice degli affetti dell'animo che col pietoso canto mosse altri al pianto." Cohen is quoted in Paola Besutti, "Da *L'Arianna* a *La Ferinda*: Giovan Battista Andreini e la 'Comedia musicale all'improviso,'" *MD* 49 (1995): 227–76, at 236, n. 30.

some have suggested, Ramponi inspired Arianna's lament, Renzi could well have inspired Ottavia's.[106]

Comedy

Monteverdi evidently found sufficient opportunity for pathos in his Venetian texts. But his three librettists conceived other ways of enabling the composer to move his listeners, and not only to tears, but to laughter as well. Indeed, some of the most striking effects in all three of these operas are created by comic characters. Once again, we are indebted to Torcigliani for focusing our attention on an issue of importance in all three works. We recall how he emphasized the delighted reception accorded Iro at the performance of *Ritorno*, and how he had been inspired to introduce his own comic character, Numano, in the hopes of encouraging the composer to match his previous success. Because he was loath to depart from his source, he said, which he was forced to do when introducing Enea's and Lavinia's monologues, and because he could not find a more suitable candidate in the *Aeneid*, he chose to focus on one aspect of Virgil's Numano: not his strength, but his swagger:

It only seems that I have altered Numano, called strong by Virgil, but also treated as a great braggart, whereby, in attaching myself to this quality of his, which doesn't usually coincide with true bravery, I am using him as a comic character, not finding any more appropriate in Virgil, and knowing the mood of many spectators, who are more pleased by such jokes than by serious things, as we see my friend's Iro to have delighted marvelously, which genre of character I truly would not have introduced in another [kind of] tragedy. (Appendix 2 [l])

---

106. Carter (*Musical Theatre*, 93–94) makes the same suggestion, but seems to contradict himself on p. 290 when he says that Ottavia does not seem to fulfill the expectations of her role for the star singer, Renzi. On Ramponi and Arianna, see ibid., p. 210; also Besutti, "Da *L'Arianna*," 227–76. Ramponi was also praised for being a remarkably quick study: she apparently learned the role of Arianna by heart in six days "and she sings it with such grace and with such manner and affect that she has amazed Madama [Grand Duchess], Signor Rinuccini, and all those lords who heard her" (Paola Bessuti, "The *Sala dei specchi* Uncovered: Monteverdi, the Gonzagas, and the Palazzo Ducale, Mantua," *EM* 27 [1999]: 451–65, at 460). Intelligence was another quality she apparently shared with Renzi. Giambattista Marino describes how she evoked sighs from her audience: "And in such a way you heard Florinda, O Manto . . . unfold the harsh torments of Arianna and draw from a thousand hearts a thousand sighs" (Carter, "Arianna," n. 30, and Fabbri, *Monteverdi*, 131; trans. Carter, 83). (If, as Besutti argues, Arianna's lament is so closely related to those sung by Ramponi in the *commedie* in which she participated, we might even give her some indirect credit for all of Arianna's operatic successors as well.) See also Besutti, "Da *L'Arianna*," 267, for Learco's lament from *La Florinda*, a kind of mixture of Arianna's and Orfeo's laments. Besutti raises issues of gesture and improvisation in connection with the performance of Arianna's lament (performative aspects), reflections of which might be seen in the formulaic nature of the imitations, especially the moment of self-consciousness just after the climax.

Iro is indeed a remarkable figure, one that stimulated the composer's most acute powers of characterization. But he is far more than a comic character. Although he surely inspired laughter and ridicule for his boorishness and false bravado, his stuttering and whining, he also evokes compassion, even horror: his actions and his fate (as we will see) underline some of the most important themes of the opera.

In attempting to replicate Iro in Numano, Turno's swaggering squire, Torcigliani had set himself an almost impossible task. That he succeeded at all is testimony to his skill as a poet. Like Iro, Numano is a descendant of the *miles gloriosus* of spoken theater. A braggart and a coward, he ridicules his master for being distracted from his martial impulses by his love for Lavinia: he himself would never be distracted by Cupid, he boasts, but would remain true to Mars:

Che frenetichi Turno,	Why are you raving, Turno,
Tu dunque innamorato?	are you in love, then?
Può far, che non diss'io, Giove scornato?	Can Giove, let me not say this, be cuckolded?
E che vuoi far d'Amore?	And what will you do with Love?
In vece d'apportar ruine, e morti	Instead of bring ruin and death
Pianger come un Bamboccio? o bell'humore.	you'll cry like a big baby? That's a laugh!
S'Amor trescasse meco	If Love messed with me,
Credi, che vorei farlo, altro che cieco.	believe me, I'd want to make him more than blind.
Amor vada in mall'hora	Let Love go to to the devil
E viva morte [Marte] ogn'hora.	and let Mars live forever.

(1.4)

The librettist takes great care in his choice of imagery and verse structure for Numano's speeches, each of them a kind of exaggerated "riff" on a comic subject. These may not all have been intended as arias, but are nonetheless substantial, prominently placed at the ends of scenes.[107] One attack of his churlish boasting begins with an effective mixture of *versi tronchi* and *piani* that is interrupted by a pair of well-placed *sdruccioli,* and culminates in a rhymed quatrain of *piani:*

Or sì contento io sto	Yes, now I am content,
Nuotando in mar di latte,	swimming in a sea of milk,
Poiché nuotar ben presto anco dovrò[108]	since soon I will also have to swim
In ampio mar di sangue	in an ample sea of blood
De le genti da me vinte e disfatte.	of the people conquered and undone by me.

---

107. Sevieri, *Le nozze,* nn. 24, 66, 83, identifies these as "tirate comiche." Some of them can be characterized as arias.

108. "poiche nuotar dovrò" (a *settenario* in the three-act libretto).

Quanto, quanto era meglio	Oh how much better it would have been
Per voi, Teucri mal pratici,	for you, inept Teucri,
Restar preda de' fochi argivi ed attici.	had you been killed by the Argives or Attici,
O tra l'onde affogati;	or drowned in the sea!
Se solo ch'io vi tocchi,	If I but touch you,
Sotto a' miei piè schiacciati	crushed under my feet,
Dovete rimaner come ranocchi.	you'll remain like frogs.
	(3.2)

Another speech, in which he encourages the Trojans, men and women alike, to fight, and then runs away, is constructed entirely of rhymed couplets in *versi piani,* once again spiced with a pair of well-placed *versi sdruccioli* in the middle:

O Troiani, o Troiani,	O Trojans, Trojans,
Or che tenete a cintola la mani?	Why are you holding your hands up?
Forse, chiusi nel vallo,	Perhaps, imprisoned on the ramparts,
Traete l'ore in lieto canto e ballo?	you're spending your hours in happy songs and dance.
Venite fuori pur pecore e buffoli,	Come out, sheep and buffalo,
Ch'io vo danzar al suon d'altro che zuffoli!	I want to dance to something besides bagpipes.
A che cingete l'armi,	Why are you girding your arms
Se credete morir solo a mirarmi?	if you think you'll die by only looking at me?
Itene a trar da le conocchie i fili,	Go spin the threads of the distaff,
Troiani no, ma Troianesse villi.	you're not Trojan men, but low Trojan girls.
	(2.8)

Finally, fearing he will be left out of the action, Numano sheds his cowardice in a brief speech—still another series of mostly rhymed couplets—and rushes off heedlessly to join the hopeless battle of his compatriots, enunciating the standard heroic battle cry to close the scene:

Fien dunque senza me guerre e perigli?	Can there be wars and danger without me?
No, no prima nel campo,	No, no, first to the field
Io volerò qual lampo,	I will fly like lightning,
E con Enea distrutti	and with Enea, destroyed,
Saranno i Teucri tutti	will all the Teucri be
Ben presto, e chi m'aspetta.	soon, and what am I waiting for.
A le straggi, a le morti, a la vendetta.	To war, to death, to vengeance.
	(4.1)

Humorous and effective as he must have been in the theater—we can imagine him brandishing his sword, mocking his master, gesturing to an imaginary army or troupe of dancers, and rapidly disappearing from the stage—Numano remains tangential to the drama. In contrast to Iro, everything he does fits well within the bounds of the traditional behavior of his character type (the *miles gloriosus*). It is difficult to imagine that any musical setting of any of his text, however skillfully structured by the librettist, could have elevated him to the status of his great predecessor. There is simply no textual equivalent for him—or for any other character in Venetian opera of the period—of the almost Shakespearean soliloquy with which Iro opens the final act of *Ritorno*.[109]

If Iro was as successful as Torcigliani reported, we can imagine that Busenello too would have sought to provide Monteverdi with a similar stimulus for his comic style. The libretto of *Incoronazione* does indeed contain several comic characters: the two nurses Arnalta and Nutrice, and the pair of servant-lovers, Valletto and Damigella. These all fall within the general category of stock comic characters, but they are treated individually, Arnalta in particular with special skill. Though none of them can be compared to Iro—or to Numano, for that matter—they share certain personality traits and dramatic functions with other characters from both *Ritorno* and *Nozze:* Arnalta and Nutrice combine elements of Ericlea and Melanto as well as Lavinia's Damigella; and Busenello's servant couple suggests a parallel with the Eurimaco/Melanto pair in *Ritorno,* though without being as integral to the plot—in fact, they are not integral at all.[110]

One of the chief functions of Busenello's comic characters is to provide contrast and relief at important junctures in the plot. Valletto crucially punctures Seneca's pedantry in his scene with Ottavia (1.6), and his love scene with Damigella brilliantly dissipates, as it cruelly contradicts, the somber mood of Seneca's suicide (2.4). This might seem analogous to the positioning of Iro's monologue immediately after the death of the Suitors, but of course his monologue is a response to their death, not a relief from it. Arnalta's running commentary on the mores of the court help to maintain the ironic tensions of the drama. But none of Busenello's characters comes any closer to resembling Iro than Numano. Nevertheless, the comic texts in all three librettos share certain striking features, some of which stand out because of the composer's response to them. Although Iro's stuttering is all Monteverdi's, he and Valletto both trade on a repertoire of physical gestures, those "words suggesting gestures, noises, or other imitative ideas," which Monteverdi

---

109. See Chap. 8, pp. 366–73. In this connection, it may be worth noting that, in contrast to Penelope's monologue, to which it bears a kind of inverted relationship, Iro's text (thirty-six lines) appears to have been virtually untouched by the composer, though of course he alters the poet's emphases with his musical setting. Badoaro obviously managed to get things magnificently right in this scene.

110. It is possible that the Elminio/Silvia duet in *Nozze* was inspired by the Melanto/Eurimaco relationship in *Ritorno*. But, as noted in Chap. 1, n. 30, these characters have little in common.

treats mimetically.[111] Iro eats, fights, drinks, whines, exhorts to battle ("Su, su dunque alla lotta, su, su"), and threatens to pull the hairs from Ulisse's beard, one by one, while Valletto laughs, sneezes, and yawns, and threatens to set Seneca on fire. He is also pinched and bitten, and his heart beats. Numano, too, is a vivid verbal actor: he swims, dismantles, touches, tramples, flies like lightning, and, like Iro, exhorts to battle: "A le straggi, a le morti, a la vendetta." We can imagine that the composer would have set his gestures similarly, with musical imitations, or exaggeratedly literal word-painting.

Monteverdi takes the same approach in his treatment of Busenello's two nurses, though not Badoaro's, a distinction owing to the librettists' very different characterizations of these ostensibly stock figures. Arnalta's comedy, like that of Valletto and Iro, is sometimes gestural: she rocks Poppea to sleep and then trips over her own feet as she chases after Ottone, who has just attempted to kill her sleeping mistress.[112] Both Arnalta and Nutrice are given multiple opportunities to express their piquant, and opposing, socio-political philosophies, to their charges as well as to the audience. That function in *Ritorno*, much less emphasized, is divided between two characters whose ultimate derivation from the *Odyssey* restricts their activities: Ericlea is sympathetic audience to Penelope's grief and facilitator of her reunion with Ulisse, while the soubrette Melanto, by actions as well as words, supplies scurrilous advice and sexual innuendo.

Monteverdi's response to his comic characters may reinforce their common elements, but he also rises to the specific challenges of his librettists' material. Iro remains unique. Arnalta, on the other hand, though likewise one of the composer's most memorable creations, finds a place within countless subsequent generations of comic nurses, in opera and spoken drama.

❦

However much they differed in literary background and experience, in poetic style and skill, Monteverdi's three Venetian librettists seem to have understood his most basic requirements. From the range of their characters to the structure of their poetry, they reveal their efforts to provide him with the opportunity for variety: characters young and old, serious and comic, poetry for song as well as speech, for soliloquy and conversation, invoking love and war-like feelings. In sum, they supplied the real men and women, entangled in believable dramatic situations, who could inspire him to enlist the full potential of his art of imitating the affections, enabling him thereby to move the affections of his audience. *Characters and situations like these pleased Monteverdi very much because they allowed him to display the marvels of his art.* That in turning them into staged musical dramas,

---

111. See letter no. 95, as discussed above.

112. Arnalta's lullaby and Poppea's response are mentioned above (p. 193). I discuss and illustrate Arnalta's pursuit of Ottone in "Monteverdi's Mimetic Art," 131–32.

the composer had to modify and edit these offerings—some more, some less—hardly comes as a surprise, not only because Torcigliani told us as much, but especially because of the notable differences between the librettos and scores (and in the case of *Nozze,* between performance and literary versions of the text). As we shall see, the enormous stylistic differences among the librettos strongly affected the nature of Monteverdi's interventions.

7

Constructions of Character

We have various ways of considering Monteverdi's interventions in his librettos—and this variety is mandated by the different source situations for the three Venetian operas. In some respects that of *Ritorno* is the simplest. There are essentially two versions of the verbal text: one transmitted in the score, which, although undated, may reflect two productions of the work (the original and the revival of 1641), the other in the eleven manuscript copies of the libretto. These all preserve virtually the same text, which is different from, and clearly earlier than, that of the score. The differences between the librettos and score, though extensive, are fairly straightforward. The major ones—a new prologue, the deletion of an entire scene—may have had to do with performance exigencies; nearly all of the smaller cuts and rearrangements can be assumed to derive from the composer's intervention.[1]

Evaluation of the composer's role in *Le nozze d'Enea* is more difficult, of course, since there is no score. But the lengthy printed description of the work by the librettist includes some very specific comments on Monteverdi's setting. And since the manuscript librettos preserve two different versions of the text, one of them evidently closer to the musical setting (and thus later) than the other, a comparison allows us a glimpse of the composer at work.

---

1. In the notes to his recording of *Ritorno*, René Jacobs distinguishes between the cuts of two editors: the first, a "good dramatist" (presumably the composer), whose cuts served to heighten the dramatic effect of certain scenes; the second, a poor dramatist, who cut some material that was necessary for the plot. Jacobs ascribes a third set of cuts—including several choruses and some entire scenes—to economic exigencies. (He overestimates the number of such cuts: as we have seen in Chap. 4, though lacking music, the choruses and ballet were intended to be performed.) See below, n. 3.

The case of *Incoronazione* is the most complicated. The sources are far more numerous and varied than those of the other two operas. We cannot simply compare one or both of the surviving scores with any of the librettos (manuscript and printed) or scenario because they all represent different stages in the evolution of the work. For one thing, only two sources can be definitively linked with the original production: the scenario and the Udine manuscript libretto. For another, Busenello's definitive text was published well after Monteverdi's death and both scores are posthumous. But, as we have seen, the two contemporary sources help us to clarify the relationship of the scores to the original production, and the nature of Busenello's printed text—its relationship to the manuscript librettos as well as to his other printed librettos—allows us to take it as essentially the text he gave to the composer. We can thus use it as a basis for comparison with the scores, which affords us a sense of the composer's impact on the work. Although we cannot document with certainty that Monteverdi himself was responsible for the many differences, their nature, the ways in which they confirm one another, and their clear kinship with Monteverdi's other works, as well as what we know about his attitude toward musical drama, all indicate the hand of the composer.

❧

Many of Monteverdi's interventions in *Ritorno* and *Incoronazione* are evident from a comparison of the textual and musical sources. But we can only imagine his influence behind the scenes, exerted before the librettos assumed the form in which we know them, the kind of influence implied by the author of *Nozze,* Michelangelo Torcigliani, when he reported that he kept his text simple and focused on portraying the affections in order to suit Monteverdi, and to please him also changed and omitted many things he had originally included.[2]

We can be sure that Giacomo Badoaro had Monteverdi's style in mind as he drafted his libretto, since he designed it specifically to tempt the composer out of his self-imposed operatic retirement. Penelope's remarkable opening monologue, for instance, was clearly intended to satisfy Monteverdi's desire for "un giusto lamento," on the model of Arianna's. The poet may also have submitted his libretto for the composer's approval before coming up with the version we know from the various manuscript copies. While some text was subjected to extensive revision in the score, most notably Penelope's lament, other apparently unedited text—particularly Iro's great monologue—may well have already been revised by the time the librettos were copied.

But in whatever ways he might have catered to Monteverdi's taste while producing his text, they were obviously insufficient, for the libretto underwent many changes in the course of being set to music. Indeed, these revisions sharpen our perceptions of the

---

2. It is difficult to imagine what kinds of things these might have been, though I speculate below, n. 9. For the relevant text in the "Letter," see Appendix 2 [n].

shortcomings of Badoaro's libretto. The poet himself, as we have already noted, acknowledged the magnitude of those revisions when he confessed, with a touch of sheepishness perhaps, that he hardly recognized his own work when he heard it in the theater (see Appendix 1).

Although Badoaro may have been indulging in hyperbole to flatter the composer, Monteverdi's impact on *Ritorno*, as on *Incoronazione*, was profound and complex, extending from the smallest to the largest elements of structure. The revisions affect everything from the articulation and development of the characters to the overall shape of the drama and, ultimately, its meaning. But the revisions are also quite different in the two works, and these differences respect, reflect, and enhance the fundamental distinctions in the nature of the two librettos.

Shaping an Epic or Rewriting Penelope

The most striking alterations in *Ritorno* strengthen the overall dramatic structure. Leaving aside for the moment the omission of one complete scene—5.2, an infernal scene for Mercury and the ghosts of the Suitors, which, as we have already suggested, may have been cut for practical reasons of staging—Monteverdi's influence on the libretto is most evident in the cutting and restructuring of individual textual passages. Several of the cuts intensify the remarkable build-up of momentum that characterizes the libretto as a whole, as Ulisse draws nearer and nearer to his goal. That momentum is gauged against Penelope's refusal to the very end to believe that the old man recently arrived in Ithaca is really Ulisse in disguise. And this despite repeated efforts to convince her of the truth, first by the swineherd Eumete, then by her son Telemaco, then her old nurse Ericlea, and finally even by Ulisse, dressed as himself. This repetition of refusal, which marks the progress of the action, renders all the more powerful Penelope's final capitulation, her recognition of Ulisse returned. (We have seen how this works in Table 7 above, Chap. 4.)

The drive toward Penelope's final capitulation is increased by the elimination of two earlier passages in the libretto. The first, in 3.6, occurs in a speech by Eumete to Ulisse, in which he describes Penelope's reaction to his report that her husband is about to return. Eumete exclaims:

> O come tosto cangia
> L'allegrezza d'un cor sembiante al vero;
> Come un torbido volto
> Presto serena i conturbati rai,
> Mostran rose i piacer, viole i guai.
> A le grate novelle
> Io vidi, o Peregrino,
> Rischiarar di Penelope il bel volto,
> E squarciando del duol la Nube oscura,

Mostrarsi come suole,
Fra torbidi d'April più chiaro il Sole.

(Oh how quickly an intimation of truth changes a heart to happiness, how quickly a cloudy visage calms its distraught looks and purpled troubles appear roseate pleasures. At the welcome news, O wanderer, I saw Penelope's beautiful face brighten, and, suppressing the dark cloud of sorrow, she revealed herself like the sun, brighter still against the storms of April.)

Eumete goes on to describe the Suitors' much more negative response to the news. Here all reference to Penelope is eliminated—the entire passage just quoted—which suggested a relaxation of her steadfastness, leaving only the description of the Suitors' reaction.

The other (related) cut occurs at the end of the very next scene (4.1), in which Penelope angrily rejects Telemaco's prediction of Ulisse's imminent return. The cut involves the final six lines of the scene, an aside in which Penelope confesses that Telemaco has inspired her with some hope:

Voglia il Ciel, che mia vita anco sostenti
Debole fil di speme,
E come picciol seme
Natura insegna ad ingrandirsi in pianta,
Così dentro al mio petto
Nasca da picciol seme alto diletto.[3]

(Heaven wills that my life still sustain a weak thread of hope, and as the little seed is taught by nature to grow into a plant, so within my breast from such a little seed is born great delight.)

The suppression of these two allusions to Penelope's softening—the only such allusions in the libretto—which confirms her moral fixity, intensifies the climactic effect of her final acceptance of her returned husband.

---

3. Jacobs believes that the omission of this passage was the work of the "poor dramatist," because it eliminates a portion of the text that was essential for the understanding of the development of Penelope's character. But I would argue the opposite. Its omission strengthens the drama. Jacobs's second example of a "poor" cut comes from act 1, scene 2; it involves a dialogue between Eurimaco and Melanto that spells out the reason why Melanto must convince Penelope to yield to a new lover. To be sure, the cut does affect the plot, but it also eliminates allusion to the noxious nature of the Eurimaco/Melanto relationship. Indeed, although Eurimaco is one of Penelope's suitors in Homer, this isn't clear in Badoaro. (He does disappear after the death of the Suitors, but it's uncertain how upset Melanto is about it.) Dubowy ("Bemerkungen," 240) argues that Melanto and Eurimaco are intended simply to balance Penelope, and that Eurimaco is not an especially evil character. If this is so, the omission is justified. The omission of this passage, by the way, may be compensated for by the addition of two lines for Penelope at the beginning of act 2, scene 1 (in the three-act version). As shown in Chap. 4, that scene originally began with Melanto urging her mistress to relinquish her loyalty to Ulisse, but two lines for Penelope were added: "Donati un giorno / contento a desir miei," lines that provoke Melanto's response. Without Eurimaco's text urging Melanto to work on her mistress, she has no excuse to initiate the subject. Penelope's added lines give her that excuse. (This scene is discussed in Chap. 4, p. 75 and n. 15, and also further below.)

Another intra-scene cut, this one in the role of the parasite Iro, affects the overall structure of the drama in a different but no less significant way. The final scene of act 4 (or act 2 of the three-act score) is the great climax of the opera, the turning point. In it, following Ulisse's resounding beating of Iro, and each Suitor's unsuccessful attempt to bend the mighty bow, the hero, still in his old man's disguise, finally takes the bow himself and, in the powerful cathartic gesture long awaited by the audience, slays the Suitors. In the libretto, the drive to this climax is interrupted by Iro, who, following the Suitors' failure, begs for a chance to test his own strength with the bow—strength that had earlier in the scene easily, and comically, yielded to Ulisse's heroic power. The interruption here is a lengthy and unfortunate one: a six-line speech for Iro, followed by Telemaco's brief, bemused approval of his request, and then Iro's extended (twenty-line) comic engagement with the bow, as he calls upon Bacchus to aid him, where Cupid and Mars had failed his predecessors. Not only does this interrupt the gathering momentum, but, by introducing a comic note, it trivializes the entire enterprise, detracting from the violent heroism of Ulisse's ultimate victory. (It is perhaps no surprise that the incident is not present in Homer.)[4]

The omission of the entire passage involving Iro eliminates the redundancy of his double failure. In the opera, Ulisse's defeat of Iro is the comic first step in his great triumph over the Suitors, the proper punishment of their hubris. Iro, a common beggar, cannot aspire to such stature. Here, as in the case of the two passages connected with Penelope, the cut tightens the drama as a whole, emphasizing aspects already present but not as strongly projected by the original text.

Admittedly, Badoaro himself could have shared responsibility for these cuts, revising his text in response to the composer. His own investment in emphasizing Penelope's virtue is clear from his depiction of the recognition scene. As we noted in Chapter 5, his version departs significantly from Homer, allowing Ulisse rather than Penelope to engineer the denouement. Rather than proffering the ruse of the immobile bed, Penelope remains steadfast until Ulisse takes the initiative by describing the coverlet on which is depicted the chaste goddess Diana. In addition to increasing the drive toward the denouement, this alteration effectively maintains the purity of Penelope's character, freeing her from any taint of deceptiveness, that quality associated with her

---

4. It also seems to undermine the effect of Iro's suicide at the beginning of the last act, which is in some sense an ironic commentary on the death of the Suitors. Another cut in Iro's role involves a six-line speech at the end of his scene with Eumete (2.3). The score ends the scene with Eumete urging Iro to go off and eat and drop dead ("crepare"). But the libretto ends with Iro's little Numano-like farewell:

Sì sì, parto hor, hor,	Yes, yes, I'm leaving right now,
Né torno più a te.	and won't return to you.
Digiuna il Pastor,	The shepherd fasts,
E mangiano i Re.	kings eat.
Tua quiete a me non piace,	I don't like your calm,
Che la guerra del ventre è la mia pace.	the war of my gut is my peace.

wily consort.[5] Significantly, too, Badoaro hardly mentions another of Penelope's most characteristic ruses: the daily weaving and unweaving of Laertes' shroud, which serves as a means of delaying her acceptance of the Suitors' proposals. His single reference to this central element of the Homeric plot, in Penelope's lament, is eliminated in the revision to the text.[6]

ACT I, SCENE I: PENELOPE AND ERICLEA

However involved the librettist may have been in revising his text, the most important intervention in Penelope's role was the composer's. Her long opening monologue, which establishes the dimensions of her character, cried out for editing. Badoaro presented Monteverdi with a sprawling text comprising 125 lines of *versi sciolti*. These are divided into four unequal sections by brief comments from Penelope's old nurse, Ericlea, and irregularly punctuated with two brief refrains (underlined), whose recurrences—the first (A) is sung twice, the second (B) three times—are so widely spaced as to be rendered ineffectual from a formal point of view (Table 16).

Monteverdi's revision exemplifies the ways in which he shaped his texts to take maximum advantage of their intrinsic structural and expressive elements. He reconfigured the speech by cutting and moving text around and exploiting the librettist's refrains to build a climax absent in the original text (Table 17). He shortened it by almost half, cutting fifty-one of Badoaro's lines (in italics in Table 16) and reducing it to three sections: he retained all of Badoaro's first section, reversed his second and third sections, omitting the second half of the former and the first half of the latter, and all but eliminated his fourth section, salvaging only four lines from the middle that contain one of the refrains (underlined) and attaching them to the end of his own third—i.e. final—section (see Figure 4). This reorganization increases the prominence of the B refrain and creates a strong sense of progression toward it.[7] We might say that Penelope runs the emotional gamut from A to B twice: first slowly, over the course of two entire sections (sixty-six lines of text), then quickly, within a mere four lines. Monteverdi enhances the structural-expressive function of both refrains by

---

5. Indeed, there is evidence in the *Odyssey* of a certain deviousness in Penelope's character, manifested in her ambivalence toward the Suitors. Marylin A. Katz, *Penelope's Renown: Meaning and Indeterminacy in the Odyssey* (Princeton: Princeton University Press, 1991), 80, points out, for instance, that in bk. 18, she *asks* the Suitors for gifts. Barbara Clayton, *A Penelopean Poetics: Reweaving the Feminine in Homer's Odyssey* (Lanham, Md., and Oxford: Lexington Books, 2003), 90–91, refers to the argument, pursued by Marie-Madeleine Mactoux (*Pénélope: Légende et mythe* [Paris: Belles Lettres, 1975], 13) that Penelope did not become synonymous with chastity until the Augustan elegiac poets.

6. The significance of Penelope's ruse in Homer is emphasized by the fact that it is (the only action) narrated three different times. See Clayton, *A Penelopean Poetics*, 23.

7. The first cut comprises eleven lines, the second part of the opening section. It amplifies the message delivered in the first lines: that Ulysses is the only thing that fails to return. "If the world is constant in its inconstancy; if every day rises, every sun sets, every winter changes to spring, everything offends fate; if the origin of

TABLE 16
Il ritorno d'Ulisse, I.1,
Badoaro's text of Penelope's lament
(Monteverdi's omissions in italics)

1   Di misera Regina

     Non terminati mai dolenti affanni!

     L'aspettato non giunge,

     E pur fuggono gl'anni.

     La serie del penar è lungi, ahi troppo!

     A chi vive in angoscia il Tempo è zoppo.

     Fallacissima speme,

     Speranze non più verdi, ma canute;

     A l'invecchiato male

     Non promettete più pace e salute.

     Scorsero quattro lustri

     Dal memorabil giorno

     In cui con sue rapine

     Il superbo Troiano

     Chiamò l'alta sua patria a le ruine.

     A ragion arsa Troia,

     Poiché l'Amor impuro,

     Ch'è un delitto di foco,

     Si purga con le fiamme.

     Ma ben contra ragion, per l'altrui fallo,

     Condannata innocente

     De l'altrui colpe io sono

     L'aflitta penitente.

     Ulisse accorto e saggio,

     Tu che punir gl'adulteri ti vanti,

     Aguzzi l'armi, e susciti le fiamme,

     Per vendicar gl'errori

     D'una profuga Greca, e in tanto lasci

     La tua casta consorte

     Fra i nemici rivali

     In dubio de l'onor, in forse a morte.

     Ogni partenza attende

     Desiato ritorno,

A   <u>Sol tu del tuo tornar perdesti il giorno.</u>

2   Torna il tranquillo al mare,

     Torna il zeffiro al prato,

     L'aurora, mentre al sol fa dolce invito,

     È un ritorno del dì, ch'è pria partito.

     Tornan le brine in terra,

(continued)

TABLE 16 *(continued)*

Tornano al centro i sassi,
E con lubrici passi
Torna a l'ocean il rivo.
L'huomo qua giù, ch'è vivo,
Lungi da suoi principi,
Porta un'alma celeste, un corpo frale.
Tosto more il mortale,
E torna l'alma in cielo,
E torna il corpo in polve,
Doppo breve soggiorni,
Nel ritorno comun tu sol non torni.
Costante è pur ne l'incostanza il mondo,
Ogni giorno s'annera,
Ogni sole tramonta,
Ogni verno si cangia in primavera.
Tutto la sorte offende
Con mobil vicende.
Han fugaci i natali,
Il pianto, il riso, i mali.
Ma perché resti eterno
Il mio danno, il mio scorno,

A   <u>*Tu sol del tuo tornar perdesti il giorno.*</u>

3   *Promettasti a la patria una vendetta.*
Già Troia è incenerita,
Ch'ha il nobil voto sciolto.
A che dunque non torni?
A che dunque non vieni?
Hai tu forse pensiero
Di disperder pria tutta
L'incenerita Troia, onde non resti
Ne l'odiato loco
L'abominando cendri del foco?
Penelope ingannata
Sì, sì, lieve cagion da me ti toglie.
Misera abbandonata,
Se pur detto infelice,
Sin che il nemico cenere si solve,
Ceder le mie ragioni anco a le polve.
Non è dunque per me varia la sorte?
Cangiò forse Fortuna
La volubile rota in stabil seggio?
E la sua pronta vela,
Ch'ogni human caso porta

TABLE 16 (continued)

Fra l'incostanza a volo,
Sol per me non raccoglie un fiato solo?
Cangian per altri pur aspetto in cielo
Le stelle erranti e fisse?

B   Torna, deh torna, Ulisse,
Penelope t'aspetta,
L'innocente respira,
Piange l'offesa, e contro
Il tenace offensor né pur s'adira.
A l'anima affannata
Porto le sue discolpe, acciò non resti
Di crudeltà macchiato,
Ma fabbro de' miei danni incolpo il Fato.
Così per tua difesa
Col destino, e col cielo
Fomento guerre, e stablisco risse.

B   Torna, deh torna, Ulisse.

4   *Torna, Ulisse, che 'l tempo*
Tosto il volto m'arriga, il pel m'inbianca.
Di tue lunghe dimore
La tela di Penelope è già stanca.
Che giova a me, le notti,
Togliendo l'hore al sonno,
Ordir menzogne, e disordir le tele
Per ingannar gl'amanti,
Se van dietro a l'eterno
I tuoi errori, i miei pianti?
Torna, che mentre porti empie dimore
Al mio fiero dolore,
Veggio del mio morir l'hore prefisse.

B   Torna, deh torna Ulisse.
L'humana vita è un lampo,
Beltà donnesca è un raggio.
D'un spatio così breve
Toglie troppo gran parte
Chi per vent'anni parte,
E che fastoso eroe
Le glorie tue con secoli misuri
Poco stimi de gl'anni
Il celeste viaggio,
Ma core innamorato anche in brev'hora
Prova tormento eterno
E formano poch'anni un lungo inferno.

TABLE 17
Il ritorno d'Ulisse, 1.1, Monteverdi's version of Penelope's lament

1	Di misera Regina	Of a miserable queen,
	Non terminati mai dolenti affanni!	anxious sorrows never end!
	L'aspettato non giunge,	The expected one does not arrive,
	E pur fuggono gl'anni.	and yet the years fly by.
	La serie del penar è lungi, ahi troppo!	The series of sufferings is, oh, too long.
	A chi vive in angoscia il Tempo è zoppo.	Time is lame for whoever lives in anguish.
	Fallacissima speme,	Most false hope,
	Speranze non più verdi, ma canute;	hopes no longer green but hoary,
	A l'invecchiato male	to my pain grown old
	Non promettete più pace e salute.	you no longer promise peace nor healing.
	Scorsero quattro lustri	Two decades have passed
	Dal memorabil giorno	since the memorable day
	In cui con sue rapine	in which, with his abduction,
	Il superbo Troiano	the proud Trojan
	Chiamò l'alta sua patria a le ruine.	brought his illustrious homeland to ruin.
	A ragion arsa Troia,	Troy burned justly,
	Poiché l'Amor impuro,	for impure love,
	Ch'è un delitto di foco,	which is a fiery crime,
	Si purga con le fiamme.	is purged by fire.
	Ma ben contra ragion, per l'altrui fallo,	But against reason, and for another's fault,
	Condannata innocente	condemned, innocent
	De l'altrui colpe io sono	for another's guilt, I am
	L'aflitta penitente.	the afflicted penitent.
	Ulisse accorto e saggio,	Shrewd, wise Ulisse,
	Tu che punir gl'adulteri ti vanti,	you who boast of punishing adulterers,
	Aguzzi l'armi, e susciti le fiamme,	sharpen your weapons and feed the flames
	Per vendicar gl'errori	to avenge the misdeeds
	D'una profuga Greca, e in tanto lasci	of a Greek refugee, and you leave
	La tua casta consorte	your own chaste wife
	Fra i nemici rivali	among enemy rivals,
	In dubio de l'onor, in forse a morte.	her honor, perhaps her life at stake.
	Ogni partenza attende	Every departure awaits
	Desiato ritorno,	the desired return.
A	<u>Sol tu del tuo tornar perdesti il giorno.</u>	<u>You alone have missed the day of your return.</u>
2	Non è dunque per me varia la sorte?	Is there then no change in my fate?
	Cangiò forse Fortuna	Did Fortune perhaps change
	La volubile rota in stabil seggio?	her turning wheel for a fixed seat?
	E la sua pronta vela,	And is her ready sail
	Ch'ogni human caso porta	that bears every human fate
	Fra l'incostanza a volo,	and all inconstancy

TABLE 17 *(continued)*

	Sol per me non raccoglie un fiato solo?	alone for me becalmed?
	Cangian per altri pur aspetto in cielo	Yet for others does the pattern in the sky
	Le stelle erranti e fisse?	of the wandering and fixed stars change?
B	<u>Torna, deh torna, Ulisse,</u>	<u>Return, oh return, Ulisse,</u>
	Penelope t'aspetta,	Penelope awaits you,
	L'innocente respira,	the innocent one sighs,
	Piange l'offesa, e contro	bewails the affront, and against
	Il tenace offensor né pur s'adira.	the unyielding offender bears no anger.
	A l'anima affannata	To my distressed soul
	Porto le sue discolpe, acciò non resti	I carry excuses, so that you will not be
	Di crudeltà macchiato,	tainted with cruelty.
	Ma fabbro de miei danni incolpo il Fato.	But as cause of my pain I blame fate.
	Così per tua difesa	Thus in your defense,
	Col destino, e col cielo	against destiny and heaven
	Fomento guerre, e stablisco risse.	I foment wars and raise quarrels.
B	<u>Torna, deh torna, Ulisse.</u>	<u>Return, oh return, Ulisse.</u>

3	Torna il tranquillo al mare,	Calm returns to the sea,
	Torna il zeffiro al prato,	the zephyr to the meadow,
	L'aurora, mentre al sol fa dolce invito,	the dawn meanwhile sweetly invites the sun
	E un ritorno del dì, ch'è pria partito.	to bring back the departed day.
	Tornan le brine in terra,	Frosts return to the earth,
	Tornano al centro i sassi,	stones return to the center,
	E con lubrici passi	and with liquid steps
	Torna a l'ocean il rivo.	the streams return to the ocean.
	L'huomo qua giù, ch'è vivo,	Man who lives below,
	Lungi da suoi principi,	far from his origins,
	Porta un'alma celeste, un corpo frale.	bears a heavenly soul and a frail body.
	Tosto more il mortale,	When the mortal dies,
	E torna l'alma in cielo,	the soul returns to heaven,
	E torna il corpo in polve,	and the body returns to dust
	Doppo breve soggiorno.	after its brief sojourn.
A	<u>Tu sol del tuo tornar perdesti il giorno.</u>	<u>You alone have missed the day of your return.</u>
	Torna, che mentre porti empie dimore	Return, for so long as you cause pitiless delays
	Al mio fiero dolore,	to my proud grief,
	Veggio del mio morir l'hore prefisse.	I see the preordained hour of my death.
B	<u>Torna, deh torna, Ulisse.</u>	<u>Return, oh return, Ulisse.</u>

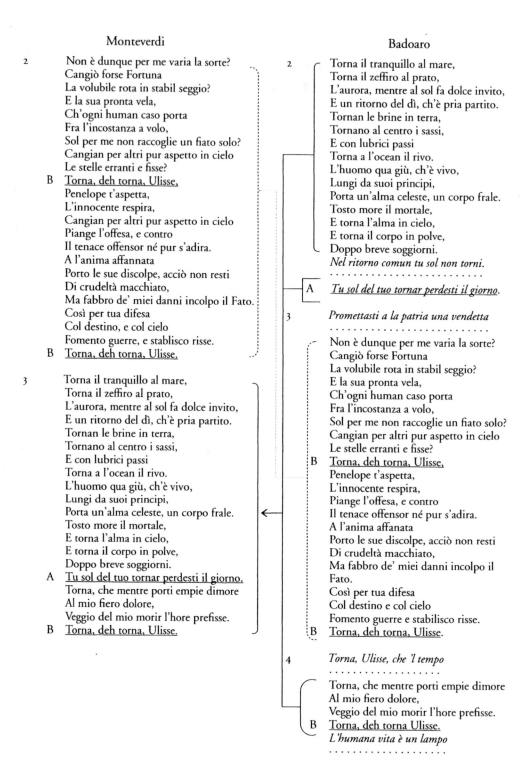

Monteverdi	Badoaro

Monteverdi

2
Non è dunque per me varia la sorte?
Cangiò forse Fortuna
La volubile rota in stabil seggio?
E la sua pronta vela,
Ch'ogni human caso porta
Fra l'incostanza a volo,
Sol per me non raccoglie un fiato solo?
Cangian per altri pur aspetto in cielo
Le stelle erranti e fisse?

B Torna, deh torna, Ulisse,
Penelope t'aspetta,
L'innocente respira,
Cangian per altri pur aspetto in cielo
Piange l'offesa, e contro
Il tenace offensor né pur s'adira.
A l'anima affannata
Porto le sue discolpe, acciò non resti
Di crudeltà macchiato,
Ma fabbro de' miei danni incolpo il Fato.
Così per tua difesa
Col destino, e col cielo
Fomento guerre, e stablisco risse.

B Torna, deh torna, Ulisse.

3
Torna il tranquillo al mare,
Torna il zeffiro al prato,
L'aurora, mentre al sol fa dolce invito,
E un ritorno del dì, ch'è pria partito.
Tornan le brine in terra,
Tornano al centro i sassi,
E con lubrici passi
Torna a l'ocean il rivo.
L'huomo qua giù, ch'è vivo,
Lungi da suoi principi,
Porta un'alma celeste, un corpo frale.
Tosto more il mortale,
E torna l'alma in cielo,
E torna il corpo in polve,
Doppo breve soggiorni.

A Tu sol del tuo tornar perdesti il giorno.
Torna, che mentre porti empie dimore
Al mio fiero dolore,
Veggio del mio morir l'hore prefisse.

B Torna, deh torna, Ulisse.

Badoaro

2
Torna il tranquillo al mare,
Torna il zeffiro al prato,
L'aurora, mentre al sol fa dolce invito,
E un ritorno del dì, ch'è pria partito.
Tornan le brine in terra,
Tornano al centro i sassi,
E con lubrici passi
Torna a l'ocean il rivo.
L'huomo qua giù, ch'è vivo,
Lungi da suoi principi,
Porta un'alma celeste, un corpo frale.
Tosto more il mortale,
E torna l'alma in cielo,
E torna il corpo in polve,
Doppo breve soggiorni.
Nel ritorno comun tu sol non torni.
. . . .

A *Tu sol del tuo tornar perdesti il giorno.*

3 *Promettasti a la patria una vendetta*
. . . .
Non è dunque per me varia la sorte?
Cangiò forse Fortuna
La volubile rota in stabil seggio?
E la sua pronta vela,
Ch'ogni human caso porta
Fra l'incostanza a volo,
Sol per me non raccoglie un fiato solo?
Cangian per altri pur aspetto in cielo
Le stelle erranti e fisse?

B Torna, deh torna, Ulisse,
Penelope t'aspetta,
L'innocente respira,
Piange l'offesa, e contro
Il tenace offensor né pur s'adira.
A l'anima affanata
Porto le sue discolpe, acciò non resti
Di crudeltà macchiato,
Ma fabbro de' miei danni incolpo il
Fato.
Così per tua difesa
Col destino e col cielo
Fomento guerre e stabilisco risse.

B Torna, deh torna, Ulisse.

4 *Torna, Ulisse, che 'l tempo*
. . . .
Torna, che mentre porti empie dimore
Al mio fiero dolore,
Veggio del mio morir l'hore prefisse.

B Torna, deh torna Ulisse.
L'humana vita è un lampo
. . . .

FIGURE 4. Monteverdi's rearrangement of Penelope's lament

setting them lyrically, with more repetition of text than normal, and in a more highly organized musical style—so that the structure is felt not only as form but as emotion.

In moving Badoaro's second section to the end of his scene and transforming it into the climax, Monteverdi was evidently inspired by the distinctive features of the text: its unusually regular structure—many of the lines form rhymed couplets—and its rhetorical emphasis, since nine different lines begin with the same key word, "torna." Both this structure and its descriptive pastoral imagery invite lyricism.

Apart from its suitability for lyrical setting, the pastoral content of this passage renders it particularly effective as the closing section of this monologue. It marks a final stage in Penelope's contemplation of her fate. In the first section Penelope is obsessed with the past; she reviews the history of her solitude, its endless length, its unjust cause, and becomes increasingly furious. Monteverdi's second section is rooted in the present; here Penelope fixates on her own feelings, her hopeless condition. In the third she moves beyond herself to a meditation on the laws of nature. Though bitter and ironic, the larger view provides a temporary respite from the personal, which makes the return to her own woes—and her old refrains—all the more poignant. The emotional arc traversed by Penelope here, in her very first scene, in which she travels far but goes nowhere, strongly establishes the image of her immutability, an image that is crucial to the structure and effect of the opera as a whole. And the trajectory of that arc is powerfully indebted to Monteverdi's textual revisions.[8] We might even think of this lament as a metaphor for Penelope's weaving and unweaving of Laertes' shroud, now otherwise absent from the opera: as we noted, Badoaro's single reference to this, the most famous of Penelope's actions, occurred in the fourth section of her lament text, which Monteverdi cut.[9] As

---

tears, laughter, and evil is fleeting; then why are my pain (*danno*) and disgrace (*scorno*) eternal?" The second, longer, cut involves sixteen lines that are concerned with Troy. "Since his aim has been accomplished, and Troy has burned to the ground, why has he not returned? Will its ashes mix with mine?" In the third excised passage, of ten lines, Penelope briefly laments her fading beauty, and then refers to the ruse of the shroud: "Time will soon wrinkle my face, my skin grows pale. What is the use of weaving and then unweaving each night to deceive the Suitors if your absence and my tears are eternal?" The final excision, of Badoaro's concluding twelve lines, eliminates a philosophical disquisition on the meaning of life and death: "Life is a mere flash of lightning, feminine beauty but a ray of sun. One who is absent for twenty years takes too much of it, you heroes who measure your glory with centuries. The heavenly voyage respects the years but little. A loving heart too, in a short time, feels eternal torment, and a few years make a long hell." Carter ("'In Love's Harmonious Consort,'" 12) notes that the cuts here and elsewhere eliminate references to Penelope's physical appearance, hence her sexuality.

8. Although Badoaro's text parallels that of Enea's long monologue in *Le nozze d'Enea,* it clearly did not meet the composer's requirements as well. The composer had to revise it substantially in order to achieve the strong emotional contrasts so effectively built into Enea's monologue. See Chap. 6.

9. As already noted, Monteverdi's cut also eliminates a long meditation on time and death. This passage resonates with Mercurio's speech in the scene following Iro's suicide, which, as we know, was also cut (the full text is in Appendix 7). "L'humana vita è un lampo / Beltà donnesca è un raggio," cut from the lament, parallels Mercurio's: "vostra vita è un passaggio. / Non ha stato, o fermezza, / Se mai giunge bellezza, / Tramonta all'hor, chà pena mostra un raggio." Both passages may qualify as the kind of "pensieri e concetti tolti di lontano" that Torcigliani avoided in *Nozze,* because they did not please Monteverdi (see Appendix 2 [n]). Indeed, the *Nozze* text is relatively free of such philosophical disquisitions.

revised, each section of the lament touches on one of the themes represented allegorically in Monteverdi's prologue: Lame Time (1), the turning wheel of Fortune (2), and Human Frailty (3), in a sense amplifying and illustrating its message.[10]

Of course we cannot pretend that Monteverdi was concerned only or even primarily with the verbal text here. His revisions of Penelope's text may have corrected weaknesses in Badoaro's original, but they also enabled a musical setting that eloquently establishes Penelope's character and position. Her ascetic rigidity, the intensity of her self-control, is embodied in her music. This is evident from the outset in the extreme constriction of her musical line. Beginning in c, low in her range, and stuck there, except to sink even lower, she seems weighed down by her grief, unable even to look up (Example 6). Centered around its opening pitch, E♭, then falling to D, the range of each successive phrase of her first section expands slightly more than its predecessor. And each phrase realizes a slightly higher goal: first F (m. 11), then A (m. 17), B♭ (m. 22), B (m. 28), C (m. 37), and finally D (m. 57). But the effort of rising is too great; each attempt culminates in a sharp dissonance and then collapses, as the undertow of her depression pulls her back down again. The gradual upward progress and subsequent collapse, painfully drawn out over the course of sixty-one measures, is summarized and re-experienced in the seven measures of the A refrain (mm. 69–75), whose own chromatic ascent, prolonged and intensified by textual repetition and unaccustomed sequential patterning, finally reaches the same high point—a D that is now consonant. It too collapses abruptly in defeat, falling back to its origins on the D an octave lower.

The same kind of depressed motion governs Penelope's second section, but the tessitura is less consistently low, the motion somewhat more hopefully diatonic, and the progress less persistently cumulative (Example 7). Although high D remains the goal, each melodic phrase wanders more, as if having lost its direction. Like the earlier A refrain, the B refrain (mm. 97–101) too recapitulates the painful upward progress of the preceding music. Again, B is more carefully shaped than the phrases that precede it. Enhanced by text repetition, strong, regular, cadential bass motion directs it to closure on A, where the section began.

The third section, with its pastoral text, brings with it a complete change of mood. Penelope begins brightly in C major, after a modulation accomplished through the offices of the nurse Ericlea (Example 8). Heightened organization is marked by reiterated melodic curves against a firmly measured and strongly directional bass, which exploits the repetitions of "torna" built into the text. The music seems almost to distance Penelope from her grief as she contemplates nature. But her song gradually disintegrates as her

---

10. "*Tempo* è zoppo" (1); "Cangio forse *Fortuna* la volubile ruota" (2); L'*huomo* porta . . . un corpo *frale* (3). The fourth allegory, which Penelope fails to mention in her lament and repeatedly rejects during the course of the opera, finally finds its place following her capitulation: "dono tutto ad *Amor* le sue ragioni" (act 5, scene 10). See below.

EXAMPLE 6. Penelope's lament (*Il ritorno d'Ulisse*, 1.1, mm. 5–75).

(continued)

EXAMPLE 6 *(continued)*

EXAMPLE 6 *(continued)*

EXAMPLE 7. Penelope's lament, continued (*Il ritorno d'Ulisse*, 1.1, mm. 83–126).

(continued)

EXAMPLE 7 *(continued)*

ne - lo - pe t'as-pet - ta, L'in - no-cen - te so - spi - ra, Pian — ge l'of - fe - sa, e con-tro Il te - na - ce of-fen -

sor né pur s'a - di - ra. Al - l'a - ni - ma_af-fan - na - ta Por-to le tue di-scol-pe, ac-ciò non re - sti Di cru-del -

tà mac - chia - to, Ma fab - bro de' miei dan - ni in - col-po_il Fa - to. Co -

si___ per tua di - fe - sa, Col de - sti - no, col Cie - lo, Fo-men-to guer - re e sta-bi - li - sco ris - se.

Tor - na, tor - na, tor - na, deh__ tor - na, tor - na_U - lis - - se!___

EXAMPLE 8. Penelope's lament, continued (*Il ritorno d'Ulisse,* I.I, mm. 135–78).

Penelope

Tor - na_il tran-quil - lo_al ma - re, Tor - na_il Ze - fi - ro_al pra - to, L'Au - ro - ra, men-tre_al

bc

EXAMPLE 8 *(continued)*

dreamy pleasure fades and harsh reality reasserts itself. The temporary brightness of C is replaced, first by g, cadencing on d (for refrain A), then by a (for refrain B). And then she is back where she started, on a single, almost unmoving reciting tone, once again contemplating her grim future.

Despite some initial references to c, Penelope's monologue centers on d and a; d, emphasized in a number of cadences and especially by the first refrain, and a, emphasized by the second refrain, establish important musical links to the prologue. There Humana Fragilità sings in d throughout, and Amore sings in a. These relationships will be played out as her drama develops.[11]

Monteverdi's setting of Penelope's opening speech, which he completely reshaped for the purpose, renders it adequate to its dramatic responsibility: as the still center toward which all of Ulisse's action is directed. Her intransigence, heroic in stature, is worthy of the energy required to overcome it. That intransigence, which persists until the final scene of the opera, is both matched and intensified by her austere and speech-like mode of expression, which suggests her reluctance (or inability) to release her voice in song.[12] And this contrasts with almost everyone she interacts with, especially Melanto and the Suitors. Until the final scene, the librettist offers her few opportunities for lyricism (structured stanzas, refrains), and the composer manages to set even those in the most austere, restrained way. Monteverdi has thus strengthened one of the most essential components of Badoaro's drama. And as I have already indicated, he reinforces his characterization of Penelope in each of her subsequent appearances (with a combination of textual manipulation and choice of musical setting).

ACT 2, SCENE I: PENELOPE AND MELANTO

As in act 1, but more directly, Penelope's stolid refusal to renounce her faith—or her recitative style—is set in relief by Melanto's exuberant lyricism,[13] and Monteverdi enhances the contrast with some careful editing. Following a brief speech by Penelope (the single couplet already mentioned), in her signature key, d, the scene comprises four speeches of diminishing length, as Melanto twice attempts to persuade her mistress to

---

11. The relationship between d and a is central to Chafe's carefully reasoned allegorical interpretation of the opera (*Tonal Language,* 261–62). Much of his chapter "Tonal Allegory in *Il ritorno d'Uisse in patria*" is devoted to a detailed exploration of the meaning of the tonal connections between the prologue and Penelope's monologue (especially pp. 276–88).

12. I develop this argument in "*Il ritorno d'Ulisse* and the Power of Music." See also Carter, " 'In Love's Harmonious Consort.' "

13. In a kind of reversal, after the Suitors' death, Melanto no longer sings.

yield and is twice rebuffed. Though consisting primarily of *versi sciolti*, both of Melanto's speeches culminate in a quatrain of four *ottonari* in *rime baciate*, a kind of varied refrain that invites lyrical setting by virtue of both its form and content. And Monteverdi obliges; following his free recitative setting of the body of Melanto's lengthy first speech, he expands the refrain to create a lovely little bipartite aria in triple meter, with each of the sections repeated (Example 9). There are four related phrases, two in each section, and most remarkably, each phrase trails off into a hedonistic melisma: pure textless music.[14] With the repeats this happens eight times.

Ama dunque, che d'Amore	Love, then, for Love's
Dolce amica è la beltà.	sweet friend is beauty.
Dal piacere il tuo dolore	From pleasure your pain
Saettato caderà.	will fall beneath his arrows.

Penelope's much shorter response, in contrast, is adamant and adamantly unmusical, an effect increased in Monteverdi's amplified version of Badoaro's first three lines (as usual, his additions are given in italics):

Amor, *Amor* è un idol vano,	Love is a frivolous idol,
Amor, Amor è'un vagabondo nume,	a roaming spirit,
Amor, Amor, all'incostanze sue non	there are wings enough for his fickleness.
mancan piume.	

Set to a sequence of rising triadic phrases articulated by rests, each initiated by a striking rhythmic motive on "Amor," these lines culminate in a long descending phrase on "Del suo dolce sereno / È misura il baleno un giorno solo," which reaches the bottom of Penelope's range, low B. Her thought is completed in the next line, "cangia il piacer *il piacer, il piacer, il piacer, il piacer* in duolo," set in triple meter to a rather circular melody. Penelope is determined. And Monteverdi makes her more so, first by repeating *Amor* in line 1, then adding the same word at the beginning of her second and third lines, repeating it both times, and finally by setting her sixth (final) line in triple meter inspired by, and entailing sixfold repetition of the very word against which she is steeling herself: *piacer*. Occasional repetition and musical depiction of individual key words mark the remainder of her speech, which ends, of course, in d.

---

14. Cf. Chap 5, p. 156 and n. 58. The meaning of the notation is ambiguous here: the melismas could have been played by strings (as they are in some recordings and in Curtis's edition), which, however, are nowhere indicated in the score. In fact, prominent slurs over the melismas seem to indicate that they were intended to be sung.

EXAMPLE 9. Melanto, "Ama dunque," and Penelope, "Amor è un idol vano" (*Il ritorno d'Ulisse,* 2.1 [or 1.10], mm. 86–116).

EXAMPLE 10. Penelope, "Non dee di nuovo amar" (*Il ritorno d'Ulisse*, 2.1 [or 1.10], mm. 161–69).

Melanto's second attempt at persuasion comprises only six *versi sciolti* plus the aforementioned *ottonario* quatrain, which reads as follows in Badoaro:

Fuggi pur del Tempo i danni,
Tosto vien nemica età
In passando i dì tiranni
Fanno oltraggio a tua beltà.

Flee then the ravages of Time,
enemy old age will soon be here,
in passing, tyrannical days
offend your beauty.

But Monteverdi replaced this second, unctuously wordy quatrain with a reprise of Melanto's first, much more direct injunction, "Ama dunque." (These words become a kind of mantra in this opera; the Suitors will chant them too.) Penelope's response this time is just as emphatic and even more concise (Example 10). She lives by rules of moral decorum, which can be expressed in a three-line apothegm: "Non dee di novo amar / Chi misera penò. / Torna stolta a penar chi prima errò" (One who has suffered affliction should not love again. She who has once erred is a fool to return to suffering). But she cannot keep her feelings from showing. Her adamant declaration, declaimed on a single repeated note, melts as she stammers on "penar" in her octave descent to the cadence on low D. Penelope's characteristic tonal space, set out in her opening lament, is maintained here, and contrasts emphatically with Melanto's. All of Penelope's speeches are in a and d, while Melanto's are in G and C.[15]

---

15. Although he does not address this particular tonal conflict, Chafe, *Tonal Language*, would perhaps associate Melanto's 'durus' keys here with the "hardness" of fiery desire, her own view of love (see p. 272). He might also explain her G as reinforcing an allegorical connection with Time and Fortune, which are also primarily in G.

Though Monteverdi's setting acknowledged the efficacy of Badoaro's dramatic structure, its increasing intensity generated by the diminishing lengths of its dialogic units, he strengthened its effect by epitomizing the confrontation between Melanto and Penelope, both musically and textually. Melanto's melodious injunction to love, heavily weighted by its expansive lyrical setting, is directly juxtaposed not once but twice with Penelope's refusal, a refusal embodied by her rejection of all lyrical impulse.

It is worth remembering that Penelope's brief opening speech in this scene, "Donate un giorno oh Dei / contenti a' desir miei," is missing from all of the librettos. Its insertion in the score allows her, rather than Melanto, to initiate the confrontation, thus strengthening her side of the argument, enabling her to stake her moral claim first.[16] The couplet sounds like the end of a speech rather than the beginning, making it seem as if Penelope is in the midst of a thought initiated in her previous appearance—long ago in act 1. It increases the impression that she has not budged since then, that she is still fixed in the same position. She is certainly still stuck in the same d tonality.[17]

ACT 3, SCENE 2: PENELOPE AND THE SUITORS

We next see Penelope in the company of the dreaded Suitors, in act 3, scene 2. Once again, by means of editorial interventions in the text as well as musical setting, the composer reinforces Penelope's adherence to her moral creed, heightening her adamant refusal to let down her guard—against love (and song). Though the means are different—a substantial cut (of some twenty lines; five-line speeches for the Suitors and Penelope) and judicious exploitation of two refrains provided by Badoaro—the result is the same: the composer manages to intensify and epitomize the opposition between Penelope and her adversaries. (See Table 8 above, Chapter 4.)

To the Suitors' first exhortation to love, "Ama dunque sì, sì / Dunque riama un dì" (ll. 5–6), which Monteverdi repeats three times in an attractive triple-meter imitative setting, Penelope responds with a curt dismissal: "Non voglio amar no, no / Ch'amando penerò" (ll. 7–8), the first two of six lines of text, likewise repeated several times in a triple-meter setting that is more forceful than lyrical (and that forcefully reverses the ascending direction of their plea—the music mimes her refusal). Rather than continuing

---

16. In Chap. 4 I pointed out that Penelope's passage was to be omitted from the three-act version. It was probably included in the five-act version because it began act 2. On a further possible reason for the insertion of this text, see above, note 3.

17. This would support Dubowy's intriguing suggestion ("Bemerkungen") that Penelope's and Ulisse's opening scenes might be thought of as taking place simultaneously in two different realms, which converge only when Eumete moves from one to the other in act 2 (Chap. 5, n. 56).

her speech, then, as Badoaro did, the composer interrupts her with a reprise of the Suitors' exhortation (italics in Table 8), after which she completes her text, closing with a repeat of her adamant couplet of refusal, not in the libretto (also italics). Having twice urged her on as a group, and been twice forcefully rejected (Badoaro had this only once, so far), the Suitors then begin their more expansive individual efforts to plead their case, each in turn using elaborate natural metaphors set to highly pictorial music (the vine, the cedar, the ivy) (ll. 13–29). At this point, rather than following Badoaro, who has Penelope reason with the Suitors and then each of them continue with a second plea (text bracketed, ll. 30–49), Monteverdi again cuts straight to their refrain, "ama dunque, sì, sì," which once again, now for the third time, is countered by Penelope's direct rejection, "Non voglio amar," though this time the textual refrain, which leads into a lengthy speech, is inexact and the musical setting consequently varied. Here the cut and the extra juxtaposition of the two extended refrains tighten the scene and help to crystallize its dramatic essence.[18]

ACT 5, SCENE 10: PENELOPE AND ULISSE

Penelope's failure to yield, either to the imprecations of the Suitors or to hope held out by Telemaco (in act 4, scene 1) and Eumete (in act 5, scene 4), persists until the final scene of the opera. Until then, both Badoaro and Monteverdi conspire to keep her from singing. The librettist provides her with nothing but *versi sciolti* and the composer withholds any musical gestures that would hint at the softening of her resolve; indeed, he even strengthens that resolve by means of pointed word repetitions or brief musical patterns, severely restricting her range and the lengths of her phrases, which, however high they may reach, invariably conclude with downward motion. And he keeps her in d, as in her scene with Eumete, 3.4, in which he sings his enthusiasm in G, and she speaks hers, succinctly, on d, rising gradually as far as a minor sixth, to B♭, but then sinking down again.

This is in contrast to Ulisse, whose recitative Monteverdi infuses with increasing lyrical ardor and shape as he nears—and earns—his goal. This trajectory is particularly striking in his opening address to Penelope in the final scene, when he first appears in his own clothes—begun startlingly high and off balance, on a first inversion of the dominant—and in his glorious description of their marital bed, which finally precipitates the denouement.

18. The cut was apparently made *after* Monteverdi's original setting, to judge from the gathering structure (Chap. 4, pp. 77–82). Might this mean that Monteverdi only recognized the redundancy of the material after it was rehearsed? Carter has pointed out that the Suitors' dialogue mimics particular Incogniti discourses (*Musical Theatre*, 245–46 and n. 4).

Penelope's capitulation, as designed by the librettist, unfolds in three stages: recitative, aria, and duet, but the text is little more than a sketch. Its overwhelming effect, all the more powerful for being so long withheld, belongs to the composer. Badoaro makes no formal distinction between her previous responses to Ulisse and this one, continuing with *versi sciolti:*

Hor sì ti riconosco, hor sì ti credo,	Now yes, I recognize you, now yes,
	I believe you,
Antico possessore	ancient possessor
Del combattuto core.	of my beleaguered heart.
Onestà mi perdoni,	Forgive my rudeness,
Dono tutte ad Amor le sue ragioni.	I lay all the blame on Love.

But text repetition, melodic patterning, and triple meter burst out in full force as Monteverdi and Penelope come alive again. The composer's setting of the first three lines grants them the weight they have earned.[19]

Hor sì, *hor sì* ti riconosco, *sì, sì, sì, sì,* hor sì ti credo, *sì, sì,*
Antico possessore
Del combattuto core.

Unlike all of her previous responses to Ulisse, though, in this one Penelope accepts C and G, his keys, though she still reverts to her d for the cadence (see Example 14 below).

Then, to Ulisse's passionate encouragement to unfetter her tongue and unleash her voice, she responds with an aria, her only aria (and one in which the orchestra plays an unusually important role, in substantial ritornellos that repeat each vocal phrase).[20] It is firmly planted from beginning to end in C major. The remarkable effect of this aria, too, is largely the composer's doing. To be sure, Badoaro has suggested lyrical setting by providing Penelope with three pairs of *versi sciolti*, alternating *settenari* and *endecasillabi*, in which she calls upon nature to rejoice with her, a pointed reference to imagery she had not used since the opening scene—to opposite effect—when she decried her estrangement from all natural laws: tranquility returns to the sea, breezes to the field, dawn to the day, salt to the earth, ocean to the shore. Only Ulisse fails to return.[21]

Though the content of Badoaro's text certainly invites lyrical setting, it is highly irregular and resistant to formal structure. To begin with, the three couplets are not strictly parallel: the first one is an invocation, urging the heavens, fields, and breezes to rejoice,

---

19. Calcagno has a beautiful analysis of this scene from the point of view of deixis ("Staging Musical Discourses," 217–20, esp. 219). See also id., "'Imitar col canto chi parla,'" 409–14.

20. The empty staves above the vocal part in the manuscript suggest that an accompaniment was intended, at least at some stage of editing. On material left to be added in rehearsal, see Chap. 4.

21. Badoaro's fourth couplet, unlike the others, is rhymed. It also lacks the *sdrucciolo* ending of the second and third; and it does not invoke nature. It suggests and receives a completely different setting.

while the second and third are descriptive of the singing birds, the murmuring streams, the greening grass and whispering waves, which now rejoice and are consoled. Nor do all three share rhyme or meter: only the second and third have an internal rhyme and end in a *sdrucciolo*. But Monteverdi regularizes (as well as expands) the text. He constructs an aria of three strophes, dividing each of them into two very unequal parts, a pair of *settenari* (taking advantage of the internal rhyme in the second and third stanzas) and a *quinario* (or in the second and third stanzas, *quinario sdrucciolo*), as follows:

Illustratevi o cieli,	Shine out, O heavens,
Rinfioratevi o prati,	bloom again, O fields,
Aure gioite.	breezes, rejoice.
Gl'augelletti cantando,	The birds singing,
I rivi mormorando	the murmuring brooks,
Hor si rallegrino.	let them now rejoice.
Quell'erbe verdeggianti,	The verdant grass,
Quell'onde sussuranti,	the whispering waves,
Hor si consolino.	let them now console themselves.

Though based on unequal textual segments, the two sections form a beautifully balanced bipartite structure (A and B), the composer compensating for the textual disparity through repetition and melismatic expansion of the B section, introducing effective text-interpretative gestures for the three final words, "gioite," "rallegrino," and "consolino." The orchestral ritornello, which echoes each section, wonderfully enacts the text: Penelope's call for nature to join in her rejoicing is answered by the string band (Example 11).

Like the imagery in Badoaro's text, Monteverdi's setting too refers back to the arioso passage in the opening scene. Both are in the key of C major, a significant departure from the key in which Penelope has found herself for most of the opera and to which she consistently returns. Only the aria stays there, the earlier arioso passage moving back to d as it dissolves in recitative. The musical material of the two movements is also similar—and significantly different. In both instances the voice outlines a descending C-major scale, but the compass of the earlier melody is restricted essentially to the fifth, G to C, while that of the later aria is more expansive, involving the entire octave C to C. (I emphasized earlier the confining limits of Penelope's melody, always falling back upon itself.) The phrase structure of the two passages also differs significantly, the initial descent of the arioso landing heavily on the tonic, where the melody waits for two beats, as if exhausted, before summoning the energy to rise back up to the fifth. The new energy is sufficient, as it turns out, to propel several more stepwise descents and ascents, but not to push the line much beyond the fifth degree, G, and never to the upper C.

The melody of the aria, on the other hand, rather than merely sinking, accomplishes its octave descent in two stages, an initial two-measure phrase balanced by a second one of

EXAMPLE 11. Penelope, "Illustratevi, o cieli" (*Il ritorno d'Ulisse,* 5.10 [or 3.10], mm. 142–95).

EXAMPLE II *(continued)*

equal length, comprised of a graceful mixture of stepwise motion and compensatory leaps. Penelope's sense of freedom or abandon is displayed in the elaborate melismatic decorations, especially in the B sections of the stanzas (but also in A, particularly on "onde sussuranti"). Whereas the earlier arioso reinforces Penelope's constraint, her inability to speak or feel expansively, the final aria has just the opposite effect: her relief seems boundless. Surface rhythm contributes to the contrast: the heavily accented, almost plodding rhythm of the arioso contrasts markedly with the dance-like rhythms of the aria, heavily accented first beats separated by decorative embellishments of the weak beats between. The regular succession of vocal and instrumental phrases conveys the sense that the entire world is infected with Penelope's joy.

Penelope shifts to a and to expressive recitative in duple meter to declaim Badoaro's final summarizing couplet: "Già ch'è sorta felice / Dal cenere troian la mia Fenice" (now that my phoenix has happily arisen from the Trojan ashes) (mm. 188–95), a conclusion that paves the way for the final duet in the same key, a, the key of Love.

Although a large-scale relationship between the first and last scenes of the opera is at least suggested by the librettist—especially through the return of nature imagery—it was the composer who made the effect palpable, through musical connections.[22] Penelope has

---

22. Calcagno ("Staging Musical Discourses," 119) points to another reminiscence of Penelope's opening monologue. Trying for the last time to deny what her heart and eyes tell her, she sings "il mio pudico letto sol d'Ulisse è ricetto" on the same contrapuntal structure and at the same pitch as the B refrain of her opening monologue: "Tu sol del tuo tornar perdesti il giorno," as if remembering it subliminally. Others have remarked on the connection between the opening and closing scenes of the opera, for instance, Dubowy, "Bemerkungen," 239.

finally learned to sing again, but she has not forgotten the travails of her past; Monteverdi has enabled her to transform them into her musical triumph, a triumph of Amor.

The Wily Hero

Whereas Penelope's defining characteristic, surely emphasized if not created by the composer in each of her appearances, is her steadfastness, her unwillingness, even inability, to change, Ulisse's is the opposite. His entire previous history has marked him as flexible and resourceful: qualities that have enabled him to adapt to his surroundings, no matter what the gods had in store for him, and brought him to the point at which we first encounter him here. The librettist and composer, as we shall see, reinforce these qualities throughout their drama.

ACT I, SCENE 7: ULISSE

Ulisse's initial appearance, in 1.7, like Penelope's six scenes earlier, is carefully orchestrated by composer and librettist to establish him as worthy of his heroic reputation and deserving, ultimately, of his wife's faith. In this case, though, the libretto served the composer better. His alterations to Ulisse's text are negligible, a few word repetitions and a single refrain; they do not entail any cuts. The scene is quite long (forty-eight lines of uninterrupted *versi sciolti*), almost balancing that of Penelope, especially after the composer's surgery (he reduced Badoaro's text from 125 lines to 74). Though his monologue lacks the expressive focus and some of the structural features of Penelope's text—the three interruptions from Ericlea, and the two recurrent refrains, which suited the composer so well—Monteverdi manages to invest Ulisse with heroic potential for action. And he does so almost exclusively through recitative, without once allowing him the relief of triple-meter arioso.

We encounter Ulisse just after he has been cast ashore, asleep, by the Phaeacians. Badoaro traces his gradual awakening and growing realization that he has been betrayed once again, and abandoned in a foreign land. Following the poet's lead, Monteverdi portrays Ulisse's increasing awareness of his situation in five distinct but interdependent musical sections. The first, treating eight lines of text, begins slowly and haltingly, in c, as Ulisse gradually awakens:

Dormo ancora, *dormo ancora* o son desto?	Do I still sleep, or am I awake?
Che contrade rimiro?	What country do I behold?
Qual aria, ohimè, respiro?	What air, alas, do I breathe?
E che Terra calpesto?	What ground do I tread upon?
Dormo ancora, dormo ancora, dormo ancora, *o son desto?*	
Chi fece in me, chi fece	Who caused in me, who caused

Il sempre dolce lusinghevol sonno,	the always sweet, beguiling slumber,
Minstro de' tormenti?	harbinger of torments?
Chi cangiò il mio riposo in ria sventura?	What has transformed my rest into dread misfortune?
Qual deità de' dormienti ha cura?	What god watches over sleepers?

His repeated questions, "Am I awake? Where am I? What air do I breathe? What has transformed my rest into misfortune?", seven in succession, inspire a brief, lower-neighbor, dotted motive that ends up pervading the entire monologue (Example 12). Monteverdi mimes Ulisse's awakening through the gradual expansion of the lower-neighbor figure from half step ("Dormo ancora"), to whole step ("Dormo ancora"—the composer's addition), to fifth ("o son desto"), the three statements separated from one another by prominent rests; this initial threefold statement, on C, is repeated in varied form on E♭ for the next three lines, and then literally, a half step higher, on F (to a reprise of the first verse, introduced by the composer, who also adds an extra repetition of "dormo ancora," increasing the urgency of its second setting by omitting one rest and shortening another).[23] Continuing to exploit the same motive, the line inches up to a high point on F in measure 14, from which it gradually descends over the course of the next seven measures, cadencing on F, an octave lower. The gradual expansion of the motive is matched by the gradual expansion of the melodic units between rests, increasing the proportion of speech to silence, from a series of one-measure units, to one and a half, to two, to three, and finally to a four-measure unit, culminating in the cadence.

Ulisse has now roused himself sufficiently to recognize that sleep has brought him his present misfortune. A shift to d initiates the second section (mm. 23–43), which comprises ten lines:

O sonno, o mortal sonno,	O sleep, o fatal sleep,
Fratello della morte altri ti chiama.	some call you the brother of death.
Solingo, e trasportato,	Alone, and forsaken,
Deluso et ingannato,	deluded and deceived,
Ti conosco ben io, Padre d'errori.	I know you well, father of my errors.
Pur de gl'errori miei son io la colpa,	Yet I alone am guilty for my errors,
che se l'ombra è del sonno	for if shadow is sleep's
Sorella, o pur compagna,	sister or companion,
Chi si confida a l'ombra,	he who entrusts himself to darkness
Perduto al fin contro ragion si lagna.	is lost and has no reason to complain.

Ulisse addresses sleep, "brother of death," "sister of shadow," and criticizes himself for having yielded to it, thus contributing to his own fate. Though still interspersed with

---

23. These are virtually the only alterations to this text on Monteverdi's part.

EXAMPLE 12. Ulisse's monologue, "Dormo ancora" (*Il ritorno d'Ulisse*, 1.7, mm. 1–88).

EXAMPLE 12 *(continued)*

ro - ri miei son io___ la col - pa,___ Che se l'Om - bra è del son - no So - rel - la, o pur com -

pa - gna, Chi si con - fi - da_al-l'Om - bra, Per - du - to_al-fin con-tro ra - gion si la - gna. O,

___ o Dei sem-pre sde - gna - ti, Nu-mi non mai___ pla - ca - ti, Con - tro_U-lis - se che dor - me,

an - che se - ve - ri! Vo - stri di-vi - ni_im-pe - ri Con-tro l'u-man vo - ler sian fer - mi_e for - ti,

Ma non tol-ghi-no,_ohi - mè, la pa - ce_ai mor - ti. Fe - a - ci_in-gan-na-to-ri! Voi,

voi, voi pur mi pro-met-te - ste Di ri-con-dur - mi sal - vo In I - ta-ca mia pa - tria, Con le ric-chez - ze

mie, co' miei te-so - ri. Fe - a - ci man-ca-to - ri, Or___ non so co-me_in-gra - ti

(continued)

EXAMPLE 12 *(continued)*

pauses, his speech is less hesitant now, less sleepy, its units longer. The lower-neighbor motive persists, but the melodic line is more mobile, centered within the fifth A to E until the point at which Ulisse acknowledges his guilt for sleeping, whereupon it descends to F, remaining stuck there, depressed, until a final descent to D at the cadence.

Ulisse then rails at the gods, against him even as he sleeps. This third section, comprising six lines (mm. 43–57), is the most active and energetic so far, and also the most tightly structured, forming a succession of rhymed couplets. Ulisse's vocal line is higher in tessitura and more dissonant, leaping up an octave to a suspension in its very first measure:

O Dei, sempre sdegnati,	O ever wrathful Gods,
Numi, non mai placati,	gods never placated,
Contro Ulisse, che dorme, anche severi,	harsh even to sleeping Ulisse,
Vostri divini imperi	let your divine authority
Contro l'human voler sian fermi, e forti,	upon the will of man be strong and resolute,
Ma non tolghino, ohimè, la pace ai morti.	But let it not deprive, alas, the dead of peace.

The persistent neighbor-note motive is now deployed in four parallel subphrases within Ulisse's line, each ending with a prominent pair of quarter notes that emphasize the important words in lines 3–5: "dorme," "severi," its rhyme "imperi," and finally "forti." The line remains stuck around high E until its final phrase, when it curls down an octave to end, exhausted, on low E, leaving the bass to cadence alone on A. But both descent and exhaustion are only temporary. The energy summoned in this section carries over into the next, longest section (section 4: seventeen lines, mm. 58–82), in which Ulisse, Arianna-like, angrily curses the Phaeacians for abandoning him:

Feaci ingannatori!	Treacherous Phaeacians!
Voi, *voi, voi* pur mi prometteste	You promised me
Di ricondurmi salvo	to take me back safely
In Itaca mia patria	to Ithaca, my homeland
Con le richezze mie, co i miei tesori.	With my riches, with my treasures.
Feaci mancatori,	Untrustworthy Phaeacians,
Or non so come, ingrati mi lasciaste	I know not how, ungratefully you could have left me
In questa riva aperta	on these bare shores
Su spiaggia erma e deserta,	on this lonely and deserted beach,
Misero, abbandonato;	miserable, abandoned;
E vi porta fastosi	and joyfully carry with you,
E per l'aure e per l'onde	with the winds and waves
Così enorme peccato?	such an enormous sin?
Se puniti non son sì gravi errori,	If such grave errors go unpunished
Lascia, Giove, deh lascia	then renounce, Jove, renounce
De' fulmini la cura,	the wielding of your thunderbolts,
Che la legge del caso è piu sicura.[24]	since the law of chance is more reliable.

Ulisse's rage explodes, ahead of the bass, as his line rises once again, this time quickly reaching its highpoint, G ("Feaci ingannatori, voi, *voi, voi* pur mi prometteste")—he (and

---

24. The text is reminiscent of Arianna's lament here, but Rinuccini's poetry is more highly structured, as is Monteverdi's setting. Chafe, *Tonal Language*, 277–78, cites Arianna's lament several times in connection with Penelope's, which he regards as a worthy successor. As already mentioned (Chap. 6, n. 80), Tomlinson would disagree (*Monteverdi and the End of the Renaissance*, 223).

Monteverdi) repeat the accusatory pronoun three times, twice on the high G—before settling lower, where a series of reiterated, percussive rhythms on the single pitch (D), utilizing the neighbor motive, finally dissolves, following a linear octave descent from E to low E that involves a sequence of 7–6 suspensions. The line rises once more, but this time only as far as D, which again is furiously reiterated with percussive sixteenth-note rhythms ("e vi porta fastosi e per l'aure e per l'onde così enorme peccato"). Thereafter it descends gradually and dejectedly to a cadence on low D, the sixteenth-note motion slowing to eighths and quarters, as Ulisse concludes despondently that Jove might as well give up his thunderbolts, since the laws of chance are more certain than those of the Gods.[25]

After a deep breath (half-note rest), Ulisse raises himself up one final time (section 5), leaping up a minor seventh to C, to curse the Phaeacians, calling on the winds to destroy their boats:

Sia de le vostre vele,	To your sails,
Falsissimi [fallacissimi] Feaci,	most treacherous Phaeacians,
Sempre Borea nemico,	may Boreas be ever an enemy,
E sian qual piume al vento, o scogli in mare,	and as feathers in the wind or reefs in the sea,
Le vostre infide navi,	let your faithless vessels be
Leggiere a gl'Aquiloni, a l'aure gravi.	light to the north winds, heavy to the breezes.

This time his line, still exploiting the neighbor motive, inches higher and remains there, leaping to the high point G four times before cadencing back in c, where he had begun so long ago.[26] The conclusiveness of this brief seven-measure passage, which effects the return to c from d in a mere two measures, is reinforced by a marked acceleration in harmonic rhythm, from the predominantly two- and one-measure units of the previous sections to half- and quarter-measure units for the final cadence.

Despite the fact that it seems tonally coherent, beginning and ending in the same key, c (with an emphasis on d and a in between), Ulisse's monologue is notable for the absence of large-scale structure. Except for the reiteration of the opening line four lines later, a repeat added by the composer, there are no refrains, and no other strong formal articulations. Although a motive introduced in the very first measure—the lower-neighbor motive—pervades all five sections, the vocal line is otherwise only loosely organized, with erratic leaps in both directions interspersed with percussive recitations on single pitches. The monologue nonetheless creates the impression of an overall increase in intensity, from its

---

25. Note that the reference to Jove's thunderbolts recurs in Ottavia's lament.

26. It is noteworthy that Ulisse begins and ends his monologue in c. Penelope began there too, but ended in a. Like Ulisse here, though, she spent most of her time in d. See Chafe, *Tonal Language,* 270–72, for an interpretation of this parallel.

halting beginnings when Ulisse, awakening, declaims in small melodic units of severely circumscribed ambitus (based on the neighbor motive) interrupted with frequent rests; this eventually builds to a climax somewhere near the middle, as Ulisse focuses his anger on the Phaeacians for having abandoned him. It is only at this point that the composer introduces a sustained expressive gesture, an extended stepwise descending sequence of 7–6 suspensions in measures 65–71, setting the enjambed text: "hor non so com'ingrati mi lasciaste in questa riva aperta su spiagga erma e deserta, misero, abbandonato," in which Ulisse's self-pity temporarily gets the better of him. Elsewhere, erratic melodic leaps, especially ascending ones, serve to highlight particularly crucial words, conveying the intensity of Ulisse's frustration. Likewise, the descending motions, whether leaps or scalar passages, communicate the depth of his despair at having squandered yet another opportunity to reach his destination. Having begun in a rather low tessitura and wandered around over the course of his monologue, he ends in a higher realm (the fifth C up to high G).

We have noted how Penelope's opening scene has managed to communicate the essential features of her character and predict her subsequent behavior. The same may be said of Ulisse's. The passionate ebb and flow of his opening monologue conveys his volatility, his potential for action. Perhaps the most striking characteristic of this monologue, though, is its unmitigated (and only loosely structured) recitative setting. Not only has the composer refrained from introducing contrast by means of triple-meter arioso passages, but he has abjured his characteristic word-painting as well as any sustained expressive text setting. As we shall see, these omissions distinguish Ulisse's first monologue from every one of his subsequent appearances. It is worth noting that this is our only view of Ulisse alone: the real Ulisse, we might say—although the full realization of his character takes place only gradually, over the course of the next four acts. In every other scene, it seems, Ulisse is acting, playing a role for someone. In contrast to his opening monologue, each step of his self-revelation, to Minerva, Eumete, Telemaco, and finally Penelope, is sealed in song, an extravagant triple-meter duet as one at a time he regains the elements of his world, coming ever closer to its center.

ACT I, SCENE 8: ULISSE AND MINERVA

The difference is apparent as soon as he interacts with Minerva in the very next scene, a scene more clearly marked by Monteverdi's characteristic intervention. For not only does it entail a major cut in the libretto, which eliminates extraneous detail and tightens the interaction between the two characters, it also involves a significant textual interpolation, as well as several long arioso expansions and abundant musical translations of textual images (and feelings).

Ulisse addresses the goddess, whom he fails to recognize in her shepherd's disguise, in a flattering tone, as "Vezzoso pastorello," with a triple-meter arioso performance of the line entailing threefold sequential repetition of "vezzoso." This is not the vulnerable, despairing Ulisse of our first acquaintance but the shrewd Ulisse of legend, using his wiles—and Monteverdi's musical art—to achieve his goal: to gain information. Thanks to a large cut, of thirteen lines, Ulisse's request that Minerva tell him where he is brings a direct answer, "Itaca è questa," rather than a series of further questions and answers tangential to the matter at hand.

As Ulisse regales the disguised Minerva with his false life story, his artistry (that is, his rhetorical effort to cover up his deception) manifests itself in the vividly exaggerated musical illustration of his textual images: a descending sixteenth-note scale on "vento," an ascending *stile concitato* sequential pattern on "a forza cacciati," another sequential pattern of syncopations against the bass on "hebbi nemico il caso," a second scalar setting of "venti," this time in eighth notes, and then, following his description of falling asleep and awakening, a final diminished fourth resolving to a fifth to overemphasize his pain.

When Minerva reveals herself, he responds with another arioso performance of two lines of text, which the composer expands through internal repetitions and by bringing the first line back at the end:

Chi crederebbe, *chi crederebbe* mai,   Who would believe it,
Le Deità vestite in human velo,   goddesses dressed in human garb!
Chi crederebbe, che crederebbe mai!

Ulisse's speech closes with a long lyrical agreement to follow the goddess's advice, again characterized by arioso expansion involving extensive textual repetition:

Hor consolato *consigliato, or consigliato, consigliato, or consigliato* seguo
I tuoi saggi consigli.

One has the feeling here that Ulisse is no longer manipulating his rhetoric but, genuinely consoled (or encouraged) by his good fortune, has found his voice. In fact, he can hardly contain himself, interrupting Minerva's next speech with an effusive arioso exclamation, "O fortunato Ulisse," before she reaches its most important part, the last two lines, after which Badoaro had originally placed his response, and where Monteverdi's Ulisse repeats it, as a refrain:

MINERVA: Incognito sarai,   Disguised will you be,
   Non conosciuto andrai sin che tu vegga   unrecognized will you go, until you see
   De' Proci tuoi rivali   the brazen impudence
   La sfaciata baldanza,   of your rivals, the Suitors,
ULISSE: *O fortunato, o fortunato Ulisse*   *O fortunate Ulisse!*
MINERVA: Di Penelope casta   the unwavering constancy
   L'immutabil costanza.   of chaste Penelope.
ULISSE: O fortunato, *o fortunato* Ulisse.

Following a brief duet with Minerva, Ulisse closes the act with a strophic aria based on the refrain material: "O fortunato Ulisse."(See Example 1 above, Chap. 5.) Although the librettist anticipated the aria refrain in the previous scene, it was the composer, by introducing it first as an interruption and then emphasizing it through arioso expansion and repetition, in that scene and in the aria as well, who rendered it emblematic of Ulisse's recovered voice—and key, now G: Fortune and Time are clearly now on his side ("Per lui guerreggiano il Tempo e la Fortuna!"). (He will use that voice more and more in his subsequent scenes with Eumete and Telemaco.) This, we hardly need reiterate, is in contrast to Penelope, who resists singing until the very end of the opera. His despondency conquered, he is already on the move toward his goal, a changed, or at least transformed, man. She stands still, waiting.

ACT 2: EUMETE, TELEMACO

Disguised as an old man, Ulisse does not reveal himself to Eumete when they first meet in act 2, scene 4, nor does he sing. The only breach in his recitative comes at the point where he assures the shepherd, in G, that Ulisse is alive ("Ulisse, Ulisse è vivo / La patria lo vedrà, / Penelope l'havrà"), an assurance underscored by highly emphatic musical setting in triple meter.[27] In 2.6 (a continuation of 2.4), they are joined by Telemaco who, in the intervening scene, probably intended to take place simultaneously with 2.4, has been brought back to Ithaca by Minerva. Here they sing not one but two duets, the first celebrating Telemaco's return, the second the prospect of Ulisse's. Though both duets are indicated in the libretto, their texts are very short, the first comprising a quatrain, the second only a tercet. It is no surprise that Monteverdi expands them by his usual means, repeating text and stretching individual words with melismatic insertions. (The first takes up thirty-six measures, the second thirty-two.) The second of the duets has the added feature of being based, initially, on the major descending tetrachord ostinato, by now a standard indicator of love. (In fact, with its two like voices overlapping, the duet recalls the final duet in *Incoronazione*, "Pur ti miro," as well as the earlier, equally sensuous duet between Nerone and Lucano.) (The conclusion of this scene, in which Telemaco sends Eumete off to advise Penelope of his return, creates a nice parallel with that of the very next scene in which Ulisse sends Telemaco off to perform the same task.)

In revealing himself to Telemaco in the following scene (2.7), Ulisse both uses and inspires song. Though Badoaro designs their dialogue strictly as recitative, culminating in a substantial duet, Monteverdi, as is his custom, highlights a few key textual passages by means of lyrical setting, passages that mark the progressive stages of Ulisse's self-revelation: Telemaco's shock at the transformation of the old man into a younger one

---

27. This measured, triple-meter emphasis on Ulisse's name is recalled several times by Eumete: in his report to Telemaco in 2.6 ("Egli, *egli* m'accerta che d'Ulisse il ritorno fia di poco lontan da questo giorno"), his subsequent declaration to Penelope ("Ulisse, *Ulisse, Ulisse* il nostro rege, il tuo consorte, è vivo, è vivo . . ."), and in his report to Ulisse of the Suitors' reponse to the news of his arrival ("il nome, *il nome, il nome* sol d'Ulisse quest'alme ree trafisse") in the final scene of act 3. These are all instances of deixis, or pointing. For a useful summary of this and other distinctive characteristics of dramatic texts as codified in contemporary linguistic theory, see Calcagno, " 'Imitar col canto,' " 386–92, esp. 390.

("Non sia più chi più chiami / Questa caduta amara / Se col morir ringiovenir s'impara"),
for instance, is set in two different musical styles, the first, for the first two lines, in triple
meter ("Non sia più chi più chiami, *non sia più, non sia più* questa caduta amara"), the
second ("Se col morir ringiovanir, *se col morir ringiovanir, ringiovanir* s'impara") in duple.
Ulisse's invitation to Telemaco to exchange his surprise for joy because an old beggar lost
is a father gained is also expanded and set in triple meter ("Telemaco, convienti / Cangiar
le meraviglie in allegrezze, *in allegrezze, in allegrezze* / Che se perdi il Mendico, il padre acquisti, *il padre, il padre, il padre acquisti*"). And finally, Ulisse's declaration of his identity
("Ulisse, Ulisse sono / Testimonio è Minerva / Quella, *quella, quella* che te portò per l'aria
a volo") is also set lyrically, in triple and then duple meter.

The climax of the scene, however, and its lyrical high point, is the duet between father
and son. More extensive than Ulisse's previous duets with Minerva and Eumete, this one
marks the most crucial stage, thus far, of his return. The formal outlines are provided by
the librettist: first father and son rejoice in finding one another, alternating in a succession of five rhyming pairs of *settenari;* then they join together for a rhymed quatrain,
abba, to enunciate the moral of the situation. Predictably, the composer's interventions
come in the first, more emotional section, where he undercuts Badoaro's strict *settenario*
alternation, breaking up some lines, repeating others, and joining some together in
passages of simultaneous singing. The result is a freedom of expression that appropriately
raises and projects the emotional temperature of the reunion.[28]

Ulisse sings another aria in G, at the end of the act ("Godo, rido") in response to Eumete's report of the Suitors' frightened reaction to the news of his arrival. As mentioned
earlier, the composer cuts and restructures Badoaro's text, eliminating all of Eumete's references to Penelope to focus on the Suitors. And he turns Badoaro's five-line aria text into a
rather substantial bipartite form, its stepwise roulades and decorative melismas mimicking
Ulisse's laughter and communicating eloquently his pleasure in hearing of the Suitors'
fear.[29] (See Example 3 above, Chap. 5.)

ACT 5: REUNION

Ulisse has repeatedly turned to song to express his growing optimism—with Minerva, with
Eumete, and with Telemaco, and in his defeat of the Suitors. His confrontation with Penelope,
so long awaited by him and by us, will be different. Resourceful Ulisse will not attempt to
reach her with music, but with speech, the mode of expression she herself had adopted, we
imagine, ever since his departure. Monteverdi takes special pains with Ulisse's speech,

---

28. This is the intercalation Carter (*Musical Theatre,* 240) points out as having been already present in the
libretto, and which he uses to support the idea that the libretto was edited from the score. But see my objec-
tions in Chap. 3, n. 40.

29. Discussed in Chap. 5, pp. 154–55.

EXAMPLE 13. Ulisse, "O delle mie fatiche" (*Il ritorno d'Ulisse*, 5.10 [or 3.10], mm. 1–6).

O del-le mie fa-ti-che Me-ta dol-ce_e so-a-ve, Por-to ca-ro,_a-mo-ro-so, Do-ve cor-ro, do-ve cor - ro_al ri-po-so,—

mustering his most carefully controlled eloquence; there is no sign of anything like Ulisse's erratic, uncontrolled anger on the Ithacan shore. Even in the scene with the Suitors, Ulisse comes across as a very well-spoken beggar; he is especially decorous and restrained when he asks for the bow, though his words are laden with meaning for the composer (and librettist, and probably the original audience).[30] Of course he is ready to burst through the constraints of decorum when he needs to: as he strings the bow and invokes the force of the *stile concitato,* first to rally the gods and then, with full orchestral reinforcement, to enact his murder of the Suitors.[31] But it is when he finally appears as himself, for the first time since his scene with Telemaco two acts earlier, that he harnesses his eloquence most effectively. Here, notably, Badoaro's libretto is adequate to the task. The composer adds very little, content to exploit rhetorical emphases—parallelisms, repetitions, enjambments, images— already built into the text.

In a series of brief speeches, each countered by Penelope's stolid denial of her feelings and refusal to trust her senses, Ulisse enlists all his powers of persuasion, an effort marked, among other things, by repeated attempts to dislodge Penelope from her fixation on d, symbol of her faith—he moves several times to a, finally to G. He presses his suit with wideranging, strongly shaped melodic lines, extended phrases, and expressive harmony. Her resistance, in contrast, is expressed in speech-like music of narrow compass placed low in her range, short phrases, strongly cadential harmony, and uniformly slow harmonic rhythm.

Ulisse's eloquence is in full flight when he first appears on stage, resplendent in his own clothes. As he has been announced by Telemaco with a strong cadence on G— "Eccolo affè"—his entrance on high E introduces an abrupt shift, with E harmonized as a first-inversion dominant of a/A (the key of Love): "O delle mie fatiche / Meta dolce e soave, / Porto caro, amoroso, / Dove corro al riposo" (Example 13). These words are beautifully performed by Ulisse's gradually unfolding melodic line, a six-measure phrase extended through a series of suspensions and secondary dominants that delay harmonic resolution until the end. The descending suspension-filled melody of his "fatiche" finally,

---

30. An argument proposed in Chap. 1, pp. 10–12.

31. He performs his defeat of the Suitors in an elaborate, aria-like triple-meter *stile concitato* passage in G major, accompanied by strings, created by Monteverdi from a single *endecasillabo,* "alle morti, alle stragi, alle rovine" (Facsimile 17).

after repeated postponement, curls briefly upward before descending once more to reach its "sweet goal" and come to rest.

Ever resourceful, in each of his subsequent attempts to move her he tries a different tack—he questions her response ("is *this* how you welcome your husband?"), he works to evoke her pity and guilt ("for you I risked death?"), and finally he asserts his identity ("I am that very Ulisse"), reminding her that he killed the Suitors—but she rejects each of his statements in turn as lies, deception, magic. Only when Ericlea, anguished witness to the scene, finally intervenes to testify on Ulisse's behalf does Penelope begin the painful process of yielding. Voicing her doubts for the first time, she struggles with the conflicting claims of love and honor. Love inspires a new key, F, but thoughts of honor lead back to d. Seizing upon the opening provided by her conflict, and especially by her poignant, provocative reference to her chaste bed, the ever wily Ulisse makes his final plea in his longest speech of the scene. Badoaro could hardly have served him better here, presenting him with ten sinewy lines almost completely devoid of rhyme and featuring a series of four consecutive enjambments:

Del tuo casto pensier io so, *io so* 'l costume,	Of your chaste thoughts I know the habit,
So che 'l letto pudico,	I know that your unsullied bed,
Che tranne Ulisse solo, altri non vide,	which none but Ulisse has ever seen,
Ogni notte da te s'adorna e copre	is adorned and covered every night by you
Con un serico drappo	with a silken cloth
Di tua man[o] conteso, in cui si vede	woven by your own hand, in which is depicted,
Col virginal suo coro	with her virginal companions,
Diana effigiata.	Diana's image.
M'accompagnò mai sempre	I was always accompanied
Memoria, *memoria* così grata.[32]	by this sweet memory.

Taking up the image of her chaste bed—an image invented by Badoaro, we remember—Ulisse begins his argument in understated prose; his simple repeated notes form tonic triads over an unmoving bass in G (Example 14a). But the enjambed lines in the middle of his speech inspire one last melodic ascent of an octave, extended over nine measures and reaching a climax on the same high E, and resolution on the same low A, as his very first speech in the scene. The tension here created dissipates in the final four-measure phrase, in which Ulisse returns calmly—and self-confidently—to G for a cadence. Recalling the passionate opening of the scene, this final burst of eloquence finds its mark: "Yes," she responds, "yes, yes, yes" (Example 14b).

---

32. Badoaro may have intended this as an allusion to Penelope's weaving (remember that his only overt reference to that ruse, in Penelope's opening monologue, was cut in Monteverdi's setting). Indeed, there is some reason for thinking that Penelope's tapestry-in-progress featured a complicated narrative design—which is why anyone could believe that it could take three years to complete (Clayton, *A Penelopean Poetics*, 34).

EXAMPLE 14. Ulisse and Penelope (*Il ritorno d'Ulisse,* 5.10 [or 3.10]).

a. Ulisse, "Del tuo casto pensiero," mm. 101–20.

b. Penelope, "Or sì ti riconosco," mm. 121–33.

I have already described Penelope's moving capitulation: her arioso, in Ulisse's key of G (though her music ends in d), and then, in response to Ulisse's urgings, her great aria "Illustratevi, o cieli." Her rediscovery of song, the language of love, inspires equal lyricism in him. Long abstemious in word repetition, they both indulge now. As he urges her to unfetter her tongue, his own tongue becomes unfettered: triple meter, expansive text repetition, and repeated emphasis on his high E warm his response: "Sciogli, *sciogli, sciogli* la lingua, deh sciogli / Per allegrezza i nodi, / *Sciogli* un sospir, *un sospir,* un'ohimè, la voce snodi."

Following her aria, their voices finally join in a duet, the first time they have sung together, sharing the language of love they have not spoken in twenty years. Rarely has an operatic duet earned its meaning so completely, so credibly. In one final editorial intervention, a thorough recasting of libretto material, Monteverdi renders this duet a fitting conclusion to all of the preceding action. Badoaro's text is rather shapeless, though one can discern an overall telescoping of verse lengths from seven syllables to five, three, and four ("Sospirato mio sole," "Non si ramenti," "Del goder," "sì, sì vita"), and finally to three-syllable lines again at the end ("sì sì sì"):

ULISSE: Sospirato mio sole	My longed-for sun,
PENELOPE: Rinovata [ritrovata] mia luce!	My refound light.
ULISSE: Porto, quiete e riposo.	Quiet and peaceful harbor.
ULISSE, PENELOPE: Bramato, sì, ma caro,	Desired and dear.
bramato sì, ma caro, caro,	
bramato sì, ma caro, caro, caro.	
PENELOPE: Per te [cui] gli andati affanni	For you I learn
A benedir imparo.	to bless my past torments.
ULISSE: Non si rammenti	No longer remember
Più de' tormenti;	the torments
PENELOPE: *sì, sì, vita, sì sì*	*yes, yes, my life, yes, yes*
ULISSE: Tutto è piacer.	All is pleasure:
PENELOPE: *sì, sì, vita, sì, sì.*	
PENELOPE: Fuggan dai petti	Let flee from our breasts
Dogliosi affetti;	all painful feelings,
ULISSE: *sì, sì, sì, core, sì sì.*	
PENELOPE: Tutto è goder.	All is joy
ULISSE: *sì, sì, sì, core, sì sì.*	
[A 2]: [Venuto è il dì]	The day is come.

Score	*Libretto*
ULISSE AND PENELOPE [A 2]: Del piacer	PENELOPE: Del goder
Del goder	ULISSE: Del piacer
Venuto è 'l dì.	
Sì, sì, *sì,* vita,	PENELOPE: Sì, sì, vita

Sì, sì *sì,* core   ULISSE: Sì, sì, core

sì, sì, sì, *sì.*   A 2: Sì, sì, sì.

The duet begins with a succession of six *settenari,* the first four for the lovers in alternation, the last two for Penelope alone. These are followed by a pair of three-line stanzas of *quinari,* one for each of the lovers, ending in a shared line, and finally four alternating *quaternari,* again ending in a shared line. Monteverdi transforms the first part of this exchange (ll. 1–3) into a well-shaped lyrical statement in which the reunited lovers first alternate (as in Badoaro), with Ulisse's ascending line mirrored by Penelope's descending one. But then, after a shift from triple to duple meter, they overlap (Penelope's line 4, repeated many times by both), creating suspensions with one another; finally joining together to sing in parallel thirds (line 4 again)—a progression that reenacts in miniature their rapprochement. As the meter moves back and forth between triple and duple, the harmony vacillates between a and d, interspersed with a few secondary dominants. Penelope then sings lines 5 and 6 alone, as in Badoaro; her music is a sequential augmentation of their previous shared material.

The final and longest section of the duet is constructed over an ostinato bass—an attenuated version of a ciaccona, extended from four to six triple-meter measures by means of a deceptive cadence. Here the composer intercalates two of Badoaro's textual units— the *quinari* and *quaternari*—so that once again the music of the lovers overlaps. First Ulisse sings his stanza ("Non si ramenti"), Penelope joining him with text taken from their later exchange ("Sì, sì, vita, sì, sì"). Then their positions are reversed: Penelope sings her stanza ("Fuggan dai petti") with Ulisse supplying counterpoint to text taken from their later exchange ("sì, sì, sì, core, sì, sì"). That later exchange never takes place: instead the lovers sing those lines together in sixths to bring the duet to a close on a. This final simultaneous passage is by far their longest in the opera. The unstable harmony, avoidance of cadences, unpredictable repetition of various textual units and irregular overlaps between voices, sometimes with different, sometimes the same text, the repetitive vocal lines and rhythmic disjunctions—repeated shifts between duple and triple meter, syncopations— create an almost dizzying effect, which does not resolve until the concluding passage of parallel sixths. Here the reunited lovers sing the same text simultaneously for the first and only time in the opera, first in C, then in a. Even the ostinato pattern dissipates here, losing itself in the bliss of their union, so long postponed, so deeply desired.

In condensing and restructuring this text, the composer has created a final duet that in many ways resembles "Pur ti miro," the final duet of *L'incoronazione di Poppea.* Clearly he had to work hard to do this, but his dramatic instinct was true. The trajectory of this long scene, with its escalating tension so wonderfully resolved in the final duet, mirrors that of the opera as a whole. Monteverdi's opera ends here, focused on the reunited lovers. It omits Badoaro's brief epilogue: Ulisse's words to Minerva, the formal renewal of the lovers' marriage vows, and the Ithacan chorus, were probably cut when the original prologue was replaced, possibly for practical reasons, or possibly because the composer was determined to save his trump card for last. Their absence, for whatever reasons, enabled Monteverdi to do what he did best: to convey the emotions of individuals, to portray a human drama.

⁊

Monteverdi's revisions to the text of *Ritorno*—his cuts, rearrangements, repetitions, and expansions—tend to heighten the most outstanding features of Badoaro's libretto: the strong, simple plot line, the powerful polar opposition of the two protagonists, and the structural integrity of the individual acts, each of which marks a distinct stage in the inevitable progress toward resolution. Character development, too, is enhanced by such revisions. One of the composer's most effective means of characterization, as we have repeatedly stressed, is his exploitation of the continuum—and contrast—between speech and song, his shift from one to the other to signal heightened feeling.[33] Often such shifts involve alterations in the text. The protagonists, as we have seen, are defined by their contrasting—and evolving—relationship to song. For Penelope (as for most of the characters), song is intimately linked to love. She does not (cannot?) sing until she accepts her husband's return. His relation to song is more complex and multifaceted: linked to enthusiasm as well as love, to pretense as well as truth, it is a means of expression that he himself controls. Like the composer, Ulisse could manipulate lyricism, using it when it served his purpose (as in his confrontation with Minerva), abjuring it when he judged speech or recitative eloquence more potent (as in his seduction of Penelope). Monteverdi's identification with his wily hero is no mere rhetorical ploy.

Deepening a Psychological Drama

Gian Francesco Busenello's libretto for *L'incoronazione di Poppea* was also radically reshaped by Monteverdi, the composer once again more fully realizing the dramatic potential latent in the text. Again he intensifies the most distinctive features of the libretto, but these are very different in the later work. *Ritorno* displayed an epic simplicity, reflected in the uncomplicated clarity of its characters, the linearity of its action. *Incoronazione* offers a more human world, a plot complicated by ambivalence and deceit, ambiguity and conflict, and a more intricate network of character interaction.

If in *Ritorno* Monteverdi emphasizes the deliberate structural pillars at beginnings and ends of acts, he increases the fluidity of *Incoronazione,* enhancing the naturalism that overrides the conventional boundaries of scene, scene group, and even act. (It is worth remembering that Busenello's libretto is already extraordinary for its *liaisons des scènes*—nine in the first act are linked). (See Table 15 above, Chap. 5.) Most important, rather

---

33. Carter makes a related point when he characterizes *Ritorno* as having "problematized the status of aria within the operatic endeavor" ("'In Love's Harmonious Consort,'" 11).

than merely strengthening the particular defining features of the characters, in opposition or contrast to one another, as he does in *Ritorno,* Monteverdi explores the special psychological complexity with which Busenello has endowed them. Both through his restructuring of the text and through the music he chooses to set it, he probes their ambivalences, their vulnerabilities, their self-doubts, and their effects on one another—that is, their humanity.

The composer's impact on Busenello's libretto is manifested in many ways, but his interventions in its actual text can be reduced to two general types, which are often used to reinforce one another: *intercalation* or displacement (rearrangement) of lines and *verbal repetitions* of various-sized units—ranging from entire lines that form refrains to single words. Although both of these techniques are certainly used in *Ritorno*—we have seen some examples in Penelope's lament, in Ulisse's "O fortunato," and in the final scene—they are much more frequent, and much more appropriate in *Incoronazione.* Intercalation, which, by definition, increases the interaction between characters, can transform stilted dialogues into more natural ones that imitate ordinary speaking. And Busenello's already naturalistic confrontations lend themselves particularly well to such treatment. (The most famous intercalation may be the one linking scenes 1 and 2 of the first act.) [34] Likewise, the psychological potential of repetition, particularly when exaggerated, finds an ideal testing ground in characters like Busenello's, whose motivations are not always on the surface. Excessive repetition of key words can sometimes go beyond the content of the text itself to reveal the speaker's deeper feelings. The rhetorical norm, for purposes of emphasis—like italics—might be a single repetition or at most two. Anything more cannot help but betray the speaker's emotional involvement in the issue.[35]

One of the simplest, yet most effective, instances of intercalation, coupled with exaggerated verbal repetition, occurs in the grand confrontation between Seneca and Nerone in act 1, scene 9, a confrontation that lies at the very heart of the drama. Although my focus for the moment is on the verbal text, the musical setting is obviously crucial to the passionate effect of this argument, particularly the *stile concitato* or warlike style of repeated notes and triadic figures setting the repeated words. Text and music portray more than an adversarial relationship here. They reveal the basic differences between the two men. Hysterical repetition of text bespeaks Nerone's excitability, and his loss of control—perhaps even his guilty conscience: he protests too much. Seneca's moral self-confidence, on the other hand, his self-righteousness, is embodied in his straightforward, conclusive responses to Nerone. He has little need to repeat text to emphasize his position. Their confrontation is energized by tonal conflict that appears finally to resolve to

---

34. See above, Chap. 6, p. 211. We should remember that the presence of intercalations in two of the *Incoronazione* librettos—Udine and Naples—are the main evidence that they were copied from scores.

35. A number of contemporary linguists have concerned themselves with the communicative functions of repetition. See, for example, Deborah Tannen, *Talking Voices: Repetition, Dialogue, and Imagery in Conversational Discourse* (Cambridge: Cambridge University Press, 1989), esp. chap. 3; and Fónagy, *La ripetizione creativa,* also chap. 3. Calcagno, "Staging Musical Discourses," 228–35, summarizes some of the issues.

TABLE 18
L'incoronazione di Poppea, 1.9, Seneca and Nerone

NERONE: Son risoluto insomma,	I am at last determined
O Seneca, o maestro,	O Seneca, my teacher,
Di rimover Ottavia	to remove Ottavia from her place
Dal posto di consorte,	as my wife
E di sposar, *e di sposar, e di sposar* Poppea.	and to marry Poppea.
SENECA: Signor, nel fondo alla maggior dolcezza	Sire, at the bottom of great sweetness
Spesso giace nascosto il pentimento.	often lies hidden regret.
Consiglier scellerato è il sentimento,	Feelings are a poor counselor;
Ch'odia le leggi, e la ragion disprezza.	They hate laws and disparage reason.
NERONE: La legge è per chi serve, e se vogl'io,	Law is for servants, and if I wish
Posso, *posso* abolir l'antica e indur la nova;	I can abolish the old and create a new one.
E partito l'imperio, e il ciel di Giove,	The universe is divided; heaven is Jupiter's,
Ma del mondo, *del mondo* terren,	but on earth I rule alone.
del mondo terren lo scettro è mio, *lo scettro è mio.*	
SENECA: Sregolato voler non è volere,	Unruled will is not law,
Ma (dirò con tua pace) egli è furor,	but (by your leave) it is madness.
egli è furor, egli è furore.	
NERONE: La ragione è misura rigorosa	Reason is a stern rule
Per chi ubbidisce et non per chi comanda.	for those who obey, but not for those who command.
SENECA: Anzi, *anzi* l'irragionevole comando	On the contrary, irrational orders
Distrugge, *distrugge* l'obbedienza.	destroy obedience.
NERONE: Lascia i discorsi, io voglio,	Cease this argument. I wish things my way.
voglio, voglio a modo mio.	
SENECA: Non irritar, *non irritar, non irritar*	Do not annoy the people and the senate.
il popol e 'l Senato.	
NERONE: Dal Senato e del popolo non curo.	What care I for people and senate?
SENECA: Cura almeno te stesso, e la tu fama.	At least think of yourself and your reputation.
NERONE: Trarrò la lingua a chi vorra biasmarmi.	I shall tear the tongue from him who speaks ill of me.
SENECA: Più muti che farai, più parleranno.	The more mutes you create, the more they will speak.
NERONE: Ottavia è infrigidita, e infeconda.	Ottavia is frigid and barren.
SENECA: Chi ragione non ha, cerca pretesti.	He who has no reasons searches for excuses.
NERONE: A chi può ciò che vuol ragion non manca.	The mighty never lack reasons.
SENECA: Manca la sicurezza all'opre ingiuste.	Unjust deeds lack conviction.
NERONE: Sarà sempre più giusto il più potente.	He who is most powerful is most just.

TABLE 18 *(continued)*

SENECA: Ma chi non sa regnar sempre può meno.	But he who cannot rule is always less powerful.
NERONE: 1 La forza, *la forza, la forza, la forza* è legge in pace,	Force is the law in peace
3 e spada, *e spada* in guerra,	and sword in war,
5 È bisogno non ha della ragione.	and has no need of reason.
SENECA: 2 La forza, *la forza* accende gl'odi,	Force kindles hate
4 e turba il sangue, *e turba il sangue;*	and excites the blood,
6 La ragione, *la ragione* regge gl'huomini e gli Dei.	Reason governs men and gods.
NERONE: Tu, *tu, tu* mi sforzi allo sdegno, *mi sforzi allo sdegno, allo sdegno, allo sdegno, allo sdegno, allo sdegno;*	You are rousing my anger;
al tuo dispetto,	despite you,
E del popol in onta, e del Senato,	and the people, the senate, despite
E d'Ottavia, e del cielo, e dell'abisso,	Ottavia and heaven and hell,
Siansi giuste od ingiuste, *siansi giuste od ingiuste* le mie voglie,	whether my wishes are just or unjust,
Hoggi, hoggi Poppea sarà mia moglie, *sarà mia moglie, sarà mia moglie.*	today, today Poppea will be my wife.

G, a key associated with Nerone throughout the opera, as the emperor asserts his ultimate victory over Seneca's C and d with threefold repetition of the key phrase "sarà mia moglie, sarà mia moglie, sarà mia moglie," leaving little doubt that he will have his way (Table 18; intercalations are numbered). But the scene ends ambiguously. Not cowed by Nerone's victorious cadence in G, Seneca initiates an epilogue of maxims—kings should be guiltless unless their guilt serve the greater glory of empire; servitude to a mere woman's wiles is base and plebian; the worst side always wins when force meets reason—returning first to his characteristic d, and thence, after Nerone reasserts G, back to the key (and mood) in which he began, C. One might well conclude that the two adversaries have finished in a draw.[36]

The effect of intercalation and word repetition is not limited to the strengthening of individual confrontations between characters, however. These techniques can contribute more globally to the shaping of the drama as a whole. One traditional interpretation of *Incoronazione* sees it as a gradual, stepwise defeat of reason by passion. Each step of the downward spiral—Nerone's sexual enslavement to Poppea, the death of Seneca, the exile of Ottavia, and the ultimate coronation of Poppea—is choreographed by Poppea herself,

---

36. See Chafe, *Musical Language*, 325–28, for a discussion of the tonal structure of this confrontation. This scene comes up again in Chap. 8 below.

and each is determined in a scene with Nerone. In each of these scenes Monteverdi's revisions of the verbal text play a crucial role.

POPPEA'S PROGRESS

In their first scene (1.3) intercalation becomes a powerful means of establishing Poppea's influence on Nerone, as Monteverdi aggressively shifts, interrupts, and transposes Busenello's text.[37] Like every other conflict in the opera, this one too is enacted in terms of tonality: in this case between her d and his F.[38]

Nerone has evidently made a move to disengage himself from Poppea's embrace, for she opens the scene by imploring him to stay (Table 19). Impatient to be gone (perhaps recognizing her power over him), he does not wait for Poppea to finish her opening speech but rather interrupts her after the first sentence (with a line taken from later in the scene), urging her to release him—and wrenching her d tonality into F: "Poppea, lascia, ch'io parta" (Poppea, let me leave). But this interruption only stimulates Poppea to try all the harder to detain him; she pulls the music back to her key as she repeats her opening line. Monteverdi makes her plea more urgent this second time by repeating words and by setting it in a higher range. Busenello's original, "Signor, deh non partire" is extended to "non partir, non partir, Signor, deh non partire." Her speech concludes with a varied development of this same textual refrain, "Deh, non dir di partir," now reaching still higher, to the high point of her melodic line, before dissolving gradually, with chromatic languor, to the low point. By using the first line of Nerone's speech too early, thereby justifying an extra repetition of Poppea's refrain in response, the composer increases the lovers' interaction at the same time as he emphasizes Poppea's persistence. Monteverdi's Poppea is even more reluctant than Busenello's to see her lover leave, a reluctance the composer will reinforce later in the scene.

Urged on by her unwillingness to release him, Nerone, trying in vain to move back to his key, F, begins to explain that it would be unwise for Rome to learn of their union until he has divorced Ottavia. Now it is Poppea who interrupts—and her interruptions too are not in the libretto. Twice she prevents Nerone from completing the sentence that will promise the very action she has been waiting for: his repudiation of Ottavia. (Her interruptions, in italics, are bracketed in the text.) After each interruption he takes up the thought again, on a higher pitch level: "In sin ch'Ottavia . . . in sin ch'Ottavia non rimane esclusa . . . in sin ch'Ottavia non rimane esclusa col repudio da me." When he finally completes his statement, it is all the more emphatic for having been delayed. Poppea engineered its delay; Monteverdi engineered her. By interrupting him, egging him on, Poppea has

---

37. Lewis, "Love as Persuasion," uses Poppea's dominance in this scene as well as others between Poppea and Nerone to argue the inauthenticity of "Pur ti miro."

38. Discussed in Chafe, *Tonal Language*, 348–59.

TABLE 19

L'incoronazione di Poppea, 1.3, Poppea and Nerone

POPPEA: Signor, deh, non partire;	My lord, please do not leave me.
Sostien che queste braccia	Let these arms
Ti circondino il collo	encircle your neck,
Come le tue bellezze	just as your charms
Circondino il cor mio.	encircle my heart.
NERONE: *Poppea, lascia ch'io parta.*	*Poppea, let me leave.*
POPPEA: *Non partir, non partir, Signor, deh*	*Do not leave, Do not leave, my lord, please*
non partire.	*do not leave.*
A pena spunta l'alba, e tu che sei	The morning has scarce begun, and you,
L'incarnato mio Sole,	my sun incarnate,
La mia palpabil luce	my tangible light,
E l'amoroso dì della mia vita,	and beloved day of my life,
Vuoi sì repente far da me partita?	do you wish to leave me so soon?
Deh, non dir	Oh, say not
Di partir,	that you are going,
Che di voce sì amara a un solo accento,	for even at the sound of these bitter words,
Ahi, perir, ahi, spirar quest'alma io sento.	ah, I feel my soul dying, breathing its last.
NERONE: [*Poppea, lascia ch'io parta.*]	[*Poppea, let me leave.*]
La nobiltà de' nascimenti tuoi	Because of your noble birth,
Non permette che Roma	Rome must not know
Sappia che siamo uniti	that we are united
In sin ch'Ottavia [P: *in sin che, in sin che?*],	until Octavia [*until what?*]
in sin ch'Ottavia non rimane esclusa	has been banished
[P: *Non rimane, non rimane*],	
in sin ch'Ottavia non rimane esclusa	
Col repudio da me.	through my repudiation.
POPPEA: Vanne, *vanne* ben mio,	Go, then, my beloved.
ben mio, vanne, vanne ben mio,	
ben mio, vanne ben mio.	

forced Nerone to repeat himself. And repetition breeds intensity and conviction. She has caused him to become more committed to the action he must take. It is Monteverdi who created this situation by adding Poppea's interruptions and by making each of Nerone's responses longer and more intense. Nerone never succeeds in reasserting his key. The scene will end in Poppea's d. Poppea's quick response to Nerone's final declaration, "in sin ch'Ottavia non rimane esclusa col ripudio da me," which now, after threefold hesitation, forcefully observes the enjambment between *endecasillabo* and final *senario*, is a masterpiece of characterization. Hardly has he finished uttering the phrase she had so long desired to hear and so effectively elicited, than she dismisses him, unceremoniously. Although their scene is far from over, this little command, "vanne, *vanne* ben mio" (you can go

TABLE 20

L'incoronazione di Poppea, 1.3, Poppea and Nerone, continued

NERONE: In un sospir, *sospir* che vien 　Dal profondo del sen, 　　*In un sospir, sospir che vien,* 　　*sospir che vien* 　　*dal profondo del sen,* 　Includo un bacio, o cara, *cara,* ed un addio. 　Si rivedrem ben tosto, *si, si rivedrem,* 　　*si rivedrem ben tosto Idolo mio,* 　　*si rivedrem ben tosto Idolo mio.*	In a sigh that comes from the depths of my breast, I enclose a kiss, o beloved, and a farewell. We will see each other soon again, 　my beloved.
POPPEA: Signor, sempre mi vedi, 　*sempre, sempre, sempre mi vedi,* 　Anzi mai non mi vedi. 　*Signor, sempre mi vedi, sempre, sempre,* 　　*sempre mi vedi, anzi mai non mi vedi,* 　Perché s'è ver, che nel tuo cor io sia, 　Entro al tuo sen celata, 　Non posso, *non posso, non posso* da tuoi 　　lumi esser mirata, 　*non posso, non posso, non posso da' tuoi* 　　*lumi esser mirata.* 　[Deh, non dir 　Di partir 　Che di voce sì amara a un solo accento, 　Ahi, perir, ahi, spirar quest'alma io sento.]	My sir, you always see me. and yet you see me not, because if it is true that I am in your heart, enclosed within your breast, I cannot be beheld by your eyes.
NERONE: Adorati miei rai, 　Deh, restatevi homai, *deh restatevi homai.* 　Rimanti, o mia Poppea, 　Cor, vezzo, e luce, *e luce* mia.	My beloved eyes, Oh, do not leave me. Remain, my Poppea, my heart, my beauty, my light.
POPPEA: *Deh, non dir* 　*Di partir* 　*Che di voce sì amara a un solo accento,* 　*Ahi, perir, ahi, spirar quest'alma io sento.*	
NERONE: Non temer, *non temer,* tu stai 　meco, *stai meco* a tutte l'hore. 　Splendor negl'occhi, e deità nel core.	Have no fear, you are 　always with me, Wondrous in my eyes and goddess in 　my heart.
POPPEA: *Tornerai?*	*Will you return?*
NERONE: Se ben io vo, 　Pur teco io stò.	Though I go, I remain with you.
POPPEA: *Tornerai?*	*Will you return?*
NERONE: Il cor dalle tue stelle 　Mai, mai non si divelle.	My heart from your stars can never, never be torn.

TABLE 20 *(continued)*

POPPEA: *Tornerai?*	*Will you return?*
NERONE: Io non posso da te,	I cannot live when I am separated from you.
non posso, non posso da te	
viver disgiunto	
Se non si smembra l'unità del punto,	unless unity can be divided.
se non si smembra l'unità del punto.	
POPPEA: Tornerai?	Will you return?
NERONE: Tornerò.	I will return.
POPPEA: Quando?	When?
NERONE: Ben tosto.	Very soon.
POPPEA: *Ben tosto,* Me 'l prometti?	*Very soon,* do you promise?
NERONE: Te 'l giuro.	I swear it.
POPPEA: E me l'osserverai?	And will you keep your oath?
NERONE: E s'a te non verrò, tu a me verrai.	If I don't come to you, then you will come to me.
POPPEA: *E me l'osserverai?*	
NERONE: *E s'a te non verrò, tu a me verrai.*	
POPPEA: A Dio,	Farewell,
NERONE: *a Dio,*	*Farewell,*
POPPEA: Nerone, *Nerone,* a Dio.	Farewell, Nerone.
NERONE: [A Dio] Poppea, *Poppea, a dio.*	Farewell, Poppea.
POPPEA: *A dio, Nerone, a dio*	
NERONE: *A dio, Poppea,* ben mio.	my beloved.

now), tacked on to the end of his *senario* to make an *endecasillabo,* conveys her intuitive response to having achieved a victory, emphasizing the nature of her agenda.[39]

There are further textual intercalations, displacements, and repetitions in this scene, all of them directed toward demonstrating Nerone's susceptibility to Poppea's charms. Finally, toward the end, having accepted the inevitability of Nerone's departure, Poppea now demands reassurance that he will return (Table 20). Four times she asks him, "Tornerai?" (Busenello has her ask only once.) Monteverdi anticipates the question, reiterating it at judicious intervals within Nerone's lengthy departure speech, and each time calling forth a different, longer response that ends on a successively higher scale degree. By splitting Nerone's single speech into three sections with Poppea's question, the composer maintains the intensity of the lovers' contact. Again, because she pushes him, his

39. Although, as already noted (Table 11, n. c, and Chap. 5, n. 95), most sources, following LV, give this command to Nerone, Np, LN, and U2 give it to Poppea, which makes more dramatic sense, particularly given Monteverdi's emphasis on Poppea's manipulation of Nerone. Indeed, the readings of LN and U2 should have greater weight because, as we have seen, they were probably copied from performance scores.

responses become increasingly ardent. Her last repetition finally elicits the concise answer provided by Busenello, "tornerò," a response whose decisiveness and conviction are strengthened by having been postponed. But it is not enough. Insatiable, she now needs to know when he will return, and is not satisfied until he swears that it will be soon.

The composer's treatment of the lovers' concluding "addio" puts the finishing psychological touch on the scene. Unwilling, almost unable to part, they stretch Busenello's mere pair of lines through passionate fragmentation and repetition into six lines of text, filling some nineteen measures of music. In this scene the relationship between the lovers portrayed in the text is enriched and intensified by the composer. His editing of the libretto, moving Busenello's text around, repeating individual words and lines, more fully realizes Poppea's power over Nerone.

She continues her emotional assault at their next meeting, several scenes later (1.10), a scene even more explicitly sensual than the one we have just considered:

POPPEA: A speranze sublime il cor m'inalzò	My heart rose to sublime hopes
Perché te lo commandi,	because you command it,
E la modestia mia riceve forza;	and my modesty is strengthened.
Ma troppo s'attraversa, ed impedisce	But too much lies in the way and prevents
Delle regie promesse il fin sovrano.	the final goal of your royal promises.
Seneca il tuo maestro,	Seneca your teacher,
Quello stoico sagace,	that wise Stoic,
Quel filosofo astuto,	that astute philosopher,
Che sempre tenta persuader altrui,	who always tries to persuade others
Che il tuo scettro, *il tuo scettro* dipenda sol da lui.	that your scepter depends on him alone.
NERONE: *Che, che?*	*What, what?*
POPPEA: *Che il tuo scettro, il tuo scettro dipenda sol da lui.*	
NERONE: Quel decrepito pazzo [P: *quel, quel]* ha tanto ardire? [P: *Ha tanto ardire.]*	That decrepit madman, has he dared so much?
NERONE: Ola, vada, *vada* un di voi	Hey, go there, one of you;
A Seneca volando, e imponga a lui,	fly to Seneca and command him
Ch'in questo giorno ei mora.	to die today.

At the end of the scene, and encouraged by Poppea's subtle insinuations regarding his failure to control his court, Nerone finally agrees, under the duress of sexual desire, to the second stage of Poppea's grand plan: to eliminate one of the chief impediments to Poppea's coronation, Seneca. Again, Poppea forces Nerone's hand. Monteverdi enhances Poppea's manipulation of Nerone through his own manipulation of text (using the same technique as he did in the previous instance). The key speech here comes at the end of the scene, after she has exploited his sexual attraction to her, bringing him to the point of ecstasy. (He was already prepared by his unsatisfactory confrontation with Seneca in the previous scene.) Here a single repetition—a slight emphasis—at the end of her speech, "Ch'il tuo scettro, *il tuo scettro*" (the only such repetition in the entire speech), has the desired effect. Monteverdi inserts some extra text here, first for Nerone: "che, che," which allows Poppea to repeat herself in a higher range; then for Poppea, to encourage him ("quel, quel"), then to confirm his own statement ("ha tanto ardire"). The careful machinations of Poppea, intensified by means of these repetitions, interruptions, and intercalations—and building upon the tension generated in the previous scene—seal Seneca's fate.

When the lovers meet again in act 3, scene 5, their first encounter since Seneca's death, Nerone has already shown himself capable of accomplishing the next step on his own. He has decided, in the previous scene, that, because she ordered Ottone to kill Poppea, Ottavia can now be legitimately banished. But before he has a chance to communicate his decision to Poppea, she makes the connection herself: "Now you have a reason to repudiate Ottavia," she declares, anticipating his conclusion. Although Busenello supplies these lines, Monteverdi adds the rhetorical emphasis, fourfold repetition of the key word "ripudio"—expressing just how great Poppea's satisfaction is:

NERONE: Non fu, non fu Drusilla, *no,*	It was not, not Drusilla
Ch'ucciderti tentò.	Who tried to kill you.
POPPEA: Chi fu, chi fu il fellone?	Who, who, then was the felon?
NERONE: Il nostro amico Ottone.	Our friend Ottone.
POPPEA: Egli da sé?	He alone?
NERONE: D'Ottavia fu il pensiero.	The idea was Ottavia's.
POPPEA: Hor hai, *hai* giusto cagione	Now you have good reason
Di passar al ripudio, *al ripudio,*	to move to repudiate her.
al ripudio, al ripudio, al ripudio.	
Hor hai, hai giusta cagione	
di passar al ripudio.	
NERONE: Hoggi, come promisi,	Today, as I promised,
Mia sposa, *mia sposa* tu sarai.	you will be my wife.
POPPEA: Sì caro dì, *sì caro dì, sì caro,*	Such a joyful day
sì caro, caro dì veder non sperò mai.	I never hoped to see.
NERONE: Per il nome di Giove, e per il mio,	In the name of Jove, and in mine
Hoggi sarai, ti giuro,	today will you be, I swear it,
Di Roma imperatrice.	empress of Rome.
In parola regal te n'assicuro.	By my royal word, I assure you.
POPPEA: *In parola, in parola*	
NERONE: *In parola regal, in parola regal te*	
n'assicuro.	
POPPEA: Idolo del cor mio, *del cor, del cor mio,*	Idol of my heart,
del cor, del cor, cor mio. Idolo del cor mio	
giunta è pur l'ora	the hour draws near
Ch'io del mio ben godrò.	when I will enjoy my beloved.

But Poppea uses her characteristic means of persuasion to close the deal. Although he has assured her that she will now be crowned empress, she questions him tremulously, echoing his own words with a mixture of calculated disbelief and, perhaps, even awe, at the imminence of her goal. Her interruptions—that is, Monteverdi's editorial intervention in the text—again lead Nerone to repeat his promise with much greater intensity.

Poppea's control over Nerone, and herself, emphasized in Monteverdi's careful editing of Busenello's text, is enacted in emphatically musical terms: her chief means of seduction is song. This is in contrast to Nerone, whose only actual victory in the opera, over Seneca, is achieved through brute force, not song: excessive text repetition and the *stile concitato,* rather than embodying self-control, demonstrate his lack of it. Even in his scene with Lucano, Nerone is eclipsed by the freedman's vocal prowess: although he initiates their singing contest, when his companion whips him up to a state of inarticulate frenzy, Nerone is reduced to brief exclamations of desire, over a descending tetrachord ostinato. (Monteverdi even increased Lucano's role by assigning him some text taken from one of the characters omitted from the scene, Petronio.) Indeed, as Poppea systematically achieves each one of her goals in turn, Nerone's singing becomes increasingly besotted—and controlled—by ostinato bass patterns: two different ones in his exchange with Poppea, beginning "Ma che dico" in 1.10; the descending tetrachord in "Bocca, bocca" in 2.5 (with Lucano); a longer, more freely structured pattern in his duet with Poppea in 3.5, "Ne più s'interporrà"; and finally, of course, in the infamous "Pur ti miro."

Although their cumulative impact on Poppea's conquest of Nerone is considerable, all the examples of text manipulation thus far considered are relatively small in scale. They involve either successive or nearly proximate lines, and very immediate effects—localized additions, echoes, and so forth. And they build on material immediately to hand in Busenello's text. But Monteverdi's editorial interventions in *Incoronazione* are occasionally much larger in scale, and they create a level of psychological complexity only suggested in the libretto. Several of these have to do with the opera's "second couple," Ottone and Drusilla.[40]

These two characters are psychologically very different from one another; at least initially they seem thoroughly incompatible. Ottone is tormented by Poppea's betrayal, introspective, and almost pathologically indecisive (and a poor dissembler), while Drusilla is positive, credulous, even self-deluding in her optimism—and unambivalent in her love: the difference is epitomized, as we shall see, in their affinity for song. She sings, even in her recitatives; he does not, even in his arias.

OTTONE'S CENTER

E pur io torno, *e pur io torno* qui, qual linea a centro,	Thus do I still return here, like a radius to its center,

---

40. Rather than merely a member of the conventional "second couple," Drusilla has been invested with central importance to the meaning of the opera by Fenlon and Miller, *Song of the Soul,* esp. 87–89, 93. According to them, the work is not a Triumph of Love, but a celebration of *constantia,* as embodied in the characters of Seneca and Drusilla. In her review of their book (*Music & Letters* 74 [1993]: 278–81), Susan McClary memorably punctured this interpretation: "Fenlon has reduced all the complex ironies . . . of the opera itself to that single theme [of constancy]. The opera Fenlon describes is not one I would ever care to hear" (p. 280).

Qual foco a sfera, e qual ruscello al mare,	like fire to the sun, and like stream to the sea.
E se ben luce, *ben luce* alcuna non m'appare,	And though I can see no light,
Ahi, *ah, ah, ah,* so ben io, che sta il mio sol	Ah, I know well that my sun is within.
qui dentro.	
E pur io torno, io torno qui, qual linea a centro.	

Ottone's very first utterance, from the balcony outside Poppea's house at dawn, establishes the nature of his commitment to her—and the nature of Monteverdi's commitment to him. Poppea is the focus of Ottone's universe, his sun, to whom he returns like a radius to a center, fire to the sun, a stream to the sea. The intensity of this attraction distorts his vision. He refuses to see the obvious, that the absence of a light outside Poppea's house means he is unwelcome; for him it is a perverse metaphor, a sun shining for him inside. In Monteverdi's setting of Ottone's opening line, centripetal force is enacted in a melody rooted to the tonic, D, weighted as if by gravity; after an initial attempt to rise to the dominant, it falls back to the tonic ("qui"—right here), where it remains virtually fixed, hardly able to move away again (Example 15). The melody embodies its text, is itself the line that returns to the center. Arrival at the center, however, is temporarily undermined by the action of the bass, which, though rising to meet the voice, passes it by deceptively, failing to cadence on the tonic until the end of the next line of poetry. Before that, the bass moves more steadily than the voice, but goes nowhere. Organized as an ostinato that hovers around—but never settles on—the dominant, it gives the illusion of movement, but by postponing cadential motion for twenty measures, it contributes a sense of restlessness.

A new, more forceful attempt to achieve the dominant, energized by a brief scalar melisma, is more successful, when Ottone notices and misinterprets the absence of the welcoming light. Does his long sighing dilation on "ah," intensified through the composer's repetition and melismatic expansion, suggest that the rationalization may have cost him some effort? His apprehension is conveyed in a pair of melismas that together elaborate an expressive scalar ascent of a ninth; their contour has been suggested by the bass in the previous passage. Ottone descends again to the tonic as he asserts that his sun must be inside—a conclusion reinforced by the return of his opening line in compressed form. This refrain was of course an insertion by the composer, the first of many to come, performing the literal meaning of "tornare" as it mimes Ottone's action. Like Ottone, the refrain returns; the music reaches out to match his actions and, finally, his feelings about Poppea. The force of her attraction is like the force of the tonic.[41]

---

41. As suggested by errors in the clef designations in Vp, this piece was originally in C major, like the ritornello that precedes and follows it; see above, Chap. 4. I discuss this passage in "Monteverdi's Mimetic Art," 119–20. Chafe, *Musical Language,* 294, points out the obvious resemblance of Ottone's stepwise scalar descent here to his later phrase "Otton, torna in te stesso" (act 2, scene 9), as well as to Penelope's "Torna il tranquillo al mare," suggesting that the descent is a musical figure (or melodic type) signifying "return to the normal, stable state of humanity." On the use of ostinato later in this scene, see Osthoff, *Monteverdistudien,* 63–65, and Reinhard Muller, "Basso Ostinato und die *imitatione del parlare* in Monteverdis *Incoronazione di Poppea,*" *AfM* 40 (1983): 1–23, esp. 4–5. This scene is discussed above, Chap. 6, pp. 209–11.

Ottone is more eloquent in this, his first utterance, and more coherent, than at any other time in the opera. Whereas later his melodic lines will have trouble exceeding the compass of a fifth, here he reaches a ninth as the culmination of a sequence of well-planned, elegant curves. If this passage bears any of the hallmarks Ottone's later rhetorical style—the restricted compass, inertia, and circularity of his melodies—in this case these qualities are rhetorically apt: they are specifically called for by the text.

In the libretto what comes next is a sequence of four poetic stanzas, suggesting a strophic aria, and in the opera a ritornello duly appears (see above, Chap. 6, pp. 209–10).

But Monteverdi sets the first of the stanzas as recitative, no doubt responding to the fact that it lacks the clear invocative charge of the others. In the series of expressively decorated strophic variations that starts with the second stanza, Ottone entreats Poppea to open the doors of her balcony, to awaken, and finally calls upon dreams to carry his sighs to her. The aria affirms the depths of his love with a certain elegance, due to a strong bass line, well-placed melismas, and careful attention to peaks and valleys in the melody—this despite the limited range and circular motion that become increasingly characteristic of Ottone's language.

All this is in complete contrast to Ottone's speech when he sees Nerone's guards: its rhythmic disjunctions, irrational, irregular text repetition, and lack of melodic or harmonic focus aptly convey Ottone's shock. Arianna-like, he questions his fate. In fact, he nearly quotes her:

Ahi, perfida Poppea,	Ah, faithless Poppea,
Son queste le promesse, e i giuramenti,	are these the promises and vows
Ch'accesero il cor mio?	that inflamed my heart?
Questa, *questa* è la fede, o dio, *dio, dio*!	Is this faith? oh God!

But his rhetoric is confused and unsteady; comprising mostly multiple sequences of repeated notes, relieved by a few large dissonant intervals, it wanders aimlessly within the interval of a perfect fourth (E to A), exceeding the lower boundary only once, with no special justification, toward the end of the speech (Example 16). Once he recognizes his betrayal Ottone loses control over his expressive language. He will not regain it for some time. He will have difficulty mounting a spirited response to any of the challenges that face him.[42]

Ottone's loss of center is increasingly evident—takes on, indeed, a pathological cast—in his dealings with others: with Poppea herself when he finally confronts her in act 1, scene 11, with Drusilla in 1.13 and 2.11, and perhaps especially with Ottavia in 2.9. In the first of these scenes, the librettist had the rather formalistic idea of providing six parallel stanzas to be shared by the former lovers in alternation (Example 17). Although the successive stanzas set up an argument between them—each of Ottone's complaints answered by a self-justification on Poppea's part—their strophic form naturally calls for strophic music.[43] Even within these constraints, however, Monteverdi manages to

---

42. For Chafe, *Monteverdi's Tonal Language*, the chief indicator of Ottone's instability is his vacillation between sharp and flat tonal regions (p. 294 and elsewhere).

43. See above, Chap. 4, pp. 120–21 and nn. 106–108, for a discussion of the apparent tonal anomalies in this scene. A number of authors, chief among them Chafe, but especially editors of the score, have gone to great lengths to rationalize (and correct) them. The problem is this: in both scores, all three of Ottone's stanzas are notated in a (though Curtis transposes them down to g); and each is preceded by a ritornello notated in g, but marked for transposition "un tuono più alto" (in Vp), which would move it to a, thereby agreeing with Ottone's stanzas. Poppea's first two stanzas, on the other hand, are in c and both are preceded by Ottone's

EXAMPLE 17. Ottone and Poppea, parallel stanzas (*L'incoronazione di Poppea*, 1.11).

a. Ottone, "Ad altri tocca," mm. 9–27.

b. Poppea, "Chi nasce sfortunato," mm. 35–51.

contrast Poppea's energetic optimism with Ottone's depression; he exploits the upper part of her range with expressive melismas and ends each of her stanzas with a definitive authentic cadence, while confining Ottone to his usual limited compass, moving repeatedly between its upper and lower limits, and ending each time on a dejected half-cadence.

Toward the end of the scene, a recitative exchange of paired couplets enlivens the unnaturally static, passive interaction established in their shared strophic aria. Ottone's incredulous interruption and repetition, added by the composer, finally provoke Poppea to terminate the scene with a forceful octave descent and a firm cadence. And Ottone is left alone to contemplate his deteriorating situation.

OTTONE: E così, *e così* l'ambitione Sovra ogni vitio tien la monarchia?	Is this how ambition above all vices attains the monarchy?
POPPEA: Così, *così* la mia ragione Incolpa i tuoi capricci di pazzia.	Thus does my reason indict your whims as madness.
OTTONE: E questo del mio amor il guiderdon?	Is this the reward for my love?
POPPEA: [Modestia] ola, non più,	No more,
OTTONE: *E questo del mio amor il guiderdone?*	
POPPEA: *Non più, non più,* son di Neron[e].[44]	I am Nerone's.

-----

ritornello, now in c, and marked "come sta." But Poppea's final stanza is in d, as is the preceding ritornello (in Vp, but not Np, where it is in c like the others). Clearly something is amiss with the transpositions. Ottone's stanzas, which end on half-cadences on a, do not lead smoothly into Poppea's ritornellos in c. When her ritornello is transposed to d, along with her final stanza, however, the fit is smoother (though the opening pitch, G, of her ritornello should probably be corrected to A in the new key). The inconsistencies in the transpositions in Vp—the miscopied clefs in Ottone's role and the numerous places in Poppea's where transpositions are indicated—makes me suspicious of these tonal relationships, especially the idea of Poppea singing two stanzas in one key and a third in another. I would suggest transposing Poppea's first two stanzas (and ritornellos) "un tuono più alto," to d, where they would accord better with Ottone's. The inconsistent rhythmic notation of the two characters, which suggests that Ottone's part was copied later (or copied from a later source), must be connected to the discrepancy of tonalities (Ottone's role was probably transposed and rewritten in more modern rhythmic notation at the same time, while Poppea's was left as it was in the exemplar). Interestingly, Chafe accepts the tonal inconsistency, rationalizing the relationships between Ottone's a and Poppea's c in terms of the durus/mollis contrast, and even finds Poppea's shift to d for her third strophe (in Vp but not Np) entirely in keeping with her closing off the discussion (*Tonal Language*, 294–97, and n. 24).

44. In Busenello, this exchange concludes with a five-line moralistic speech for Ottone:

Ahi, chi ripon sua fede in un bel volto
Predestina se stesso a reo tormento,
Fabrica in aria, e sopra il vacuo fonda,
Tenta palpare il vento
Ed immobili afferma il fumo, e l'onda.

Though cut in Vp, the speech, modified, is set in Np, but the music does not seem much like Monteverdi. A further speech, for Arnalta, is also cut in Vp, but not in Np. (See Chap. 4, n. 49 and Table 9, item 2.)

The effect of this confrontation on Ottone's sense of self is expressed in his subsequent soliloquy in scene 12. As with "E pur io torno" at the beginning of the opera, Monteverdi makes a refrain out of the opening line, "Otton, torna in te stesso," this time not only in order to mirror the text but also to inject energy and structure into the librettist's long passage of *versi sciolti*. He brings Ottone's opening line back twice within the first six lines, distinguishing it from the remainder of the speech by setting it in triple meter, to music that matches both the sense of the text and its structural function as a returning refrain. Each time, though slightly varied, the music of the refrain twice travels the distance from the dominant to land solidly on the tonic, C, with a strong authentic cadence. And each time it anchors harmony that had drifted elsewhere in the interim—first to a, then to V of a (Example 18a).

Otton, *Otton*, torna, *torna* in te stesso.	Ottone, return to your senses.
Il più imperfetto sesso	The more imperfect sex
Non ha per sua natura	has in its nature
Altro di humano in sé, che la figura.	nothing human except its shape.
Mio cor, mio cor torna, torna in te stesso,	
Costei pensa al commando, e se ci arriva,	This one thinks only of ruling, and if that happens
se ci arriva	
La mia vita è perduta. *Otton, torna,*	my life is lost,
torna in te stesso, ella temendo,	she, fearing
Che risappia Nerone	that Nerone will learn
I miei passati amori,	of my former love,
Ordirà insidie all'innocenza mia . . .	will plot to ensnare my innocence . . .

But Ottone cannot keep himself anchored. Following the third statement of the refrain, he embarks on a paranoid adventure, filled with dissonant intervals, cross-relations, and suspensions and finally cadencing on B-flat, after he has convinced himself that Poppea's ambition will bring about his destruction. This prompts him to conclude that his only recourse is to kill her. Marked by an abrupt (and, for him, very unusual) harmonic shift, from b-flat to G, this decision is enunciated in the triadic language of the *stile concitato*. But his decisiveness unravels almost immediately, and his speech ends weakly, with two prolonged suspensions leading to a hollow cadence on C (Example 18b).

༄

It is on this false note that Ottone's relationship with Drusilla is founded. She opens the next scene, their first together—and the first time we have seen her—by letting us (and Ottone) know that she is aware of his obsession with Poppea. (Directors have been known to show her overhearing his soliloquy.) Deluding herself, she pursues him all the same; dissembling, he tells her he loves her. Their interaction reaches a critical point toward the end of the scene, where the nature of their underlying feelings is emphasized by

EXAMPLE 18. Ottone's soliloquy (*L'incoronazione di Poppea*, I.12).

a. "Otton, torna in te stesso," mm. 1–26.

b. "Indurà con la forza," mm. 26–47.

EXAMPLE 18 *(continued)*

the composer's repetitions: three times Drusilla asks Ottone if he loves her, seeking to re-assure herself, and three times he responds, albeit indirectly, in the affirmative. (Busenello stated the question and answer only once, though he brings the exchange back five lines later, giving Monteverdi the opportunity for one more repetition.) Repetition emphasizes her doubts; repetition emphasizes his efforts to hide his:[45]

DRUSILLA: Già l'oblio sepellì	Has oblivion already buried
Gl'andati dispiacer?	the past displeasures?
È ver Ottone, *Otton* è ver,	Is it true, is it true
Che [a] questo fido cor il tuo s'uni?	That to my faithful heart yours is
	united?
OTTONE: È *ver* Drusilla, *Drusilla,*	It's true, Drusilla, yes, yes.
è ver sì, sì.	
DRUSILLA: Temo, *temo* che tu mi dica	I fear that you are lying to me.
la bugia.	
OTTONE: *No, no, Drusilla, Drusilla, no.*	*No, no, Drusilla, Drusilla, no.*
DRUSILLA: *Otton, Otton, Otton,*	*Ottone, Ottone, Ottone, Ottone,*
Otton, non so.	*I don't know.*

45. See Chap. 6, p. 223.

OTTONE: Teco non può mentir la fede mia.

My faith cannot lie to you.

DRUSILLA: M'ami [adunque]

You love me then?

OTTONE: Ti bramo,

                    I desire you.

DRUSILLA: *M'ami, m'ami?*

OTTONE: *Ti bramo, ti bramo.*

DRUSILLA: E come in un momento?

And how so suddenly?

OTTONE: Amor è foco, e subito s'accende.

Love is a fire and is kindled immediately.

DRUSILLA: Sì subite dolcezze

Such sudden sweetness

  [Hora] gode, *gode lieto* il mio cor, *lieto,*

my heart happily enjoys,

    lieto gode il mio cor ma non le intende,

    but does not understand.

  M'ami [adunque], *m'ami?*

Do you love me then?

OTTONE: Ti bramo, *ti bramo.*

                    I desire you.

  [Ti] E dican l'amor mio le tue bellezze,

Your beauties assure my love.

  Per te nel cor ho nova forma impressa,

For you a new form impresses my heart.

  I miracoli tuoi, *miracoli tuoi* credi a te stessa.

Believe the miracles you have yourself created.

DRUSILLA: Lieta, *lieta* men vado, *m'en vado,*

Happy, I leave;

  lieta, lieta m'en vado, m'en vado.

       Ottone, *Otton* resta felice,

       Ottone, be happy.

    resta, resta, resta felice

  [Hor hora] [*M'indirizzo*] a visitar

Now, I go to wait upon the Empress.

  l'imperatrice.

OTTONE: Le tempeste del cor,

She calms the tempests in my heart.

  le tempeste del cor tutte tranquilla.

  D'altri Otton non sarà, *d'altri Otton*

Otho will belong to no one but Drusilla.

  non sarà che di Drusilla;

  E pure al mio dispetto, iniquo Amore,

And yet, in spite of myself, cruel Love,

  Drusilla ho in bocca, ed ho Poppea,

I have Drusilla on my lips, but Poppea

  ho Poppea nel core.

  in my heart.

These feelings are intensified in Monteverdi's setting by Drusilla's readiness to burst into effusive song, and Ottone's characteristically labored speech. Even his attempts at lyricism are restricted in range and unfocused. The contrast, evident from the beginning of the scene, is especially striking at the end: the first line of Drusilla's final couplet ("Lieta m'en vado, Otton resta felice") is set as an expansive, patterned, triple-meter arioso, shifting between C and a, the second as a shapely descending recitative line in duple meter, cadencing firmly in C major. Ottone's final quatrain, in contrast, makes use of disparate styles: first the *stile concitato*—a sequence of six ascending broken thirds in even quarter notes depicting the tempests in his heart, rather than the calming of them that the text describes, then another equally frenetic and equally restricted rising sequence, this one based on a dotted rhythmic figure ("D'altri Otton non sarà che di Drusilla"). In both of these passages, Ottone's vocal line is pitted contrapuntally against the bass. A third, speech-like recitative passage expresses the pathetic oxymoron of the final couplet

by means of dissonance and sharp rhythmic contrast. The first two passages cadence in d; the third moves dissonantly from d to cadence on e (Example 19).

Monteverdi's interpolations and repetitions in this scene help define the essential dynamic between the two lovers, a dynamic that he pursues and develops with more extensive interventions in their subsequent interactions. They establish Drusilla as all too ready to believe Ottone and they confirm the power of Ottone's conscience.

Their next scene will be preceded by another traumatic event, one even more unsettling to Ottone than his confrontation with Poppea. Ottavia's order that he kill Poppea comes directly on the heels of another of Ottone's soliloquies (his third), comprising a long recitative followed by an aria of three stanzas. The recitative, in which Ottone admonishes himself for having entertained the possibility of killing his beloved, reveals perhaps more than any other speech the crippling extent of his depression. The music is utterly shapeless: a succession of unintegrated, unpredictable phrases, a tortuously static vocal line interrupted by an occasional leap or chromatic inflection leading nowhere in particular. Rhythm is completely dominated by the unarticulated unfolding of the text; hardly a word or thought gains rhetorical emphasis through repetition or sequence. A weak, if distinct harmonic shift, from d to C halfway through the speech, coincides with a shift in Ottone's focus from the shame of his guilt to a more active effort to purge the memory of his murderous thoughts—as he says, by recounting them. But even the strophic aria in which he addresses the absent Poppea, masochistically promising to love her no matter how much she torments him, depicts his depression by means of its awkwardly circular melody and bass line. Only in the last stanza does the music assume any kind of structural coherence, thanks to a well-integrated, shapely melisma that culminates in a satisfying closing gesture based on sequential repetition of the final line of text: can he regain his center this way? (Example 20).

When Ottavia thus comes upon him, lost in the contemplation of his beloved, he is in no condition to react, though he manages to mouth some typically rambling and incoherent response to her general request for help. But he completely fails to understand when she spells out the specific nature of her request. Once again the situation is exacerbated by the composer's intercalations and repetitions:

OTTAVIA: Voglio, *voglio, voglio* che la tua spada	I wish your sword
Scriva gl'obblighi miei	to write its debts to me
[Alla tua cortesía]	[with your courtesy]
Col sangue, *col sangue* di Poppea;	with Poppea's blood.
Vuò che l'uccida, *vuò che l'uccida, vuò che l'uccida.*	I wish you to kill her.
OTTONE: Che uccida chi? *Che uccida chi? Chi?*	That I should kill whom?
OTTAVIA: Poppea.	Poppea.
OTTONE: *Che uccida, che uccida, che uccida chi?*	
OTTAVIA: *Poppea, Poppea,*	
OTTONE: Poppea? *Poppea? Che uccida Poppea?*	Poppea.
OTTAVIA: Poppea, *Poppea* [perché] dunque ricusi	Poppea, then you refuse
Quel che già promettesti?	What you promised me?
OTTONE: Io ciò promisi?	I promised you?
Urbanità di complimento humile,	O urbanity of humble complements,
Modestia di parole costumate,	modesty of well-mannered words,
A che penna mortal mi condannate?	To what mortal punishment do you condemn me?

EXAMPLE 20. Ottone's aria "Sprezzami" (*L'incoronazione di Poppea*, 2.8, mm. 42–62 and 67–87).

The *stile concitato* setting of her opening speech, with its exaggerated text repetition of the single word "voglio" and the phrase "vuò che l'uccida," leaves no doubt as to what Ottavia wants—except to Ottone. He responds as if in a daze, answering her strong cadence to G with a tentative repeated question, whose harmonic instability communicates his complete disorientation. Though Ottavia answers his question, he continues to ask it, three more times, in a succession of ever more unstable harmonies. When he hears her answer finally and repeats it, his lack of comprehension persists in the wandering harmony of his speech. (His inability to grasp Ottavia's order is slightly ironic, given the fact that he himself had so recently considered—and rejected—the same action.) Infuriated, she harangues him in *stile concitato,* reminding him of his earlier promise. But having failed to understand the nature of that promise, he responds once again with incomprehension. This time his unstable harmony is more actively disso-nant, and instability also characterizes the rhythmic relationship between voice and bass. His vocal line, a series of brief, irregular, mostly descending phrases interspersed with rests, wavers indecisively within the octave above middle C. The dialogue contin-ues, she in harsh, firmly harmonic *stile concitato,* he in brief, disconnected, and har-monically unstable descending phrases, until he finally agrees, unwillingly, to do her bidding. But the trauma must be all the greater for his having expunged it from his mind so recently—and with such great effort. His only partially regained sense of self is definitively shattered here. This is emphasized by one final intervention on Mon-teverdi's part: to conclude the scene, he replaces Ottavia's gratuitous long-winded rhetor-ical dismissal ("Vattene pure; la vendetta e un cibo . . .") with a reprise of Ottone's earlier desperate plea to the gods: "O Cielo, o Dei, / In questo punto horrendo / Ritoglietevi i giorni, e i spiriti mie" (O heaven, O gods, in this horrible moment, take back my days and powers).[46]

Monteverdi cannot have enough of Ottone's depression; he picks it up again at his next appearance, two scenes later (it's actually the next scene, but the librettist shows us Drusilla in the interim). Ottone describes the somatic effect of his emotions:

Io non so, *non so* dov'io vada;	I know not where I go;
Il palpitar del core,	the beating of my heart
E il moto del piè non van d'accordo.	and the movement of my feet do not agree.
L'aria, che m'entra in sen, quand'io,	The air that enters my breast when
quand'io respiro,	I breathe
Trova il cor mio sì afflitto, *sì afflitto,*	finds my heart so afflicted that,
[che pietosa]	moved by pity,
*Ch'*ella si cangia in subitaneo pianto;	it turns itself at once into tears;
E così mentr'io peno	and thus, while I suffer,
L'aria per compassion mi piange	the air in sympathy laments within my
in seno.	breast.

Monteverdi's wandering melodic line, like Ottone, knows not where it goes (Example 21). Wavering back and forth within his typically narrow range, the line is fragmented unpredictably by rests of varying lengths. The rhythm is erratic, sixteenth, eighth, and

---

46. Ottavia's rejected text is as follows:

Vattene pure; la vendetta è un cibo,
Che col sangue inimico si condisce.
Della spenta Poppea fu 'l monumento
Quasi a felice mensa
Prenderò così nobile alimento.

quarter notes succeeding one another seemingly at random—though the succession of steady quarter notes on "palpitar del core" imitates the beating of Ottone's heart. Harmonic motion is suspended: the vacillating bass hovers around A, which, however, never achieves full status as a tonic (a strong cadence occurs only at the end of the passage, but it is on E, not A). The bass line is also shapeless, wavering half-steps at the opening of the passage yielding to equally unpredictable leaps and shifts of direction at the end. Voice and bass—heart and feet—are unsynchronized, their few simultaneities occurring only at the final cadence. (Ottone's music is completely ruled by his mood, even as it projects it. The very air he breathes imitates his emotions.) If one thinks of Ottone's opening speech at the very start of the opera, the contrast is remarkable. There his melodic line was obsessively centered on d, miming Poppea's centrality to him. Here it has no center at all, moving irresolutely from its beginning on a to a weak final cadence on E.

It is in this disoriented state that Drusilla finds him—she seems always to be seeking him out, even here, where she was on stage first, though he will pretend to be looking for her. (This is another example of two actions occurring simultaneously: while she was with Valletto and Nutrice, he was with Ottavia.)[47] Through intercalation and repetition of text, Monteverdi gives Ottone time to come up with a response to her. This scene, act 2, scene 11, is the site of one of Monteverdi's boldest and most effective textual interventions. He inserts material borrowed from the preceding scene for Drusilla, Valletto, and Nutrice, material that is already prominent at its original appearance, textually as well as musically:

<u>Felice cor mio</u>
<u>Festeggiami in seno</u>, *festeggiami in seno, festeggiami in seno.*
Doppo i nembi, e gl'horror, *doppo i nembi e l'horror* godrò il sereno.
Hoggi *hoggi* spero, che Ottone, *hoggi, hoggi spero, che Ottone*
Mi riconfermi il suo *promesso* [primiero] Amore.
Hoggi, hoggi spero, che Ottone
Mi riconfermi il suo perduto amore.
Felice core mio,
Festeggiami in seno, festeggiami in seno, festeggiami in seno,
<u>Festeggiami nel sen</u>, *festeggiami nel sen, festeggiam, festeggiami nel sen,* <u>lieto mio core.</u>

(Oh my happy heart, rejoice in my breast. After clouds and horrors I will enjoy serenity. To-day I hope that Ottone will reconfirm his promised love. Rejoice in my breast, my happy heart.)

In Monteverdi's setting, it exemplifies that special quality of Drusilla, her blind optimism, manifested in her predilection for song. The speech is enclosed by an inexact textual refrain (underlined). Inspired perhaps by the suggestion of closure provided by that refrain, as well as by the sentiments expressed, Monteverdi sets the speech in a song-like manner; he regularizes Busenello's inexact refrain and emphasizes its importance by musical expansion based on extensive word repetition as well as lengthy melismas. (If the repetition sounds somewhat exaggerated, an overreaction to Ottone's promise, that may be because it signals the persistence of some subliminal doubts.)

When Ottone joins Drusilla, he reveals that he seeks her aid and assures her that she has no further need to be jealous of Poppea (an assurance that rings particularly hollow, especially since he repeats it). In response, Monteverdi's Drusilla (but not Busenello's) attempts only too impetuously to repeat her refrain from the previous scene (in brackets and italics, underlined). Monteverdi's Ottone interrupts several times, as he begs her to listen while he explains the help he needs from her in killing Poppea. He wishes to disguise himself in her clothes:

---

47. Cf. Table 15, Chap. 5 (*Incoronazione* structure), and recall Dubowy's comment on simultaneous action in *Ritorno* ("Bemerkungen").

OTTONE: Non esser più gelosa, *no, non esser più gelosa*

  Di Poppea *[D: no no] [O: Di Poppea] [D: Felice cor mio, felice core mio, festeggiami in seno]*

     Senti, senti *[D: Festeggiami in seno, festeggiami in seno, festeggiami] [O: senti, senti]*,

       io devo

  Hor, hora per terribile commando

  Immergerle [li] nel sen questo mio brando.

  Per ricoprir me stesso

  In misfatto sì grande,

  Io vorrei le tue vesti.

  . . . .

DRUSILLA: E le vesti, e le vene

  Ti darò volontieri, *volontieri ti darò, ti darò volontieri, volontier,*

  Ma circonspetto va, cauto procedi,

  Nel rimanente, *nel rimanente* sappi

  Che le fortune, e le richezze mie

  Ti saran tributarie in ogni loco,

  E proverai Drusilla

  Nobile amante, e tale,

  Che mai, *mai* l'antica età non n'ebbe eguale.

  Andiam, *andiam* pur, *[Felice cor mio, festeggiami in seno, festeggiami in seno, festeggiami in seno], andiam, andiam pur* ch'io mi spoglio,

  E di mia man[o], *di mia man, di mia man* travestirti io voglio . . .

(Be jealous no longer of Poppea. Now I must, by terrible command, thrust my dagger in her heart. To cover myself for such a great misdeed, I would need your clothes . . . . My clothes and my life I willingly give you. But be circumspect, proceed with caution. And remember that all my fortune and riches will be at your disposal everywhere, and you will find Drusilla a noble lover, such that was never equaled in ancient times. Let's go so that I can undress. With my hand I would like to dress you.)

Having been short-circuited twice, the refrain returns a third time, in its complete expanded form (and full glory) toward the end, sealing Drusilla's agreement. This linkage between scenes 10 and 11 is completely Monteverdi's doing. The threefold recurrence of Drusilla's refrain in a scene from which it was completely absent, to interrupt a speech by Ottone, not only heightens the casual naturalism of the characters' interaction but injects a powerful element of irony that is only hinted at in Busenello's original. Particularly in Monteverdi's expansive setting, the refrain emphasizes Drusilla's overwhelming but ironically inappropriate happiness; the audience knows that she should not believe Ottone, and they certainly suspect that he is exploiting her love. Although the means are initially textual, involving repetition and rearrangement of Busenello's words, it is primarily the repetitions and intercalations of Monteverdi's setting of the text that gives this exchange its dramatic edge. We recall how Poppea's carefully calculated interruptions goaded Nerone into doing her will, and while Drusilla's interruptions appear far more spontaneous, they too accomplish her goal. Her steadfast love, expressed in her recurrent refrain, will eventually win over Ottone.[48]

Just as Poppea's manipulative behavior forms an essential aspect of her character, informing all of her confrontations with Nerone, Drusilla's credulity and her inclination to self-deception are among her most distinctive personality traits. She succumbs almost fatally to this tendency in the opening scene of act 3, as she awaits the arrival of Ottone and the news that he has killed Poppea. Her anticipation is given voice in an extended three-part aria setting of her entire text, in which another musical refrain, initially accompanying words that echo her much belabored refrain in the previous act, "O felice cor mio," is heard three times. Once again the exaggerated repetition of key words—"felice," "corre," morirò," "mio"—underscores the irony of Drusilla's position: her happiness is an illusion, her anticipation vain. She alone is unaware that the assassination attempt was unsuccessful, that she herself has been accused of the crime, and that she is further than ever from realizing her desires.

As it turns out, though, she is closer than we might think. Her relationship to Ottone is about to undergo a change, one that her characteristic impetuousness finally precipitates. In scene 4, the lovers' final appearance in the opera, Drusilla twice repeats three lines she had used in her false confession to Nerone in the previous scene in attempts to preempt Ottone's own admission of guilt (underlined B1, B2, B3). Each time, her refrain interrupts a longer speech by Ottone, and has the effect of deepening the interaction between them:

Scene 3		Scene 4	
<u>Signor, io fui la rea,</u>		OTTONE: No, no questa sentenza	
<u>Che uccidere tentò</u>	**B1**	Cada sopra di me, che ne son degno;	
<u>L'innocente Poppea.</u>		DRUSILLA: *Io, io fui la rea*	**B2**
[Quest'alma, e questa mano	**A**	*Ch'uccider volli l'innocente Poppea*	
Fur le complici sole;		OTTONE: Siate voi testimonio, O Cieli,	
		O Dei,	
A ciò m'indusse un'odio occulto antico;		Innocente è costei.	
Non cercar più la verità ti dico.]		DRUSILLA: *Quest'alma e questa mano*	**A**
		Fur le complici sole;	
		A ciò m'indusse un odio occult'antico;	
		Non cercar più la verità ti dico.	
		OTTONE: *Innocente, innocente è costei.*	
		Io, *io* con le vesti di Drusilla andai	
		Per ordine d'Ottavia l'imperatrice	
		Ad attentar la morte di Poppea.	
		[Giove, Nemesi, Astrea	**C**
		Fulminate il mio capo,	
		Che per giusta vendetta	

---

48. Drusilla's inappropriate use of song in her refrain here is an example of irony. I discuss this passage in "Monteverdi's Mimetic Art," 122–23.

Il patibolo horrendo a me s'aspetta.]
Dammi, *dammi* Signor, con la tua
man la morte.

DRUSILLA: *Io fui, io fui la rea*   B₃
    Ch'uccider volli l'innocente Poppea.

OTTONE: *Giove, Nemesi, Astrea*   C
    Fulminate il mio capo,
    Che per giusta vendetta
    Il patibolo horrendo a me s'aspetta.

DRUSILLA: *A me s'aspetta,* O: *A me*
    s'aspetta, D: *A me,* O: *A me,* D: *A me,*
    O: *A me, a me s'aspetta.*
    Dammi signor con la tua man la morte.
    E se non vuoi, che la tua mano adorni
    Di decoro il mio fine,
    Mentre della tua gratia io resto privo
    All'infelicità lasciami vivo,
    Se tu vuoi tormentarmi
    La mia coscienza ti darà i flagelli;
    Se a Leoni, ed agl'Orsi espor mi vuoi,
    Dammi in preda al pensier delle
      mie colpe,
    Ch'ei mi divorerà l'ossa, e le polpe . . .

(DRUSILLA: Sire, I was the wicked one who tried to kill the innocent Poppea. This soul and this hand were the only accomplices; an old hidden hatred pushed me to it. Do not seek the truth any further. OTTONE: No, no, let this sentence fall on me, since I deserve it. Let you be witness, O heavens, o gods, that she is innocent. I went with Drusilla's clothes, on the empress Ottavia's orders, to attempt to kill Poppea. Jove, Nemesis, Astrea, strike my head with lightning, for in just revenge the horrendous gallows awaits me. And if you do not wish to adorn my proper end with your hand, and if I am to be deprived of your pardon, let me live unhappily. If you wish to torment me, my conscience will provide the whips. If you wish to expose me to lions and bears, deliver me to the thought of my guilt, which will devour my bones and flesh.)

The four remaining (final) lines of Drusilla's scene-3 speech (A) also recur in scene 4 (A), though separated from the first three, and in this case not to preempt but to counteract Ottone's admission of guilt.[49] Like the other intercalations and displacements, this one too

---

49. A certain ambiguity surrounds this passage, however: although it appears twice in the Naples score—in scenes 3 and 4—with different music, it appears only once in the Venetian manuscript (and in the various librettos), in scene 4. Evidently it was intended to be omitted from scene 3, but was left in the Naples score by mistake. The differences in the two settings of the Naples score seem random, as if the composer simply forgot that he already had set the same text in the previous scene. The music in the Venice score is like the second version in Naples, which suggests that the first version should probably have been cut.

breaks up a lengthy speech for Ottone, again energizing the interaction between the characters and emphasizing Drusilla's commitment to her lover. The very speech that it interrupts, incidentally, is edited in a similar way and for similar purposes: four of Ottone's last five lines (**C**) are displaced so as to occur in a separate speech, after Drusilla's final statement of her refrain (**B3**).

Here, for the first time, it is Ottone who seeks out Drusilla, as he rushes in to deny her guilt and claim his own. Recognizing her self-sacrifice, Ottone is finally able to commit himself to her. (Some interpretations place a high value on Nerone's magnanimity in pardoning the guilty couple and emphasize Drusilla's self-sacrifice as a manifestation of the virtue of constancy, a virtue recognized by Nerone, though he himself has none.[50] But the focus belongs on Ottone, who is the last to speak before the two are ushered off.) Ottone may have relatively little to say in the third act, yet we realize that his harmonies are now palpably stronger, his melodies more sequential, less chromatic, less wandering, more rhythmically structured, often spanning an octave rather than concentrated within a fourth. His speeches, brief as they are, end in authentic cadences; voice and bass move decisively in tandem. In his final speech, in which he thanks Nerone for sending him into exile with Drusilla, he even borrows her characteristic rhetoric of excessive repetition to emphasize his emotions:

Signor, *signor* non son punito, *non son punito.*	Sire, I am not punished, but blessed.
no, *non son punito* anzi beato, *anzi beato,*	
anzi beato.	
Le virtù di costei	The virtues of this woman
Sara[n] richezza[e], e gloria, *le virtù di costei*	will be the riches and glory of my days.
saran ricchezze e gloria a giorni miei.	

His melody in these lines is carefully shaped and rhythmically and melodically decisive; it moves now in contrary motion, now in imitation against a rhythmically active bass. The two parts cadence together confidently (Example 22).

What can we make of this transformation in Ottone's music? Can we not say that his center has been restored?

∂⬥

Contrary to some recent critics, who find Ottone's characterization so weak as to doubt the authenticity of his music, I would argue that he is the most complex character in the drama, that his ambivalence and psychological vulnerability presented a special challenge to the composer—a greater challenge than the stronger, more focused and goal-directed

---

50. See Fenlon and Miller, *Song of the Soul,* 88.

EXAMPLE 22. Ottone, "Signor, non son punito" (*L'incoronazione di Poppea*, 3.4, mm. 105–18).

feelings of the other characters.[51] Poppea's overweening ambition, Nerone's perversity, Drusilla's optimism, and Ottavia's angry bitterness are far more readily projected than Ottone's vacillating emotions and his dangerously undramatic inaction. Unlike the others, he is deeply introspective; his three soliloquies provide ample opportunity for him to reveal himself, but what he reveals is his vulnerability, his fragile ego.[52] Like his emotions, Ottone's music often lacks focus, almost as if Monteverdi were stymied by his ambivalence. And yet that very ambivalence is enacted in the music, which vacillates consistently between sharp and flat harmonic regions. One has to bear in mind the possibility that

---

51. The critics, primarily Curtis, who have questioned the authenticity of Ottone's music, have done so on the basis of manuscript evidence, which, as I have shown, is at best inconclusive. Chafe, emphatically not among Ottone's negative critics, credits him with having perhaps the strongest claim to audience sympathy of any of the characters, and he essentially affirms his authenticity on the basis of the tonal areas in which he sings (*Tonal Language*, 290–97). Along the same lines, Giulio Ongaro (paper presented at the meeting of the Society for Seventeenth-Century Music, Princeton, 2003) argues that Ottone is actually the main character in the opera, the one most likely to strike a responsive chord in a large segment of the public. In confirmation of this status, it is probably worth noting that in the scenario Ottone is described as "cavalliero principalissimo," as opposed to the more clearly historical Nerone, "Imperator Romano," Seneca, "Filosofo Maestro di Nerone," Ottavia, "Imperatrice Regnante,"and Poppea, "Dama Nobilissima" (see Appendix 4, B).

52. Ottone actually appears in as many scenes as all but one of the other main characters, nine: four in acts 1 and 2, one in act 3. Poppea likewise appears in four scenes in acts 1 and 2, but two in act 3, for a total of ten. Nerone appears in nine scenes, three in act 1, two in act 2, and four in act 3. As for soliloquies, with three he exceeds all other characters—Ottavia has two, while Seneca, Arnalta, and Drusilla have one each.

some dire emergency may have confronted the composer with a singer with a very limited vocal range.[53] But if so he seems to have exploited the limitation to dramatic effect. Monteverdi surely knew how to write coherent and shapely music, whether aria or recitative. That he obviously did not do so with Ottone seems purposeful, crucial to his conception of the character.

It was also Busenello's conception: Ottone, we recall, is not developed in any of the historical sources that he adapted, where Otho appears merely as Poppaea's former husband or lover, in some sort of competition with Nero. We must assume that the librettist conceived him with some purpose in mind—arguably to provide a counterpoint to the immoral story of Poppea and Nerone, almost certainly as a device to keep the opera going after Seneca has left it. His featured position in the very concise synopsis in the scenario may be due to his almost wholly invented status. The opening sentence summarizes the situation in Tacitus, the rest describes the plot:

> Nero enamored of Poppaea, who was the wife of Otho, sent the latter, under the pretext of embassy, to Lusitania, so that he could take his pleasure with her. . . . But here we represent these actions differently. Ottone, desperate at seeing himself deprived of Poppea, gives himself over to frenzy and exclamations. Ottavia, wife of Nerone, orders Ottone to kill Poppea. Ottone promises to do it; but lacking the spirit to deprive his adored Poppea of life, he dresses in the clothes of Drusilla, who was in love with him. Thus disguised, he enters the garden of Poppea. Love disturbs and prevents that death. Nerone repudiates Ottavia, in spite of the counsel of Seneca, and takes Poppea to wife. Seneca dies, and Ottavia is expelled from Rome. (Appendix 4, A)

Even in this briefest of plot outlines, Ottone is distinguished from the other characters by the detailing of his actions, and especially his emotions: his desperation, frenzy and exclamations, his lack of spirit—not perhaps *those changes of affection that pleased our Signor Monteverdi very much because they allow him to display the marvels of his art,* but emotions nonetheless. Monteverdi's portrayal is particularly compelling when the text offers him strong metaphors or concrete imagery, as when he depicts Ottone's focus on Poppea as his center, or the disjunction between his beating heart and his feet, and his labored breathing, or else when he can reveal Ottone's insecurity in dynamic interactions with other, contrasting characters. The imagery stands for deep psychological currents. Ottone's vulnerability to a loss of self and his emotional dependence on Poppea for validation expose a psychic wound not easily healed. Monteverdi's characteristic approach to text setting, learned as a composer of madrigals, his development of concrete images as metaphors of psychological states, fully conveys Ottone's emotional turmoil and its resolution.

---

53. Ottone was one of the few roles of the period written for what we would call an alto (as opposed to soprano) castrato; today, unless the part is transposed upward, only female alto voices are adequate to the role.

Most important of all, the healing of Ottone's wound, the restoration of his center through a new relationship, with Drusilla, serves to mitigate the effect of Poppea's triumph, lending a positive note to the immoral ending of the opera itself. In the *mondo alla rovescia* of *L'incoronazione di Poppea,* a world of intrigue, perversion, and inversion, where vice triumphs over virtue, weak and vacillating and suffering Ottone, more than any other character in the opera, represents the human condition—or, as Badoaro had figured it, *humana fragilità.*[54]

⁂

Although I have discussed only a limited number of characters and examples in detail, they illustrate the fundamental difference in the composer's approach to the two librettos. Many of Monteverdi's interventions in *Ritorno* are on a large scale. They involve extended segments of text, the wholesale restructuring of entire speeches and scenes; and they have an impact on the overall shape of the drama. The interventions in *Incoronazione* are on a smaller scale, more concerned with details. But although their individual impact may be more limited and subtle—an emphasis here, a motivation there—their cumulative effect is profound (at least as significant to the opera as a whole as those in *Ritorno*).

In part the character of the alterations is determined by the nature of the raw material: the structural sweep of Badoaro's classical tragedy made different demands on the composer than the mosaic of individual situations, the quicksilver shifts of perspective, in Busenello's psychological drama. In *Ritorno* Monteverdi felt impelled to reinforce the steady, inevitable act-by-act progress of the drama and to strengthen the contrasts between the modally distinct characters: between faithful Penelope, wise Ulisse, lascivious Melanto, treacherous Eurimaco, and so on;[55] in *Incoronazione,* on the other hand, he was attracted by the possibility of constructing more complex characters, who revealed different aspects of themselves in their various confrontations with others. The different level of intervention may also be partly a function of the disparate skills of the poets. Badoaro was a self-confessed neophyte, and his text is on the whole much weaker than Busenello's; it labors under the weight of heavy philosophical issues and long-winded speeches that lend themselves poorly to dramatic performance. Busenello, in contrast, was already an experienced dramatist with several librettos to his credit. If he too was occasionally prone to excessive formalism or vacuous philosophizing, *Incoronazione* in particular shows that he had a keen appreciation

54. Chafe, *Tonal Language,* 331 arrives at a similar conclusion: "Within a world of rapidly declining virtue as set up in the prologue . . . Otho, the weakest of the principle [*sic*] characters in terms of political power and singleness of purpose, is to a great extent the representative of the human predicament, victim of both Love and Fortune. In this respect he is the successor to the idea of Human Frailty in *Ulisse.*"

55. As already noted, Torcigliani described just such modal characters in his preface to *Nozze:* "Enea è forte, e pio Ascanio generoso, Turno fuorché quando parla con Lavinia furibondo. La medesima Lavinia modesta anco nell'amore. Amata colerica . . ." (Appendix 2 [k]); also above, Chap. 5, p. 132.

of the requirements of theatrical performance: both characters and dramatic situations are shaped economically but fully.[56]

It is apparent, in any case, that the composer's editorial interventions in the two works took place at different stages in the creative process. The *Ritorno* revisions are cool, careful, considered—and corrective: they presuppose a general analysis of the text as drama, an overall conception and appreciation of its potential symmetries and overall shape; and they are distinct from the musical setting. (Indeed, some of the cuts I discussed have no bearing whatever on the music—since they were not set—though they significantly affect the drama.) These revisions must have taken place at a pre-compositional stage—a planning stage, before Monteverdi ever set pen to music paper. The revisions in *Incoronazione,* on the other hand, still glow with the heat of inspiration. They give every indication of having occurred during the very act of composition, as the composer, in a kind of *raptus poeticus,* became ever more deeply immersed in the conflicts and confrontations he was bringing to life.

---

56. One other partial explanation for the disparity may be that we are observing the poets' works at different stages—our source for Busenello's text is a libretto he published fourteen years after the first performance of the opera, after he had time to reconsider it, whereas Badoaro's text is known only from manuscripts that represent an earlier version than Monteverdi's setting. We have no analogous sources for *Incoronazione.*

8

The Philosopher and the Parasite

The analysis I have developed over the course of the previous chapters, notably in Chapters 5 and 7, suggests a broad conclusion: *Ritorno* and *Incoronazione* stand on opposite sides of an aesthetic divide, constituting a kind of debate between tradition and innovation, or between classicism and modernism (ancients and moderns). Such a debate would have been fully in keeping with those engaged in by members of the Accademia degli Incogniti. This divide is personified by two characters: Seneca, the stoic philosopher, and Iro, the gluttonous parasite. Though at first they may seem an unlikely duo, a perverse pairing of the sublime and the ridiculous, these two characters offer themselves as emblematic of their respective operas. In unexpectedly related ways, they are surely Monteverdi's most problematic and disturbing creations: problematic in their ambiguity, disturbing in their deaths. Close attention to them, both individually and comparatively, will serve to bring into clearer focus some of the most challenging interpretive questions raised by the two operas. These questions, which have come up sporadically during the course of the preceding chapters, now finally beg for fuller consideration.

A philosopher and a parasite are the opposing voices in *The Parasite*, a dialogue by the second-century Greek satirist Lucian, whose works were very much part of the classical heritage of the Renaissance.[1] In this work, Tychiades the philosopher and Simon the parasite debate the distinctions between their professions, after Simon has been challenged to demonstrate that sponging *is* in fact a profession—which he does, predictably, by recourse

---

1. Christopher Robinson, *Lucian and His Influence in Europe* (London: Duckworth, 1979).

to infallible logic.[2] Lucian's interlocutors stand as predecessors to the *personaggi* of the Venetian librettists, and some of his arguments are indeed suggestive for their characterization of Iro and Seneca. Two in particular concern the contrasting responses of the interlocutors to battle and to death, as we will see.

Heroic Pedant, Ambiguous Philosopher

Of the two operatic characters, Seneca makes more obvious claim to a signifying role, a key to meaning in his opera.[3] Unlike Iro, he is a main character—even, one could argue, the main character of *Incoronazione*, the moral fulcrum of the work.[4] He makes two appearances, in two groups of scenes: act 1, scenes 6–9 (out of a total of thirteen) and act 2, scenes 1–4 (of fifteen), and his death at the precise midpoint of the opera bisects the drama and sets its moral opening against its immoral conclusion.[5] While alive, Seneca seems the only bulwark against decadence, sustaining conscience in others: Ottavia's piety initially prevents her from avenging herself, despite her rage against Nerone. "If there were neither honor nor God," she declares, "I would be my own god and would punish the wrongs done to me with my own hand." Ottone's self-respect initially keeps him from yielding to his anger against Poppea. "Ottone, return to your senses," he tells himself, pulling back from the urge to kill her. Even Arnalta's conscience initially bothers her. She cannot condone Poppea's immoral ambition and feels a certain pity for Ottone: "Unhappy boy. The wretch moves me to compassion." It is Nerone who confronts Seneca's moral force most directly; but despite his struggle, even he cannot counter the moral logic of his old tutor.

Once Seneca is dead, morality is undone and immorality runs rampant, gradually and systematically infecting the entire world of the opera. Ottavia can now plan a murder and become a blackmailer; Ottone can agree to kill Poppea, and exploit Drusilla by making her an accessory to the murder. Arnalta can accept Poppea's ambitious expediency, and look forward to the rewards of her new status. Nerone, justified by the failed murder attempt, can feel free to repudiate Ottavia, the very action Seneca had refused to countenance.[6]

2. *The Works of Lucian of Samosata*, trans. H. W. Fowler and F. G. Fowler, Loeb Classical Library (Oxford: Clarendon Press, 1905), 3:167–90.

3. Some of this section may be familiar from my article "Seneca," from which it is adapted.

4. Among the other candidates to have been proposed are Nerone, Drusilla, Poppea, and, more recently, by Eric Chafe as well as Giulio Ongaro, Ottone—that is, virtually everyone except for Ottavia.

5. Chafe (*Tonal Language*, 312–13) remarks on the symmetrical placement of Seneca's scenes in act 1, which is illustrated in his figure 14.1. It is worth noting that, although Busenello mentions Seneca's death in his summary of the plot, he fails to mention that it occurs midway through the drama. Rather, he associates it with Ottavia's exile at the end, following the coronation. Moving it to the middle, among other things, gives Poppea a more active role in the drama: it is one of her accomplishments (see Appendix 4, A).

6. Heller ("Tacitus Incognito") links Seneca with Agrippina, whose death in Tacitus seems to have had an effect similar to that of Busenello's Seneca on Roman life under Nero, at least as summarized in *Le vite de gli imperadori romani da Giulio Cesare sino a Massimiliano, tratte per M. Lodovico Dolce dal libro spagnolo del*

The importance of Seneca's death for Busenello's drama is underscored, obviously enough, by two identical references to it at the beginning of act 2, scenes 6 and 12: "Hor che Seneca è morto," sings Nerone to Lucano; "Hor che Seneca è morto," sings Poppea to Arnalta—his death is very much on all their minds, on the tip of their tongues.[7] But the meaning of that death is inflected by the ambiguity of Seneca's character, as portrayed by the librettist. Ambiguity is carefully established from the very beginning, as Seneca gradually reveals a mixture of admirable and less admirable traits.

We first encounter the stoic philosopher through the eyes of Nerone's soldiers, who indict him for failing to follow his own precepts, calling him not only a pedant, but a greedy old man, a cunning fox, a villainous flatterer who increases his earnings by betraying his friends, an evil architect who builds his own house on other men's graves.[8] Valletto's evaluation of him is hardly more flattering. He calls him a Jove-cheater, a philosophical miniaturist of pretty notions who lines his pockets on others' ignorance and does the opposite of what he preaches;[9] he disparages Seneca's philosophical advice to Ottavia as empty—an opinion she herself echoes—accusing him of impotence, and labeling his promises specious, affected, and useless. Though comic characters such as Valletto and the Soldiers are traditionally prized for their ready realism, disinterest, and objectivity, for seeing things as they are rather than as they ought to be, we may be forgiven for not taking their exaggerated observations too seriously—until they are confirmed by Ottavia.[10] For Ottavia, Seneca's stoicism is patently ineffective; it can offer her no solace.

Although he subsequently reveals himself a worthy antagonist of Nerone and a committed champion of philosophical principle, even Seneca's most heroic act, his suicide, is tainted by ambivalence, for his eloquent plea to his followers and students to accept his death as the natural culmination of his life's work falls on deaf ears. It is a famously unsettling scene. Not only do the *famigliari* refuse to accept his stoic gesture, urging him to

Signor Pietro Messia (Venice: Turrini e Brigonci, 1664), 211: "[Nero] ove egli veggendosi libero dalla grave autorità della madre, che mai non restò di esser grande appresso di lui, finì affatto di perder la vergogna, e sciolse compiutamente la briglia a suoi rei e bestiali desideri. Laonde senz'alcuno impedimento a freno sciolto si diede a tutte le maniere di lorde e scellerate lussurie, le quali furono tanto orribili, che per riguardo dell'onestà, che alla nostra istoria richiede, e per non offender le orecchie di chi legge, ho proposto di non volerle scrivere."

7. This repetition also suggests that the two scenes might have been conceived as taking place simultaneously, a point already raised, among other places, in Chap. 5 with respect to _Ritorno_.

8. Lucian's philosopher is a "slave of vanity, reputation, and . . . money" (_Works_, 186).

9. The reference to lining his pockets is another allusion to money, and Seneca's suspicious financial practices.

10. Although Holzer (Review of _The Song of the Soul_), 86, 89, and 91, discounts their remarks as unreliable, they are clearly derived from the historical tradition of Seneca reception. Fenlon and Miller (_Song of the Soul_), 63, speak of Ottavia's mind in disarray in her lament, and interpret her failure to accept Seneca's advice as a rejection of stoicism (cf. Holzer, Review, 90).

rescind it, but they are unconvinced by its meaning. They would not do the same, they say; life is too sweet, there is nothing worth dying for.[11]

Their reaction casts doubt on the very foundations of Stoicism, and the doubt is not theirs alone. Seneca's *famigliari* speak for the librettist. Busenello's skepticism is aired not only throughout this libretto, but in a number of his other writings. A particularly caustic passage from one of his dialect poems, "Do brazzolari in man ha la natura," sounds as if it could even have been spoken by Seneca's *famigliari*:

Sbeletta Ciceron le Toscolane,	Cicero polishes his little Tusculans,
Boetio Severin vende balotte	Severinus Boethius sells ballot-balls (or testicles)
E Plutarco e Zenon cazza carotte	And Plutarch and Zeno chase carrots (penises)
E Seneca vien via con le merdane.	And Seneca comes away with the turds(?).
Ei dise che la morte sia 'il Bobò'	He said that death was the bogeyman(?)
Che non diè spaurir noma i putini;	That ought not to frighten even children;
Con bona gratia de i so concetini	With respect to his little ideas
Mi volontiera mai non morirò.[12]	I shall never die willingly.

And yet of course Busenello also casts a strong positive light on Seneca's suicide. In the scene following his farewell, Seneca prepares to ascend to heaven accompanied by a chorus of Virtues, having earned his apotheosis through his courageous act. As the philosopher himself predicts: the knife that opened his veins on earth unlocks the doors of eternity in heaven. We will say more about this scene—which Monteverdi seems not to have set—later in this chapter.

THE HISTORICAL SENECA

Naturally enough, Busenello's characterization of Seneca reflects the common view of the historical Seneca, as derived from the various Roman histories widely read at the

---

11. Monteverdi's interpretation (inverting the followers' two lines so that they always read: "Non morir / Io per me morir non vò," and setting them to wildly contrasting music) emphasizes their rejection of stoicism; cf. Tim Carter, "Re-reading *Poppea*: Some Thoughts on Music and Meaning in Monteverdi's Last Opera," *JRMA* 122 (1997): 173–204; esp. 189–98. See further discussion below.

12. Quoted in Francesco Degrada, "Il teatro di Claudio Monteverdi: Gli studi sullo stile," in *Claudio Monteverdi: Studi e prospettive. Atti del convegno, Mantova 21–24 ottobre 1993*, ed. Paola Besutti, Teresa M. Gialdroni, and Rodolfo Baroncini (Florence: Olschki, 1998), 263–83, at 278. For a further discussion of Busenello's poetry, see id., "Gian Francesco Busenello e il libretto dell'*Incoronazione di Poppea*," in *Congresso internazionale sul tema "Claudio Monteverdi e il suo tempo,"* ed. Rafaello Monterosso (Verona: Stamperia Valdonega, 1969), 81–102. I am grateful to Leofranc Holford-Strevens for the translation.

time: Tacitus, Suetonius, and Dio Cassius.[13] Certainly his ambivalence toward Seneca was shared by his colleagues in the Accademia degli Incogniti. In addition to the numerous occasions when his rules as a dramatist are quoted and dismissed, Seneca turns up frequently in their *novelle* and political writings.[14] One such work that has already been mentioned several times is *L'imperatrice ambiziosa* by Federico Malipiero. In this moral-essay-cum-prose-romance on the life of Nero's mother, Agrippina, Seneca comes off as a consummate politician, a prime supporter of Agrippina's claim to the Roman throne and an eloquent orator whose forensic gifts convince Claudius to adopt Nero as his son and heir, displacing his own son Britannicus. For Malipiero, Seneca was a cunning and clever man, a great philosopher, valorous, with an enviable intelligence, but one who used that intelligence for political gain that was not always legitimate. Although entrusted with the education of the emperor, Malipiero's Seneca does not hesitate to lie, cheat, and even pimp in the service of his charge.[15]

To Malipiero and Busenello, then, the stoic philosopher was morally suspect, a smooth-talking opportunist whose actions did not always match his professed ideals. This view of Seneca has ample support in history and the traditions of reception of the time. The tradition had been neatly summed up several centuries earlier by Petrarch, in his *Epistolae familiares:* his letter to Seneca (bk. 24) explicitly addresses the dichotomy between the philosopher's life and his thought, the one worthy of reproof, the other of praise (*Ad Anneo*

---

13. On Seneca's involvement in covering up Nero's crimes, particularly his justification of Agrippina's murder, see Champlin, *Nero,* 89.

14. For instance, Seneca plays a major role in Ferrante Pallavicino's novella *Le due Agrippine* (Venice: Guerigli, 1642); Giovan Francesco Loredano, founder of the Incogniti, devoted one of the dialogues in his *Scherzi geniali* (Venice: Guerigli, 1632) to him: "Seneca prudente," which was based on Tacitus's account of the philosopher's response to the accusations brought against him in the presence of Nero (Fenlon and Miller, *Song of the Soul,* 32). Loredano's collection also includes a dialogue entitled "Poppea supplichevole," a reworking of the speech in *Annals* 14.61 in which Poppaea begs Nero to send Octavia back into exile (Holzer, Review, p. 87; Fenlon and Miller, *Song of the Soul,* 47).

15. In describing Nero's tastelessly eloquent oration on the death of Claudius, whom he murdered, Malipiero attributes both the idea and the speech itself to Seneca, as evidence of his political acumen (Malipiero, *L'imperatrice ambiziosa,* 114). Seneca's services to Nero are discussed on p. 127. Seneca's ambiguous reputation among the Incogniti is fully in evidence in Henri de Boulay, "Il Nerone difeso di Luciano," in *Tre discorsi di Henri de Bullay, gentil'huomo francese* (Venice: Deuchino, 1627), a work first introduced into the discussion of *Incoronazione* by Tim Carter ("Re-reading *Poppea*," 180–82). Boulay, a Frenchman, was a tutor to the sons of Venetian patricians during this period. His text, which represents itself as an Italian translation of a dialogue by the Greek poet Lucian supposedly in defense of Nero, takes place in the Underworld, where Nero, attempting to justify himself before Minos, the judge, asks that Seneca be called a witness and then systematically blames him for encouraging his crimes and benefiting financially from them (p. 144). Minos raises the issue of the contrast between Seneca's works and life when he wonders how such a distinguished philosopher could have been so evil: "Ma il suo sembiante tutto Filosofico, e tanti libri da lui lasciati sono molto lontani da tal calunnia, a da quello che il volgo ne parla, e giudica" (p. 129). Carter, *Musical Theatre,* 276 identifies the genre of Boulay's dialogue as a paradoxical encomium and offers the plausible suggestion that this tradition might be relevant to the interpretation of *Incoronazione.* He also points out that some of the accusations leveled at Seneca by Boulay's Nero closely resemble the critical remarks of Valletto and the Soldiers. See also Carter, "Re-reading *Poppea*," 178–86.

Seneca, lettera di rampogna per quel che riguarda la sua vita, e invece di elogio per il suo pensiero). It is a view articulated almost verbatim by the soldiers in *Incoronazione*.[16]

The earlier historians, Tacitus and Suetonius, emphasize Seneca's role as teacher and advisor to Nero without dwelling on the unsavory aspects of that role, though Tacitus hints at some scandal, mentioning an episode of adultery and some suspicious financial dealings (*Annals*, 13.42). It is left to Dio Cassius to draw the obvious conclusion from these reports, namely, that Seneca did not live up to his reputation as a stoic:

> Seneca now found himself under accusation, one of the charges against him being that he was intimate with Agrippina. It had not been enough for him, it seems, to commit adultery with Julia, nor had he become wiser as a result of his banishment, but he must establish improper relations with Agrippina, in spite of the kind of woman she was and the kind of son she had. Nor was this the only instance in which his conduct was seen to be diametrically opposed to the teachings of his philosophy. For while denouncing tyranny, he was making himself the teacher of a tyrant; while inveighing against the associates of the powerful, he did not hold aloof from the palace himself. . . . Though finding fault with the rich, he himself acquired a fortune of 300,000,000 sesterces; and though he censured the extravagances of others, he had five hundred tables of citrus wood with legs of ivory, all identically alike, and he served banquets on them. In stating this much I have also made clear what naturally went with it—the licentiousness in which he indulged at the very time that he contracted the most brilliant marriage, and the delight he took in boys past their prime, a practice which he also taught Nero to follow.[17]

BUSENELLO'S SENECA

Seneca the playwright naturally looms large in Busenello's aesthetics. Like most serious dramatists of the time, he regarded Seneca the tragedian as an important model, but he accepted his dramaturgical precepts with more than a grain of salt. His preface to the libretto *La prosperità infelice di Giulio Cesare dittatore*, for instance, invokes Senecan authority in two distinct, even contradictory, contexts. On the one hand, Seneca as dramatist justifies Busenello's choice of the orthodox format of five acts for *Giulio Cesare*, the format he implicitly rejected in all of his previous librettos, including, of course, *Incoronazione*.[18] But while Seneca the dramatist provides authority for a return to orthodoxy and the rules,

---

16. The specific biographical details that contributed to this view are summarized in *Seneca: Mostra bibliografica e iconografica*, ed. Francesca Niutta and Carmela Santucci (Rome: Fratelli Palombi, 1999), 23 and n. 36, with further bibliography.

17. Dio Cassius, *Dio's Roman History*, Epitome of Book 61.10.1–4, trans. Earnest Cary, Loeb Classical Library (Cambridge, MA: Harvard University Press, 1961), 8: 55–57; see also n. 21 regarding the support for Dio's version by other authors.

18. Also the later *Statira*. "If the acts are five and not three, remember that all ancient dramas, and particularly the tragedies of Seneca, are divided into five acts" (Se gli atti sono cinque e non tre, rammentati che tutti i drammi antichi e particolarmente le tragedie di Seneca sono distinte in cinque atti); Gian Francesco Busenello, *La prosperità infelice di Giulio Cesare dittatore*, preface, p. x, in *Delle hore ociose*.

Seneca the man provides authority for just the opposite, a lenient attitude toward modern taste: "It is necessary to satisfy modern taste to some extent, always keeping in mind the praise that Tacitus bestowed on Seneca, that is, that he had an imagination made to order for the taste of his times."[19] And once again, in his letter to Giovanni Grimani concerning his libretto *La Statira*, Busenello explicitly rejects Seneca's dramatic practice because it fails to conform to modern taste: "Seneca, in his tragedies, most of the time confines an act to a single scene and a chorus. If anyone were to do such a thing today, that is, with Senecan authority to form a tragedy according to that ancient rule, I leave it to those with wit to imagine how much would be said against him. Therefore, the customs and teachings of antiquity are not articles of faith for our efforts."[20]

As to *Incoronazione* itself, it is important to remember that Seneca was thought to be the author of the *Octavia*, one of the most important—if unacknowledged—sources of Busenello's libretto. Given the obvious parallels between the two texts, Busenello's failure to cite the *Octavia* as a source is certainly noteworthy, though the way in which he used the play, like his other sources, was a matter of expediency: he took what he needed, disguising or altering it according to his aesthetic or philosophical aims as an Incognito dramatist.[21] Although their political purpose and interpretation of historical events are very different, play and libretto share many features, including characters, dramatic situations, and even poetic language—all of which are features unique to these two sources.[22] Within the nearly identical dramatis personae—only Otho and Drusilla are missing from the play—possibly the most telling parallel involves the nurses of Poppaea and Octavia, who behave in much the same way in both texts. In the *Octavia*, as in *Incoronazione*, Octavia's most impassioned lament is prompted by imminent exile and is generally similar in mood and even imagery to Busenello's "Addio Roma." Finally, in the play, as in the libretto, Nero announces to Seneca his plan to marry Poppaea and engages him in a stichomythic contest. This Busenello seems to have lifted directly into his text.[23] The big

---

19. "Bisogna in qualche parte dilettare i gusti correnti, ricordando sempre della lode che diede Tacito a Seneca, cioè che haveva un ingegno fatto a posta per i gusti di quei tempi" (ibid.).

20. "Seneca nelle tragedie il più delle volte chiude un atto in una scena sola et un choro. Chi facesse così al dì d'oggi mi rimetto a' bel ingegni di quanto sarebbe detto contro chi con l'autorità di Seneca formasse la tragedia a quell'antico prescritto. Adunque gl'usi e gl'insegnamenti antichi non sono destini et articoli di religione alle nostre fatiche"; cited in Livingston, *La vita veneziana*, 373.

21. The only source he actually cites is Tacitus, but he also makes some use of Suetonius and Dio Cassius, in addition to the *Octavia*, as noted in Chap. 5, p. 177 and n. 103. On Dolce's translation of the *Octavia*, see Chap. 5, n. 104. For an up-to-date bibliography regarding the attribution of the play, see *Seneca. Mostra bibliografica*, 131, n. 11, and especially the new edition by Rolando Ferri, *Octavia, a Play Attributed to Seneca* (Cambridge: Cambridge University Press, 2003), reviewed by Emily Wilson, in *Times Literary Supplement*, 16 April 2004, pp. 4–6.

22. Heller, "Tacitus Incognito," 69–73, summarizes the relationship of the *Octavia* to *Incoronazione*, noting the differences in their political messages. She points out that the play predates and is therefore not influenced by Tacitus, that it does not manipulate chronology, that its author was an admirer of Seneca and his play a "diatribe against Nero" (p. 70).

23. Dolce's translation of the *Octavia* makes Busenello's indebtedness all the more apparent. See Chap. 5, pp. 177–78.

difference between the two works involves Seneca's death, which is absent in the ancient play. (Had it been included, of course, the *Octavia* could never have been ascribed to Seneca in the first place.) But its absence in this source—and the lengths Busenello had to go to include it in his text—highlights the importance of the event to him.[24]

That Busenello intended his depiction to reflect the historical Seneca, warts and all, is affirmed by the dialogue he gives him, which is laced with expressions borrowed from a variety of Senecan texts. So, for example, in reminding Ottavia that "the vanity of tears is unworthy of imperial eyes," he is paraphrasing a passage from the *Consolatio ad Polybium,* in which the philosopher counseled the emperor Claudius's powerful adviser not to cry for his dead brother: "though you have equal grief, you do not have the same liberty as your brothers. There are many things that the opinion which others have formed of your learning and your character does not permit you to do . . . Men demand much of you, expect much . . . You may not weep beyond measure" (6.3–4). A passage from *De providentia,* in which Seneca asked his friend Lucilius "You are a great man; but how do I know it if Fortune gives you no opportunity of showing your worth?" seems to be echoed when Busenello's Seneca urges Ottavia to "thank fortune who with its strokes increases your ornaments: an unstruck flint cannot give sparks" (La cote non percossa non può mandar faville). A more striking echo of *De providentia* is found in Seneca's description of death as a "breve angoscia" ("so brief that its fleetness cannot come within the ken"). There are several allusions to the *Consolatio ad Helviam,* in Seneca's reference to the unhappiness of the rich (1.7), and in the exiled Ottavia's expression of hope that the air will send her breath to her beloved Rome. One particular formulation from the *Epistulae morales,* "Ungoverned anger begets madness," and a number of passages from *De ira* resonate in Seneca's confrontation with Nero in 1.9.[25]

There is another important point to be made about Busenello and Seneca. While the characterization may be justified by history, Busenello's manipulation of the facts, especially his treatment of Seneca's suicide, indicates a more pointed Venetian political agenda. The very fact that he included it at all, let alone his readiness to alter the historical record to do so, was a polemical gesture: suicide is a sin in the eyes of the Church,[26] and Busenello's dramatization of Seneca's act would have been interpreted—especially in post-Tridentine Italy, and coming from an Incognito—as an anti-clerical statement, a deliberate affront to

---

24. The most substantial of several chronological rearrangements in the libretto is the anticipation of Seneca's death by three years, from A.D. 65 to A.D. 62, so that it coincides with the other events in the opera (Ottavia was murdered in A.D. 62, Poppea in A.D. 65). This point in is made in Chap. 5, p. 176; see also Heller, "Tacitus Incognito," 65. Busenello's chronological rearrangement is also discussed in Holzer, Review, p. 80. Heller, p. 73, argues that the distortion of history involved in Busenello's handling of Lucano is even bolder than that involving Seneca.

25. The preceding paragraph is based on Holzer, Review, pp. 89–91.

26. See Daniel Rolfs, *The Last Cross: A History of the Suicide Theme in Italian Literature* (Ravenna: Longo, 1981), chap. 4: "From the Counter-Reformation Era to the Age of Enlightenment," and Elizabeth G. Dickenson and James M. Boyden, "Ambivalence toward Suicide in Early Modern Spain," in *From Sin to Insanity: Suicide in Early Modern Europe,* ed. Jeffrey R. Watt (Ithaca: Cornell University Press), 100–15.

established religion.[27] Such a statement was permissible in the theater perhaps only in Venice, which had asserted its independence from Rome with increasing energy from the late sixteenth century onward: following the papal interdict of 1606–1607, Venice famously defied Rome by expelling the Jesuits from Venetian territories for a period of nearly fifty years. (That such an overt anti-ecclesiastical gesture might not have been tolerated in staunchly Catholic Naples could certainly explain the absence of the death scene in the Naples libretto of the opera, whether or not the reasons were practical as well.)[28] But, as we have seen, even as Busenello changed history to include Seneca's suicide in his drama, he undermined its heroic potential by focusing on the *famigliari*'s casual rejection of its significance.

Seneca's contradictory combination of qualities epitomizes the shifting morality of *Incoronazione*. His ambiguity matches that of the opera as a whole, which depicts a world shaped by the turning wheel of fortune, the kaleidoscopic, conflicting claims of love and lust, politics and ethics, and the deconstruction of absolute heroism and moral clarity.

Tragic Buffoon

As inarticulate as Seneca is eloquent, Iro would appear in no position to sustain a debate of any kind, or even to bear the interpretive weight of the libretto in which he seems to play such a minor, if vivid, part. And yet, though it cannot derive from his history—Iro hardly has a history—his characterization is comparably fraught with ambiguity. That ambiguity is at root generic: comic characters do not die.[29]

To be sure, Iro, variously identified as "parte redicola" or "persona giocosa," never quite fits the pattern of a conventional comic character, even in the scenes leading up to his suicide. That sort of character had only recently emigrated to Venetian opera from the realm of spoken comedy.[30] One year before *Ritorno*, in 1639, a "personaggio gio-

---

27. Possibly the direct association between the suicidal knife and the key to Heaven in Seneca's scene with the Virtues was considered too blasphemous to be articulated on stage, and was therefore cut. On this scene, see below.

28. See above, Chap. 4, p. 97 for the issue of censorship as it might have affected the Naples libretto.

29. There may be some ambiguity as to whether Iro actually dies or not. And although he lacks successors in Venetian opera, one may perhaps identify ancestors within the plays of Ruzzante: Menego, in the *Dialogo facetissimo [Menego]* (1529), for instance, delivers what Nancy Dersofi (*Arcadia and the Stage* [Madrid: Turanzas, 1978], 75) has characterized as "a harrowing soliloquy or mock debate on the subject of suicide," for which she provides a translation (pp. 77–78). Iro's soliloquy might well be characterized similarly. It may hardly be a coincidence that the *Dialogo* takes place in a year of famine and that, like Iro, all the characters, including Menego, risk dying of hunger. Menego even threatens to eat himself. A similar soliloquy, delivered by Ruzzante playing himself, occurs in *La moscheta* (3.6; *Ruzzante: Teatro*, ed. Lodovico Zorzi [Turin: Einaudi, 1967], 634–36).

30. Paolo Fabbri, *Il secolo cantante: Per una storia del libretto d'opera nel Seicento*, 2nd ed. (Rome: Bulzoni, 2003), 92, rightly notes that conventional comic characters in Venetian opera had Roman precedents.

coso" called Ermafrodite had appeared in *La Delia,* a libretto by Giulio Strozzi, set to music by Francesco Manelli. Strozzi emphasized the novelty of this character in his preface: "I have introduced the Hilarode of the Greeks in the person of the cheerful Hermaphrodite, a novel character, who, between the severity of the tragic and the facetiousness of the comic stands out to advantage upon our stage."[31] But the character him/herself belies its creator's claim of novelty, disclosing its true lineage in its first solo scene, at the end of act 1: there, in a strophic poem of three stanzas, s/he reveals herself as resembling the old nurse Scarabea, featured in Benedetto Ferrari's *La maga fulminata* of the previous year, 1638, only the second opera to have been performed in Venice.[32] The cast of every Venetian opera following *La maga fulminata* included such a Scarabean descendant, now often identified as a comic role. Arnalta in *Incoronazione* is another one of these old nurses who, with their scurrilous sensibilities and witty repartee, serve as procuresses for their mistresses.[33]

The nurse was one of the comic types drawn directly from the realm of spoken theater into opera; others included the astute page, like Busenello's Valletto, who gives advice or comfort to his aristocratic master or mistress, and the *miles gloriosus,* like Iro and Numano, whose blustering bravado served as a foil to his master.[34] The structural/dramatic function of these characters in opera was the same as that in spoken drama: to bridge the gap between the fictional world and reality by commenting on the stage action, both from within as participants and as outside observers, in the form of direct

---

31. "Ho introdotto quì l'Hilaredo de' Greci, e questi sarà il giocoso Ermafrodito, personaggio nuovo che tra la severità del Tragico, e la facetiae del Comico campeggia molto bene sù le nostre Scene" (Giulio Strozzi, *La Delia,* preface, p. 7).

32. Con lusinghe ladre
    Mercurio mio padre
    Venere assaggiò:
    Nacqui di bella Dea;
    E la nudrice mia fù Scarabea.
    L'han già molti udita
    Vecchia rimbambita
    D'Amore cantar,
    Ma non è meraviglia:
    D'una tiorba e d'un poeta è figlia.
    Latte Scarabeo
    Mi fece un Orfeo,
    Sì lungo e sottil;
    Son di Venere figlio
    Ma nel restante à Scarabea simiglio.

This text is discussed and translated in Rosand, "Iro," 145–46.

33. Penelope's nurse Ericlea does not share these qualities; she is too serious and important to the plot. The characteristic scurrility is taken over by Penelope's younger companion Melanto.

34. The pedant philosopher (resembling Seneca?) was another one. The various comic types in early Venetian opera are surveyed in Fabbri, *Il secolo cantante,* 92–114. Another Iro type is Giroldo, from *Gli amori di Isifile e Giasone* of 1642.

address to the audience. Precisely because they stood apart from the narrative action, their ironic and humorous remarks were often cast in strict poetic forms (like Ermafrodite's strophes mentioned above) and set as songs or arias. Arnalta and Valletto offer typical examples.[35]

The comedy of these conventional characters resides in what they say, their quips and clever, pointed dialogue, their enunciation of clichés, maxims, proverbs, sexual innuendo, and social satire. Iro, however, though he falls into the general category of *miles gloriosus,* conforms to his comic type only in part. He may bluster, threaten, and ape his masters, but he does not simply react, foil, and provoke; he feels and he acts. He challenges Ulisse to a duel. He kills himself. Most disturbingly, heartless as it may seem to say so, he does not sing: a matter of no small importance that we will take up later.

A revealing sign of the significance of Iro's suicide, like Seneca's, lies in its relation— or rather lack of relation—to the source material of the libretto. Just as Busenello had to alter the course of Roman history to include Seneca's death, so too Badoaro had to reach beyond Homer for Iro's. It is the only major event in the libretto, a libretto almost pedantically faithful to its source, that is completely absent from the *Odyssey*. The character, to be sure, is based on Homer's Irus, also known as Arnaios, but Irus appears only once in the epic, at the opening of book 18 (ll. 1–107). After foolishly challenging him to a fight, he is viciously beaten by Odysseus, who props his mangled body against the courtyard wall, staff in hand, to scare away the dogs and stray pigs.

Iro receives slightly more emphasis in Dolce's "rifacimento" of the *Odyssey*. Though still appearing in only one canto (canto 16), he is deemed worthy of two allegorical glosses, something that distinguishes him from all but one of the other secondary characters in the canto.[36] Significantly, we recall that the first allegory describes him as a parasite—Badoaro's term, as well, though Homer does not use it nor, it seems, does any other translation.[37] "From Iro, who fights with Ulisse, one understands the nature of parasites, who, in order to please their supporters, will commit every insolence and make it their business to injure anyone, no matter how honored." Dolce's second allegory turns Iro into a kind of cautionary exemplar: "And in the same Iro, who is nearly killed by Ulisse, one comes to understand how those who boldly attempt to test their strength against adversaries unknown to them will be punished." That Dolce considers Iro worthy of two allegorical glosses, however generalized, raises him to a level of significance he may

---

35. Melanto is somewhat less typical. Though she repeatedly urges her mistress to forsake her marital vows, extolling the pleasures of sexual freedom, she is too personally implicated: she stands to retain her own lover, Eurimaco, if Penelope accedes to the Suitors.

36. Eumete is the other one. This parallel is one of the indications that Dolce was probably a source for Badoaro. See Chap. 5, pp. 136–37, and Appendix 5.

37. As mentioned above, in Dolce, the Iro scene, culminating in the fight with Ulisse, takes up canto 16, ottave 12–30 (=Homer 18.1–107). By introducing the epithet parasite, Dolce (and Badoaro) emphasize the link to Lucian. He is a buffoon in Malipiero and a beggar in most other authors (including Della Porta). Cf. Chap. 5, n. 19.

not have had in the *Odyssey,* a suggestive precedent perhaps for Badoaro's use of the parasite for his own allegorical purposes.[38]

Iro's role is greatly expanded in the opera, where he appears in three different scenes, one in each of Monteverdi's three acts: in 1.12, with the shepherd Eumete, who sends him off to eat; in 2.12, which enacts the Odyssean beating; and, most extensively by far, alone in the scene that culminates in his suicide, 3.1.[39] The first added scene is dramatically redundant, obviously put in to bolster the role. But it helps to establish Iro as a comic character whose guttural stuttering contrasts markedly with Eumete's musical eloquence.

The second added scene, the suicide, is shocking in its suddenness and shockingly inappropriate for a character of Iro's stature. Placed just after the long-awaited climax of the opera, it is an unexpected and unexpectedly pathetic echo of Ulisse's violent slaying of the Suitors. It gives the impression of being impulsive, a desperate last-minute decision—by Iro, perhaps even by Badoaro (or even the composer): it is certainly worth noting that the Argomento, given in two of the manuscript librettos of *Ritorno,* fails completely to mention this scene.[40]

Seneca's death, the inevitable, appropriate culmination of a stoic's life, has been prepared and anticipated, almost from the beginning of the drama;[41] the philosopher goes to his death with determination, after having bid farewell to his followers. In contrast, the parasite falls almost accidentally into his, at the close of a long monologue that began like a comic lament, a parodic response to the defeat of his hosts that had promised to end very differently. Yet in a sense Iro's death is as inevitable as Seneca's, for neither character can exist in the new world order that has emerged around them. In the Venetian librettos, both philosopher and parasite have been rendered irrelevant, the former by corrupt political power, the latter by its defeat.

The two deaths parallel one another in other interesting ways. Occurring as it does at the beginning of the final act (in both three- and five-act versions), Iro's monologue has a structural function analogous to that of Seneca's farewell to his followers, especially within the five-act drama. Instead of providing the fulcrum, however, it serves as a balancing counterweight to Penelope's opening lament—ironically, almost the only other

---

38. The texts of the two allegories for Iro are given in Appendix 5, A.

39. As noted in Chap. 7, Badoaro includes him once more, in the scene of the Suitors' slaughter, but this is omitted in the score.

40. The argomento is reproduced in Appendix 5, A. Other scenes go unmentioned in the argomento as well, such as Ericlea's monologue. Whether or not this indicates last-minute insertion, however, is impossible to determine. In the scenario for *Incoronazione,* the omission of reference to "Pur ti miro" was once—but is no longer—considered evidence of its absence from the first production. One other contemporary operatic suicide comes to mind: that of Aristeo, one of the protagonists in *Orfeo* by Francesco Buti and Luigi Rossi, performed in Paris in 1647. Aristeo's suicide, like Iro's the culmination of an extended mad scene (act 3, scene 4), is particularly shocking because it begins on stage—he jumps off a cliff. Iro and Seneca conform to the more circumspect classical tradition by disposing of themselves behind the scenes, though directors have been known to allow their audiences to observe Iro stabbing himself.

41. Not only is it probable that a knowledgeable reader would have known of Seneca's ultimate fate, it is mentioned in the scenario, which prepares the audience.

substantial soliloquy in the opera.[42] By claiming the stage for such an extended, incongruous scene, Iro affirms his importance to the drama as a whole.

The significance of parasite and philosopher for the meaning of their respective operas is reinforced by a final parallel between them, one that has seldom been noted: both of their deaths are followed directly by substantial supernatural scenes, scenes in neither case set by Monteverdi.[43]

The scene in *Ritorno*—dismissed in Monteverdi's score, as we have noted, for being "troppo maninconico"—comprises an extended meditation by Mercurio on the meaning of death—of the Suitors and, by implication, of Iro. The first part is addressed to the Suitors' ghosts:

Of a human tragedy this is the end.
Kingdoms, beauties, Love
in transience dissolve,
the spirit flies away, and nothing remains but dust.
Death is a powerful Goddess,
who defeats every living thing,
denying even cruel hope.
He who disbelieves the evidence
in the end cannot deny the proof.
You, once proud suitors, now dark souls,
by the hand of Ulysses the strong,
great minister of heaven, were rendered extinct.
And now, having tasted
the wandering freedom of death,
you will be submerged in the kingdom
of him who teaches cruelty.
Your sins demand
the precipices of Avernus,
the chasms of Hell,
reserved for perfidious and cruel souls
when heaven has ordained eternal damnation.
Thus opens the abyss.

At this point, Hell opens and the ghosts disappear into it. Mercurio then directs his attention to the audience, admonishing:

Learn, then, ye mortals,
that the punishments of your briefest pleasures

---

42. Ulisse has a soliloquy, of course, but it lacks the structural prominence or significance of Penelope's and Iro's.

43. Carter mentions the parallelism, but without exploring its implications (*Musical Theatre*, 287).

are eternal.
Proud while you live,
your human delights
will reign in dust.
While they may indulge in the flesh and the senses,
when you are dead
your spirit will suffer immortal torment.
A hard and unfortunate exchange it is
of a butterfly of joy for a Phoenix of suffering.
Life is but a passage,
it has neither state nor firmness;
if beauty ever arises
it fades as soon as it begins to shine forth.
Live cautiously, O mortals,
for life marches on and time has wings.
And where hope grows greedy
it cannot be sated.
Of human madness, this is the desert.[44]

Mercurio's—and Badoaro's—message is clear (and familiar, from text Monteverdi cut from Penelope's lament): the punishment of passing delight is eternal; indulging in pleasures of the flesh will reap everlasting torment; life is but a brief passage on the road to eternal death. This moral, spelled out with considerable rhetorical flourish, may have been central to the significance of the drama for Badoaro—but evidently not for the opera, since, as we have noted several times, Monteverdi cut the scene.[45]

The parallel scene, for Seneca's ghost and a chorus of Virtues, presents the obverse of the situation:

Lieto, e ridente	Happy and smiling,
Al fin t'affretta,	Hurry, finally,
Che il Ciel t'aspetta.	for heaven awaits you.
Breve coltello,	A short knife,
Ferro minuto	a minute sword
Sarà la chiave,	will be the key
Che m'aprirà	that will open
Le vene in terra,	my veins on earth,
E in Ciel le porte dell'eternità.	and in heaven the doors of eternity.
Lieto e ridente. Ecc.	

---

44. Italian text in Appendix 7, A.
45. The issue is discussed in Chap. 4, nn. 18–19. On the cut in Penelope's lament, see Chap. 7, n. 9.

A Dio grandezze,	Farewell greatness,
Pompe di vetro,	pomp of glass,
Glorie di polve,	glories of dust,
Larve d'error.	shadows of error,
Che in un momento	which at the same time
Affascinate, assassinate il cor.	fascinate and assassinate the heart.
<u>Lieto ridente.</u>	
Già, già dispiego il volo	Already I launch the flight
Da questa mia decrepita mortale,	from this, my mortal decay
E verso il choro vostro	and toward your choir,
Adorate virtudi inalzo l'ale.	adored virtues, I raise my wings.

Seneca's ghost is headed in the opposite direction: not to Hell with the Suitors, but to Heaven. The philosopher's self-sacrifice earns Virtue's reward: the knife that opened earthly veins is the key to the doors of eternity. Bidding farewell to greatness, pomp, and glory, which are of glass and dust, the source of error, and fascinate as they assassinate the heart, Seneca ascends on wings to the seat of Virtue. These two supernatural scenes set up a contrast between Vice and Virtue, the one to be punished with eternal suffering, the other rewarded with eternal salvation. Yet once again, of course, like its dark twin, a scene intrinsic to the librettist's conception of his drama, emphasizing one of its central themes, was deemed extraneous to the opera (or at least dispensable): Monteverdi did not set it. In recompense, however, as we shall see, the composer endowed both Iro and Seneca with sufficient musical substance to enable them to shoulder the full weight of interpretation on their own.[46]

Critics and Directors

The ambiguities surrounding both Iro and Seneca, particularly as regards their suicides, have consistently challenged interpreters of the operas. This is evident not only in the musicological literature, but in the divergent ways these characters have been portrayed in performance. In Jean-Pierre Ponelle's classic and widely circulated versions of the operas, both deaths occur onstage (contradicting the normal expectations of classical drama, whereby such events were usually reported rather than witnessed). This interpretation

---

46. Carter, "Re-reading *Poppea*," 202–203, suggests that the supernatural scene was never intended to be set to music. "It is religiously suspect, the jogging *quinari* are unamenable to music, and one wonders how such a curiously banal apotheosis would have been staged." His main argument against its inclusion, however, is based on its subject matter: it stages the triumph of Virtue, whereas it is Love that is the subject of the opera. I see no contradiction here. Love's triumph over Virtue and Fortune is all the stronger (and more shocking) for Seneca's apotheosis. Carter's is an interesting argument, but it flattens the work. Perhaps both supernatural scenes were cut for the same reason: difficulties in staging.

heightens the shock of Iro's suicide, but undercuts the tragic effect of Seneca's—especially since his corpse remains on stage for the remainder of act 2.

Although traditionally accepted as a thoroughly serious character, over the past quarter century Seneca has inspired an enormous range of interpretations: from tragic and moving to pompous and incompetent. On the positive side, Eric Chafe regards Seneca as the embodiment of Virtue, emphasizing his isolation from surrounding events, and crediting his bass voice for the "tone of gravity that tends toward the pompous at times."[47] Peter Miller and Iain Fenlon, too, are convinced of his seriousness: Seneca's lack of efficacy, according to Miller, is a failure of others to understand him, a rejection of Stoicism rather than a failure of communication on his part. He terms him a perfect embodiment of Neostoic constancy, which is defeated by Love (appearances) in the opera.[48] Robert Holzer advocates a still more serious reading of Seneca, discounting the critical remarks of the soldiers and the page because, as inferior characters, they are untrustworthy; and he likens them to the unreliable witnesses in Tacitus's rendering of the events.[49]

Other critics, however, focus on Seneca's weakness rather than his strength. Susan McClary, for instance, characterizes him, along with the other males in the opera—"the traditional repositories of patriarchal authority"—as profoundly passive and impotent; and she accuses him of habitually reverting "to silly madrigalisms, which destroy the rhetorical effect of most of his statements." This, according to McClary, is in contrast to Poppea, "who usurps and perverts to her own ends the tools of patriarchal persuasion," thereby indicating a historically significant shift in gender representation in the work.[50]

Wendy Heller, too, views Seneca as pompous and ineffective. She is struck by his "inability to muster his famed rhetorical powers in the service of a coherent oration. . . . Seneca, oblivious to the nature of beauty, is an incompetent rhetorician and musician. Unable to coordinate word and sound," she concludes, "he is thus an unlikely hero for an opera by Monteverdi." She criticizes his language as contrived and academic. "Such blatant contrivances as the melisma on 'faville,' the syncopations on 'colpita,' and the ascent illustrating 'Glorie' seem more like academic exercises in madrigalesque imitation."[51]

Tim Carter reluctantly acknowledges an ambiguous Seneca, but he is not sure whom to credit, librettist or composer: "These two sides to Seneca [pompous and heroic] are certainly present in the libretto of *Incoronazione* and perhaps even in the music," he says. But in the end, Carter minimizes the heroic side by deliberately denying the effect of his death. (I shall return to this.)[52]

---

47. Chafe, *Tonal Language*, 313.

48. Fenlon and Miller, *Song of the Soul, passim*, esp. chap. 7.

49. Holzer, Review; cf. above, n. 10.

50. Susan McClary, "Constructions of Gender in Monteverdi's Dramatic Music," in *Feminine Endings: Music, Gender, and Sexuality* (Minneapolis: University of Minnesota Press, 1991), 49.

51. Heller, "Tacitus Incognito," 67.

52. Carter, "Re-reading *Poppea*," 179.

Divergent, or at least perplexed, interpretations of Iro have a longer history. Most writers on the opera have had something to say about him. They typically comment on the realistic, comic, or parodic aspects of his character. Hans Redlich mentions him only in passing: he calls him a clown and characterizes his monologue as a "comic air," though he refers to "Chi lo consola" as a "tragi-comic outburst."[53] Luigi Dallapiccola dubs Iro a Falstaff *avant la lettre*.[54] Anna Amalie Abert, who regards Iro as the "Stammvater" of the comic servant tradition of Venetian opera, quotes Robert Haas's description of the lament as a "Kabinettstuck musikalischer Realistik." Noting its mixture of parody elements with comic exaggeration, she praises the scene as a point of repose for the listener, following the catastrophe of act 2.[55] Leo Schrade focuses on the lament's ridiculousness: "The first scene [of the final act] with Iro's solo has special interest . . . , for Iro's aria is marked as a *parte ridicola*. . . . To make this lament ridiculous, Monteverdi parodies every feature of his noble madrigalesque style . . . It is the first aria in which exaggeration of the new distinguished, serious style is used for comic effect."[56] Paolo Fabbri judges Iro's scenes worthy of special notice because they represented Monteverdi's first attempt at the comic style, remarking on the aspects of caricature in his music: "the role of Iro is characterized as caricature in the sense that stylistic elements are pushed to the point of exaggeration, that is overloaded with expression";[57] and Silke Leopold regards the lament as pure parody: "It is hilarious, when Iro, in the exalted language of lament poems, reflects on food and drink rather than upon crown and scepter when he is abandoned . . . by his provender."[58]

Only a few commentators remark on the serious turn at the end of the lament scene. Domenico De' Paoli mentions a change in mood, but interprets it as part of the comedy: "Arrived almost at the point of paroxysm, excitation yields to a depression that is even more comic, when prostrate, the parasite decides: 'Let my body go feed my tomb.'"[59] But Claudio Gallico, in his exemplary discussion, focuses on the change in Iro's demeanor toward the end of his scene, a greater seriousness and sense of compassion, a complexity and grandeur of Shakespearean proportions. After likening Iro to Falstaff, he continues:

And yet a new tolerant cordiality flowers in this final scene, in comparison with the sarcastic and dismissive negative images in his previous appearances. There is a sense of

---

53. Redlich, *Monteverdi*, 112, pronounces the monologue authentic because it quotes the ciaccona from Monteverdi's "Zefiro torna."

54. Dallapiccola, "Per una rappresentazione," 128–29.

55. Abert, *Monteverdi*, 56.

56. Schrade, *Monteverdi*, 356.

57. "La parte di Iro si caratterizza come caricaturale nel senso che vi appaiono stilemi spinti fino all'esagerazione, all'espressione appunto 'caricata'"; Fabbri, *Monteverdi*, 327 (not in the English translation).

58. Leopold, *Monteverdi*, 145.

59. "Giunta quasi al parossismo, l'eccitazione cede a una depressione anche più comica, quando il parassita, prostrato, decide: 'Vad'il mio corpo a disfamar la tomba'"; De' Paoli, *Monteverdi*, 482–83.

comprehension, perhaps compassion, that tempers the mockery and leads to observation more familiar and articulate, and less schematic on the part of the character. This seems ready to rise to a Shakespearean complexity and grandeur at the end, when contrasting impulses and interpretations are mixed in. At this moment he has expressions of stoicism, which rectify with seriousness earlier meanings; and the final "motto" is an extreme flash of grotesque and mournful ambiguity, inflated by exaggerated, conceit-filled solemnity.[60]

Portrayals of Iro on stage have registered his ambiguity, ranging from the exceedingly, exclusively comic, almost slapstick (Ponelle), to ironic and even tragic (Christie); some directors emphasize his growing insanity as he shifts from one topic to another and laments his abandonment by the Suitors. Some interpretations have not seemed to take his suicide seriously, even ignoring it completely, whereas others, such as Ponelle, have focused on it.[61]

Music and Text

The meaningful contrast between our two emblematic characters extends to their textual and musical personae. As a pair, philosopher and parasite call forth special—even opposite—treatment, together illustrating the full range of their creators' expressive resources. Once again, a comparison of ridiculous and sublime is instructive; this time in revealing the shared responsibility of librettist and composer in the shaping of these memorable characters.

Of course the two speak very differently. Busenello's Seneca is especially long-winded, and repeatedly delivers himself of extended precepts, while Badoaro's Iro can barely form a sentence. But although the two kinds of speech naturally inspire very different responses on the part of the composer, his means of expression are the same: repetition of text, interpolation of song-like passages, harmonic and melodic shape, sequences, melismatic expansions, madrigalisms, are all chosen with an eye toward portraying, enhancing, and developing the characters offered to him by his poets.

---

60. "Affiora in quest'ultima scena una nuova cordialità tollerante, a confronto con la pittura sarcastica e sprezzante del carattere negativo nelle sue passate apparizioni; c'è un senso di comprensione, forse di compassione, che tempera lo scherno e conduce a un'osservazione più accostata e articolata, e meno schematica del personaggio. Il quale pare fatto ascendere a una complessità e grandezza shakesperiane nel finale, allorquando s'annodano e si mescolano impulse e interpretazioni contrastanti. In questo momento ha espressioni di stoicismo, che rettificano seriamente i connotati precedenti; e il motto finale è un estremo guizzo di ambiguità grottesca e funebre, paludata di esagerata concettosa solennità." Claudio Gallico, *Monteverdi: Poesia musicale, teatro, e musica sacra* (Turin: Einaudi, 1979), 89.

61. The contrast is evident in the two most recent videos of the opera. In the production conducted by Christophe Rousset, Iro simply walks off the stage; in that of William Christie, he entombs himself in a monumental urn.

Seneca expounds his precepts almost exclusively in lengthy passages of *versi sciolti*. (The single potential formal aria in his entire role, two stanzas of *quinari*, occurs in the scene following his death, the one that was not set to music.) Although an occasional rhymed couplet, especially at the end of a speech, may add emphasis to a particularly pertinent— often literally Senecan—formulation, his texts are generally prose-like, surprisingly lacking in rhyme. More than half of his twenty-four-line speech to Ottavia is without rhyme—the first rhyme does not come until lines 16–17 (rhymes are underlined in Table 21 below)—and equivalent unrhymed passages can be found in several of his later speeches as well; even when rhyme does occur more frequently, as in his soliloquy in 1.7, Busenello minimizes its effect by avoiding paired lines of equal lengths. In addition to mimicking prose, the infrequency of rhyme or other potential devices of closure tends to leave it up to the composer to find occasions for lyricism. Significantly, as we shall see, for Seneca such occasions are limited.

However infrequent in most of his long speeches, though, rhyme works well in punctuating some of Seneca's shorter exchanges. For example, to Nerone's declaration, in seven unrhymed *settenari*, that he wishes to divorce Ottavia and marry Poppea, Seneca responds with a rhymed hendecasyllabic quatrain, immediately establishing his calm control over the situation. Then, after having parried Nerone, line for unrhymed line, as their confrontation proceeds, he effectively closes off the debate with a sententious rhymed couplet of hendecasyllables. (See Table 18 above, Chap. 7.)

Rhymed or not, Seneca's language remains excessively formal, even pompous in its tone and verbosity. This is particularly evident in his frequent recourse to concrete, abstract imagery, sometimes forming sentientious generalizations that paraphrase, if they do not replicate, actual Senecan texts, some of them mentioned earlier. Especially in the scene with Ottavia and the following one, he expresses himself in long, convoluted sentences in which adjective and noun tend to be awkwardly separated (Table 21): lines 3–4: "o gloriosa / Del mondo Imperatrice," and lines 5–6: "sovra i titoli eccelsi / Degl'insigni avi tuoi conspicua e grande"; or where a succession of modifiers repeatedly postpones the point until the end ("La vaghezza del volto, i lineamenti, / Che'in apparenza illustre / Risplendon coloriti e delicati, / Da pochi ladri dì *ci son rubati*"). Such stilted rhetoric bespeaks a lack of personal engagement with Ottavia, an aloofness emphasized by his adoption of synecdoche in his fruitless efforts to comfort her: "La vanità del pianto / Degl'occhi imperiali, è ufficio indegno." But even first-person address fails to bridge the gap between them. His objective attempt to preach stoicism above personal feeling, to encourage her to thank Fortune for her suffering and to accept her harsh destiny as a means of achieving glory, fails utterly to move her: she rejects his advice as specious vanities.[62] (This is one of those Senecan precepts mentioned earlier.)

---

62. As we cannot fail to remember, the Valletto thinks even less of Seneca's preaching.

TABLE 21

L'incoronazione di Poppea, 1.6, Seneca with Ottavia

1 (Ecco la sconsolata	(Behold the disconsolate
c: 1	
2 Donna assunta all'impero	lady, raised to an imperial throne
3 5	
3 Per patir il servaggio.) O gloriosa	only to suffer slavery.) O glorious
1 ↓ 5 1 d:1 3	
4 Del mondo Imperatrice,	empress of the world,
5	
5 Sovra i titoli eccelsi	even above the exalted ranks
6 Degl'insigni avi tuoi conspicua, e grande,	of your illustrious forebears, renowned
8 1 3 1 5	and great,
7 La vanità del pianto	the indulgence of tears
8 Degl'occhi imperiali è ufficio indegno.	is unworthy of imperial eyes.
1 ↓ 5 1	
9 Ringratia *ringratia* la fortuna,	Give thanks to Fortune,
c: 5 8	
10 Che con i colpi, *i colpi* suoi	whose blows
11 Ti cresce gl'ornamenti.	do but add to your graces.
12 La cote non percossa, *non percossa*	An unstruck flint
13 Non può mandar, *non può mandar* faville:	cannot give forth sparks.
14 Tu dal destin colpita, *dal destin colpita*	You, by fate struck,
15 Produci a te medesma alti splendori	shall yourself produce the exalted splendors
16 Di vigor, di fort<u>ezza</u>,	of strength, of fortitude,
17 Glorie maggiori assai, che la bell<u>ezza</u>.	glories much greater than beauty.
18 La vaghezza del volto, i lineamenti,	The charm of face and figure
19 Che in apparenza illustre	that in illustrious appearance
20 Risplendon coloriti e deli<u>cati,</u>	shine, colored and delicate,
21 Da pochi ladri di ci son rub<u>bati.</u>	by a few thieving days is stolen from us.
22 Ma la virtù costante	But virtue that stands firm,
23 Usa bravar le stelle, il fatto, e 'l <u>caso,</u>	employed to defy the stars, fate, and
	chance,
24 Giamai non vede, *non vede* oc<u>caso.</u>	will never be eclipsed.

NOTE: Interlinear notations for lines 1–9 indicate scale degrees.

Seneca continues to deliver stiff philosophical platitudes in his soliloquy in the following scene, as he "speculates on the transitory grandeur of this world." Note here how the verb of the sentence is withheld until the end (italicized):

Le porpore regali, e imperatrici	The purple, royal and imperial,
D'acute spine e triboli conteste	composed of sharp thorns and tribulations

| Sotto forma di veste | in the form of clothing |
| *Son* il martirio a Prencipi infelici. | are the torments of unhappy princes. |

But when Minerva appears to warn him of his imminent death (1.8), Seneca for once responds directly and personally, vowing to overcome his fear with strength and constancy ("costante, e forte vincerò gli accidenti, e le paure"), only to conclude the scene in his more characteristic, objective mode with a typically convoluted generalization: "Doppo il girar delle giornate oscure / È di giorno infinito alba la morte." His subsequent confrontation with Nerone (in 1.9) is likewise filled with sententious proverbs. Only rarely addressing the emperor personally, he deflects each of Nerone's angry thrusts with a generalization, the philosopher's cool reason contrasting strongly with the emperor's passionate fury. His concluding eleven-line address has but a single personal pronoun (italicized), introduced after a lengthy series of objective statements:[63]

SENECA: Siano innocenti i regi,	Rulers are innocent
O s'aggravino sol di colpe illustri;	if they're concerned alone with glorious thrusts;
S'innocenza si perde,	if innocence is lost
Perdasi sol per guadagnar i regni.	it's only lost to gain kingdoms.
Ch'il peccato commesso,	Sins committed
Per aggrandir l'impero,	to expand the empire
Si assolve da sé stesso;	are absolved by themselves.
Ma ch'una femminella abbia possanza	But that a woman has the power
Di condur*ti* agli orrori,	to lead *you* to horror
Non è colpa da rege o semideo.	is no fault of a ruler or demigod.
È un misfatto plebeo.	It's a plebeian misdeed.
NERONE: Levamiti dinanzi	Be gone from me,
Maestro impertinente,	impertinent teacher,
Filosofo insolente.	insolent philosopher.
SENECA: Il partito peggior sempre sovrasta	The worse always prevails
Quando la forza a la ragion contrasta.	when force opposes reason.

Seneca's final rhymed couplet effectively extracts the meaning of the scene, reducing all of its tensions to a single objective sentence.[64]

---

63. Heller, "Tacitus Incognito," 72, draws attention to Seneca's use of the word "feminella" in this passage: it is a word dripping with disdain both for Poppea and for Nerone's vulnerability to her.

64. The first part of this scene is discussed above, Chap. 7, pp. 295–97.

Following his confrontation with Nerone in act 1, scene 9, Seneca is not heard from again until the beginning of act 2 (scenes 1–4). Over the course of these four scenes, alone, with Mercurio, with Liberto, and finally with his followers, Seneca's language becomes consistently more direct and more personal. As he faces the looming prospect of death, he undergoes a pronoun conversion, and begins increasingly to speak of (and to) himself in the first person, and to others in the second. He opens the act with a prayer to solitude: "A *te* [solitudine amata] l'anima *mia* lieta sen viene . . . la Corte . . . insolente, e superba fa della *mia* patienza anotomia." "*M*'assido in grembo della pace *mia*." His response to Mercurio's warning that death is near is immediate and direct: "O *me* felice," he says, and then proceeds to explain why he welcomes death: "hor confermo i *miei* scritti, / Autentico i *miei* studi." When Liberto arrives to deliver Nerone's actual death decree, Seneca jumps in and anticipates the message, thanks the unwilling messenger, and joyfully embraces his fate: "Se *m*'arrechi la morte, / Non *mi* chieder perdono. / Rido, mentre *mi* porti un sì bel dono." The aloof objectivity of his earlier interactions is replaced by genuine compassion, a quality that reaches its apex in the scene of farewell to his followers, when he explains proudly to them, as he did to Mercurio, that dying will enable him to realize his philosophy, to fulfill his stoical aspirations. If he resorts once more, temporarily, to the formal language of Senecan precepts—death is but a brief anguish (which echoes a passage from ancient Seneca's *De providentia*)—his personal belief in them is clear: the stòic philosopher realizes himself in the dying man:

Amici, *amici*, è giunta, *è giunta* l'ora	My friends, the hour has come
Di praticar infatti	to put into practice
Quella virtù che tanto celebrai.	the virtue I have always praised so highly.
Breve angoscia è la morte:	Death is a momentary anguish:
Un sospir peregrino esce dal core,	a wandering sigh emerges from the breast
Ove è stato molt'anni	where for many years it has sojourned
Quasi in ospizio come forestiero,	like a visitor in a wayside hostel,
E se ne vola all'Olimpo,	and wings its way to Olympus,
Della felicità soggiorno vero.	the true abode of joy.

Although he cannot resist one final rhetorical analogy of life to a flowing stream, his last words direct his followers to prepare *his* bath, explaining that he wishes *his* flowing blood to purple *his* path to death:

Itene tutti a preparmi il bagno,	Go all of you to prepare my bath,
Che se la vita core	for since life flows
Come rivo fluente,	like a river,
In un tepido rivo	I wish the warm current
Questo sangue innocente io vo', *vo'* che vada	of my guiltless blood

A imporporarmi del morir, *del morir* la strada.   to paint my road to death with royal
purple.

I have gone on at length here because the change in Seneca's behavior and language incorporated in Busenello's text surely affected the character as conceived and portrayed by Monteverdi, and it helps to explain the wide disparity of interpretations of Seneca in recent literature on the opera, mentioned above. Some years ago, I argued that the difficulties of interpreting the opera as a whole could be traced in part to ambiguities in Seneca's character, at once impotent philosopher, miner of pretty notions, and martyred hero, willing to die for his beliefs. These ambiguities, I suggested, could be ascribed to differing attitudes toward Seneca on the part of librettist and composer.[65] Upon further reflection, it now appears to me that neither my original interpretation, nor those advanced over the past two decades by other critics, has given adequate weight to a *change* in Seneca's character as depicted in both text and music. For Monteverdi seems to have responded differently to two Senecas: the pompous and impotent philosopher who speaks in proverbs and the defeated hero who proudly embraces his own death. And these two Senecas form part of a single character who develops over the course of the opera, a development strengthened by Monteverdi's musical setting of his words.

SENECA'S MUSIC

The composer's interpretation of his characters is usually revealed in the words he chooses to emphasize—and the ways he does so. Emphasis can take the form of simple repetition, and/or the application of a madrigalism; or it can involve more complex musical choices: a shift in meter, for instance, or in melodic style—from conjunct to disjunct motion—can highlight a particular textual passage. To judge from the ways in which he chose to set the text, Monteverdi would seem to have been initially uninspired by Seneca. Undoubtedly constrained by the range and physiognomy of the bass voice—and especially its vulnerability to being doubled by the basso continuo—the composer reacts rather formulaically to Seneca's generally formulaic text. Four different speeches begin similarly, in duple meter, on a single reciting tone—usually D—doubled in the bass, which is extended over the course of several measures before rising to the fifth above, and then falling back to the tonic. This initial gesture is usually balanced by a symmetrical motion in the opposite direction, a stepwise descent to the lower fifth, which then returns to the tonic for a cadence, and the whole formula may then be repeated in its entirety or in an expanded form.

---

65. Rosand, "Seneca."

Act 1, scene 6, Seneca and Ottavia

This pattern is established in Seneca's very first speech, in 1.6, the offending address to Ottavia (see Table 21 above), and recurs in his subsequent reflection on that speech (see above: "Le porpore regali") in 1.7, in his longest response to Nerone (see above: "Siano innocenti i regi"), in 1.9, and in his soliloquy ("Solitudine amata") at the beginning of act 2. Although significantly elaborated, it even forms the basis of his final speech of farewell to his followers, in 2.3: "Amici, è giunta l'ora."

In the speech to Ottavia, the standard formula, on C, lays out the tonal and melodic space of an opening section of nineteen measures, setting the first eight lines of text (bracketed in Table 21 as section 1, with numbers beneath the text outlining the formula by scale degree). The formula is reiterated (in m. 8) on a second tonal level, D, to distinguish the lines actually addressed to Ottavia (beginning in l. 3, "O gloriosa del mondo") from the previous aside ("Ecco la sconsolata donna"), although the distinction is not maintained, and the speech soon reverts to C, the key of the "aside" (at l. 9), where it remains. When the bass is not completely stationary, it merely doubles the only slightly more rhythmically active vocal line.

In contrast to the rather austere declamation of this opening section, the remainder of the setting, some forty measures, is remarkably active—too active, one might say—and discontinuous. Though it remains centered on C, the music meanders disconcertingly back and forth between extremes of range, and is frequently stalled by authentic cadences involving large leaps of fourths, fifths, and octaves. Continuity is further undermined by several metric shifts, by phrases that vary unpredictably between extremes of brevity and length (from two to ten measures), and by a succession of exaggerated, excessively literal musical imitations of various kinds. Several disparate images involving conflict, opposition, or force ("i *colpi* suoi," "La cote non *percossa*," "dal destin *colpita*") are enacted in conflicts between voice and bass—syncopations, accent displacement. Verbs or phrases describing increase or growth ("Ti *cresce* gl'ornamenti," "Tu . . . produci . . . alti splendori / Di vigor, di fortezza, / Glorie maggiori") are accompanied by ascending linear motion; and melismas decorate a number of expressive—and some not so expressive—words: "faville," glorie." The composer finds occasions for other isolated, conventional madrigalisms as well—reiterated long notes on "costante," an ascending leap to a melodic high point on "stelle"—before reaching a final cadence that involves the largest leap of the speech, a descending major ninth. There are numerous other conventional madrigalisms, some more fitting than others. For instance, the most extended melisma of all occurs on the article, "la," in line 17, instead of on the following noun "bellezza," where it belongs. And likewise the setting of line 18, "la vaghezza del volto," places an offending melisma on the noun "volto," instead of on the preceding noun, "vaghezza." But even those musical images that do reflect the accompanying text are poorly integrated with one another. As a result, they fail to contribute a coherent message.

The impression of superficiality or disjunction in the relationship of music to text in this speech is heightened by the ineffective use of two of the composer's most trusted expressive techniques: the repetition of key words to encapsulate the essence of an argument, and the shift to song-like triple meter to convey moments of heightened feeling. The many words and phrases chosen for repetition here (in italics in Table 21) are neither rhetorically nor dramatically important. Emphasizing individual words at the expense of thought, the sheer density of these repetitions (five different text fragments are repeated within a six-line passage of text) makes their artificiality plain indeed, almost comical. (One remembers nostalgically Nerone's powerful use of this device when he concludes his confrontation with Seneca by declaring: "Poppea sarà mia moglie, *sarà mia moglie, sarà mia moglie.*") And the two brief triple-meter passages (the first beginning at line 9, "Ringratia la fortuna," the second at line 18, "la vaghezza del volto") seem unmotivated: generalized responses to mere words rather than expressions of feeling. Indeed, because it is so fragmented by the succession of musical images, and so unjustified, song here ironically seems to reflect the very opposite of feeling: cold calculation, mere words.

The composer's setting emphasizes Seneca's worst qualities: his pedantry, reliance on formulas and clichés, and especially his lack of personal engagement. The absence of an overall controlling structure in the setting of this speech, its halting syntax, heightens the artificiality of Seneca's words and undermines his message. His failure to comfort Ottavia is musical as well as textual.

This setting is hardly eloquent; but it eloquently justifies Gary Tomlinson's disparaging critique of Monteverdi's late style as Marinist, or rather for the ways in which individual words and images tend to be singled out by abrupt changes of style to produce a disjointed succession of discrete images and emotions.[66] It is no wonder that, whether explicitly or implicitly, just about every negative assessment of Seneca focuses on this speech. I quote again from Heller, this time more fully:

> Seneca fails to persuade or comfort Ottavia not only because of the apparent futility of his arguments, but also by his utter inability to muster his famed rhetorical powers in the service of a coherent oration. Such blatant contrivances as the melisma on "faville," the syncopations on "colpita," and the ascent illustrating "Glorie" seem [more] like academic exercises in madrigalesque imitation. This catalogue of musical devices dissuades rather than persuades, distracting the listener from the intention of the speech as a whole, raising suspicions not only about Seneca's oratory but also about the validity of his philosophical stance. The meaninglessness and inappropriateness of such gestures is particularly apparent in the absurdly long melisma . . . placed on the article "la" rather than on the noun "bellezza." Seneca, oblivious to the nature of beauty, is an incompetent rhetorician and musician. Unable to coordinate word and sound, he is thus an unlikely hero for an opera by Monteverdi.[67]

---

66. Tomlinson, "Music and the Claims of Text," 285–87; and *Monteverdi,* 205 and especially 218. To be fair, Tomlinson's formulation is more nuanced than this. He characterized Monteverdi's late style as caught between his and his librettists' tendencies toward the disjointed images of Marinism and his own clear recollection of different kinds of affective imitation practiced in his earlier works.

67. Heller, "Tacitus Incognito," 67.

EXAMPLE 23. Seneca, "Il partito peggior" (*L'incoronazione di Poppea*, 1.9, mm. 153–63).

Carter, too, is disturbed by the rhetoric of this speech, citing it as evidence of Seneca's "worrying tendency to engage in vapid musical gestures, whether to support his words (a melisma on 'faville', 'sparks') or even to contradict them (more than three bars of running semiquavers on the definite article 'la')."[68] Perhaps the most telling critique, however, comes from John Elliot Gardiner, who introduces a big cut in his performance of this speech (ll. 14–17), eliminating, among other things, the melisma on "la."[69]

Of course, as we shall see, there are places in Seneca's subsequent music when the very same techniques that fragment the syntax of his speech to Ottavia—frequent authentic cadences, excessively literal imitations—are used to specific dramatic effect. Indeed, sometimes the very isolation rather than integration of a literal imitation makes a particular expressive point. In Seneca's confrontation with Nerone, for example, such isolated gestures strengthen the two sides of the argument (cf. Table 18 above, Chap. 7). Frequent cadences emphasize Seneca's decisiveness; threefold repetition of "egli è furor," set to an eighth-note sequence culminating in a long melisma on "furor" emphasizes his criticism of Nerone; and finally, the kind of rhythmic dissonance between voice and bass that in his speech to Ottavia seemed so artificial, dutiful, and distracting in translating images of conflict here effectively communicates the punch line of Seneca's final couplet: "quando la forza alla ragion contrasta" (Example 23).

In fact, all of the elements that misfire in Seneca's address to Ottavia are deployed more effectively in his later speeches. In response to the change in rhetoric introduced by the librettist, Monteverdi combines a variety of structural and expressive devices to shape the philosopher's successive responses to Minerva, Mercurio, Liberto, and finally to his follow-

---

68. Carter, *Musical Theatre*, 282.
69. Gardiner, Archiv, 1996.

ers. As he becomes increasingly involved in his personal fate, Seneca's music becomes more highly organized and expressively focused: melodies are more carefully controlled with respect to high and low points; words are selected for repetition and other special treatment in order to encapsulate the central theme or emotional core of the speech; musical images are appropriate to the meaning of the text and are integrated within the overall dramatic context; and triple meter is deployed for its expressive effect, to communicate intensified feeling. Seneca's increased personal involvement is matched by Monteverdi's. The composer warms to Seneca the martyr, who heroically—and alone—welcomes death.[70]

Act I, scene 8, Seneca and Minerva

Several of these features are already evident in Seneca's brief speech to Minerva in act I, scene 8, setting a quatrain of *endecasillabi* rhyming abba. The overall point of the speech, Seneca's willing acceptance of death, is underlined by the repetition of key words, a characteristic technique of the composer that was sorely missing in the speech to Ottavia. "Venga, *venga* [la morte]," "let death come," Seneca says; "e forte, *e forte*"; "vincerò, *vincerò, vincerò* [gl'accidenti e paure]" (I will be strong, and I will vanquish all misfortune and fear). Repetition involving the entire final line of this speech is structural as well as expressive: "E di giorno infinito, *infinito* alba la morte" (Example 24).

Beautifully shaped and remarkably expressive, the music falls into two nearly equal but contrasting sections (eleven and ten bars). The first, strongly in d, is underpinned by a rhythmically active, strongly cadential two-bar ostinato pattern heard five times in the bass; the second, which begins on C and moves through several tonal centers before returning to d, features a carefully calibrated series of expressive linear ascents and descents, melismatic as well as syllabic.

In both sections, the choice of musical materials is clearly linked to text interpretation. The eighth-note ostinato sets up a rhythmic conflict with sustained half-notes in the voice part that effectively portrays three different textual images: the voice is "costante" against the moving bass; it is also "forte," holding its own; and in its steadiness it also represents the victory over "le paure," fear. In the second section each of the melodic motions likewise portrays a verbal image: the ascending melisma reaching up to a high point on "girar," the answering descent by leap and step to a low point on "delle giornate oscure," and in the setting of the final, epitomizing line, a more subtle as well as a more extended kind of interpretation. Beginning at the highpoint of the speech, high D, touched here for only the second—and last—time, the final line is set to a scalar syllabic descent of a seventh, repeated sequentially (and now melismatically) down a step. This descent is balanced by two ascending sequential curves that span a shorter distance—a mere fourth, which brings the speech to a peaceful close on the tonic. Here the balanced phrases, shapely melody with

---

70. This Seneca is not accompanied by his wife and family, the way the historical Seneca was.

carefully plotted high and low points, and especially the concinnity of text-imitative and sheer musical decisions, effectively communicate Seneca's desire for death.

Act 2, scene 1, Seneca alone

Text interpretation is also effectively synchronized with musical structure in Seneca's soliloquy at the opening of act 2, prior to the entrance of Mercurio. Carefully plotted melodic extremes coincide with appropriate textual passages. High C, the culmination of a rising octave scale on "imagini celesti," is balanced by low A a moment later on "ignobili terene"; and the key word, "lieta," which encapsulates Seneca's emotional state, receives a long melisma that is gracefully extended in the repetition by the most supple of sequences, eased along by a freshly chromatic bass.

It is worth noting that, ever since Seneca's misappropriation of song in his speech to Ottavia, Monteverdi has not allowed him to express himself in triple meter. The ban is finally lifted in his response to Mercurio's announcement of his imminent death. In the shaping of this speech, metric contrast, sequence, melodic structure, and expressive text repetition all play an important role. Once Mercurio delivers his message, Seneca immediately breaks into triple meter for a joyful fourfold repetition of the key phrase "o me felice," set to a gently descending series of melodic curves in d (Example 25). They are all the more moving for being melodically distinct. A shift to duple meter and a more sober, speech-like style culminates in a strongly cadential statement over a rhythmically active bass, as Seneca explains his welcome embrace of death: "Or confermo i miei scritti, / Autentico i miei studi," he declares (a passage notable, as we have seen, for its first-person affirmation). Seneca's final peroration on his happiness brings with it a return to triple meter and expansive song style. The sequential melismas here are expressively suitable, if not specifically word-inspired.

Act 2, scene 2, Seneca and Liberto

Equally fitting, triple meter once again combines with mimetic text setting and a beautifully curved melody in Seneca's reaction to Liberto's reluctant message in the next scene (2.2). Not only is he expecting his fate, he welcomes it. Recitative setting of the first seven lines of his speech culminates in a concise but telling setting of the final line in triple meter. "Rido, mentre mi porti un sì bel dono" is initiated by a descending mimetic melisma on "rido" that is balanced by another shorter melisma at the end, the phrase returning to the high point, high C, before settling on the cadence on d (Example 26).[71]

It has to be said that Monteverdi hardly distinguishes himself in setting the remainder of Seneca's text in this scene, one of those shapeless textual passages (twenty-two lines) of *versi sciolti*, articulated by only three irregularly spaced and widely separated rhymed couplets. Like the speech to Ottavia, this one too seems more empty rhetoric than focused communication, an extended explanation of the philosophical necessity of his death, which culminates in one of those Senecan proverbs, though this time even the proverb itself is redundant: "L'alimento d'un vitio all'altro è fame; / Il varco ad'un eccesso a mille è strada; / Et è là sù prefisso, / Che cento abissi chiami un sol abisso" (The feeding of one vice is the hunger for another; the opening to one excess is the road to thousands, and it is written up

---

71. Compare Ulisse's laugh in "Rido, né so perché" (Example 5.c). The cadence is in fact ambiguous, as indicated in the example, where I have followed Curtis in calling for a shrpened third.

EXAMPLE 25. Seneca, "Oh me felice" (*L'incoronazione di Poppea*, 2.1, mm. 51–81).

EXAMPLE 26. Seneca, "Rido" (*L'incoronazione di Poppea*, 2.2, mm. 41–48).

there that just one abyss summons a hundred abysses). Like the earlier setting, this one too is musically wayward, tonally, melodically, and rhythmically discontinuous, moving desultorily between a, d, and G, with a few localized madrigalisms that are far more interruptive than expressive. Finally, the closing passage in triple-meter song style is shapeless and affectively gratuitous, introduced, it would seem, merely to emphasize the final proverb.

The similarities with the Ottavia speech suggest a common source. It as if Seneca forgets that he is speaking to another person and becomes entangled in Senecan philosophy, carried away by the sound of his own rhetoric. It is no wonder this speech is shortened (by some fifteen lines of text, forty measures of music) in nearly every recording of the opera.[72] Once again, the composer reacts to the absence of personal involvement in the text, and to the lack of any kind of formal cues—such as rhymes or refrains—that might suggest significant musical punctuation. Fortunately for the drama, however, despite an even more redundant and vacuous response by Liberto, Monteverdi ends the scene powerfully: he sets Seneca's final directive sending Liberto back to Nerone to report his death in a strongly articulated, rhetorically emphatic phrase whose melodic direction and halting rhythm elegantly convey the meaning of the text: "Vanne, vattene o mai / E se parli a Nerone avanti sera, / Ch'io son morto, e sepolto gli dirai" (Go, then, and if you speak with Nerone before evening, you can tell him that I am dead and buried).[73]

Act 2, scene 3, Seneca and his followers

Seneca finally finds his singing voice in his farewell address to his followers in the next scene, act 2, scene 3. Monteverdi sets his sequence of nine *versi sciolti*, "Amici, è giunta l'ora," not as recitative, but as an aria—Seneca's only aria in the score.[74] Here, triple meter finally matches Seneca's feelings. Song aptly conveys his joy at the prospect of achieving the goal of his philosophy, and dying for his beliefs. In just over twenty measures, the aria displays all the hallmarks of a rhetorically convincing, musically coherent farewell. Music

---

72. Hickox, Vartolo, and Harnoncourt are the only ones to include this whole passage.

73. Some of Liberto's even wordier response to this speech is cut from the Venice score as well as from the short librettos (Udine, Florence, and Treviso).

74. Recall that his one strophic aria is in the apotheosis scene, which was cut.

EXAMPLE 27. Seneca, "E se ne vola" (*L'incoronazione di Poppea*, 2.3, mm. 17–21).

and text meet more closely, and in a more sustained way, than in any of Seneca's previous speeches. Taking as its structural foundation the basic formula that underlies most of Seneca's earlier speeches in recitative, centering around d, the aria is nonetheless highly effective. Seneca's eagerness to communicate with his followers is figured by word repetition at the outset, "Amici, *amici,* è giunta, *è giunta* l'ora."

A balanced pair of phrases (mm. 1–8, 9–16), the first tracing a double ascending curve, the second a triple descending one, leads to a third and final phrase, setting the two concluding lines of text (Example 27). Here Seneca's eloquence reaches its apex. Text painting is calibrated to coincide with melodic and rhythmic structure so that his music actually enacts his ascent to and then his sojourn on Olympus. A long rising melisma on "vola" culminates on a high point on "Olimpo," which is then just slightly surpassed by an upper-neighbor B♭ on "soggiorno," emphasized by a little expressive melismatic turn before resolving, in Seneca's characteristic fashion, by descending fifth leap to the cadence.

Equal eloquence marks Seneca's final utterance, his directive to his followers to prepare his fatal bath.[75] His line is constructed so that the high point, C, is touched twice, the first time as the start of a rapid stepwise linear descent of an eleventh that poignantly anticipates (as it imitates) the flowing of blood from Seneca's open veins (Example 28). The second time it at once caps an ascent and initiates another descent, which is both more gradual and more abrupt than the first one, since it occurs in three stages, each involving a descending fourth leap. Two small word repetitions (vo', *vo'* and del morir, *del morir*) capture the essence of Seneca's message, his desire to die, and the enactment of that death is mimed in the second melodic descent, slowed by a built-in retard from eighth-note to quarter-note, and finally half- and whole-note motion suggesting his gradual weakening.

The followers' uncomprehending response to Seneca's gesture has already been mentioned. After urging him to reconsider ("Non morir, Seneca"), they dissociate themselves

---

75. These are the final six of the sixteen *versi sciolti* with which Busenello's scene ends. They are the only ones set to music in the Venice score, whereas the Naples score has the entire passage. Carter, "Re-reading *Poppea*," n. 46, argues convincingly that the fuller Naples version was the earlier one and uses this as evidence that the Naples score preserves some earlier (more authentic?) readings than the Venice score. The fuller version does not appear in the Udine libretto, however, which suggests that, though Monteverdi may originally have set the entire speech, it was already shortened for the first performance. (The Naples libretto cannot help us here because, as already noted, this entire scene is notably absent.)

EXAMPLE 28. Seneca, "Itene tutti" (*L'incoronazione di Poppea*, 2.3, mm. 95–109).

from the act ("Io per me morir non vuò"), in a reaction that would seem to be a rejection of Stoicism.

FAMIGLIARI: <u>Non morir Seneca, no,</u>	<u>Do not die, Seneca, no.</u>
<u>Io per me morir non vuò.</u>	*<u>I myself would not die.</u>*
[UNO]: Questa vita è dolce troppo,	This life is too sweet,
Questo ciel troppo sereno,	this sky too serene,
Ogni amaro, ogni veneno	every bitterness, every poison
Finalmente è lieve intoppo	is in the end a trifling obstacle.
[Io per me morir non vuò.]	
[FAMIGLIARI: <u>Non morir, Seneca, no.</u>]	
[UNO]: Se mi corco al sonno lieve	If I lie down for a light sleep,
Mi risveglio in sul mattino,	I awaken in the morning.
Ma un avel di marmo fino	But a tomb of fine marble
Mai non dà quell che riceve.	never gives up what it receives.
[FAMIGLIARI]: <u>Io per me morir non vuò.</u>	<u>I myself would not die.</u>
FAMIGLIARI: <u>Non morir Seneca, no.</u>	<u>Do not die, Seneca, no.</u>

Monteverdi's extraordinary setting of this text has often been noted. To begin with, he does away with Busenello's distinction between chorus and solo, casting the entire text for the Famigliari as a group (of three): two tenors and bass. Then, he emphasizes the refrain. This single verse, expanded through internal repetition, is heard a total of nine times, increasing in urgency as the voices enter one by one in imitation with a chromatically ascending scale passage, begging Seneca not to die. Although in the libretto the refrain line appears three times, Monteverdi sets it only twice, at the beginning and the end, linking it both times to a line drawn from later in the text, "Io per me morir non vuò," which expresses the opposite affect: the disciples desire to distance themselves from Seneca's act. Monteverdi's cheerful canzonetta-like setting of this second line contrasts strongly with that of the refrain—so strongly that it erases the memory of the earlier chromaticism. The effect is reversed at the end. Although he uses the same two lines to round out the disciples' response, he inverts them, now following Busenello, and concludes with the chromatic refrain, leaving us—and Seneca—with the sound of their urgent plea.

In attempting to assess the dramatic function and meaning of this scene, Carter has pointed to the stylistic similarity between the setting of "Non morir Seneca" and a frankly lascivious madrigal in Monteverdi's Eighth Book, "Non partir ritrosetta" (both drawing on the *giustiniana* tradition), as undermining the seriousness of Seneca's death.[76] But if anything, the inter-textual connection to a trivial love song actually increases the effect of Seneca's gesture. It emphasizes even further the gulf between the philosopher and his followers, the heroic loneliness of the practicing Stoic. The indifference of Seneca's followers is a major irony. It heightens the nobility and pathos of the philosopher's final act.

There is strong evidence, in fact, that contemporary audiences were impressed by Seneca's high seriousness. In describing the action of the opera, the scenario of *Incoronazione* is unambiguous with respect to his character (see Appendix 4, B). In the first act Seneca *consoles* Ottavia, urging her to be constant. He then *muses on the transitory greatness of the world.* When Pallade appears to predict his death, she promises him that when it becomes imminent, she will send Mercurio to warn him, because, *as a virtuous man, he is dear and beloved to her.* When Nerone tells Seneca of his plan to divorce Ottavia and marry Poppea, Seneca *morally and politically answers him, trying to dissuade him.* Nerone *disdains* the philosopher, and dismisses him. The second act shifts to Seneca's villa, where Mercurio, sent by Pallade, announces to Seneca that he will surely die that very day. The philosopher, *without at all losing sight of the horrors of death,* renders thanks to heaven. He then receives Nerone's death decree from Liberto, captain of the guards, and *with constancy,* prepares to depart from life. Finally, he consoles his *famigliari,* who [try to] dissuade him, and orders them to prepare the bath so that he can die. As depicted in the scenario, then, Seneca is constant, moral, virtuous, and beloved by the gods: a character of heroic stature.

---

76. The relationship, first pointed out by Osthoff (*Monteverdistudien,* 98), is more fully explored by Carter, "Re-reading *Poppea,*" 194–98. Even if the different stylistic, generic, and textual environments are taken into account, Carter suggests, "at the very least there now is the possibility of playing 'Non morir Seneca' not so seriously" (p. 198). "The connection," he concludes, "works against Rosand's [serious] reading of the scene and therefore, perhaps, of Monteverdi's Seneca as a whole: the composer may be no less detached from, or even cynical about, the character than some of his colleagues in the Accademia degli Incogniti" (p. 201).

Monteverdi's character is more nuanced and more profound. Seneca's philosophy of stoicism is ineffectual when preached to others: it cannot comfort Ottavia, it cannot save the Roman Empire from decay, and it cannot convince his *famigliari* to follow him. But it is revealed as supremely effective as a code for living—or dying—as a hero. The philosopher earns his heroic status gradually over the course of his lifetime in the opera, through both text and music. He develops from an impotent and pompous rhetorician who speaks in proverbs to a tragic and increasingly isolated hero, willing to die for his beliefs; befriended by the gods, but abandoned by his followers: the insufferable philosopher becomes a suffering man. By exacerbating Seneca's pomposity with unintegrated, exaggerated text setting and withholding sustained, expressive lyricism until his final tragic gesture, the composer created music that compassionately represented the complex historical and moral ambiguity of Busenello's philosopher.

In order to understand our response to this character, our impatience with his early behavior, and our compassion for his death, we have to accept that Monteverdi could have chosen to write *bad* music some of the time, shapeless music that purposely fails to "cohere" according to the standards he himself has provided elsewhere. (Busenello encourages him in this by offering few opportunities for emotional expression and only one occasion for an aria, late in the role.) One key to Seneca's early failure and late success in moving his audience lies in his use and abuse of song. His fleeting, intermittent lyrical excursions in act I are disconnected from his emotions and fail to persuade. Only when song and feeling finally coincide in him can Seneca engage our sympathies and become a hero.

IRO'S TEXT AND MUSIC

The composer faced a completely different set of problems with the parasite. For one thing, rather than resolving over the course of the opera, Iro's ambiguity does not even manifest itself until the very end of his final scene. But the musical seeds of that ambiguity are planted at his very first appearance. Their persistence, indeed exaggeration, at the end communicates (if it does not cause) the transformation from hilarious comic character to shocking moral symbol, in fact, mouthpiece of meaning. While the composer controls his use of lyricism and integrated musical imagery as a means of depicting different aspects of Seneca, he withholds lyricism completely from Iro. In Iro's case, Monteverdi's stylistic choices are transparent; there is no question about their purpose: musical discontinuity, exaggerated, unintegrated text setting, and the absence of lyricism—i.e., bad music—are intrinsic to Iro's character. The contrast between smooth-talking Seneca and inarticulate Iro is played out musically.

Act 2, scene 3, Iro and Eumete

Iro's distinctive voice, distinctively unmusical, is already evident at his first appearance, in a scene with Eumete (2.3/1.12). The gentle shepherd, completely at home with nature and his flock, sings with natural lyricism; he is one of Monteverdi's most musical characters. Iro, the alien outsider, can only sputter and stutter. (The contrast is announced by the abrupt tonal juxtaposition between Eumete's song, ending on a, and Iro's music, beginning on g.) Badoaro introduces the parasite with two five-verse stanzas of poetry, indicating an aria (Example 29):

Pastor d'armenti può	The keeper of the flocks can
Prati e boschi lodar,	praise the fields and woods,
Avezzo nelle mandre a conversar.	accustomed to converse with his herds.
Quest'herbe che tu nomini	These plants you name
Sono cibo di be– *di be– pastor,*	are food for beasts and not for men.
di be, di be pastor	
*di be*stie e non degl'huomini.	
Colà fra regi io sto,	I live among kings there,
Tu fra gli armenti qui;	you, here, among the herds.
Tu godi e tu conversi tutto il dì.	You are happy and you converse all day.
Amicizie selvatiche,	Sylvan friendships,
Io mangio i tuoi compagni *pastor,*	I eat your companions, and all your work.
i tuoi compagni pastor,	
e le tue pratiche.	

Responding to the awkwardness of this text—the variety of verse length, the unbalanced rhymes, and especially the contrast of *tronchi* and *sdruccioli* endings—Monteverdi not only eschews all lyricism; he disguises some of the structural parallels between the two stanzas. (This is the inverse of what he does for Ulisse in "O fortunato.")

Iro's music is intermittent, interrupted, melodically and harmonically static; frequent metric shifts, irregular alternation of short syllabic and melismatic passages, and the obstinate repetition of brief rhythmic units lend his utterances a distinctly non-musical quality. Like the stuck, repeated syllables that postpone the completion of "bestie" ("di be–, di be– pastor, di be–, di be– pastor") in stanza 1, directionless melismatic lines, circling around without resolving, create an uncertain text flow that mimes stuttering. The unpredictable phrases fail to rhyme musically: not surprisingly, they also fail to confirm the rhyme scheme of the text.[77]

It is important to emphasize that Iro stutters because Monteverdi wants him to. It is the composer, not the librettist, who deconstructs the text to make Iro stutter, even repeating the opening word of the text, "pastor," as an insert in line 5 to enhance the ef-

---

77. As noted in connection with Seneca's poetry, the pairing of lines of disparate length tends to minimize the punctuating or interruptive effect of rhyme.

EXAMPLE 29. Iro's strophic aria "Pastor" (*Il ritorno d'Ulisse*, 2.3 [or 1.12], mm. 1–26 and 27–52).

fect in both stanzas.[78] In his stuttering declamation of "bestie," Iro becomes bestial, as he bahs like a sheep. The composer distinguishes the second stanza from the first only minimally, but with special care, introducing slight melodic and rhythmic differences that respect new accentuation and meaning—the subtle variety in the melismas in the first two lines give the effect of improvisation. The most significant change involves the final line where, instead of repeating and fragmenting a single word ("bestie") to mimic one kind of stuttering, he repeats an incomplete phrase of music and text ("i tuoi compagni, pastor") to mimic another.

78. This is not the case with opera's later stutterers, where the dialogue is set up to include repeated syllables—the stuttering hunchback Dema from Cavalli's *Giasone* comes to mind. There the composer follows the librettist; here he leads him.

Act 4, scene 4, Iro, the Suitors, and Ulisse

Similar musical (or anti-musical) features characterize Iro's second appearance in 2.11 (or 4.4). Crowned with Homeric epithets, the "huomo di grosso taglio, di larga prospettiva," the "mostruoso animale," comically echoes the Suitors' denigration of the disguised Ulisse, exchanging insults with him, threatening, Valletto-like, to pluck the hairs from his beard, one by one ("E che si rimbambito guerriero, vecchio importuno, che ti strappo i peli della barba ad uno ad uno"),[79] and challenging him to a fight. His ignominious thrashing at Ulisse's hands, taken straight from Homer, comically anticipates the cataclysmic defeat of the Suitors in the following scene.[80] Once again, Monteverdi provides Iro with music that mimes stuttering: clipped, interrupted phrases, reiterated single pitches, rapid metric shifts, abrupt tempo changes, exaggerated sequences, and *stile concitato* arpeggios for his fight with Ulisse. His defeat is marked by the only smooth linear descent in his entire role. (He has been in G the whole time, but ends in f—a shift from durus to mollis with clear allegorical significance.)[81]

Act 5, scene 1: Soliloquy

Brilliant as we may judge Monteverdi's characterization thus far, until his final appearance in the last act Iro's actions fall within the norms of comic behavior. He stutters, boasts, and taunts his betters; his humor derives from his physical being, his speech defect, and his monstrous size and appetites. His physical awkwardness is mirrored in his music in ways we have seen. Iro's congenital unmusicality and the mimetic (gestural) component reach an apex in his final speech, the famous lament, where his inability to express himself—or to sustain an independent existence, musical or otherwise—assumes tragic proportions.

Nothing in Iro's past behavior (or in opera history, for that matter) has prepared us for this monologue. In its length, variety of expression, and dramatic impact it far exceeds any expectation an audience might have for Iro's comportment. For once, the librettist might claim credit (though the composer's pre-compositional influence on the text may be suspected, not only from its quality, but because, uncharacteristically, his only alterations involve standard ones of word and phrase repetition). Ostensibly, his lament is focused on the death of the Suitors, the parasite's host, but the loss is far greater than that. We can

---

79. Valletto similarly threatens to set Seneca's toga on fire and burn his books, in a gradually rising, sequential, scalar passage spanning a twelfth that mimes the igniting of a fire (mentioned above, Chap. 6, p. 247). The composer's setting of Valletto's text in this scene resembles his treatment of Iro in other respects as well: Valletto sneezes, yawns, and laughs; and he enacts his most damning critique of Seneca's morals—"sempre al contrario fa di quell ch'insegna"—by singing in contrary motion against the bass.

80. As we have already noted (Chap. 7, p. 253), a third appearance, in that very scene in which, following the Suitors' failure, Iro attempts to string Ulisse's bow, is eliminated in Monteverdi's setting.

81. See Chafe, *Tonal Language*, 274–75. Earlier (p. 262), Chafe points out that recurrences of the three main keys of the prologue, d (Humana Fragilità), G (Tempo and Fortuna), and a (Amore), usually reflect their initial associations. Iro's G, then, the key of most of his music, could be associated with Fortuna.

extrapolate once again from the ancient satirical dialogue. As Lucian's Simon argued, in response to his interlocutor's query as to whether the parasite will feel pain if his supplies run short, "he is not a parasite if that happens." Iro has lost his identity. And this is evident in his text. Speaking now to the audience, now to himself, Iro shifts erratically between first-, second-, and third-person address; he infantilizes himself by referring to the Suitors as his fathers—earlier he was a sheep, now he is a baby who has to be fed and clothed; he is an I ("io"), stomach, throat, body ("ventre," "gola," "corpo"), a you ("tu"), an Iro, and a starving man ("digiun").

Near the end he is even a philosopher ("chi si toglie al nemico ha gran vittoria"). (In addition to refrains, other built-in structural elements are underlined.)

1 Oh dolor, o martir che l'alma attrista!	Oh pain, oh martyrdom that saddens the soul,
Honesta [Oh mesta] rimembranza	honest memory
Di dolorosa vista!	of a painful sight;
Io vidi i proci estinti, estinti, estinti, i proci	I saw the Suitors dead,
5 I proci furo uccisi, i proci furo uccisi,	the Suitors were killed,
i porci, i porci furo uccisi, ah, ah, ah,	
ah, ah, ah, ch'io perdei	alas, and I lost
Le delizie del ventre, e della gola!	the delights of the stomach and the throat.
Chi soccorre il digiun, chi, chi lo consola?	Who will save the starving one,
lo consola, chi lo consola, chi lo consola,	who will console him?
chi, chi, chi, chi, chi, chi lo consola?	
O flebile parola!	O pitiful word,
I proci, Iro perdesti!	you have lost the Suitors, Iro!
10 I proci, i padri tuoi.	The Suitors, your fathers.
Sgorga pur quanto puoi	Shed as much as you can
Lacrime amare e meste,	bitter, mournful tears,
Che padre, che padre è chi ti ciba, e	for a father is the one who feeds you
chi ti veste.	and dresses you.
Chi più della tua fame	Who now will satiate
15 Satollerà le brame?	your hungry yearnings?
Non troverai no, no, no, no non	You won't find anyone to
troverai chi goda	enjoy
Empir del vasto ventre	filling the ravenous caverns
L'affamate caverne.	of your vast stomach.
Non troverai no, no, no, no, non troverai	You won't find anyone to
chi rida, rida, rida, rida	laugh
20 Del ghiotto trionfar della tua gola.	at the gluttonous triumph of your gullet.
Chi soccorre il digiun, chi, chi lo consola?	Who will save the starving one, who
lo consola, chi lo consola, chi lo consola, chi,	will console him?
chi lo consola?	
Infausto giorno, a mie ruine armato:	Unlucky day armed for my ruin!

Poco dianzi mi vinse *il vecchio antico*	A short time ago the old
[*un vecchio ardito*],	man conquered me.
Or m'abbate *m'abbatte* la fame,	Now hunger prostrates me.
m'abbatte, m'abbatte la fame.	
25 Dal ci<u>bo abba</u>ndonato.	Abandoned by food,
L'<u>hebbi</u> già per nemica,	it was once my enemy
l'hebbi già per nemica	
L'<u>ho</u> distrutta, *l'ho distrutta, l'ho distrutta,*	and I destroyed it,
l'ho distrutta, l'ho distrutta, l'ho distrutta,	
l'ho distrutta, l'ho distrutta, l'ho distrutta,	
l'ho distrutta, l'ho distrutta, <u>l'ho</u>	
vinta; hor troppo fora	I conquered it. Now it would be too painful
Vederla vincitrice.	to see it victorious.
Voglio uccider me stesso,	I want to kill myself
voglio uccider me stesso e non vo' mai,	so that it never
mai, mai, mai, mai, mai, mai	
30 Ch'ella porti di me trionfo, e gloria;	shall triumph or glory over me.
Chi si toglie al nemico, *chi si toglie al nemico*	He who removes himself from his enemy
ha gran vittoria.	earns a great victory.
<u>Coraggioso mio core,</u>	Be courageous, my heart!
<u>Mio core coraggioso,</u> *coraggioso mio core,*	My heart, be courageous!
Vinci, *vinci* il dolore, e pria	Vanquish your pain, and before
35 Ch'alla fame nemica egli soccomba,	it succumbs to inimical hunger
Vada il mio corpo, *vada, vada, vada*	let my body go feed my tomb.
il mio corpo a disfamar la tomba.	

Such loss of identity bespeaks the disintegration of a personality, a comic character gone berserk. It leads directly to Iro's suicide.[82]

The irregularity of Badoaro's long sequence of thirty-six *versi sciolti,* especially the paucity of formal articulations, contributes to Iro's psychological precariousness. It provides him with very little to hold on to: but single irregular refrain—at lines 7 and 21— some irregularly placed rhymed couplets, and a number of built-in rhetorical emphases (underlined).[83]

---

82. Though admittedly different from that of the philosopher, Iro's death is not quite as pleasant as the one Lucian describes for his parasite (*Works*, 88–89): "Now I suppose you will tell me that the sponger's life may be better than theirs [the philosophers], but his death is worse. Not a bit of it; it is a far happier one. We know very well that all or most philosophers have had the wretched fate they deserved, some by poison after condemnation for heinous crimes, some by burning alive, some by *strangling,* some in exile. No one can adduce a sponger's death to match these; he eats and drinks, and dies a blissful death. If you are told that any died a violent one, be sure it was nothing worse than indigestion."

83. In addition, two fairly long stretches of consecutive *settenari* (ll. 8–12 and 14–19) might have had formal implications, but Monteverdi chose to ignore or override them.

The composer responds to most of the librettist's rhetorical emphases—most notably the refrain in lines 7 and 21 and the anaphora in 16 and 18—but adds many more of his own, and sometimes in places not signaled by the librettist. (These are indicated by the pas-. sages in italics in the text above.) Most of Monteverdi's techniques are familiar from his other music, perhaps especially from Seneca's. As usual, we can read his emphases and understand his interpretation through the words he chooses to repeat, and his setting of them.

Iro's music involves a tremendous amount of text repetition—more possibly than anywhere else in Monteverdi's oeuvre—of individual words as well as longer phrases. Much of it, of course, is a natural manifestation of Iro's stuttering, but it performs other, more objective mimetic functions as well, and also expressive ones. For instance, "Estinti" (l. 4), sung three times to a disjunct sequence of three descending thirds separated by rests, does indeed finally extinguish itself. The repetition also signals Iro's strong affective identification with the Suitors' death. "M'abbatte" (l 24), heard four times, predictably pits voice against bass, but this fight involves a third party, the meter: the two overlapping five-beat melodic figures in the voice and bass overlap a six-beat measure; the three patterns literally "beat" against one another, creating palpable conflict—not the least by the jarring incongruities of text and musical accent. (Iro experiences the textual image physically, somatically.) And Iro's imitation of laughter, on "rida," also sung four times to a melodic sequence, is exaggerated and stylized to the point of hysteria—the last laugh is extended fourfold, finally disintegrating into the mimetic repeated notes of a goat trill. (Now he's a goat! Note the contrast with Seneca's much more decorous—and less natural—laugh, and also Ulisse's.) Here, though, the text ascribes the [missing] action to others—"you won't find anyone to laugh"—it is Iro who laughs—though he has nothing to laugh about. The perversity of his taking it upon himself to act out a word that expresses the opposite of what he feels is one more symptom of his breakdown.

There are many others. When his initial bestial whine on a single pitch, unmeasured and unaccompanied, is joined by a fast-moving ostinato bass repeated no fewer than six times, it suggests a kind of splitting, as if Iro is being propelled by a motoric inner compulsion. (Can it be hunger?)

His most poignant cry for help, in the refrain, "chi soccorre il digiun, chi lo consola," disintegrates into frenetic parody. It will be worth analyzing this music closely. Badoaro's single hendecasyllabic line forms a couplet with its predecessor, but the composer's setting overrides the rhyme, extending the single refrain line so that it becomes the longest single phrase in the lament thus far—twelve measures. (In its next appearance the refrain stretches to sixteen measures.) The words "Chi soccorre il digiun," hesitant and hollow, recall the opening whine: the voice, alone, declaiming each word separately on D (Example 30). These words are interspersed with long rests, during which the bass sounds the root, G; the voice delivers Iro's weak cry for help unsupported by the bass. The following phrase, "chi lo consola," in contrast, is frantic with activity; following a shift to triple meter, the voice declaims and stutters the much repeated text over and over again in scalar passages of eighth-notes, supported by a ciaccona bass. Having begged for consolation,

EXAMPLE 30. Iro's lament, refrain (*Il ritorno d'Ulisse*, 5.1 [or 3.1], mm. 31–42).

EXAMPLE 31. Iro's lament, "Chi soccorre il digiun" (*Il ritorno d'Ulisse*, 5.1 [or 3.1], mm. 72–87).

Iro seems to have found it in song—the regularity of triple meter and ciaccona bass support him. But it is a chimera, a quick fix: short-lived, gone in a flash. Once again there is a disjunction between what text and music say, an ironic distance. Iro is deceived by song. He himself is forced to supply the consolation he begs for.

When the refrain returns later in the scene, the ciaccona is extended from a single repetition to five, promising even greater consolation, but Iro, instead of continuing to move in tandem with the dancing bass, suddenly pauses on his usual D—yet another reminder of his opening whine—letting the ciaccona bass run on and on before winding down to a cadence (Example 31). It is as if Iro can no longer expect consolation from song and is reduced to a mere observer, watching the mechanical activity of the bass from a distance; another instance of splitting.

Nearing the end of his rope (and the lament), Iro remembers that he once defeated hunger, an enemy every bit as palpable as the old man at whose hands he has just suffered a traumatic beating. Hunger literally attacked him—an attack he reenacts in *stile concitato*, rendered especially potent by the three-layered conflict between voice, bass, and meter already mentioned—but he destroyed it (Example 32). In describing his metaphoric victory, he re-experiences it, repeating the verb of action, "l'ho distrutta" *ten* times in a rapid sequence of uninterrupted eighth notes that, in leaving him no time to catch his breath, turns against him to become the agent of his defeat. The contrast between that past victory and his inability to replicate it in the present pushes him over the edge. Monteverdi's treatment of the text, his concrete setting of inanimate imagery, seduces Iro into conflating Ulisse and hunger, his outer and inner enemies. (Monteverdi makes the inner conflict stronger than the outer one.) Here, rather than splitting, Iro overidentifies, as he at once describes and experiences his metaphoric struggle.

Though the idea of suicide seems to have emerged suddenly, almost inadvertently, as the only permanent solution to hunger, Iro faces the prospect seriously. Having stuttered his way through his monologue, exaggerating, repeating, and decontextualizing individual words, he now changes pace. He declaims his final lines clearly and directly, in a perfectly well-shaped line characterized by carefully plotted peaks and a gradual descent to the end. His few repetitions and pauses no longer interrupt and distort but emphasize the seriousness of his intentions; that is, they serve their normal rhetorical purpose. His final cadence

EXAMPLE 32. Iro's lament, "Or m'abbate la fame" (*Il ritorno d'Ulisse*, 5.1 [or 3.1], mm. 92–142).

(continued)

EXAMPLE 32 *(continued)*

l'ho di-strut-ta, l'ho di-strut-ta, l'ho vin-ta, l'ho vin-ta; or trop-po fo-ra Ve-der la vin-ci-

tri - ce. Vo-glio_uc-ci-der me stes-so, vo-glio_uc-ci-der me stes-so e non vo' ma-i, ma-i,

ma-i, ma-i, ma-i, ma-i, ma-i, Ch'el-la por-ti di me tri-on-fo_e glo-ria;__ Chi si to-glie_al ne-

mi-co, chi si to-glie_al ne-mi-co ha gran vit-to - ria. Co-rag-gio-so mio co-re, mio

co - re co-rag-gio-so, co-rag-gio-so mio co-re, Vin-ci, vin-ci_il do-lo-re, e pri-a Ch'al-la fa-me ne-mi-ca

e-gli soc-com-ba Va-da_il mio cor-po, va-da, va-da, va-da_il mio cor-po a di-sfa-mar___ la tom-ba.

is incomplete. In a gesture reminiscent of Seneca's projection of his death, instead of rising from leading tone to tonic he sinks, defeated, to the fifth degree.

Monteverdi's exceedingly discontinuous, splintered setting of Iro's monologue up to this point—the sudden shifts of meter, sporadic text flow, rapid changes in musical style, and relationship between voice and bass—brilliantly captures the effect of Badoaro's shifting "io." That effect is further embodied in suggestive links between Iro's gestures and those of other characters in the opera. His exaggerated and protracted whine parodies Ulisse's heartfelt expression of heroic emotion at the news that he will soon see his son (1.9) as well as Eumete's joyful reaction to the prospect of his master's return (2.4) and Telemaco's response to the actual event (2.7); his hysterical laugh ironically recalls Ulisse's more noble laugh in 3.7 (as well as Seneca's). And his lapse into a frenetic ciaccona at the refrain "Chi mi consola" recalls Eumete's dance (which begins as a passacaglia), welcoming Telemaco (2.6).[84] The one thing Iro is denied is song. His only real lyricism comes within the monologue's refrain, but it is an illusion, cut short. He is thus deprived of the possibility of fully expressing his feelings. Given the function of song in this opera, this is a real deprivation, perhaps the biggest tragedy of all: Iro cannot live in the opera because he cannot sing.

Post Mortem

The fact that Iro's death is so sudden, because it is so completely unprepared, means either that we dismiss it as entirely gratuitous and meaningless, or else conclude that so deliberate a gesture must be somehow critical to the interpretation of the work. Seneca's death is completely expected, having become increasingly inevitable during the preceding action, and there can be no question as to its central importance for the drama. In light of the thesis of the present chapter, of course, the two deaths appear complementary and mutually clarifying. Each provides a key to the interpretation of the opera in which it occurs.

Seneca's death, inserted into *Incoronazione* by virtue of an anachronism and placed in a manifestly pivotal position, calls attention to a subject that was fundamental to Busenello's libertine philosophy, a philosophy he shared with Badoaro and with the Accademia degli Incogniti. That by now familiar group of politically influential libertine skeptics, educated at Padua under the tutelage of the arch-Aristotelian Cesare Cremonini, questioned, among many other things, the immortality of the soul and the existence of an afterlife. Their regular academy debates aired skepticism on this and other matters relating to Christian doctrine—such as the nature of morality, salvation, and the providence of God. The figure of Seneca embodied many of these issues and served as a

---

84. It also resembles Valletto's ciaccona, of course. In availing himself of the rhetoric of his superiors, Iro reveals a kinship with one of the most renowned mad characters of commedia dell'arte, the Isabella of *La pazzia d'Isabella*—the most famous vehicle of the great actress Isabella Andreini. See Rosand, "Iro," 155–57 and nn. 23 and 24.

focus for the Incogniti's related concerns with the nature and rewards of the moral life and the tension between the senses and ethical values.

Iro raises some of the same issues, though from the opposite side, as though in a debate—a characteristic Incognito debate between body and soul. For whereas Seneca's reasons for dying are philosophical (death represents a fulfillment of his stoic creed), Iro's are physical (he dies because he has no more food). The argument is epitomized, as I have suggested, in the two supernatural scenes immediately following: Mercury and the Suitors' ghosts in *Ritorno*, the Virtues and Seneca's ghost in *Incoronazione*. Attached to his suitor-hosts, the parasite is doomed to share their fate, which is damnation. That punishment is for sins of the flesh, their lust, his gluttony: as Mercury makes clear, the punishment in Hell of even the briefest of pleasures will be eternal. Mindless indulgence of the senses will reap everlasting torment. Seneca's heroic act, in contrast, leads to an apotheosis earned when he leaves his body behind, escorted to heaven by a chorus of Virtues. Immortality is Seneca's reward for hewing to his virtue: his Stoicism. Iro is punished for hewing to his vice: his gluttony. By choosing death, then, Seneca asserts victory of the spirit over the senses, affirming the stoic value of suppression of instinct. Iro, who chooses death to save himself from hunger, asserts the opposite, the power of the body, of base appetite over mind.

Body and soul may have stood as opposite poles of an Incogniti debate, but in the end they remain inextricably linked. The dialogue form so favored by these academicians allowed the airing of all sides of such questions, and the dialectic could find synthesis in the acceptance of their very complexity. Although Iro and Seneca are led in different directions, the moral lessons of their deaths strike a similar theme—the theme of life's fragility, portrayed so memorably by the *Ritorno* prologue as set by Monteverdi. The philosopher suffers a kind of moral martyrdom: Seneca's apotheosis, the reward of the virtuous soul, follows the sacrifice of his body to a vicious reality. Iro, slave to his own body, is ultimately mastered by its reality as hunger forces the parasite to destroy the self he can no longer nourish. Seneca the suicide is led up to Heaven by the Virtues—which, had Monteverdi set the scene, would have been an affirmation on stage of the immortality of the soul. Iro's post-suicide fate may be less clear. If in death, as in life, he follows the Suitors, he follows them down to Hell. But we cannot be sure that there is indeed anything of the spirit to survive the death of this gluttonous body, whose self-indulgence and self-destruction seem almost an ironic commentary on the lessons of Cremonini. The ultimate fate of this character without status, neither purely comic nor heroic, must somehow remain open—a perfectly appropriate Incognito situation.

Iro and Seneca may indeed have epitomized an Incognito debate, but they represent much more than two sides of an intellectual argument—or two manifestations of earthly *vanitas*. Their deaths were unusually final: neither seems to have produced any heirs in the operatic canon. In transcending his genre, Iro stands out as a unique figure, worlds apart from the long line of comic characters that succeeded him. Papageno, we remember, jokes with the audience about his suicide and is only too easily dissuaded. Iro's unusual depth may be due in part to the message he carried, but it is also a function of Monteverdi's unique ability to endow the most unlikely of characters with human qualities. Seneca, too, is uniquely complex. What other moral personage dies halfway through his opera and reverses the action? And while that complexity may also be a response to a philosophical message, once again, it is also a testament to the composer's grand ambition to present fully rounded human beings on the stage. The parasite and the philosopher are the composer's most arresting and original creations.

⅌

The debate epitomized by Iro and Seneca is, of course, the very one that underlies and energizes *L'incoronazione di Poppea* as a whole: Seneca's moral arguments are powerfully opposed—and defeated—by the sensual ones of Nerone and Poppea, his Virtue by their Love. A similar opposition also shapes *Il ritorno d'Ulisse*, more subtly, no doubt, but just as clearly.[85] Iro's body, representing the weakness of the flesh, is set against the moral strength of Penelope. Base appetite is pitted against chaste love. The same essential polarities thus operate in the two works, but the values are reversed: love in *Ritorno* is a matter of the spirit, in *Incoronazione* of the body. We might say that Iro's suicide is to Seneca's as the love between Poppea and Nerone is to that of Ulisse and Penelope. Indeed, not only does such moral conflict—of spirit and body, reason and sense—underlie both operas, but the opposition sheds light on the relationship between them.

Some time ago I raised the possibility of viewing the two operas as a grand Incognito debate on the nature of love. The debaters, Badoaro and Busenello, address the question of which kind of love is superior: the chaste, faithful, marital love that triumphs in *Ritorno* or the illicit passion, adulterous and sensual, that claims victory in *Incoronazione*.[86] Penelope is an emblem of chastity (Malipiero's *casta Penelope*), a chastity that is heightened in the libretto and even more so in the score (recall how Badoaro makes her less conniving

<hr>

85. Once again, the debate between spirit and sense, chastity and lust, evokes an explicit Incognito agenda. The skepticism promulgated by Cremonini's teaching regarding the immortality of the soul sanctioned a moral relativism and permissiveness. The corollary of the argument that the soul was not demonstrably immortal was the denial of carnal sin. Why, then, should not bodily appetites be indulged rather than denied? In preaching the value of physical pleasure over the restraint of conventional Christian morality, Cremonini may be said to have set the stage for the morality of *L'incoronazione di Poppea*—as well as for that of *Il ritorno d'Ulisse*.

86. Such a debate would have been fully at home in the precincts of the Accademia degli Incogniti, though admittedly the subject has greater resonance than such typical Incognito subjects as whether tears or song are more powerful in inspiring love, whether a beloved should be beautiful or ugly, or whether one or many beloveds are preferable. It is even tempting to see this debate continued in their later works, *Ulisse errante*, Badoaro's much freer Homeric adaptation (1644), and *La prosperità infelice di Giulio Cesare dittatore*, Busenello's imitation of Seneca in five acts (1646). This is the kind of "intertextuality" that would aid immeasurably to our understanding of these works, but which is difficult to recover from mere historical documentation. I have already referred to an analogous relationship—a kind of aesthetic debate—between the librettos of Badoaro and Torcigliani, as demonstrated in a recent article by Michelassi ("Michelangelo Torcigliani è l'Incognito autore delle *Nozze di Enea con Lavinia*"). *Le nozze d'Enea* (1641) is in some sense a response to *Il ritorno d'Ulisse* (1640), and it is answered in turn by *Ulisse errante* (1644).

than Homer and Dolce and how Monteverdi strengthened this portrayal by his editing and by his withholding of lyricism). In contrast, we might characterize Poppea (and Nerone) as an emblem of dissipation (Malipiero might have called her *Poppea impudica*), the very opposite of chastity, an interpretation that Monteverdi underscores by a super-abundance of the kind of sensual music he so conspicuously denies Penelope.

The debate is adumbrated in the two prologues, whose shared allegorical figures under-line their common psychomachic theme: a battle of Love. In *Ritorno,* where Human Frailty stands for the condition of the protagonist, Love's adversaries are Fortune and Time; in *Incoronazione* they are Fortune and Virtue. Love finally triumphs in Ithaca over the vicissi-tudes of Fortune and Time, which together had long effectively conspired to keep Ulisse from Penelope. In Rome, that same blind god, having first thwarted Fortune by saving Pop-pea from certain death, gradually and inevitably obliterates Virtue, undermining her even in her most ardent representatives, Ottavia and Seneca.

Though essential to the meaning of *Incoronazione,* Virtue is absent from *Ritorno;* she is not represented in the prologue. But she does play a role in the prologue of our third opera, *Le nozze d'Enea;* indeed, as the sole allegorical figure, she is the moving force of the prologue—and the opera. And this suggests the possibility of an as yet unexamined the-matic link between *Incoronazione* and *Nozze*—and another debate, this one on the subject of Virtue rather than Love. (Love, we recall, completely absent from the portion of the *Aeneid* used for *Nozze,* was conspicuously added by the librettist.)

Defeated by Love (and Fortune) in *Incoronazione,* Virtue reigns triumphant in *Nozze,* embodied in the happy outcome, the marriage of Enea and Lavinia. That Virtue, who once defended Troy, assuring its victims eternal life as spirits, now bids them arise from the Un-derworld to learn of Enea's successful landing in Italy. There, she tells them, she will assure Enea's victory over Fortune (though that cruel, blind goddess will not cease to tremble; de-feated by Virtue, she will fall at Enea's feet ("Ben l'empia e cieca Dea / Fremer non cesserà. / Ma tosto a piè d'Enea / Per me vinta cadrà"). Under Virtue's auspices, Enea's happy and holy marriage will consecrate "Troia novella" ("Qui dove il Tebro adorno / Feconda i prati e le campagne intorno, / Più che mai vaga e bella / Rinascer si vedrà Troia novella"). Virtue's victory in *Nozze* will not survive her defeat in *Incoronazione.* The victorious repre-sentative of marriage in the one becomes a victim of sensual love in the other.

The victory of Virtue in Italy, with its implications for Venice, is a political one. Indeed, we are indebted once again to our middle opera for revealing—and contributing—a further dimension to the debate on love in the other two works. That dimension, proclaimed by its title, is marriage—a marriage, it is worth reiterating, that does not figure in the Virgilian source of the libretto.[87] The culminating action of *Nozze* is at once moral and politically necessary for the founding of Rome and, ultimately, Venice. This presents a powerful

---

87. "Ma Virgilio se ben predice le nozze d'Enea, non le fa però attualmente seguire, terminando l'Eneide con la morte di Turno. La dove volend'io, ch'effettivamente si veda questo maritaggio per terminar con esso l'opera con fine molto proprio ad un tal Poema . . ." (Appendix 2 [j]).

contrast to *Incoronazione,* which also revolves around a marriage of state. But this marriage, rather than culminating the action of the opera, dissolves relentlessly over its course, and that dissolution, toward which all the other actions in the opera are specifically directed, is the single necessary prerequisite to Poppea's coronation. This, in turn will lead to the downfall of Rome—notionally, at least, though we are spared the spectacle in the theater. We might frame this contrast between *Nozze* and *Incoronazione* as still another debate, on the relation of marriage to the well-being of the state. The implication is that, while a virtuous marriage assures the flourishing of a nation, a union built on lust invites the decay of empire.[88]

This debate, finally, engages the trilogy as a whole. *Ritorno* represents a third position here, for its marriage, which provides the substructure of the entire work and is renewed at the end, would seem to be exclusively personal, apparently uncontaminated, we might say, by concerns of state. But the preservation of marriage in *Ritorno* is also linked to the preservation of the state. Ulisse's realm is maintained rather than divided when his marriage to Penelope is reaffirmed. This aspect of the marriage theme has strong resonance within Venetian society, in which kinship and marriage ties assured patrician economic and political fortune.[89]

However politically motivated, though, the preservation of marriage in *Ritorno* is personally costly—attained through great personal effort and sacrifice, only secondarily because it is preordained by the gods. That personal aspect, in turn, indicts the absence of human emotion in *Nozze* as a whole. No matter what the librettist tried to add in the way of emotional depth to Lavinia's character, or to Enea's, he could not match the feeling in his model, *Ritorno,* feeling personified allegorically by the highly unusual figure of Humana Fragilità.

Taken together, then, the three operas offer, in effect, a complex commentary on marriage: personal in *Ritorno,* political in *Nozze,* and in *Incoronazione* a powerful conflict between the two. Affirming chaste marriage as political necessity, prerequisite to the founding of the state, *Nozze* betrays the fuller implications of the decadence of *Incoronazione.* On the other hand, slighting the personal for the public, *Nozze* also underscores the deeper emotional bond between individuals that defines the meaning of *Ritorno. Le nozze d'Enea,* our missing opera, thus offers a lens through which *Ritorno* and *Incoronazione* reveal further dimensions of themselves.

---

88. This state marriage, this Virtù, is under siege from the outset of *Incoronazione.* Ottavia herself, the rejected wife, and Virtue's emblem, is an unlikely but powerful spokesman for its defeat. For her, "Il matrimonio c'incatena serve." The notion of marriage as an exalted state and its connection to good government was very much part of the Incogniti debates on female chastity. See Heller, *Emblems,* chap. 1, especially pp. 32 ff., and nn. 21–23; also ead., "*O delle donne miserabil sesso:* Tarabotti, Ottavia, and *L'incoronazione di Poppea,*" *Saggiatore musicale* 7 (2000): 5–46.

89. On this theme, see Margaret Leah King, "Caldiera and the Barbaros on Marriage and the Family: Humanist Reflections of Venetian Realities," *Journal of Medieval and Renaissance Studies* 6 (1975): 19–50; also Stanley Chojnacki, *Women and Men in Renaissance Venice: Twelve Essays on Patrician Society* (Baltimore: Johns Hopkins University Press, 2000); id., "Identity and Ideology in Renaissance Venice," in *Venice Reconsidered: The History and Civilization of an Italian City-State, 1297–1797,* ed. John Martin and Dennis Romano (Baltimore: Johns Hopkins University Press, 2000), 264–94.

EPILOGUE

In the end, though the thematic interrelationships among the three operas may emphasize political meanings that were of real relevance to their librettists—as well as to their patrons and at least some parts of their audience—these are not primarily political dramas. Rather, they are human ones, forming a substantial, sustained platform for Monteverdi's culminating contribution to musical theater. Together, they confirm their librettists' concerted effort—initiated by Badoaro—to lure the composer out of operatic retirement with subjects that would inspire him ("eccitare" his "virtù") "to make known to this city that in warming the affections there is a great difference between a real sun and a painted one." They amply display their authors' appreciation of Monteverdi's tastes (his dislike of "thoughts and concepts taken from afar") and skills (his ability to depict the affections, especially rapidly changing ones, which provide him with the opportunity for demonstrating, with "una varia patetica," the marvels of his art). Finally, while celebrating his stature, they challenge him to transcend it. As Torcigliani concluded in the letter to his friends, eloquently demonstrating his understanding of the composer's achievements— and the power of his music—"Monteverdi was born to demonstrate his mastery over the emotions of others, there being no soul so impervious that he could not turn and move with his art, adapting musical notes to words and passions in such a way that the singer seems to laugh, cry, become angry and feel pity, and do everything else that they [music, words, passions] command, the listener by the same impetus being no less carried away by the variety and force of the same perturbations" (Appendix 2 [u]).

Torcigliani's final peroration proclaims that the composer had already entered the pantheon of the immortals: "To that truly great man, this noble art of music, especially the theatrical kind, acknowledges itself so indebted that it can confess that thanks to him it has been restored to the world more effective and perfect than ever it was in ancient Greece or wherever else the fine arts [*belle discipline*] were admired. For this Signor Monteverdi, known in the most distant parts, and wherever music is understood, will be longed for in future ages, in so much as they can be consoled by his most noble compositions, which are made to resist the ravages of time, inasmuch as they are the most prized and estimable fruits of one who is the most memorable genius of his profession" (Appendix 2 [v]). We may dismiss this as hyperbole, perhaps, reflecting the librettist's desire to associate himself with greatness, but it is sprinkled with more than a grain of verisimilitude.

The Venetian trilogy was Monteverdi's great final act, the remarkable distillation, in just three brief years, of a lifetime devoted to the exploration of text and music in every genre available to him, but most especially the young art of opera. None of his immediate successors in the opera house—Cavalli, Ziani, Cesti, and others—could have aspired to match him, for none of them shared either the breadth or the depth of his experience or his ambition. Or his historical moment. By the time they came upon the scene operatic conventions had begun to shift. The most notable of his successors, his former student Cavalli, whose works dominated the stages of Venice for the next three decades, was a superb operatic craftsman and entrepreneur. He (and his chief librettist Giovanni Faustini) helped to forge a style well suited to the developing genre of public opera, a style that was flexible enough to respond to the changing demands of the marketplace. The style could accommodate any subject: pastoral, tragicomedy, romance, history—all were interchangeable. But audience taste for novelty rendered these works transient, ephemeral, to be replaced by new ones each season: only their published librettos remained as public testimony to their past existence. Cavalli's own contemporaries and followers, and the librettists with whom they worked—likewise responsive to market demands—continued along the same path, supplying audiences with works that appealed, featuring their preferred singers in situations at once novel and yet comfortably familiar. Within a few years of Monteverdi's death in 1643, Venetian public opera had become a business, ready for export throughout the Italian peninsula and beyond.

The ambitions of Monteverdi's Venetian librettists were especially lofty, even more so than those of the humanist "creators" of opera at the beginning of the century. They aimed at nothing less than the recreation of ancient drama, the particular power of which they understood to have been conveyed by music. Such ambition endowed Monteverdi's trilogy with a special stature, distinguishing his operas from more purely commercially motivated works that were explicitly designed to meet the requirements of the public stage. However much these may have been inconceivable without his example, Monteverdi's true heirs were not his immediate Venetian successors. Rather, they are those later composers bold enough to claim the genre of opera for their own art, who shared his belief that words essentially opened a way to a deeper world of feeling only fully attainable through music, and for whom the libretto was something to be actively molded to serve the higher ambitions of musical drama. These are the composers who shaped the subsequent history of opera: Handel, Gluck, Mozart, Wagner, Verdi.

Above all, it is that other grand old man of Italian opera, Giuseppe Verdi, whose achievement reflects most brilliantly back to the "true sun" of Venice. Like Monteverdi, Verdi was effectively recalled to his art following a long hiatus. Having retired from the operatic stage which they had so dominated, both were lured out of retirement by clever librettists fully cognizant of their creative requirements and proclivities. As septuagenarians both took on the challenge of monumental literature—Homer and Virgil, Shakespeare—and both met that challenge on their own terms, with musical responses of corresponding power. Both were notorious for intervening in their librettos—amply demonstrated in correspondence with poets, impresarios, and patrons. And both produced remarkable late-style works— indeed, at the same age, of seventy-four: Monteverdi, *L'incoronazione di Poppea;* Verdi, *Otello*. And just as Monteverdi's three late operas reveal their richness of meaning when considered together, so do Verdi's last two operas, *Otello* and *Falstaff,* setting in relief their common themes and musical correspondences—love, jealousy, evil, gossip, human fallibility.

The late efforts of both composers transcended the accomplishments of their earlier works, though these provided the essential preparation—Monteverdi's late madrigals, Verdi's previous engagement with Shakespeare. These old men discovered new expressive depth and complexity in the art they had made very much their own. And although the modern Monteverdi revival came long after his death, Verdi, by the example of his last operas, may have prepared the way for that new appreciation, reaffirming the dramatic power of music that his Venetian predecessor had first demonstrated over three centuries earlier. Although both changed the course of opera, their late works were without direct heirs. Fiercely independent, to the point of arrogance, these two great musical dramatists end up speaking to one another over the centuries, each one by the example of his art teaching us how to listen to the other.

Giacomo Badoaro,
Il ritorno d'Ulisse, Preface

Al molt'Illustre e molto Reverendo Signor Claudio Monte Verdi. Gran maestro di Musica. Non per farmi concorrente di quelli ingegni, che ne gli anni ad esso hanno publicato le loro compositioni ne' Veneti Teatri, ma per eccitare la virtù di V.S. a far conoscer a questa Città che nel calore degl'affetti vi è gran differenza da un sol vero a un sol depinto, mi diedi da principio a compore il ritorno d'Ulisse in Patria. Le amabilissime lusinghe delli Ill.mi Ss.ri Pietro Loredano et Gasparo Malipiero d'avantaggio me n'invogli[ar]ono; mentre confermi ad essi le prime scene, restai con poco meno, che con violenza incaricato a prosseguire. Perfetionate al fine, a lei le donai, acciò con il mio poetico [furore] perfetionasse, sfogasse il suo [*was* mio] musicale furore; sapevo che anco i vapori aerei colà su vestono l'espressi habiti di stelle, da che sperai i miei versi racoloriti dall'Armonia di lei fossero portati a passare per riguardevole. Ad ogni modo il mondo sa che la mia penna combatte per vincer l'otio, e non per guadagnar gloria. Hora veduta rappresentar l'opera dieci volte sempre con eguale concorso della Città convengo affermativamente, et vivamente affermare, che il mio Ulisse è più obbligato a V.S. che non fu il vero Ulisse alla sempre Gratiosa Minerva. Questa, superando i favori delle disdegnose Deità lo condusse alla Reggia, e V.S., confuse le dettrationi, l'ha condotto in Gloria, Patria più naturale delle più gloriose fatiche. Ammiriamo con grandissima maraviglia i concetti così pieni, non senza qualche conturbatione, mentre non so più conoscere per mia quest'opera, che conferma per contrasti al suo merito gli applausi, l'acompagna il grado molto universale mi fa conoscere che i parti dei Monti sono anco tal volta amirabili per l'eccesso, et che quel monte, che abbellisse le proprie altezze col verde avicina i fiori alle stelle che vuol dire unire le belle lettere della terra con le pompe del Cielo. E chi potrà condannar la mia Musa, se per natura habitatrice de Parnasi ha per habitatione scelto l'eminenza d'un Monte, che opprime le forze di lei essaltate nelle fiamme d'un insidioso sdegno ne fattori [negatore]. Mentre ho fatto universalmente alla Città tutti i più saporosi sali, che l'arte musicale trovasse mai, è vero, che ne pur di questo posso vantarmi, senza nota di fraude poi che dall'honore che ho ricevuto dalla sua musica, son stati promotivi non che mezani quelli Ill.mi Ss.ri, i quali poi addotando per proprii fig[uo]li i miei partini, hanno datto a vedere, che più . . . che in natura è violente amore. Gl'habiti ben intesi, le numerose comparse studiosamente elaborate dall'Ill.mo Malipiero han condotto col maggior segno il possibile di private persone, cosiché per l'avenire s'affaticherà forse indarno, chi senza le Prottetioni havute dal mio Ulisse cercherà d'uguagliarlo. Quest'opera è nata con i primi buoni auspicii del fatto non potrà haver Giove, che favorevole, mentre chi nacque dal Capo di lui drizzava con particolar cura i suoi sfortunati eccessi. Io me ne chiamo sodisf[at]issimo et ella deve restarne contenta poi che ha fatto conoscere al Mondo qual sia il vero spirito della Musica teatrale non bene intesa da Moderni compositioni. Con che auguro a V.S. felice e longo corso d'anni per Gloria del nostro secolo.

Argomento et Scenario delle
Nozze d'Enea in Lavinia
Tragedia di lieto fine. Da rappresentarsi in Musica

Lettera dell'auttore ad alcuni suoi Amici.

[a] Illustrissimi Signori: Già s'avicina il finir dell'anno che fu la prima volta recitata la bellissima tragedia del Ritorno d'Ulisse in patria del nostro illustrissimo e virtuosissimo amico. Con quest'occasione, voi sapete, come per scherzo io formassi l'argomento delle Nozze d'Enea in Lavinia. *Il quale mostraste gradir in modo, che voleste, ch'io vi fabbricassi sù alcune scene, e di poi andassi dietro al rimanente, perché posto in musica ci servisse per diporto il presente anno. Aria queta, e serena vogliono i cigni, e se freme, e fulmina il Cielo già non cantano gli usignuoli: onde per me stesso (2) inabile a formar suono, che dolce fosse, che meraviglia poi s'in tal caso sono riuscite al tutto le mie voci stridule, e dissonanti?* [b] Qual nondimeno si fosse quel mio aborto di pochissimi mesi, voi pur voleste fosse posto in musica dal Signor Monteverde senza riguardo, ch'a quel grand'huomo altra compositione fosse dovuta, perché tra la Musica e Poesia non fosse una sproportion infinita: aggiungendosi la mia opera dover recitarsi dopo nuova rappresentatione di quella dell'amico, di cui chi non sa i meritissimi applausi della Città tutta, e de forastieri a segno, che soggetti Eminentissimi l'hanno ricercata per vederla e udirla altrove [in Bologna]: onde s'è vero, che le cose più chiare appariscano in paragone, certo la mia Opera priva d'ogni ornamento potrà malagevolmente esser tollerata, là dove io che ciò molto ben conosco mi sarei volontieri rimaso ad applauder co' gli altri a chi tanto amo, le cui lodi più mi piacciono delle mie, perché sono più meritate. Ma volendo voi altrimenti, io non posso che protestarmi, che il solo desiderio di compiacervi mi condusse a quello, che per me stesso non (3) haverei fatto, e molto meno publicato giamai, essendo vero, che [c] se ben rapito dal Genio alla poesia ho composte molte cose, nondimeno

---

Passages not referred to in the text are given in italics. Numbers in parentheses are those of the original pages.

atterito dalla malagevolenza d'una tal facoltà divina, e più dalla debolezza del proprio ingegno ho in maniera occultate le mie compositioni alle viste altrui, ch'altri che pochi, e confidentissimi non hanno saputo, ch'io habbi composto un verso. *Or chiedendomi voi l'argomento dell'Opera per communicarlo a gli altri amici, io con questi intendo passar prima alcune giustificationi, non già con voi conscii della mia intentione, perché dove io non son in stato di conseguir loda, almeno m'allontani quanto più posso dalle riprensioni.*

La Tragedia secondo la sua più general divisione è di due sorti, come voi sapete. L'una terminante in mestitia, e l'altra in allegrezza. Ma perché fine della stessa Tragedia si è per mezzo del terrore, e della compassione purgar gli animi de medesimi affetti, prestando ciò meglio quella del fin funesto, che del contrario, per tanto parve, che li compositori lasciando l'altra, più s'appigliassero alla (4) prima come più perfetta, e chiamata da Aristotile tragichissima. Ond'è avenuto, che questa voce di Tragedia, ch'importa attione di persona illustre, con quel, che segue nella sua diffinitione, sia stata volgarmente presa per cosa miserabile ed atroce contro il suo proprio significato. Ma come sia vero, che la Tragedia d'esito lugubre sia migliore dell'altra, non è però, ch'anco questa non sia atta all'eccitamento delle passioni, partorendo ella poi il diletto maggiore, il quale se non è il fin principale, come l'utile dovuto alla Poesia, deve tuttavia dal Poeta esser molto ricercato; massime così richiedendo la conditione de' tempi, a quali si sono sempre li Poeti grandemente accomodati. Chi non vede ora non solo non piacer le cose spaventevoli, e miserande come i casi de Tiesti, de gli Edipi, e d'Atrei, ma esser esse oltre modo aborrite ed abominate? . . . io per accomodarmi al gusto corrente, mi son eletto più tosto Tragedia di lieto fine, ch'altrimenti, (5) aggiungendosi che dovendo ella cantarsi, e non semplicemente esser recitata più mi parve propria in sì fatto modo, non già, ch'io non sappi ch'anticamente anco le malinconiche tragedie erano cantate, e per lo meno la parte corica, ma certo è, che un tal uso s'andò tralasciando, in modo, ch'anco alle liete parve che la melodia fosse restata solo per un così fatto estrinseco ornamento. Per suggetto poi stimai d'ellegger le nozze d'Enea in Lavinia, non sapendo che d'altri fossero state drammaticamente trattate. Ben me fu detto poscia esser elleno d'altri prese, ma havendo sino il Carnoval passato mostrato il modello della mia Opera, e poi tosto sù fabbricatovi l'edificio, non mi parve d'abbandonarlo, rallegrandomi più tosto che l'esser la stessa materia in mano di nobilissimo e virtuosissimo Cavalliere, mostrava, ch'io havea havuto buon giudicio della scielta. Sono le favole come i campi aperti del commune, de' quali chiunque vuole senz'onta altrui a suo agio si può servire. Tanto più, che non è la favola, che costituisca l'uniformità della Tragedia, ma l'altre sue parti, e (6) particolarmente l'andamento e disciogliemento, come in molte delle già fatte si può vedere. [d] Tolso io dunque un così fatto soggetto, ancorché in alcune rappresentationi moderne si veda qualche alteratione da quello, che già si costumava, non stimai però esser sciolto dalle leggi imposte, da chi tutto ottimamente ha saputo. Et però quant'al loco dove per me havrei eletta una Città, o una parte d'essa come fanno li buoni tragici ed amici antichi, e moderni, per dilettar nondimeno li spettatori con le variationi mi son preso una poca parte del Latio picciola portione d'Italia, perché si mostri or in reggia, or in boscareccia, ed in altro modo, che portano l'occasioni. Ma quanto al tempo non ho voluto dipartirmi dalla Regola tante volte commandata dal maestro del vero sapere, che statuisce alla Tragedia lo spatio d'una giornata, o poco più; con che pene una essential differenza tra essa, e l'Epopeia, alla quale non è prescritta quantità di tempo. *Et certo, che per me anco havrei indrizzata la favola in altra guisa; ma dovendo dilettar con le già dette variationi per venir alle nozze d'Enea ho (7) cominciato dalla sua giunta in Italia intrecciando tutti quegli accidenti, che non sono al tutto incompatibili nello spatio sudetto, li* quali se ben succedendo da dovero sarebbero in più lungo corso distesi, a me non importa, essendo la favola poetica imitatione d'attione, e non l'istessa attione, e l'imitatione non è lo stesso vero, ma in qualche parte mancante, altrimenti non sarebbe imitatione: ond'è necessario, ch'alcune cose si facciano imitando, che con le imitate pienamente non concordino. Et perché la necessità non ha legge gli spettatori discreti donano volontieri tutto quello, che ricerca l'arte dell'imitare, conoscendo, che senza questo l'imitatione non havrebbe luogo, e conseguentemente essi rimarebbero privi di quel diletto. Ma già non concedono quegli alontanamenti dal vero, e verisimile, che non sono necessarii, come i passaggi d'età, non che d'anni, e remotissimi viaggi insegnati da Spagnuoli, e prima appresi da loro da Mori, i quali come nella Poetica siano buoni auttori classici io mi rimetto a chi tien buon senno; dovendo sempre il Poeta camminar co 'l (8) filo del naturale e verisimile, anzi convenendo a lui l'ammirabile non però gli viene permesso, se non quando scaturisce in modo, che paia, ch'altrimenti non possi essere. Ne perché nella mia Tragedia intervengano più accidenti è però impedito l'unità dell'attione dovuta non pur alla Tragedia, ma ancora all'Epopeia, percioché tutto è indirizzato alle nozze d'Enea, per le quali egli vien in Italia, seguono i turbamenti della Furia, le battaglie, ed altre cose, che si vedono. Succedendo ciò com'in un naufragio dipinto, nel quale ancorché sia espresso il mare, i scogli, i naviganti, e l'altre cose, che vi concorrono, non è pero che ritratta una sola attione, la dove se v'intervenisse una battaglia, o altro di diversa natura sarebbero doi cose fra se separate. La qual moltiplicità d'attione vien tanto da Aristotile detestata, come non meno chiama vitiosissime le favole episodiche, cioè composte d'episodi fra loro disgiunti senza riguardo ad una primaria attione. Non già che non convengano i medesimi Episodi all'augumento della favola, ma sì come non ogni cibo è abile a far crescer l'huomo, ma (9) solo il reso idoneo dalla natura, così non ogni aggiungimento fa l'officio d'Episodio per ingrandimento della favola, ma solo quelli, che con la medesima hanno affinità. [e] Non essendo altro l'Episodio che quell'attione, ch'alla principal si congiunge, che se bene non l'è intrinseca, nondimeno vien a far il corpo di quella maggiore con la mira ad un medesimo fine. E tal Episodio dev'esser grande quanto comporta la sua natura, altrimenti egli stesso si può dir una favola, e disdice nell'Epopeia, non che nella Tragedia, a cui pare tanto sia assignato per conveniente lunghezza, quanto basti a far seguir il trapassamento da fortuna a fortuna. Et come sconverebbe al Poema Epico esser ristretto tra confini tragici, così non meno dispare al Tragico l'estendersi nell'Epica licenza. Essendo vero, che la bellezza consista in una dovuta proportion di parti disposte in modo, che ne risulti un tutto non eccedente la sua natura, come il cavallo non dev'esser grande quanto un elefante. Et il medesimo Filosofo asserisce dall'Iliade, e dall'Odissea poter cavarsi più Tragedie, come si può far dal nostro Virgilio (10) in Priamo, in Ecuba, in Didone, e nell'altre persone primarie, e particolarmente nell'istesso Enea, che facendo più attioni principali può esser soggetto di più Tragedie. Il qual [f] Enea è veramente personaggio tragico, per esser molto noto, come ricerca la Tragedia; parendo che movano assai più gli affetti le cose credute vere, che le stimate imaginarie, le quali meno anco si fermano nella memoria dell'altre; onde vien dato il nome d'imperfetta alla Tragedia di tutta inventione, la quale più conviene alla Comedia. Et s'è vero, che come la Tragedia non vuole li scelerati per esser a pena degni di svegliar alle lor miserie un tal senso d'umanità, così sbandisca li perfetti per meritar essi più che compassione, odio, ed abominatione del loro male, ma solo ricerchi fra questi una sì fatta mezanità; parendo, ch'Enea sia un perfetto Eroe ne seguirebbe, che non fosse un convenevol soggetto tragico. Ma in fatti Virgilio decorandolo di pietà, di fortezza, e d'altre virtù, nel caso tuttavia di Didone lo fa decadere dalla sublimità della perfettione, non già che mancando per cagione amorosa non sia degno di scusa in (13; recte 11) quel modo, che devon'esser *gli errori tragici non per pravità e malitia, ma per fragilità, e certo inconsiderato trascorso. Oltre che sì fatte perfette persone per le cagioni sudette sono particolarmente escluse dalle Tragedie di mesto fine, nelle quali più propriamente cade il terrore, e la compassione, il che tanto non aviene nelle contrarie, dove succedendo il fin felice, pare a punto, ch'egli convenga a chi tiene in sé stesso una gran bontà.* [g] Ma perché non solo la persona d'Enea, ma tutta l'Eneide è cosa notissima, così per Virgilio, come per altri, che ne fanno mentione, essendo regola inviolabile che sì fatte istorie, o favole non s'alterino, io devo render conto di due cose, che paiono diversificate da ciò, che ne dice il medesimo Poeta, che tuttavia non sono l'attion principale, le quali intendo accennare, acciò non si creda che siano in tutto fuor di ragioni. La prima nell'apparitione del Tebro, la dove secondo Virgilio Enea, intesi li rumori contro lui de Latini, stanco e faticato dalle cure si pone a dormir in riva del medesimo Fiume, il quale apparendogli lo consola (14), ed inanima, onde svegliandosi allegro si pone ad esseguire le cose raccordate. Ma ciò fa seguir il Poeta di notte in tempo, ch'ogn'uno quantunque travagliato finalmente riposa; onde ciò non è fuori del costume d'Eroe, anzi che quel dormire come vien detto *Gelidi sub aeteris axe* è a punto da guerriero. [h] Io mò volendo per vaghezza dell'Opera, e per la sua importanza non lasciar la sudetta apparitione, e dovendo per necessità farla seguire di giorno, non ho stimato decoro conveniente a saggio Capitano, che ricevendo nuove sinistre ed impensate si ponga fuori de padiglioni a dormire, dove più tosto vegliando dovea preparar li rimedii a così fatti mali. Per tanto io più tosto figuro Enea, che di loro ignaro, e lieto per le novelle di pace, ma pur stanco per li stenti passati, invitato dall'amenità del luogo si ponga a riposare su 'l margine del sudetto Tebro, il quale dovendo da lui esser reso famoso, come amico lo avisa de vicini perigli invigorendolo a sostenerli. . . . [i] Così per quella inopinata novella Enea si sveglia turbato, e dolendosi della continuatione di sì malvagia fortuna, va toccando (15) le passate disgratie, ch'in parte almeno dovevano esser notte a' Spettatori. Indi com'huomo forte rinvigorisce se stesso, così passando dalla quiete, al travaglio, e da questo all'allegrezza per la comparse della Madre. Le quali mutationi d'affetti, come in sì fatti poemi paiano sempre bene, piacciono poi molto al nostro Signor Monteverde per haver egli campo con una varia patetica di mostrar li stupori dell'arte sua. La seconda alteratione è ne gli amori di Lavinia, la quale se bene secondo Virgilio non è apertamente inamorata di Turno, si vede tuttavia ella al medesimo molto inclinata e niente propensa ad Enea. Così dovendo il medesimo Turno duellar co 'l detto Enea con pianti pietosi seconda le preghiere della Madre, perché non s'esponga a tanto pericolo, e succedendo la general battaglia se ne va con l'altre Latine nel tempio a pregar li Dei per la perdita de Troiani. [j] Ma Virgilio se ben predice le nozze d'Enea, non le fa però attualmente seguire, terminando l'Eneide con la morte di Turno. La dove volend'io, ch'effettivamente si veda questo maritaggio per terminar con esso (16) l'opera con fine molto proprio ad un tal Poema, ho stimato convenevole il far preceder l'amor di Lavinia verso Enea veduto da lei nella Battaglia. Ma perché Lavinia è regia vergine, essendo che la mutation d'amori darebbe segno di poca onestà per serbar la convenevolezza dovuta alla persona introdotta, io faccio, che non badi a Turno per serbarsi co 'l cuore intatto ad Enea, il quale dovendole esser Sposo può bene esser amato da lei senza che ne resti offesa la pudicitia dovuta a così gran nozze, tanto più che per la nascita di Roma essend'elleno fatali anco fatale si può dir la vicendevolezza di tali Amori, com'accenna il medesimo Enea in parlando la prima fiata con Lavinia. *Queste sono le scuse delle doi diversificationi; che quanto all'Anatopismo della fucina di Vulcano non posta da Virgilio nel Latio, resta con ciò risoluto, ch'il Fabbro de' Dei per le molte sue facende havesse più luoghi; dove per se stesso, e per li suoi ministri essercitasse l'arte sua: e l'alteratione del nome d'Almone in Elmino più dicevole ad un pastorello, come sconverrebbe in persona (17) principale, cosi in lui ch'è delle minori pochissimo importa.* [k] Del resto ho più tosto lasciato molto del posto da Virgilio per la strettezza del luogo, e tempo, che diversificatolo. Il costume è considerabilissimo dal Poeta, e specialmente la parte in lui della convenevolezza nominato decoro, con cui è mestieri, ch'ogn'uno parli e opri conforme a quanto la conditione, sesso, età, tempo, congiuntura, e altre circostanze richiedono. E come il Pittore nello spiegare co' colori le cose, convien che s'accommodi alle più vere forme e idee loro, così di pari il Poeta deve fare nell'espressione de gli affetti facendo altri in quel modo, ch'idealmente dovrebbe essere: In questo io mi son ingegnato, che li personaggi introdotti parlino ed oprino secondo a loro conviene. Così Enea è forte, e pio Ascanio generoso, Turno fuorché quando parla con Lavinia furibondo. La medesima Lavinia modesta anco nell'amore. Amata colerica, e l'altre persone si conservano nelle sue conditioni, che sono le medesime poste da Virgilio, non per altro Silvia pastorella dolendosi ugualmente della morte del Cervo, e (18) d'Elmino, se non per esser questo a punto costume di fanciulli, a quali anco più spiace talvolta qualche picciola perdita, che quella del medesimo Padre. [l] Solo pare, che vi sia mutatione in Numano, nominato da Virgilio forte, ma insieme reso un grandissimo parabolano, la dove attaccandomi a questa sua qualità, che non suol stare con la vera bravura, mi son servito di costui, come di persona giocosa, non trovando nell'Autore altri più a proposito, e sapendo l'umore di molti Spettatori, a' quali più piacciono così fatti scherzi, che le cose serie, come vediamo l'Iro dell'amico haver maravigliosamente dilettato, al qual genere di personaggio io veramente in altra Tragedia non havrei dato luogo. [m] Et così per accomodarmi alle persone ed a gli affetti, che devono da loro esprimersi, mi son servito di più metri di versi, com'a dire dando lo sdrucciolo a persone basse, ed il breve, e tronco ad adirati, ben sapendo, che li buoni tragici toscani non hanno usato altro, che l'epmsillabo [eptasillabo?], Endecasillabo, e tal volta il pentasillabo, se bene, c'havendo gli antichi Greci e Latini nelle lor Tragedie adoperati, oltre (19) il Iambo, il trimeno, tetrameno ed altri, io non so perch'a noi sia proibito almeno ne così il essiliabo ed optosillabo; oltre che alle Tragedie musicali si deve quella licenza, che non hanno l'altre semplicemente rappresentate. *Et se in tali versi vi bisogna quella leggiadria e maestà, ch'io confesso di non havere è ben questo mancamento d'ingegno, ma insieme strettezza di tempo e moltiplicità d'occupationi, che non m'hanno lasciato applicar lo studio necessario per trovar le parole, leggiadre, e peregrine, e considerar le metafore perché riescano con la loro dovuta proportione; contentandomi più tosto di riuscire umile e basso, che troppo tumido, come porta in gran parte il moderno uso.* Oltre che [n] se la musica vuol leggiadria, ricerca anco chiarezza perché usando quelle sue divisioni e partimenti, con li molti translati ed altre figure si vien a render il sentimento oscuro; per la qual cagione ho io schifati li pensieri e concetti tolti di lontano, e più tosto atteso a gli affetti, come vuole il Signor Monteverde, al quale per compiacere ho anco mutate e lasciate molte cose di (20) quelle, ch'io havea poste prima. *Quant'alle sentenze io son stato scarso, parendomi, che nel formarle troppo vi voglia di consideratione, perché non riescano cose in aria, e stiano come si suol dir a martello.* [o] Il Prologo dell'antiche Tragedie s'intendeva tutta la parte instruttiva della favola avanti il canto del Coro, ma poi s'è posto in uso il farlo in certo modo staccato, con quei personaggi, che non han luogo nel rimanente dell'Opera. Tuttavia resta a lui il suo officio d'aprir un tal poco il soggetto, e non spanderlo totalmente. *Per questo volev'io tradur l'ombra di Creusa, stimata da me molt'a proposito a tal effetto, ma avertito, ch'oltre l'esser una sola voce continuata, la comparsa in su 'l primo sarebbe stata molto povera, ho aggiunta la virtù, con altre tre ombre invitate da lei a venir a godere delle nozze d'Enea. Et certo mertamente essendo a lui tutte congiuntissime, e di già instrutte della promessa de' Fati per la sua venuta in Italia. Imperoché Ettore e Creusa nell'ultima notte di Troia ne parlano ad Enea ed Anchise non solo in vita, ma nell'apparitioni, e poi nell'Inferno tien colui (21), un lungo proposito, dovendosi credere, che per quel, che ne predisse Cassandra anco Priamo ne havesse sentore.* [p] Et se paresse che con quest'ombre il principio fosse malinconico, io dico, che forse non sta male in questo modo per far tanto maggior il passaggio all'allegrezza del fine, come essendo il fin funesto sta bene cominciar dalla letitia, perché sortisca più miserabile la decaduta. Oltre che se bene queste son ombre de morti, sono nondimeno felici, venendo da campi Elisi, e cantano assai lietamente. . . . (22) [q] Et se bene modernamente si usa il divider anco le cose recitate in tre Atti, a me è più piaciuto il far ciò in cinque, perché con più posate possano li Spettatori respirare dalla fatica della mente in tener dietro ad una serie d'accidenti rappresentati, al qual fine fu ritrovato un così fatto spartimento. Et anco per accomodar almeno in apparenza il tempo dell'imitatione a quello della cosa imitata. Perciochè essendo lo spatio dell'attione un giorno, tanto a punto parerebbe, che dovesse durar la rappresentatione, ma perché ciò riuscirebbe con troppo incommodo e tedio de Spettatori, perciò si divide la medesima attione in [cinque] Atti, perché tra l'uno e l'altro si presupponga correr più tempo di quello, che corre, sì che in tutto si giunga allo spatio della giornata. S'aggiunge che le catastrofe non paiono bene nel mezzo degli Atti, onde [r] nel primo atto delle nozze d'Enea, resta egli queto con la pace di Latino. Nel secondo (23) sparge la Furia i semi della discordia. Nel terzo e quarto ne seguono gli effetti, terminando con la morte di Turno con l'altra catastrofe contraria in miglioramento di Fortuna; succedendo più peripetie non solo in Enea, ma in Lavinia, in Turno ed in Amata. Cadendo poi l'Essodo nel Quinto Atto co 'l riconoscimento d'Enea per quello veramente, ch'era destinato da' Fati per gloria d'Italia: onde più caramente vien accolto da Latino, acclamato da gli altri prima suoi nemici, e concorrendo la stessa Giunone dianzi contraria è da Himeneo Dio delle Nozze conchiuso lo Sponsalitio, tacendosi il fine d'Amata per non intorbidar funestamente una tanta allegrezza, [s] non vedendosi l'altre morti di Turno, d'Elminio, e di Numano, com'è gia noto il precetto dell'arte di bandire la rappresentatione dell'atrocità anco dalle più malinconiche Tragedie, bastando per intelligenza degli uditori siano semplicemente riferite. [t] Dal qual maritaggio prende il medesimo Himeneo occasione di ritoccar l'origine e grandezza di Roma, accennata prima dalla Virtù nel Prologo, e poi il nascimento (24) della nostra Venetia, non certo di soverchio lontano, e con sforzato stiramento, essendo che questa nobilissima Città all'hora cominciò, che si vide cader Roma sotto il giogo de Barbari, li quali invadendo l'Italia, spinsero molti suoi abitanti non mica ignobili per sottrarsi al loro furore a ricoverare in queste Lacune, dando in sì fatto modo principio alla Città, dopoi con la caduta principalmente d'Alsino ed'Aquileia andò crescendo sino, che co 'l valore de' nostri padri pervenne alla grandezza, in cui la miriamo, e piaccia a Dio, ch'ella si conservi, come mediante il sostegno della virtù non è dubbio, che sia per essere. . . .

[u] Or voi signori miei tollerando l'imperfettione (25) della mia poesia godete allegramente la soavità della Musica del non mai a bastanza lodato Monteverde, nato al Mondo per la patronia sopra gli altrui affetti, non essendo sì duro animo ch'egli non volga e commova a talento suo, adattando in tal modo le note musicali alle parole, ed alle passioni, che chi canta convien che rida, pianga, s'adiri, e s'impietisca, e faccia tutto il resto, ch'esse commandano, essendo non meno l'uditore dal medesimo impeto portato nella varietà, e forza delle stesse perturbationi. [v] Al qual huomo veramente grande quest'arte nobilissima della Musica si conosce tanto debbitrice, ed

in particolare la Teatrale, che può confessar la mercè di lui esser ravivata al mondo più efficace e perfetta di ciò che nell'antica Grecia, o altrove che s'habbino havuto in pregio le belle discipline ella sia stata giamai. Che però esso signor Monteverde conosciuto in lontanissime parti, e dovunque si conosce Musica sarà sospirato nell'età future, se non in quanto potranno esse consolarsi con li suoi nobilissimi componimenti, che sono per durar quanto (26) più possa resister alla violenza del tempo qualsivoglia più pregiato e stimabil frutto di chi si sia memorabil ingegno nella sua professione.

Quanto all'argomento dell'Opera io potrei far di meno d'apportarlo, apparendo egli espresso nella diceria sudetta. Ma perché non tutti gli amici voranno questa briga di svoglierlo da tante parole, per questo mi risolvo di repplicarlo più tosto in forma di Scenario, che disteso, credendo che ciò possa esser più sodisfattione de' Lettori.

Giacomo Badoaro,
Ulisse errante, Preface

Al Signor Michelangelo Torcigliani l'Assicurato Academico Incognito

[a] Feci già molti anni rappresentare il ritorno d'Ulisse in Patria, Drama cavato di punto da Homero, e raccordato per ottimo da Aristotile nella sua Poetica, e pur anco all'hora udii abbaiar qualche cane. Hora fo vedere l'Ulisse Errante, ch'è in sostanza dodici libri dell'Odissea d'Homero: in parte ho diminuiti gli Episodii, in parte ho aggrandito il soggetto con inventioni per quanto mi parve il bisogno, non dilungandomi però nell'essenza dalla rappresentata Historia. . . . In riguardo agli accidenti, che occorrono viaggiando ad Ulisse, sono, è vero, più attioni; ma in riguardo alla intentione del Viatore, che è di girne in Patria, non è che una sola. (6–7)

[b] Se vorrà affermar un bell'Ingegno, che di questo suggetto poteva farne cinque Opere; io le rispondo, ch'è vero, ma non le ho fatte, perché ho voluto, e saputo farne una sola. Replicherà, che il soggetto è più da Epopeia, che da Tragedia, io le dico, che chi vorrà leggerlo in Epopeia anderà nell'Odissea d'Homero, e chi vorrà sentirlo in Tragedia, venirà nel Theatro dell'Illustrissimo Signor Giovanni Grimani, dove in poco tempo, e con minor fatica lo vedrà più pomposo comparire sopra le Scene. (9–10)

[c] Niente si cura al presente per accrescer diletto agli Spettatori il dar luogo a qualche inverisimile, che non deturpi la Attione: onde vedemo, che per dar più tempo alle Mutationi delle Scene, habbiamo introdotta la musica, nella quale non possiamo fuggire un'inverisimile, che gli huomini trattino i loro più importanti negotii cantando. . . . (11–12)

[d] Sapeva Monsignor Leoni (soggetto di molta dottrina, e gran stima) che stando nelle propositioni degli antichi non poteva comporre una Tragisatiricomica, e pure stampò la Roselmina, e ne riportò molta lode; ciò ch'egli fece dire in sua difesa, vedasi nel Prologo della detta, che servirà anco al presente mio caso. E V.S. parimente, in quel suo Drama, di cui mi communicò

alquante Scene, tenendo un sentiero, né da alcuno de gli Antichi, né de Moderni calcato, con nuovo e maraviglioso ritrovamento non fa vedere, che un Componimento Tragico, che pure ha per suggetto il lagrimevole, può esser lieto in se stesso, mentre, oltre l'aspettatione, e quasi che non dissi il possibile, fa risultare dall'horrido il dilettevole? (12–13)

[e] Vedasi dunque l'Opera, e quando habbia fortuna ella di bene incontrare, non mi tassi altri con le regole; poiché la vera regola è sodisfare a chi ascolta. Se gl'Ingegni ritroveranno qualche intoppo, ne incolpino la strada non piana, per non esser battuta dagl'altri: ma non restarono gli Antichi di adorare quegl'Idoli, che tenevano i loro Tempii sopra le cime de' Monti. Fù il Ritorno d'Ulisse in Patria decorato dalla Musica del Signor Claudio Monteverde soggetto di tutta fama, e perpetuità di nome; hora mancherà questo condimento, poiché è andato il Gran Maestro ad intuonar la Musica degli angeli a Dio. Si goderanno in sua vece le gloriose fatiche del Signor Francesco Sacrati, e ben'era di dovere, che per veder gli splendori di questa Luna tramontasse prima quel Sole. . . . Nel resto se per il mio particolare si ritroverà qualche sconcio, sappia ognuno, che a comporre m'invita non l'altrui lode, ma il mio proprio trattenimento, e di mille pensieri, che del continuo m'agitano la mente non mai otiosa, questo è il minore. Ella intanto, per (18) esser meco uniforme di sentimenti, sostenga le mie con le sue proprie opinioni, pregandola per ovviare a disordini, che suol portar seco la Scena, che voglia involar tanto di tempo alle sue virtuose occupationi, onde resti favorita l'Opera della sua assistenza; come in quella parimente di me stesso, riconosca la stima, ch'io faccio della sua virtù, e l'affetto insieme, di cui sono tenuto alla gentilezza di V.S. Alla qual bacio cordialissimamente la mano. (16–18)

L'incoronazione di Poppea:
Argomento, Scenario, Preface

A. Busenello Libretto, Argomento

Nerone inamorato di Poppea, ch'era moglie di Ottone, lo mandò sotto pretesto d'Ambasciaria in Lusitania per godersi la cara diletta, così rappresenta Cornelio Tacito. Ma qui si rappresenta il fatto diverso. Ottone disperato nel vedersi privo di Poppea dà nei delirii e nelle esclamationi. Ottavia Moglie di Nerone ordina ad Ottone, che sveni Poppea. Ottone promette farlo; Ma non bastandogli l'animo di levar la vita all'adorata Poppea, si traveste con l'habito di Drusilla, ch'era inamorata di lui. Così travestito entra nel Giardino di Poppea. Amore disturba ed impedisce quella morte. Nerone ripudia Ottavia, non ostante i consigli di Seneca, e prende per moglie Poppea. Seneca more, e Ottavia vien discacciata da Roma.

B. Scenario

Prologo: Scena aerea con orizonti bassi. Fortuna, Virtù, e Amor in Aria sopra nuvole. (*nell'aria contrastano di superiorità, e ne riceve la preminenza, Amore*).

1.1 **Si muta la scena nel pallazzo di Poppea.** Ottone, e due soldati della guardia di Nerone, che dormono. *Ottone amante di Poppea al schiarir dell'alba visita l'albergo della sua amata, esagerando le sue passioni amorose, e vedendo addormentate in strada le guardie di Nerone, che in casa di Poppea dimora in contenti [sic], compiange le sue miserie.* [Florence

---

Roman type for Udine libretto only; italics for scenario only; boldface for shared material; pertinent descriptions are underlined.

manuscript: La scena rappresenta il cortile di Poppea. Ottone e due soldati della guardia di Nerone, che dormono].

1.2 **Soldati si destano.** *Soldati di Nerone si svegliano, e da patimenti sofferti in quella notte maledicono gl'Amori di Poppea, e di Nerone, e mormorano della corte.*

1.3 **Poppea e Nerone.** *Poppea, e Nerone escono al far del giorno amorosamente abbracciati, prendendo comiato l'uno dall'altro con tenerezze affettuose.*

1.4 **Poppea, Arnalta vecchia sua consigliera.** *Poppea con Arnalta Vecchia sua Consigliera discorre della Speranza sua alle grandezze; Arnalta la documenta ed ammaestra a non fidarsi tanto de' grandi, né di confidar tanto nella fortuna.*

1.5 **Si muta la scena in città di Roma. Ottavia Imperatrice, e Nutrice.** *Ottavia Imperatrice esagera gl'affanni suoi con la Nutrice, detestando i mancamenti di Nerone suo Consorte. La Nutrice scherza seco sopra novelli Amori per traviarla da cupi pensieri; Ottavia resistendo constantemente persevera nell'afflittioni.*

1.6 **Seneca, Ottavia, Valletto paggio d'Ottavia.** *Seneca consola Ottavia ad'esser constante. Valetto Paggio d'Ottavia per trattenimento dell'Imperatrice burla Seneca al quale Ottavia si raccomanda, e va a porger preghiere al Tempio.*

1.7 **Seneca solo.** *Seneca fa considerazione sopra le grandezze transitorie del Mondo.*

1.8 **Pallade, e Seneca.** *Pallade in aria predice la morte a Seneca, promettendogli che se doverà certo morire, glielo farà di novo intender per bocca di Mercurio, e ciò per esser come huomo virtuoso suo caro e diletto; venendo ringratiata sommamente da Seneca.*

1.9 **Neron, e Seneca.** *Nerone con Seneca discorre, dicendo voler adempire alle sue voglie. Seneca moralmente e politicamente gli risponde dissuadendolo, Nerone si sdegna, e lo scaccia dalla sua presenza.*

1.10 **Poppea, Nerone, e Ottone in disparte.** *Poppea con Nerone discorrono de' contenti passati, restando Nerone preda delle bellezze di Poppea, promettendoli volerla crear Imperatrice, e da Poppea venendo messo in disgratia di lui Seneca, Nerone adirato gli decreta la morte. Poppea fa voto ad'Amore per l'esaltatione delle sue Grandezze, e da Otthone, che se ne sta in disparte vien inteso, ed osservato il tutto.*

1.11 **Ottone, e Poppea.** *Otthone con Poppea palesa le sue morte speranze con lei, da passione amorosa la rinfacia, Poppea si sdegna, e sprezzandolo parte dicendo esser soggetta a Nerone.*

1.12 **Ottone solo.** *Otthone Amante disperato imperversa con l'animo contro Poppea.*

1.13 **Drusilla ed Ottone.** *Otthone di già amante di Drusilla Dama di Corte, vedendosi sprezzato da Poppea rinova seco gl'Amori promettendoli lealtà. Drusilla resta consolata del ricuperato suo affetto, fornisse l'Atto Primo.*

Fine dell'Atto Primo

2.1 **Si muta la scena nella villa di Seneca. Seneca, e Mercurio in Terra.** *Mercurio in terra mandato da Pallade annuntia a Seneca dover egli certo morire in quel giorno, il quale senza punto smarirsi degl'orrori della morte, rende gratie al Cielo, e Mercurio doppo fatta l'ambasciata se ne vola al Cielo.*

2.2 **Liberto Capitano de la guardia de' pretoriani, e Seneca.** *Seneca riceve da Liberto Capitano della Guardia di Nerone l'annuntio di morte d'ordine di Nerone, Seneca constante si prepara all'uscir di vita.*

2.3 **Seneca e suoi famigliari.** *Seneca consola i suoi familiari, quali lo dissuadono a morire, e ordina a quelli di prepararli il bagno per ricever la morte.*

2.4 **Si muta la scena nella città di Roma.** Valletto, e Damigella. *Valletto Paggio, e Damigella dell'Imperatrice scherzano amorosamente insieme.*

2.5 Nerone e Lucano, Poeta. *Nerone intesa la morte di Seneca <u>canta amorosamente</u> con Lucano Poeta suo familiare <u>deliriando</u> nell'amor di Poppea.*

2.6 Nerone e Poppea. *Nerone e Poppea <u>esaltano</u> i loro Amori dimostrandosi l'uno dell'altro <u>ardentemente accesi.</u>*

2.7 Ottone solo. *Otthone <u>s'adira</u> contra a sé medesimo delli pensieri havuti di voler offendere Poppea nel disperato affetto della quale si contenta viver soggetto.*

2.8 Ottavia, e Ottone. *Ottavia Imperatrice comanda ad Otthone, che uccida Poppea sotto pena della sua indignatione, e che per sua salvezza si ponga in habito feminile. Otthone tutto si contrista e <u>parte confuso.</u>*

2.9 Drusilla, Valletto, Nutrice. *Drusilla vive consolata dalle promesse amorose di Otthone, e Valletto <u>scherza</u> con la Nutrice sopra la sua Vecchiaia.*

2.10 Ottone, Drusilla. *Otthone palesa a Drusilla dover egli uccider Poppea per commissione d'Ottavia Imperatrice, chiede per andar sconosciuto all'Impresa gl'habiti di lei la quale promette non meno gl'habiti che secretezza, ed aiuto.*

2.11 **Si muta la scena nel giardin di Poppea.** Poppea, Arnalta. *<u>Poppea godendo della morte di Seneca perturbatore delle sue Grandezze</u> prega Amor, che prosperi le sue fortune, e promette ad Arnalta sua Nutrice continovato affetto, ed'essendo colta dal sonno se fa adagiar riposo nel giardino, dove da Arnalta <u>con nanna soave</u> vien adormentata.*

2.12 **Amor scende dal Cielo mentre lei [Poppea] dorme** *per impedirli la morte, e si nasconde vicino a lei.*

2.13 **Ottone travestito da Drusilla.** Amor, Poppea, Arnalta. *Otthone travestito da Drusilla capita nel Giardino dove sta addormentata Poppea per ucciderla, Amor lo vieta. Poppea nel fatto si sveglia, ed <u>inseguito</u> (Ottone creduto Drusilla) <u>dalle serventi di Poppea fugge.</u> Amor protestando voler oltre la diffesa di Poppea incoronarla <u>in quel giorno</u> Imperatrice se ne vola al Cielo, e finisse l'Atto Secondo.*

Fine dell'Atto 2do

3.1 **Si muta la scena nella città di Roma.** Scena prima: Drusilla sola. *Drusilla <u>gioisce</u> sperando di breve intender la morte di Poppea sua rivale per goder degl'Amori di Otthone.*

3.2 Arnalta, Littori e Drusilla. *Arnalta Nutrice di Poppea, con Littori fa prender Drusilla, la quale <u>si duole</u> di sé medesma.*

3.3 Arnalta, Nerone, Drusilla, Littori. *Nerone interroga Drusilla del tentato homicidio, Lei per salvar <u>dall'ira di Nerone</u> Otthone suo Amante, confessa per odio antico (benché innocente) haver voluto uccider Poppea, dove da Nerone vien sententiata a morte.*

3.4 Ottone, Nerone, Drusilla. *Otthone vedendo Rea l'innocente Drusilla palesa se medesimo, colpevole del fatto confessando haver voluto commettere il delitto per commissione d'Ottavia Imperatrice, Nerone inteso ciò li salva la vita, dandoli l'esilio, e spogliandolo di fortune, Drusilla chiede in gratia d'andar in esilio seco e partono <u>consolati</u>, Nerone decreta <u>il repudio d'Ottavia Imperatrice</u>, e <u>che oltre all'esilio sia posta in una barca nel Mare a discrettione de venti.</u>*

3.5 Poppea, e Nerone. *Nerone giura a Poppea, che sarà <u>in quel giorno</u> sua sposa.*

3.6 Si vede Ottavia, che se ne va in barca all'essiglio. *Ottavia repudiata da Nerone <u>deposto l'habito Imperiale</u> parte sola miseramente <u>piangendo in abbandonare la Patria; ed i Parenti.</u>*

3.7 Si serra il prospetto e torna Roma. Arnalta sola. *Arnalta Nutrice e Consigliera di Poppea, gode in vedersi assunta al grado di confidente d'una Imperatrice, e giubila de suoi contenti.*

3.8 **Si muta la scena nella** città di Roma con lontananza. Neron, Poppea, Consoli Tribuni, Amor, Choro d'Amori[ni], Venere e choro delle gratie. **Si muta la Scena nella** *Reggia di Nerone. Nerone sollennemente assiste alla CORONATIONE DI POPPEA, la quale a nome del Popolo, e del Senato Romano vien indiademata da Consoli e Tribuni. Amor parimenti calla dal Cielo con Venere, Gratie ed'Amori, e medesimamente incorona Poppea come Dea delle bellezze in Terra, e fornisse l'opera.*

C. Naples Libretto, Preface

Il Nerone overo L'incoronatione di Poppea, Drama musicale dedicato all'Illustriss. e Eccellentiss. Sig. D. Inigo de Guevara. Et Tassis, Conte de Onate, e Villamediana, etc. Vicerè, Luogotenente, e Capitan Generale del presente Regno. In Napoli, Per Roberto Mollo 1651. *Con licenza de' Superiori*

Abbandonata nel cumolo delle sue felicità l'imperatrice Ottavia, e repudiata da quel Nerone, che per anche ne' lussi amorosi volle dimostrarsi crudele: non sa dove ricettarsi, dalle sponde dell'-Adria redutasi su le rive del Tirreno, viene a prostrarsi a' piedi di questa gran Reina Partenope; ma non havendo seco nessuna conoscenza, non isdegna humiliarsi à V.E, solito sempre a risorger corone. L'autorità di così inclito Principe gioverà di mezzo per avventurare le sue disavventure. Di grazia, Eccellentissimo Signore, vagliami il credere, che la sua intercessione sia bastevole per ricondurla nel suo pristino soglio, co 'l difenderla similmente da quei biasmi tutti, ne' quali sogliono proromper le lingue de' malevoli. Non v'è dubbio alcuno, che la potenza d'un Grande, non giunga a sedare ogni animo: perché se Popoli stuzzicano loro la benignità, ne provano poi l'intenirirsi della giustizia; onde per ogni capo è bisogno, o credere, o cedere. Intanto con più coraggio m'inoltrerò a nuovi trattenimenti, palesandomi sempre servitore di V.E. A chi senza più riverentemente m'inchino. Di V.E. Humiliss. E devotiss. serv. Curtio Manara.

POSTSCRIPT

Le voci occorse in quest'opera, come sono Deità, Fato, Fortuna, Cielo, Anima, Paradiso, e simili, l'Autore se n'ha avvaluto o piuttosto per ischerzo della Poesia, che per altro fine, già che con vero sentimento si sottomette alla censura, e corettione della Santa Romana Chiesa.

Il ritorno d'Ulisse: Badoaro's Argomento Compared with Dolce's *Allegorie* and Dolce's Argomenti Compared with Badoaro's Structure

A. Argomento, with Dolce's *Allegorie*

Badoaro, Argomento (scenario)

Ulisse, dopo aver con gl'altri Greci sepolta nelle ceneri l'inimica Troia, fu nel ritorno alla patria dalla violenza degl'accidenti condotto a vagar lungamente, ne' quali errori inimicossi la Deità di Nettuno, mentre per fuggire dall'antro, dove stava con i compagni in prigione, privò dell'unico suo lume Polifemo figlio di quella Deità; per il che sdegnato Nettuno destinò di prolungargli a tutto suo potere il ritorno in patria. Dopo il corso di *quattro lustri,* e le variationi di molti accidenti, fu Ulisse dalle fortune di mare, solo e semivivo, risospinto nelle rive de' Feaci, popoli che per naturale inclinazione favorivano i destinati viaggi de' passaggieri. Fu da questi accolto e consolato con promessa di ricondurlo in sua patria, *e ciò eseguirono in tempo, che il predetto Ulisse, stanco da sostenuti disagi, profondamente dormiva.*

Dolce, *Allegorie*

Allegory headings and relevant scene numbers are in bold. Relevant plot elements are italicized.

Per Ulisse, che dormendo arriva alla sua patria, si comprende la conditione di colui, ch'è amato dalla fortuna; percioché l'huomo fortunato conseguisce molti beni senza cercarli.

Varcò tacita la nave il quieto seno del mare, e giunta alle rive d'Itaca, sbarcarono i Feaci col suo bagaglio sopra la spiaggia l'addormentato Ulisse (1.4). Nettuno avvedutosi e sdegnato del fatto, con che tornavano pieni d'allegrezza per segno della loro temerità, fermò, così permettendo Giove, la nave, convertendola in uno scoglio (1.5, 6). Svegliatosi Ulisse dal sonno, né riconoscendo la patria, doleva de' Feaci che dormendo l'avessero posto sopra una riva aperta non conosciuta (1.7),

quando Minerva, che aveva sempre protetto i viaggi e distornato i pericoli dell'amato Ulisse, in abito di pastorello consolandolo, e gli mostrò ed ammaestrandolo di ciò che operare doveva, per assicurar il buon esito de' suoi disegni, lo trasformò in sembianza di vecchio mendico (1.8), sotto la quale apparenza fu caramente raccolto da *Eumete pastore*. (2.4)

Per Minerva che tramuta Ulisse in habito di povero, si conosce la prudenza e saviezza d'un huomo, che non volendo esser conosciuto, si trasforma, e finge d'esser persona abbieta e vile, le quali sorti di persone ordinariamente non sono osservate. (13)

Nel Porcaro, che mantenne sempre l'amore verso Ulisse . . . si comprende, che nelle corti de' Principi, si trova più affetione e fede nelle persone semplici e basse, che ne' Cortigiani ambitiosi e superbi, che tanto mostrano affetto al lor Signore, quanto vedono il lor utile e commodo; mà mutandosi la fortuna, si mutan d'animo *come i Parasiti e come le Mosche*, le quali tolto via il mangiare, volan via ancor esse. (13)

Per Ulisse che sconosciuto ragiona piacevolmente col suo Porcaro, si comprende la gentilezza d'un signor ben creato, che quantunque si trovi poveramente alloggiato per qualche accidente, non ritiene la gravità severa di Principe, ma si mostra affabile e benigno, con che secondo la sua possibilità cortesemente l'alloggia. (14)

Intanto affannata la moglie Penelope per la lunga assenza del marito e per l'infesta servitù de' proci amatori, passava dogliosa e lamentevole la vita (**1.1: Ericlea added**), altrettanto scontenta, quanto del continuo sollecitata non solo nell'amoroso assedio de' proci ma anco dagl'interessati consigli di Melanto sua damigella, la quale per aver compagna nelle lascivie, tentava di condur la regina alla corrispondenza de' proci, esortandola di rimetter il pensiero di fedeltà alle memorie d'Ulisse. (**1.1, 2**)

Telemaco il figlio, che peregrinando ricercava del sì lungamente smarrito padre qualche novella, fu da Minerva nel proprio carro ricondotto (**2.5**) là dove il vecchio mendico dimorava e con bell'artificio fu da lui riconosciuto per padre (**2.6, 7**). Eumete fatto araldo della venuta di Telemaco divulge l'arrivo alla corte (**3.4**). Per il che i proci intimoriti e sorpresi consultavano d'uccider Telemaco, prima del suo arrivo alla reggia, quando sovrappresi e spaventati dal volo d'un aquila disisterono dal concertato omicidio, risolvendosi per miglior partito d'assalire con doni Penelope e cimentar al tocco dell'oro la di lei onestà. (**3.5**)

Per Telemaco, il qual se ne torna a casa avvisato da Minerva, si conosce la saviezza d'un huomo, il quale havendo lungamente e con diligenza cercato una cosa da lui molto desiderata, si risolve con prudenza di non perder tempo in quel che gli par impossibil da ritrovarsi. (**14**)

In Ulisse, che tiene gli occhi fermi nel figliuolo, si conosce l'affetto paterno, che non havendo più cara cosa un padre ch'il figliuolo, dopo un lungo esilio, non si satia di mirarlo, e di compiacersi in lui. (**14**)

In Ulisse che si lascia conoscer dal suo figliuolo, si comprende l'affetto paterno verso il figlio, mercè del quale, si scuoprono quelle cose a lui, che si sono con molta Prudenza celate ad altre. (**15**)

In Telemaco, che racconta al padre l'ingiurie fatte da' proci in casa sua, si nota l'accortezza d'un savio figliuolo, che narra al padre le

Consolò con il suo arrivo Telemaco l'affanata madre, e tra gli accidenti de' suoi viaggi le raccontò ch'Elena greca, famosa indovinatrice del volo di certi augelli, aveva predetto ch'Ulisse in patria tornar doveva e che averebbe stabilito le sue glorie con la strage de' suoi nemici. (4.1)

Ulisse, ammaestrato prima da Minerva del modo che doveva tenere per uccider il proci (3.6), fu da Eumete condotto nell'abito di mendico alla corte (3.7), dove Antino principale fra' proci villaneggiandolo lo discacciava, *ma per la vittoria avuta da lui contro Iro famoso parassita*, fu da Penelope fermato in corte. (4.2)

I proci che già avevano consultato di vincer con doni Penelope, le offriscono ori, manti, e corone ed ella così inspirata da Minerva, promise d'eleggere per marito quello di loro che più valoroso, l'arco d'Ulisse trattando, saettasse. (4.2)

cose che l'offendono più nell'honore che nel resto . . . (15)

Nel medesimo Telemaco, che non discuopra alla madre la venuta d'Ulisse, si conosce che le cose d'importanza non si debbono manifestar alle donne, quantunque siano in concetto di sagge e prudenti, così in un subito, ma aspettar tempo ed occasione. (15)

Ne' Proci che si burlan d'Ulisse, e gli fanno anche oltraggio, si nota l'insolenza di coloro che essendo in prosperità, non considerano la miseria altrui; anzi si fanno la calamità d'altri il bersaglio della lor lingua e delle loro insolenze e bestialità, non avvertendo ch'un huomo quantunque felice, può cascar.

Nel Porcaro, che mena Ulisse in habito di povero alla presenza di tanti Signori . . . si nota la semplicità d'un servo, che eseguisce il commandamento del padrone, senza avvertire s'è bene o male quel che gli vien commandato. (15)

In Penelope, che si lamenta, che Ulisse sconosciuto in habito di povero sia stato in casa sua oltraggiato, si conosce la nobilità dell'animo d'una gentildonna e principessa honorata, la qual ha per male che sia fatto torto a persona, quantunque di bassa conditione, massimamente in casa sua. (16)

In Iro, che si burla d'Ulisse, si comprende la natura de' parasiti . . . (16)

Nel medesimo Iro, che resta quasi morto da Ulisse, si comprende come meritano d'esser gastigati coloro che temerariamente si mettono a esperimentar le lor forze con le persone che non conoscono. (16)

Nel Proco, che tira un colpa ad Ulisse, si comprende la natura d'alcuni nobili insolenti, i quali più per faccenteria che per giuditio si mettono a offender le persone, non sapendo chi son coloro, a chi fanno l'offesa . . . (16)

Vennero alla prova, ne potendo alcuno di loro caricar il detto arco, disperarono la vittoria ed il premio (4.3). Ulisse, che assisteva in sembianza di vecchio, ricercò anch'egli d'esser ammesso alla prova. Il che, per maggior rossore de' Proci, gli fu da Penelope conceduto. Carica Ulisse con facilità l'arco, ed assistendolo Minerva e tuonando Giove, uccise i proci (4.3), le anime de' quali, come alloggianti in corpi insidiosi, furono da Mercurio, esecutor de' divini decreti, condotte alle pene delle infernali fiamme. (5.2)

Minerva che previdde il pericolo d'Ulisse nella sollevazione de' parenti de Proci da lui uccisi, fece ricorso a Giunone, perché unita con lei intercedesse appresso Giove la sicurezza di quell'Ulisse che aveva oppresso l'ardire di Paride e superate le nemiche protezioni di Venere (5.6) Giove pregato dalla moglie acconsentì, e placate l'ire di Nettuno spedì Minerva con ordine d'acquietar gl'Achivi e di commandar loro, conforme il celeste stabilmento, la pace. (5.7)

Intanto Penelope, avvisata che il mendico uccisore de' proci era stato il suo consorte Ulisse, non consentiva di prestar fede all'avviso, che però ostinata rimproverò Eumete, sgridò Telemaco, rise d'Ericlea (5.9) e non credè alla protezione di Minerva. (5.9)

Sopraggiuntogli Ulisse in sua propria forma, lo discacciò, trattandolo da mago ed incantatore. Ma alla fine, palesandole Ulisse il modo che era fatto il suo letto, non mai d'altra persona veduto, cede la sua lunga ostinazione, e riconosciutolo caramente l'abracciò, per il che cantossi la rinnovazione delle nozze con allegrezza. (5.10)

In Penelope, che propone il partito de l'arco d'Ulisse, si comprenda la grandezza del l'anima d'una gentildonna, laqual conoscendosi altamente maritata, poi ch'ella è costretta per la morte del primo, a pigliar il secondo marito, non vuol accompagnarsi con persona men degna e men valorosa del primo. (18)

Ne' Proci che restano ingannati della loro speranza, si conosce la temerità di coloro, che si mettono a certe imprese, le quali, quando si viene a l'esperienza della virtù, non eran da loro meritate, ne si confacevano con le forze loro. (18)

In Penelope che non crede ch'Ulisse sia venuto et habbia ucciso i Proci, si conosce la inresollution d'un'animo dubbioso, che tenendo una cosa quasi per certa, non crede così subito al contrario, quando gli è detto. (19)

Nella medesima che accarezza il marito, si comprende l'affetto d'una pudica moglie, che stata lungamente aspettando il ritorno del suo consorte, mostra co' fatti, di fuori, quanto sia stato grande l'affetto intrinseco del core, ed il desiderio di rivederlo. (19)

B. Dolce's Argomenti and Badoaro's Structure

Dolce, Argomenti	Badoaro

<table>
<tbody>
<tr><td></td><td>I.I (Penelope, Ericlea)</td></tr>
<tr><td></td><td>I.2 (Melanto, Eurimaco)</td></tr>
<tr><td></td><td>I.3 (Nereidi)</td></tr>
<tr><td></td><td>I.4 (Feaci)</td></tr>
<tr><td></td><td>I.5 (Nettuno)</td></tr>
<tr><td></td><td>I.6 (Feaci)</td></tr>
</tbody>
</table>

13, p. 109 (Homer 13.1–20; 14.21–62)   I.7 (Ulisse)

                                                   I.8 (Ulisse, Minerva)

In Itaca dormendo Ulisse giunto
Gli appar Minerva e lo consiglia quanto
Ei far doveva, e lo tramuta a punto
Come huom che sempre ha la miseria
    a canto.
Poi qual povero va tutto consunto   2.4
Dal suo Porcaro, il qual l'amava tanto,
E quivi dice al vecchio (che credeva
Ch'Ulisse fusse morto) ch'ei viveva.

14, p. 118 (Homer 15)

Mentre col suo Porcar s'adagia Ulisse   2.5
Minerva in Argo in sonno al figlio   (in 15?)
    apparve
E ch'ei tornasse in Itaca gli disse
E dal Porcaro andasse, e poi disparve.
Tornato, al padre parla, ch'avea fisse   2.6
Le luci in lui, ma le divine larve
Lo facevan parer vil forestiero,
Ma finalmente Palla aperse il vero.

15, p. 127 (Homer 16.1–23; 17.24–69)

Conosce al fin Telemaco suo padre   2.7
E gli narra de' Proci i fatti indegni.
Tornato in casa poi, dice a sua madre   4.1
Quanti paesi ha cercò, e quanti regni.
Entra Ulisse la dove eran le ladre   4.2
Turbe de' Proci, e par ch'ogniun lo sdegni
Perché d'huom vil mendico havea
    sembiante,
Et oltraggiato vien come furfante.

16, p. 136 (Homer 17.1–12; 18.12–6)   4.2

Lamentasi Penelope ch'a torto
In casa sua sia stato un vecchio offesi.
Le dice il figlio, che sarà di corto
A chi l'oltraggio fece, il premio reso.
Fu con un pugno quasi estinto e morto
Iro dal grande Ulisse, e d'ira acceso
Un de' Proci gli tira un colpo, e coglie
Un servo. Ulisse poi entra alla moglie.

17, p. 145 (Homer 19.1–68)

Risponde a le parole di Melanto
Ulisse, ch'era a la Reina ancella,
Parla alla moglie, e le da speme Melanto
Di riveder il suo marito, ed ella   5.8
Fa che la Balia il lava, la qual tanto
Lo mira che 'l conosce, ed egli a quella
Si scuopre, e nel convito un piè gli tira
Di bue Ctesippo, e 'l figlio se n'adira.

18, p. 154 (Homer 20.1–12; 21.13–60;
    22.60–68)

Penelope se stessa per consorte   4.2
Offerisce a colui che tirar l'arco
Potrà d'Ulisse: ognun tenta la sorte
E ciascun resta di valore scarco.
Ulisse intanto fa serrar le porte
Del suo palazzo, e coglie ogniun al varco,
Et ucciso un de' Proci di saetta
E intento a far de gli altri aspra vendetta.

19, p. 164 (Homer 22.1–38; 23.39–67)

Ch[i]edon mercede i Proci al grande   4.3
    Ulisse
Et egli ad un ad un tutti gli uccide,
Dodici ancelle poi (come gli disse
La balia) dishoneste, appese vide.
Va la nuova a Penelope, che fisse   5.10
Le luci havea nel sonno, e se ne ride
Perché lo credea morto, e finalmente
Conosciuto, l'abbraccia caramente.

20, p. 172 (Homer 24)

Mena Mercurio l'anime all'Inferno   5.2
De' morti Proci; Ulisse intanto arriva
A casa il padre e con un gaudio interno
Mostra il piacer ch'egli ha, ch'il vecchio
    viva
Impeto contra Ulisse, i figli ferno
De' Morti, ed egli lor di vita priva,
Palla l'esorta poi che con amore
Perdon a tutti, e lor l'han per Signore.

Le nozze d'Enea e Lavinia:
Scenario Compared with Dolce's *Allegorie*

Scenario	Dolce, *Allegorie*
Prologue(s)	
Act 1	
1: Latino Re del Latio dubbioso del matrimonio della figliuola Lavinia ricorre per consiglio all'Oracolo di Fauno suo padre, ottenendo per risposta esser quella destinata ad uno straniero.	**41: Per il Re Latino,** il qual havendo nel bosco intesa l'opinione de' Fati, propone di maritar Lavinia ad Enea e non a Turno.
2: Le Nereidi e Tritoni fanno festa alla venuta d'Enea, il quale sbarcato alla Foce del Tebro si rallegra d'esser giunto in Italia. Et apparendo alcuni auguri, invita li Troiani ad applauder a loro, com'essi fanno, inviando dopo ambasciatori a Latino, ed altri alla caccia per difetto de' cibi.	
3: Turno mostrandosi innamorato vien ripreso da Numano milantatore di bravura: il quale dopo si parte al comparir di Lavinia.	

Allegory headings are in bold.

4: Lavinia biasma Amore, dal che Turno prende occasione di parlare dell'Amor suo, e n'ottien risposta molto severa.

5: Ilioneo ambasciator d'Enea dimanda sicurezza a Latino, il quale non solo gliela concede, ma le dà intentione delle nozze della figliuola co 'l sudetto Enea, facendo rappresentar a' forestieri alcuni giuochi, che servono per intermedio del Primo Atto.

42: **Per il Re Latino**, che con liete accoglienze abbraccia gli oratori mandatigli da Enea, offrendogli gratiosamente quanto era in poter suo.

Act 2

1: Giunone sdegnata per lo arrivo d'Enea in Italia chiama dall'Inferno la Furia Aletto per por discordia tra Latini e Troiani, il che prontamente eseguisce.

42: **Per Giunone**, che ancor non satia di perseguitar Enea va nell'inferno a ritrovar Aletto, per metter discordia tra i Latini, ed infiammar il petto d'Amata.

2: Elminio e Silvia pastorelli cantano lietamente, e sopragiunti da Ascanio ed altri cacciatori si ritirano fuggendo.

3: Uscito Ascanio alla caccia ferisce il bel cervo di Silvia figliuola di Torreo [*sic*], il quale accorso al rumore con altri pastori, attacca zuffa con li Troiani, e si ritirano combattendo.

42: **Per Silvia**, che come forsennata ad alta voce grida vendetta del cervo feritole.

4: Turno ed Amata inveiscono contro Latino e Troiani, esprimendo con parole gli effetti cagionati dalla Furia. Aletto, mentre invisibilmente infiamma all'uno il cuore con la face, ed all'altra con un serpe avelena il seno, onde divengono furibondi.

42: **Per Amata**, che come pazza disprezza la deliberatione del marito. **Per Turno**, che di subito infiammato di sdegno, cerca in tutti modi, che Enea non ottenga Lavinia per mogliera.

5: Aletto riferisce a Gionone [*sic*] i semi delle discordie per la morte del cervo, ed Elminio, e per le concitationi di Turno ed Amata. Ed essendole imposto il ritornar all'Inferno, chiama prima l'altre Furie compagne, e mostri a far un ballo per allegrezza de' mali futuri, il quale serve per intermedio dell'Atto Secondo.

Act 3

1: Venere per li nuovi pericoli d'Enea suo figliuolo prega Vulcano suo marito a fornirlo di fine armi, al che egli prontamente obbedisce.

44: **Per Venere**, che induce Vulcano a far l'armatura ad Enea. **Per Vulcano**, che a' prieghi di Venere fabrica di subito a l'armi ad Enea, s'intende, come sono d'Amor le forze tanto potenti, che ancor infiammano quei, che per natura sono freddi, e contrarii alle fiamme amorose.

2: Mentre Latino sta consolato per la pace con li Troiani, e sperato matrimonio di Lavinia, giunge Tirreo, dimandando vendetta del figliuolo ucciso. Amata grida contro li Troiani, Turno ricerca, che s'apra il Tempio di Giano per denuntiarli la guerra. Il che negando Latino di fare co 'l ritirarsi nel suo Pallazzo, scende Giunone, e spalanca il Tempio sudetto. Turno e li suoi gridano guerra, facendone festa Numano per dover uccider tutti li Troiani.

3: Lavinia udito lo strepito dell'intimation della guerra, dubita di qualche suo futuro accidente, ritirandosi sopra le muraglie per veder Enea nel combattimento.

4: Enea non per anco sapendo li rumori contro di lui de' Latini, invitato dall'amenità del luogo si pone a dormir su la sponda del Fiume Tebro, il quale avisandolo de' vicini perigli, lo inanima alla battaglia. Enea svegliato si duole de' novi travagli, e rammemora le passate disgratie, ma tosto anco torna a rinvigorirsi.

5: Venere lietamente cantando presenta in una nube l'armi ad Enea. Et sopragiungendo Turno il campo Troiano dà all'armi, uscendo Acate ad avisarne Enea, il quale entra ne' padiglioni ad armarsi.

6: Turno inanima li suoi soldati; et Numano chiama li suoi soldati alla Battaglia, li quali comparendo egli si pone in fugga. Combattono le squadre, e retiratisi li capitani, li soldati battono una moresca in modo di Battaglia per intermedio dell'Atto Terzo.

Act 4

1: Parendo a Turno, ch'a lui sia rimproverata la cagione de' mali, propone a Latino il duello con Enea, procurando in vano dissuaderlo.

43: **Per li pastori,** che per la morte d'alcuni di loro corrono a dimandarne vendetta al Re Latino; **Per Latino,** che sta costante in dar la figliuola ad Enea. **Per Turno,** che sprezzato il consiglio di Latino prepara a Guerra contro Enea.

43: **Per il dio del Tebro,** che consigliando Enea l'assicura della guerra con Turno . . .

45

47

50: **Per Turno,** che sprezzando il parer d'ognuno, vuol combater in tutti modi.

Amata, perch'egli spedisce un Araldo nel campo inimico, Numano afferma vuol esser il primo a combatter con Troiani.

2: Amata vuol che Lavinia arresti Turno dalla Battaglia con Enea, ma mostrandosene ella renitente, se ne va come furiosa.

3: Lavinia havendo veduto Enea a combattere, stando ella sopra le mura della Città, dopo varii dubii si confessa inamorata di lui, e dalla sua Damigella vien rincorata al proseguimento di tal Amore, sperando ambedue il fine felice.

4: Giove consiglia Venere e Giunone alla concordia, mentre l'una parla in furore [favore] d'Enea, e l'altra contro; proponendo il futuro duello per decisione delle loro liti.

5: Ascanio desidera, che giunga il tempo per acquistarsi fama. Torna Numano a villaneggiar i Troiani, e ferito da Ascanio si ritira fuggendo.

6: Enea ricevuta la disfida di Turno esce al certame con lui, uscendo questi dall'altra parte. Latino venuto come per forza si ritira avanti il cominciar della pugna. Tolunnio augure all'apparir dell'augurio del cigno procura sturbar il duello con l'attaccar la battaglia universale. Enea si duole, e chiama Turno a combatter seco. A questi cade la spada, onde si pone a fuggire, e seguitato da Enea resta fuori di scena ucciso. Il che veduto dalli Troiani celebrano la vittoria del lor Principe co 'l canto, e con un ballo, che serve per intermedio dell'Atto Quarto.

Act 5

1: Esce Enea trionfante inanimando il figliuolo alla gloria con mostrarle le spoglie del vinto inimico, cantando intanto il coro in suo onore.

52: **Per Amata,** che dissuadendo Turno da combatter, gli promette di non dar mai Lavinia ad Enea.

2: Drante Ambasciator di Latino venendo dalla Città invita Enea ad entrarsene in quella, e sposar Lavinia, com'egli eseguisce seguitato dalli Troiani.

3: Giove essorta Giunone a placarsi verso Enea, acconsentendo ella agevolmente di già affettionata al valore del medesimo Enea.

4: Enea entrato nella Città, ed incontrata Lavinia passa con lei amoroso ragionamento.

5: Sopragiunge Latino, ed accogliendo Enea le riconferma la figliuola per moglie, eccitando li Troiani e Latini ad invocar Himeneo, il quale con Venere e Giunone comparendo congiunge li Sposi felici, presagiendo da tal maritaggio le grandezze di Roma, e la nascita e maraviglie della Città di Venetia. Qui restando terminata l'opera.

50: **Per Drance,** che propone, et persuade nel consiglio, che ad Enea senza contesa si dia Lavinia.

55: **Per Enea,** che mirando l'infinita et singolar bellezza di Lavinia, iscusa Turno per haver egli prese armi per cagion sua.

55

Supernatural Scenes

A. *Il ritorno d'Ulisse,* 5.2. Mercurio e i spiriti de' Proci

MERCURIO: Dell'humana tragedia è questo il fine.

Regni, bellezze, amore

Nel transito dissolve;

Lo spirto vola, e non riman, che polve.

La Morte è Dea possente,

Abbatte ogni vivente,

Né ria speranza giova.

Chi non crede all'esempio,

Al fin non può negar fede alla prova.

Voi già Proci superbi, hor placid'ombre,

Prima Prencipi illustri, hor alme oscure,

Per man d'Ulisse il forte

Gran ministro del Ciel estinti foste.

Et hor doppo goduta

La vagabonda libertà di morte,

Andrete profondati, ove chi regna

A incrudelir insegna.

Chiaman le vostre colpe

Precipitii d'Averno,

Voragini d'Inferno,

Ch'a perfide, e crudele,

Quando l'eterno danno ha il ciel prefisso,
S'apre così l'abisso.

Imparate, mortali,
Son di vostri brevissimi piaceri
I castighi immortali,
Stolti, sin che vivete
Vostri humani diletti:
Hanno la Reggia in polve,
Mentre godono sol la carne, e i sensi,
E poi che morti siete,
Passa allo spirto un immortal tormento.

Duro cambio infelice,
Gioir farfalla, e tormentar fenice,
Vostra vita è un passaggio,
Non ha stato, o fermezza,
Se mai giunge bellezza,
Tramonta all'hor, ch'a pena mostra un raggio.
Vivi cauti, o Mortale,
Che camina la vita, e 'l tempo ha l'ale,
E dove ingorda speme
Vivendo non s'acqueta,
De l'humane pazzie quest'è la meta.

B. *L'incoronazione di Poppea,* 2.4. La Virtù con un Coro di Virtù, Seneca

CORO: [*Rit.*] Lieto e ridente
Alfin t'affretta,
Che il Ciel t'aspetta.

SENECA: [1.] Breve coltello,
Ferro minuto
Sarà la chiave
Che m'aprirà
Le vene in terra
E in Ciel le porte dell'eternità.

CORO: Lieto e ridente
Alfin t'affretta,
Che il Ciel t'aspetta.

SENECA: [2.] Addio grandezze,
Pompe di vetro,
Glorie di polve,
Larve d'error,

Che in un momento
Affascinate, assassinate il cor.

CORO: Lieto e ridente
Alfin t'affretta
Che il Ciel t'aspetta.

SENECA: Già, già dispiego il volo
Da questa mia decrepità mortale,
E verso il coro vostro,
Adorate Virtudi, inalzo l'ale.

Singers

A. Poppea

"Idilio per la S.ra Cantatrice unica, ed insigne nel Teatro dell'Ill.mo Sig.r Gio: Grimani Rapresentante Poppea" (Udine, Biblioteca comunale, Fondo Joppi 496)

Qual Miracolo novo
Per gl'attoniti orrecchi
Entra e trapassa a instupidirmi 'l core?
Qual invisibil forza,
Qual ignota violenza
Trattand'armi canore
Mi vince i sensi e con catena d'oro
M'avvinciglia i pensieri?
Chi fu, che la mia mente
Carcere di sé stessa
Dentro un'inamorata meraviglia
Mentre tace ed ascolta,
Quasi riman sepolta?
Qual impeto Amoroso
Gli spiriti mi turba ond'io rimango
Indiferente a i marmi? e son a punto
Ammirato, e immoto.
All'altar d'un bel volto appena si noto?
Aura glorificata

Dal labro ch'a te s'apre
Da la bocca gentil che si respira
Porta a gl'habiti miei
Picciola parte almeno
De la soavità ch'in te ricevi.
E s'ami le armonie
Addaggiasi cortese
In bocca a la mia musa
Vieni, vieni a bearmi.
Per la bella Poppea compongo i carmi.
O come, o come a rimirar è vaga
Questa dolce sirena
Che per rendersi eterna
Ne le memorie humane
Adormenta l'obblio.
Ella è sirena e mare
Ondeggia con la voce
E viene e va con musici riflessi,
D'alta dolcezza ad imitar i cori
Inamora col volto in cui rimiro
Negre lasciviggiar due ladre stelle,
E riconosco al fine
Che s'usano anco in Ciel furti e rapine,
Gravi accenti ed accuti
Con diversi trapassi
Entrano per l'udito in voci pure
Ed arrivar al cuor dolci punture.
Basse notte alte corde
All'alternar d'inimitabil arte
Oprano sì che l'uditor rapito
Al proprio cuor nel sen non trova sito.
I forti, i piani accenti
Confondendo in un canto Abbissi e Cieli,
Movon sontuose i petti semivivi
A palpitar se ben di cor son privi.
O come, o come, o dolce
Sentir le voci care ond'ella forma
Laberinti sonori
Ch'implicando di gruppi
Il respirato vento
E carcerando l'Aria
In angustie canore
Con dolce Tirania
Dona, e tronca i passaggi all'armonia?

Esce del bel rubino
Dell'amorosa bocca
Quasi da Paradiso
L'Angelico parto del caro labro,
L'adorabile voce,
E per linea diretta
Vene a ferir la diletosa piaga.
L'attonito auditore
E la bella cantante
Ch'in dolce melodie tradduce i fiati
Aspreggia falsi in modo
Liber gorghe n' guisa
Sviene e rinforza a' segno
Che lo stupor caduto e soprafatto
Dall'oggetto mirabile e divino
Tessiglia 'l piacere
Col piagnere e tacere.
Move 'labro celeste
Se stesso a cominciar musici accenti,
E la divinità riddotta in lingua
Circondatta di perle
Movesi rubiconda
Vipereggiando in amoroso gesto
E la voce cantata
Si sdegna uscir da l'amorosa bocca.
L'anima che l'ascolta
Non promette raccorla
Qual reliquia d'Amore
Nel sacrario del core.
Cara voce 'l ciel vole
Che tu gemi invisibile, e se mai
Tua forma spiritual prendesse corpo,
Destituiti gl'altari,
Abbandonati i tempi,
Vedriano pullular per ogni via
A te per te novella idolatria.
O il so s'è così dolce
Quel labro ove in un punto
Inibriando l'estingue
Quella voce beata,
Qual dolcezza sana in te l'anima pura
Che la concesse e instilla
All'organo lascivo
Del loquace coral ch'a noi la suona?

Ch'inefabil principio,
Ch'origine sublime ha la tua voce,
Pelegrina Amorosa?
Se il labro ove finisce
Tanto nettare stilla,
Tanta mana fluisce,
Son i principii tuoi più che divini.
Se son beati i fini
Quanta beatitudine dimora,
Ove tua voce nasce
Se 'l tuo morir di balsamo ci parve?
Se rimanesse impressa
Nell'aria vagabonda
Di tua celesta voce alcuna imago
Volarebbero i giorni
A farsi luminosi
Del tuo cantar ne le sembianze belle
E l'alto firmamento
Rinegare le stelle
Insidiarebbe d'imprimerti ed ornarti
D'altri tanti ritratti
Della tua cara voce
Che viva oltre ogni stima
In nuda povertà di paragoni,
In penuria di titoli riddotta.
Attributi non ha non trova nomi
E come va invisibile de gl'occhi
Così va infigurabile da i carmi
E sì come non puote esser mirata
Cosi ricerca indarno esser lodata.
Aria più non respiro,
Ma respiro armonie.
Chi beve ad una fonte
Limpida e cristallina
Vede apparir in lei la propria imago,
E mentr'appressa il labro
A gl'ondosi cristali
Perché beva l'effiggie su se stesso
E in un medesmo issa
La propria imago e 'l dolce fonte asuagge
Io respirar non posso
Se non ricevo entr' a miei propri fiati
Gl'accenti tuoi, Poppea,
Che trascendendo 'l nome de beati

E tanto ti trasformi
Con affetto amoroso
Nel canto dilettoso
Che 'l tuo canto a tua imago
E l'ambiente impresso ed arrichito
Di tue rare virtù,
Di tue bellezze insigni
Porta a respiri miei
Di virtù di beltà genuina gloria,
Ond'in un fiato solo
Porto al cor mio per meraviglia attratto
Di te, bella Poppea doppio ritratto.
Non hò piu caro 'l core
Come fonte di vita
Come sede dell'alma
Ma sol come tabella in cui si pinge
Di così bell'imagine l'tesoro.
Luminoso tesoro
Che nel mezo a le tenebre del petto
Con vivace splendor s'apre le vie
Ne gli è d'huopo di sole
Per fabricar a te medesmo 'l die.
Vivi, bella Poppea,
Anni in numero pari a' merti tuoi
Che vuol dir infiniti.
Viverà sopra i secoli venturi
Ne i Veneti Teatri 'l tuo bel nome,
Non stelle o bronzi o marmi,
Triviali strumenti
Di commun riccordanza
Esposti al tempo e sogiacenti a gl'anni
Ti mostreran bella a gl'occhi altrui.
Ma immortali memorie
Che son opre di Dio
Ma le vergate carte
Figlie de' sacri ingegni
Ma le glorie miei
Emule de l'eterno
Del tuo nome gentil havran la cura.
Né mai tua pura ed'honorata lode
Può soccomber a morte, o sepoltura.
Se transformar potessi
Quest'anima in inchiostro
Porrei fermar con oro

Dell'eccelse sue musiche le noti,
Acciò che tu cantando
Vedessi riverenti
Sotto forma d'inchiostri i pensier miei
Tutti diretti a publicar al mondo
Che chi si tramortisce di dolcezza
Quando la bocca tua gorgheggia e canta
Di esser huom, d'esser vivo indarno vanta.

B. Giulia Saus Paolelli

1. Fulvio Testi, *Lettere*, 1: 495–96; letter to Francesco d'Este, Rome, 3 December 1633.

La Signora Paolella . . . canta isquisitamente, suona di spinetta, di liuto e di tromba in eccellenza; ha marito . . . è donna fatta e adesso porta buon nome. Si disse una volta un non so che d'un tale Duca di Montalto e fors'anche di alcuni altri, che non erano duchi, ma questo non ha a che fare col canto e non si mette a conto qui in Roma. Se V.A. ricerca una perfetta onestà nelle Sue cantatrici, non si volti a questo cielo. Qui le cantatrici si prendono qualche piacevole licenza, e moltissime dell'altre donne ancora, che non sanno cantare, diventano cantatrici in questa parte.

2. Vincenzo Nolfi, *Descrittione de gli apparati del Bellerofonte di Giulio del Colle* (Venice: n.p., 1642).

Signora Giulia Saus Paolelli Romana . . . [rappresentò] la regina Anthia . . . non s'inoltra con descrittioni la penna poiché da tre anni in qua ha questa Patria con l'honore del suo soggiorno bastevol cognitione de' suoi talenti, e quel favor divoto che alla sua prima venuta rubbarno dolcemente i suoi sembianti e rare virtù a gl'animi più nobili e qualificati, tanto va prendendo per giornata d'alteratione, che posso dire gl'affetti sollevarsi in ammirationi, e quasi toccar dell'adorationi i confini. . . . (*OSV*, 418).

3. *Panegirici, epitalami, discorsi accademici, novella, et lettere amorose di Ferrante Pallavicino* (Venice: Gio: Battista Cester, 1652), 184–88; another edition (Venice: Turrini, 1652), 162–65. Letter no. 9: "Alla sig. Giulia Paulelli [*sic*] Romana. Per vaga cantatrice." (The text is a collation of the two editions, paginated according to the Cester edition. Important points, such as references to various roles played by Paolelli, are italicized.)

Mentre a niuno è prohibito l'adito ne' Tempii, per esporre gl'osequi d'animo devoto alle Deità, ch'ivi s'adorano, non dovrete, o Signora, rimpoverarmi, come temerario, se vengo anch'io, senza precedenza di cognitione, a tributare alla vostra virtù, i parti della mia ammiratione. Nel punto, in cui, lusingandomi l'occhio, le apparenze di bellissimo theatro, m'obligò allo stupore la soavità del vostro canto, stimai quegl'edificii, eretti, e regolati dalla vostra voce; perché sapevo, qualmente con molto minor concerto havea Anfione edificate le mura di [p. 185] Thebe. Ma suggerrirmi un pensiero, che anzi quelli erano apparecchi, ordinati a ricevere l'harmonia de' cieli, ch'animata in voi era venuta ad honorare la terra. Gl'eccessi però del vostro merito mi necessitarono a rigettare questi concetti, mentre mi ricordarono che, se così soave fosse stata l'harmonia di quelle Sfere, i

Dei non havrebbero havuto bisogno di chiamare colà su Apollo, e le Muse; acciocché con concertata melodia, accordassero i loro sconcertati voleri. Credetti bensì, che havrebbero volontieri le Deità suscitate nuove discordie, perché l'occasione di rappacificarle, attraesse al suo trono la dolcezza del vostro canto, per cui sarebbe trascurato Apollo, sarebbe negletta ogni musa. Ma confiderai, ch'i vanti delle vostre glorie, havrebbero in quella suprema magione generati nuovi contrasti, o di rivalità, o d'invidia. I vostri raggi seguir non possono ad altro, che ad abbruggiare [bruciare] anco in Cielo. Cessai ben sì di stupirmi nella simplicità di colui, il quale posto in non cale il fuoco, che ardeva la propria casa, attendeva al formare per suo compiacimento, delle altrui sregolate grida, un regolato concerto. Ecco moltiplicati questi tali, anche nel numero de' più saggi; mentre non evvi chi volentieri non permetta fomentati dalla vostra [p. 186] presenza gl'incendi nel proprio petto, pur che goda la melodia de' vosti canori accenti. Per questa parte però giudicai mal collocata in voi la musica, come che suole esser compagna della medicina, onde Apollo dell'una, e dell'altra professione è Dio; anzi lei medesma tal hora serve di medicamento, come a morsi della tarantola in Puglia, et altri simili, e voi all'incontro, cantando, ferite et uccidete i cuori. *Quindi più ragionevolmente nel personaggio di Scilla, che in quello d'Armida, dovevate far pompa delle vostre glorie, mentre anco quello nelle straggi di Roma, accompagnava la crudeltà, con l'Harmonia del canto.*

E quali affetti (diceano tra sé stessi i miei pensieri) non si muoverebbero a pietà nel vedere le anime di chi v'ode, rapite già del vostro concento, *hora essere strascinate in una veloce fuga, hora sospese in un sospiro, hora ristrette in un groppo di ben articolato passaggio, hora combattute dell'ordinanza di Musiche voci; hora finalmente tormentate in varie guise, mentre, e d'improviso si fermano, e impetuosamente si spingono, gravamente si liberano e precipitosamente si lasciano, s'obligano in somma al seguito, di chi con variati artificij, ha per regola l'esser sempre incostante et inquieta?* Chiamarei queste [p. 187] pene, pene d'Inferno, se su vostr'occhi, e nell'udirsi i vostri soavi accenti, credessi possibile, il provar altro che delitie di Paradiso. Restai stupido, al vedervi cinta di fiamme, dalle quali si tramandavano ad ogni cuori intolerabili ardori; sapendo, che le Sirene sogliono viver nelle acque. Ma connobbi, che non meritava stupore, la vita miracolosa, di chi è un compendiato prodigio della natura, e dell'arte. *Giurai, che la constanza d'Ulisse havrebbe sicuramente ceduto a vostri soavi concenti ne i suoi legami, forano stati bastevoli ritegni, per impedire a chiunque ha senso, il correre volontaria preda del vostro merito.* Chi già biasmò la Musica, condannarebbe hora sé stesso, come sacrilego nell'offendere i pregi della vostra Divinità, e chi ne vietò la professione, ritrattarebbe i suoi divieti per non esser empio contro tutto il mondo, nel privarlo della felicità, che si gusta in udirvi. Nella confusione di simili concetti fu absorta la mia mente, sin che mi trattene estatico la vostra Angelica voce; e per certo, se non rapito in estasi, goder potevo la melodia d'un Angelo. Ho voluto notificarvi, o Signora, ciò che d'improviso pensai, perche possa annoverarsi tra le vostre glorie questo trofeo, d'haver [p. 188] aggiunto un'Idolo a quelli dell'Antichità, proponendo cioè per adorabile anco una voce. In più longa consideratione, oppressi gli spiriti dal vostro merito, non hanno havuta forza per palesare altri sentimenti, che di maraviglia. Questa finalmente, è il centro, in cui fermandosi col silentio, terminano le linee di quella penna, o di quella lingua, che volle ostendersi in lodarvi.

4. *Le glorie della musica celebrate dalla sorella poesia Rappresentandosi in Bologna la Delia, e l'Ulisse Nel Teatro de gl'Illustriss. Guastavillani.* (Bologna: Ferroni, 1640), 19. Five of the remaining fifteen sonnets in the same volume (far more than for any other figure) refer to Paolelli in the title role of Manelli and Strozzi's *La Delia*, which shared the Bologna stage with *Ulisse* in 1640. Others are addressed to Guastavillani, Monteverdi, Badoaro, Ferrari as theorbo player, and Maddalena

Manelli as Venere in *Delia* and Minerva in *Ulisse*, and there are two brief poems (the only non-sonnets) for Costantino Manelli (the Manelli's son) as Amore in *Delia*. Other relevant passages about the performance of *Ulisse* in Bologna include the following sonnets:

"Per l'Ulisse, Opera Musicale del Sig. Claudio Monteverdi" (p. 6):

> Scioglie vela al gioir, se spiega un foglio
> Claudio, che in mar canoro affetti scrisse.
> Ah stanchezza non è, non è cordoglio,
> Ma melodia, se s'addormenta Ulisse.
>
> Non gl'incanta i sentieri al regio Soglio
> Il suon, ch'a l'alme una magia prescrisse;
> Anzi placa Nettun l'ira, e l'orgoglio,
> Come se di Sirene il canto udisse.
>
> A tender l'arco arma d'Ulisse intatta,
> Mentr'ei l'incurva a sostener lo scettro,
> Proci, la vostra man non ben s'adatta.
>
> Claudio, a cui ride il lauro, a cui l'elettro
> Sudan le pioppe, e i pini, oggi non tratta
> Alcuno eguale a voi l'arco del plettro.
>
> (Ber. Mar.)

"Per l'Ulisse, Dramma dell'Illustrimo Sig. Giacomo Badoero, e Musica del Sig. Claudio Monteverdi" (p. 7):

> De l'Itaco Guerriero il bel ritorno
> Giacomo canti, e di tua Cetra al tuono
> Tace il Cieco di Smirna, e ti fa dono
> Del serto, che gli tende il capo adorno.
>
> Claudio se già de le Sirene a scorno
> Varco di Circe a l'amoroso Trono
> L'astuto Greco, de' tuoi canti al suono
> Fermaria la sua prora ad Adria intorno.
>
> S'i termini passo, ch'altrui prescrisse
> Meta del folle ardire Alcide il forte
> Di veder vago, e di sapere Ulisse;
>
> A voi passar la Fama è dato in sorte,
> Ch'a le glorie di quegli ah non prefisse
> Termine il Ciel, che sa domar la Morte.
>
> (Clotildo Artemii)

"Per la Sig. Maddalena Manelli, Che cantò da Venere nella Delia, e da Minerva nell'Ulisse" (p. 13):

> O Degna solo in quelle Scene, e in queste
> Che silenzio ti lodi, e meraviglia,
> Donna, il cui petto a l'armonia celeste

Un'augelliera d'angioli somiglia.

   O se Pallade giri occhiate oneste,
O se fatta Ciprigna alzi le ciglia,
Sempre con giusta, e meritata veste
Forma di Deità da te si piglia.

   Anzi che d'ogni Musico perfetto
Vincendo il suon, tu non difformi intanto,
Qual già Minerva, il riverito aspetto.

   E senza perder di pudica il vanto,
Tu porgi, colme di maggior diletto,
Le dolcezze di Venere col canto.

(A.S.)

C. Anna Renzi

1. Giulio Strozzi, *Le glorie della signora Anna Renzi romana* (Venice: Surian, 1644), pp. 6–10.

L'azione con la quale si da l'anima, lo spirito, e l'essere alle cose, deve esser governata dal movimento del corpo, dal gesto, dal volto, e dalla voce, hora innalzandola, hora abbassandola, sdegnandosi, e tornando subito a pacificarsi: una volta parlando in fretta, un'altra adagio, movendo il corpo hor a questa, hor a quella parte, raccogliendo le braccia, e distendendole, ridendo, e piangendo, hora con poca, hora con molta agitatione di mani: la nostra Signora Anna è dotata d'una espressione sì viva, che paiono le risposte, e i discorsi non appresi dalla memoria, ma nati all'hora. In somma ella si trasforma tutta nella persona che rappresenta. . . . Padroneggia la Scena, intende quel che proferisce, e lo proferisce sì chiaramente, che non hanno l'orecchie, che desiderare: Ha una lingua sciolta, una pronuntia suave, non affettata, non presta, una voce piena, sonora, non aspra, non roca, né che ti offenda con la soverchia sottigliezza; il che nasce dal temperamento del petto, e della gola. . . . Ella ha il passaggio felice, e 'l trillo gagliardo, doppio, e rinforzato. . . . Ella va tacitamente osservando le azzioni altrui, e quando poi ha da rapresentarle, aiutata dal sangue, del quale ella è copiosissima, e dalla bile, che se le accende . . . mostra lo spirito, e valor suo appreso con lo studio delle osservationi fatte.

2. *Abozzo di veraci lodi. Alla Signora Anna Renzi Cantatrice singolare, Idilio d'incerto Autore* (Venice, Surian: 1644), 47.

> Ti conducesti al fine,
> Pur nella stessa scena,
> Sotto nome mentito
> D'Ottavia Imperatrice,
> Di tue gratie, e vaghezze
> A far leggiadra, ed amorosa mostra.
> Attione adeguata
> A tuoi saggi costumi,
> Al tuo degno, e honesto,

E puro, e grave, e gratioso gesto.

E mentre fuori uscivi

Col tuo languido volto,

Pria, che snodasi il canto,

Con dolci ricercate

De' sommessi sospiri,

Palesavi ad'ogn'uno i tuoi martiri.

    Poi cominciasti afflitta

Tue querele Canore

Con tua voce divina,

Disprezzata Regina,

E seguendo il lamento

Facevi di dolore

Stillar in pianto, e sospirar Amore.

So ben'io, che se vero

Fosse statto il cordoglio,

E l'historia funesta,

Alla tua voce mesta,

Alle dolci parole, ai cari detti.

Sì come i nostri petti

Colmaro di pietade, ah so ben'io,

Neron s'haverebbe fatto humile, e pio.

    Al tuo sommo valor palme immortali,

Si videro produr, Anna, le scene,

E parean le rivali

Di tue virtuti emulatrici belle

appresso al chiaro sol picciole stelle.

    Soprafatta dal sdegno

Contro l'empio marito

Per satollar col sangue

Di Poppea tua nemica

Tue giustissime brame,

Commettesti ad Ottone,

Ch'era suo fido Amante,

Per sua cattiva sorte

Con le sue proprie man la di lei morte.

    Quella voce imperiosa,

Che con grave sembiante

Essercitava un barbaro talento,

Parea che a noi medesmi

L'annuntio del morir anco apportasse,

Ma con tale dolcezza,

E tanta tenerezza,

Ch'anco recava aita,

E quella morte al fin era la Vita.
    Ecco in esilio, ahi lasso,
Al mar volgesti il passo,
E mentre in cavo pino
Dall'impero marino,
Acceso quasi d'amorose fiamme,
Eri abbracciata, e colta,
L'Anima nostra sciolta
Dal legame vital pur ti seguia
Che in perigliosa via
Non si stancava mai
Del tuo giorno seguir la luce, e i rai.

BIBLIOGRAPHY

MANUSCRIPT SOURCES

Scores

A-Wn Mus. Ms. 18763: *Il ritorno d'Ulisse in patria*
I-Nc Rari 6, 4, 1: [*L'incoronazione di Poppea*]
I-Vnm It. IV, 439 (= 9963): *Il Nerone*

Librettos

I-Fn Magl. VII. 66: *La Coronatione di Poppea*
I-Fn Magl. VII. 129: *La Didone*, fragment
I-Mb 3077: *Il ritorno d'Ulisse in patria*
I-Mb 4457: *Le nozze d'Enea con Lavinia*
I-Mb 5672: *Il ritorno d'Ulisse in patria*
I-Pci H 48575: *Il ritorno d'Ulisse in patria*
I-Pci H 48576: *Le nozze d'Enea con Lavinia*
I-Pu MS 40: *La Dafne opera che si rapresentò in musica nel teattro di San Cassano, L'Anno 1639*
    [sic], *del Eccmo Sig. Gio: Francesco Businello, honorata con la musica del Ille & Illto Rdo*
    Sig. [blank] *in Venetia.*
I-Rig Rar. Lib. Ven 13: *Il ritorno d'Ulisse in patria*
I-Rig Rar. Lib. Ven 14: *Le nozze d'Enea con Lavinia*
I-RVI Silvestriani 239: *La Coronatione di Poppea*
I-RVI Silvestriani 244 (Cod. 7–1-30), Mazzatini no. 66: *Gl'Amori d'Apollo e Dafne del Businello.*
    Rappresentata in musica nel' Theatro di S. Cassano di Venetia Anno 1640

I-TVco Cod. Rossi 29: *Gli Amori d'Apollo e di Dafne Opera recitata in musica nel Theatro di S. Cassano In Venetia l'Anno 1640.*

I-Tvco Cod. Rossi 83: *La Popea*

I-UDc 55: *La Coronatione di Poppea,* fragment

I-UDc Fondo Joppi 496: *Coronatione di Poppea*

I-Vcg S. Cassiano I.5: *Il ritorno d'Ulisse in patria*

I-Vmc 564: [*Il ritorno d'Ulisse*]

I-Vmc 3330 (191.1): *Il ritorno d'Ulisse in patria*

I-Vmc 3330 (192.1): *Le nozze d'Enea e Lavinia*

I-Vmc 3331: *Le nozze d'Enea e Lavinia*

I-Vmc 3332: *Le nozze d'Enea con Lavinia*

I-Vmc Cicogna 585: *La Popea*

I-Vmc Cicogna 220.1: *Il ritorno d'Ulisse in patria*

I-Vmc Cicogna 1229 (fols. 216–19): *La Didone,* fragment (act 3, scene 7)

I-Vmc Correr 270 (fols. 394–403): *La Didone,* fragment

I-Vnm 909.2: *Il ritorno d'Ulisse in patria*

I-Vnm 909.4: *Le nozze d'Enea con Lavinia*

I-Vnm 1294.1: *Il ritorno d'Ulisse in patria*

I-Vnm 1294. 2, 3: *Le nozze d'Enea con Lavinia*

I-Vnm 3449.9: *Il ritorno d'Ulisse in patria*

I-Vnm 3449.11: *Le nozze d'Enea con Lavinia*

I-Vnm It. IX, 591 (=10407): *Apollo e Dafne*

I-Vnm It. IX, 465 (=6386): *La Didone*

I-Vnm It. IX, 493 (=6660): *Enea nell'inferno*

PL-Wn BOZ 1043: *Nerone*

US-LAu II, 17: *Il ritorno d'Ulisse in patria*

US-LAu II, 18: *Le nozze d'Enea con Lavinia*

US-Wc Schatz 6596.12: *Le nozze d'Enea con Lavinia*

PRINTED SOURCES

Abert, Anna Amalie. *Monteverdi und das musikalische Drama.* Lippstadt: Kistner & Siegel, 1954.

Abozzo di veraci lodi. Alla signora Anna Renzi cantatrice singolare, Idilio d'incerto autore. In Giulio Strozzi, *Le glorie della signora Anna Renzi romana.* Venice: Surian, 1644.

Accorsi, Maria Grazia. "Varietà: Problemi testuali dei libretti d'opera fra Sei e Settecento." *Giornale storico della letteratura italiana* 166 (1989): 212–25.

Allacci, Leone. *Drammaturgia di Leone Allacci accresciuta e continuata fino all'anno MDCCLV.* Venice: Giambattista Pasquali, 1755.

Alm, Irene. *Catalogue of Venetian Librettos at the University of California, Los Angeles.* Berkeley: University of California Press, 1993.

———. "Theatrical Dance in Seventeenth-Century Venetian Opera." Ph.D. diss., University of California, Los Angeles, 1993.

———. "Winged Feet and Mute Eloquence: Dance in Seventeenth-Century Venetian Opera," *COJ* 15 (2003): 216–80.

Amato, Mario. "Le antologie di arie e cantate tardo-seicentesche alla Biblioteca del Conservatorio S. Pietro a Majella di Napoli." Ph.D. diss., Scuola di Paleografia Musicale di Cremona, a.a. 1996–97, 2 vols.

Ambros, August Wilhelm. *Geschichte der Musik,* second ed., ed. Hugo Leichtentritt. Leipzig, 1881; third ed., Leipzig, 1909.

Argomento et scenario delle Nozze d'Enea in Lavinia. Tragedia di lieto fine. Da rappresentarsi in musica. Venice: n.p., 1640.

Aristotle. *The Complete Works of Aristotle.* Edited by Jonathan Barnes. Princeton: Princeton University Press, 1985.

Arnold, Denis. *Monteverdi.* London: Dent, 1960; 3rd ed., rev. Tim Carter. London: Dent, 1990.

Arnold, Denis, and Nigel Fortune, eds. *The New Monteverdi Companion.* London: Faber and Faber, 1985.

Badoaro, Giacomo. *Ulisse errante.* Venice: Pinelli, 1644.

Barlow, Jeremy. "The Revival of Monteverdi's Operas in the Twentieth Century." In *The Operas of Monteverdi,* ed. Nicholas John, pp. 193–203. English National Opera Guide 45. London: John Calder, 1992.

Bégaud, Josée, and Germain Fauquet. "L'oeuvre à l'affiche." In *Monteverdi: Le retour d'Ulysse. L'Avant-scène opéra* 159 (1994): 128–33.

Benvenuti, Giacomo. "Il manoscritto veneziano della *Incoronazione di Poppea.*" *RMI* 41 (1937): 176–84.

———. "Il ritorno d'Ulisse non è di Monteverdi." *Il Gazzettino,* 7 May 1942.

Besutti, Paola. "Da *L'Arianna* a *La Ferinda:* Giovanni Battista Andreini e la 'Comedia musicale all'improviso.'" *MD* 49 (1995): 227–76.

———. "The *Sala dei specchi* Uncovered: Monteverdi, the Gonzagas, and the Palazzo Ducale, Mantua." *EM* 27 (1999): 451–65.

———, Teresa M. Gialdroni, and Rodolfo Baroncini, eds. *Claudio Monteverdi: Studi e prospettive. Atti del convegno, Mantova, 21–24 ottobre 1993.* Accademia Nazionale Virgiliana di Scienze, Lettere, e Arti: Miscellanea 5. Florence: Olschki, 1998.

Bianconi, Lorenzo. "La finta pazza." *NGO,* 2: 213.

———. "La finta pazza ritrovata." In *La finta pazza, Gran Teatro La Fenice, programma di sala,* 967–82. Venice: Stamperia di Venezia, 1987.

———. "Funktionen des Operntheaters in Neapel bis 1700 und die Rolle Alessandro Scarlattis." In *Colloquium Alessandro Scarlatti. Würzburg 1975,* ed. Wolfgang Osthoff, 13–116. Tutzing: Hans Schneider, 1979.

———. "Hors-d'oeuvre alla filologia dei libretti." *Saggiatore musicale* 2 (1995): 143–54.

———. *Music in the Seventeenth Century.* Translated by David Bryant. Cambridge: Cambridge University Press, 1987.

———, and Giorgio Pestelli, ed. *Opera on Stage.* The History of Italian Opera 5. Chicago: University of Chicago Press, 2002.

———, and Thomas Walker. "Dalla *Finta pazza* alla *Veremonda:* Storie di Febiarmonici." *RIM* 10 (1975): 379–454.

Bolgar, R. R. *The Classical Heritage.* New York: Harper, 1954.

Bonarelli, Prospero. *Il Solimano di Prospero Bonarelli,* ed. Roberto Cincarelli. Rome: E&A, 1992.

Bongi, Salvatore. *Annali di Gabriel Giolito de' Ferrari da Trino di Monferrato, stampatore in Venezia.* 2 vols. Rome: Presso i principali librai, 1890–95.

[Bonlini, Carlo.] *Le glorie della poesia e della musica contenute nell'esatta notitia de teatri della città di Venezia.* Venice: Bonarigo, 1730; repr. Bologna: Forni, 1979.

Bossarelli, Anna Mondolfi. "Ancora intorno al codice napolitano della *Incoronazione di Poppea.*" *RIM* 2 (1967): 294–313.

Boulay, Henri de. "Il Nerone difeso di Luciano." In *Tre discorsi di Henri de Bullay, gentil'huomo francese.* Venice: Deuchino, 1627.

Bouwsma, William J. *Venice and the Defense of Republican Liberty: Renaissance Values in the Age of the Counter-Reformation.* Berkeley and Los Angeles: University of California Press, 1968.

Bozza, Tomasso. *Scrittori politici italiani dal 1550 al 1650: Saggio di bibliografia.* Storia e letteratura 23. Rome: Edizioni di "Storia e letteratura," 1949.

Braden, Gordon. *Renaissance Tragedy and the Senecan Tradition: Anger's Privilege.* New Haven: Yale University Press, 1985.

Brizzi, Bruno. "Teoria e prassi melodrammatica di G. F. Busenello e *L'Incoronazione di Poppea.*" In *Venezia e il melodrama nel Seicento,* ed. Maria Teresa Muraro, 51–74. Florence: Olschki, 1976.

Brown, Patricia Fortini. *Venice and Antiquity: The Venetian Sense of the Past.* New Haven and London: Yale University Press, 1996.

Bujić, Bojan. "Rinuccini the Craftsman: A View of His *L'Arianna.*" *EMH* 18 (1999): 75–117.

Burney, Charles. *A General History of Music, from the Earliest Ages to the Present Period (1789).* Edited by Frank Mercer. New York: Dover, 1935.

Busenello, Francesco. *Delle hore ociosi.* Venice: Giuliani, 1656.

———. *L'incoronazione di Poppea.* Edited by Paolo Fabbri. In *Libretti d'opera italiani dal Seicento al Novecento,* ed. Giovanna Gronda and Paolo Fabbri, 1: 49–105. Milan: Mondadori, 1997.

———. *La prosperità infelice di Giulio Cesare dittatore.* In *Delle hore ociosi.*

Caberloti, Matteo. "Laconismo delle alte qualità di Claudio Monteverdi." In *Fiori poetici raccolti nel funerale del . . . signor Claudio Monteverde . . . ,* ed. Giovanni Battista Marinoni. Venice: Miloco, 1644.

Calcagno, Mauro. "Fonti, ricezione e ruolo della committenza nell'*Eliogabalo* musicato da F. Cavalli, G. A. Boretti e T. Orgiani (1667–1687)." In *Francesco Cavalli: La circolazione dell'opera veneziana nel Seicento,* ed. Dinko Fabris, 77–99. Naples: Turchini edizioni, 2005.

———. "'Imitar col canto chi parla': Monteverdi and the Creation of a Language for Musical Theater." *JAMS* 55 (2002): 383–431.

———. "Signifying Nothing: On the Aesthetics of Pure Voice in Early Venetian Opera." *JM* 20 (2004): 461–97.

———. "Staging Musical Discourses in Seventeenth-Century Venice: Francesco Cavalli's *Eliogabalo.*" Ph.D. diss., Yale University, 2000.

Camerini, Paolo. *Piazzola.* Milan: Alfieri & Lacroix, 1925.

———. *Piazzola.* Milan: Hoepli, 1929.

Cannizzaro, Nina. "Studies on Guido Casoni (1561–1642) and Venetian Academies." Ph.D. diss., Harvard University, 2001.

Capacci, Christophe. "Discographie." In *Monteverdi: Le Couronnement de Poppée. L'Avant-scène opéra* 115 (December 1988): 154–61.

Carter, Tim. "'In Love's Harmonious Consort'? Penelope and the Interpretation of *Il ritorno d'Ulisse in patria.*" *COJ* 5 (1993): 517–23.

———. "Lamenting Ariadne?" *EM* 27 (1999): 395–405.

———. *Monteverdi's Musical Theatre.* New Haven and London: Yale University Press, 2002.

———. "Re-reading *Poppea*: Some Thoughts on Music and Meaning in Monteverdi's Last Opera." *JRMA* 122 (1997): 173–204.

Chafe, Eric. *Monteverdi's Tonal Language*. New York: Schirmer, 1992.

Champlin, Edward. *Nero*. Cambridge, MA: Harvard University Press, 2003.

Chiarelli, Alessandra. "*L'incoronazione di Poppea* o *Il Nerone*: Problemi di filologia testuale." *RIM* 9 (1974): 117–51.

Chiarelli, Alessandra, and Angelo Pompilio. "*Or vaghi or fieri*": *Cenni di poetica nei libretti veneziani (circa 1640–1740)*. Bologna: CLUEB, 2004.

Chojnacki, Stanley. "Identity and Ideology in Renaissance Venice." In *Venice Reconsidered: The History and Civilization of an Italian City-State, 1297–1797*, ed. John Martin and Dennis Romano, 264–94. Baltimore: Johns Hopkins University Press, 2000.

———. *Women and Men in Renaissance Venice: Twelve Essays on Patrician Society*. Baltimore: Johns Hopkins University Press, 2000.

Clarke, Howard. *Homer's Readers: A Historical Introduction to the Iliad and the Odyssey*. London: Associated University Presses, 1981.

Clayton, Barbara. *A Penelopean Poetics: Reweaving the Feminine in Homer's Odyssey*. Lanham, MD and Oxford: Lexington Books, c. 2004.

Clubb, Louise George. *Giambattista Della Porta, Dramatist*. Princeton: Princeton University Press, 1965.

Cohen, Judith. "Giovan-Battista Andreini's Dramas and the Beginnings of Opera." In *La musique et le rite sacré et profane: Actes du XIIIe Congrès de la Société Internationale de Musicologie*, ed. Marc Honegger and Paul Prevost, 2: 423–32. Strasbourg: Université de Strasbourg, 1986.

Composing Opera: From Dafne to Ulisse Errante. Edited by Tim Carter and Zygmunt M. Szweykowski. Kraków: Musica Iagellonica Katedra Historii i Teorii Muzyki Uniwersytetu Jagiellonskiego, 1994.

Croce, Benedetto. *I teatri di Napoli*. Naples: Pierro, 1891.

Curtis, Alan. "*La Poppea impasticciata*, or, Who Wrote the Music to *L'Incoronazione* (1643)?" *JAMS* 42 (1989): 23–54.

Cusick, Suzanne. "'There Was not One Lady who Failed to Shed a Tear': Arianna's Lament and the Construction of Modern Womanhood." *EM* 22 (1994): 21–41.

D'Alessandro, Domenico Antonio. "L'opera in musica a Napoli dal 1650 al 1670." In *Seicento napolitano: Arte, costume e ambiente*, ed. Roberto Pane, 409–30. Milan: Edizioni di Comunità, 1984.

D'Alessandro, Domenico Antonio, and Agostino Ziino, eds. *La musica a Napoli durante il Seicento. Atti del convegno internazionale di studi: Napoli, 11–14 aprile 1985*. Rome: Edizioni Torre d'Orfeo, 1987.

Dallapiccola, Luigi. "Per una rappresentazione de *Il ritorno di Ulisse in patria* di Claudio Monteverdi." *Musica* 2 (1943): 121–36.

Damerini, Adelmo. "Aspetti dell'VIII Maggio musicale fiorentino." *Musica* 2 (1943): 207–13.

Day, Christine J. "The Theater of SS. Giovanni e Paolo and Monteverdi's *L'incoronazione di Poppea*." *CM* 25 (1978): 22–38.

Degrada, Francesco. "Gian Francesco Busenello e il libretto dell'*Incoronazione di Poppea*." In *Congresso internazionale sul tema "Claudio Monteverdi e il suo tempo*," ed. Rafaello Monterosso, 81–102. Verona: Stamperia Valdonega, 1969.

———. "Il teatro di Claudio Monteverdi: Gli studi sullo stile." In *Claudio Monteverdi: studi e prospettive. Atti del convegno, Mantova 21–24 ottobre 1993*, ed. Paola Besutti, Teresa M. Gialdroni, and Rodolfo Baroncini, 263–83. Florence: Olschki, 1998.

Della Porta, Giambattista. *Teatro.* Vol. 1, *Le tragedie,* ed. Rafaelle Siri. Naples: Istituto Universitario Orientale, 1978.

De' Paoli, Domenico. *Monteverdi.* Milan: U. Hoepli, 1945.

Dersofi, Nancy. *Arcadia and the Stage.* Madrid: Turanzas, 1978.

Dickenson, Elizabeth G., and James M. Boyden. "Ambivalence toward Suicide in Early Modern Spain." In *From Sin to Insanity: Suicide in Early Modern Europe,* ed. Jeffrey R. Watt, 100–115. Ithaca: Cornell University Press, 2004.

Dio Cassius. *Dio's Roman History.* Translated by Earnest Cary. Loeb Classical Library. Cambridge, MA: Harvard University Press, 1968.

Dolce, Lodovico. *L'Achille et l'Enea . . . .* Venice: Giolito, 1570.

———. *L'Achille et l'Enea di Messer Lodovico Dolce . . . .* Venice: Giolito, 1571.

———. *Dialogo della institutione delle donne.* Venice: Giolito, 1547.

———. *L'Enea di M. Lodovico Dolce, tratta dall'Eneide di Vergilio, all'illustrissimo et eccellentissimo signor Don Francesco de Medici principe di Fiorenze & di Siena.* Venice: Varisco & compagni, 1568.

———. *Le tragedie di Seneca tradotte da M. Lodovico Dolce.* Venice: Gio. Battista et Marchion Sessa, 1560.

———. *L'Ulisse.* Venice: Gabriel Giolito de' Ferrari, 1573.

———. *Le vite di tutti gl'imperadori romani da Giulio Cesare insino a Massimiliano. Tratte per M. Lodovico Dolce dal libro spagnuolo del nobile cavaliere Pietro Messia, con alcune utili cose in diversi luoghi aggiunte.* Venice: Giolito, 1558.

———. *Le vite de gli imperadori romani da Cesare sino a Massimiliano, tratte per M. Lodovico Dolce dal libro spagnolo del signor Pietro Messia.* Venice: Turrini e Brigonci, 1664.

Drammi per musica dal Rinuccini allo Zeno, ed. Andrea della Corte. Turin: Unione tipografico-editrice Torinese, 1958; 2nd ed., 1970.

Dubowy, Norbert. "Bemerkungen zu einigen Ulisse-Opern des 17. Jahrhunderts." In *Claudio Monteverdi und die Folgen. Bericht über das Internationale Symposium Detmold 1993,* ed. Silke Leopold and Joachim Steinheuer, 215–43. Kassel: Bärenreiter, 1998.

Elam, Keir. *The Semiotics of Theatre and Drama.* London and New York: Methuen, 1980.

Evelyn, John. *Diaries.* Edited by E. S. de Beer, 6 vols. Oxford: Clarendon Press, 1955.

———. *The Memoires of John Evelyn.* 2 vols. Edited by W. Bray. London: H. Colburn, 1918.

Fabbri, Paolo. *Monteverdi.* Turin: EDT, 1985. Translated by Tim Carter. Cambridge: Cambridge University Press, 1994.

———. "New Sources for *Poppea.*" *ML* 74 (1993): 16–23.

———. "On the Origins of an Operatic Topos: The Mad Scene." In *Con che soavità: Essays in Italian Opera, Song, and Dance, 1580–1740,* ed. Tim Carter and Iain Fenlon, 157–95. Oxford: Clarendon Press, 1995.

———. *Il secolo cantante: Per una storia del libretto d'opera nel Seicento.* Bologna: Il Mulino, 1990; 2nd ed. Rome: Bulzoni, 2003.

Fabris, Dinko. *Mecenati e musici: Documenti sul patronato artistico dei Bentivoglio di Ferrara nell'epoca di Monteverdi (1585–1645).* Lucca: Libreria italiana musicale: 1999.

———. "*Statira* da Venezia a Napoli." In *Francesco Cavalli: La circolazione dell'opera veneziana nel Seicento,* ed. Dinko Fabris, 165–94. Naples: Turchini edizioni, 2005.

Fenlon, Iain, and Peter Miller. *The Song of the Soul: Understanding Poppea.* London: Royal Musical Association, 1992.

Ferrari, Benedetto. *Musiche varie a voce sola, libri I, II, III,* ed. Alessandro Magini. Florence: Studio per edizioni scelte, 1985.

Fiori poetici raccolti nel funerale del. . . signor Clavdio Monteverde. . . . Edited by Giovanni Battista Marinoni. Venice: Miloco, 1644.

Follino, Federico. *Compendio delle sontuose feste fatte l'anno MDCVIII nella città di Mantova, per le reali nozze del serenissimo prencipe d. Francesco Gonzaga con la serenissima infante Margherita di Savoia.* Mantua: Aurelio & Lodovico Osanna, 1608.

Fónagy, Ivan. *La repetizione creativa: Ridondanze espressive nell'opera poetica.* Bari: Dedalo, 1982.

Freitas, Roger. "The Eroticism of Emasculation: Confronting the Baroque Body of the Castrato." *JM* 20 (2000): 196–249.

Gallico, Claudio. *Monteverdi: Poesia musicale, teatro, e musica sacra.* Turin: Einaudi, 1979.

Gasperini, Guido, and Franca Gallo. *Catalogo delle opere musicali: Città di Napoli, Biblioteca del R. Conservatorio di Musica di S. Pietro a Majella.* Pubblicazioni dell'Associazione dei musicologi italiani, serie 10. Parma: Officina grafica Fresching, 1934.

Genette, Gérard. *Palimpsestes.* Paris: Éditions du Seuil, 1982; Eng. ed., *Palimpsests: Literature in the Second Degree.* Lincoln: University of Nebraska Press, 1997.

Gerber, Ernst Ludwig. *Neue-historisch-biographisches Lexikon der Tonkünstler.* Leipzig: A. Kühnel, 1812–14.

Getrevi, Paolo. *Le labbra baroche.* Verona: Essedue, 1987.

Ghilini, Girolamo. *Teatro aperto d'huomini letterati.* Venice: Guerigli, 1647.

Giacobello, Sebastiano. "Giovan Domenico Ottonelli sulle donne cantatrice." *SM* 26 (1997): 297–311.

Giazotto, Remo. *La musica a Genova nella vita pubblica e privata dal XIII al XVIII secolo.* Genoa: Società industrie grafiche e lavorazioni affini, 1951.

Giordani, Gaetano. *Intorno al Gran Teatro del Comune e ad altri minori in Bologna.* Bologna: Società tipografica bolognese e Ditta Sassi, 1855.

Giraldi Cinthio, Giambattista. *Discorsi . . . intorno al comporre de i romanzi, delle comedie, e delle tragedie, e di altre maniere di poesie.* Venice: Giolitti, 1554.

Giuliani, Roberto. "Monteverdi Opera on DVD." *EM* 34 (2006): 702–706.

Giuntini, Francesco. "L'Amore trionfante nell'*Incoronazione di Poppea.*" In *Claudio Monteverdi: Studi e prospettive. Atti del convegno, Mantova, 21–24 ottobre 1993,* ed. Teresa M. Gialdroni and Rodolfo Baroncini, 347–56. Accademia Nazionale Virgiliana di Scienze, Lettere, e Arti: Miscellanea 5. Florence: Olschki, 1998.

Glixon, Beth L. "Private Lives of Public Women: Prima Donnas in Mid-Seventeenth-Century Venice." *ML* 76 (1995): 509–31.

———. Review of *Emblems of Eloquence: Opera and Women's Voices in Seventeenth-Century Venice* by Wendy Heller. *Journal of the Society for Seventeenth-Century Music* 12, no. 1 (2006), www.sscm-jscm.org/jscm/.

———. "Scenes from the Life of Silvia Gailarti Manni, a Seventeenth-Century *Virtuosa.*" *EMH* 15 (1996): 97–146.

————, and Jonathan E. Glixon. *Inventing the Business of Opera: The Impresario and His World in Seventeenth-Century Venice*. New York: Oxford University Press, 2006.

Le glorie degli Incogniti o vero gli huomini illustri dell'Accademia de' Signori Incogniti di Venetia. Venice: Valvasense, 1647.

Le glorie della musica celebrate dalla sorella poesia rappresentandosi in Bologna la Delia, e l'Ulisse nel Teatro de gl'illustriss. Guastavillani. Bologna: Ferroni, 1640.

Glover, Jane. *Cavalli*. London: Batsford, 1978.

————. "The Teatro Sant'Apollinare and the Development of Seventeenth-Century Venetian Opera." Ph.D. diss., Oxford University, 1975.

Gmeiner, Josef. "Die Schlafkammerbibliothek Kaiser Leopolds I." *Biblios* 43 (1994): 3–4.

Goldschmidt, Hugo. "Monteverdi's *Ritorno d'Ulisse*." *SIMG* 4 (1902–1903): 671–76, and 9 (1907): 570–92.

————. *Studien zur Geschichte der italienischen Oper im 17. Jahrhundert*. 2 vols. Leipzig: Breitkopf & Härtel, 1901–1904.

Gordon, Bonnie. *Monteverdi's Unruly Women*. Cambridge: Cambridge University Press, 2004.

Groppo, Antonio. *Catalogo di tutti i drammi per musica recitati ne' teatri di Venezia dall'anno 1637 in cui ebbero principio le pubbliche rappresentazioni de' medesimi, fin all'anno presente 1745*. Venice: Groppo, 1745; repr. Bologna: Forni, 1977.

Haas, Robert. "Zur Neuausgabe von Claudio Monteverdis *Il Ritorno d'Ulisse in patria*." *Studien zur Musikwissenschaft* 9 (1922): 3–42.

Heller, Wendy. "Chastity, Heroism, and Allure: Women in the Opera of Seventeenth-Century Venice." Ph.D. diss., Brandeis University, 1995.

————. *Emblems of Eloquence: Opera and Women's Voices in Seventeenth-Century Venice*. Berkeley and Los Angeles: University of California Press, 2003.

————. "*O delle donne miserabil sesso:* Tarabotti, Ottavia, and *L'incoronazione di Poppea*." *Saggiatore musicale* 7 (2000): 5–46.

————. "Tacitus Incognito: Opera as History in *L'incoronazione di Poppea*." *JAMS* 52 (1999): 39–96.

Holzer, Robert. "*Ma invan lo tento, impossibil mi pare,* or How *Guerrieri* are Monteverdi's *Madrigali guerrieri?*" In *The Sense of Marino: Literature, Fine Arts, and Music of the Italian Baroque*, ed. Francesco Guardiani, 429–50. Ottawa: Legas, 1994.

————. "Monteverdi's *Rerum vulgarium fragmenta:* The Italian-Texted Pieces of the *Selva morale et spirituale*." Unpublished typescript, 2000.

————. Review of *The Song of the Soul: Understanding Poppea*, by Peter Miller and Iain Fenlon. *COJ* 5 (1993): 79–92.

Homer. *The Odyssey*. Translated with an Introduction by Richmond Lattimore. New York: Harper & Row, 1965.

————. *The Odyssey*. Translated by A. T. Murray. Loeb Classical Library. Cambridge, MA: Harvard University Press, 1980.

Infelise, Mario. "*Ex ignoto notus?* Note sul tipografo Sarzina e l'Accademia degli Incogniti." In *Libri, tipografi, biblioteche: Ricerche storiche dedicate a Luigi Balsamo*, ed. Istituto di Biblioteconomia e Paleografia, 207–23. Florence: Olschki, 1997.

Ivanovich, Cristoforo. "Memorie teatrali di Venezia." In *Minerva al tavolino*. Venice: Pezzana, 1681. Second edition (1688) repr. *Memorie teatrali di Venezia*, ed. Norbert Dubowy. Lucca: Libreria musicale italiana, 1993.

Jakobson, Roman. "Closing Statement: Linguistics and Poetics." In *Style in Language,* ed. Thomas A. Sebeok, 350–77. New York: Wiley, 1960.

Jeffery, Peter. "The Autograph Manuscripts of Francesco Cavalli." Ph.D. diss., Princeton University, 1980.

John, Nicholas, ed. *The Operas of Monteverdi.* ENO Guides, 45. London, New York, and Paris: Calder, 1992.

Jungheinrich, Hans-Klaus. "Arrivi e partenze: Hans Werner Henze e la sua elaborazione del *Ritorno d'Ulisse in patria* di Monteverdi." In *Il ritorno d'Ulisse in patria,* program book, 50th Maggio Musicale. Florence: Cassa di Risparmio, 1987.

Kallendorf, Craig. *Virgil and the Myth of Venice: Books and Readers in the Italian Renaissance.* Oxford: Oxford University Press, 1999.

Kapp, Volker, "Liebeswahn und Staatsräson in der Oper *L'incoronazione di Poppea:* Zur Verarbeitung von Seneca und Tacitus durch Monteverdis Text-Dichter Giovanni Francesco Busenello." In *Italia viva: Studien zur Sprache und Literatur Italiens. Festschrift für Hans Ludwig Scheel,* ed. Willi Hirdt and Reinhard Kleczewski, 213–24. Tübingen: Gunter Narr, 1983.

Katz, Marylin A. *Penelope's Renown: Meaning and Indeterminacy in the Odyssey.* Princeton: Princeton University Press, 1991.

Kerman, Joseph. "The Full Monte." Review in the *New York Review of Books* 49, no. 10 (13 June 2002): 36–38.

Ketterer, Robert. "*Militat omnis amans:* Ovidian Elegy in *L'incoronazione di Poppea.*" *International Journal of the Classical Tradition* 4 (1998): 381–95.

———. "Neoplatonic Light and Dramatic Genre in Busenello's *L'Incoronazione di Poppea* and Noris's *Il Ripudio d'Ottavia.*" *ML* 80 (1999): 1–22.

King, Margaret Leah. "Caldiera and the Barbaros on Marriage and the Family: Humanist Reflections of Venetian Realities." *Journal of Medieval and Renaissance Studies* 6 (1975): 19–50.

Kretzschmar, Hermann. *Geschichte der Oper.* Leipzig: Breitkopf & Härtel, 1919.

———. "Monteverdi's *Incoronazione di Poppea.*" *VfMw* 10 (1894): 483–530.

Laini, Marinella. *La raccolta zeniana di drammi per musica veneziani della Biblioteca nazionale marciana, 1637–1700.* Lucca: Libreria musicale italiana, 1995.

Laurenzi, Filiberto. *Musiche per La finta savia e concerti et arie,* ed. Alessandro Magini. Florence: Studio per edizioni scelte, 2000.

Leopold, Silke. *Monteverdi und seine Zeit.* Laaber: Laaber-Verlag, 1982. Translated by Anne Smith as *Monteverdi: Music in Transition.* Oxford: Clarendon Press, 1991.

Lewis, Rachel A. "Love as Persuasion in Monteverdi's *L'incoronazione di Poppea:* New Thoughts on the Authorship Question." *ML* 86 (2005): 16–41.

Libretti d'opera italiani dal Seicento al Novecento, ed. Giovanna Gronda and Paolo Fabbri. Milan: Mondadori, 1997.

Livingston, Arthur. *La vita veneziana nelle opere di Gian Francesco Busenello.* Venice: V. Callegari, 1913.

Lorandi, Marco. *Il mito di Ulisse nella pittura a fresco del Cinquecento italiano,* con la collaborazione di Orietta Pinessi. Milan: Jaca, 1995.

Loredano, Giovan Francesco. *Scherzi geniali.* Venice: Guerigli, 1632.

Lucian. *Satirical Sketches.* Translated and with an Introduction by Paul Turner. Bloomington: Indiana University Press, 1990.

———. *The Works of Lucian of Samosata*. Translated by H. W. Fowler and F. G. Fowler. Loeb Classical Library. Oxford: Clarendon Press, 1905.

Mactoux, Marie-Madeleine. *Pénélope: Légende et mythe*. Paris: Belles Lettres, 1975.

Magini, Alessandro. "Le monodie di Benedetto Ferrari e *L'incoronazione di Poppea*: Un rilevamento stilistico comparativo." *RIM* 21 (1987): 266–99.

Malipiero, Federico. *L'Iliada d'Omero trapportata dalla greca nella toscana lingua da Federico Malipiero*. Venice: Baglioni, 1642.

———. *L'imperatrice ambiziosa*. Venice: Surian, 1642.

———. *L'Odissea d'Omero trapportata dalla greca nella toscana favella*. Venice: Corradicci, 1643.

———. *La peripezia d'Ulisse overo la casta Penelope*. Venice: Surian, 1640.

McClary, Susan. "Constructions of Gender in Monteverdi's Dramatic Music." *COJ* 1 (1989): 203–32; also in McClary, *Feminine Endings: Music, Gender, and Sexuality*, 35–53. Minneapolis: University of Minnesota Press, 1991.

———. Review of *The Song of the Soul* by Iain Fenlon and Peter Miller. *ML* 74 (1993): 278–81.

Menegatti, Tiziana. *Ex Ignoto Notus: Bibliografia delle opere a stampa del Principe degli Incogniti: Giovan Francesco Loredano*. Padua: Il Poligrafo, 2000.

Miato, Monica. *L'Accademia degli Incogniti di Giovan Francesco Loredan, Venezia (1630–1661)*. Accademia Toscana di scienze e lettere "La Colombaria," Studi, no. 172. Florence: Olschki, 1998.

Michelassi, Nicola. "Michelangelo Torcigliani è l'Incognito autore delle *Nozze di Enea con Lavinia*." *Studi secenteschi* 48 (2007): 381–86.

———. " 'Musici di fortuna' e 'pellegrini architetti': *La Finta pazza* tra Venezia e l'Europa." Introduction to *La doppia Finta pazza: Un dramma veneziano in viaggio nell'Europa del Seicento*, ed. Nicola Michelassi. 2 vols. Florence: Olschki, 2008.

Michot, Pierre. "Discographie-Vidéographie." In *Monteverdi: Le retour d'Ulysse, L'Avant-scène opéra* 159 (1994): 120–26.

Monaldini, Sergio. *L'orto dell'Esperidi: Musici, attori e artisti nel patrocinio della famiglia Bentivoglio (1646–1685)*. Lucca: Libreria italiana musicale, 2000.

Monteverdi, Claudio. *Le couronnement de Poppée (1908)*, ed. Vincent d'Indy. Paris: Rouart, Lerolle, c. 1922.

———. *L'incoronazione di Poppea*, ed. Gian Francesco Malipiero. *Tutte le opere*, vol. 13. Asolo: the author, 1931. 2nd rev. ed., Vienna: Universal Edition, 1954–68.

———. *L'incoronazione di Poppea*, ed. Giacomo Benvenuti. Milan: Suvini Zerboni, 1937.

———. *L'incoronazione di Poppea*, facsimile del manoscritto It. cl. 4. n. 439 della Biblioteca nazionale di S. Marco in Venezia, ed. Giacomo Benvenuti. Milan: Fratelli Bocca, 1938; repr. Bologna: Forni, 1969.

———. *L'incoronazione di Poppea*, ed. Alan Curtis. London: Novello, 1989.

———. *Claudio Monteverdi and Giovanni Francesco Busenello, L'incoronazione di Poppea*. Performing edition by Jane Glover. London: Cantata Editions, 2003.

———. *Lettere*, ed. Éva Lax. Florence: Olschki, 1994.

———. *The Letters of Claudio Monteverdi*. Edited and translated by Denis Stevens. London: Faber, 1980; rev. ed. Oxford: Clarendon Press, 1995.

———. *Ritorno d'Ulisse in patria*, ed. Robert Haas. DTÖ, Jahrgang 29, Band 57. Vienna: Universal-Edition; Leipzig: Breitkopf & Härtel, 1922.

———. *Le retour d'Ulysse*, ed. Vincent d'Indy. Traduction française de Xavier de Courville. Paris: Heugel, c. 1926.

————. *Il ritorno d'Ulisse in patria*, ed. Gian Francesco Malipiero. *Tutte le opere*, vol. 12. Asolo: the author, 1931. 2nd rev. ed., Vienna: Universal Edition, 1954–68.

————. *Monteverdi, Il ritorno d'Ulisse in patria*. Performing edition by Jane Glover, based on the transcription by Clifford Bartlett. Huntingdon, GB: King's Music, c. 1998.

————. *Il ritorno d'Ulisse in patria*. Performing edition by Jane Glover. London: Cantata Editions, 2006.

————. *Il ritorno d'Ulisse in patria*, ed. Alan Curtis. London: Novello, 2002.

————. *Il ritorno d'Ulisse in patria*, facsimile, ed. Sergio Vartolo. Florence: SPES, 2007.

Monteverdi: Le couronnement de Poppée, L'Avant-scène opéra 115 (1988).

Monteverdi: Le retour d'Ulysse, L'Avant-scène opéra 159 (1994).

Moore, James. Review of *The Letters of Claudio Monteverdi*, ed. Denis Stevens. *JAMS* 35 (1982): 562–64.

Morelli, Giovanni. "*Il filo di Poppea:* Il soggetto antico-romano nell'opera veneziana del Seicento, osservazioni." In *Venezia e la Roma del Papa*, 245–74. Milan: Banca cattolica del Veneto, 1987.

Morini, Agnès. "Sous le signe de l'inconstance, la vie et l'oeuvre de Giovan Francesco Loredano (1606–61)." Thèse de Doctorat d'État, University of Paris, 1994.

Morrier, Denis. "Un retour aux sources d'*Ulysse*." In *Monteverdi: Le Retour d'Ulysse, L'Avant-scène opéra* 159 (1994): 110–15.

Muir, Edward. *Civic Ritual in Renaissance Venice*. Princeton: Princeton University Press, 1981.

————. *The Culture Wars of the Late Renaissance: Skeptics, Libertines, and Opera*. Cambridge MA: Harvard University Press, 2007.

Muller, Reinhard. "Basso Ostinato und die *Imitatione del parlare* in Monteverdis *Incoronazione di Poppea*." *AfM* 40 (1983): 1–23.

Murata, Margaret. "Why the First Opera Given in Paris Wasn't Roman." *COJ* 7 (1995): 87–106.

Il Nerone overo L'incoronatione di Poppea. Naples: Roberto Mollo, 1651.

Nolfi, Vincenzo, *Descrittione de gli apparati del Bellerofonte di Giulio del Colle* (Venice: n.p. 1642).

Octavia, a Play Attributed to Seneca, ed. Rolando Ferri. Cambridge: Cambridge University Press, 2003.

Ongaro, Giulio. "E pur io torno qui': Sixteenth-Century Literary Debates, the Audience's View, and the Interpretation of *Poppea*." Paper presented at the Tenth Annual Conference of the Society of Seventeenth-Century Music, Princeton, 4–7 April 2002.

Ossi, Massimo. *Divining the Oracle: Monteverdi's 'Seconda Prattica'*. Chicago: University of Chicago Press, 2003.

Osthoff, Wolfgang. "Filiberto Laurenzis Musik zu *La finta savia* in Zusammenhang der frühvenezianischen Oper." In *Venezia e il melodramma nel Seicento*, ed. Maria Teresa Muraro, 173–97. Florence: Olschki, 1976.

————. "Maschera e musica." *NRMI* 1 (1967): 16–44.

————. *Monteverdistudien: Das dramatische Spätwerk Claudio Monteverdis*. Tutzing: Schneider, 1960.

————. "Neue Beobachtungen zu Quellen und Geschichte von Monteverdis *Incoronazione di Poppea*." *Mf* 11 (1958): 129–38.

————. "Trombe sordine." *AMw* 13 (1956): 77–95.

————. "Die venezianische und neapolitanische Fassung von Monteverdis *Incoronazione di Poppea*." *AcM* 26 (1954): 88–113.

————. "Zu den Quellen von Monteverdis *Ritorno di Ulisse in patria*." *Studien zur Musikwissenschaft* 24 (1956): 67–78.

———. "Zur Bologneser Aufführung von Monteverdis *Ritorno di Ulisse* im Jahre 1640." Oester-reichische Akademie der Wissenschaften. Anzeiger der phil-hist. Klasse 1958. *Mitteilungen der Kommission für Musikforschung* 11 (1958): 155–60.

Pallavicino, Ferrante. *Le due Agrippine.* Venice: Guerigli, 1642.

———. *Panegirici, epitalami, discorsi accademici, novella, et lettere amorose di Ferrante Pallavicino.* Venice: Gio. Battista Cester, 1652; another ed. Venice: Turrini, 1652.

Pannain, Guido. "Claudio Monteverdi nell'opera in musica." *Musica* 2 (1943): 35–50.

Pass, Walter. "Monteverdis Il ritorno d'Ulisse in patria." In *Performing Practice in Monteverdi's Music,* ed. Rafaello Monterosso, 175–81. Cremona: Fondazione Claudio Monteverdi, 1995.

Passi, Giuseppe. *I donneschi difetti.* Venice: Somascho, 1599.

Pazdro, Michel. "L'oeuvre à l'affiche." In *Monteverdi: Le Couronnement de Poppée, L'Avant-scène opéra* 115 (1988): 162–65.

Pertusi, Agostino. *Leonzio Pilato fra Petrarca e Boccaccio: Le sue versioni omeriche negli autografi di Venezia e la cultura greca del primo Umanesimo* (Venice and Rome: Istituto per la collaborazione culturale, 1964).

Pirrotta, Nino. "Early Venetian Libretti at Los Angeles." In *Essays in Musicology in Honor of Dragan Plamenac,* ed. Gustave Reese and Robert Snow, 233–43. Pittsburgh: University of Pittsburgh Press, 1969; repr. in *Essays,* 317–24; translated as "Antichi libretti d'opera veneziani a Los Angeles," in *Scelte poetiche,* 243–54.

———. *Music and Culture in Italy from the Middle Ages to the Baroque: A Collection of Essays.* Cambridge, MA: Harvard University Press, 1984 (cited as *Essays*).

———. "Forse Nerone cantò da tenore." In *Musica senza oggettivi: Studi per Fedele D'Amico,* ed. Agostino Ziino, 1: 47–60. Florence: Olschki, 1991; repr. in *Poesia e musica e altri saggi,* 179–94.

———. "Monteverdi e i problemi dell'opera." In *Studi sul teatro veneto fra Rinascimento ed età barocco,* ed. Maria Teresa Muraro, 321–43. Florence: Olschki, 1971; repr. in *Scelte poetiche di musicisti,* 197–218; translated as "Monteverdi and the Problems of Opera," in *Essays,* 235–53.

———. *Poesia e musica e altri saggi.* Florence: La Nuova Italia, 1994.

———. *Scelte poetiche di musicisti.* Venice: Marsilio, 1987.

———. "Teatro, scene e musica nelle opere di Monteverdi." In *Claudio Monteverdi e il suo tempo,* ed. Rafaello Monterosso, 45–67. Verona: Stamperia Valdonega, 1969; trans. as "Theater, Sets, and Music in Monteverdi's Operas," in *Essays,* 271–316.

——— and Elena Povoledo, *Li due Orfei.* Turin: Eri, 1969; 2nd ed., Turin: Einaudi, 1975. Translated as *Music and Theatre from Poliziano to Monteverdi.* Cambridge: Cambridge University Press, 1982.

Poe, Joe Park. "Octavia Praetexta and Its Senecan Model." *American Journal of Philology* 110 (1989): 434–59.

Povoledo, Elena. "Controversie monteverdiane: Spazi teatrali e immagini presunte." In *Claudio Monteverdi: Studi e prospettive,* ed. Paola Besutti, Maria Teresa Gialdroni, and Rodolfo Baroncini, 357–89. Florence: Olschki, 1998.

Prota-Giurleo, Ulisse. *Francesco Cirillo e l'introduzione del melodramma a Napoli.* Grumo Nevano: a cura del comune, 1952.

———. *Il teatro di corte del Palazzo Reale di Napoli.* Naples: L'Arte tipografica, 1952.

Prunières, Henry. *L'opéra en France avant Lulli.* Paris: H. Champion, 1913.

———. *La vie et l'œuvre de Claudio Monteverdi.* Paris: Librairie de France, 1926; *Monteverdi: His Life and Work.* Translated by Marie D. Mackie. New York: Dutton, 1926.

Pryer, Anthony. "Authentic Performance, Authentic Experience, and *Pur ti Miro* from *Poppea*." In *Performing Practice in Monteverdi's Music*, ed. Rafaello Monterosso, 191–213. Cremona: Fondazione Claudio Monteverdi, 1995.

Questa, Cesare. *L'aquila a due teste: Immagini di Roma e dei romani*. Urbino: Quattro Venti, 1998.

———. "Presenze di Tacito nel Seicento veneziano." In *Musica, scienza e idee nella Serenissima durante il Seicento: Atti del convegno internazionale di studi, Venezia – Palazzo Giustinian Lolin, 13–15 dicembre 1993*, ed. Francesco Passadore and Franco Rossi, 317–24. Venice: Fondazione Levi, 1996.

Quirini, Leonardo. *I vezzi d'Erato, poesie liriche di Leonardo Quirini*. Venice: Hertz, 1649.

Redlich, Hans Ferdinand. *Claudio Monteverdi, Leben und Werk*. Olten: O. Walter, 1949; *Claudio Monteverdi: Life and Works*. Translated by Kathleen Dale. London: Oxford University Press, 1952; repr. Westport: Greenwood Press, 1970.

Riemann, Hugo. *Handbuch der Musikgeschichte*. Leipzig: Breitkopf & Härtel, 1904–23.

Ringer, Mark. *Opera's First Master: The Musical Dramas of Claudio Monteverdi*. Pompton Plains, NJ: Amadeus Press, 2006.

Ripa, Cesare. *Iconologia overo descrittione di diverse imagini cavate dall'antichità, & di propria inventione, trovate, & dichiarate da Cesare Ripa*. Rome: Lepido Faeii, 1603; orig ed., Rome, 1593.

Robinson, Christopher. *Lucian and His Influence in Europe*. London: Duckworth, 1979.

Rolfs, Daniel. *The Last Cross: A History of the Suicide Theme in Italian Literature*. Ravenna: Longo, 1981.

Rosand, Ellen. "Barbara Strozzi, *Virtuosissima cantatrice:* The Composer's Voice." *JAMS* 31 (1978): 241–81.

———. "The Bow of Ulysses." *JM* 12 (1994): 376–95.

———. "Did Monteverdi Write *L'incoronazione di Poppea* and Does It Matter?" *Opera News* 59, no. 1 (July 1994): 20–23.

———. "L'incoronazione di Poppea di Francesco Cavalli." In *Francesco Cavalli: La circolazione dell'opera veneziana nel Seicento*, ed. Dinko Fabris, 119–46. Naples: Turchini edizioni, 2005.

———. "Iro and the Interpretation of *Il ritorno d'Ulisse in patria*." *JM* 7 (1989): 141–64.

———. "Monteverdi's *Il ritorno d'Ulisse in patria* and the Power of Music." *COJ* 4 (1992): 75–80.

———. "Monteverdi's Mimetic Art: *L'Incoronazione di Poppea*." *COJ* 1 (1989): 113–37.

———. *Opera in Seventeenth-Century Venice: The Creation of a Genre* (Berkeley and Los Angeles: University of California Press, 1991.

———. "The Opera Scenario, 1638–1655: A Preliminary Survey." In *In Cantu et in Sermone: For Nino Pirrotta on His 80th Birthday*, ed. Fabrizio Della Seta and Franco Piperno, 335–46. Florence: Olschki, 1989.

———. "Seneca and the Interpretation of *L'incoronazione di Poppea*." *JAMS* 38 (1985): 34–71.

Rossi, Giuseppe. "Il taccuino del discofilo." In *Program Book for Maggio musicale 63*, 151–63. Florence: Teatro del maggio musicale fiorentino, 2000.

Ruzzante. *Teatro*. Edited by Lodovico Zorzi. Turin: Einaudi, 1967.

Salvioli, Giovanni, and Carlo Salvioli. *Biblioteca universale del teatro drammatico con particolare riguardo alla storia della musica italiana*. Venice: Ferrari, 1903.

Sartori, Claudio. *Claudio Monteverdi*. Brescia: La Scuola, 1953.

———. *I libretti italiani a stampa dalle origini al 1800: Catalogo analitico con 16 indici*. Cuneo: Bertola & Locatelli, c. 1990–c. 1994.

Scaramella, Pierroberto. "L'Italia dei trionfi e dei contrasti." In *Humana Fragilitas: I temi della morte in Europa tra Duecento e Settecento,* ed. Alberto Tenenti, 25–98. Clusone: Ferrari, 2000.

Scenario dell'opera reggia intitolata La Coronatione di Poppea che si rappresenta in musica nel theatro dell'Illustr. Sig. Giovanni Grimani. Venice: Pinelli, 1643.

Schneider, Louis. *Un précurseur de la musique italienne aux XVIe et XVIIe siècles. Claudio Monteverdi. L'homme et son temps.* Paris: Perrin, 1921.

Schrade, Leo. *Monteverdi, the Creator of Modern Music.* New York: Norton, 1950; repr. 1979.

Schulze, Hendrik. "Cavalli Manuscript Scores and Performance Practice." In *Francesco Cavalli: La circolazione dell'opera veneziana nel Seicento,* ed. Dinko Fabris, 39–58. Naples: Turchini edizioni, 2005.

———. *Odysseus in Venedig: Sujetwahl und Rollenkonzeption in der venezianischen Oper des 17. Jahrhundert.* Frankfurt am Main: Lang, 2004.

Segal, Charles. *Singers, Heroes, and Gods in the Odyssey.* Ithaca: Cornell University Press, 1994.

Seneca: Mostra bibliografica e iconografica. Edited by Francesca Niutta and Carmela Santucci. Rome: Fratelli Palombi, 1999.

Sevieri, Maria Paola. *Le nozze d'Enea con Lavinia: Dal testo alla scena dell'opera veneziana di Claudio Monteverdi.* Recco: De Ferrari, 1997.

Shotter, David. *Nero.* London: Routledge, 1997.

Solerti, Angelo. "Feste musicali alla corte di Savoia nella prima metà del secolo XVII." *RMI* 11 (1904): 675–724.

———. *Gli albori del melodramma.* 3 vols. Milan, Palermo, and Naples: Sandron, 1904–1905; repr. Hildesheim: Olms, 1969.

Sorenson, Villy. *Seneca: The Humanist at the Court of Nero.* Trans. W. Glyn Jones. Chicago: University of Chicago Press, 1984.

Spini, Giorgio. *Ricerca dei libertini: La teoria dell'impostura delle religioni nel Seicento italiano.* Rome: Editrice universale, 1950; 2nd ed. Florence: La nuova Italia, 1983.

Staffieri, Gloria. "Lo scenario nell'opera in musica del XVII secolo." In *Le parole della musica* II: *Studi sul lessico della letteratura critica del teatro musicale in onore di Gianfranco Folena,* ed. Maria Teresa Muraro, 3–31. Florence: Olschki, 1995.

Stenzl, Jürg. "Claudio Monteverdi nell'epoca della riproducibilità tecnica." In *Rezeptionsästhetik und Rezeptionsgeschichte in der Musikwissenschaft,* 269–306. Laaber: Laaber-Verlag, 1991. Expanded version in *L'esperienza musicale: Teoria e storia della recezione,* ed. Gianmario Borio and Michela Garda, 166–84. Turin: EDT, 1989.

Strozzi, Giulio. *La Delia.* Venice: Pinelli, 1639.

———. *La finta pazza.* Venice: Surian, 1641; terza impressione, 1644.

———. *La finta savia.* Venice: Leni e Vecellio, 1643.

———. *Le glorie della signora Anna Renzi romana.* Venice: Surian, 1644.

———. *Romolo e Remo.* Venice: Surian, 1645.

———. *La Venetia edificata.* Venice: Pinelli, 1624.

Suetonius. *The Twelve Caesars.* Translated by Robert Graves. London: Penguin Books, 1957.

Sullivan, J. P. *Literature and Politics in the Age of Nero.* Ithaca: Cornell University Press, 1985.

Szweykowska, Anna. "Le due poetiche venete e le ultime opere di Claudio Monteverdi." *Quadrivium* 18 (1977): 145–57.

Tacitus, Gaius [Publius] Cornelius. *The Annals of Imperial Rome.* Revised Edition. Translated and with an Introduction by Michael Grant. Harmondsworth: Penguin Books, 1977.

————. *Histories.* Translated by W. H. Fyfe; revised and edited by D. S. Levine. Oxford: Oxford University Press, 1997.

Taddeo, Edoardo. "La cetra e l'arpa: Studio su Michelangelo Torcigliani." *Studi secenteschi* 34 (1992): 3–60.

————. "Torcigliani e Delfino, patriarca atomista." Ibid. 40 (1999): 83–95.

————. "Torcigliani fra gli astri e l'alchimia." Ibid. 35 (1993): 233–39.

Tannen, Deborah. *Talking Voices: Repetition, Dialogue, and Imagery in Conversational Discourse.* Cambridge: Cambridge University Press, 1989.

Tarr, Edward, and Thomas Walker. "*Bellici carmi, festivo fragor:* Die Verwendung der Trompete in der italienischen Oper des 17. Jahrhunderts." *Hamburger Jahrbuch der Musikwissenschaft* 3 (1978): 154–56.

Taruskin, Richard. *Text and Act: Essays on Music and Performance.* New York: Oxford University Press, 1995.

Termini, Olga. "From God to a Servant: The Bass Voice in Seventeenth-Century Venetian Opera." *CM* 44 (1990): 38–60.

Terpening, Ronnie H. *Lodovico Dolce, Renaissance Man of Letters.* Toronto: University of Toronto Press, 1997.

Tessiers, André. "Les deux styles de Monteverdi." *Revue musicale* 3 (1922): 223–54.

Testi, Fulvio. *Lettere.* Edited by Maria Luisa Doglio. Bari: Laterza, 1967.

Tomlinson, Gary. "Madrigal, Monody, and Monteverdi's *Via naturale alla immitatione.*" *JAMS* 34 (1981): 60–108.

————. *Monteverdi and the End of the Renaissance.* Berkeley and Los Angeles: University of California Press, 1987.

————. "Music and the Claims of Text: Monteverdi, Rinuccini, and Marino." *Critical Inquiry* 8 (1982): 565–89.

————. "Twice Bitten, Thrice Shy: Monteverdi's 'finta' *Finta pazza.*" *JAMS* 36 (1983): 303–11.

Torcigliani, Michelangelo. *Echo cortese o vero resposte date da più, e diversi Signori a M. A. T. con altre Lettere ecc. publicate da Salvestro Torcigliani suo fratello.* Lucca: S. Marescandoli, 1680.

————. *Echo cortese parte seconda con l'Iride posthuma o vero veri residui di diversi componimenti di M. A. T. publicati . . .* Lucca: Marescandoli, 1681.

————. *Echo cortese parte terza con la parte seconda dell'Iride posthuma.* Lucca: I Paci, 1683.

Van den Borren, Charles. "Il ritorno d'Ulisse in patria." *Revue de l'Université de Bruxelles* 30 (1924–25): 353–87.

Vio, Gastone. "Musici veneziani dei primi decenni del Seicento: Discordie e bustarelle." *Rassegna veneta di studi musicali* 5–6 (1989–90): 375–85.

————. "Ultimi ragguagli monteverdiani." *Rassegna veneta di studi musicali* 2–3 (1986–87): 347–64.

Virgil. *Aeneid.* Translated by H. R. Fairclough. Loeb Classical Library. Cambridge, MA: Harvard University Press, 1978.

Vogel, Emil. "Claudio Monteverdi: Leben, Wirken, im Lichte der zeitgenössischen Kritik und Verzeichniss seiner im Druck erschienenen Werke." *VfMw* 3 (1887): 315–450.

Walker, Thomas, ed. *Gianfrancesco Busenello, L'incoronazione di Poppea. A Comparative Edition of Text Sources.* Unpublished typescript, Yale Music Library, n.d.

———. "Gli errori di *Minerva al tavolino:* Osservazioni sulla cronologia delle prime opere veneziane." In *Venezia e il melodrama del Seicento,* ed. Maria Teresa Muraro, 7–20. Florence: Olschki, 1976.

———. "*Ubi Lucius:* Thoughts on Reading *Medoro.*" In Francesco Lucio, *Medoro.* Drammaturgia musicale veneta, 4, cxxxi–clxiv. Milan: Ricordi, 1984.

Wallace, Richard. "Salvator Rosa's *Democritus* and *L'Umana Fragilità.*" *Art Bulletin* 50 (1968): 21–32.

Warner, Marina. Review of *The Myths of Rome* by T. P. Wiseman. *Times Literary Supplement* (15 April 2005): 8.

Westrup, Jack. "Monteverdi's *Il ritorno d'Ulisse in patria.*" *Monthly Musical Record* (2 April 1928): 106–7.

Whenham, John. *Duet and Dialogue in the Age of Monteverdi.* 2 vols. Ann Arbor: UMI, 1982.

———. "Perspectives on the Chronology of the First Decade of Public Opera at Venice." *Saggiatore musicale* 11 (2004): 253–302.

Wiel, Taddeo. *I Codici musicali contariniani del secolo XVII nella R. Biblioteca di San Marco in Venezia.* Venice: F. Ongania, 1888; repr. Bologna: Forni, 1969.

———. "Francesco Cavalli (1602–1676) e la sua musica scenica." *Nuovo archivio veneto,* 3rd ser., 18 (1914): 106–50.

Wilson, Emily. Review of *Octavia, A Play Attributed to Seneca,* ed. Rolando Ferri. *Times Literary Supplement* (16 April 2004): 4–6.

Wiseman, P. T. *The Myths of Rome.* Exeter: University of Exeter Press, 2004.

Wistreich, Richard. "'La voce è grata assai, ma': Monteverdi on Singing." *EM* 22 (1994): 7–19.

———. *Warrior, Courtier, Singer: Giulio Cesare Brancaccio and the Performance of Identity in the Late Renaissance.* Aldershot: Ashgate, 2007.

Zaguri, Pietr'Angelo. *Le gelosie politiche.* Venice: Pinelli, 1657.

Zeno, Pietro Angelo. *Memoria de' scrittori veneti patritii.* Venice: Baglioni, 1662.

Zoppelli, Luca. "Il rapto perfettissimo: Un'inedita testimonianza sulla *Proserpina* di Monteverdi." *Rassegna veneta di studi musicali* 3 (1987): 343–45.

INDEX

Abert, Anna Amalie, 345

Aeneid, 9, 12, 17, 132, 144, 146, 148–49, 161, 163, 234, 243, 376. *See also* Virgil

Agnelli, Scipione, *Le nozze di Tetide*, 188–89. *See also under* Monteverdi, Claudio

Agrippina, 16, 20–21, 180; and Seneca, 179–80, 333–34; and Tacitus, 176

Aletto (in *Le nozze d'Enea*), and Giunone, 164, 167, 173

Allacci, Leone, 26, 48n

Amata (in *Le nozze d'Enea*), 132, 147, 149, 165; and Lavinia, 145, 159; and Turno, 145, 164, 167

Ambros, August Wilhelm, 26–29

Andreini, Giovanni Battista, 242

Andreini Ramponi, Virginia, as Arianna, 238, 242–43

Arianna (in *L'Arianna*), 189, 199, 238, 242; Martinelli as, 238; Ramponi as, 238, 242–43. *See also under* lament

Ariosto, Lodovico, 13

Aristotle, 9, 131–32, 143–44, 149, 175, 180–81, 373

Arnalta (in *L'incoronazione di Poppea*), 97, 107, 204, 222, 246–47, 338–39; and Poppea, 64, 117, 181, 183, 193, 330–31; same singer as Nutrice, 97, 100; transpositions for, 117, 119, 121. *See also* comic characters

authenticity, 3, 37, 49; in performance, 42–44, 62, 65–68. *See also under L'incoronazione di Poppea; Il ritorno d'Ulisse in patria*

Baccelli, Girolamo, 140

Badoaro, Giacomo: aristocratic neophyte, 3–4, 8, 48, 50, 185, 327; and Dolce, 134–38, 339–40; erroneous author of *Le nozze d'Enea*, 24–26, 49, 59; Incognito, 48, 375; letter to Monteverdi, 3–4, 6–7, 48; lure for Monteverdi, 3, 5–6, 10, 48, 185, 250, 379; and Malipiero, 140–43; model for Torcigliani, 8–12, 149; and *Odyssey*, 12, 132–36, 143–44, 247, 253–54, 339–40; *Ulisse errante*, 17, 48, 143–44. *See also Il ritorno d'Ulisse in patria*

Basile, Margherita, 196

Bentivoglio, Cornelio, 126

Benvenuti, Giacomo, 31, 89, 105–6

Bianconi, Lorenzo, 36–37, 65, 125

Bolton, Ivor, 40–41

Bonlini, Carlo, 26, 47, 49

Boretti, Giovanni Antonio, *Ercole in Tebe*, 73n

Burney, Charles, 25

Busenello, Gian Francesco: aesthetics of, 133, 175, 180–81, 183, 334–35; and Badoaro, 17, 19, 175, 339; and Cavalli, 10, 50–51, 64–65; and Dolce,

Busenello, Gian Francesco *(continued)*
177–80; Incognito, 19n, 336, 373–75; and
Malipiero, 333; and *Octavia*, 335–36; and
Seneca, 331–37, 339, 346–47, 351, 361–63; and
Suetonius, 177; and Tacitus, 175–77, 179,
336–37. WORKS: *Gli amori di Apollo e di
Dafne*, 33, 50, 65, 87; *Didone*, 17–18, 50, 65,
89, 99, 180; *Le hore ociose*, 47, 50–51, 64–66,
90, 125, 198, 250; *La Statira*, 334n, 335. See also
L'incoronazione di Poppea
Buti, Francesco, *Orfeo*, 126, 340n

Caberloti, Matteo, 197
Carter, Tim, 38, 344, 354, 362
cast changes: in *Incoronazione*, 72–73, 97, 117; in
Ritorno, 7, 116–17
castrato, 38, 42, 126, 186
Cavalli, Francesco, 4, 7, 25, 57, 67, 73, 88, 92, 99,
107, 380; and Busenello, 10, 50, 64–65; as
editor/owner/producer of *Incoronazione*, 35,
46, 62, 65–66, 89, 97, 100, 106, 108–10, 113–18,
120, 122, 125–28; manuscript scores of, 33, 42n,
46, 69, 73, 87, 89, 125–26, 198; music in
Incoronazione, 65–66, 125. WORKS: *Amore
inamorato*, 18; *Gli amori di Apollo e di Dafne*,
33, 50, 65, 87; *Artemisia*, 105n, 106n, 113n;
Calisto, 87, 89; *Didone*, 17–18, 50, 65, 89, 99,
180; *Doriclea*, 19; *Egisto*, 28, 87, 89, 99; *Ercole
amante*, 114n; *Eritrea*, 73n; *Giasone*, 7n, 89,
94n, 365n; *Le nozze di Teti e di Peleo*, 17, 73n;
Orimonte, 96n; *Oristeo*, 72, 87, 119n; *La
prosperità infelice di Giulio Cesare dittatore*,
125, 334, 375n; *Rosinda*, 72, 89; *Scipione
affricano*, 72; *Veremonda*, 89, 114n; *La virtù
de strali d'Amore*, 18; *Xerse*, 105n, 113n, 114n
Cavalli, Maria, 35, 46, 87, 89, 105–7, 119–21, 126
censorship, 97, 122, 336
Cesti, Antonio, 380
Chafe, Eric, 67–68, 344
Chiarelli, Alessandra, 36–37, 65–66, 93, 96, 102
Christie, William, 40, 346
ciaccona, 293, 369–70, 373
comic characters, 243–47, 337–39, 364, 365n. *See
also* Arnalta; Iro; Numano; Nutrice; Valletto
Contarini Collection, 29, 30n, 33, 65n, 76n, 87n,
89, 90n, 106n
Costa, Anna Francesca, 126
Costa, Margherita, 126
Costa, Stefano, 126–27, 186n
Cremonini, Cesare, 239n, 373–74

Curtis, Alan, 29, 37–42, 44, 57, 66–67, 69, 88,
90, 93, 121

Dallapiccola, Luigi, 24, 29, 31, 39, 345
Damerini, Adelmo, 32
Damigella (in *L'incoronazione di Poppea*), and
Valletto, 42, 44, 93, 101–3, 108, 110, 220, 246
Damigella (in *Le nozze d'Enea*), 172, 174, 233;
and Lavinia, 215, 234, 246
Della Porta, Giambattista, 130n
De' Paoli, Domenico, 32–33, 345
D'Indy, Vincent, 24, 28–29
Dio Cassius, 177, 333–34
Dolce, Lodovico, 133–43, 146–49, 177–80,
339–40, 376. WORKS: *Achille ed Enea*, 146;
Dialogo della institutione delle donne, 136n;
Iliade, 139; *Octavia*, 177–78; *Ulisse*, 133, 143; *Le
vite di tutti gl'imperadori . . . di Pietro Messia*,
178–79. *See also under* Badoaro, Giacomo;
Busenello, Gian Francesco; Torcigliani,
Michelangelo
Doni, Giovanni Battista, 224
Drusilla (in *L'incoronazione di Poppea*), 116–17,
119, 181, 318; in Busenello, 176; emblem of
constancy, 304n; and Nerone, 322; and Ottone,
175–76, 183, 223, 304, 307, 311–15, 319–24, 327,
330; predilection for song, 181, 320–21
Dubowy, Norbert, 69, 76, 77, 158

Enea (in *Le nozze d'Enea*), 132, 145, 163–64, 213,
216; and Giunone, 164; and Lavinia, 165, 173,
183, 215; love duet, 173, 215; and marriage, 144,
147–48, 164, 376–77; and Turno, 144, 146,
161, 164–65, 216, 229, 232–33; and Venere,
145, 164, 226, 229. *See also under* lament;
soliloquy
Ericlea (in *Il ritorno d'Ulisse*), 84–85, 135,
200–203, 246–47, 278; and Penelope, 225,
247, 251, 254, 262; and Ulisse, 142–43, 200,
290
Eumete (in *Il ritorno d'Ulisse*): cast change
involving, 72–75; and Iro, 136, 340, 363–64;
libretto material cut in score, 251–52; musical
eloquence of, 340, 364; and Penelope, 251, 273;
performance indications for, 83; and
Telemaco, 287, 373; and Ulisse, 285, 287–88
Eurimaco (in *Il ritorno d'Ulisse*), 83, 327; and
Melanto, 135, 157, 199, 218–20, 246
Evelyn, John, 125
Êwerhart, Rudolf, 39, 40, 42

magnanimity of, 324, 353; and Ottavia, 178, 181, 183, 234–38, 330; and Ottone, 326, 362; in performance, 39, 178–79, 186n; and Poppea, 181, 222–23, 296–304, 321–22, 375–76; as protagonist, 43; and Seneca, 118, 176–77, 179, 181, 223, 295–98, 302–4, 330–31, 347, 349–50, 352–54, 362; transpositions affecting, 116–18; in Venice score, 110–16

Il Nerone, as title of *Incoronazione,* 29, 43, 122, 126–27

Le nozze d'Enea e Lavinia (Torcigliani/ Monteverdi): argomento e scenario of, 8, 12, 26, 48, 55, 59, 129, 147, 157–59, 161–63, 165, 170; arias in, 211–15; author of, 8, 48–49, 59; and Dolce, 143, 146–49; libretto of, 50, 59–61; —, discrepancies with scenario, 159, 161; —, editing of, 158, 166–67; —, literary vs. performance versions of, 158–59, 162–63, 170, 172–73, 248; metric variety in, 216; modeled on *Ritorno,* 8–10, 12, 130; and myth of Venice, 15–17, 162, 376; oral components in, 172; plot summary of, 145–46; and rules of tragedy, 130, 132, 144, 149–50, 196; structure of, 149, 160, 164–68; and Virgil, 9, 132. *See also* Aletto; Amata; Damigella; Enea; Giunone; Latino; Lavinia; Numano; Silvia; Turno; Venere; Vulcano

Numano (in *Le nozze d'Enea*), 170–71, 215–16; and Iro *(Ritorno),* 9, 243–44, 246–47, 338; and Turno, 164–65, 244. *See also* comic characters

Nutrice (in *L'incoronazione di Poppea*), 97, 117–18, 121, 204–6, 211, 220–23, 246–47, 320. *See also* comic characters; intercalation

Octavia, in Tacitus, 176, 178

Octavia: and Busenello, 17; influence on *Incoronazione* 335–36; misattributed to Seneca, 335

Odyssey, 9–10, 12, 20–21, 43, 132–33, 135, 137, 140, 143–44, 247, 339–40. *See also* Homer

Orpheus, 199, 224. *See also* Monteverdi, Claudio: *Orfeo*

Osthoff, Wolfgang, 24n, 33–36, 55, 65–66, 69, 87, 102, 106n

Ottavia (in *L'incoronazione di Poppea*): absence of arias for, 204; in Busenello, 175–76, 179, 181, 235–36; exile of, 296; and Nerone, 178, 181, 183, 234–38, 330; and Ottone, 92, 223, 307, 315–18; Renzi as, 240–42; role

expanded for Naples, 92, 95, 122; and Seneca, 331, 336, 347–48, 352–53. *See also under* lament

Ottoboni, Cardinal Pietro, 50

Ottone (in *L'incoronazione di Poppea*): as alto, 39; authenticity of music for, 66–68, 93, 95, 324–26; in Busenello, 175–76, 179–80, 183, 326; and Drusilla, 175–76, 183, 223, 304, 307, 311–15, 320–324, 327, 330; historical sources for, 326, 335; as mezzo-soprano, 125; and Ottavia, 92, 223, 307, 315–18; and Poppea, 120, 304, 307, 309–10; role in Venice score, 109; soliloquies for, 325; strophic arias for, 204; transpositions for, 116–21, 125, 305n, 307n, 310n

Pallavicino, Ferrante: *Le due Agrippine,* 180; Incognito, 240

Pannain, Guido, 31

Paolelli, Giulia Saus, as Penelope, 238–40

passacaglia, 73, 107, 373

Passi, Giuseppe, *I donneschi difetti,* 136n

Penelope (in *Il ritorno d'Ulisse*), 225, 229, 235; aria for, 274–77; chastity of, 136, 141, 254n, 290, 375; distrust of singing, 155–56, 203, 220, 268, 272, 285, 287, 294, 376; and Ericlea, 225, 247, 251, 254, 262; and Eumete, 251, 273; and Melanto, 75, 140–41, 156, 235, 268–73; Monteverdi's editing of, 235, 251, 253; Paolelli as, 238–40; and Suitors, 77, 156, 254, 272–73; and Telemaco, 135, 157, 251–52, 273; and Ulisse, 53, 151, 157, 288, 292–93. *See also* intercalation; lament

Petrarch, 184

Pirrotta, Nino, 2, 55

Ponelle, Jean-Pierre, 39, 343, 346

Poppea (in *L'incoronazione di Poppea*), 21, 63, 344, 376; and Amore, 43; and Arnalta, 64, 117, 181, 183, 193, 330–31; in Busenello, 175–76, 179–80; and Nerone, 181, 222–23, 297–304, 321–22, 375–76; and Ottone, 120, 304, 307, 309–10; and Seneca, 181, 302; strophic texts for, 204; transpositions in role of, 117–18, 120. *See also* intercalation; repetition

Pritchard, John, 38

Pryer, Anthony, 37–38

"Pur ti miro" (*L'incoronazione di Poppea*), 34, 36–38, 43–44, 66, 68, 91, 95, 110, 122, 124, 287, 293, 304; missing from Busenello, 36, 99, 104, 127

Ramponi, Virginia Andreini, as Arianna, 238, 242–43

Rapallino, 196

Redlich, Hans, 32, 345

Renzi, Anna: as Ottavia, 240–42; as singing actress, 242–43

repetition, as expressive device, 153, 168, 184, 200, 205, 221, 223, 225, 236 et passim. *See also* intercalation

Riemann, Hugo, 26, 28

Rinuccini, Ottavio, 184–86, 191, 224–25. *See also* Monteverdi, Claudio: *Arianna*

Ripa, Cesare, *Iconologia*, 137. *See also* Humana Fragilità

Il ritorno d'Ulisse in patria (Badoaro/Monteverdi)
—authenticity of, 27–34, 52–55
—characters. *See* Ericlea; Eumete; Eurimaco; Iro; Melanto; Minerva; Penelope; Suitors; Telemaco; Ulisse; *and under* —prologue(s)
—chronology of performances of, 7, 31, 46, 54–57, 59, 86–97, 174, 249
—and classicism, 130, 132, 149–50
—librettos, 27, 33, 46, 48–49, 52–59. *See also under* —score
—as model for *Le nozze d'Enea*, 7–10, 12, 15, 59, 130
—prologue(s), 53, 70, 77, 138–39, 150, 249, 374; allegorical characters in, 53, 137–40
—score: cuts in, 27, 50, 76–82; discrepancies with librettos, 27, 50, 52–54, 58, 70–71, 76–77, 86, 150–51, 198, 249, 251–53, 294, 342; performance indications in, 76–77, 83–86; revisions, to Penelope's lament, 250, 254–61; structure and copying of, 69–75, 86–87

Rossi, Luigi, *Orfeo*, 126, 340n

Rossini, Gioacchino, 38

Sacrati, Francesco, 7, 25, 37, 66–67, 195–96; *Bellerofonte*, 239n; and *Incoronazione*, 35, 65, 67

Sartori, Claudio, 32, 34

scenarios: commedia dell'arte, 130; vs. librettos, 45–47. See also under *L'incoronazione di Poppea; Le nozze d'Enea e Lavinia*

Schrade, Leo, 34, 345

Seneca: ambiguity of, 344–45; and censorship, 336; death of, 176; as historical figure, 332–36; and *Octavia*, 335; in Petrarch, 333–34; as playwright, 334–35; and stoicism, 331–32, 362–63. WORKS: *Consolatio ad Helviam*, 336; *Consolatio ad Polybium*, 336; *De providentia*, 336, 350; *Epistolae morales*, 336. *See also* Busenello, Gian Francesco; Seneca (in *L'incoronazione di Poppea*)

Seneca (in *L'incoronazione di Poppea*): death of, 44, 175–76, 180–81, 246, 330–32, 336–37, 374; and followers, 44, 97, 332, 337, 350–51, 359–62; and Nerone, 118, 176–77, 179, 181, 223, 295–98, 302–4, 330–31, 347, 349–50, 362; and Ottavia, 331, 336, 347–48, 352–53; and Poppea, 181, 302; and song, 357–60; and Valletto, 246–47. *See also* intercalation

Shakespeare, William, 246, 345

Silvia (in *Le nozze d'Enea*), 148, 171–72

soliloquy: Enea's, 159, 167, 174, 183, 225–29, 235; Ericlea's, 142; Iro's, 246, 341; Lavinia's, 229–31, 236; Ottavia's, 338; Ottone's, 311, 325; Seneca's, 347–48, 352–56, 366. *See also* lament; suicide

song: Drusilla's predilection for, 181, 320–21; and Iro, 370; and love, 294; and Penelope, 156, 203, 220, 268, 272, 285, 287, 294, 376; and Seneca, 353, 357, 359; and speech, 203;

stichomythia, 165, 177, 223; in *Octavia*, 335

stile concitato, 154, 192, 233–35, 237, 286, 289, 295, 304, 311, 314, 317–18, 366, 371

Stoicism. *See* Seneca

Striggio, Alessandro, 184, 187, 190, 194, 196, 224, 236n. *See also under* Monteverdi, Claudio

Strozzi, Giulio, 13–14, 19, 51, 56, 184, 190–192, 196, 242; *La Delia*, 18, 33, 56, 195, 239n, 338; *Ersilda*, 195; *La finta pazza*, 13–14, 17–18, 51, 65, 67, 195–96; —, in Paris, 127; *La finta pazza Licori*, 188–97, 227; *La finta savia*, 13–15, 37, 67, 126; *Il Romolo e Remo*, 14–15; *Venetia edificata*, 19; *La Veremonda*, 89, 114n. *See also* Incogniti, Accademia degli; *and under* Monteverdi, Claudio

Suetonius, 177, 333–34

suicide: of Iro, 339–40, 343–44, 346, 368, 371, 374–75; of Seneca, 97, 118, 176, 246, 331–32, 336–37, 374

Suitors (in *Il ritorno d'Ulisse*): arias for, 199; death of, 155, 253, 340–43, 362, 374; and Iro, 246, 366–67, 369; and Penelope, 77, 156, 254,

272–73; score material cut, 76–81, 140, 252; and Ulisse, 366

Tacitus, Cornelius, 175, 177–78, 333–34
Telemaco (in *Il ritorno d'Ulisse*); and Eumete, 287, 373; and Minerva, 288; and Penelope, 135, 157, 251–52, 273; and Ulisse, 151, 286–89
theaters: Novissimo, 8n, 15n, 17, 125, 195; S. Cassiano, 4, 17, 55–57, 125; —, as venue for *Ritorno*, 55–56; S. Moise, 17, 56, 125, 225; SS. Giovanni e Paolo, 4–6, 14, 17, 55–57, 59, 67–68, 125–26, 158, 163, 195; —, and *Incoronazione*, 62, 68; —, and *Ritorno*, 55–56; —, two operas per season in, 56–57
Tomlinson, Gary, 186, 196, 353
Torcigliani, Michelangelo, 8–10, 19, 183, 195, 197, 231, 235, 244, 379; and act division, 132, 150, 157; and *Aeneid*, 132; and Aristotle, 144; author of *Le nozze d'Enea*, 8, 48–49, 59; and classicism, 183; and Dolce, 146–47; letter to friends, 8, 15, 19, 48–50, 55, 59, 131–32, 183, 225, 379, 380; and meter, 216–17; and rules of tragedy, 131–32. *See also* Badoaro, Giacomo; Incogniti, Accademia degli; *Le nozze d'Enea e Lavinia*
tragedy, rules of. *See* Aristotle
trilogy: Monteverdi's, 3, 15–17, 21, 129–30, 195; political significance of, 377; Strozzi's, 13–15, 195; Zaguri's, 21
Il trionfo della fatica, 36. *See also* Laurenzi, Filiberto
Tron, owners of Teatro S. Cassiano, 4
Turno (in *Le nozze d'Enea*), 132, 145, 147, 149, 163, 214; and Amata, 145, 164, 167; death of, 149; and Enea, 144, 146, 161, 164–65, 216, 229, 232–33; and Lavinia, 145, 147, 165; and Numano, 164–65, 244

Ulisse (in *Il ritorno d'Ulisse*): and Ericlea, 142–43, 200, 290; and Eumete, 285, 287–88; and human frailty, 137–39; and Iro, 253, 339; and Minerva, 139, 285–88, 293–94; monologue of, 278–85; and Penelope, 53, 151, 157, 288, 292–93; and prudence, 139; and song, 151–55, 200, 294; and Suitors, 366; and Telemaco, 151, 286–89. *See also stile concitato*
unities, 180–81. *See also* Aristotle

Valletto (in *L'incoronazione di Poppea*), 101–3, 107–10, 117, 125, 204, 220, 320, 331, 338–39, 366; and Damigella, 42, 44, 93, 101–3, 108, 110, 220; and Seneca, 246–47
Van den Borren, Charles, 28, 30
Vartolo, Sergio, 41
Venere (in *Le nozze d'Enea*), 164, 212, 215; and Enea, 145, 164, 226, 229; and Giunone, 145–46, 159; and Lavinia, 237; and Vulcano, 145, 214, 217
Venetian opera, chronology of, 18–19, 125
Venice, myth of, 12–22; and *Le nozze d'Enea*, 13, 162
Verdi, Giuseppe, 34, 38, 381
Virgil, 131–32, 183, 226, 381. See also *Aeneid*
virgolette, 97
Vogel, Emil, 27–28, 33
Vulcano (in *Le nozze d'Enea*), and Venere, 145, 214, 217

Wagner, Richard, 381
Walker, Thomas, 25–26, 125
watermarks, 33n, 87n, 89–90, 94n, 121
Westrup, Jack, 30
Whenham, John, 125n
Wiel, Taddeo, 29, 89n

Zaguri, Pietro Angelo, 21
Ziani, Pietro Andrea, 88, 380

TEXT: 10.25/14 ADOBE GARAMOND

DISPLAY: ADOBE GARAMOND

COMPOSITOR: BINGHAMTON VALLEY COMPOSITION

MUSIC ENGRAVER: NATHAN LINK